Table of Contents

Introduction

1   A HISTORICAL PERSPECTIVE

The human search for pure water supplies must have begun in prehistoric times. Much of that earliest activity is subject to speculation. Some individuals may have conveyed water through trenches dug in the earth. They may have used a hollow log as the first water pipe. Thousands of years probably passed before our more recent ancestors learned to build cities and enjoy the convenience of water piped into houses and wastes carried away by water. Our earliest archeological records of central water supply and wastewater disposal date back about 5000 years, to the city of Nippur, in Sumeria. In the ruins of Nippur there is an arched drain, each stone being a wedge tapering downward into place [1]. Water was drawn from wells and cisterns. An extensive system of drainage conveyed the wastes from the palaces and residential districts of the city.

The earliest recorded knowledge of water treatment is in Sanskrit medical lore and Egyptian wall inscriptions [2]. Sanskrit writings dating to about 2000 B.C. tell how to purify foul water by boiling it in copper vessels, exposing it to sunlight, filtering it through charcoal, and cooling it in an earthen vessel.

Nothing is written about water treatment in the biblical sanitary and hygienic code of the early Hebrews, although three incidents may be cited as examples of the importance of fresh water. At Morah, Moses is said to have sweetened bitter waters by casting into them a tree shown him by God [3]. When the Israelites were wandering in the wilderness, the Lord commanded Moses to bring forth water by smiting a rock [4]. At a much later date, Elisha is said to have "healed unto this day" the spring water of Jericho by casting "salt" into it [5].

The earliest known apparatus for clarifying liquids was pictured on Egyptian walls in the fifteenth and thirteenth centuries B.C. The first picture, in a tomb of the reign of Amenhotep II (1447–1420 B.C.), represents the siphoning of either water or settled wine. A second picture, in the tomb of Rameses II (1300–1223 B.C.), shows the use of wick siphons in an Egyptian kitchen.

The first engineering report on water supply and treatment was written in A.D. 98 by Sextus Julius Frontinus, water commissioner of Rome. He produced two books on the water supply of Rome. In these, he described a settling reservoir at the head of one of the aqueducts and pebble catchers built into most of the aqueducts. His writings were first translated into English by the noted hydraulic engineer Clemens Herschel in 1899 [2].

In the eighth century A.D., an Arabian alchemist named Geber wrote a treatise on distillation that included various stills for water and other liquids. In the seventeenth century, the English philosopher Sir Francis Bacon wrote of his experiments on the purification of water by filtration, boiling, distillation, and clarification by coagulation. This work was published in 1627, one year after his death. Bacon also noted that clarifying water tends to improve health and increase the "pleasure of the eye."

The first known illustrated description of sand filters was published in 1685 by Luc Antonio Porzio, an Italian physician. He wrote a book on conserving the health of soldiers in camps based on his experience in the Austro-Turkish War. This was probably the earliest published work on mass sanitation. Porzio described and illustrated the use of sand filters and sedimentation. He also stated that his filtration method was the same as that of "those who built the Wells in the Palace of the Doges in Venice and in the Palace of Cardinal Sachette, at Rome" [2].

The oldest known archeological examples of water filtration are in Venice and the colonies it ruled. The ornate heads on the cisterns bear dates, but it is not known when the filters were placed. Venice, built on a series of islands, depended on catching and storing rainwater for its principal freshwater supply for over 1300 years. Cisterns were built and many were connected with sand filters. The rainwater ran off the house tops to the streets, where it was collected in stone-grated catch basins and then filtered through sand into cisterns.

A comprehensive article on the water supply of Venice appeared in the *Practical Mechanics Journal* in 1863 [6]. The land area of Venice was 12.85 acres and the average yearly rainfall was 32 inches. Nearly all of this rainfall was collected in 177 public and 1900 private cisterns. These cisterns provided a daily average supply of about 4.2 gallons per capita per day (gpcd). This low consumption was due in part to the absence of sewers, the practice of washing clothes in the lagoon, and the universal drinking of wine. The article explained in detail the construction of the cisterns. The cisterns were usually 10 to 12 feet deep. The earth was first excavated to the shape of a truncated inverted pyramid. Well-puddled clay was placed against the sides of the pit. A flat stone was placed in the bottom, and a cylinder was built in the center from brick laid with open joints. The space between the clay walls and the central brick cylinder was filled with sand. The stone surfaces of the courtyards were sloped toward the cistern, where perforated stone blocks collected the water at the lowest point and discharged it to the filter sand. This water was always fresh and cool, with a temperature of about 52°F. These cisterns continued to be the principal water supply of Venice until about the sixteenth century.

Many experiments on water filtration were conducted in the eighteenth and nineteenth centuries in England, France, Germany, and Russia. Henry Darcy patented filters in France and England in 1856, anticipating all aspects of the American rapid-sand filter except for coagulation. He appears to have been the first to apply the laws of hydraulics to filter design [7]. The first filter to supply water to a whole town was completed at Paisley, Scotland, in 1804, but this water was carted to consumers [2]. Filtered water was first piped to consumers in 1807 in Glasgow, Scotland [8].

In the United States, where turbidity was not as urgent a problem as it was in Europe, little attention was given to water treatment until after the Civil War. The first filters were of the slow-sand type, similar to British design. Around 1890, rapid-sand filters were developed in the United States, and coagulants were later introduced to increase their efficiency. These filters soon evolved into our present rapid-sand filters.

The drains and sewers of Nippur and Rome are among the great structures of antiquity. These drains were intended primarily to carry away runoff from storms and to flush streets. There are specific instances where direct connections were made to private homes and palaces, but these were the exceptions, for most of the houses did not have such connections. The need for regular cleansing of the city and flushing of the sewers was well recognized by commissioner Frontinus of Rome, as indicated in his statement, "I desire that nobody shall conduct away any excess water without having received my permission or that of my representatives, for it is necessary that a part of the supply flowing from the water-castles shall be utilized not only for cleaning our city, but also for flushing the sewers."

It is astonishing to note that from the days of Frontinus to the middle of the nineteenth century there was no marked progress in sewerage. In 1842, after a fire destroyed the old section of the city of Hamburg, Germany, it was decided to rebuild it according to modern ideas of convenience. The work was entrusted to an English engineer, W. Lindley, who was far ahead of his time. He designed an excellent collection system that included many of the ideas now in use. Unfortunately, the ideas of Lindley and their influence on public health were not then widely recognized.

The history of the progress of sanitation in London probably offers a more typical picture of what took place in the middle of the nineteenth century. In 1847, following an outbreak of cholera in India that had begun to work westward, a royal commission was appointed to look into London's sanitary conditions. This royal commission found that one of the major obstacles was the political structure, especially the lack of a central authority. The city of London was only a small part of the metropolitan area, comprising approximately 9.5% of the land area and less than 6% of the total population of approximately 2.5 million. This lack of a central authority made the execution of sewerage works all but impossible. The existing sewers were at different elevations, and in some instances the wastes would have had to flow uphill. In 1848, Parliament followed the advice of this commission and created the Metropolitan Commission of Sewers. That body and its successors produced reports that clearly showed the need for extensive sewerage works and other sanitary conditions [9]. Cholera appeared in London during the summer of 1848, and 14,600 deaths were recorded during 1849. In 1854, cholera killed 10,675 people in London. The connection was established between a contaminated water supply and the spread of the disease, and it was determined that the absence of effective sewerage was a major hindrance in combating the problem.

In 1855, Parliament passed an act "for the better local management of the metropolis," thereby providing the basis for the subsequent work of the Metropolitan Commission of Sewers, which soon after undertook the development of an adequate sewerage system. It is notable that the sewerage system of London, like that of Paris, was a result of the cholera epidemic.

Due to the concerns over disease, human excrement was discharged into the existing storm sewers and additional collection systems were installed. These measures removed wastes from the more inhabited areas of cities and also created the combined sewers of many older metropolitan areas. These storm drains had been constructed to discharge into the nearest watercourse. The addition of wastes to the small streams overtaxed the receiving capacities of the waters, and many of them were covered and converted into sewers. Much of the material was carried away from the point of entry into the drains, which in turn overtaxed the receiving waters. First the smaller and then the larger bodies of water began to ferment, creating a general health problem, especially during dry, hot weather.

The work on storm drainage in the United States closely paralleled that in Europe, especially England. Some difficulty was experienced because of the differences between rainfall patterns in the United States and England. Rains in England are more frequent but less intense. In the United States, storm drains must usually be larger for the same topographical conditions.

2   A CURRENT GLOBAL ISSUE

The enormous demands being placed on water supply and wastewater facilities have necessitated the development and implementation of far broader concepts, management scenarios, and technologies than those envisioned only a few years ago. Environmental engineers must address water as part of a complex natural system that is subject to both microscopic and planetary dynamics. This system is made up not only of complex chemical and physical realities but also of biological ones. The standards for water quality have increased significantly concurrent with a marked decrease in raw-water quality. Evidence of water supply contamination by toxic and hazardous materials has become common and worry over broad water-related environmental issues has heightened. As human populations throughout the world multiply at an alarming rate, environmental control becomes a critical factor. Many European and Asian nations have reached or exceeded the maximum populations their lands can comfortably support. These nations must now find innovative ways to provide for more people than their lands can conveniently support. Furthermore, scientists and engineers throughout the world are facing the realities of global climate change and working with the social, economic, and political complexities of the problem. To compound this issue, political and social unrest throughout the world has made water supply an urgent security issue. The lesson is that populations increase, but natural resources do not. Consequently, the use, management, and control of these resources must be sustainable.

3   A LOOK TO THE FUTURE

The physical and dynamic nature of our natural world demands that the engineers and scientists of tomorrow excel not only technically, but also in their ability to see beyond the political, social, legal, and economic constraints of the problems they will face. Tomorrow's technical leaders must shape the policies that will ultimately prescribe the types of solutions that will be accepted by society and that will effectively address the world's water needs. Imaginative and creative engineers who can perceive, address, and communicate issues related to the natural world are needed. These experts must set forth and assess viable alternatives and understand the differences between what is realistic to implement and what is not. The future of this "one world" rests upon the decisions that environmental scientists, engineers, and others will contribute to and on the actions that will flow from these decisions. These environmental engineers and scientists are embarking on an important mission, a mission that will shape life for future generations.

REFERENCES

[1] W. Durant, *Our Oriental Heritage* (New York: Simon & Schuster, 1954), 132.

[2] M. N. Baker, *The Quest for Pure Water* (New York: American Water Works Association, 1949), 1–3, 6–11.

[3] Exodus 15:22–27.

[4] Exodus 17:1–7.

[5] 2 Kings 2:19–22 (King James Version).

[6] "The Water Cistern in Venice," *J. Franklin Inst.*, 3rd ser., 70 (1860): 372–373.

[7] H. Darcy, *Les Fontaines Publiques de la Ville de Dijon; Distribution d'Eau et Filtrage des Eaux* (Paris: Victor Dalmont, 1856).

[8] D. Mackain, "On the Supply of Water to the City of Glasgow," *Proc. Inst. Civil Engrs.* (London) 2 (1842–1843): 134–136.

[9] First Report of the Metropolitan Sanitary Commission (London: 1848).

Water Resources Planning and Management

Water Resources Planning and Management

Water resources planning and management are multidimensional and dynamic endeavors. They must be conducted within the constraints of technology, social goals, laws and regulations, political viewpoints, environmental concerns, and economic realities. To be effective, those responsible for water planning and management must recognize and take advantage of interconnections between surface and groundwater; exploit the potential for coordinated use of existing facilities; acknowledge that water quantity and quality are a single issue; devise new ways to operate old systems; blend structural and nonstructural approaches; accept that the nature of water resources systems may require regional rather than local solutions to problems; and provide equity, as far as possible, if not on a monetary basis at least on a service basis, to all those affected. In concept, water planning and management is simple; the trouble is that the boundaries of the physical systems that must be dealt with often differ markedly from the political boundaries that affect how water is used and developed. Furthermore, many historical, social, legal, and political factors have been narrowly focused and constrain, if not preclude, good water management.

1 ENVIRONMENTAL REGULATION AND PROTECTION

In the early twentieth century in the United States, the major focus was on constructing dams, waterways, water treatment plants, and wastewater treatment facilities. Irrigation works helped settle the West. Improvements to waterways encouraged commerce and industry in populous areas of the East, South, and Midwest. Municipal water and wastewater systems provided the basis for increasing urbanization and industrial growth in many localities. Now, however, most of the nation's rivers have been subjected to engineering controls, and many old water policies are no longer valid. Furthermore, numerous facilities constructed in the past are reaching the end of their design lives, and the question of how to rehabilitate them is now urgent.

The maturity of our water infrastructure suggests that good management practices should be followed in correcting deficiencies and making improvements. Broad issues rather than the local interests that historically have been satisfied on a project-by-project basis are moving to the forefront. A transition is under way. The question is whether this new outlook can hurdle the barriers created over the years while effectively dealing with the newer complexities.

Water pollution legislation originated in 1886 when Congress passed a bill forbidding the dumping of impediments to navigation into New York Harbor. In 1899, Congress passed the Rivers and Harbors Act, which prohibited depositing solid wastes into navigable waters. These early concerns with water pollution were strictly in the interests of navigation. The Public Health Service Act of 1912 included a section on waterborne diseases, and the Oil Pollution Act of 1924 was designed to prevent oil discharges from vessels into coastal waters; such discharges could damage aquatic life. This act gave pollution enforcement authority to the federal government if local efforts failed, and it included a provision for matching grants for waste-treatment facilities. Policy was strengthened with the Water Quality Act of 1965, which set water quality standards for interstate waters.

In 1966 attention to water quality heightened, owing to the efforts of President Johnson. It was his position that entire river basins rather than localities should be considered in pollution control efforts. He proposed a "clean rivers demonstration program" in which the federal government would provide funds to interstate and regional water pollution control authorities on a first-ready, first-served basis. Those participating in the program would be required to have permanent water quality planning organizations, water quality standards, and implementation plans in effect for all waters of the designated basin.

The Clean Rivers Restoration Act of 1966 provided for a substantial increase in the level of funding appropriated for the construction of wastewater treatment facilities. Due to the Vietnam War, however, the construction grant program was not funded at the levels authorized.

After the Nixon administration took office in 1969, Congress prodded it to take action in the areas of water pollution control and environmental policy. This prodding was supported by the strong, and growing, environmental movement of the late 1960s. By 1970 the Nixon administration became convinced that there was a need for a massive federal investment in sewage treatment plant construction. In his February 1970 message on environmental quality, President Nixon proposed a four-year, $10-billion program of state, federal, and local investment in wastewater treatment facilities. The federal share of this investment was to be $1 billion per year. While this amount lagged behind actual authorized funding levels and was less than many environmental advocates desired, it was much more than any previous presidential request [1].

The intended result of congressional passage of pollution control laws was for the EPA and the states to issue enforceable regulations to improve the quality of the nation's waters. Pollution control programs were generated at every level of government to implement regulations, issue permits, inspect regulated facilities, and enforce established rules. In response, industries and municipalities organized internal pollution control programs to stay abreast of regulatory requirements, worked with plant personnel to attain compliance with regulations, learned about environmental monitoring and sampling techniques, and worked with the regulatory agencies to obtain permits. In a sense, the 1970s was a period of institutionalization of the ideals of the environmental movement prevalent in the 1960s.

In 1970 the National Environmental Policy Act (NEPA) was passed. The act was praised by President Nixon, who proclaimed that the three-member Council on Environmental Quality (CEQ) would be a great asset in keeping the President informed on important environmental issues. The Nixon administration promptly put the provisions of NEPA into effect. NEPA was significant in that it required the federal government to report on environmental impacts related to its activities. On March 5, 1970, the President issued an executive order instructing all federal agencies to report on possible variances of their authorities and policies with NEPA's purposes. Then on April 30, 1970, the CEQ issued interim guidelines for the preparation of environmental impact statements.

In December 1970, as an outgrowth of the administration's environmental interests, a new independent body, the Environmental Protection Agency (EPA), was created. This organization assumed the functions of several existing agencies in matters of environmental management. It brought together under one roof all of the pollution-control programs related to water, air, solid wastes, pesticides, and radiation. The EPA was seen by the administration as the most effective way of recognizing that the environment should be considered as a single, interrelated system. It is noteworthy, however, that the creation of the EPA made the separation of water quality programs from other water programs even more pronounced.

Even with the enactment of NEPA, it was clear that a comprehensive response to water pollution issues was still lacking. During Congressional hearings in 1971 it became evident that, relative to the construction grants program, the program was underfunded. To rectify this situation, Congress passed the Water Pollution Control Act Amendments of 1972 (P.L. 92-500). Responding to public demand for cleaner water, the law ended two years of intense debate, negotiation, and compromise and resulted in the most assertive step in the history of national water pollution control activities.

The act departed in several ways from previous water pollution control legislation. It expanded the federal role in water-pollution control, increased the level of federal funding for construction of publicly owned waste treatment works, elevated planning to a new level of significance, opened new avenues for public participation, and created a regulatory mechanism requiring uniform technology-based effluent standards together with a national permit system for all point-source dischargers as the means of enforcement.

In the strategy for implementation, Congress stated requirements for achieving specific goals and objectives within specified time frames. The objective of the act was to restore and maintain the chemical, physical, and biological integrity of the nation's waters. Two goals and eight policies were articulated:

Goals

1. To reach, wherever attainable, a water quality that provides for the protection and propagation of fish, shellfish, and wildlife and for recreation in and on the water.
2. To eliminate the discharge of pollutants into navigable waters.

Policies

1. To prohibit the discharge of pollutants in toxic amounts.
2. To provide federal financial assistance for construction of publicly owned treatment works.
3. To develop and implement area-wide waste treatment management planning.
4. To mount a major research and demonstration effort in wastewater treatment technology.
5. To recognize, preserve, and protect the primary responsibilities and roles of the states to prevent, reduce, and eliminate pollution.
6. To ensure, where possible, that foreign nations act to prevent, reduce, and eliminate pollution in international waters.
7. To provide for, encourage, and assist public participation in executing the Act.
8. To pursue procedures that dramatically diminishes paperwork and prevents needless duplication and unnecessary delays at all levels of government.

The act provided for achievement of its goals and objectives in phases, with accompanying requirements and deadlines. It was intended to be more than a mandate for point-source discharge control: it embodied an entirely new approach to the traditional way Americans had managed their water resources.

The 1972 amendments recognized the importance and urgency of the water quality management problem. The National League of Cities and the U.S. Conference of Mayors estimated, for example, that a financial commitment of from $33 billion to $37 billion would be needed for water pollution control programs during the rest of the 1970s [2]. The 1972 act committed the federal government to covering 75% of the costs associated with the construction of wastewater treatment facilities and authorized $18 billion of contract authority.

After passage of Public Law 92-500, there was a transition from researching the water pollution problem to implementing solutions [3]. For example, Section 101 of the act states goals for fishable and swimmable waters and the prohibition of toxic discharges. These goals required that programs be implemented to reverse the threats that scientists had identified. The 1972 Clean Water Act provided the framework for a concerted effort to control water pollution. Contract authority to construct treatment facilities combined with meaningful enforcement procedures set in motion a policy to reverse the water-quality-degrading practices of the past.

Not long after passage of the 1972 Clean Water Act, the Safe Drinking Water Act (SDWA) was passed (December 16, 1974). The purpose of that legislation was to ensure that water supply systems serving the public would meet minimum standards for the protection of public health. The act was designed to achieve uniform safety and quality of drinking water in the United States by identifying contaminants and establishing maximum acceptable levels. Before the SDWA it was possible to prescribe federal drinking water standards only for water supplies used by interstate carriers. After the act was passed, the EPA established federal standards to control the levels of harmful contaminants in drinking water supplied by all public water systems. It also established a joint federal–state system for ensuring compliance with these standards, with the following major provisions:

1. Establishment of primary regulations for the protection of the public health.
2. Establishment of secondary regulations related to taste, odor, and appearance of drinking water.
3. Establishment of regulations to protect underground drinking water sources by the control of surface injection.
4. Initiation of research on health, economic, and technological problems related to drinking water supplies.
5. Initiation of a survey of rural water supplies.
6. Allocation of funds to states for improving their drinking water programs through technical assistance, training of personnel, and grant support.

In 1977, in response to an obvious need to address deficiencies in the 1972 act, the Clean Water Act was revised. The salient points of the 1977 act included the following:

1. States were specifically mandated primacy over water quality and water use issues.
2. Municipalities were given evidence of a federal commitment in the form of construction grants and training assistance.
3. The public received assurances of the importance of water quality in the form of effective enforcement and incentive provisions for governments and industries to achieve the goal of fishable and swimmable waters.
4. Industry received the necessary extensions of compliance deadlines under the effluent discharge limitations provision.
5. Environmental groups witnessed the incorporation of a Resource Defense Council/EPA consent decree into the law that established toxic effluent standards and set forth a comprehensible process to implement effluent limitations [4].

In 1986, the Safe Drinking Water Act of 1974 was amended [5]. The principal changes were focused on groundwater protection. A wellhead protection program was established. The program provides that states undertaking wellhead protection efforts are eligible to receive federal grants to aid them in these endeavors. The EPA guidelines for wellhead protection are unique in that they allow regional flexibility rather than prescribe uniform national standards. The act also provides for sole-source aquifer protection. The objective is to protect from contamination recharge areas that are primary sources of drinking water. Drinking water standards apply to these areas, and underground injection of effluent is regulated. Enforcement provisions of the act are strong, and in 1987 the first criminal conviction under the act was obtained [6]. The act was again amended in 1996. The changes focused water program spending on the contaminants that pose the greatest risk to human health and that are most likely to occur in a specified water system. Rather than focusing on certain contaminants, the law gives the EPA more authority to determine which contaminants to regulate. The amendments require that the best available scientific information and objective practices be used when proposing drinking water standards and they require that the EPA and the states begin to emphasize protection of source waters.

The Clean Water Act was reauthorized in 1987 as the Water Quality Act of 1987 [7]. A major feature of the 1987 act was the addition of the goal of controlling nonpoint sources of pollution. This was the most pronounced federal excursion into this important aspect of water-quality management. Agricultural fields, feedlots, and urban areas, including streets, were addressed. And while mandatory controls were not authorized, Congress did direct the states to conduct planning studies for developing strategies for abating water pollution associated with nonpoint sources. A total of $400 million of federal funds was authorized to be used by the states to implement cleanup programs, with priority to be given to regulatory programs, innovative practices, and strategies that deal with groundwater contamination. The 1987 act provided for creation, by the states, of revolving funds to facilitate low-interest loans to local governments for sewage treatment improvements. It also provided more options for state and federal sharing of programs under the National Pollution Discharge Elimination System (NPDES). The EPA and the states could now divide the categories of discharges regulated within each state.

During the Reagan administration, regulations and regulatory practices were reviewed to determine whether costs of pollution control could be reduced by modifying the regulatory approach [2]. This led to a debate about the relative merits of water-quality standards versus technology-based standards. Water-quality standards establish a designated use for a specified section of a water body, which is then balanced with the maximum amount of waste the water body can assimilate. Technology-based standards are effluent limitations based on the levels of pollutant removal that can be achieved by modern wastewater treatment technology. Since 1972, technology-based standards had been the keystone of the Clean Water Act.

By law, all waters must have designated "beneficial uses" that must be protected and met. These uses establish the water-quality criteria that must be considered in pollution control efforts. Using EPA guidelines, states apply a range of chemical, biological, habitat, and other parameters to establish criteria to protect specific designated uses. The EPA must approve the water-quality standards that result and the states then apply them to determine the quality of their waters, consistent with supported uses. In 1990, it was reported that of 519,000 miles of streams assessed in 1988, 30% did not meet, or partially did not meet, the standards for their designated uses [4, 8, 9].

Congress initiated the technology-based approach in 1972 because the water-quality-based approach of the 1960s had failed due to difficulties of enforcement and the limited availability of data for use in water-quality models. The following arguments were put forth in favor of a technology-based approach:

1. Technology-based standards are easy to enforce. This is important from an institutional perspective.
2. These standards are the first step toward the ultimate goal of zero discharge of pollutants to natural waters, as opposed to merely cleaning up waters to suit human objectives (the basis for water-quality standards).

3. Knowledge and resources to set water-quality standards for all pollutants and locations are insufficient. Technology-based standards are an interim approach to avoiding pollution.

4. Nationwide uniformity in treatment standards minimizes economic dislocations.

5. The approach promotes equity among dischargers. No one should have the right to discharge more into the environment simply because of geographic location.

The Reagan administration, however, contended that while technology-based standards had been important in the past to provide impetus for local governments and industry to clean up pollution from their treatment facilities, the EPA now had the ability and sophistication to regulate discharged pollutants under water-quality standards. The administration stated that the Clean Water Act should be amended accordingly and noted the following advantages of water-quality standards [2]:

1. Water-quality standards and the process by which they are adopted inherently encourage an assessment of costs and benefits, which is absent in the adoption and application of technology-based standards.

2. These standards foster scientific debate, which accelerates the advancement of the state of the art in predicting the fate and effect of pollutants.

3. The debate takes place in a local and state arena and heightens awareness on the part of local government, policy makers, and the public of the importance of water-pollution control in their communities.

4. The assertion of the primary right and responsibility of states to regulate pollutants is essential to establishing the appropriate balance of power between federal and state governments.

5. Water-quality-based decisions avoid requiring treatment for treatment's sake, which can result from applying technology-based standards [10].

For the present, it appears that technology-based effluent standards will continue to be the norm, even though they may be economically and socially inefficient [11]. But someday, a shift to water-quality standards may gain stronger support, particularly as holistic water management becomes reality.

Despite subsequent efforts to revise it, the Clean Water Act was last amended in 1987. During the 104th Congress, the Republican majority worked with business and industry lobbyists to write a bill that would ease restrictions on the discharge of a wide variety of industrial pollutants, but environmentalists and the Clinton administration opposed this thrust. Many complex issues surround amendment of the act, a particularly significant one being the control of nonpoint pollution. About two-thirds of all pollution stems from farms, construction sites, mining, forestry, and urban runoff (nonpoint sources). Solutions to the nonpoint problem may require tougher regulations on the use of pesticides and fertilizers, as well as new land use controls to protect watersheds [12].

Another major issue that must be addressed is that of the storage, treatment, and disposal of the hazardous and toxic wastes generated by our industrial society. Even though many manufacturers have reduced their use of hazardous and toxic materials, the volume of such wastes continues to increase. According to one source, the cleanup of all civilian and military hazardous waste sites could cost over $750 billion over the next 30 years [13].

It appears that the American public is strongly committed to the goal of clean water. Billions of dollars have already been invested in water-quality control programs, and this trend is expected to continue. Many of the easiest problems have been solved, however, and the future agenda will pose some significant political, legal, social, and economic challenges.

The Pollution Prevention Act of 1990 (P.L. 101–508) established the Office of Pollution Prevention within the EPA to coordinate agency efforts at source reduction. It created a volunteer program to improve lighting efficiency, thereby reducing energy consumption, and stated that waste minimization was to be the primary means of hazardous waste management. It also promoted voluntary industry reduction of hazardous waste and mandated a source reduction and recycling report to accompany the annual toxic release inventories.

In 1996, the Safe Drinking Water Act was again reauthorized. This was the first major revision to the act in 10 years. Upon signing the bill, President Clinton said the law "replaces an inflexible approach with the authority to act on contaminants of greatest risk and to analyze costs and benefits, while retaining public health as the paramount value. Americans do have a right to know what's in their drinking water, where it comes from, before turning on their taps. Americans have a right to trust that every precaution is being taken to protect their families from dangerous, and sometimes even deadly contaminants." The SDWA amendments focus on funding related to contaminants that pose the greatest risk to human health and that are most likely to occur in a given water system. Rather than prescribe the contaminants that the EPA is to focus on, the law gives the EPA latitude to select which contaminants to regulate, but requires it to use the best available scientific information and objective practices when proposing drinking water standards. The act also establishes a self-revolving trust fund for drinking water systems, requires that water system operators be certified, maintains requirements for setting both a maximum contaminant level and a maximum contaminant level goal for regulated contaminants based on health risk reduction and cost/benefit analyses, and requires the EPA to establish a database to monitor the presence of unregulated contaminants in water.

As a result of water pollution control efforts since the late 1960s, the once-rising tide of pollution has diminished. But there is still much to be done, particularly in the field of nonpoint pollution control. Table 1 summarizes federal statutes governing or affecting water-quality protection.

2   SECURITY OF WATER RESOURCES SYSTEMS

Following the September 11, 2001 terrorist attacks, protecting our water resources systems became increasingly important, adding yet another dimension to water planning and management. In the United States, a number of federal agencies are responsible for one or more aspects of water resources development and management. The EPA (www.epa.gov), for example, has major responsibility for water quality, while the U.S. Army Corps of Engineers (USACE, www.usace.army.mil), the

TABLE 1   A Summary of Federal Environmental Legislation: 1948–1996

Year	Act
1948	Federal Water Pollution Control Act
1968	Wild and Scenic Rivers Act
1969	National Environmental Policy Act
1972	Federal Water Pollution Control Act Amendments
1972	Marine Protection, Research and Sanctuaries Act
1973	Endangered Species Act
1974	Safe Drinking Water Act
1976	Resources Conservation and Recovery Act
1976	Toxic Substances Control Act
1977	Clean Water Act
1980	Comprehensive Environmental Response, Compensation, and Liability Act
1984	Resources Conservation and Recovery Act Amendments
1986	Superfund Amendment and Reauthorization Act
1986	Federal Safe Drinking Water Act Amendments
1987	Clean Water Act Amendments
1990	Pollution Prevention Act
1996	Safe Drinking Water Act Amendments
2002	Public Health Security and Bioterrorism Preparedness and Response Act

U.S. Bureau of Reclamation (USBR), the Natural Resources Conservation Service (NRCS, www.nrcs.usda.gov), and the Tennessee Valley Authority (TVA, www.tva. gov) have significant roles in water supply. The Water Resources Council (WRC) was, until its demise in 1982, the principal body for coordinating federal and state water programs and assessing the state of the nation's waters. Several other agencies—the Economic Development Administration (EDA), the Small Business Administration (SBA), the Farmers Home Administration (FmHA), and the Department of Housing and Urban Development (HUD)—help rural and economically depressed areas build and maintain adequate water supply and wastewater disposal facilities. Table 2 briefly describes each agency's role.

The Public Health Security and Bioterrorism Preparedness and Response Act of 2002 was enacted in response to growing concerns over the safety of the U.S. water supply. This act was preceded by an amendment to the Safe Drinking Water Act that includes a section addressing Terrorism and Other Intentional Acts. The Bioterrorism Act required that community water systems complete vulnerability assessments by the end of 2004. These assessments were used to shape emergency response plans six months after the completion of the vulnerability assessments. This act continues to support research and new technologies related to water security—including advanced water distribution modeling and water-quality monitoring [14].

TABLE 2   Principal United States Water Resources Planning and Development Agencies

Agency	Mission
Army Corps of Engineers (CE)	Planning, constructing, operating, and maintaining a wide variety of water resources facilities, including those for navigation, flood control, water supply, recreation, hydroelectric power generation, water quality control, and other purposes. Nationwide activities.
Economic Development Administration (EDA), Small Business Administration (SBA), Farmers Home Administration (FmHA), and the Department of Housing and Urban Development (HUD)	Assist rural and economically depressed areas to develop and maintain water and wastewater conveyance, processing, and other related facilities. This is accomplished mainly through grant and loan programs.
Natural Resources Conservation Service (NRCS)	Carries out a national soil and water conservation program. Provides technical and financial assistance for flood prevention, recreation, and water supply development in small watersheds (fewer than 250,000 acres). Also appraises the nation's soil, water, and related resources.
Tennessee Valley Authority (TVA)	Planning, constructing, operating, and maintaining facilities in the Tennessee River Basin for navigation, flood control, and the generation of electricity. The TVA is a unique regional organization that has worked well in the United States.
U.S. Bureau of Reclamation (USBR)	Planning, constructing, operating, and maintaining facilities for irrigation, power generation, recreation, fish and wildlife preservation, and municipal water supply. Most activities are confined to the 17 western states. Original efforts were concentrated on irrigation.
U.S. Environmental Protection Agency (EPA)	Abatement and control of pollution. Provision of financial and technical assistance to states and local governments for constructing wastewater treatment facilities and for water quality management planning. Coordination of national programs and policies relating to water quality. Its principal role is regulatory.
U.S. Water Resources Council (WRC)	Principal role was the coordination of regional and river basin plans, assessing the adequacy of the nation's water and related land resources, suggesting changes in national policy related to water matters, and assisting the states in developing water planning capability. Although terminated in 1982, the WRC exemplified the long-sought mechanism for water program coordination and water policy analysis that was recommended by many study commissions since the early 1900s. A new organization with many of the WRC's roles is almost sure to be formed.

3   WATERSHED MANAGEMENT

Since the late 1980s, the concept of "watershed management" has been a guiding principle for water resources planners and engineers. The National Water Commission's 1973 report, "Water Policies for the Future," and the many studies that preceded and followed it argued for integrated watershed management to be the foundation for managing water resources on all geographic scales [15–18]. Consistent with this notion, there has been a broadening of state water planning practices in the United States [19].

Many water problems cannot be solved in the context of traditional spatial and institutional boundaries. Recognizing this, several states have taken regional or watershed management approaches. Nebraska and Florida have established regional management districts that have broad powers to manage water resources.

The 23 Nebraska Natural Resources Districts and the five Florida Water Management Districts blanket their states and have similar powers, including the authority to levy property taxes [2, 20]. Some federal, state, and local government agencies are beginning to adopt and implement holistic water management practices. These watershed-oriented approaches are based on flexible frameworks that specify guidelines, define the roles and responsibilities of key players, and permit the unique attributes of the watershed to dictate appropriate actions [21]. The watershed-oriented approaches are analogous to ecosystem approaches in that they consider the linkages among air, water, land, and the biological elements within the systems' boundaries. *Integrated watershed management* means focusing on the appropriate spatial configuration (the right watershed), using solid science and credible data, involving the key stakeholders in decision-making processes, and applying the concepts of "sustainable development" [20].

4   INTEGRATED WATER MANAGEMENT

Integrated water management is conceptually sound and should be the goal of water planners and managers. It requires full recognition of the true spatial, environmental, and institutional dimensions of water management. Key stakeholders must be involved in the planning process and the approach must be as holistic as possible. Plans for integrated water management should drive water resources decision-making processes and serve as the basis for developing regulatory programs. Preventive rather than remedial actions should be emphasized. Unfortunately, adoption of integrated water resources planning processes is hampered by a number of constraints:

- Complexities associated with holistic water management planning; agency, interest group, and political boundaries of authority and space.
- Government, agency, and professional biases and traditions.
- The lack of effective forums for assembling and retaining stakeholders.
- The narrow focus, lack of implementation capability, poor public involvement, and limited coordination attributes of many water resources planning and management processes.
- The separation of land and water management, water-quantity and water-quality management, surface water and groundwater management, and other directly linked elements.
- Poor coordination and collaboration among state, local, and federal water-related agencies.
- Limited ability to value environmental systems on monetary or other scales.
- The public's perception of risk as opposed to the reality of risk associated with water-management options.
- Suspicion regarding the formation of partnerships and poor communications links among planners, managers, stakeholders, and others.

5   ROLE OF GEOGRAPHIC INFORMATION SYSTEMS

Since the rise of computers in the 1970s, Geographic Information Systems (GIS) have added a new, exciting dimension to water resources planning processes. This shift is characterized by viewing water projects in an integrated manner as opposed to considering them discrete elements. Textbooks usually define GIS as a combination of hardware and software that allows data to be managed, developed, analyzed, and maintained in a spatial context. GIS has also been defined in many other ways that are perhaps more helpful in understanding what it is and how it can successfully be applied to water resources projects. At a 1998 conference, Jack Dangermond, the President of the Environmental Systems Research Institute (ESRI), noted that GIS is a visual language, a framework for studying complex systems, integrating our knowledge about places, and helping us to organize our institutions [22]. We can add to this definition that GIS helps us do a better job of managing water resources, enhances the life of the public, increases efficiency, decreases time spent on repetitious tasks, and ensures the success of ecological restoration efforts.

GIS is routinely used in a variety of water supply, wastewater, and stormwater planning and management projects and can help with water-use projections, permit preparation and tracking, watershed assessments, master planning, conceptual design and development of alternatives, model development and enhancement, floodplain creation and modernization, decision support, construction management, infrastructure and asset management, and disaster prediction and emergency management.

Before GIS, engineers and hydrologists parameterized their hydrologic and hydraulic models using hard-copy maps, a planimeter, and perhaps a spreadsheet. If the modeler made an error on a hard-copy map, the modeler would manually erase the information or use another map. Once the hard-copy information was correct, a planimeter was used to calculate areas for several model parameters. This process was usually lengthy for larger models and was limited by the accuracy of the planimeter. GIS displays the information in a dynamic, visual, and interactive environment and modelers can now delineate large watersheds in a fraction of the time that it used to take—with a much higher level of accuracy. A simple command or the push of a button can calculate areas for a virtually limitless number of watersheds in a GIS and provide levels of precision that were previously unattainable. Many modelers also overlay data layers in GIS and parameterize important parts of models such as the longest flowpath, runoff coefficients, and stage-area relationships. This same GIS is then used to check models and develop floodplains and, because of the strong visual component, it is much easier to see where data anomalies may exist. Today, virtually all hydrologic and hydraulic model parameterization tasks can be completed using automated GIS tools that significantly increase model accuracy and the overall efficiency of planning efforts [23].

GIS is a powerful tool for water resources engineers and planners because it is spatially correct (often referred to as being cartographically correct) and contains sound analytical components that can be used to examine the many nonlinear and multidimensional aspects of water management. And while nothing can replace sound engineering and scientific judgment, GIS can be used to enhance and expedite almost any water planning or management effort.

6 CONCLUSIONS

The need for water planning and management has long been recognized and continues to increase in complexity. At the most basic level, successful planning and management require a strong working knowledge of the political, legal, social, and regulatory context of the planning region. *Individual, agency, government*, and *special-group* interests must be coordinated and conflicts among them must be resolved. Water resources planners must apply their technology effectively to address the views of society if their plans are ever to be implemented.

PROBLEMS

1 Do your state's water planning agencies take an integrated approach to water resources planning? Explain.

2 What are the principal statutes under which the EPA controls water pollution? Which aspects of water pollution may be regulated under each act?

3 Define point and nonpoint water pollution sources. Give five examples of each.

4 List three adverse health effects of toxic chemical pollutants.

5 Identify the agencies in your state responsible for managing (a) water quality and (b) water quantity.

6 Do you believe the primary responsibility for pollution control should rest with the states, the federal government, or some mix? Explain your viewpoint.

7 Why do you think that integrated water management is difficult to achieve?

8 Do you think GIS has advanced integrated water management or is GIS being used to provide localized, project-specific evaluations? Use the Internet to find three examples of how GIS is being used to support your argument.

REFERENCES

[1] B. H. Holmes, *History of Federal Water Resources Programs and Policies, 1961–1970*, U.S. Department of Agriculture Misc. Publ. No. 1379 (Washington, DC: U.S. Government Printing Office, September 1979).

[2] W. Viessman, Jr., and C. Welty, *Water Management: Technology and Institutions* (New York: Harper & Row, 1985).

[3] R. M. Linton, "The Politics of Clean Water," *Chemtech* (July 1982).

[4] U. S. Environmental Protection Agency, "National Water Quality Inventory: 1988 Report to Congress," Report No. EPA 440-4-90-003, Office of Water (Washington, DC, April 1990).

[5] 42 U.S.C. 300(f) et seq.

[6] *United States v. Jay Woods Oil Co. Inc.* (ED Mich. No. 87 CR20012 BC), unreported opinion cited in *Environmental Reporter*, 18, no. 6 (June 5, 1987): 502.

[7] Public Law 100-4: (Feb. 4, 1987).

[8] D. H. Moreau, "The Clean Water Act in Retrospect," *Water Resources Update,* Universities Council on Water Resources (Winter 1991), no. 84 (Carbondale, IL): 5–12.

[9] R. Savage, "The Clean Water Act: Accomplishments," *Water Resources Update,* Universities Council on Water Resources (Winter 1991), no. 84 (Carbondale, IL): 30–34.

[10] B. H. Holmes, *History of Federal Water Resources Programs and Policies, 1961–1970,* U.S. Department of Agriculture Misc. Publ. No. 1379 (Washington, DC: U.S. Government Printing Office, September 1979).

[11] L. J. MacDonnell, "Restoring and Maintaining the Integrity of the Nation's Water: An Assessment of the Clean Water Act," *Water Resources Update,* Universities Council on Water Resources (Winter 1991), no. 84 (Carbondale, IL): 19–23.

[12] N. J. Vig and M. E. Kraft, eds., "The New Environmental Agenda," Chap. 17 in *Environmental Policy in the 1990s,* 3rd ed. (Washington, DC: CQ Press, 1997).

[13] M. Russell, E. W. Colglazier, and B. E. Tonn, "The U.S. Hazardous Waste Legacy," *Environment* 34 (July–August 1992): 12–14, 34–39.

[14] 42 U.S.C. 300i-2 et seq.

[15] J. A. Ballweber, "Prospects for Comprehensive, Integrated Watershed Management Under Existing Law," *Water Resources Update,* Universities Council on Water Resources (Summer 1995), no. 100 (Carbondale, IL), 19–23.

[16] J. W. Bulkley, "Integrated Water Management: Past, Present, and Future," *Water Resources Update,* Universities Council on Water Resources (Summer 1995), no. 100 (Carbondale, IL): 7–18.

[17] R. E. Deyle, "Integrated Water Management: Contending with Garbage Can Decision Making in Organized Anarchies," *Water Resources Bulletin* (American Water Resources Association), 31, no. 3 (June 1995): 387–398.

[18] M. W. Hall, "A Conceptual Model for Integrated Water Management" (paper prepared for the workshop "Total Water Environment Management for Military Installations," U.S. Army Environmental Policy Institute, Atlanta, GA, 1996).

[19] W. Viessman and T. D. Feather, eds., *State Water Resources Planning in the United States,* (Reston, VA: ASCE Press, 2006).

[20] A. Kovar, "Natural Resource Districts and Groundwater Quality Protection: An Evolving Role," in *Redefining National Water Policy: New Roles and Directions,* ed. Stephen M. Born, Special Publication No. 89-1 of the American Water Resources Association (1989): 51–72.

[21] L. P. Wise and J. Pawlukiewicz, "The Watershed Approach: An Institutional Framework for Action" (paper prepared for the workshop "Total Water Environment Management for Military Installations," U.S. Army Environmental Policy Institute, Atlanta, GA, 1996).

[22] U. M. Shamsi, *GIS Tools for Water, Wastewater, and Stormwater Systems* (Reston, VA: ASCE Press, 2002).

[23] D. Maidment and D. Djokic, eds., *Hydrologic and Hydraulic Modeling Support with Geographic Information Systems* (Redlands, CA: ESRI Press, 2000).

The Hydrologic Cycle and Natural Water Sources

The Hydrologic Cycle and Natural Water Sources

Since water surrounds us in many parts of the world, water supply would appear to be a simple matter. The reality, however, is that the distribution, quality, quantity, and mode of occurrence are highly variable from one location to another. The oceans, containing about 1060 trillion acre · ft of water, are the greatest source of water, but they are saline [1]. The planet's freshwater resources, contained in the atmosphere, on the earth's surface, and underground, are the principal source of supply for a spectrum of human needs but only amount to about 3% of the volume of water in the oceans.

Not many years ago, water resources management focused almost exclusively on water supply, flood control, and navigation. The primary goal was usually to convey wastewater and stormwater away from populated areas as quickly as possible. Today, protecting the environment, ensuring safe drinking water, and providing aesthetic and recreational experiences compete equally for water resources and for funds for water management and development. An environmentally conscious public is pressing for improved management practices with fewer structural components to address the nation's water problems. The notion of continually striving to provide access to more water has been replaced by one of husbanding this precious resource.

Water resources planners and managers are now confronted with tough issues of allocating limited water supply and are faced with multiple management objectives, and this problem has become more severe as a result of society's desire to allocate a share of the waters to ecosystem restoration, environmental protection, and other traditional purposes such as municipal water supply and irrigation. To effectively address the complexities of these management objectives, modern water professionals must have a basic understanding of the physical, chemical, and biological aspects of the hydrologic cycle and natural water sources.

1   THE HYDROLOGIC CYCLE

Water resources vary widely in regional and local patterns of availability. The supply depends on the influence of topographic, geographic, and meteorological conditions on precipitation and evapotranspiration. Quantities of water stored depend to a large extent on the physical features of the Earth and on the Earth's geological structure. Table 1 shows the major components of the water resources of the continental United States.

In theory, accounting for the water resources of an area is simple. The basic procedure involves evaluating each component of the water budget so that the amount of available water resources can be compared with the known or anticipated water requirements of the area Figure 1 is a simplified diagram of the hydrologic cycle. In general, the hydrologic cycle is made up of surface water flow, groundwater flow, evapotranspiration, evaporation, infiltration, and precipitation. In practice, however, the evaluation of a water budget is often quite complex, and extensive and time-consuming investigations are generally required [2].

Natural as well as human-induced gains and losses in water sources must be considered. The principal natural gains to surface water bodies are those resulting from direct runoff caused by precipitation and seepage of groundwater. Evapotranspiration (combined losses from evaporation from open water and transpiration from plants and soils) and unrecovered infiltration are the major natural losses. Dependable dry-season supplies can be increased through diversion from other areas, through low-flow augmentation, through saline-water conversion, and perhaps, in the future, through induced precipitation. The major human-induced losses are from diversion of flows out of the watershed.

Once the gross dependable water supply has been estimated, the net dependable supply can be determined by subtracting the quantity of water used, detained, or lost as a result of human activities from the gross supply. When water is withdrawn from a flowing

TABLE 1   Summary Data Concerning Water Resources of the Continental United States

	Square Miles	Acre · Feet ($\times 10^6$)
Gross area of continental United States	3,080,809	—
Land area, excluding inland water	2,974,726	—
Volume of average annual precipitation	—	4,750
Volume of average annual runoff (discharge to sea)	—	1,372
Estimated total usable groundwater	—	47,500
Average amount of soil moisture	—	635
Estimated total lake storage	—	13,000
Total reservoir storage (capacity of 5000 acre · ft or more)	—	365

Source: E. A. Ackerman and G. O. Löf, *Technology in American Water Development* (Baltimore, MD: The Johns Hopkins University Press, 1959).

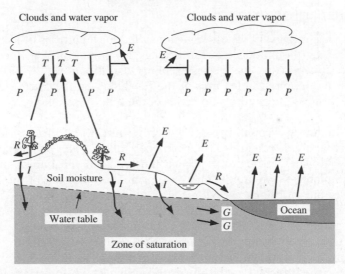

FIGURE 1   The hydrologic cycle.

stream, a decrease in flow between the point of withdrawal and the point of return is experienced. As the water is used, part of it is lost to the atmosphere through various consumptive uses that are cumulative downstream. Decreases in dependable water supply along a watercourse are the result of withdrawals of water that occur upstream.

THE WATER BUDGET

Although a water supply may be adequate for present needs, it may not be able to support future demands. Forecasts of future water requirements are needed, as are forecasts of changes in dependable water supplies. The factors that affect water requirements include population, industrial development, agricultural practices, water policy, technology, and water management practices. Very crudely, the water budget may be represented by the following mass balance equation:

$$I - O = \Delta S \tag{1}$$

where the inflows (I) are all sources of water, natural and human-made, entering the region; the outflows (O) are all movements of water out of the region, including evaporation, evapotranspiration, groundwater flow, and surface water flow; and the change in storage (ΔS) is the increase or decrease in storage over time for all natural (surface and underground) and all artificial reservoirs.

Consumption use has been defined by the American Water Works Association as water used in connection with vegetative growth or food processing, or water that is incidental to an industrial process, which is discharged to the atmosphere or incorporated in the products of the process [3]. In short, it is water that is not returned to the watershed for potential reuse.

Withdrawal use is the use of water for any purpose that requires it to be physically removed from the source. Depending on the use to which the water is put, some of it may be returned after use to the original source and be available for reuse.

Nonwithdrawal use is the use of water for any purpose that does not require it to be removed from the original source. Use for navigation and to support fish and wildlife are examples.

Certain water losses, although not "consumptive" by definition, may reduce an available water supply. For example, dead storage (storage below control or outlet elevations) in impoundments is unavailable for downstream use. Diversion of water from one drainage basin to another represents an additional form of *nonconsumptive loss*. An example of this is the use of Delaware River basin water for the municipal supply of New York City. This decreases the total flow in the Delaware River below the point of diversion. (New York is required, however, to augment low flows by compensating the downstream interests for diversion losses.) Water contaminated or polluted during use to the extent that it cannot be economically treated for reuse also constitutes a real loss from the total water supply.

2   MATHEMATICS OF HYDROLOGY

Like all natural systems, the hydrologic cycle can be defined by a number of complex and interconnected variables. These complexities are so great that it is sometimes difficult to define all of the parameters when studying a hydrologic system. These parameters relate to various chemical, physical, thermodynamic, temporal, spatial, and biological phenomena that are interconnected at various scales. For example, rainfall is a parameter that is commonly measured and used by water managers. This highly observable parameter is easy for us to understand at a basic level. However, rainfall is highly variable over time and space and the mathematical aspects of rainfall are not always easy to define with simple equations.

Smaller, less-observable parameters play an equally important role in the hydrologic cycle. Some of these less obvious parameters are considered when evapotranspiration must be estimated. For example, plant physiology brings a biological dimension to hydrology that is of critical importance in water budget analysis. In cases where rigorous, continuous simulation is needed, evapotranspiration becomes a critical loss term and vegetation must be considered at various scales.

Many hydrologists and engineers have used physical equations with great success when studying or modeling the hydrologic cycle. The speed of modern computers has increased our ability to use more complex multidimensional physical equations in a timely manner. However, for the majority of engineers and researchers, a number of simplified mathematical, probabilistic, and statistical methods are available to effectively manage the many complexities that are inherent to hydrology. These methods do not require the use of supercomputers, but they do require a strong understanding of the governing equations and assumptions behind them. Whenever a hydrologic method is employed, it is critical to understand how the method was derived and when it is appropriate to use — or not use — the method.

One important and common use of probability is in defining the frequency of extreme events. If a hydrologic event has a true recurrence interval of T_R years, the probability that this magnitude will be equaled or exceeded in any particular year is

$$P = \frac{1}{T_R} \tag{2}$$

Recurrence interval is defined as the average interval in years between the occurrence of an event of stated magnitude and an equal or more serious event.

Annual series and partial duration series are both used in estimating the recurrence intervals of extreme events [2]. An annual series is composed of one significant event for each year of record. The nature of the event depends on the object of the study. Usually the event will be a maximum or minimum flow. A partial duration series consists of all events exceeding a base value in significance. The two series compare favorably at the larger recurrence intervals, but for the smaller recurrence intervals the partial duration series will normally indicate events of greater magnitude.

There are two possibilities regarding an event: It either will or will not occur in a specified year. The probability that at least one event of equal or greater significance than the T_R-year event will occur in any series of N years is shown in Table 2. For example, there exists a probability of 0.22 that the 100-year event will occur in a design period of 25 years.

Table 2 was derived by means of the binomial distribution, which gives the probability $p(X:N)$ that a particular event will occur X times out of N trials as

$$p(X:N) = \binom{N}{X} P^X (1 - P)^{N-X}$$

$$\binom{N}{X} = \frac{N!}{X!(N - X)!} \tag{3}$$

TABLE 2   Probability That an Event Having a Prescribed Recurrence Interval
Will Be Equaled or Exceeded During a Specified Design Period

T_R (yr)	Design Period (yr)					
	1	5	10	25	50	100
1	1.0	1.0	1.0	1.0	1.0	1.0
2	0.5	0.97	0.999	1.0[a]	1.0[a]	1.0[a]
5	0.2	0.67	0.89	0.996	1.0[a]	1.0[a]
10	0.1	0.41	0.65	0.93	0.995	1.0[a]
50	0.02	0.10	0.18	0.40	0.64	0.87
100	0.01	0.05	0.10	0.22	0.40	0.63
200	0.005	0.02	0.05	0.12	0.22	0.39

[a]Values are approximate.

where P is the probability that an event will occur in each individual trial ($P = 1/T_R$ in this case). Now, if we let the number of occurrences equal zero ($X = 0$) in a given period of years N (number of trials) and substitute this value in Eq. (3) the result is

$$p(0:N) = (1 - P)^N \qquad (4)$$

This is the probability of zero events equal to or greater than the T_R-year event. The probability Z that at least one event equal to or greater than the T_R-year event will occur in a sequence of N years is then given by

$$Z = 1 - \left(1 - \frac{1}{T_R}\right)^N \qquad (5)$$

Solving Eq. (5) for various values of N and T_R provided the data for Table 2. This was a simplified discussion but probabilities and statistics provide a convenient and common way to study and analyze hydrology. Relationships among hydrology measurements, probability, and statistics are the subject of much research and analysis.

3   WATER QUALITY

Although water quality and water quantity are inextricably linked, water quality deserves special attention because of its effect on public health and the environment. Even with the large federal investments in pollution control since 1972, President George H. W. Bush's Council on Environmental Quality reported that the nation's waters continue to be damaged by pollution and misuse. Pollutants reach water bodies from both point and nonpoint sources. Municipal wastes, urban and agricultural runoff, and industrial wastes are principal offenders. Of special importance are the vestiges of past toxic and hazardous materials that are now being transported by surface water and groundwater systems. The impacts of polluting activities are widespread and they affect the public health, the economy, and the environment [4, 5].

In 1991, the United States Geological Survey (USGS) established a National Water Quality Assessment (NAWQA) Program to develop long-term consistent and comparable science-based information on national water-quality conditions. As of 2002, NAWQA assessments indicate that the waters in the United States are generally suitable as drinking water supplies, for other human and recreational uses, and for irrigation. Nevertheless, there are trouble spots. Protecting the nation's water resources from nonpoint sources emanating from pesticides, nutrients, metals, volatile organic chemicals, naturally occurring pollutants, and other contaminants remains a major problem [6].

Waterborne pathogenic microbes (Table 3) and pharmaceuticals are also potential threats to our water supplies. Various instances of gastrointestinal illnesses have been blamed on microbial pathogens in drinking water. In 1998, the Centers for Disease Control and Prevention estimated that the annual number of deaths related to microbial illnesses associated with drinking water ranges from about 900 to 1000, suggesting the existence of a serious problem [7]. Microbial contaminants such as *Cryptosporidium, Giardia, Legionella*, and the Norwalk virus are among the culprits.

TABLE 3   Some Waterborne Diseases of Concern in the United States

Disease	Microbial Agent	General Symptoms
Amebiasis	Protozoan (*Entamoeba histolytica*)	Abdominal discomfort, fatigue, diarrhea, flatulence, weight loss
Campylobacteriosis	Bacterium (*Campylobacter jejuni*)	Fever, abdominal pain, diarrhea
Cholera	Bacterium (*Vibrio cholerae*)	Watery diarrhea, vomiting, occasional muscle cramps
Cryptosporidiosis	Protozoan (*Cryptosporidium parvum*)	Diarrhea, abdominal discomfort
Giardiasis	Protozoan (*Giardia lomblia*)	Diarrhea, abdominal discomfort
Hepatitis	Virus (hepatitis A)	Fever, chills, abdominal discomfort, jaundice, dark urine
Shigellosis	Bacterium (*Shigella* species)	Fever, diarrhea, bloody stool
Typhoid fever	Bacterium (*Salmonella typhi*)	Fever, headache, constipation, appetite loss, nausea, diarrhea, vomiting, appearance of abdominal rash
Viral gastroenteritis	Viruses (Norwalk, rotavirus, and other types)	Fever, headache, gastrointestinal discomfort, vomiting, diarrhea

Source: Courtesy of the Water Resources Research Center, University of Arizona, Tucson, AZ. Table appeared in *Arroyo* 10, no. 2 (March 1998).

Pharmaceuticals have also been identified as a source of water pollution. Antibiotics, antidepressants, hormones, painkillers, steroids, and many other drugs have been identified in water bodies. Concern about these potential contaminants emerged in Europe in the 1980s, and during the 1990s it surfaced in the United States as well. As a result, the USGS has included the occurrence of human and veterinary pharmaceuticals in its assessment of emerging contaminants found in selected streams. The extent of the threat these contaminants pose to humans and animals is not well known, but research is underway to better define the scale of this problem [8].

Some of these substances, in particular those that are hormones or those that may interfere with the endocrine systems of humans and other vertebrates, are called *endocrine disruptors*. This aspect of water quality is relatively new, although previous regulations such as the Safe Drinking Water Act may provide limited authority to address endocrine disruptors. Significant research on the subject is being carried out by various universities, the Environmental Protection Agency, and the Centers for Disease Control and Prevention, among others [9]. Finally, the threat of the introduction of harmful substances into water supplies through acts of terrorism must be considered. Safeguards are needed for water treatment plants and water supply reservoirs. Both surface and groundwater quality are critical aspects of water supply and pollution control, and will be discussed more as part of this and subsequent chapters.

4   SOIL MOISTURE

Soil moisture is the most broadly used water source on the Earth's surface. Agriculture and natural plant life depend on it for sustenance, and there are countless links between soil science and water resources. The quantity of water stored as soil moisture at any specified time is small, however. Estimates indicate that it is equivalent to a layer of about 4.6 inches distributed over 57 million square miles of land surface. This in itself would be insufficient to support adequate plant growth without renewal. It is therefore important to know the frequency with which this supply is renewed and the length of time it remains available. The supply of soil moisture depends on geographical location, climatic conditions, geologic structure, and soil type. Variations may be experienced seasonally, weekly, or even daily.

The natural supply of soil moisture in most of the agricultural areas of this country is considered less than optimal for crop growth during an average year. It is evident, then, that we must have a greater understanding of optimal water requirements for crops if we are to supply water economically and efficiently to overcome natural soil moisture deficiencies.

GROUNDWATER

5   AN INTRODUCTION TO GROUNDWATER QUANTITY AND QUALITY

Groundwater is a major source of fresh water for public consumption, industrial uses, and crop irrigation. For example, more than half of the fresh water used in Florida for all purposes comes from groundwater sources, and about 90% of the state's population depends on groundwater for its potable water supply. The need to husband this resource is clear and quantity and quality dimensions are both very important.

The need for an adequate database to determine the quantity of groundwater and to estimate its change over time is very great because groundwater systems are not as easily defined as those for surface water. Groundwater storage volumes and transmission rates are affected by soil properties and geologic conditions, and these are often highly variable and not amenable to simple quantification.

Groundwater supplies are much more widely distributed than surface waters, but local variations are found as a result of the variety of soils and geologic structures beneath the land surface. The usable groundwater storage in the United States is estimated to be about 48 billion acre · ft. This vast reservoir is distributed across the nation in quantities determined primarily by precipitation, evapotranspiration, and geologic structure. There are two components to this supply: One is a part of the hydrologic cycle; the other is water trapped underground in past ages which is no longer naturally circulated in the cycle.

Figure 2 shows the principal groundwater areas of the United States as depicted by Thomas [10]. Generally, it is evident that the mountain regions in the East and West, the northern Great Plains, and the granitic and metamorphic rock areas of New England and the southern Piedmont do not contain important groundwater supplies.

Groundwater quality is influenced by the quality of its source. Changes in aquifer waters or declines in the quality of source supplies may seriously impair the quality of the groundwater supply. Municipal, commercial, and industrial wastes entering an aquifer are major sources of pollution. Large-scale organic pollution of groundwaters is infrequent, however, since significant quantities of organic wastes usually cannot be easily introduced underground. The problem is quite different with inorganic solutions, since these move easily through the soil and once introduced are removed only with great difficulty. In addition, the effects of such pollution may continue for indefinite

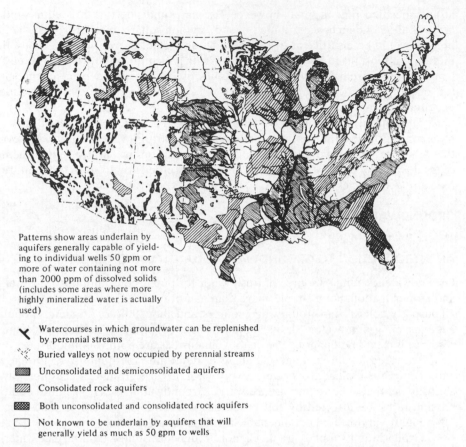

Patterns show areas underlain by
aquifers generally capable of yielding to individual wells 50 gpm or
more of water containing not more
than 2000 ppm of dissolved solids
(includes some areas where more
highly mineralized water is actually
used)

⟋ Watercourses in which groundwater can be replenished
    by perennial streams

⟋ Buried valleys not now occupied by perennial streams

▨ Unconsolidated and semiconsolidated aquifers

▨ Consolidated rock aquifers

▨ Both unconsolidated and consolidated rock aquifers

☐ Not known to be underlain by aquifers that will
    generally yield as much as 50 gpm to wells

FIGURE 2   Groundwater areas in the United States. [From H.E. Thomas, "Underground
Sources of Water," *The Yearbook of Agriculture, 1955* (Washington, DC: U.S. Government
Printing Office, 1956).]

periods since natural dilution is slow and artificial flushing or treatment is generally
impractical or too expensive.

The number of harmful enteric organisms is generally reduced to tolerable levels
by the percolation of water through 6 or 7 feet of fine-grained soil [11]. However, as the
water passes through the soil, the amounts of dissolved salts may increase significantly.
These salts are added by soluble products of soil weathering and of erosion by rainfall
and flowing water. Locations downstream of heavily irrigated areas may find that the
water they are receiving is too saline for satisfactory crop production. These saline contaminants are difficult to control because removal methods are very expensive. A possible solution is to dilute the saline-contaminated water with water of lower salt
concentration (wastewater treatment plant effluent, for example) so that the average
water produced by mixing will be suitable for use. This is a highly specialized and
important aspect of hydrogeology and environmental engineering and is the focus of
much research.

6   THE SUBSURFACE DISTRIBUTION OF WATER

Groundwater distribution may be generally categorized into zones of aeration and saturation. The *saturation zone* is one in which all the soil voids are filled with water under hydrostatic pressure. The *aeration zone*, a zone in which the interstices are filled partly with air and partly with water, may be subdivided into several subzones. Todd classifies these as follows [12]:

1. The *soil–water zone* begins at the ground surface and extends downward through the major root zone. Its total depth is variable and dependent on soil type and vegetation. The zone is unsaturated except during periods of heavy infiltration. Water is placed into three categories in this region: *hygroscopic water*, which is adsorbed from the air; *capillary water*, which is held by surface tension; and *gravitational water*, which is excess soil water draining through the soil.

2. The *intermediate zone* extends from the bottom of the soil–water zone to the top of the capillary fringe and may vary from being nonexistent to being several hundred feet thick. The zone is essentially a connecting link between the near-ground surface region and the near-water table region through which infiltrating waters must pass.

3. The *capillary zone* extends from the water table to a height determined by the capillary rise that can be generated in the soil. The capillary zone thickness is a function of soil texture and may vary not only from region to region but also within a local area.

4. At the *groundwater zone,* groundwater fills the pore spaces completely, and porosity is therefore a direct measure of storage volume. Part of this water (*specific retention*) cannot be removed by pumping or draining because of molecular and surface-tension forces. The specific retention is the ratio of the volume of water retained against gravity drainage to the gross volume of the soil.

The water that can be drained from a soil by gravity is known as the *specific yield*. It is expressed as the ratio of the volume of water that can be drained by gravity to the gross volume of the soil. Values of specific yield depend on soil particle size, shape and distribution of pores, and degree of compaction of the soil. Average values of specific yield for alluvial aquifers range from 10% to 20%. Meinzer and others have proposed numerous procedures for determining specific yield [13].

7   AQUIFERS

An *aquifer* is a water-bearing stratum capable of transmitting water in quantities sufficient to permit development of a water supply. Aquifers may be classified into four categories:

1. Those directly connected to surface supplies that are replenished by gravitational flow. Gravels found in floodplains or river valleys are examples.

2. "Regional" aquifers occurring east of the 100th meridian. These aquifers produce some of the largest permanent groundwater yields and have moderate to high rates of recharge. Good examples are found in the Atlantic and Gulf coastal plain areas.

3. Low recharge aquifers between the 100th and 120th meridians. These aquifers have relatively little inflow compared to potential or actual withdrawals. Although storage volumes are often large, the low rate of replenishment indicates that the water must be considered a nonrenewable resource—similar to mined materials. This possible "limited life" category poses significant questions related to developing and managing these aquifers for water supply.

4. Aquifers subject to saline-water intrusion. These are usually found in coastal regions, but inland saline waters also exist, primarily in the western states.

Groundwater storage is considerably greater than all artificial and natural surface storage in the United States, including the Great Lakes [4, 14]. This enormous groundwater reserve sustains the continuing outflow of streams and lakes during periods that follow storms. The relation between groundwater and surface water is one of mutual interdependence. Groundwater intercepted by a well as it moves toward a stream is the same as a diversion from the stream, for example. Developing and using surface water and groundwater sources jointly can optimize opportunities for making water available for various uses.

Aquifers may be classified as *confined* or *unconfined* depending on whether or not a water table or free water surface exists under atmospheric pressure. The storage volume within an aquifer is changed whenever water is recharged to or discharged from it. In the case of an unconfined aquifer, this may be determined using the equation

$$\Delta S = S_y \, \Delta V \tag{6}$$

where ΔS = change in storage volume, S_y = average specific yield of the aquifer, and ΔV = volume of the aquifer lying between the original water table and the water table at a later, specified time.

For saturated, confined aquifers, pressure changes produce only slight changes in storage volume. In this case, the weight of the overburden is supported partly by hydrostatic pressure and partly by the solid material in the aquifer. When the hydrostatic pressure in a confined aquifer is reduced by pumping or other means, the load on the aquifer increases, causing its compression, with the result that some water is forced from it. Decreasing the hydrostatic pressure also causes a small expansion, which in turn produces an additional release of water. For confined aquifers, the water yield is expressed in terms of a storage coefficient, S_c. This storage coefficient may be defined as the volume of water that an aquifer takes in or releases per unit surface area of aquifer per unit change in head normal to the surface. Figure 3 illustrates the classifications of aquifers.

In addition to water-bearing strata exhibiting satisfactory rates of yield, there are also non-water-bearing and impermeable strata. An *aquiclude* is an impermeable stratum that may contain large quantities of water but whose transmission rates are not high enough to permit effective development. An *aquifuge* is a formation that is impermeable and devoid of water.

Any circumstance that alters the pressure imposed on underground water will also cause a variation in the groundwater level. Seasonal factors, changes in stream and river stages, evapotranspiration, atmospheric pressure changes, winds, tides, external

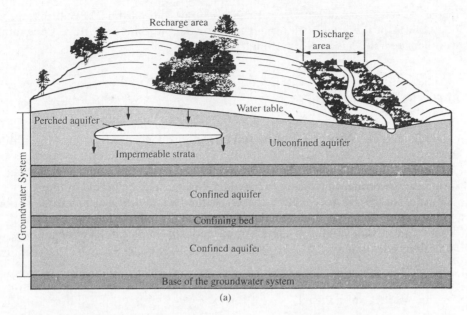

(a)

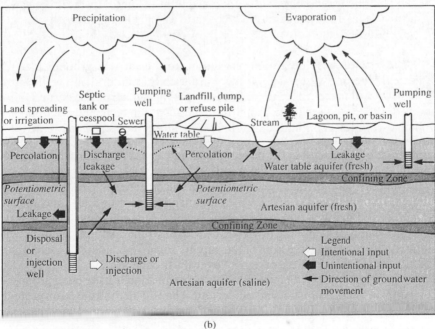

(b)

FIGURE 3   Definition sketches of groundwater systems and mechanisms for recharge and withdrawal. (a) Aquifer notation [15]. (b) Components of the hydrologic cycle affecting groundwater [16].

loads, various forms of withdrawal and recharge, and earthquakes all may produce fluctuations in the level of the water table or the piezometric surface, depending on whether the aquifer is free or confined [12].

8   SAFE YIELD OF AN AQUIFER

Before a groundwater source is developed for use, the quantity of water that it can be expected to deliver must be estimated. This is known as the *safe yield* of the aquifer — the quantity of water that can be withdrawn annually without the aquifer's being depleted. Other related terms are defined as follows:

1. The *maximum sustained yield* is the maximum rate at which water can be continuously withdrawn from a given source.
2. The *permissive sustained yield* is the maximum rate at which continuous withdrawals can be made legally and economically for beneficial use without undesired results.
3. The *maximum mining yield* is the total storage volume in a given source that can be withdrawn and used.
4. The *permissive mining yield* is the maximum volume of water that can be withdrawn legally and economically to be used for beneficial purposes without causing an undesired result.

A review of these definitions should make it clear that groundwater resources are finite. If the drafts imposed on them are such that natural and artificial recharge mechanisms will make up for these losses over time, no harm will occur. On the other hand, if drafts exceed recharge, groundwater storage can be mined out or depleted to a level below which economic development is infeasible. Some areas in the United States where perennial overdrafts occur are shown in Figure 4 [4, 12].

Hill, Harding, Simpson, and others [12] have proposed methods for determining safe yield. The Hill method is based on groundwater studies in southern California and Arizona. In this method, the annual change in the elevation of the groundwater table or piezometric surface is plotted against the annual draft. The data points can be fitted by a straight line, provided that the water supply to the basin is fairly uniform.

The draft that corresponds to zero change in elevation is considered to be the safe yield. The period of record should be such that the supply during this period approximates the long-time average supply. Even though the draft during the period of record may be an overdraft, the safe yield can be determined by extending the line of best fit to an intersection with the zero change in elevation line. An example of this procedure is given in Figure 5.

It is important to understand that the safe yield of an aquifer can change over time if the conditions under which it was determined do not remain constant. This requires drafts, recharge rates, and other conditions affecting the safe yield to be monitored.

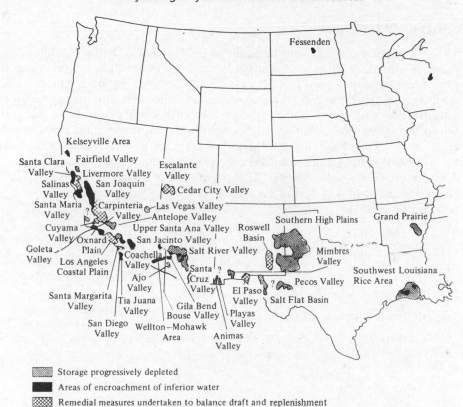

FIGURE 4   Groundwater reservoirs with perennial overdraft. [From H. E. Thomas, "Underground Sources of Water," *The Yearbook of Agriculture, 1955* (Washington, DC: U.S. Government Printing Office, 1956).]

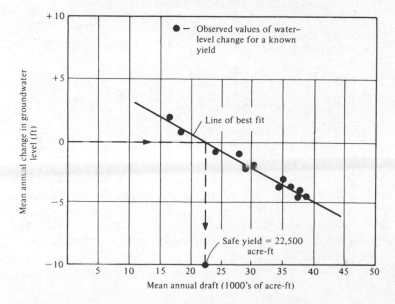

FIGURE 5   Example of determination of the safe yield by the Hill method.

9   GROUNDWATER FLOW

The rate of movement of water through the ground is of an entirely different magnitude from that through natural or artificial channels or conduits. Typical values range from 5 feet per day to a few feet per year. Groundwater in motion can be described as saturated or unsaturated. *Saturated groundwater flow* refers to situations in which water fills all void spaces of the porous media that is being considered. *Unsaturated flow* refers to flow in which both water and air are present within the porous media in question [17]. Only simplified examples of saturated flow will be discussed in this text.

For one-dimensional saturated flow, a classical empirical equation can be used to describe the flow of groundwater. This equation was developed by Henry Darcy in Dijon, France in 1856 as part of his famous laboratory experiments [17]. *Darcy's law* [18] may be stated as

$$Q = -KA\frac{dh}{dx} \tag{7}$$

where

Q = flow across the control area A

K = hydraulic conductivity of the material

A = total cross-sectional area, including the space occupied by the porous material

In Eq. (7),

$$h = z + \frac{p}{\gamma} + C \tag{8}$$

where

h = piezometric head

z = elevation above a datum

p = hydrostatic pressure

C = an arbitrary constant

γ = specific weight of water

If the specific discharge $q = Q/A$ is substituted into Eq. (7), then

$$q = -K\frac{d}{dx}\left(z + \frac{p}{\gamma}\right) \tag{9}$$

Note that q also equals the porosity n multiplied by the pore velocity V_p. Darcy's law is widely used in groundwater flow problems. Applications are illustrated later in this chapter.

Darcy's law is limited in its applicability to flow in the laminar region. To determine whether laminar flow is taking place, the *Reynolds number* must be checked:

$$N_R = Vd/v \tag{10}$$

In this equation,

$$V = \text{flow velocity}$$
$$d = \text{mean grain diameter}$$
$$v = \text{kinematic viscosity}$$

Groundwater flow may be considered laminar for Reynolds numbers less than 1. Departure from laminar conditions normally occurs within the range of Reynolds numbers from 1 to 10, depending on grain size and shape. Under most conditions encountered, with the exception of regions close to collecting devices, the flow of groundwater is laminar and Darcy's law applies.

Example 1

1. Find the Reynolds number for the portion of an aquifer distant from any collection device where water temperature is 50°F ($v = 1.41 \times 10^{-5}$ ft²/s), flow velocity is 1.0 ft/day, and mean grain diameter is 0.09 in.
2. Find the Reynolds number for a flow 4 ft from the centerline of a well being pumped at a rate of 3800 gpm if the well completely penetrates a confined aquifer 28 ft thick. Assume a mean grain diameter of 0.10 in, a porosity of 35%, and $v = 1.41 \times 10^{-5}$ ft²/s.

Solution:

1. Using Eq. (10), we obtain

$$N_R = \frac{Vd}{v}$$

where

$$V = \frac{1.0}{86,400} \text{ fps} \qquad d = \frac{0.09}{12} \text{ ft}$$

$$N_R = \frac{1.0}{86,400} \times \frac{0.09}{12} \times \frac{1}{1.41 \times 10^{-5}}$$

$$= 0.0062 \text{ (indicating laminar flow)}$$

2. Using Eq. (10) yields

$$N_R = \frac{Vd}{v} = \frac{Q}{A} \frac{d}{v}$$

$$Q = 3800 \times 2.23 \times 10^{-3} = 8.46 \text{ cfs}$$

$$V = 8.46/2\pi \, rh \times \text{porosity}$$

$$= 8.46/8\pi \times 28 \times 0.35$$

$$= 0.0344 \text{ fps}$$

$$N_R = \frac{0.0344 \times 0.10}{1.41 \times 10^{-5} \times 12} = 20.3 \text{ (beyond Darcy's law range)}$$

To compute discharge, Eq. (7) can be used. Note that this equation may also be stated as

$$Q = pAkS \qquad (11)$$

where

p = porosity or ratio of void volume to total volume of the mass

A = gross cross-sectional area

k = intrinsic permeability

S = slope of hydraulic gradient

By combining k and p into a single term, Eq. (11) may be written in its most common form,

$$Q = KAS \qquad (12)$$

Several ways of expressing *hydraulic conductivity* K may be found in the literature. The USGS defines *standard hydraulic conductivity* K_S as the number of gallons of water per day that will flow through a medium of 1-ft^2 cross-sectional area under a hydraulic gradient of unity at 60°F. The field coefficient of permeability is obtained directly from the standard coefficient by correcting for temperature:

$$K_f = K_s \, (\mu_{60}/\mu_f) \qquad (13)$$

Here,

K_f = field coefficient

μ_{60} = dynamic viscosity at 60°F

μ_f = dynamic viscosity at field temperature

An additional term that is much used in groundwater computations is the *coefficient of transmissibility*, T. It is equal to the field coefficient of permeability multiplied by the saturated thickness of the aquifer in feet. Using this terminology, Eq. (11) may also be written

$$Q = T \times \text{section width} \times S \qquad (14)$$

Table 4 gives typical values of the standard hydraulic conductivity for a range of sedimentary materials. It should be noted that the permeabilities for specific materials vary widely. Traces of silt and clay can significantly decrease the permeability of an aquifer. Differences in particle orientation and shape can cause striking changes in permeability within aquifers composed of the same material. Careful evaluation of geologic and geotechnical information is essential if realistic values of permeability are to be identified for use in groundwater flow computations.

TABLE 4   Some Values of the Standard Hydraulic Conductivity and Intrinsic Permeability for Several
Classes of Materials

Material	Approximate Range K_s (gpd/ft^2)	Approximate Range k (darcys)
Clean gravel	10^6–10^4	10^5–10^3
Clean sands; mixtures of clean gravels and sands	10^4–10	10^3–1
Very fine sands; silts; mixtures of sands, silts, clays; stratified clays	10–10^{-3}	1–10^{-4}
Unweathered clays	10^{-3}–10^{-4}	10^{-4}–10^{-5}

Example 2

Laboratory tests on an aquifer material indicate a standard hydraulic conductivity $K_s = 1.08 \times 10^3$ gpd/ft^2. If the field temperature is 70°F, find the field hydraulic conductivity K_f.

Solution: Using Eq. (13),

$$K_f = K_s\left(\frac{\mu_{60}}{\mu_f}\right)$$

and using the values of the kinematic viscosity given in Table 8 in the Appendix for 60 and 70°F, 1.21×10^{-5} and 1.06×10^{-5}, respectively, we get

$$K_f = \frac{1.08 \times 10^3 \times 1.21 \times 10^{-5}}{1.06 \times 10^{-5}} = 1232.8 \text{ gpd/ft}^2$$

Note that the absolute viscosity and the kinematic viscosity are related as

$$v = \frac{\mu}{\rho} \tag{15}$$

and given that the density of water over the range of temperatures in this case is virtually constant, values for the kinematic viscosity may be used in place of those for the absolute velocity in Eq. (13).

10   HYDRAULICS OF WELLS

The collection of groundwater is accomplished mainly through the use of wells or infiltration galleries. Numerous factors affect the performance of these collection works and they must be taken into account when mathematical models are used to make estimates. Some cases are amenable to solution through the use of relatively simple mathematical expressions; others require the use of sophisticated mathematical models. Several approaches will be discussed here. The reader is cautioned not to be misled by the simplicity of some of the solutions presented and should understand that many of these are special-case solutions and are not applicable to all groundwater flow problems. A more complete treatment of groundwater and seepage problems may be found in numerous sources [12, 14, 17, 19, 20].

The structure of wells as well as construction techniques for drilling and completing wells are covered in many specialty publications. Well systems generally have three components—well structure, pump, and discharge piping. The well itself contains an open section through which water enters and a casing through which the flow is transported to the ground surface. The open section is usually a perforated casing, or a slotted metal screen, that permits water to enter and at the same time prevents the hole from collapsing. Occasionally gravel is placed at the bottom of the well casing around the screen. Only vertical wells will be discussed in this section, although horizontal wells are gaining popularity for some specialty water supply applications.

When a well is pumped, water is removed from the aquifer immediately adjacent to the screen. To replenish this withdrawal, flow then becomes established at locations some distance from the well. Owing to the resistance to flow offered by the soil, a head loss is encountered and the piezometric surface next to the well is depressed. This is known as the *cone of depression* (Figure 6). The cone of depression spreads until a condition of equilibrium is reached and steady-state conditions are established.

The hydraulic characteristics of an aquifer (which are described by the storage coefficient and the aquifer permeability) can be determined by laboratory or field tests. The three most commonly used field methods are the application of tracers, use of field permeameters, and aquifer performance tests [4, 14]. Aquifer performance tests are discussed here along with the development of flow equations for wells. Aquifer performance tests are classified as equilibrium or nonequilibrium. For equilibrium tests, the cone of depression must be stabilized for the flow equation to be derived. The first performance tests based on equilibrium conditions were published by Thiem in 1906 [21]. In nonequilibrium

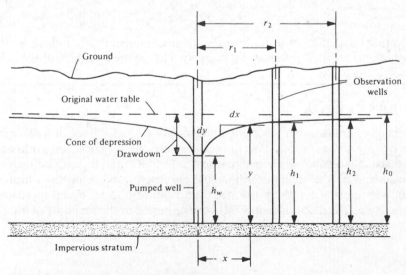

FIGURE 6   Well in an unconfined aquifer.

tests the derivation of the flow equation takes into consideration the condition that steady-state conditions have not been reached.

The basic equilibrium equation for an unconfined aquifer can be derived using the notation of Figure 6. In this case, the flow is assumed to be radial, the original water table is considered to be horizontal, the well is considered to fully penetrate an aquifer of infinite areal extent, and steady-state conditions are considered to prevail. Using these assumptions, the flow toward a well at any location x from the well equals the product of the cylindrical element of area at that section and the flow velocity. Using Darcy's law, this becomes

$$Q = 2\pi x y K_f \frac{dy}{dx} \tag{16}$$

where

$$2\pi x y = \text{area at any section}$$

$$K_f dy/dx = \text{flow velocity}$$

$$Q = \text{discharge, cfs}$$

Integrating over the limits specified below yields

$$\int_{r_2}^{r_2} Q \frac{dx}{x} = 2\pi K_f \int_{h_2}^{h_1} y \, dy \tag{17}$$

$$Q \ln\left(\frac{r_2}{r_1}\right) = \frac{2\pi K_f(h_2^2 - h_1^2)}{2} \tag{18}$$

and

$$Q = \frac{\pi K_f(h_2^2 - h_1^2)}{\ln(r_2/r_1)} \tag{19}$$

This equation may then be solved for K_f to yield

$$K_f = \frac{1055Q \log(r_2/r_1)}{h_2^2 - h_1^2} \tag{20}$$

where ln has been converted to log, K_f is in gallons per day per square foot, Q is in gallons per minute, and r and h are measured in feet. If the drawdown is small compared with the total aquifer thickness, an approximate formula for the discharge of the pumped well can be obtained by inserting h_w for h_1 and the height of the aquifer for h_2 in Eq. (19).

The basic equilibrium equation for a confined aquifer can be obtained in a similar manner, using the notation of Figure 7. The same assumptions apply. Mathematically, the flow in cubic feet per second may be determined as follows:

$$Q = 2\pi x m K_f \frac{dy}{dx} \tag{21}$$

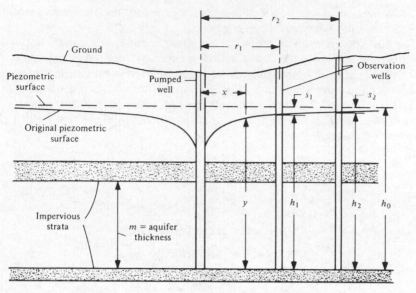

FIGURE 7   Radial flow to a well in a confined aquifer.

Integrating, we obtain

$$Q = 2\pi K_f m \frac{h_2 - h_1}{\ln(r_2/r_1)} \tag{22}$$

The coefficient of permeability may be determined by rearranging Eq. (22) to the form

$$K_f = \frac{528Q \log(r_2/r_1)}{m(h_2 - h_1)} \tag{23}$$

where Q is in gallons per minute, K_f is the permeability in gallons per day per square foot, and r and h are measured in feet.

Example 3

Find the hydraulic conductivity of an artesian aquifer being pumped by a fully penetrating well. The aquifer is 100 ft thick and composed of medium sand. The steady-state pumping rate is 1000 gpm. The drawdown at an observation well 50 ft away is 10 ft; in a second observation well 500 ft away it is 1 ft.

Solution: Using Eq. (23), we obtain

$$K_f = \frac{528Q \log(r_2/r_1)}{m(h_2 - h_1)}$$

$$= \frac{528 \times 1000 \times 10}{100 \times (10 - 1)}$$

$$= 586.7 \text{ gpd/ft}^2$$

Example 4

A 20-in. well fully penetrates an unconfined aquifer of 100-ft depth. Two observation wells located 90 and 240 ft from the pumped well are known to have drawdowns of 23 and 21.5 ft respectively. If the flow is steady and $K_f = 1400$ gpd/ft^2, find the discharge from the well.

Solution: Eq. (20) is applicable, and for the given units this is

$$Q = \frac{K(h_2^2 - h_1^2)}{1055 \log(r_2/r_1)}$$

$$\text{Log}(r_2/r_1) = \log(240/90) = 0.42651$$

$$h_2 = 100 - 21.5 = 78.5 \text{ ft}$$

$$h_1 = 100 - 23 = 77 \text{ ft}$$

$$Q = \frac{1400(78.5^2 - 77^2)}{1055 \times 0.42651}$$

$$= 725.7 \text{ gpm}$$

For a steady-state well in a uniform flow field where the original piezometric surface is not horizontal, a somewhat different situation from that previously assumed prevails. Consider the artesian aquifer shown in Figure 8. The previously assumed circular area of influence becomes distorted in this case. This problem may be solved by applying potential theory or by graphical means, or, if the slope of the piezometric surface is very slight, Eq. (22) may be applied without serious error.

Referring to the definition sketch of Figure 8, a graphical solution to this type of problem will be discussed. First, an orthogonal flow net consisting of flow lines and equipotential lines must be constructed. The construction should be performed so that the completed flow net will be composed of a number of elements that approach little squares in shape. A comprehensive discussion cannot be provided here, but Harr [19] is a good source of information on this subject for the interested reader.

Once the net is complete, it may be analyzed by considering the net geometry and using Darcy's law in the manner of Todd [12]. In the definition sketch of Figure 8, the hydraulic gradient is

$$h_g = \frac{\Delta h}{\Delta s} \tag{24}$$

and the flow increment between adjacent flow lines is

$$\Delta q = K \frac{\Delta h}{\Delta s} \Delta m \tag{25}$$

where, for a unit thickness, Δm represents the cross-sectional area. If the flow net is properly constructed so that it is orthogonal and composed of little square elements,

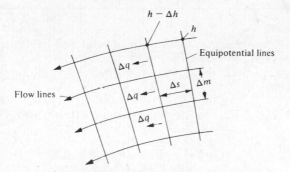

Definition Sketch of a Segment of a Flow Net

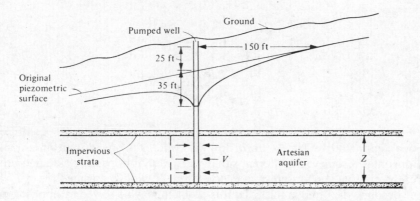

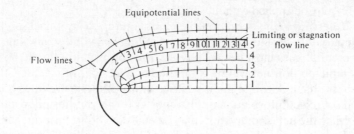

FIGURE 8   Well in a uniform flow field and flow-net definition.

then

$$\Delta m \approx \Delta s \qquad (26)$$

and

$$\Delta q = K \Delta h \qquad (27)$$

Now consider the entire flow net,

$$\Delta h = \frac{h}{n} \tag{28}$$

where n is the number of subdivisions between equipotential lines. If the flow is divided into m sections by the flow lines, the discharge per unit width of the aquifer will be

$$q = \frac{Kmh}{n} \tag{29}$$

Knowledge of the aquifer permeability and the flow-net geometry permits solution of Eq. (29).

Example 5

Find the discharge to the well in Figure 8 by using the applicable flow net. Consider that the aquifer is 35 ft thick, K_f is 3.65×10^{-4} fps, and the other dimensions are as shown.

Solution: Using Eq. (29),

$$q = \frac{Kmh}{n}$$

where

$$h = (35 + 25) = 60 \text{ feet}$$
$$m = 2 \times 5 = 10$$
$$n = 14$$

we obtain
$$q = \frac{3.65 \times 10^{-4} \times 60 \times 10}{14}$$
$$= 0.0156 \text{ cfs per unit thickness of the aquifer}$$

The total discharge Q is thus

$$Q = 0.0156 \times 35 = 0.55 \text{ cfs} \qquad \text{or} \qquad 245 \text{ gpm}$$

When a new well is first pumped, a large portion of the discharge is produced directly from the storage volume released as the cone of depression develops. Under these circumstances, the equilibrium equations overestimate permeability and therefore the yield of the well. Where steady-state conditions are not encountered—as is usually the case in practice—a nonequilibrium equation must be used. Two approaches can be taken, the rather rigorous method of Theis or a simplified procedure such as that proposed by Cooper and Jacob [22, 23].

In 1935, Theis published a nonequilibrium approach that takes into consideration time and the storage characteristics of an aquifer. Application of the method is appropriate for confined aquifers of constant thickness. For use under conditions of unconfined flow, vertical components of flow must be negligible, and changes in aquifer storage through water expansion and aquifer compression must also be negligible relative to the gravity drainage of pores as the water table drops as a result of pumping.

Theis states that the drawdown in an observation well located at a distance r from the pumped well is given by

$$s = \frac{Q}{4\pi T} \int_u^\infty \frac{e^{-u}}{u} du \qquad (30)$$

where Q = constant pumping rate ($L^3 T^{-1}$ units), T = aquifer transmissivity ($L^2 T^{-1}$ units), and u is a dimensionless variable defined by

$$u = r^2 \frac{S_c}{4tT} \qquad (31)$$

where r is the radial distance from the pumping well to an observation well, S_c is the aquifer storativity (dimensionless), and t is time. The integral in Eq. (30) is commonly called the *well function of u* and is written as $W(u)$. It can be evaluated from the infinite series

$$W(u) = -0.577216 - \ln u + u - \frac{u^2}{2 \times 2!} + \frac{u^3}{3 \times 3!} \cdots \qquad (32)$$

Using this notation, Eq. (30) may be written as

$$s = \frac{QW(u)}{4\pi T} \qquad (33)$$

The basic assumptions of the Theis equation are generally the same as those in Eq. (23) except for the non-steady-state condition. Some values of the well function of u are given in Table 5.

In U.S. practice, Eqs. (30) and (31) commonly appear in the form

$$s = \frac{114.6Q}{T} \int_u^\infty \frac{e^{-u}}{u} du \qquad (34)$$

$$u = \frac{1.87r^2 S_c}{Tt} \qquad (35)$$

where T is in units of gpd/ft, Q has units of gpm, and t is the time in days since the start of pumping.

Equations (30) and (31) can be solved by comparing a log–log plot of u versus $W(u)$, known as a "type curve," with a log–log plot of the observed data r^2/t versus s. In plotting the type curve, $W(u)$ is the ordinate and u is the abscissa. The two curves are superimposed and moved about until some of their segments coincide. In doing this, the axes must be maintained parallel. A coincident point is then selected on the matched curves and both plots are marked. The type curve then yields values of u and $W(u)$ for

TABLE 5   Values of $W(u)$ for Various Values of u

u	1.0	2.0	3.0	4.0	5.0	6.0	7.0	8.0	9.0
$\times 1$	0.219	0.049	0.013	0.0038	0.0011	0.00036	0.000038	0.000012	0.000012
$\times 10^{-1}$	1.82	1.22	0.91	0.70	0.56	0.45	0.37	0.31	0.26
$\times 10^{-2}$	4.04	3.35	2.96	2.68	2.47	2.30	2.15	2.03	1.92
$\times 10^{-3}$	6.33	5.64	5.23	4.95	4.73	4.54	4.39	4.26	4.14
$\times 10^{-4}$	8.63	7.94	7.53	7.25	7.02	6.84	6.69	6.55	6.44
$\times 10^{-5}$	10.94	10.24	9.84	9.55	9.33	9.14	8.99	8.86	8.74
$\times 10^{-6}$	13.24	12.55	12.14	11.85	11.63	11.45	11.29	11.16	11.04
$\times 10^{-7}$	15.54	14.85	14.44	14.15	13.93	13.75	13.60	13.46	13.34
$\times 10^{-8}$	17.84	17.15	16.74	16.46	16.23	16.05	15.90	15.76	15.65
$\times 10^{-9}$	20.15	19.45	19.05	18.76	18.54	18.35	18.20	18.07	17.95
$\times 10^{-10}$	22.45	21.76	21.35	21.06	20.84	20.66	20.50	20.37	20.25
$\times 10^{-11}$	24.75	24.06	23.65	23.36	23.14	22.96	22.81	22.67	22.55
$\times 10^{-12}$	27.05	26.36	25.96	25.67	25.44	25.26	25.11	24.97	24.86
$\times 10^{-13}$	29.36	28.66	28.26	27.97	27.75	27.56	27.41	27.28	27.16
$\times 10^{-14}$	31.66	30.97	30.56	30.27	30.05	29.87	29.71	29.58	29.46
$\times 10^{-15}$	33.96	33.27	32.86	32.58	32.35	32.17	32.02	31.88	31.76

Source: After L. K. Wenzel, "Methods for Determining Permeability of Water Bearing Materials with Special Reference to Discharging Well Methods," U.S. Geological Survey, Water-Supply Paper 887, Washington, DC, 1942.

the selected point. Corresponding values of s and r^2/t are determined from the plot of the observed data. Inserting these values into Eqs. (30) and (31) and rearranging the equations yields values for the transmissibility T and the storage coefficient S_c.

This procedure can often be shortened and simplified. When r is small and t large, Jacob found that values of u are generally small [23]. Thus, the terms in the series of Eq. (32) beyond the second term become negligible and the expression for T becomes

$$T = \frac{264Q(\log t_2 - \log t_1)}{h_0 - h} \qquad (36)$$

which can be further reduced to

$$T = \frac{264Q}{\Delta h} \qquad (37)$$

where

Δh = drawdown per log cycle of time, $(h_0 - h)/(\log t_2 - \log t_1)$

Q = well discharge, gpm

h_0 and h are defined as shown in Figure 7, and T is the transmissibility in gallons per day per foot. Field data on drawdown $h_0 - h$ versus t are plotted on semilogarithmic paper. The drawdown is plotted on the arithmetic scale as shown in Figure 9. This plot

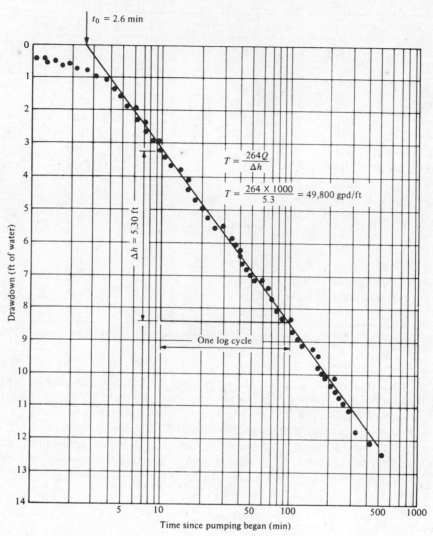

FIGURE 9   Pumping test data.

forms a straight line, the slope of which permits the determination of the formation constants using Eq. (37) and

$$S_c = \frac{0.3Tt_0}{r^2}$$ (38)

where t_0 is the time that corresponds to zero drawdown.

Example 6

Using the data given in Figure 9, find the coefficient of transmissibility T and the storage coefficient S_c for the aquifer, given $Q = 1000$ gpm and $r = 300$ ft.

Solution: Find the value of Δh from the graph. This is 5.3 ft. Then, using Eq. (37), we obtain

$$T = \frac{264Q}{\Delta h} = \frac{264 \times 1000}{5.3}$$
$$= 49{,}800 \text{ gpd/ft}$$

Using Eq. (38) yields

$$S_c = \frac{0.3Tt_0}{r^2}$$

Note from Figure 9 that $t_0 = 2.6$ min. Converting to days, this becomes

$$t_0 = 1.81 \times 10^{-3} \text{ days}$$

and

$$S_c = \frac{0.3 \times 49.800 \times 1.81 \times 10^{-3}}{(300)^2}$$
$$= 0.0003$$

Example 7

Find the drawdown at an observation point 300 ft away from a pumping well. It has been found that $T = 2.8 \times 10^4$ gpd/ft, the pumping time is 15 days, the storativity is $= 2.7 \times 10^{-4}$, and $Q = 275$ gpm.

Solution: From Eq. (35), u can be computed as

$$u = \frac{1.87r^2 S_c}{Tt}$$

$$u = [1.87 \times (300)^2 \times 2.7 \times 10^{-4}]/[2.8 \times 10^4 \times 15] = 1.08 \times 10^{-4}$$

Referring to Table 5 and interpolating, we estimate $W(u)$ to be 8.62. Using Eq. (34), the drawdown is then found to be

$$s = \frac{114.6Q}{T} \int\limits_u^\infty \frac{e^{-u}}{u} du$$

$$s = \frac{[114.6 \times 275 \times 8.62]}{[2.8 \times 10^4]} = 9.70 \text{ ft}$$

Example 8

A well is being pumped at a constant rate of 0.004 m³/s. Given that $T = 0.0025$ m²/s, $r = 100$ meters, and the storage coefficient $= 0.00087$, find the drawdown in the observation well for a period of (a) 15 min, and (b) 20 hr.

Solution: (a) Using Eq. (31), u can be computed as follows:

$$u = \frac{r^2 S_c}{4tT}$$

$$u = [100 \times 100 \times 0.00087]/[4 \times 15 \times 60 \times 0.0025]$$

$$u = 0.97$$

Then, from Table 4, $W(u)$ is found to be 0.23.
Applying Eq. (33), the drawdown can be determined:

$$s = \frac{QW(u)}{4\pi t}$$

$$s = [0.004 \times 0.23]/[4 \times \pi \times 0.0025]$$

$$s = 0.029 \text{ m}$$

(b) Follow the procedure used in (a):

$$u = [100 \times 100 \times 0.00087]/[4 \times 72{,}000 \times 0.0025]$$

$$u = 0.0121$$

From Table 4, $W(u)$ is found to be 8.49.
Applying Eq. (33), the drawdown can be determined:

$$s = [0.0004 \times 8.49]/[4 \times \pi \times 0.0025]$$

$$s = 1.08 \text{ m}$$

11 BOUNDARY EFFECTS

Only the effect of pumping a single well has been considered here. But if more than one well is pumped in a region, a composite effect (interference) due to the overlap of the cones of depression of the individual will result. In this case, the drawdown at any location is obtained by summing the individual drawdowns of the various wells involved. An additional problem is that of boundary conditions. The previous derivations have been based on the supposition of a homogeneous aquifer of infinite areal extent. A situation such as this is rarely encountered in practice. Computations based on this assumption are often sufficiently accurate, however, provided that field conditions closely approximate the basic hypotheses. Boundary effects may be evaluated by using the theory of image wells proposed by Lord Kelvin, through the use of electrical and membrane analogies, and through the use of relaxation procedures. For a detailed discussion of these topics, the reader is referred to the many references on groundwater flow [12, 14, 17].

12 REGIONAL GROUNDWATER SYSTEMS

Methods discussed so far have related mostly to the flow of water to individual wells. But regional well fields are common, and analysis of these systems is complex. An in-depth treatment of this subject is beyond the scope of this book, but some basic concepts related to analyzing regional groundwater systems can be introduced [2, 14, 17, 24–34].

In almost all cases, regional groundwater systems are analyzed using mathematical models. These models consist of sets of equations representing the physical, chemical, biological, and other processes that occur in an aquifer. The models may be deterministic, probabilistic (also called *stochastic*), or a combination of the two. The discussions that follow are limited to deterministic mathematical models. These models describe physical relationships stemming from known features of the system under study. Figure 10 characterizes the procedure for developing a deterministic mathematical model. First, a

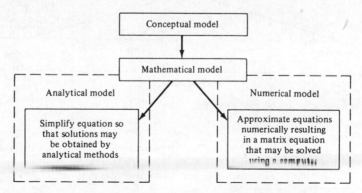

FIGURE 10   Logic diagram for developing a mathematical model.
(Courtesy of the National Water Well Association, Worthington, OH.)

conceptual model is formulated that is based on a study of the region of interest and that takes into consideration the mechanics of groundwater flow. This is translated into a mathematical model of the system, which usually consists of a set of partial differential equations accompanied by appropriate boundary and initial conditions. Continuity and conservation of momentum considerations are featured in the model and are represented over the extent of the region of concern. Darcy's law, discussed earlier, is widely used to describe conservation of momentum. Other model features include artesian or water table condition designation and a dimensionality that is one-, two-, or three-dimensional. Where the modeling objective includes water quality or heat transport considerations, other equations describing conservation of mass for the chemical constituents involved and conservation of energy are required. Typically used relationships are Fick's law for chemical diffusion and Fourier's law for heat transport.

Once a conceptual model has been designed, the next step is to translate it into a workable model by introducing needed assumptions. The model is then formulated for solution using numerical methods such as finite difference or finite elements to represent the governing partial differential equations. When the finite difference approach is used, the groundwater region is divided into grid elements and the continuous variables are represented as discrete variables at nodal points in the grid. In this way the continuous differential equation defining head or other features is replaced by a finite number of algebraic equations that define the head or other variables at nodal points. Such models find wide application in predicting site-specific aquifer behavior. Although a choice of model should be based on the study involved, numerical models have proven to be effective where irregular boundaries, heterogeneities, or highly variable pumping or recharge rates are expected [24]. Figure 11 indicates four types of groundwater models and their application.

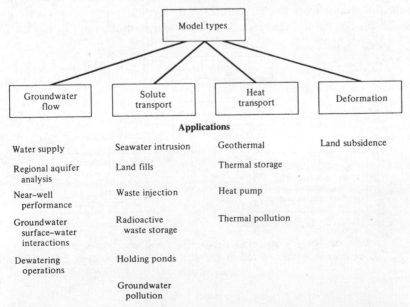

FIGURE 11   Types of groundwater models and typical applications. (Courtesy of the National Water Well Association, Worthington, OH.)

Normally, several steps are involved in the modeling process. These include data collection and preparation, matching of observed histories, and predictive simulation. The first step in data preparation involves specifying the region's boundaries. These may be physical, such as an impervious layer, or arbitrary, such as the choice of some small subregion. Once the overall boundaries have been defined, the region is divided into discrete elements by superimposing a rectangular or polygonal grid (see Figure 12).

After the grid type has been selected, the modeler must specify the controlling aquifer parameters (such as storage coefficients, transmissivities, etc.) and set initial conditions. This must be accomplished for each grid element. Where solute transport models are required, additional parameters such as hydrodynamic dispersion properties must also be specified. Results of model runs include determination of hydraulic heads at node points for each time step during the period of interest. Where solute and

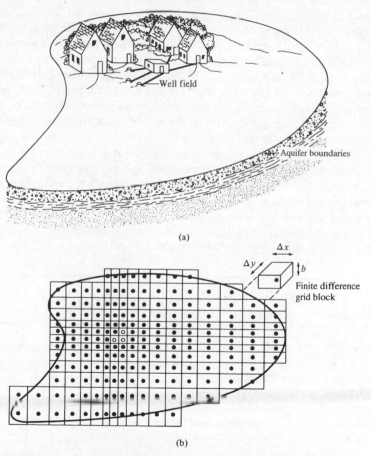

(a)

(b)

FIGURE 12   (a) Map view of aquifer showing well field and boundaries. (b) Finite difference grid for aquifer study, where Δx is the spacing in the x direction, Δy is the spacing in the y direction, and b is the aquifer thickness. Solid dots: block-center nodes; open circles: source-sink nodes. (Courtesy of the National Water Well Association, Worthington, OH.)

heat transport are involved, concentrations of constituents and temperatures may also be determined at the nodes for each time interval.

After the aquifer parameters have been set, the model is operated using the initial values and the output is checked with recorded history. This process is known as *history matching* and is used to refine parameter values and to determine boundaries and flow conditions at the boundaries. Historic conditions and modeled conditions are compared and parameters adjusted until satisfactory fits are obtained. This is known as the *calibration process*. There is, however, no rule that specifies when adequate matching is achieved. This determination must be made by the modeler based on an understanding of the problem and the use to which the model's results are to be put.

Once calibration is completed, the model can be used to analyze many types of management and development options so that the outcomes of these courses of action can be assessed. Observing model performance under varying conditions is an asset in determining courses of action to be prescribed for future aquifer operation or development. Groundwater models may be used to estimate natural and artificial recharge, effects of boundaries, effects of well location and spacing, effects of varying rates of drawdown and recharge, rates of movement of hazardous wastes, and saltwater intrusion [24].

Although groundwater models have much to recommend them, caution must be exercised if the models are not to be misused. According to Prickett, there are three common ways to misuse models [25]: overkill, inappropriate prediction, and misinterpretation. To avoid such pitfalls, the modeler and model user must be fully aware of the limitations and sources of errors in the model used. In particular, they should understand the underlying assumptions.

Several public domain computer codes for solving groundwater flow problems are referenced in Table 6. These codes become models when the groundwater system being studied is described to the code by inputting the system geometry and known internal operandi (aquifer and flow field parameters, initial and boundary conditions, and water use and flow stresses applied over time to all or parts of the system). Codes fall generally into four major categories: groundwater flow codes, solute transport codes, particle tracking codes, and aquifer test data analysis programs [29].

TABLE 6   Public Domain Computer Codes for Groundwater Modeling

Acronym for Code	Description	Source	Year
Groundwater flow models			
PLASM	Two-dimensional finite difference	Ill. SWS	1971
MODFLOW	Three-dimensional finite difference	USGS	1988
AQUIFEM-1	Two- and three-dimensional finite element	MIT	1979
GWFLOW	Package of seven analytical solutions	IGWMC	1975
GWSIM-II	Storage and movement model	TDWR	1981
GWFL3D	Three-dimensional finite difference	TDWR	1991
MODRET	Seepage from retention ponds	USGS	1992

Solute transport models

SUTRA	Dissolved substance transport model	USGS	1980
RANDOMWALK	Two-dimensional transient model	Ill. SWS	1981
MT3D	Three-dimensional solute transport	EPA	1990
AT123D	Analytical solution package	DOE	1981
MOC	Two-dimensional solute transport	USGS	1978
HST3D	3-D heat and solute transport model	USGS	1992

Particle tracking models

FLOWPATH	Two-dimensional steady state	SSG	1990
PATH3D	Three-dimensional transient solutions	Wisc. GS	1989
MODPATH	Three-dimensional transient solutions	USGS	1991
WHPA	Analytical solution package	EPA	1990

Aquifer test analyses

TECTYPE	Pump and slug test by curve matching	SSG	1988
PUMPTEST	Pumping and slug test	IGWMC	1980
THCVFIT	Pumping and slug test	IGWMC	1989
TGUESS	Specific capacity determination	IGWMC	1990

Note: IGWMC = International Groundwater Modeling Center; Ill. SWS = Illinois State Water Survey; SSG = Scientific Software Group; EPA = Environmental Protection Agency; USGS = U.S. Geological Survey; Wisc. GS = Wisconsin Geological Survey; MIT = Massachusetts Institute of Technology; TDWR = Texas Department of Water Resources; DOE = Department of Energy.

13   SALTWATER INTRUSION

Saltwater contamination of freshwater aquifers can be a major water quality problem in island locations; in coastal areas; and occasionally inland, as in Arizona, where some aquifers contain highly saline waters. Because freshwater is lighter than saltwater (specific gravity of seawater is about 1.025), it will usually float above a layer of saltwater. When an aquifer is pumped, the original equilibrium is disturbed and saltwater replaces the freshwater. Under equilibrium conditions, a drawdown of 1 foot in the freshwater table will result in a rise in the saltwater of approximately 40 feet. Pumping rates of wells subject to saltwater intrusion must therefore be strictly controlled. In coastal areas, recharge wells are sometimes used to maintain a sufficient head to prevent seawater intrusion. Injection wells have been used effectively in this manner in southern California.

A prime example of freshwater contamination by seawater was recorded in Long Island, New York [35]. During the first part of the 20th century, the rate of pumping far exceeded the natural recharge rate. The problem was further complicated because stormwater runoff from the highly developed land areas was transported directly to the sea. This precluded the opportunity for this water to return to the ground. As pumping continued, the water table dropped well below sea level and saline water entered the aquifer. The result was such a serious impairment of local water quality that Long Island was forced to transport its water supply from upper New York State.

14   GROUNDWATER RECHARGE

The volumes of groundwater replaced annually through natural mechanisms are relatively small because of the slow rates of movement of groundwater and the limited opportunity for surface water to penetrate the earth's surface. Artificial recharge has been used to supplement this natural recharge process since the turn of the last century. As early as the mid-1950s, over 700 million gallons of water per day were being artificially recharged in the United States [36]. This water was derived from natural surface sources and returns from air conditioning, industrial wastes, and municipal water supplies. The total recharge volume was, however, equal to only about 1.5% of the groundwater withdrawn that year. In California, artificial recharge is at present a primary method of water conservation. During 1957 and 1958, a daily recharge volume of about 560 million gallons was reported for 63 projects in that state alone [36].

Numerous methods are employed in artificial recharge operations. One of the most common is the use of holding basins. The usual practice is to impound the water in a series of reservoirs arranged so that the overflow of one will enter the next, and so on. These artificial storage works are generally formed by constructing dikes or levees. A second method is the modified streambed, which makes use of the natural water supply. The stream channel is widened, leveled, scarified, or treated by a combination of methods to increase its recharge capabilities. Ditches and furrows are also used. The basic types of arrangement are the contour type, in which the ditch follows the contour of the ground; the lateral type, in which water is diverted into a number of small furrows from the main canal or channel; and the tree-shaped or branching type, in which water is diverted from the primary channel into successively smaller canals and ditches. Where slopes are relatively flat and uniform, flooding provides an economical means of recharge. The normal practice is to spread the recharge water over the ground at relatively shallow depths so as not to disturb the soil or native vegetation. An additional method is to use injection wells. Recharge rates are normally lower than pumping rates for the same head conditions, however, because of the clogging that is often encountered in the area next to the well casing. Clogging may result from the entrapment of fine aquifer particles, from suspended material in the recharge water that is subsequently strained out and deposited in the vicinity of the well screen, from air binding, from chemical reactions between recharge and natural waters, and from bacteria. For best results, the recharge water should be clear, contain little or no sodium, and be chlorinated.

15   CONCURRENT DEVELOPMENT OF GROUNDWATER AND SURFACE WATER SOURCES

The maximum practical conservation of our water resources depends on the coordinated development of groundwater and surface water supplies. Geologic, hydrologic, economic, and legal factors affect the process.

Concurrent use is primarily founded on the premise of transference of impounded surface water to groundwater storage at optimal rates [37, 38]. Annual water requirements are generally met by surface storage, while groundwater storage is used to meet cyclic requirements covering periods of dry years. The operational procedure involves a lowering of groundwater levels during periods of below-average precipitation and a subsequent raising of levels during wet years. Transfer rates of surface waters to underground storage must be large enough to ensure that surface water reservoirs will be drawn down sufficiently to permit impounding significant volumes during periods of high runoff. To provide the required maximum transfer capacity, methods of artificial recharge such as spreading, ponding, injecting, or returning flows from irrigation must be used.

The coordinated use of groundwater and surface water sources results in the provision of larger quantities of water at lower costs. As an example, it has been found that the conjunctive operation of the Folsom Reservoir (California) and its groundwater basin yields a conservation and utilization efficiency of approximately 82% compared with about 51% efficiency for the operation of the surface reservoir alone [39]. There is little doubt that groundwater resources should be considered very carefully in planning for large-scale water development projects.

In general, the analysis of a conjunctive system consisting of a dam and an aquifer requires solving three fundamental problems. The first is to establish the design criteria for the dam and the recharge facilities. The second is to determine the service area for the combined system. The third is to develop a set of operating rules that defines the reservoir drafts and pumpages to be taken from the aquifer. A mathematical model for an analysis such as this has been proposed by Buras [37].

SURFACE WATER

16   AN INTRODUCTION TO SURFACE WATER QUANTITY AND QUALITY

Surface waters are nonuniformly distributed over the earth's surface. Of the U.S. land mass, only about 4% is covered by rivers, lakes, and streams. The volumes of these freshwater sources depend on geographic, landscape, and temporal variations and on the impact of human activities.

For surface waters, historic records of stream flows, lake levels, and climatic data are used to identify trends and to indicate deficiencies in databases. Since surface water supplies are always in transition, models become valuable tools for estimating future water supply scenarios based on assumed sequences of hydrologic variables, such as precipitation, temperature, and evapotranspiration and for projected physical manipulations of the surface water containment system. The verification of hydrologic models depends heavily on adequate historic data for calibration, and, where data voids and errors exist, every effort should be made to fill them.

Surface water supplies may be categorized as *perennial* or *continuous* unregulated rivers, rivers or streams containing impoundments, or natural lakes. Evaluating the capability of a region's surface water resources to sustain various uses requires assembling data on the climate, hydrology, water quality, geology, and topography of the area. Information on industrial, agricultural, and residential development (population centers) is also needed, as are forecasts of future changes in these categories. An assessment of the region's natural resources and the impact their development would have on the watershed's hydrology and economy is also of value.

Approximately 30% of the average annual rainfall in the United States becomes surface runoff. The allocation of this water is directly related to precipitation patterns and thus to meteorologic, geographic, topographic, and geologic conditions. In the West, large regions are devoid of permanent runoff, and some localities, such as Death Valley, California, receive no runoff for years at a time. In contrast, some areas in the Pacific Northwest average about 6 feet of runoff annually. Mountain regions are usually the most productive of runoff, whereas flat areas, especially those experiencing less precipitation, generally produce relatively little runoff.

Runoff is distributed nonuniformly over the continental United States. It is subject to seasonal and annual variations influenced by climate and weather. For example, about 75% of the runoff in the semiarid and arid regions of the United States occurs during the few weeks following snowmelt in the upper portion of the watershed. Even in the well-watered East, an uneven distribution of runoff prevails, and this has an impact on the availability of water for various competing uses. The four major runoff regions in the United States are depicted in Figure 13.

The primary causes of deterioration of surface water quality are municipal and domestic wastewater, industrial and agricultural wastes (organic, inorganic, heat), solid/semisolid refuse, and non-point-source pollution. Since the passage of the Clean Water Act, many of the pollution point sources in the United States have been addressed. Since non-point-source pollution results from almost any human activity, reduction of non-point-source pollution still remains one of the most challenging aspects of surface water management.

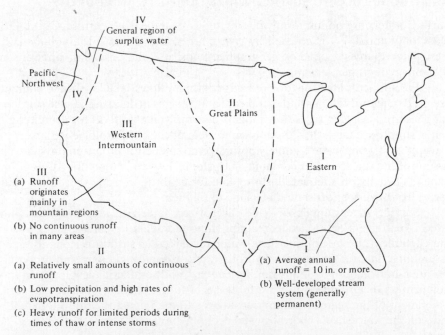

FIGURE 13   Major runoff regions of the United States.

17   SURFACE WATER STORAGE

Water may be stored for single or multiple purposes such as navigation, flood control, hydroelectric power, irrigation, municipal water supply, pollution abatement, recreation, and flow augmentation. Either surface or subsurface storage can be used, but both require the use of a reservoir or reservoirs.

Reservoirs regulate stream flow for beneficial use by storing water for later release. *Regulation* can be defined as the amount of water stored or released from storage in a period of time, usually one year. The ability of a reservoir to regulate river flow depends on the ratio of its capacity to the volume of flow in the river. The regulation provided by existing storage facilities can be evaluated by studying the records of typical reservoirs. Information on the usable capacity, detention period, and annual regulation of a number of reservoirs having detention periods from 0.01 of a year to 20 years is given by Langbein [40].

About 190 million acre · ft of water, representing approximately 13% of the total river flow, has been made available through reservoir storage development in the United States [38]. The degree of storage development is variable but is generally greatest in the Colorado River basin and least in the Ohio River basin. Substantial increases in water supply can be attained by developing additional storage, but water regulation of this type follows a law of diminishing returns. There are limitations on the amount of storage that can be used. The storage development of the Colorado River basin, for example, may be approaching (if not already in excess of) the maximum useful limit.

18   RESERVOIRS

Where natural storage in the form of ponds or lakes is not available, artificial impoundments or reservoirs can sometimes be built to optimize the development of surface water flows. The amount of storage needed is a function of expected demands and the quantity of inflow to the impoundment. Mathematically this may be stated as

$$\Delta S = I - O \tag{39}$$

where ΔS = change in storage volume during a specified time interval, I = total inflow volume during this period, and O = total outflow volume during this period. Normally, O is the draft requirement imposed by the various uses, but it may also include evaporation, flood discharges during periods of high runoff, and seepage from the bottom or sides of the reservoir. It is also important to note the similarity of Eq. (39) to Eq. (1). Both equations point to the importance of the use of control volumes and the conservation of mass in water resources.

Because the natural inflow to any impoundment area is often highly variable from year to year, season to season, or even day to day, the reservoir function must be that of redistributing inflow with respect to time so that projected demands are satisfied. Several approaches may be taken to calculate reservoir capacities. Actual or synthetic records of stream flow and a knowledge of the proposed operating rules of the reservoir are fundamental to all solutions. Storage may be determined by graphical or analytical techniques. With the speed of modern computers, a continuous simulation is almost always the preferred method for reservoir design when adequate resources are available. *Continuous simulation* refers to the use of a dataset that is many years in duration (usually more than 10) that must include extreme hydrologic conditions such as large floods and droughts. Reservoirs may be simulated by third-party software packages or spreadsheets. The most important factor in selecting these models is to ensure that the model uses appropriate governing equations and assumptions for the situation that is being modeled.

Commonly, storage calculations are based on comparing demands with a critical low flow period such as the most severe drought on record. Once the critical period is chosen, the required storage is usually determined using a mass-curve analysis introduced in 1883 by Rippl [41]. This method evaluates the cumulative deficiency between outflow and inflow $(O - I)$ and selects the maximum cumulative value as the required storage. Examples 9 and 10 illustrate the procedure.

Example 9

Find the storage capacity required to provide a safe yield of 67,000 acre·ft/yr for the data given in Figure 14.

Solution: Construct tangents at *A, B*, and *C* having slopes equal to 67,000 acre·ft/yr. Find the maximum vertical ordinate between the inflow mass curve and the constructed draft rates. From Figure 14, the maximum ordinate is 38,000 acre·ft, which is the required capacity.

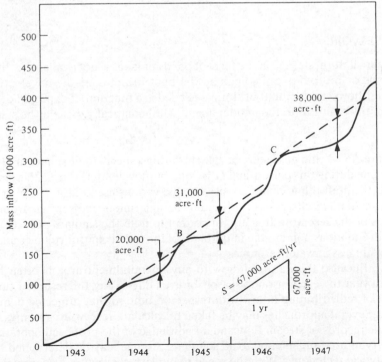

FIGURE 14   Reservoir capacity for a specified yield as determined by use of a mass curve.

This example shows that the magnitude of the required storage capacity depends entirely on the time period chosen. Since the period of record given covers only 5.5 years, it is clear that a design storage of 38,000 acre · ft might be totally inadequate for the next 3 years, for example. Unless the frequency of the flow conditions used in the design is known, little can be said regarding the long- or short-term adequacy of the design.

Example 9 also illustrates the fact that the period during which storage must be provided depends on hydrologic conditions. Since *reservoir yield* is defined as the amount of water that can be supplied during a specific interval, choice of the interval is critical. For distribution reservoirs, one day is often sufficient. For large impounding reservoirs, several months, a year, or several years may be required.

Example 10

Consider an impounding reservoir that is expected to provide for a constant draft of 637 million gallons (mil gal)/mi^2/yr. The following record of monthly mean inflow values represents the critical or design period. Find the storage requirement. Data on monthly inflows are given in Table 7 in Column 2.

Solution: The calculations are shown on the spreadsheet given in Table 7. It can be seen that the maximum cumulative deficiency is 202.2 mil gal/mi^2, which occurs in September. The number of months of draft is 202.2/53.1 = 3.8, or, stated differently, enough water must be stored to supply the region for about 3.8 months.

This example gives a numerical answer to the question posed in determining a storage design. It does not, however, give an expression for the probabilities of the shortages or excesses that may result from this design. Past practice has been to use the

TABLE 7 Spreadsheet Storage Requirement Calculations

Month	Inflow (*I*)	Draft (*O*)	Inflows Sum Of ΣI	Deficiency (*O* − *I*)	Deficiency[a] Cumulative $\Sigma(I - O)$
J	37.2	53.1	37.2	15.9	15.9
F	64.8	53.1	102	−11.7	0
M	108	53.1	210	−54.9	0
A	12	53.1	222	41.1	41.1
M	8.4	53.1	230.4	44.7	85.8
J	9.6	53.1	240	43.5	129.3
J	2.4	53.1	242.4	50.7	180
A	33.6	53.1	276	19.5	199.5
S	50.4	53.1	326.4	2.7	202.2
O	129.6	53.1	456	−76.5	0
N	117.6	53.1	573.6	−64.5	0
D	26.4	53.1	600	26.7	26.7
J	60	53.1	660	−6.9	0

[a]Only positive values of cumulative deficiency are tabulated.

lowest recorded flow of the stream as the critical period. Obviously, this approach overlooks the possibility that a more serious drought might occur, with a resultant yield less than the anticipated safe yield.

19   LOSSES FROM STORAGE

The availability of water impounded in a reservoir is affected by losses in storage that result from natural or artificial phenomena. Natural losses occur through evaporation, seepage, and siltation, while artificial losses result from withdrawals.

After a dam has been built and the impoundment filled, the exposed water surface area is increased significantly over that of the natural stream. The result is a greatly increased opportunity for evaporation. The opportunity for generation of runoff from the flooded land is also eliminated, but this loss is countered by gains made through the catchment of direct precipitation. These *water surface effects* tend to result in net gains in well-watered regions, but in arid lands losses are typical, since evaporation generally exceeds precipitation.

The magnitude of seepage losses depends mainly on the geology of the region. If porous strata underlie the reservoir valley, considerable losses can occur. On the other hand, where permeability is low, seepage may be negligible. A thorough geotechnical investigation is a prerequisite to the adequate evaluation of such losses and should certainly be a significant part of the design of any reservoir or impoundment. Also, since the useful life of a reservoir can be significantly affected by the deposition of sediment, a knowledge of sedimentation rates is important in reaching a decision regarding the feasibility of its construction [4, 40].

The rate and characteristics of the sediment inflow can be controlled by using sedimentation basins, providing vegetative screens, and employing various erosion control techniques [4]. Dams can also be designed so that part of the sediment load can be passed through or over them. A last resort is the physical removal of sediment deposits. Normally this is not economically feasible.

Example 11

Determine the expected life of the Lost Valley Reservoir. The initial capacity of the reservoir is 45,000 acre · ft. and the average annual inflow is 76,000 acre · ft. A sediment inflow of 176 acre · ft/yr is reported. Assume that the useful life of the reservoir is exceeded when 77.8% of the original capacity is lost.

Solution: The solution is obtained through application of the data given in Figure 14. The results are tabulated in Table 8.

TABLE 8   Determination of Probable Life of the Lost Valley Reservoir

(1)	(2)	(3)	(4)	(5)	(6)	(7)
Reservoir Capacity (acre · ft)	Volume Increment (acre · ft)	Capacity Inflow Ratio: (1) ÷ 76,000	Percent Sediment Trapped, from Fig. 4	Percent Sediment Trapped per Volume Increment	Average Acre-Ft Sediment Trapped Annually: (5) × 176	Number of Years Required to Fill the Volume Increment: (2) ÷ (6)
45,000	5000	0.59	96.5			
40,000	5000	0.52	96.1	96.3	169	30
35,000	5000	0.46	95.8	95.9	169	30
30,000	5000	0.39	95.0	95.4	168	30
25,000	5000	0.33	94.5	94.7	167	30
20,000	5000	0.26	93.0	93.8	165	30
15,000	5000	0.20	92.0	92.5	163	31
10,000	5000	0.13	88.0	90.0	158	32
Total number of years of useful life						213

Problems of the type illustrated in Examples 10 and 11 are especially suited to the use of spreadsheet analyses. These and analytic tools offer opportunity for quick adjustments to parameters and speedy recalculation of values.

20   IMPACTS OF CLIMATE CHANGE ON GLOBAL HYDROLOGY

Traditionally, engineers did not consider the impacts of climate change on the systems they designed. This approach is now being reconsidered in many parts of the world as the evidence of climate change mounts and the widespread effects on water resources and the environment become more apparent. In many parts of the world, definitive actions have been taken to address this topic. In the United States, climate change remains a somewhat controversial topic in some circles.

Many questions related to climate change and global hydrology must be answered. At the most basic level, is it going to be warmer or cooler and will storm intensities increase or decrease? Also to be considered are the impact of temperature on the amount of water that will be available to the region and the time when this water will be available. For example, if a temperature increase were to occur with no change in precipitation, the net water availability would be reduced as a result of higher rates of evapotranspiration. Furthermore, water managers must consider many important and complicated aspects of water quality in relation to climate change.

The many reports by the Intergovernmental Panel on Climate Change (IPCC) are good sources of information on potential climate change impacts. The Panel's many working groups regularly report on a variety of climate change topics, including mitigation of potential impacts. Their *Climate Change 2007: Impacts, Adaptation and Vulnerability Summary for Policymakers* noted many issues related to global hydrology.

The report notes that all continents and most oceans are being affected by the impacts of climate change. Among these effects are changes in snow, ice, and permafrost related to higher temperatures. These changes (loss of glacial ice, rock avalanches in colder mountainous regions, etc.) are also reported along with changes to Arctic and Antarctic ecosystems [42]. The IPCC's website at http://www.ipcc.ch/, in addition to the many online scientific resources dedicated to climate change, is an excellent source of information on this topic.

Changes in soil moisture and runoff resulting from increased or decreased precipitation could significantly affect water supplies for municipalities, agriculture, industry, environmental protection, and other purposes. Changes in precipitation would certainly increase the uncertainty of frequency analysis. Since these return frequencies are based on historical data and are used to design infrastructure, the potential impacts to both humans and the environment would be significant. The five major global climate prediction models all predict an increase in average worldwide precipitation. This would also be associated with soil moisture increases. However, the precipitation increase is not projected to be uniform across the world [43]. In fact, some regions are projected to have decreases in precipitation and thereby decreased soil moisture. Some inconsistencies are apparent in the analyses of climate change model results, and it is clear that the predictions of changes in local and regional hydrology are far from perfect.

It can be argued that the potential effects of global climate change on water resources could be more serious than the actual warming of the earth. This is particularly true for regions where surface water supplies are generated from water stored in snowpacks in the mountains. Such a situation exists in the southwestern United States where the Colorado River is a major source of water supply for cities in Southern California and Arizona. The Colorado River Basin covers southwestern Wyoming, western Colorado, eastern Utah, all of Arizona, and small portions of southern Nevada, northwestern New Mexico, and southeastern California. In those regions, even if total precipitation does not change while temperatures rise, a decreasing water supply would be the outcome.

Our climate predictions are not perfect, but model results provide an insight into what might be expected under a variety of global change scenarios. The water policy implications of global climate change are significant and must be taken into account in planning for water resources development and management. Actions should be taken now to reduce the potential impacts of climate change. Many of these actions relate to improving water use efficiency and considering environmental impacts during all of our professional and personal activities. These are wise courses of action even if unfavorable climate change scenarios do not unfold.

PROBLEMS

1 Compare the amounts of water required by the various users in your state. What is the relative worth of water in its various uses?

2 A flow of 100 mgd is to be developed from a 190-mi^2 watershed. At the flow line the area's reservoir is estimated to cover 3900 acres. The annual rainfall is 40 in, the annual runoff is 14 in, and the annual evaporation is 49 in. Find the net gain or loss in storage this represents. Calculate the volume of water evaporated in acre · ft and cubic meters.

3 A flow of 4.8 m^3/s is to be developed from a 500-km^2 watershed. At the flow line, the area's reservoir is estimated to cover 1700 hectares. The annual rainfall is 97 cm, the annual runoff is 30 cm, and the annual evaporation is 120 cm. Find the net gain or loss in storage this represents. Calculate the volume of water evaporated in cubic meters.

4 Discuss how you would go about collecting data for an analysis of the water budget of a region. What agencies would you contact? What other sources of information would you seek out?

5 For an area of your choice, make a plot of mean monthly precipitation versus time. Explain how this fits the pattern of seasonal water uses for the area. Will the form of precipitation be an important consideration?

6 Given the following 10-yr record of annual precipitation, plot a rough precipitation frequency curve. Tabulate the data to be plotted and show the method of computation. The data are annual precipitation in inches: 28, 21, 33, 26, 29, 27, 19, 28, 18, 22. (*Note:* The frequency in percent of years is $1/T_R \times 100$.)

7 Given the 10-yr record of annual precipitation that follows, develop and plot a precipitation frequency curve. The precipitation values in cm are 70, 54, 89, 66, 75, 69, 48, 72, 46, and 56.

8 An impounding reservoir is expected to provide a constant draft of 448 million gallons per square mile per year. The following record of monthly mean inflow values (mg per sq. mi. per month) represents the critical or design period. Find the storage required.

Mo	F	M	A	M	J	J	A	S	O	N	D	J	F
In	31	54	90	10	7	8	2	28	42	108	98	22	50

9 Over a 100-mi^2 surface area, the average level of the water table for an unconfined aquifer has dropped 10 ft due to the removal of 128,000 acre $\cdot$ ft of water from the aquifer. Determine the storage coefficient. The specific yield is 0.2 and the porosity is 0.22.

10 Over a 100-mi^2 surface area, the average level of the piezometric surface for a confined aquifer has dropped 400 ft due to long-term pumping. Determine the volume of water, in acre-feet, pumped from the aquifer. The porosity is 0.3 and the coefficient of storage is 0.0002.

11 Find a maximum reservoir storage requirement if a uniform draft of 726,000 gpd/mi^2 from a river is to be maintained. The following record of average monthly runoff values is given (mg per sq. mi. per month):

Mo	A	M	J	J	A	S	O	N	D	J	F	M	A	M	J
R	97	136	59	14	6	5	3	7	19	13	74	96	37	63	49

12 Using the information given in Table 2, plot recurrence interval in years as the ordinate and the design period in years as the abscissa and construct a series of recurrence interval–design period probabilities that an event will not be exceeded during the design period. Use arithmetic coordinate paper. [*Note:* For use in this problem, probabilities in the table must be subtracted from 1.0. Where sufficient information is not provided by the table, probabilities may be computed using $P_n = (1 - 1/T_R)^n$, *where n is the design period in years.*]

13 Given the following 50-month record of mean monthly discharge, find the magnitude of the 20-month low flow. The consecutive average monthly flows (cfs) were 14, 17, 19, 21, 18, 16, 18, 25, 29, 32, 34, 33, 30, 28, 20, 23, 16, 14, 12, 13, 16, 13, 12, 12, 13, 14, 16, 13, 12, 11, 10, 12, 10, 9, 8, 7, 6, 4, 6, 7, 8, 9, 11, 9, 8, 6, 7, 9, 13, 17.

14 Given the following data relating mean annual change in groundwater level in ft to mean annual draft in thousands of acre-feet, find the safe yield.

Change in GW level	+1	+2	−1	−3	−4	+1.5	+1.2	−2.6
Mean annual draft	23	19	31	42	44	21	19	33

15 Given the following data relating mean annual change in groundwater level in ft to mean annual draft in thousands of acre-feet, find the safe yield.

GW level	−2	+2.5	−4	+0.5	−3	+2	−2.5	−0.5	+0.5	−2
Annual draft	26	14	36	21.5	32	13	32.5	26	19	28

16 What would the maximum continuous constant yield be from a reservoir having a storage capacity of 750 acre · ft? Give your results in acre · ft/yr and m^3/yr.

17 If a constant annual yield rate of 1500 gpm was required, what reservoir capacity would be needed to sustain it? Give the capacity in acre · ft/yr.

18 A mean draft of 100 mgd is to be developed from a 150 mi^2 catchment area. At the flow line, the reservoir is estimated to be 4000 acres. The annual rainfall is 38 in, the mean annual runoff is 13 in, and the mean annual evaporation is 49 in. Find the net gain or loss in storage that this represents. Compute the volume of water evaporated. State this figure in a form such as the number of years the volume could supply a given community.

19 For the following data and using the well and flow-net configuration of Figure 8, find the discharge using a flow-net solution. The well is fully penetrating; $K = 2.87 \times 10^{-4}$ ft/s, $(a) = 180$ ft, $(b) = 43$ ft, and $(c) = 50$ ft.

20 Rework Problem 19 using $K = 8.4 \times 10^{-5}$ m/s, (a) = 100 m, (b) = 22 m, and $(c) = 35$ m.

21 Use the following data: $Q = 60,000$ ft^3/day, $T = 6200$ ft^3/day, $t = 30$ days, $t = 1$ ft, and $S_c = 6.4 \times 10^{-4}$. Consider this a nonequilibrium problem. Find the drawdown s. Note that for

$$u = 8.0 \times 10^{-10} \qquad W(u) = 20.37$$
$$u = 9.0 \times 10^{-10} \qquad W(u) = 20.25$$

22 Determine the permeability of an artesian aquifer being pumped by a fully penetrating well. The aquifer is composed of medium sand and is 90 ft thick. The steady-state pumping rate is 850 gpm. The drawdown of an observation well 50 ft away is 10 ft, and the drawdown in a second observation well 500 ft away is 1 ft.

23 An 18-in well fully penetrates an unconfined aquifer of 100-ft depth. Two observation wells located 100 and 235 ft from the pumped well have drawdowns of 22.2 and 21 ft, respectively. If the flow is steady and $K_f = 1320$ gpd/ft^2, what is the discharge?

24 Find the drawdown at an observation point 200 ft away from a pumping well, given that $T = 3.0 \times 10^4$ gpd/ft, the pumping time is 12 days, $S_c = 3.0 \times 10^{-4}$, and $Q = 300$ gpm.

25 A well is being pumped at a constant rate of 0.0038 cubic meters per second. Given that $T = 0.0028$ m^2/s, $r = 90$ m, and the storage coefficient $= 0.00098$, find the drawdown in the observation well for a time period of (a) 1000 s and (b) 20 hr.

26 A well is being pumped at a constant rate of 0.004 m^3/s. Given that $T = 0.0028$ m^3/s, $r = 100$ m, and the storage coefficient $= 0.001$, find the drawdown in the observation well for a time period of (a) 1 hr and (b) 24 hr.

27 A well is being pumped at a constant rate of 0.003 m^3/s. Given that $T = 0.0028$ m^3/s, the storage coefficient $= 0.001$, and the time since pumping began is 12 hr, find the drawdown in an observation well for a radial distance of (a) 150 m and (b) 500 m.

28 A 12-in well fully penetrates a confined aquifer 100 ft thick. The coefficient of permeability is 600 gpd/ft^2. The difference in drawdown between two test wells 45 and 120 ft away is 8 ft. Find the rate of flow delivered by the well.

29 Determine the permeability of an artesian aquifer being pumped by a fully penetrating well. The aquifer is composed of medium sand and is 100 ft thick. The steady-state pumping rate is 1200 gpm. The drawdown in an observation well 75 ft away is 14 ft, and the drawdown in a second observation well 500 ft away is 1.2 ft. Find K_f in gpd/ft^2.

30 Consider a confined aquifer with a coefficient of transmissibility $T = 680$ ft^3/day/ft. At $t = 5$ min, the drawdown $s = 5.6$ ft; at 50 min, $s = 23.1$ ft; and at 100 min, $s = 28.2$ ft. The observation well is 75 ft away from the pumping well. Find the discharge of the well.

31 Assume that an aquifer is being pumped at a rate of 300 gpm. The aquifer is confined and the pumping test data are given below. Find the coefficient of transmissibility T and the storage coefficient S for $r = 60$ ft.

Time since pumping started (min)	1.3	2.5	4.2	8.0	11.0	100.0
Drawdown s (ft)	4.6	8.1	9.3	12.0	15.1	29.0

32 Find the drawdown at an observation point 250 ft away from a pumping well, given that $T = 3.1 \times 10^4$ gpd/ft, the pumping time is 10 days, $S_c = 3 \times 10^{-4}$, and $Q = 280$ gpm.

33 A 12-in. well fully penetrates a confined aquifer 100 ft thick. The coefficient of permeability is 600 gpd/ft^2. The difference in drawdown between two test wells 40 and 120 ft away is 9 ft. Find the rate of flow delivered by the well.

34 Find the permeability of an artesian aquifer being pumped by a fully penetrating well. The aquifer is 130 ft thick and is composed of medium sand. The steady-state pumping rate is 1300 gpm. The drawdown in an observation well 65 ft away is 12 ft and in a second well 500 ft away it is 1.2 ft. Find K_f in gpd/ft^2.

35 Consider a confined aquifer with a coefficient of transmissibility of 700 ft^3/day/ft. At $t = 5$ min, the drawdown is 5.1 ft; at 50 min, $s = 20.0$ ft; at 100 min, $s = 26.2$ ft. The observation well is 60 ft from the pumping well. Find the discharge from the well.

36 An 18-in well fully penetrates an unconfined aquifer 100 ft deep. Two observation wells 90 and 235 ft from the pumped well are known to have drawdowns of 22.5 ft and 20.6 ft, respectively. If the flow is steady and $K_f = 1300$ gpd/ft^2, what is the discharge?

37 A well is pumped at the rate of 500 gpm under nonequilibrium conditions. For the data given below, find the formation constants S and T. Use the Theis method.

r^2/t	Average Drawdown H (ft)
1,250	3.24
5,000	2.18
11,250	1.93
20,000	1.28
45,000	0.80
80,000	0.56
125,000	0.38
180,000	0.22
245,000	0.15
320,000	0.10

38 A well fully penetrates the 100-ft depth of a saturated unconfined aquifer. The drawdown at the well casing is 40 ft when equilibrium conditions are established using a constant discharge of 50 gpm. What is the drawdown when equilibrium is established using a constant discharge of 66 gpm?

39 A confined aquifer 80 ft deep is being pumped under equilibrium conditions at a rate of 700 gpm. The well fully penetrates the aquifer. Water levels in observation wells 150 and 230 ft from the pumped well are 95 and 97 ft, respectively. Find the field coefficient of permeability.

REFERENCES

[1] E. A. Ackerman and G. O. Löf, *Technology in American Water Development* (Baltimore: The Johns Hopkins Press, 1959).

[2] W. Viessman, Jr., and G. L. Lewis, *Introduction to Hydrology*, 5th ed. (Upper Saddle River, NJ: Prentice Hall, 2003).

[3] Task Group A4, D1, "Water Conservation in Industry," *J. Am. Water Works Assoc.* 45 (December 1958).

[4] W. Viessman, Jr., and C. Welty, *Water Management: Technology and Institutions* (New York: Harper & Row, 1985), 44–45.

[5] W. Viessman, Jr., "United States Water Resources Development," *Natl. Forum* 69, (1) (Winter 1989): 6, 7.

[6] P. A. Hamilton, "Water-Quality Patterns in Some of the Nation's Major River Basins and Aquifers," *Water Resources Impact*, 4, no. 4 (July 2002).

[7] J. Gelt, "Microbes Increasingly Viewed as Water Quality Threat," *Arroyo* 10, no. 2, Water Resources Research Center, University of Arizona, Tucson, AZ (March 1998).

[8] "Pharmaceuticals in Our Water Supplies," *Arizona Water Resource*, Water Resources Research Center, University of Arizona, Tucson, AZ (July–August 2000).

[9] http://www.epa.gov/scipoly/oscpendo/pubs/edspoverview/primer.htm

[10] H. E. Thomas, "Underground Sources of Water," *The Yearbook of Agriculture, 1955* (Washington, DC: U.S. Government Printing Office, 1956).

[11] J. Hirshleifer, J. DeHaven, and J. Milliman, *Water Supply—Economics, Technology, and Policy* (Chicago: University of Chicago Press, 1960).

[12] D. K. Todd, *Ground Water Hydrology* (New York: Wiley, 1960).

[13] O. E. Meinzer, "Outline of Methods of Estimating Ground Water Supplies," U.S. Geological Survey Water Supply Paper No. 638C (Washington, DC: U.S. Government Printing Office, 1932).

[14] R. A. Freeze and J. A. Cherry, *Groundwater* (Englewood Cliffs, NJ: Prentice-Hall, 1979).

[15] R. C. Heath, "Groundwater Regions of the United States," U.S. Geological Survey Water Supply Paper No. 2242 (Washington, DC: U.S. Government Printing Office, 1984).

[16] U.S. Environmental Protection Agency, "The Report to Congress: Waste Disposal Practices and Their Effects on Groundwater," Executive Summary, U.S. EPA, PB 265–364 (1977).

[17] J. Bear, *Hydraulics of Groundwater* (Mineola, NY: Dover Publications. Mineola, 2007).

[18] Henri Darcy, *Les fontaines publiques de la ville de Dijon* (Paris: V. Dalmont, 1856).

[19] M. E. Harr, *Groundwater and Seepage* (New York: McGraw-Hill, 1962).

[20] M. Muskat, *The Flow of Homogeneous Fluids Through Porous Media* (Ann Arbor, MI: J. W. Edwards, 1946).

[21] G. Thiem, *Hydrologische Methoden* (Leipzig: Gebhart, 1906), 56.

[22] C. V. Theis, "The Relation Between the Lowering of the Piezometric Surface and the Rate and Duration of Discharge of a Well Using Ground Water Storage," *Trans. Am. Geophys. Union* 16 (1935): 519–524.

[23] H. H. Cooper, Jr., and C. E. Jacob, "A Generalized Graphical Method for Evaluating Formation Constants and Summarizing Well-Field History," *Trans. Am. Geophys. Union* 27 (1946): 526–534.

[24] J. W. Mercer and C. R. Faust, *Ground-Water Modeling* (Worthington, OH: National Water Well Association, 1981).

[25] T. A. Prickett, "Ground-water Computer Models—State of the Art," *Ground Water* 17 (2) (1979): 121–128.

[26] C. A. Appel and J. D. Bredehoeft, "Status of Groundwater Modeling in the U.S. Geological Survey," *U.S. Geol. Survey Circular* 737 (1976).

[27] Y. Bachmat, B. Andres, D. Holta, and S. Sebastian. *Utilization of Numerical Groundwater Models for Water Resource Management*, U.S. Environmental Protection Agency Report EPA-600/8-78-012.

[28] J. E. Moore, "Contribution of Ground-Water Modeling to Planning," *J. Hydrol.* 43 (October 1979).

[29] National Research Council, *Ground Water Models—Scientific and Regulatory Applications*, Water Science and Technology Board, Commission on Physical Sciences, Mathematics, and Resources (Washington, DC: National Academy Press, 1990).

[30] R. J. Charbeneau, *Groundwater Hydraulics and Pollutant Transport* (Upper Saddle River, NJ: Prentice Hall, 2000).

[31] M. McDonald and A. Harbaugh, *A Modular Three-Dimensional Finite-Difference Ground-Water Flow Model Book 6 Modeling Techniques* (Washington, DC: Scientific Software Group, 1988).

[32] M. P. Anderson and W. W. Woessner, *Applied Groundwater Modeling: Simulation of Flow and Advective Transport* (Orlando, FL: Academic Press, 1992).

[33] J. Istok, *Groundwater Modeling by the Finite Element Method*, Monograph 13 (Washington, DC: American Geophysical Union, 1989).

[34] H. F. Wang and M. P. Anderson, *Introduction to Groundwater Modeling: Finite Difference and Finite Element Methods* (San Francisco: W. H. Freeman, 1982).

[35] J. F. Hoffman, "How Underground Reservoirs Provide Cool Water for Industrial Uses," *Heating, Piping, Air Conditioning* (October 1960).

[36] R. C. Richter and R. Y. D. Chun, "Artificial Recharge of Ground Water Reservoirs in California," *Proc. Am. Soc. Civil Engrs., J. Irrigation Drainage Div.* 85 (IR4) (December 1959).

[37] N. Buras, "Conjunctive Operation of Dams and Aquifers," *Proc. Am. Soc. Civil Engrs., J. Hydraulics Div.* 89 (HY6) (November 1963).

[38] F. B. Clendenen, "A Comprehensive Plan for the Conjunctive Utilization of a Surface Reservoir with Underground Storage for Basin-wide Water Supply Development: Solano Project, California" (D. Eng. thesis, University of California, Berkeley, 1959), 160.

[39] "Ground Water Basin Management," *Manual of Engineering Practice*, no. 40 (New York: American Society of Civil Engineers, 1961).

[40] W. B. Langbein, "Water Yield and Reservoir Storage in the United States," *U.S. Geol. Survey Circular* (1959).

[41] W. Rippl, "The Capacity of Storage Reservoirs for Water Supply," *Proc. Inst. Civil Engrs.* (London) 71 (1883): 270.

[42] Intergovernmental Panel on Climate Change, *Climate Change 2007: Impacts, Adaptation, and Vulnerability, Summary for Policymakers*, Working Group II Contribution to the Intergovernmental Panel on Climate Change Fourth Assessment Report (Geneva, Switzerland, 2007).

[43] R. M. White, "The Great Climate Debate," *Scientific American* 263 (July 1990).

Alternative Sources of Water Supply

The global surge in population has strained water supplies and threatened the ecology of the earth. In 2000, 1.1 billion people (or 18% of the world's population) did not have access to clean drinking water, and 2.4 billion did not have access to adequate sanitation services [1]. Water shortages and poor water quality have caused and will continue to cause some of the most serious problems throughout the world. A 2003 joint report by 23 United Nations agencies found that improved water management could assist with global issues such as poverty, hunger, universal primary education, gender equality, child mortality, maternal mortality, major diseases, and environmental sustainability. The agencies also reported that approximately 6000 people (primarily children under the age of five) die each day from water-related diseases [2].

As long as demands increase, humans will continue to search for new ways to create safe and adequate water supplies. For seasoned professionals, the many sources of raw water are not new. However, as traditional water supplies are depleted many alternative and nontraditional water supplies have started to gain more attention from the public and from policy makers. As a result, water professionals have started to implement more alternative, or nontraditional, water supply projects on a broader scale. This chapter will briefly discuss many of these alternative technologies.

Although the majority of raw water is still withdrawn from ground or surface waters and then treated and distributed, many agencies and utilities have started augmenting their supplies with treated wastewater, brackish or saline water, and stormwater. New technologies such as cloud seeding and aquifer storage and recovery are also being used to create and store these supplies. Using a number of management practices, raw water sources, treatment technologies, and storage techniques to create an adequate water supply is called a *portfolio approach* to water supply planning and is becoming more common as traditional water supplies are depleted in many parts of the world. Water supply planners must now tap into a variety of sources, methods, and technologies to meet growing needs [3].

1   WATER CONSERVATION

While most water supply problems are solved on the supply side, water conservation is a way to create more supply by addressing the demand side. Many conservation measures are fairly easy to implement but may be overlooked until comprehensive planning is undertaken. Water conservation can take place in any of the water use sectors (urban, agricultural, industrial, municipal) and is among the most environmentally friendly of all of the alternative water supply options. Conservation is generally broken into *soft measures* such as public educations programs and *hard measures* such as regulations and mandatory watering bans [3].

California has been using conservation measures since the early 1990s and has employed both soft and hard measures to address its water supply needs. Public education campaigns throughout the United States often encourage the use of low-flow showerheads and toilets in addition to general messages related to efficient use of water in home appliances (primarily dishwashers and washing machines). However, efficient outdoor use of water has proved more challenging. In California, more than half of residential water use is outdoors. To reduce outdoor water use, California water managers have encouraged the use of sensors on sprinkler systems and reduced landscaping in front yards [3]. Other outdoor conservation measures include *xeriscaping* (the use of native, water-efficient vegetation). When soft measures do not bring about needed results in urban areas, measures such as watering restrictions and increased fees are implemented.

Conservation can also be employed in the agricultural and industrial sectors. The success of agricultural water conservation is more difficult to quantify than the success of urban conservation. In the case of agricultural conservation in California, only net flows can be quantified and the costs to create higher net flows usually result in a need to subsidize those employing the conservation measures [3].

Regardless of the measures employed and the water use sector involved, water conservation measures must be employed in a targeted, proactive, and organized manner. The political and public response to conservation measures can significantly slow or even halt the progress of a program. The decision makers and the public must understand why the conservation measures are needed and the case must be made effectively and consistently. Unfortunately, many conservation measures are implemented during drought—these reactive measures generally prove to be more difficult to enforce than proactive measures that are implemented during normal conditions.

2   WASTEWATER REUSE

Reclamation, recycling, and reuse of water that has been used for a variety of purposes offers an attractive alternative to the development or expansion of natural water sources. Although the terms *reclamation, recycling,* and *reuse* are similar and used almost interchangeably by practicing engineers, *water reclamation* refers to the treatment of water to meet predefined water quality criteria, whereas *water reuse* refers to the use of treated wastewater for beneficial uses. These terms usually refer to municipal wastewater that is used to supplement irrigation needs for agriculture or urban uses [1]. If viewed in terms of popular environmental themes, it makes sense that water should be used more than once. In other words, water can and should be recycled. Wanielista notes that the reasons for implementing reuse projects are many [4]:

1. To maintain natural hydrologic conditions and balance the water budget.
2. To improve water quality in natural waterbodies.
3. To meet regulatory criteria.
4. To conserve water.
5. To reduce saltwater intrusion in coastal areas.
6. To take advantage of the potential ease of permitting.
7. To reduce costs.

Municipal wastewater reuse is common, especially in the more arid western and southwestern states. In California and Texas, for example, there are numerous reuse projects. Wastewater reuse appears to be particularly attractive in areas where rainfall is low, evaporation is high, irrigation water use is intense, and interbasin transfers of water are being practiced or planned. Environmental regulations, water scarcity, and economic factors are expected to increase the popularity of reuse. This will undoubtedly affect water use trends in the future, especially in the industrial and agricultural sectors. Figure 1 gives a good indication of the significance of wastewater reclamation to the

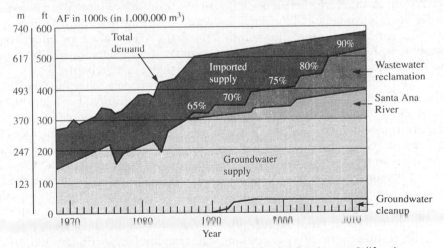

FIGURE 1 Projected distribution of source waters for Orange County, California, water supply to the year 2010. *Source:* From L. W. Owen and W. R. Mills, "California's Orange County Water District: A Model for Comprehensive Water Resources Management," in *Water Resources: Planning and Management and Urban Water Resources,* Proceedings of the 18th Annual Conference and Symposium of the Water Resources Planning and Management Division of ASCE, New York, NY, May 1991, p. 5.

water supply future of Orange County, California. By 2010, it is projected that about 20% of the Orange County Water District's water needs will be met by reclaimed wastewater. Benefits of wastewater reuse include improved quality of surface waters, preservation of higher-quality water for potable consumption, and added recreational opportunities [5].

Treated wastewater may be used directly or indirectly. In direct reuse, wastewater is treated and then delivered to a user without intervening travel dilution in natural surface water or groundwater bodies [6]. Connection of a municipal wastewater plant to an irrigation site provides a direct water supply to that site. Indirect reuse involves a middle step between the generation of reclaimed water and its reuse. This middle step commonly includes discharge, retention, and mixing with another water source before reuse. *Recycling* refers to two or more consecutive uses of water by the same business, industry, or person in a coordinated, planned manner, sometimes with partial treatment between uses.

The most widely available and least variable source of wastewater for reuse is municipal wastewater. It can be relied on to provide a dependable continuous flow having fairly stable physical, chemical, and biological characteristics. Reuse of municipal wastewater may be accomplished in a number of ways, with treatment ranging from none to the most advanced systems available, depending on the end use of the water. Municipal wastewater reuses are varied. In California, municipal wastewaters are reused for irrigation of fiber and seed crops, landscapes, orchards and vineyards, and processed, and nonprocessed food crops; restricted and unrestricted recreational impoundments; pasture for dairy animals; and groundwater recharge [7].

Manufacturing processes can contribute significantly to the amount of wastewater generated in an area. However, the constituents in industrial wastes may limit options for reusing them. Nevertheless, on-site wastewater reuse by industry has become more prevalent as environmental standards set by regulatory agencies have tightened.

In agriculture, return flows from irrigation projects are a potential source of reusable water. These flows are often contaminated with salts leached from the soil, however, and treatment is often required before they can be reused.

The objective of wastewater reclamation is to provide a water supply of adequate quality to meet the standards of the proposed reuse application. For municipal wastewater flows that have been subjected to secondary treatment, pollutants that may still require removal include nitrates, phosphates, total dissolved solids, microorganisms, and refractory organics such as trace levels of pesticides [6, 8]. Depending on the type of reuse, some of these constituents may enhance the value of the product water and should remain. For example, phosphates and nitrates are desirable in reclaimed water scheduled for reuse in irrigation because they are useful nutrients for the crops that are to be grown. A number of states, including California, have established water-quality standards for various types of reuse [9].

To restore wastewaters to drinking water quality, *tertiary* or advanced treatment processes are usually required. These proven wastewater reclamation technologies are widely used. Regardless of the methods used, reuse projects should be viewed as an extension of conservation plans. The new text *Water Reuse: Issues, Technologies, and Applications* provides a thorough treatment of this topic [1].

3 STORMWATER REUSE

Stormwater reuse or *stormwater harvesting* refers to the capture, treatment, and use of stormwater to augment water supplies. The reasons for the reuse of stormwater are the same as those for the reuse of wastewater, but stormwater reuse is less common in the United States. However, rain has always generally been seen as a valuable source of clean water and manmade structures have been used to capture rain since the beginning of civilization. In many parts of the developing world, *cisterns* (a structure or barrel used to store captured stormwater) are a primary source of domestic potable water. However, using stormwater in the framework of developing an urban alternative water supply in an industrialized country can be fairly complex.

Stormwater reuse, like wastewater reuse, is commonly considered abroad and in some parts of the United States as a way to supplement water supply for nonpotable uses. For all reuse projects, chemical composition of the stormwater is important. Like wastewater, stormwater may contain valuable nutrients that can aid in the growth of vegetation while providing a potential source of biological treatment for the stormwater. The desirable constituents usually include nitrogen and phosporus. Stormwater can also contain constituents that should not be released to the environment in the high concentrations that tend to be present in untreated stormwater (heavy metals, microorganisms, pesticides, and herbicides to name a few). Stormwater is also more variable than wastewater in terms of quantity and quality.

Australia and some European countries have implemented many successful stormwater reuse projects, including aquifer storage and recovery (ASR, see Section 6), lakes, wetlands, rainwater storage tanks, water sensitive urban design, industrial reuse, and urban reuse [10]. The storage of surface water is also fairly common in the United States in facilities variously called *irrigation ponds, reuse ponds,* or *recycling ponds.* In Florida, over 300 stormwater reuse projects have been implemented. Most of these projects use stormwater for irrigation purposes [4]. Regardless of where the stormwater is stored, it is usually used to meet local irrigation needs. If a rainwater tank or cistern is used, stormwater may also be used for potable uses. Whenever stormwater is used for potable uses, it is important to monitor water quality and public health.

Given the availability of stormwater in many areas, reuse of this valuable resource is one of the best sources of alternative water supply for nonpotable uses. When undertaking a reuse project, it is critical that project costs do not outweigh the useful life of the project. Maintenance, environmental integrity, and public health are also critical issues that must be addressed during the planning process.

4 BRACKISH AND SALINE WATER CONVERSION

In coastal areas the conversion of brackish and saline water into a viable water supply is becoming more popular. Broadly speaking, desalination includes the treatment of all impaired waters. For water supply engineers, the term *desalination* refers to the removal of salts from brackish water and seawater [11]. The sources of water in this category include brackish groundwater and water from seas and oceans (usually generically referred to as *seawater desalination*). As with other sources of water, this alternative has a number of advantages and disadvantages. When considered as part of a planning process, the source water should be carefully analyzed. Some parameters of interest include total suspended solids, silt density index, temperature, chemical constituents, and bacteriological quality [12]. In addition, potential environmental impacts must be carefully considered. Generally, the withdrawal of the source water and the disposal of the wastes are significant hurdles in implementing a desalination project.

Conventional water treatment techniques such as coagulation, sedimentation, and filtration are not adequate to remove dissolved solids in brackish water and sea-water [11]. However, the following treatment techniques are effective at converting brackish or saline water [12, 13, 14]:

1. *Distillation/Condensation* or *Thermal Treatment* is the most developed form of desalination throughout the world. This is a well-understood unit operation and is the most common method of desalination. Some types of thermal treatment include solar distillation, multistage-flash, multiple effect evaporation, thermal vapor compression, mechanical vapor compression, and adsorption vapor compression.

2. *Membrane Filtration* is a term used to describe a variety of membrane-based technologies that can be used for desalination. Membrane-based technologies generally include electrodialysis, electrodialysis-reversal, reverse osmosis (also referred to as hyperfiltration), nanofiltration, ultrafiltration, and microfiltration. Membrane filtration is the most common form of desalination in the United States.

3. *Ion Exchange* describes processes that exchange one type of ion for another of the same charge.

Pretreatment and posttreatment must be considered with each process. For example, degasification must be considered for waters that were produced via reverse osmosis. For waters produced from electrodialysis-reversal processes, small suspended material must be removed during post-treatment processing. As with all water treatment facilities, residual disinfection must also be carefully timed for each type of treatment process [12].

The most common disadvantages of brackish and saline water conversion are power costs and disposal of wastes (usually referred to as *brine* or *concentrate*) that accumulate during treatment processes. Energy is one of the most important cost-related concerns related to desalination. Energy consumption is closely linked to the qualities of the source water and the selected treatment technologies. Generally, reverse osmosis facilities consume more energy than other types of desalination facilities. A relatively high level of energy is usually needed to drive pumps that create the needed pressures. Electrodialysis is only economically feasible for brackish waters due to the energy that is needed to reduce dissolved solids concentrations. It is simply too expensive to create the energy needed to desalinate seawater using electrodialysis [15].

Desalination facilities are potential sources of environmental degradation during and after construction. General environmental concerns include but are not limited to plant location, construction materials, air pollution, onsite chemical management, ecological impacts near the intake, and groundwater contamination. Perhaps most common are concerns related to management and disposal of concentrate. Environmental concerns related to desalination are well documented in Younos [16]. Ultimately, desalination remains one of the more expensive sources of alternative water supplies, but many utilities continue to consider desalination because of the relatively high reliability of the supply compared with other sources [2].

5   INTERBASIN TRANSFERS

The option of transporting water from another region is also considered a viable source of alternative water supply—although it can be among the most politically difficult and environmentally harmful options. These transfers must also include a careful economic and environmental analysis. The primary concern, besides the negotiations with the parties involved in the transfer, is the harm that can occur to third parties once the transfer begins. Usually, the third party of greatest concern is the environment and the wildlife that rely on the water source [3]. Other impacted parties can include agricultural and commercial interests. Although water transfer can sometimes appear relatively low in cost compared with other sources of water, it is important to consider the costs to third parties as well.

6   OTHER RELEVANT TECHNOLOGIES

Many technologies are relevant to the development of alternative water supplies. Some of these technologies include *aquifer storage and recovery* (ASR) and *cloud seeding*. In fact, what is considered an alternative source of water supply in one region may be considered a traditional source of water supply in another region. For example, in Florida surface water is usually considered an alternative source of water supply, while in the neighboring state of Georgia, surface water is a traditional source of water.

ASR is a process involving storing water in an aquifer (by recharge) during wet periods and removing it during dry periods when it is needed. The underground storage basin can be operated like a surface water reservoir, but it eliminates evaporative losses, which can be significant, and it does not require inundating the large land areas that are associated with surface water reservoirs. ASR systems can also be called upon to support water supply needs during severe multiyear droughts. The concept is not new, having been used in the United States for over 30 years. Figure 2 illustrates the typical ASR facility.

As with all water technologies, ASR facilities must meet stringent water quality regulations. Recently, concerns about arsenic have slowed ASR implementation in some parts of Florida. It is currently thought that the bulk matrix of the limestone in some parts of Florida may contain low concentrations of arsenic, which is a natural but troublesome, phenomenon. As a result, arsenic levels have exceeded maximum contaminant levels of 10 ug/L at many ASR facilities and this has slowed the implementation of ASR projects throughout the state. Research is underway to find ways to strip arsenic from groundwater using a variety of methods. Norton and researchers at the University of Florida are investigating this topic in cooperation with the City of Bradenton, Florida [17].

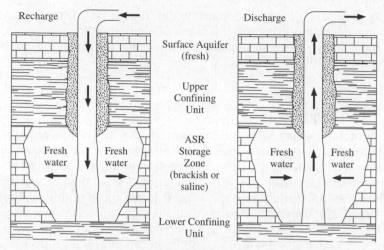

FIGURE 2   Schematic diagram of an aquifer storage and recovery
system. (Everglades Restoration Plan, www.evergladesplan.org/docs/
asr_whitepaper.pdf.)

Cloud seeding, a method of increasing rainfall, is perhaps the rarest source of water supply. Many parts of the United States are experimenting with technologies to increase rainfall. In fact, there are approximately a dozen active seeding projects in the Sierra Nevada foothills. There is no concensus in the scientific community about the effectiveness of cloud-seeding technology [3].

PROBLEMS

1 Investigate the sources of water in your area. What technologies are being used to create the potable water supply you use?

2 Investigate a current water conflict that is occurring within your country, using the Internet. Discuss the nature of the conflict and the measures and technologies that are being considered to address it. Discuss why you think these measures will or will not be effective.

3 Investigate an international water conflict using the Internet. Discuss the nature of the conflict and the measures and technologies that are being considered to address it. Discuss why you think these measures will or will not be effective.

4 List 10 ways you can conserve water in your home.

REFERENCES

[1] Metcalf & Eddy, Inc., *Water Reuse: Issues, Technologies, and Applications* (New York: McGraw-Hill, 2007).

[2] United Nations World Water Assessment Programme, *Water for People Water for Life: The United Nations World Water Development Report* (Barcelona: United Nations Educational, Scientific, and Cultural Organization and Berghahn Books, 2003).

[3] E. Hanak, "Finding Water for Growth: New Sources, New Tools, New Challenges," *Journal of the American Water Resources Association* 43, no. 4 (August 2007).

[4] M. Wanielista, "Stormwater—An Alternative Water Supply in Florida," *Proceedings of the Florida Water Environment Association's Fall Seminar Series* (September 2007).

[5] R. Von Dohren, "Consider the Many Reasons for Reuse," *Water and Wastes Eng.* 17, no. 9 (1980): 7478.

[6] SCS Engineers, Inc., "Contaminants Associated with Direct and Indirect Reuse of Municipal Wastewater," U.S. EPA Report No. EPA600/178019, NTIS No. PB 280 482 (March 1978).

[7] J. Crook, "Reliability of Wastewater Reclamation Facilities" (Berkeley, CA: California Department of Health, Water Sanitation Section, 1976).

[8] W. E. Garrison and R. P. Miele, "Current Trends in Water Reclamation Technology," *J. Am. Water Works Assoc.* 69, no. 7 (1977): 364–369.

[9] California Department of Health, "Wastewater Reclamation Criteria," California Administrative Code, Title 22, Division 4, Water Sanitation Section (Berkeley, CA, 1975).

[10] T. McAlister, "Stormwater Reuse—A Balanced Assessment," *Proceedings of the Stormwater Industry Association's Conference* (Sydney, Australia, 1999).

[11] T. Younos, "Desalination: Supplementing Freshwater Supplies Approaches and Challenges," *Journal of Contemporary Water Research and Education*, Issue 132, 1–2 (December 2005).

[12] U.S. Army, *Water Desalination* (Honolulu: University Press of the Pacific, 2005).

[13] K. S. Spiegler and Y. M. El-Sayed, *A Desalination Primer* (Santa Maria Imbaro, Italy: Balaban Desalination Publications, 1994).

[14] T. Younos and K. E. Tolou, "Overview of Desalination Techniques," *Journal of Contemporary Water Research and Education*, Issue 132, 3–10 (December 2005).

[15] T. Younos and K. E. Tolou, "Energy Needs, Consumption and Sources," *Journal of Contemporary Water Research and Education*, Issue 132, 27–38 (December 2005).

[16] T. Younos, "Environmental Issues of Desalination," *Journal of Contemporary Water Research and Education*, Issue 132, 11–18 (December 2005).

[17] S. B. Norton, *Quantifying the Near-Borehole Geochemical Response During Aquifer Storage and Recovery: Application of "Push-Pull" Analytical Techniques to ASR Cycle Testing,* A Thesis Presented to the Unviersity of Florida in Partial Fulfillment of the Requirements for the Degree of Master of Science (Gainesville: University of Florida, 2007).

Water Use Trends
and Forecasting

Water Use Trends and Forecasting

The water supply problem is one of balancing supply and demand. The geographical and temporal availability of water sources, the quality of these resources, the rates at which they are replenished and depleted, and the demands placed upon them by water users are determining factors in water management strategies. Estimates of future water uses, uncertain as they might be, are fundamental to efficient and equitable allocation of water supplies. These estimates depend on an ability to forecast changes in population, agricultural and industrial activity, ecologic and economic conditions, technology, and social and other related factors.

1 WATER USE SECTORS

Decisions on developing and allocating water resources must be based on availability, quality, type, and rate of use of the resource. A complication is that source waters must usually be allocated to numerous competing uses. When supplies are limited, conflicts among users may become intense and tradeoffs must be made.

Community water use projections are always needed for distribution system and treatment plant design, in addition to information on the timing of these demands. More detailed information on individual water use sectors is provided throughout the remainder of this section. Demand parameters, critical to the design and operation of water treatment facilities, are usually expressed as the following parameters:

- *Average day demand* is calculated by dividing the total annual amount of water produced by 365.
- *Maximum day demand* is the highest water demand for any 24-hour period.
- *Peak hour demand* is the highest demand for water for a 1-hour period.

- *Peak factors* are common and important terms used in the design and description of water systems. These are usually multiples of the average day demand and are used to describe maximum day or peak hour demands [1].

Agriculture

Water is critical to agriculture. In arid and semiarid regions without a dependable water supply, there is little chance of achieving success in agricultural operations. In humid areas rainfall is often adequate to produce good crops, but even in these areas supplemental irrigation is increasingly relied upon to prevent crop failures and to improve the quality of the products produced. In the eastern United States, the increasing use of supplemental irrigation highlights the importance of sustainable water supplies for crop production [2].

Irrigation water requirements are generally seasonal, varying with climate and type of crop. In humid regions, water withdrawals for irrigation may range from about 10% of the total annual demand in May to 30% in September, while in arid and semi-arid locations rates of withdrawal are nearly uniform during the irrigation season. The quantities and timing of water uses for irrigation conflict with many other uses. This creates special problems in arid regions. Irrigators promote storing as much water as possible during the winter when hydropower producers are eager to release flows into their turbines to generate electricity, for example. Of considerable importance is the fact the water used for irrigation (about 40% of U.S. freshwater use in 2000) is consumptively used (evaporated or transpired) and is thus unavailable for reuse in the region.

Thermoelectric Power

The principal use of water in power-generating facilities is for cooling to dissipate rejected heat. The amount of cooling water withdrawn depends on plant size, generator thermal efficiency, cooling heat transfer efficiency, and institutionally regulated limits on effluent temperatures. In 2000, generation of electricity ranked first in total water withdrawals in the United States (fresh plus saline water). About 70% of the amount used was from freshwater sources [3]. If the demands for cooling water increase, limitations on freshwater resources will probably stimulate even greater interest in developing coastal sites with their potential for once-through cooling using saline water. *Once-through cooling* is the passage of water through cooling units followed by direct release to a receiving body of water without any recycling through water-cooling facilities. Withdrawals for once-through cooling are large, but little water is used consumptively.

Cities and Other Communities

In 2000, central water supply systems furnished water to about 285 million people residing in municipal areas of the United States [3]. Approximately 45.2 million people living outside of these service areas had their own domestic systems. The principal domestic and commercial water uses are for drinking, cooking, sanitation, lawn watering, swimming pool maintenance, street cleaning, firefighting, and various aspects of city and park maintenance. Although the public water use sector is vital to our well-being, since it furnishes much of our drinking water, the total amount of water used by this sector is small when compared to water-using sectors such as irrigation and thermoelectric cooling. In 2000, the

USGS reported that this sector represented about 12.5% of the nation's freshwater withdrawals. In 1975, the national average daily per capita use from public supplies was about 170 gallons per capita per day (gpcd); in 1990, it had increased to about 184 gpcd [2, 3]. It is noteworthy that total public water withdrawals declined to about 180 gpcd in 2000. Since 1990, public per capita water use has been declining slightly even though the population has been increasing. Average domestic water use from self-supplied systems averaged about 79 gpcd in 2000. As a result of more conservative water use and more efficient plumbing fixtures, per capita water use may show further declines in the future. Note that the unit of measurement in the SI system is liters per capita per day (lpcd).

Residential water use rates are continually fluctuating, from hour to hour, from day to day, and from season to season. Average daily winter consumption is only about 80% of the annual daily average, whereas summer consumption averages are about 25% greater than the annual daily average. Figure 1 compares a typical winter day with a typical maximum summer day in Baltimore, Maryland. Note the hourly fluctuations and the tendency toward two peaks. Studies by Wolff indicate that hydrographs of systems serving predominantly residential communities generally show two peaks, the first between 7 A.M. and 1 P.M., the second betweeen 5 P.M. and 9 P.M. [4]. During the

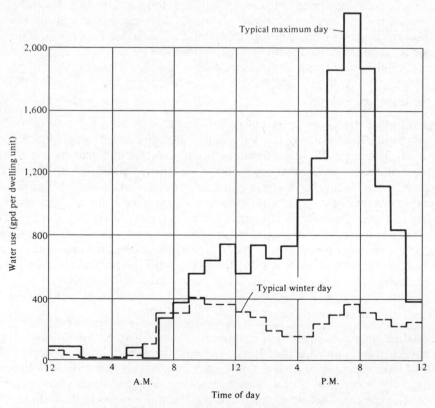

FIGURE 1   Daily water use patterns, maximum day and winter day. *Source:* Residential Water-Use Research Project, Johns Hopkins University and Federal Housing Administration, 1963.

summer, when lawn irrigation demands are high, the second peak is usually the greatest, while during the colder months or during periods of high rainfall, the morning peak is commonly the larger of the two.

Variations in water use within homes are a function of the type of development, its age, geographic location, and extent of conservation practices. Lawn irrigation has been found to represent as much as 75% of total daily volumes and as much as 95% of peak hourly demands where large residential lots are involved [5]. Peak hourly demands have been found to vary from average daily demands by as much as 1500% [4], but there is no rule that can be universally applied to predetermine variations. Table 1 summarizes water usage within the home and Table 2 summarizes water usage by household size.

Fire demands must also be considered in municipal water system design. Design requirements vary by municipality and must be designed according to those guidelines [1]. The annual volumes required for firefighting are small, but during periods of need the short-term demand may be large and may govern the design of distribution systems, distribution storage, and pumping equipment [6].

Firefighting requirements for residential areas vary from 500 to 15000 gpm, the required rate being a function of population density and land use [1]. Hydrant pressures should generally exceed 20 psi where motor pumpers are used; otherwise, pressures in excess of 100 psi might be required. If recommended fire flows cannot be maintained for the indicated time periods, community fire insurance rates may rise.

In addition to supplying water for homes, firefighting, and perhaps some industrial purposes, most communities also must meet the needs of various commercial establishments. In considering commercial requirements, it is important to know both the magnitude and time of occurrence of peak flow. Table 3 provides some insight into the relative magnitudes and timing of water uses by several commercial sectors. The table provides a guide to water requirements and periods of maximum demand for apartments, motels, hotels, office buildings, shopping centers, laundromats, and gas stations [7]. Note that commercial uses may also include civilian and military installations and public supplies delivered to golf courses. In 1995 the USGS reported that commercial uses constituted about 3% of all freshwater uses [3]. Generally, it can be stated that commercial water users do not materially affect peak municipal demands. In fact, peak hours for many commercial

TABLE 1   A Summary of Residential Water Use in the United States

Water Use	Without Water Conservation (gpcd)	With Water Conservation (gpcd)
Bathing	1.3	1.3
Faucets	11.4	11.1
Leaks	9.4	4.7
Showers	13.2	11.1
Toilets	19.3	9.3
Washing Clothes	16.8	11.8
Washing Dishes	1.0	1.0
Miscellaneous Other Uses	1.6	1.6
Total	74	51.9

Source: Adapted from the American Water Works Association (AWWA), *1998 Residential Water Use Survey*, Denver, CO and as shown in Metcalf & Eddy, Inc., 2003 [7].

TABLE 2   A Summary of Water Usage by Household Size

Number of Persons in Household	Water Usage/Wastewater Flowrate (gpcd)	Typical Water Usage/Wastewater Flowrate (gpcd)
1	75–130	97
2	68–81	76
3	54–70	66
4	41–71	53
5	40–68	51
6	39–67	50
7	37–64	48
8	36–62	46

Source: Adapted from the American Water Works Association Research Foundation (AWWARF), *Residential End Uses of Water*, Denver, CO and as shown in Metcalf & Eddy, Inc. 2003 [7].

TABLE 3   Commercial Water Use

	Unit	Range of Average Daily Demand (gpd)	Typical Daily Demand (gpd)	Hour of Peak Usage
Airport	Passenger	3–5	4	
Apartment building	Bedroom	100–150	120	5–6 P.M.
Gas Station	Vehicle Served	8–15	10	
Motel	Guest	50–90	60	
Hotel				
Guest	Person	65–75	70	9–10 A.M.
Employee	Person	8–15	10	
Mobile Home Park	Unit	125–150	140	
Movie Theater	Seat	2–4	3	
Office Buildings	Employee	7–16	13	10–11 A.M.
Restaurant	Customer	7–12	9	
Shopping Center	Parking Space	1–3	2	2–3 P.M.
Laundromat				
Machine	Unit	400–550	450	
Customer	Person	45–55	50	11–12 A.M.

Source: Residential Water Use Research Project of The Johns Hopkins University and the Office of Technical Studies of the Architectural Standards Division of the Federal Housing Administration, 1963 and Metcalf & Eddy, Inc., 2003 [7].

establishments tend to coincide with the secondary residential peak period. Because many commercial activities end at about 6 P.M., they do not contribute to demands in the early evening, when lawn irrigation demands are often high.

The many factors affecting municipal water use preclude any generalization that could apply to all areas. General trends and representative figures are useful, but it should be understood that local usage may vary considerably from reported averages. For design purposes, past records of the type and pattern of community water use, the physical and climatic characteristics of the area, expected trends in development, projected population values, and other pertinent factors must be thoroughly studied.

Example 1

Given a residential area encompassing 500 acres with a housing density of six houses per acre, assume a high-value residence with a fire flow requirement of 1000 gpm. Find (a) the combined draft and (b) the peak hourly demand. Use Figures 2 and 3 to solve the problem.

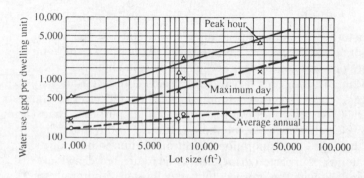

FIGURE 2   Relationship of lot size to water use. *Source:* The Residential Water-Use Research Project of The Johns Hopkins University and the Office of Technical Studies of the Architectural Standards Division of the Federal Housing Administration, 1963.

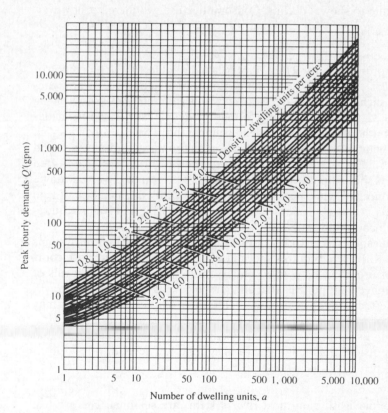

FIGURE 3   Relation of total peak hourly demands to number of dwelling units in terms of housing density. *Source:* The Residential Water-Use Research Project of The Johns Hopkins University and the Office of Technical Studies of the Architectural Standards Division of the Federal Housing Administration, 1963.

Solution: (a) Given that 1 acre contains 43,560 ft^2, each lot will be about 7000 ft^2 in size. From Figure 2, this value produces a maximum day value of 700 gpd per dwelling unit. For the 3000 dwelling units, this would be 3000 × 700 = 2,100,000 gpd or 1458 gpm. The combined draft is thus 1458 + 1000 = 2458 gpm. (b) From Figure 3, for 3000 dwelling units and a density of 6.0, find a peak hourly demand of 2500 gpm. The peak hourly flow would control since it exceeds the combined flow estimate.

Industry

From 1970 to 1980 manufacturing accounted for about 17% of total U.S. freshwater withdrawals. In 1995, industrial withdrawals represented only about 7% of the total withdrawals for all categories of water use [3]. This decline is attributed mainly to recycling and process changes. Manufacturing uses vary with the product produced, but they generally include both process waters and cooling waters. From about 1955 to 1975 the amount of freshwater and saline water withdrawn for manufacturing purposes almost doubled. This water was recycled about twice before being returned to the source and diminished somewhat less than 10% by evaporation and incorporation into products. Although manufacturing water use is expected to increase in the future, recycling is also predicted to increase substantially, with the prospect that actual water withdrawals for this purpose will continue to show a decline. Consumptive use will increase, however.

Natural Systems

Providing water for the preservation and benefit of fish and wildlife, for the protection of marshes and estuary areas, and for other environmentally oriented purposes is now considered a necessity. But such water uses often conflict with traditional uses, and resolving these conflicts is destined to become an increasingly common task. The Everglades restoration project in South Florida is an excellent example (http://www.evergladesplan. org). Estimating the quantities of water needed for environmental protection and restoration is difficult. Scientific data needed to make good determinations are often lacking, and this presents special problems since the quantities of water involved can be substantial. Topics of concern include instream flow requirements, maintenance of lake levels, wetland hydration, freshwater releases to bays and estuaries, and water requirements for protecting fish and wildlife.

The water-related aspects of restoring, protecting, and managing natural systems are abundant. Dealing with them requires special policies, good data, and close coordination with a host of programs conducted under the auspices of various levels of government. Water management policies that encourage or result in excessive growth may trigger unwanted effects on the environment. Draining and reclaiming lands may provide additional opportunity for economic development, for example, but not without paying a price in disrupting ecosystems. Growth management policies that embrace the many dimensions of managing natural systems are needed.

Navigation

Water requirements for navigation on most river systems are seasonal. The greatest demands usually occur during the driest months of the year. Flows released for navigation limit the availability of water for irrigation and hydropower generation and for recreational uses at reservoir sites. They do, however, complement other instream uses. Where navigation depths are maintained by low dams, there is usually little effect on other water uses in a river. These structures do not impound large volumes of water; rather, they provide greater uniformity of flows. Many advantages result from this type of operation, including benefits to fish and other wildlife, recreation, pollution control, and aesthetics.

Large multipurpose reservoirs, such as those on the main stem of the Missouri River, also provide storage to meet periodic navigational flows. In such cases, reservoir operating policies must be designed to accommodate the conflicting requirements of other water uses for which storage is provided.

Hydroelectric Power Generation

In the past, requirements for hydroelectric power were usually heaviest during the peak winter heating months, but with the increased use of air conditioning, demands for electricity are less seasonal and in some cases the summer months are the most demanding. The use of hydroelectric facilities to provide peak power, as opposed to furnishing base load, is also becoming more common. Unfortunately, this type of operation increases conflicts with recreational users and others who favor little or no short-term fluctuations in reservoir levels. In general, conflicts between water use for electric power generation and use for other purposes stem from opposing seasonal requirements. For example, heavy summertime releases for navigation dictate maximizing storage during the winter, a situation in conflict with discharging from storage during the same period to produce electricity. Hydroelectric production does not adversely affect all water uses, however; for example, water passed through turbines can also be used downstream for navigation, flow augmentation, and other purposes. It is worth noting that the largest hydroelectric project in the world is under construction in China. The Three Gorges Dam project, scheduled for completion in 2009, is projected to produce 18 gigawatts of electrical energy, approximately 10% of China's total capacity in 1993. The project has been widely criticized on technical and environmental grounds, but proponents state that the project will decrease atmospheric pollution and eliminate the burning of 40 to 50 million tons of coal each year.

Recreation

About a fourth of the nation's outdoor recreation activity depends on water. In 1975, swimming, fishing, boating, water skiing, and ice skating accounted for about 3 billion activity days. By 2000, this figure had increased to about 8 billion [2]. Water requirements for recreation are normally greatest in the summer. The sports enthusiast and vacationer desire substantial stream flows and unvarying reservoir levels during this period. Such conditions are optimal for water-based recreation activities but conflict with many withdrawal uses.

Energy Resource Development

Water can be used to produce energy via turbines driving electric generators. It can also be used to process energy-producing resources such as coal and oil shale and to help restore lands despoiled during mining operations. The water requirements for extraction of coal, oil shale, uranium, and oil gas are not great, but secondary recovery operations for oil require large quantities of water. Substantial quantities of water may be used in coal slurry pipelines and for retorting oil shale. Synfuels conversion processes also require large quantities of water, and, as stated earlier, withdrawal of water for cooling thermal electric plants is the largest category of total water use in the United States.

The availability of water is a factor in the location and design of energy conversion facilities, but these users can generally afford to pay high prices for water. Securing legal rights to water, rather than increasing its availability, is often the critical issue in dry regions.

2   FACTORS AFFECTING WATER USE

Many factors affect the amount and timing of water use: population size and character; climate; the types of water uses in the region; the cost of water; public commitment to environmental protection and restoration; public attitude toward conservation and wastewater reuse; water management practices; federal, state, local government laws and ordinances; and tourism.

Population.   The amount of water used in a locality is directly related to the size, distribution, and composition of the local population. Forecasts of future water use depend, in part, on population forecasts as well. Much more will be said about this in Section 4.

Climate.   The amount of water used in a locality is influenced by its climate. Lawn irrigation, gardening, bathing, irrigation, cooling, and many other water uses are directly affected.

Types of Water Uses.   The type and scale of residential, commercial, industrial, and agricultural development in an area define the levels and timing of water uses.

Economic Conditions.   Economic health is reflected in all aspects of resource management and development. Inflation and other economic trends influence the availability of funds for water supply, wastewater treatment, and environmental and other programs, and they affect the attitudes of individuals as well.

Environmental Protection.   Social attitudes toward environmental protection and enhancement strongly affect water allocation and use. Water use forecasts must take into account the amount of water that is to be dedicated to environmental protection and restoration. This quantity can be substantial.

Conservation.   Attractive alternatives to developing new water supplies are conservation practices and the reuse of wastewater and stormwater. These approaches, although not a panacea, can at least delay the need for additional water supplies and/or the development of new facilities.

Management Practices.   Water management practices, including interbasin transfers, saline water conversion, water reclamation and reuse, and many other practices influence water use trends [8–16]. The impact of technological change on water use can be significant.

Tourism.   Some states, such as Florida, have annual tourist populations that significantly exceed their resident populations. The impacts of such occurrences must be recognized when forecasting future water demands.

3   WATER USE TRENDS

Analyses of water use projections made since 1970 show that a rapidly increasing rate of per capita water use is less likely than estimators of the 1960s would have believed. Another point is that national or regional trends are not always indicative of state and local trends. Thus, planners must be equipped to deal with development and management options at several geographic levels to accommodate special local and regional influences.

Every five years the U.S. Geological Survey publishes a pamphlet, "Estimated Water Use in the United States" [3]. This publication summarizes water use in each major water-using category and indicates trends over time. The data are available by state and by region (http://water.usgs.gov/watuse/). Although the overall tendency in water use to 2000 appears to be more conservative than that of the past, striking local variances can be expected. Table 4 provides water usage information by state for 2000 and Table 5 provides snapshots of water usage over time. Note that the total offstream water withdrawal declined from 440 bgd in 1980 to 408 bgd in 1990 (fresh and saline water). During the 10-year period from 1980 to 1990 there was an overall reduction in total withdrawals of about 7% even though the U.S. population increased almost 19% during that same period. The shift in trend that occurred in 1980 suggests that a more conservative approach to water use and water resources development is beginning to take hold. The USGS data also shows that public water use increased about 27% from 1980 to 2000. This is not surprising, since the public sector is strongly associated with population growth, and as long as the population continues to increase water use in that sector can be expected to increase, although not necessarily at the same per capita rate. About 70% of the water withdrawn is returned to the source after use, about 5% is lost in irrigation conveyances, and about 25% is consumptively used (evaporated or transpired). Of the amount of water consumptively used, irrigated agriculture is responsible for the lion's share (about 80%).

4   POPULATION

Generally, the more people residing in an area, the more water that will be used. But it is not only the number of people that is important but also their ages, level of education, social background, field of employment, religious beliefs, and other factors. Factors that must be considered include the geographic distribution and growth rate of the population; measures that might be taken to influence the growth rate; and the impact of population changes on the regional economy, natural resources, labor force, energy requirements, urban infrastructure, and so on.

Historical data are basic to estimating future levels of population, but these data are not always available. Even in the United States where the Bureau of the Census

TABLE 4 Total Water Withdrawals by Water Use Category and State, 2000

State	Public Supply	Domestic	Irrigation	Livestock	Aquaculture	Industrial		Mining		Thermoelectric Power		Total		Total
	Fresh	Fresh	Fresh	Fresh	Fresh	Fresh	Saline	Fresh	Saline	Fresh	Saline	Fresh	Saline	Total
Alabama	834	78.9	43.1	—	10.4	833	0	—	—	8,190	0	9990	0	9990
Alaska	80.0	11.2	1.01	—	—	8.12	3.86	27.4	140	33.6	0	161	144	305
Arizona	1080	28.9	5400	—	—	19.8	0.08	85.7	8.17	100	0	6720	8.17	6730
Arkansas	421	28.5	7910	—	198	134	13.6	2.78	0	2180	0	10,900	0.08	10,900
California	6120	286	30,500	409	537	188	13.6	23.7	153	352	12,600	38,400	12,800	51,200
Colorado	899	66.8	11,400	—	—	120	0	—	—	138	0	12,600	0	12,600
Connecticut	424	56.2	30.4	—	—	10.7	0	—	—	187	3440	708	3440	4150
Delaware	94.9	13.3	43.5	3.92	0.07	59.4	3.25	—	—	366	738	582	741	1320
District of Columbia	0	0	0.18	—	—	0	0	—	—	9.69	0	9.87	0	9.87
Florida	2440	199	4290	32.5	8.02	291	1.18	217	0	658	12,000	8140	12,000	20,100
Georgia	1250	110	1140	19.4	15.4	622	30.0	9.80	0	3250	61.7	6410	91.7	6500
Hawaii	250	12.0	364	—	—	14.5	0.85	—	—	0	0	640	0.85	641
Idaho	244	85.2	17,100	34.9	1,970	55.5	0	—	—	0	0	19,500	0	19,500
Illinois	1760	135	154	37.6	—	391	0	—	—	11,300	0	13,700	0	13,700
Indiana	670	122	101	41.9	—	2,400	0	82.5	0	6700	0	10,100	0	10,100
Iowa	383	33.2	21.5	109	—	237	0	32.8	0	2540	0	3360	0	3360
Kansas	416	21.6	3710	111	5.60	53.3	0	31.4	0	2260	0	6610	0	6610
Kentucky	525	27.5	29.3	—	—	317	0	—	—	3260	0	4160	0	4160
Louisiana	753	41.2	1020	7.34	243	2680	0	—	—	5610	0	10,400	0	10,400
Maine	102	35.7	5.84	—	—	247	0	—	—	113	295	504	295	799
Maryland	824	77.1	42.4	10.4	19.6	65.8	227	8.31	0.02	379	6260	1430	6490	7910
Massachusetts	739	42.2	126	—	—	36.8	0	—	—	108	3610	1050	3610	4660
Michigan	1140	239	201	11.3	—	698	0	—	—	7710	0	10,000	0	10,000
Minnesota	500	80.8	227	52.8	—	154	0	588	0	2270	0	3870	0	3870
Mississippi	359	69.3	1410	—	371	242	0	—	—	362	148	2810	148	2960
Missouri	872	53.6	1430	72.4	83.3	62.7	0	16.9	0	5640	0	8230	0	8230
Montana	149	18.6	7950	—	—	61.3	0	—	—	110	0	8290	0	8290

Nebraska	330	48.4	8790	93.4	—	38.1	0	128	4.552	820	0	12,200	4.55	12,300
Nevada	629	22.4	2110	—	—	10.3	0	—	—	36.7	0	2810	0	2810
New Hampshire	97.1	41.0	—	—	16.3	44.9	0	6.80	0	236	761	447	761	1210
New Jersey	1050	79.7	4.75	1.68	6.46	132	0	110	0	650	3390	2170	3390	5560
New Mexico	296	31.4	2860	—	—	10.5	0	—	—	56.4	0	3260	0	3260
New York	2570	270	35.5	—	—	297	0	—	—	4040	5010	7210	5010	12,200
North Carolina	945	189	287	121	7.88	293	0	36.4	0	7850	1620	9730	1620	11,400
North Dakota	63.6	11.9	145	—	—	17.6	0	—	—	902	0	1140	0	1140
Ohio	1470	134	31.7	25.3	1.36	807	0	88.5	0	8590	0	11,100	0	11,100
Oklahoma	675	25.5	718	151	16.4	25.9	0	2.48	256	146	256	1760	256	2020
Oregon	566	76.2	6080	—	—	195	0	182	—	15.30	0	6930	0	6930
Pennsylvania	1460	132	13.9	—	—	1190	0	—	0	6980	0	9950	0	9950
Rhode Island	119	8.99	3.45	—	—	4.28	0	—	—	2.40	290	138	290	429
South Carolina	566	63.5	267	—	—	565	0	—	—	5710	0	7170	0	7170
South Dakota	93.3	9.53	373	42.0	—	5.12	0	—	—	5.24	0	528	0	528
Tennessee	890	32.6	22.4	—	—	842	0	—	—	9040	0	10,800	0	10,800
Texas	4230	131	8630	308	—	1450	907	220	504	9820	3440	24,800	4,850	29,600
Utah	638	16.1	3860	—	116	42.7	5.08	26.3	198	62.20	0	4760	203	4970
Vermont	60.1	21.0	3.78	—	—	6.91	0	—	—	355	0	447	0	447
Virginia	720	133	26.4	—	—	470	53.3	—	—	3850	3580	5200	3,640	8830
Washington	1020	125	3040	—	—	577	39.9	—	—	519	0	5270	39.9	5310
West Virginia	190	40.4	0.04	—	—	968	0	—	—	3950	0	5150	0	5150
Wisconsin	623	96.3	196	66.3	70.2	447	0	—	—	6090	0	7590	0	7590
Wyoming	107	6.57	4500	—	—	5.78	0	79.5	222	243	0	4940	222	5170
Puerto Rico	513	0.88	94.5	—	—	11.2	0	—	—	0	2190	620	2,190	2810
U.S. Virgin Islands	6.09	1.69	0.50	—	—	3.34	0	—	—	0	136	11.6	136	148
Total	~3,300	3720	137,000	1760	3700	18,500	1280	2010	1490	136,000	59,500	346,000	62,300	408,000

[Figures may not sum to totals because of independent rounding. All values in million gallons per day. —, data not collected]

Source: U.S. Geological Survey, http://water.usgs.gov/pubs/circ/2004/circ1268/htdocs/table02.html

TABLE 5 Trends of Estimated Water Use in the United States. 1950–1995

| | Year | | | | | | | | | | Percentage Change |
	1950[a]	1955[a]	1960[b]	1965[b]	1970[c]	1975[d]	1980[d]	1985[d]	1990[d]	1995[d]	1990–95
Population, in millions	150.7	164.0	179.3	193.8	205.9	216.4	229.6	242.4	252.3	267.1	+6
Offstream use											
Total withdrawals	180	240	270	310	370	420	440[e]	399	408	402	−2
Public supply	14	17	21	24	27	29	34	36.5	38.5	40.2	+4
Rural domestic and livestock	3.6	3.6	3.6	4.0	4.5	4.9	5.6	7.79	7.89	8.89	+13
Irrigation	89	110	110	120	130	140	150	137	137	134	−2
Industrial											
Thermoelectric power use	40	72	100	130	170	200	210	187	195	190	−3
Other industrial use	37	39	38	46	47	45	45	30.5	29.9	29.1	−3
Source of water											
Ground:											
Fresh	34	47	50	60	68	82	83[e]	73.2	79.4	76.4	−4
Saline	(f)	.6	.4	.5	1	1	.9	.652	1.22	1.11	−9
Surface:											
Fresh	140	180	190	210	250	260	290	265	259	264	+2
Saline	10	18	31	43	53	69	71	59.6	68.2	59.7	−12
Reclaimed wastewater	(f)	.2	.6	.7	.5	.5	.5	.579	.750	1.02	+36
Consumptive use	(f)	(f)	61	77	87[g]	96[g]	100[g]	92.3[g]	94.0[g]	100[g]	+6
Instream use											
Hydroelectric power	1100	1500	2000	2300	2800	3300	3300	3050	3290	3160	−4

[a] 48 states and District of Columbia

[b] 50 states and District of Columbia

[c] 50 states and District of Columbia, and Puerto Rico

[d] 50 states and District of Columbia, Puerto Rico, and Virgin Islands

[e] Revised

[f] Data not available

[g] Freshwater only

Source: USGS 2004 [3]. [Data for 1950–1980 adapted from MacKichan (1951, 1957), MacKichan and Kammerer (1961), Murray (1968), Murray and Reeves (1972, 1977), and Solley and others (1983, 1988). The water use data are in thousands of million gallons per day and are rounded to two significant figures for 1950–1980 and to three significant figures for 1985–1990; percentage change is calculated from unrounded numbers.]

(http://www.census.gov) maintains historic records and forecasts, errors in estimates sometime occur [17, 18]. Because many uncertain factors affect population change (fertility, mortality, and migration, for example), most forecasters suggest exploring at least three trends in population growth based on plausible mixes of influencing factors.

Population Trends

There have been some notable trends in population change in the United States during the last part of the twentieth century. They include internal migration from the Northeast and other areas to the South and West and out-migration from central cities. The U.S. Census Bureau projects that during the first quarter of the twenty-first century, net population change will be most evident in three states—California, Texas, and Florida [17]. It has also been projected that the fastest growth will be in the West.

Cities confronted with declines in population often experience shifts in the character of their residents as well. In general, the more affluent residents move out, thus reducing the tax base and leaving a less-well-off population to shoulder tax burdens and maintain water and other municipal services. An associated problem can be that of maintaining a larger-than-needed infrastructure with fewer resources.

Rural migration, fueled by the belief of many urban dwellers that rural locations are more attractive and in some cases less expensive, accounts for some of the loss of population by central cities. The shifting of population to sparsely settled areas can create problems in water supply and wastewater treatment services. Factors that could counter this trend include escalating energy prices, which make transportation to jobs more costly; traffic problems associated with large numbers of commuters from rural areas; and urban renewal projects in downtown areas offering modern accommodations combined with convenience to city attractions.

Since the 1960s, movement to the sunbelt has brought about regional population shifts. The population in some northeastern and north-central states has been declining, whereas growth in the South and West has been accelerating.

Planners and developers must recognize and carefully consider current and emerging population trends. The impacts of these trends on water requirements can be significant, and, if ignored, can result in costly deficit or excess capacities of proposed facilities.

It must be recognized, however, that rates of change in population are not necessarily the same as those for water use. Per capita water use can remain constant, increase, or decrease during the period of the forecast. The rate of water use could mirror the rate of population change or be more or less than that rate.

Population Forecasting

Population estimates required for designing and operating water supply and waste treatment works may be (1) short-term estimates in the range of one to 10 years, and (2) long-term estimates of 10 to 50 years or more. The prediction of future population is at best complex. It should be emphasized that there is no exact solution, although sophisticated mathematical equations are often used. War, technological developments, new scientific discoveries, government operations, and a whole host of other factors can drastically disrupt population trends. There is no surefire way to predict many of these occurrences; thus, their impact can only be estimated to the best of current ability.

Mathematical and graphical methods are both used. Forecasts are often based on past census records for the area or on the records of what are considered to be similar communities. But extrapolations of past trends do not consider such factors as the influx of workers when new industries settle in the area, the loss of residents due to curtailment of military activities, or changes in business or transportation facilities. To optimize estimates, all possible information regarding anticipated industrial growth, local birth and death rates, government activities, and other related factors should be obtained and used. The local census bureau, planning commissions, the bureau of vital statistics, local utility companies, movers, and the chamber of commerce are all sources of information.

Trend-Based Methods

Trend-based methods assume that population growth follows natural growth patterns and can, therefore, be represented in mathematical or graphic form. Usually the approach is that of extending past trends into the future. Linear, geometric, exponential, logarithmic, and other mathematical tools have been used. These methods are easy to use but they neglect to consider that past trends are not necessarily sustained.

Most short-term estimates (one to 10 years) are made using trend-based methods. They often follow segments of a typical population growth curve as shown in Figure 4. This S curve can be considered to consist of geometric, arithmetic, and decreasing rates of increase segments.

Arithmetical Progression   This method of estimation is based on a constant increment of increase and may be stated as

$$\frac{dY}{dt} = K_u \tag{1}$$

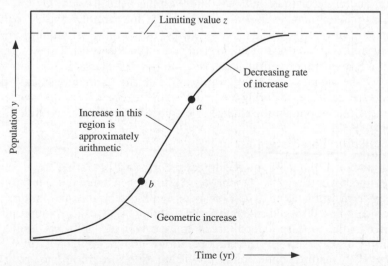

FIGURE 4   Population growth curve.

where

Y = population

t = time (usually years)

K_u = uniform growth-rate constant

If Y_1 represents the population at the census preceding the last census (time t_1), and Y_2 represents the population at the last census (time t_2), then

$$\int_{Y_1}^{Y_2} dY = \int_{t_1}^{t_2} dt$$

Integrating and inserting the limits, we obtain

$$Y_2 - Y_1 = K_u(t_2 - t_1)$$

Therefore,

$$K_u = \frac{Y_2 - Y_1}{t_2 - t_1} \tag{2}$$

We use Eq. (2) to write an expression for short-term arithmetic estimates of population growth:

$$Y = Y_2 + \frac{Y_2 - Y_1}{t_2 - t_1}(t - t_2) \tag{3}$$

Here, t represents the end of the forecast period.

Constant-Percentage Growth Rate   For equal periods of time, this procedure assumes constant growth percentages. If the population increased from 90,000 to 100,000 in the past 10 years, it would be estimated that the growth in the ensuing decade would be to $100,000 + 0.11 \times 100,000$, or 111,000. Mathematically, this may be formulated as

$$\frac{dY}{dt} = K_p Y \tag{4}$$

where the variables are defined as before, except that K_p represents a constant percentage increase per unit time. Integrating this expression and setting the limits yields

$$K_p = \frac{\log_e Y_2 - \log_e Y_1}{t_2 - t_1} \tag{5}$$

A short-term geometric estimate of population growth is thus given by

$$\log_e Y = \log_e Y_2 + K_p(t - t_2) \tag{6}$$

Note that base 10 logs may also be used in Eqs. (5) and (6).

Decreasing Rate of Increase   Estimates made on the basis of a decreasing rate of increase assume a variable rate of change. Mathematically, this may be formulated as

$$\frac{dY}{dt} = K(Z - Y) \tag{7}$$

where Z is the saturation or limiting value that must be estimated and the other variables are as previously defined. Then,

$$\int_{y_1}^{y_2} \frac{dY}{(Z - Y)} = K_D \int_{t_1}^{t_2} dt \tag{8}$$

and upon integration,

$$-\log_e \frac{Z - Y_2}{Z - Y_1} = K_D(t_2 - t_1) \tag{9}$$

Rearranging yields

$$Z - Y_2 = (Z - Y)e^{-K_D \Delta t} \tag{10}$$

Then, subtracting both sides of the equation from $(Z - Y_1)$, we obtain

$$(Z - Y_1) - (Z - Y_2) = (Z - Y_1) - (Z - Y_1)e_-^{K_D \Delta t} \tag{11}$$

and

$$Y_2 - Y_1 = (Z - Y_1)(1 - e^{-K_D \Delta t}) \tag{12}$$

Equation (12) may be used to make short-term estimates in the limiting region.

Curve Fitting   Population data are also used to derive equations that fit observed trends or to select a mathematical function that appears to fit the data and then use that relationship for extrapolating into the future [19]. In general, mathematical curve fitting has its greatest utility in the study of large population centers or nations. The Gompertz curve and the logistic curve are both used in establishing long-term population trends. Both curves are S-shaped and have upper and lower asymptotes, with the lower asymptotes being equal to zero.

The logistic curve in its simplest form is [19]

$$Y_c = \frac{K}{1 + 10^{a+bX}} \tag{13}$$

where

$$Y_c = \text{ordinate of the curve}$$
$$X = \text{time period in years (10-year intervals are frequently chosen)}$$
$$K, a, b = \text{constants}$$

Short-term, trend-based forecasts are more reliable than long-term, trend-based forecasts since over long periods there is considerable opportunity for unpredictable factors to affect the forecasted trend.

Methods Based on Relationship of Growth in One Area to That of Another

Long-term predictions are sometimes made by graphical comparison with growth rates of similar and larger cities. The population–time curve of a given community can be extrapolated on the basis of trends experienced by similar and larger communities. Population trends are plotted in such a manner that all the curves are coincident at the present population value of the city being studied (see Figure 5). The cities selected for comparison should not have reached the reference population value too far in the past since the historical periods involved may be considerably different. It should be understood that the future growth of a city may digress significantly from the observed development of communities of similar size. In making the final projection, consideration should be given to conditions that are anticipated for the growth of the community in question. With the exercise of due caution, this method could give reasonable results.

The population growth in an area may also be estimated from the growth of a larger area of which it is a part, such as a state, geographical region, or nation. The procedure used is to compute the ratio of the population of the area of interest to the population of the larger area at the time of the most recent census [20]. Then, using a projection of the growth of the larger area, an estimate of growth for the study area may be made by applying the population ratio. This is known as the *ratio method*. Ratios may also be computed over time and the time series of ratios extrapolated using techniques for projecting trends discussed earlier. The ratio projected for a

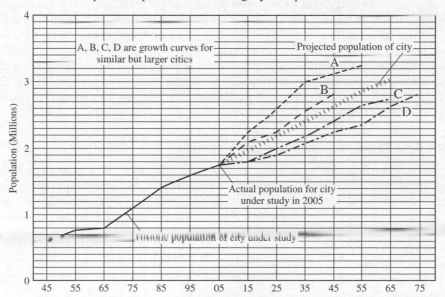

FIGURE 5   Graphical prediction of population by comparison.

future date is then applied to the forecasted population of the larger area for that time. Ratio methods should be used with caution because historic relationships between the area of concern and the larger area may change as well as other influencing factors.

Component Methods

The rate of population change at any location at any time is determined by many factors, some of which are interactive. They include birth rate, death rate, immigration, emigration, government policies, societal attitudes, religious beliefs, education, technological change, and war. The components of population change (births, deaths, net migration) can be linked to form the fundamental population equation:

$$P_2 = P_1 + B - D \pm M \tag{14}$$

where

P_2 = the population at the end of the time interval
P_1 = the population at the beginning of the time interval
B = number of births occurring in the population during the time interval
D = number of deaths occurring in the population during the time interval
M = net number of migrants moving to or away from the region during the time interval

The component method is widely used by population forecasters. For most areas and municipalities, it should provide better forecasts than those that would be obtained using the trend and ratio methods described earlier. Component methods take into account the size of the study area at the start of the forecast period and the effects of births, deaths, and migration on a population of that size. The procedure also requires the forecaster to take into account the influences on the components of Eq. (14) of events (industrial growth, regulatory policies, etc.) that may be expected to occur during the forecast period.

Forecasts Based on Estimates of Employment

Population growth in a locality depends on the ability of that location to provide jobs for the people living there. Forecasts of the labor force required to support local commercial, industrial, and institutional needs can thus be used as the basis for making population projections. Usually a labor-force-to-population ratio is computed and used. Procedures based on a single indicator like this are subject to errors that result from the failure to consider other influences on population change. They should be used with caution.

Population Density

Knowing the total population of a region makes it possible to estimate the total volume of water supply or wastewater generated. To design conveyance systems for such

TABLE 6   Guide to Population Density

Area Type	Number of Persons per Acre
Residential — single-family units	5–35
Residential — multiple-family units	30–100
Apartments	100–1000
Commercial areas	15–30
Industrial areas	5–15

flows, additional information regarding the physical distribution of the population to be served must be obtained. It is important to know the population density as well as the total population. Population densities may be estimated from data collected on existing areas and from zoning master plans for undeveloped areas. Table 6 may be used as a guide if more reliable local data are not available.

Example 4

A community that had a population of 250,000 in 2000 estimates that its population will increase to 400,000 by 2020. The water treatment facilities in place can process up to 55 million gallons per day (mgd). The 2000 per capita water use rate was found to be 160 gpcd. Estimate the water requirements for the community in 2020 assuming that the per capita use rate remains unchanged. Will new treatment facilities be needed to accommodate this growth in population? If revised plumbing codes were adopted during the period of growth and if these changes resulted in an overall reduction in the community's water use by 15%, what would the water requirement be in 2020? Could expansion of treatment facilities be deferred until after 2020 under these conditions?

Solution:

1. The water requirement in 2020 for a population of 400,000 and a per capita use rate of 160 gpcd would be

$$400,000 \times 160 = 64 \text{ mgd}$$

2. Since 64 mgd exceeds the 2000 treatment capacity of 55 mgd, new facilities would be needed before 2020.

3. For a 15% reduction in water use, the per capita water requirements would be

$$160 \times 0.85 = 136 \text{ gpcd}$$

Water use in 2020 would be

$$136 \times 400,000 = 54.4 \text{ mgd}$$

4. Under these conditions, expansion of water treatment facilities could be deferred until after 2020, since the demand of 54.4 mgd is less than the treatment plant capacity of 55 mgd.

This example illustrates that an alternative to providing new facilities to meet expanding water needs could be more efficient use of the water already at hand.

Example 5

Consider that in 2000 a state had a total water withdrawal of 8 billion gallons per day (bgd) distributed as follows: municipal water use, 1 bgd; steam electric generation, 5 bgd; and irrigated agriculture, 2 bgd. The 2000 population was 11.7 million, and by 2020 it is expected that the population will increase to 13.2 million. Furthermore, it is estimated that 4000 megawatts (MW) of new electricity-generating capacity will be installed by 2020 and that irrigated acreage will expand by 500,000 acres. Estimate the total water withdrawal in 2020 and the withdrawal for each of the three sectors.

Solution:

1. Estimated water use in the municipal sector can be obtained by using the projected change in population and an estimate of per capita water use in 2020. Assume the latter to be 140 gpcd. Change in population 2000 to 2020 = 13.2 − 11.7 = 1.5 million. 1.5 × 140 = 210 mgd = 0.21 bgd increase in municipal water use from 2000 to 2020.

2. Assume that the water requirements for the crops to be raised average 3 acre · ft per acre. 500,000 (acres) × 3 (acre · ft/per acre) = 1,500,000 acre · ft irrigation water needed annually in 2020. Since 1.12 million acre · ft/yr = 1 bgd, 1.5/1.12 = 1.34 bgd, the added irrigation water requirement in 2020.

3. Assume that the plant capacity factor for the steam electric facilities to be built is 60% (this measures the percentage of the nameplate, or installed capacity, of generating facilities that is actually realized in operation). At a 60% capacity factor, one kilowatt of installed capacity would produce 14.4 kilowatt-hours (kWh) of electrical energy each day. Note also that the WRC indicates that new steam electric facilities using once-through cooling (which we shall assume here) will require about 50 gallons of water per kilowatt-hour. Then 4000 MW × 1000 (kW/MW) × 14.4 = 57,600,000 kWh per day $57.6 \times 10^6 \times 50$ (gal/kWh) = 2880 mgd or 2.88 bgd, the water requirement for steam electric cooling to be added from 2000 to 2020.

4. The added water requirements to 2020 are thus obtained by totaling the incremental increases for the three sectors: 0.21 + 1.34 + 2.88 = 4.43 bgd increase; thus, the total water withdrawal in 2020 would be 4.43 + 8.00 = 12.43 bgd. The combined withdrawal use in 2020 would thus be about 1.6 times that of 2000.

5   LONG-TERM WATER USE FORECASTING

Forecasting is the art and science of looking ahead; it is the core of planning processes. Options for selecting a forecasting procedure range from the exercise of judgment to the use of complex mathematical models. Forecasts are required for periods varying from less than a day to more than 50 years. Unfortunately, the more distant the planning horizon, the more questionable the forecast. It is therefore important to exercise great care in selecting a forecasting technique and to understand the limitations of the method selected. Furthermore, an array of alternative futures, rather than a single projection, should be used to make decisions. Forecasts should be recognized for being approximations of what might occur, not accurate portrayals of what will be. Commonly used forecasting methods include projections based on historic data, the use of models and simulation, and qualitative and holistic techniques [21].

The Delphi technique and scenario writing are examples of qualitative/holistic approaches, while trend extrapolation and trend impact analysis are history-based procedures [21]. Simulation is the process of mimicking the dynamic behavior of a system over time. A simulation (or model) is a surrogate of the real-world system it is designed to represent. Model results are widely used to describe (forecast) the future states of water or other systems being studied.

Many types of forecasting models have been used in water supply planning. They range from rough trend extrapolations and crude correlations of variables to complex mathematical representations of the dynamics of land and water use. Historically, future water requirements were determined as the product of a projected service area population and an anticipated per capita water use rate. Such an approach employs only two of the determinants of water use. Furthermore, per capita water use rates generally vary within and among communities and over time. The bottom line, however, is that long-term planning for public water supply systems depends on reliable forecasts of water demands and on identifying and assessing demand-side alternatives. Demand-reduction options must be considered because they can increase the efficiency of water use, thereby increasing the likelihood that future water supplies and demands will be balanced at a cost below the economic, social, and environmental costs of developing new water sources.

IWR-MAIN Water Demand Analysis Software

IWR-MAIN is a computerized water use forecasting system that includes a range of forecasting models and data management techniques [22–29]. The IWR-MAIN Water Demand Management Suite © (DMS, 1999) operates in the Windows environment using an open architecture in which the user inputs the forecasting model and specific variables into the model. The software features a high level of disaggregation of water use categories and user flexibility in selecting forecasting methods and assumptions. It is designed to deal principally with urban water uses: residential, commercial/institutional, manufacturing, and uses not accounted for in other sectors. The model also provides for forecasts of water use recognizing the influences of conservation policies, indicates the disaggregation of urban water use, summarizes estimation methods, and indicates the IWR-MAIN model inputs and outputs. The narrative presentation of the IWR-MAIN model given in this chapter follows that of Planning and Management Consultants, Ltd. [22, 23].

The water demand management models described here are effective predictive models developed for IWR-MAIN Version 6.1 ©. They have three major components: forecasting water use, estimating conservation water savings, and performing benefit/cost analyses. IWR-MAIN uses econometric water demand models for translating the existing demographic, housing, and business statistics into estimates of existing water demands. These estimates are used to fine-tune the water use equations for translating the long-term projections of population, housing, and employment into disaggregated forecasts of water use. An extensive analysis of existing and projected demands, disaggregated by season, sector, and purpose, is conducted to generate estimates of water conservation savings from efficient technologies and plumbing codes as well as from utility-sponsored programs such as retrofits, water audits, financial incentives, and public education and information initiatives. Estimates of water savings can also be used in analyzing the economic effectiveness of demand-side alternatives.

The IWR-MAIN software disaggregates total urban water use by customer sectors, time periods, spatial study areas, and end-use purposes. Water demands of various parts of a service area are disaggregated according to their seasonal variation and the relative needs of various customer classes and sectors (e.g., residential single-family, residential multifamily, commercial, manufacturing, and government). The water demands of each sector in a given area and period are expressed as a product of (1) the number of users (i.e., demand drivers such as the number of residents, housing units, employees, and parkways) and (2) the average rate of water use (e.g., per household or per employee) as determined by a set of explanatory variables for a given sector. In the residential sector, the set of explanatory variables may include income, price of water and wastewater services, household size, housing density, air temperature, and rainfall. The seasonality of water use may be represented by including a set of binary variables for months (or seasons) of the year. In the nonresidential sector, these factors may include employment by industry type, labor productivity, weather conditions, and the price of water and wastewater services. Separate forecasts can be made for each identified sector; for specific study areas such as cities, counties, and load zones; for summer and winter daily water use; and for average daily, annual, and peak-day water use. In addition, the software provides for the inclusion of a variety of demand management or conservation practices. The conservation savings component of IWR-MAIN distinguishes among passive, active, and emergency (i.e., temporary) conservation effects. *Passive* conservation effects are represented by shifts in end-use consumption from less-efficient fixtures/practices to more-efficient fixtures/practices brought about mainly through plumbing codes for new construction or improved water-use technologies. The conservation savings of *active* programs are estimated by noted changes in water use efficiency classes brought about by participation in a utility-sponsored program in which inefficient or standard end uses are replaced or retrofitted. These water savings can be incorporated into long-term forecasts of water demand.

IWR-MAIN can also help the user conduct *benefit/cost analyses of demand management alternatives*, that is, of the active conservation programs for which water savings have been estimated. A number of economic feasibility tests are used to evaluate the economic merits of conservation programs, including net present value, discounted payback period, benefit/cost ratio, levelized cost, and life-cycle revenue impact. The results of the benefit/cost component of IWR-MAIN can be used to compare supply augmentation alternatives with demand management alternatives using the same economic criteria.

IWR-MAIN also offers the ability to conduct *sensitivity analyses*, or what-if scenarios, regarding projected changes in the determinants of water demand and to assess the impact of these changes on long-term water demands. Thus, water planners may evaluate the impact of changes in socioeconomic conditions, weather patterns, water pricing, or alternative conservation programs.

Residential Sector Forecasting

Within the residential sector of IWR-MAIN there are seven subsectors available for forecasting water demands: (1) single family—single attached or detached units; (2) multifamily low density—two, three, or four units per structure; (3) multifamily high density—five or more units per structure; (4) mobile homes; (5) nonurban; (6) user added; and (7) total residential. These categories correspond to the housing types used by the U.S. Bureau of the Census. One or more of the seven subsectors may be used, depending on the characteristics of the service area. The DMS allows the user to select the subsectors to be evaluated and allows the user to define new subsectors. The residential water demand model described here may be entered into the IWR-MAIN DMS for residential subsectors.

Average rates of water use within each residential subsector are estimated using causal water demand models, which take the following theoretical form [22, 23]:

$$q_{c,s,t} = \alpha I^{\beta 1} H^{\beta 2} L^{\beta 3}\, T^{\beta 4} R^{\beta 5} P^{\beta 6} e^{b7B} \tag{15}$$

where

$q_{c,s,t}$ = predicted water use in sector c, during year s, in year t

I = median household income

H = average household size (persons)

L = average household density (units per acre)

T = average maximum daily temperature

R = rainfall

P = marginal price of water (including sewer charges related to water use)

B = fixed charge or rate premium

α = constant

β_i = constant elasticities of explanatory variables

The season, sectoral, and temporal indices of the explanatory variables in the above equation are suppressed for clarity. This water demand model conforms to economic theory and may be considered causal since the explanatory variables can be shown to cause the demand. For example, "income" measures the consumer's ability to pay for water and "price" influences the amount of water the consumer is willing to purchase.

The default elasticities of the explanatory variables of residential household water use are derived from econometric studies of water demand through a rigorous statistical analysis of empirical data. Multiple regression is used to explain the variance in the values of reported elasticities due to interstudy differences. Note that elasticity is interpreted as the percent change in quantity (e.g., water use) that is expected from a 1% change in the explanatory variable [23].

Nonresidential Sector Forecasting

The nonresidential sector of IWR-MAIN addresses water uses within the following major industry groups: (1) construction; (2) manufacturing; (3) transportation, communications, and utilities (TCU); (4) wholesale trade; (5) retail trade; (6) finance, insurance, and real estate (FIRE); (7) services; and (8) public administration. The DMS has default nonresidential subsectors for commercial, industrial, and government, yet allows the user to add additional subsectors as needed for the analysis of a given study area. The eight major industry groups are classified according to Department of Commerce Standard Industrial Classification (SIC) codes (note that in 1997, the U.S. Office of Management and Budget issued the North American Industry Classification System [NAICS] to replace the SIC classification system). The conceptual model of water use in the nonresidential (commercial/industrial) sector is [22, 23]

$$Q_i = f(GED_i, E_i, L_i, P_i, CDD, O_i) \tag{16}$$

where

$$Q_i = \text{category-wide water use in gallons per day}$$
$$GED_i = \text{gallon per employee per day water use}$$
$$E_i = \text{category-wide employment}$$
$$L_i = \text{average productivity (of labor) in category I}$$
$$P_i = \text{marginal price of water and wastewater services in category I}$$
$$CDD = \text{cooling degree days}$$
$$O_i = \text{other variables known to affect commercial/industrial water use}$$

Although this theoretical model is fully operational within IWR-MAIN, there are no currently available econometric (and generally applicable) models that contain model elasticities for price, productivity, cooling degree days, or the other variables for nonresidential water uses. Such models of nonresidential use may be estimated for the given study area from historic water use and economic and climatic data. The IWR-MAIN system is designed, however, to accommodate the above model specifications once data regarding the responsiveness of nonresidential water use to such variables become available. Thus, Version 6.1 of IWR-MAIN calculates commercial/industrial water use based upon gallon-per-employee-per-day coefficients for SIC categories and groups [22, 23]:

$$Q_i = (GED_i \cdot E_i) \tag{17}$$

The water-use-per-employee coefficients contained within IWR-MAIN are the result of extensive research devoted to collecting data on employment and water use for various establishments throughout the United States. The water use coefficients within IWR-MAIN are based on the analysis of water use and employment relationships in over 7000 establishments. Table 7 shows the water-use-per-employee coefficients for the eight major industry groups.

The appropriate SIC level to be used should be based on the structure of employment in the community, the availability of employment data at the various levels, and the need for sensitivity analyses regarding potential water use impacts.

TABLE 7   Nonresidential Water Use Coefficients Contained in TWR-MAIN Version 6 (1995)

Major Industry Group	SIC Codes	Water Use Coefficient (gallons/employee/day)[a]	
Construction	15–17	20.7	(244)
Manufacturing	20–39	132.5	(2784)
Transportation, communications, utilities (TCU)	40–49	49.3	(225)
Wholesale trade	50–51	42.8	(750)
Retail trade	52–59	93.1	(1041)
Finance, insurance, real estate (FIRE)	60–67	70.8	(233)
Services	70–89	137.5	(1870)
Public administration	91–97	105.7	(25)

[a]The numbers in parentheses represent the sample number of establishments from which the water use coefficient was calculated.

Source: Planning and Management Consultants, Ltd., Carbondale, Il. [33]

Additional Sector Forecasting

IWR-MAIN can be used to address water uses in a service area not accounted for by the other sectors. Water use in these special categories must be expressed as a function of a single explanatory variable (such as the number of acres or number of facilities). Water-use coefficients (expressed in gallons per day per selected unit) must also be provided. Forecasts for these uses can be made by projecting the number of units into the future and multiplying them by the appropriate water-use coefficients. The following examples of uses and defining parameters fall under this classification: (1) irrigation of public parks and medians (acres), (2) make-up water for public swimming pools (number of pools), and (3) irrigation of golf courses (acres) [22, 23].

Other/Unaccounted-for Sector Forecasts

The difference between the total quantity of water produced (treated and delivered) and the quantity of water sold to customers is referred to as *unaccounted-for water use*. This sector may include the following types of uses/losses: (1) distribution system leakage, (2) meter slippage, (3) hydrant flushing, (4) major line breaks, (5) firefighting, (6) unmetered or nonbilled customers, (7) illegal connections, and (8) street washing/construction water [23]. Water utilities generally record unaccounted-for water use as the percentage difference between total quantity of water delivered to the distribution system and total metered sales. In the IWR-MAIN model, users specify a percentage rate for each base and forecast year to estimate the amount of unaccounted-for water.

Socioeconomic Input Data Requirements

Two types of data are required for generating water use estimates from the IWR-MAIN system: (1) actual values of demographic and socioeconomic determinants (or parameters) of water use for the base year and (2) projected values of selected determinants for each forecast year [22]. IWR-MAIN can accommodate a variable degree of data availability. The amount of time and effort required to prepare a forecast depends on the chosen level of detail of the input data and the chosen level of disaggregation of the user sectors. Base year input data for the IWR-MAIN system may be used to estimate current water requirements and may also be used as a reference for projections of future parameter values.

Water Conservation Savings Methods

The conservation savings module of the IWR-MAIN system further disaggregates seasonal demands of various water use sectors into a number of specific end uses such as dishwashing, toilet flushing, lawn watering, cooling, and others. This high level of disaggregation is designed to accommodate the evaluation of various demand management (conservation) measures that usually target specific end uses. The IWR-MAIN conservation savings module uses an end-use accounting system that disaggregates the seasonal demands of various water use sectors into as many as 16 end uses [22]. A rational representation of each end use is made using a structural end-use equation. Given parameters of local end-use conditions, the equation predicts the average quantity of water for each end use as a function of (1) the distribution of end uses among three classes of efficiency (nonconserving, standard, and ultraconserving), (2) average usage rate or intensity of use, (3) leakage rate and incidence of leaks, and (4) presence of end use within a given customer sector. The structure of the end use equation allows the planner to estimate the net effects of long-term conservation programs by tracking the values of each end-use parameter over time. The end-use relationship is expressed as [22, 23]

$$q_i = [(M_1 S_1 + M_2 S_2 + M_3 S_3) \cdot U_N + K \cdot F_N] \cdot A_N \qquad (18)$$

where

q_i = quantity of water used by end use i, gpd/unit

M_{1-3} = mechanical parameter (e.g., volume per use, flow rate per minute)

S_{1-3} = fraction of the sector for end use that is nonconserving, standard, and ultraconserving

U_N = intensity of use parameters (e.g., flushes per day/unit, minutes of use per day/unit)

K = mechanical parameter representing the rate of leakage

F_N = fraction of end uses with leakage

A_N = fraction of units in which end use i is present

N = normal use or nondrought/nonemergency

$1-3$ = end use or group that is nonconserving, standard, and ultraconserving 1 signifying the lowest level of efficiency

Long-term conservation savings may be achieved by increasing the fractions S_2 and S_3, which is accomplished by moving customers from one efficiency class to another. For example, for each end use, a fraction of the water users would be shifted from nonconserving to ultra-conserving or from standard to ultra-conserving. The quantifiable effect of the program is accounted for directly by the numerical shift in the customer pools and the change in the fractions of customers in each efficiency class.

The conservation savings module distinguishes among passive, active, and emergency (i.e., temporary) conservation effects. Passive conservation effects are represented by shifts in end-use consumption from less efficient fixtures to more-efficient fixtures brought about primarily by plumbing codes for new construction (e.g., the toilet end use moves from the inefficient 5.5-gallon-per-flush toilet to the standard 3.5-gallon toilet, or the highly efficient 1.6-gallon toilet). The conservation savings of active programs are estimated by noting changes in the distribution of efficiency classes brought about by the participation in a utility-sponsored program whose inefficient or standard end uses were replaced or retrofitted.

Applications

Output from the IWR-MAIN model can be used to aid in the following:

- Planning to meet future water supply needs.
- Sizing and expanding distribution systems.
- Preparing contingency plans for water shortages.
- Evaluating the effectiveness of conservation practices.
- Performing sensitivity analyses using varying assumptions about water prices, climatic factors, and other determinants of water use.
- Assessing utility revenues with improved precision.

The IWR-MAIN model has been used in Arizona, Illinois, Texas, Oklahoma, California, Nevada, Massachusetts, Oregon, and Florida [22, 23]. To obtain more information on the IWR-MAIN system or to find out how to obtain software, the reader should visit http://www.iwrmain.com/.

There are numerous models for forecasting water use. The prediction equations for many of these models are empirical and have been derived using regression analysis or related techniques [30–34]. Most models developed since 1970 also include the cost of supplying water as a parameter [22, 24–29, 34–37]. The IWR-MAIN model is typical of the types of approaches that can be taken in water-use forecasting. Further information on forecasting models may be found in the references at the end of the chapter [38–48].

Example 6

The Planning Council of the City of Gladston, Florida is facing problems of population growth and increasing stress on the city's public water supply system. To provide guidance for the council, a consulting firm has been hired to (1) prepare three alternative population forecasts for the years 2010 and 2020, (2) prepare three alternative average annual water use forecasts for estimating the demands that may be placed on the city's public water supply system for the same time frame, and (3) estimate the 2010 and 2020 water demands (million gallons per day) that would result for the three alternative population forecasts and the three average annual water demand forecasts.

Solution:

1. It is decided that one of the forecasts should be based on a linear regression of the Gladston historic population data (see Table 8). Software for making such forecasts is abundant, but the software used here is the WinQSB forecasting tool for linear regression [49]. Figure 6 shows the high-degree of correlation of the forecasted linear trend with the actual data. Table 9 shows the linear regression forecast results. Note the high value of R-squared. These forecasted populations, for 2010 and 2020, are identified as Population 1 and shown on Table 10.

A review of population growth statistics for several cities about the size of Gladston (U.S. Census Data, reveals that an annual rate of growth of 2%

TABLE 8	Historic Population for Gladston
Year	Population Millions
1930	0.578
1940	0.689
1950	0.837
1960	1.024
1970	1.263
1980	1.546
1990	1.731
2000	1.847

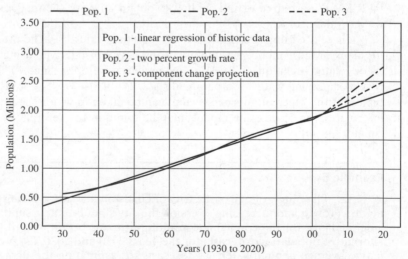

FIGURE 6   Gladston population, actual and forecast, from 1930 to 2020 (Example 6).

TABLE 9 Linear Regression Forecast Results

03-20-2007 10 years	Actual Data	Forecast by LR
1	0.5780	0.5036
2	0.6890	0.6995
3	0.8370	0.8955
4	1.0240	1.0914
5	1.2630	1.2873
6	1.5460	1.4833
7	1.7310	1.6792
8	1.8470	1.8752
9		2.0711
10		2.2670
CFE		0.0000
MAD		0.0472
MSE		0.0027
MAPE		4.8087
Trk. Signal		0.0000
R-square		0.9868
		Y-intercept = 0.3076
		Slope = 0.1959

TABLE 10 Gladston Population Forecasts for 2010 and 2020

Population 1–Linear Regression of Historic Data		
2000	2010	2020
1.85 million	2.07 million	2.27 million
Population 2–Two Percent Growth Rate		
2000	2010	2020
1.85 million	2.25 million	2.74 million
Population 3–Component Projection		
2000	2010	2020
1.85 million	2.17 million	2.48 million

would be highly likely. Using this information, population forecasts for 2010 and 2020 were estimated with the equation

$$P_2 = P_1(1 + i)^n$$

where P_2 is the population at time 2, P_1 is the population at time 1 (Year 2000, population = 1,847), i = percent as a decimal, and n = the number of years into the future. Thus,

i. $P_{2010} = 1.847(1 + 0.02)^{10} = 2.25$ million
ii. $P_{2020} = 1.847(1 + 0.02)^{20} = 2.74$ million

These forecasted populations, identified as Population 2, are shown in Table 10.

The third population forecast is made via the component method (Equation 14),

iii. $P_2 = P_1 + B - D \pm M$

where P_2 is future population to be determined, P_1 is the base population (known), B is the number of births in the period between P_1 and P_2, D is the number of deaths between P_1 and P_2, and M is the net migration during the time interval. In this case, P_1 is the population in 2000 (1.847). The Office of Vital Statistics in Florida provides data on B, D, and M for various political jurisdictions. The data used to forecast the component values were obtained from that agency for a number of years of record. The historic data and forecasts on births, deaths, and net migration are shown in Table 11. In the table, in the year columns for births and deaths, Year 11 is 2000, Year 21 is 2010, and Year 31 is 2020. In the year column for net migration, Year 5 is 2005, Year 10 is 2010, and Year 20 is 2020. To solve the component equations, the cumulative number of births, deaths, and net migrants must be calculated. For births the totals are 0.235 (2010) and 0.271 (2020), for deaths the totals are 0.170 (2010) and 0.184 (2020), and for net migration the totals are 0.257 (2010) and 0.226 (2020), all in thousands. The component equations to be solved are

iv. $P_{2010} = P_{2000} + B - D \pm M$

v. $P_{2010} = 1.847 + 0.235 - 0.170 + 0.257 = 2.17$ million

$P_{2020} = P_{2010} + B - D \pm M$

vi. $P_{2020} = 2.17 + 0.271 - 0.184 + 0.226 = 2.48$ million

These forecasted populations, identified as Population 3, are shown in Table 10.

Having completed the population forecasts, the next task is to prepare three alternative annual average per capita water use forecasts for 2010 and 2020. Based on current USGS water use figures which suggest a leveling off of per capita water use for public water supply systems, one alternative selected was based on the extension of the Gladston Year 2000 demand (179 gpcd) without change until 2020. This option is identified as Demand Forecast 1 (see Table 12).

2. A second alternative indicating a reduction of the Year 2000 demand by 10% in 2010 and 20% in 2020 was selected based on the emergence of new plumbing regulations and the expansion of other water-conservation methods. Under this option the average annual demands are 161.1 gpcd in 2010 and 143.2 gpcd in 2020. This option is identified as Demand Forecast 2 (see Table 12).

3. The third alternative considers a slow increase in per capita water use from public water supply systems. A plausible forecast was based on a growth of the Year 2000 demand by 2.5% in 2010 and 5% in 2020. Under this option, the average annual demands are 183.5 gpcd in 2010 and 188 gpcd in 2020. This option is identified as Demand Forecast 3 (see Table 12).

The final task is to estimate the 2010 and 2020 water demands (million gallons per day) that would result for the three alternative population forecasts and the three average annual per capita water demand forecasts. These calculations are made by

TABLE 11 Linear Regression Forecasts of Births, Deaths, and Net Migration

	Deaths			Births			Net Migration	
03-21-2007 Year	Actual Data	Forecast by LR	03-21-2007 Year	Actual Data	Forecast by LR	03-21-2007 Year	Actual Data	Forecast by LR
1	14352.0000	14751.2300	1	18738.0000	18079.6800	1	27056.0000	27074.4000
2	14586.0000	14893.5100	2	18033.0000	18428.3100	2	26786.0000	26768.9000
3	15071.0000	15035.7900	3	18317.0000	18776.9400	3	26467.0000	26463.4000
4	15628.0000	15178.0700	4	19312.0000	19125.5600	4	26173.0000	26157.9000
5	15519.0000	15320.3600	5	19488.0000	19474.1900	5	25835.0000	25852.4000
6	15804.0000	15462.6400	6	20059.0000	19822.8200	6		25546.9000
7	15921.0000	15604.9200	7	19927.0000	20171.4500	7		25241.4000
8	15579.0000	15747.2000	8	20417.0000	20520.0700	8		24935.9000
9	15633.0000	15889.4800	9	20647.0000	20868.7000	9		24630.4000
10	16215.0000	16031.7600	10	21033.0000	21217.3300	10		24324.9000
11	15781.0000	16174.0400	11	22080.0000	21565.9500	11		24019.4000
12		16316.3300	12		21914.5800	12		23713.8900
13		16458.6100	13		22263.2100	13		23408.3900
14		16600.8900	14		22611.8400	14		23102.8900
15		16743.1700	15		22960.4600	15		22797.3900
16		16885.4500	16		23309.0900	16		22491.8900
17		17027.7300	17		23657.7200	17		22186.3900
18		17170.0200	18		24006.3400	18		21880.8900
19		17312.3000	19		24354.9700	19		21575.3900
20		17454.5800	20		24703.6000	20		21269.8900
21		17596.8600	21		25052.2200	CFE		−0.0039
22		17739.1400	22		25400.8500	MAD		14.3203
23		17881.4200	23		25749.4800	MSE		234.9544
24		18023.7100	24		26098.1100	MAPE		0.0541
25		18165.9900	25		26446.7300	Trk.Signal		−0.0003
26		18308.2700	26		26795.3600	R-square		0.9987
27		18450.5500	27		27143.9900			
28		18592.8300	28		27492.6200			
29		18735.1100	29		27841.2400			
30		18877.3900	30		28189.8700			
31		19019.6800	31		28538.5000			
CFE		−0.0059	CFE		0.0059			
MAD		277.1751	MAD		292.5073			
MSE		90513.6000	MSE		119061.1000			
MAPE		1.7972	MAPE		1.4945			
Trk.Signal		0.0000	Trk.Signal		0.0000			
R-square		0.6910	R-square		0.9108			

TABLE 12   Public Water Supply Forecasts for 2010 and 2020

Demand Forecast–1, Based on 179 gpcd sustained from 2000 to 2020

	2010 Demand - mgd	2020 Demand - mgd
Pop. 1	370.5	406.3
Pop. 2	402.8	490.5
Pop. 3	388.4	443.9

Demand Forecast–2, Based on 179 gpcd decreased by 10% in 2010 and 20% in 2020

	2010 Demand - mgd	2020 Demand - mgd
Pop. 1	333.5	325.1
Pop. 2	362.5	392.4
Pop. 3	349.6	356.6

Demand Forecast–3, Based on 179 gpcd increased by 2.5% in 2010 and 5% in 2020

	2010 Demand - mgd	2020 Demand - mgd
Pop. 1	379.8	426.8
Pop. 2	412.9	515.1
Pop. 3	398.2	466.2

multiplying the alternative demands by the population options. For example, the 2010 demand for Demand Forecast 1 and Population Option 1 would be $179 \times 2.07 = 370.5$ mgd. The results of the demand computations are given in Table 12.

Armed with the consultant's findings, the Planning Council is ready to present the options to the City Council for their selection. The City Council will have to consider the ability of the current infrastructure to meet the forecasted demands of the alternatives presented. If all of the alternative demand forecasts can be met with existing facilities and water sources, there is no need for further deliberation. But if some or all of the forecasted demands cannot be met, then one of the alternative forecasts will have to be chosen to guide development of new facilities and/or sources of water supply. A reasonable selection might be Population 3 associated with Demand Forecast 1. Table 12 shows that this choice falls between the others, representing an approximate median forecast. If the City Council is very conservative, however, it might opt for the Population 2 and Demand Forecast 3 option (high forecast).

PROBLEMS

1 A reservoir has a capacity of 2.75 acre-ft. How many years would this supply a city of 100,000 if evaporation is neglected? Assume a use rate of 180 gpcd.

2 If the minimum flow of a stream having a 200-mi^2 watershed is 0.10 cfs/mi^2, what population could be supplied continuously from the stream? Assume that there is only distribution storage (maximum withdrawal = stream flow) and that the water use rate is 175 gpcd.

3 Estimate the 2010 and 2015 population of your community by plotting the historic data and extrapolating the trend. How reliable do you think this estimate would be?

4 Given the population, public water withdrawal, and total freshwater withdrawal for the states shown in Table 4 in 2000, calculate the percent of freshwater withdrawn by the public sector and the per capita water use of the freshwater for your state and the surrounding states.

5 Given the population, public water withdrawal, and total freshwater withdrawal for the states shown in Table 4 in 2000, calculate the percent of freshwater withdrawn by the public sector and the per capita water use of the freshwater for 10 states of your choice and state why you think these percentages differ.

6 Compare the annual water requirements of a 1500-acre irrigated farm and a city with a population of 130,000. Assume an irrigation requirement of 3 acre · ft/yr/acre and a per capita water use rate of 180 gpcd.

7 For the region in which you reside, determine which water-using sectors are most dominant. How did you arrive at this determination? Do you think the past trends will continue? If so, why? If not, why not? Are there water supply problems in the region? If so, could these be alleviated by modifying water use rates in one or more of the water-using sectors? How much of a reduction below current rates of use do you think could be achieved? What revision in facilities or systems operation would be required to bring about this reduction?

8 Obtain historic and projected population data on the municipality in which you reside. Consult your local water department and obtain historic and projected water use trends for your city. Estimate the current per capita water-use rate. Use this figure to project water requirements to 2010. How does your projection compare with that of the water department? By how much could the per capita water use rate be reduced, if any, by 2010?

9 Given a residential area encompassing 1100 acres with a housing density of four houses per acre and assuming a high-value residence with a fire flow requirement of 1000 gpm, find (a) the combined draft and (b) the peak hourly demand.

10 Given that a residential community has an area of 10 mi^2, assume a population density and calculate the required fire flow. Give results in gpm and lpm.

11 Consider a 1000-acre residential area with a housing density of four dwellings per acre. Estimate the peak hourly water-use requirement.

12 If 100 acres of farmland were developed for urban housing (four houses per acre), what would be the difference in average annual water requirements after the changeover? Assume that the irrigation requirement is 2.5 acre-ft of water for a growing season of six months.

13 The population of a state was 7 million in 2000. Consider that by 2015, it is expected to increase to 9 million. Consider that the amount of freshwater withdrawn in 2000 was 2.5 bgd. Estimate the amount of freshwater that might be withdrawn in 2015. State your assumptions.

14 A community had a population of 200,000 in 2000 and it is expected that this will increase to 260,000 by 2015. The water treatment capacity in 2000 was 43 mgd. A survey showed that the average per capita water use rate was 180 gpcd. Estimate the community's water requirements in 2015, and state whether expanded treatment facilities will be needed by that date, assuming (a) no change in use rate and (b) a reduced rate of 130 gpcd.

15 For the community described in Problem 14, assume that the treatment plant capacity in 2000 was 35 mgd. If the water use rate in 2015 is 140 gpcd, will expanded treatment facilities be needed by 2015? In about what year would they be needed if so? What reduction in water use rate would be needed to delay the need for new facilities until 2015? Is a reduction of this magnitude attainable?

16 Consider a state with a total water withdrawal of 4.5 bgd in 2000. This was distributed as follows: municipal use 1.0 bgd, industrial use 1.5 bgd, and steam electric cooling 2 bgd. Assume a 2000 population of 10 million and a projection of 12 million for 2015. It is estimated that an additional 3000 MW of electric-generating capacity will be required by 2015 and that the cooling water requirements will be 50 gal/kWh. An industrial expansion of 10% is also expected. Estimate the total water that will be withdrawn in 2015 for each sector and for all sectors combined. State your assumptions. Assume a plant capacity factor of 0.6 (water use will relate to 3000 MW × 0.6).

17 Given a residential community with an area of 26 km², assume a population density and calculate the required fire flow. Give results in lpm.

18 Consider a 450-acre residential area with a housing density of four dwellings per acre. Estimate the peak hourly water use requirement and the peak hourly sewage flow.

REFERENCES

[1] L. W. Mays, *Water Distribution Systems Handbook* (New York: McGraw-Hill, 2000).

[2] U.S. Water Resources Council, *The Nation's Water Resources 1975 to 2000* (Washington, DC: U.S. Government Printing Office, December 1978).

[3] "Estimated Water Use in the United States, 2000," U.S. Geological Survey Circular 1268 (2004).

[4] J. B. Wolff, "Peak Demands in Residential Areas," *J. Am. Water Works Assoc.* 87 (October 1961).

[5] F. P. Linaweaver, Jr., "Report on Phase One, Residential Water Use Research Project" (Baltimore: The Johns Hopkins University, Department of Sanitary Engineering, October 1963).

[6] *Standard Schedule for Grading Cities and Towns of the United States with Reference to Their Fire Defenses and Physical Conditions* (New York: National Board of Fire Underwriters, 1956).

[7] Metcalf & Eddy, Inc., *Wastewater Engineering: Treatment and Reuse* (New York: McGraw-Hill, 2003).

[8] S. W. Work, M. R. Rothberg, and K. J. Miller, "Denver's Potable Reuse Project: Pathway to Public Acceptance," *J. Am. Water Works Assoc.* 72, no. 8 (1980): 435–440.

[9] U.S. Congress, "Water Reuse Project Underway in Denver," *Congressional Record*, pp. E5191, E5192, (October 22, 1979).

[10] J. E. Matthews, "Industrial Reuse and Recycle of Wastewaters: Literature Review," EPA Report No. EPA/600/280183, U.S. EPA, Ada, OK (1980).

[11] B. A. Carnes, J. M. Eller, and J. C. Martin, "Reuse of Refinery and Petrochemical Wastewaters," *Ind. Water Eng.* 9, no. 4 (1979): 25.

[12] L. E. Streebin, L. W. Canter, and J. R. Palafox, "Water Conservation and Reuse in the Canning Industry" (proceedings of the 26th Industrial Waste Conference, Purdue University, Lafayette, IN, Part II 1971): 766.

[13] C. A. Caswell, "Water Reuse in the Steel Industry," *Complete Water Reuse: Industry's Opportunity* (New York: American Institute of Chemical Engineers, 1973); 384.

[14] R. Field and C. Fan, "Recycling Urban Stormwater for Profit," *Water/Eng. Management* 128, no. 4 (1981).

[15] J. Merrell and R. Stoyer, "Reclaimed Sewage Becomes a Community," *American City* (April 1964): 97.

[16] J. C. Merrell, Jr., W. F. Jopling, R. F. Bott, A. Katko, and H. E. Pintler, "Santee Recreational Project, Santee, California, Final Report," FWPCA Report WP-20-7 (Cincinnati: Publication Office, Ohio Basin Region, Federal Water Pollution Control Administration, 1967).

[17] P. Campbell, *Population Projections: States, 1995–2025*, Current Population Reports, Bureau of the Census, U.S. Department of Commerce, P25–1131 (Washington, DC, May 1997).

[18] F. W. Hollmann, T. J. Mulder, and J. E. Kallan, *Methodology and Assumptions for the Population Projections of the United States: 1999 to 2100*, Bureau of the Census, U.S. Department of Commerce, Washington, DC, January 2000.

[19] F. E. Croxton and D. J. Cowden, *Applied General Statistics* (Englewood Cliffs, NJ: Prentice-Hall, 1960).

[20] R. C. Schmitt, "Forecasting Population by the Ratio Method," *J. Am. Water Works Assoc.* 46 (1954): 960.

[21] W. Viessman, Jr. and C. Welty, *Water Management: Technology and Institutions* (New York: Harper & Row, 1985).

[22] Planning and Management Consultants, Ltd. "IWR-MAIN, Version 6.1 ©, Water Demand Analysis Software, Technical Overview" (Carbondale, IL, 1994).

[23] E. M. Opitz, B. Dziegielewski, and J. R. M. Steinbeck, "Water Use Forecasts and Conservation Evaluations for the Eugene Water and Electric Board" (Carbondale, IL; Technical Report, Planning and Management Consultants, Ltd., November 1995).

[24] J. J. Boland, "IWR-MAIN System Improvements: Phase III—Growth Models, Consultant Report," Contract DACW72-84-C-0004 (Fort Belvoir, VA: U.S. Army Engineer Institute for Water Resources, 1987).

[25] B. Dziegielewski, "The IWR-MAIN Disaggregate Water Use Model" (proceedings of the 1987 Annual UCOWR Meeting, UCOWR, Southern Illinois University, Carbondale, IL, 1987).

[26] Planning and Management Consultants, Ltd., "A Disaggregate Water Use Forecast for the Phoenix Water Service Area" (report presented to City of Phoenix, Water and Wastewater Department, March 1986).

[27] Planning and Management Consultants, Ltd., "IWR-Main Water Use Forecasting System, System Description," Carbondale, IL (January 1987).

[28] Planning and Management Consultants, Ltd., "Municipal and Industrial Water Use in the Metropolitan Water District Service Area," Carbondale, IL (November 1987).

[29] D. D. Baumann, J. J. Boland, and W. M. Hanemann, *Urban Water Demand Management and Planning*, (New York: McGraw-Hill, 1998).

[30] AWWA Committee on Water Use, "Review of The Johns Hopkins University Research Project Method for Estimating Residential Water Use," *J. Am. Water Works Assoc.* 65, no. 5 (1973): 300–301.

[31] J. P. Heaney, G. D. Lynne, N. Khanal, W. C. Martin, C. L. Sova, and R. Dickinson "Agricultural and Municipal Water Demand Projection Models" (University of Florida, Gainesville, FL, March 1981).

[32] B. Dziegielewski, J. J. Boland, and D. D. Baumann, "An Annotated Bibliography on Techniques of Forecasting Demand for Water," IWR Contract Report 81-C03 (Fort Belvoir, VA: U.S. Army Corps of Engineers, 1981).

[33] J. J. Boland, D. D. Baumann, and B. Dziegielewski, "An Assessment of Municipal and Industrial Water Use Forecasting Approaches," IWR Contract Report 81-C05 (Fort Belvoir, VA: Army Corps of Engineers, 1981).

[34] B. T. Bower, I. Gouevsky, D. R. Maidment, and W. R. D. Sewell, *Modeling Water Demands* (New York: Academic, 1984).

[35] Comptroller General, "Water Supply for Urban Areas: Problems in Meeting Future Demand," Report to the Congress of the United States, CED-79-56, June 15, 1979.

[36] Congressional Research Service, Library of Congress, *State and National Water Use Trends to the Year 2000*, Serial No. 96-12 (Washington, DC: U.S. Government Printing Office, May 1980).

[37] J. R. Kim and R. H. McCuen, "Factors for Predicting Commercial Water Use," *Water Resources Bull.* 15, no. 4 (1979): 1073–1080.

[38] D. R. Maidment and S. Miaou, "Daily Water Use in Nine Cities," *Water Resources Res.* 22, no. 6 (1986): 845–851.

[39] C. T. Osborn, J. E. Schefter, and L. Shabman, "The Accuracy of Water Use Forecasts: Evaluation and Implications," *Water Resources Bull.*, Paper No. 84245, Am. Water Resources Assoc. 22, no. 1 (February 1986).

[40] J. J. Boland, E. M. Opitz, B. Dziegielewski, and D. D. Baumann, *IWR MAIN Modifications, Technical Consultant Report,* Contract DACW-72-84-C-0004, Task 2 (Fort Belvoir, VA: U.S. Army Engineer Institute for Water Resources, 1985).

[41] Y. L. Chang, *WinQSB Version 2.0* (New York, NY, John Wiley & Sons, Inc., ISBN 0-471-40672-4, 2003).

Conveying and Distributing Water

Designing conveyance systems for water requires engineers to consider a variety of details, including projected demands on these systems, mathematical sizing of the system elements, engineering details involved in the plans and project documents, constructability, testing, permitting of the system, and ease of future operations and maintenance. This chapter will focus on the mathematical analyses and design considerations for water distribution systems.

HYDRAULICS

1   INTRODUCTION TO HYDRAULICS

Before designing a water distribution system or conveyance system of any type, it is critical to understand the mathematics of how water will behave in these systems. Regardless of the system, some form of the continuity equation is usually used.

- Hydrology should not be confused with hydraulics. Most simply, *hydrology* is the study of the many physical, chemical, and biological factors involved in water's interaction with natural and manmade environments. Hydrology is an interdisciplinary science that can involve climate, soils, geography, oceanography, ecology, fluid mechanics, and classic civil engineering, among other areas of study [1]. In a practical sense for engineers doing design, hydrologic routing is usually completed before hydraulic calculations as part of a site design or stormwater investigation. Hydrology can also be a factor when water or wastewater infrastructure ages, as with inflow and infiltration (also commonly referred to as I&I).

- *Hydraulics* is the study of mechanical properties of fluids and is a common subdiscipline within many types of engineering. The remainder of this chapter will focus on hydraulics as it pertains to water distribution. Hydraulics is a complex topic and only a brief introduction is provided in this text. As particular topics within hydraulics are covered throughout this and the next chapter, additional references will be provided that can provide a more detailed treatment of each topic.

Engineers investigate hydraulics problems in a number of ways:

1. Dimensions of the system—Flow can be defined in one or more dimensions. Most water distribution and conveyance systems are designed while only considering one-dimensional flow, although many engineers now consider two-dimensional flow for some applications. At this time, three-dimensional flow is only considered for a small minority of hydraulic questions and primarily remains an academic endeavor. As computational speed increases and as more modelers adjust to using three-dimensional equations, there may be an increase in number of dimensions considered by practicing engineers.

2. Changes over time—Flow can be examined with regard to its change over time. Although unsteady flow (flow that changes over time) is common, it is only briefly covered in this text. For many water and wastewater applications, steady flow (flow that does not change over time) is an appropriate assumption. However, engineers should be cautious about assuming steady flow, as steady flow is far less common in natural systems. A number of excellent models exist to investigate both unsteady and steady flow, although these models can never replace a firm understanding of hydraulics.

3. Pressures within the system—When solving water problems, engineers often define *flow* as "pressurized flow" or "open-channel flow." The primary difference between the two terms is whether the flow is **above** atmospheric pressure (commonly referred to as "pressurized flow") or whether the flow is **at** atmospheric pressure (as in open-channel flow or systems that are flowing under gravity). Both types of flow will be discussed in this chapter.

4. Energy involved in flow—Many energy variables can be used to describe flow. A common energy term used in open channel hydraulics is "specific energy." More will be said about specific energy in this chapter.

5. Spatial variations of the flow—This concept will be revisited throughout this and the next chapter. The most common consideration of spatial variation is gradually varied flow.

6. Velocity and acceleration.

2   UNIFORM FLOW

Many practicing engineers assume uniform flow, a situation where the cross-sectional velocity and depth do not change in the direction of flow [2]. For uniform flow, the velocity in an open channel is usually determined by Manning's equation:

$$V = 1.49R^{0.66}S^{0.5}/n \tag{1}$$

where

V = velocity of flow, fps
n = coefficient of roughness
R = hydraulic radius, ft
S = slope of energy grade line

In metric units

$$V = R^{0.66}S^{0.5}/n$$

where

V = velocity of flow, m/s
n = coefficient of roughness
R = hydraulic radius, m
S = slope of energy grade line

The equation is applicable as long as S does not significantly exceed 0.10. In channels having no uniform roughness, an average value of n is selected. Where the cross-sectional roughness changes considerably, as in a channel with a paved center section and grassed outer sections, it is common practice to compute the flow for each section independently and sum these flows to obtain the total. For most purposes, n is considered a constant. It is actually a function of several factors, however, and should be adjusted for pipe diameters exceeding five or more feet. As with the Hazen–Williams equation (see Section 7), nomographs are available to allow rapid computation (see Figure 1). Values of n for use in Manning's equation are provided in Table 1.

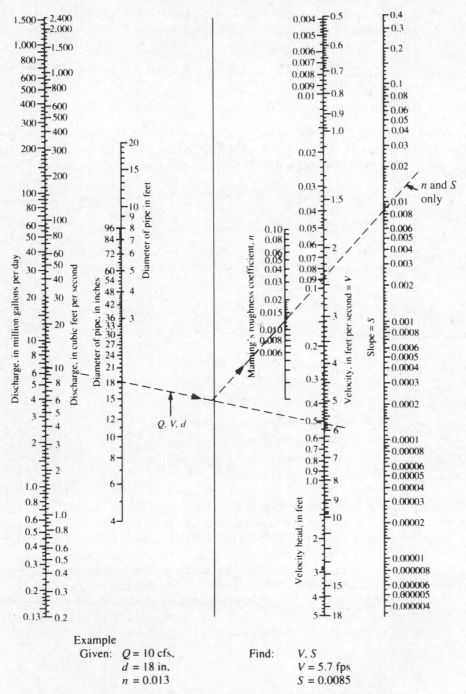

Example
Given: $Q = 10$ cfs,   Find: V, S
         $d = 18$ in, $V = 5.7$ fps
         $n = 0.013$ $S = 0.0085$

FIGURE 1   Nomograph based on Manning's formula for circular pipes flowing full.

TABLE 1 Roughness Coefficients

Material	Hazen–Williams, C	Manning, n
New pipes:		
Cast iron	130–140	0.012–0.015
Concrete	120–140	0.012–0.017
Concrete-lined galvanized iron	120	0.015–0.017
Plastic	140–150	0.011–0.015
Steel	140–150	0.015–0.017
Vitrified clay	110	0.013–0.015
Welded steel	120	—
Older pipes and other materials:		
5-yr-old cast iron	120	—
20-yr-old cast iron	100	—
Asbestos cement	140	—
Brick	—	0.016
Corrugated metal pipc	—	0.022
Bituminous concrete	—	0.015
Uniform, firm sodded earth	—	0.025

Example 1

Determine the discharge of a trapezoidal channel having a brick bottom and grassy sides, and with the following dimensions: depth—6 ft, bottom width—12 ft, top width—18 ft. Assume $S = 0.002$.

Solution:

1. Using Eq. (1) and noting that $Q = AV$, calculate the discharge for the portion of flow in the rectangular subsection. From Table 1, choose $n = 0.017$.

$$R = (6)(12)/(12) = 6.0 \text{ ft}$$

$$Q = (1.49/0.017)(72)(6)^{2/3}(0.002)^{1/2} = 930.75 \text{ cfs}$$

2. Calculate the discharge for the portion of flow in the grassy subsections of the channel. From Table 1, choose $n = 0.025$. Then for each side

$$A = (0.5)(3)(6) = 9 \text{ ft}^2$$
$$R = 9/6.7 = 1.35 \text{ ft}$$

For both sides,

$$Q = 2[(1.49/0.025)(9)(1.35)^{2/3}(0.002)^{1/2}] = 58.59 \text{ cfs}$$

3. The total discharge for the channel is thus
$$Q = 930.75 + 58.59 = 989.34 \text{ cfs}$$

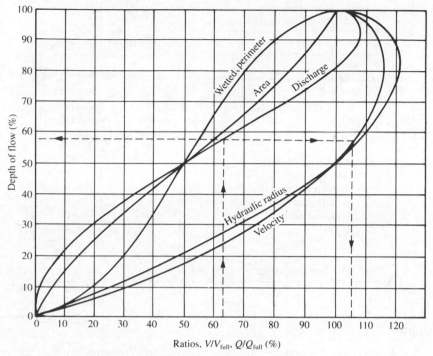

FIGURE 2   Hydraulic elements of a circular section for constant n.

For open channels consisting of circular pipes or tunnels flowing partly full, calculating the hydraulic radius and cross-sectional area of flow can be cumbersome. Figure 2 facilitates these calculations by showing the relation between the hydraulic elements of a circular pipe, which allows the conditions of a pipe flowing partly full to be calculated from the conditions of the full-flowing pipe.

Example 2

Given a pipe discharge flowing full of 16 cfs and a velocity of 8 fps, find the velocity and depth of flow when $Q = 10$ cfs.

Solution: Enter Figure 2 at 10/16 = 62.5% of value for full section. Obtain a depth of flow of 57.5% of full-flow depth and a velocity of $1.05 \times 8 = 8.4$ fps.

The depth at which uniform flow occurs in an open channel is termed the *normal depth* d_n. This depth can be computed by using Manning's equation for discharge after the cross-sectional area A and the hydraulic radius R have been translated into functions of depth. For those solving the equation without the aid of a computer, the solution for d_n is often obtained by trial and error.

For a specified channel cross section and discharge, there are three possible values for the normal depth, all dependent on the channel slope. Uniform flow for a given discharge may occur at critical depth, at less than critical depth, or at greater than critical depth. Critical depth occurs when the specific energy is at a minimum. Specific energy is defined as

$$E_s = d + V^2/2g \qquad (2)$$

where

$$d = \text{depth of flow}$$
$$V = \text{mean velocity}$$

Flow at critical depth is highly unstable, and designs indicating flow at or near critical depth should be avoided. For any value of E_s above the minimum, two alternative depths of flow are possible—greater than critical depth or less than critical depth. The former case indicates subcritical flow, the latter supercritical flow. The critical depth for a channel can be found by taking the derivative of Eq. (2) with respect to depth, setting this equal to zero, and solving for d_c. For mild slopes, the normal depth is greater than d_c and subcritical flow prevails. On steep slopes, the normal depth is less than the critical depth and flow is supercritical. Once the critical depth has been computed, critical velocity is easily obtained. The critical velocity for a channel of any cross section can be shown to be

$$V_c = \sqrt{g\frac{A}{B}} \qquad (3)$$

where

$$V_c = \text{critical velocity}$$
$$A = \text{cross-sectional area of the channel}$$
$$B = \text{width of the channel at the water surface}$$

The critical slope can then be found by using Manning's equation.

In practice, uniform flows are encountered only in long channels after a transition from nonuniform conditions. Nevertheless, knowledge of uniform flow hydraulics is important, as numerous varied flow problems are solved through partial applications of uniform flow theory. A basic assumption in gradually varied flow analyses, for example, is that energy losses are considered the same as for uniform flow at the average depth between two sections along the channel that are closely spaced.

3   GRADUALLY VARIED FLOW AND SURFACE PROFILES

Gradually varied flow results from gradual changes in depth that take place over long reaches. Abrupt changes in the flow regime are classified as "rapidly varied flow." Problems in gradually varied flow are common and represent the majority of flows in natural open channels and many of the flows in manmade channels. They can be caused by such factors as change in channel slope, cross-sectional area, or roughness, or by obstructions to flow, such as dams, gates, culverts, and bridges. The pressure distribution in gradually varied flow is hydrostatic and the streamlines are considered approximately parallel.

The significance of gradually varied flow problems may be illustrated by considering the following case. Assume that the maximum design flow for a uniform rectangular canal will occur at a depth of 8 ft under uniform flow conditions. For these circumstances, the requisite canal depth, including 1 ft of freeboard, will be 9 ft. Now consider that a gate is placed at the lower end of this canal. Assume that at maximum flow the depth immediately upstream of the gate will have to be 12 ft to produce the required flow through the gate. The depth of flow will then begin decreasing gradually in an upstream direction and approach the uniform depth of 8 ft. Obviously, unless the depth of flow is known all along the channel, the channel design depth cannot be determined.

In an open channel the water surface profile for a given discharge must be determined to solve many engineering problems. There are 12 classifications of water surface profiles, or *backwater curves* [3]. Figure 3 illustrates several of these and also a typical change that might take place in the transition from one type of flow regime to another. For any channel the applicable backwater curve will be a function of the relationship between the actual depth of flow and the normal and critical depths of the channel. Often it is helpful to sketch the curves for a given problem before attempting an actual solution. The curves given in Figure 3 are useful in sketching the curves for a given problem. Woodward and Posey provide additional curves [3].

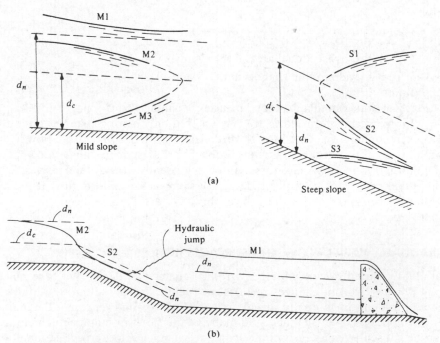

FIGURE 3   Gradually varied flow profiles.

Numerous procedures have been proposed for computing backwater curves. The direct-step method is discussed here. Referring to Figure 4, the energy equation may be written as

$$Z_1' + d_1 + \frac{V_1^2}{2g} = d_2 + \frac{V_2^2}{2g} + H_f$$

A rearrangement of this equation yields

$$\left(\frac{V_2^2}{2g} + d_2\right) - \left(\frac{V_1^2}{2g} + d_1\right) = Z_1' - H_f$$

or

$$E_2 - E_1 = S_c L - \bar{S}_e L$$

$$L = \frac{E_2 - E_1}{S_c - \bar{S}_e} \tag{4}$$

where

$$E_2, E_1 = \text{values of specific energy at sections 1 and 2}$$
$$S_c = \text{slope of the channel bottom}$$
$$\bar{S}_e = \text{slope of the energy gradient}$$

The value of $\bar{S}_e$ is obtained by assuming that (1) the actual energy gradient is the same as that obtained for uniform flow at a velocity equal to the average of the velocities at Sections 1 and 2 (this can be found using Manning's equation) or (2) the slope of the energy gradient is equal to the mean of the slopes of the energy gradients for uniform

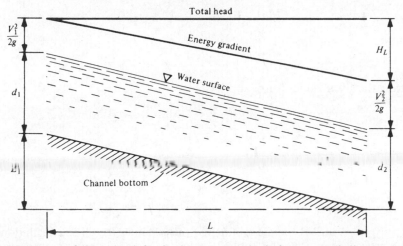

FIGURE 4 Definition sketch for the direct-step method of computing backwater curves.

flow at the two sections. The procedure in using Eq. (4) is to select some starting point where the depth of flow is known. Then select second depth in an upstream or downstream direction, and compute the distance from the known depth to this point. Then, using the second depth as a reference, select a third and calculate another length increment, and so on. The results obtained will be reasonably accurate provided the selected depth increments are small, since the energy-loss assumptions are fairly accurate under these conditions.

Example 3

Water flows in a rectangular concrete channel 10 ft wide, 8 ft deep, and inclined at a grade of 0.10%. The channel carries a flow of 245 cfs and has a roughness coefficient n of 0.013. At the intersection of this channel with a canal, the depth of flow is 7.5 ft. Find the distance upstream to a point where normal depth prevails and determine the surface profile.

Solution: Using Manning's equation and the given value of discharge, the normal depth is found to be 4 ft. Critical depth y_c is determined by solving Eq. (3) after rearranging and substituting by_c for A and b for B, where b equals the width of the rectangular channel.

Then

$$V_c = \sqrt{g\left(\frac{bv_c}{b}\right)}$$

$$= \sqrt{gy_c}$$

$$y_c = \frac{V_c^2}{g} = \frac{Q^2}{A^2 g} \tag{5}$$

$$y_c^3 = \frac{Q^2}{gb^2}$$

Substituting the given values for Q and b yields

$$y_c = \sqrt[3]{\frac{(245)^2}{32.2 \times (10)^2}}$$

and

$$y_c = 2.65 \text{ ft}$$

Since $y > y_n > y_c$, an M1 profile will depict the water surface. The calculations then follow the procedure indicated in Table 2.

TABLE 2 Calculation for the Surface Profile of Example 3

y	A	V	$\dfrac{V^2}{2g}$	$E = d + \dfrac{V^2}{2g}$	P	R	$R^{4/3}$	$S_e = \dfrac{V^2}{(1.49)^2 R^{4/3}/n^2}$	$\bar{S}_e$	ΔE	$S_c - \bar{S}_e$	$\Delta L = \dfrac{\Delta E}{S_c - \bar{S}_e}$
7.5	75	3.27	0.166	7.666	25	3.0	4.33	0.000188				
									0.000207	0.475	0.000793	598
7.0	70	3.50	0.191	7.191	24	2.91	4.15	0.000225				
									0.000279	0.932	0.000721	1292
6.0	60	4.08	0.259	6.259	22	2.73	3.82	0.000333				
									0.000436	0.885	0.000564	1570
5.0	50	4.90	0.374	5.374	20	2.50	3.40	0.000539				
									0.000762	0.792	0.000238	3328
4.0	40	6.12	0.582	4.582	18	2.22	2.90	0.000984				

$$L = \Sigma \, \Delta L = \overline{6788}$$

The distance upstream from the junction to the point of normal depth is 6788 ft. The surface profile can be plotted by using the values in Table 2 for y and ΔL. In practice, greater accuracy could be obtained by using smaller depth increments, such as 0.25 ft, but the computational procedure would be the same.

---

4   VELOCITY

Maximum and minimum velocities are both prescribed for water transportation systems. Minimum velocities are set to ensure that suspended matter does not settle out in the conduit, while maximum velocities are set to prevent erosion of the channel. Normally, velocities in excess of 20 fps should be avoided in concrete or tile sewers, and whenever possible velocities of 10 fps or less should be used. Specially lined inverts (pipe bottoms) are sometimes employed to combat channel erosion. The average value of the channel shearing stress is related to erosion and to sediment deposition.

Using the Chézy equation for velocity, Fair and Geyer [4] have shown that the minimum velocity for self-cleansing V_m can be determined according to

$$V_m = C\sqrt{\frac{K(\gamma_s - \gamma)}{\gamma}}\, d \qquad (6)$$

where γ_s is the specific weight of the particles, γ is the specific weight of water, d is the particle diameter, and C is the Chézy coefficient (equal to $1.49R^{1/6}/n$ as evaluated by Manning). The value of C is selected with consideration given to the containment of solids in the flow. The value of K must be found experimentally and appears to range from 0.04 for the initiation of scour to more than 0.8 for effective cleansing [4].

If nonflocculating particles have mean diameters between 0.05 and 0.5 mm, the minimum velocity may be determined [5] using

$$V_m = \left[25.3 \times 10^{-3}\, g\, \frac{d(\rho_s - \rho)}{\rho} \right]^{0.816} \left(\frac{D\rho_m}{\mu_m} \right)^{0.633} \qquad (7)$$

where

$$
\begin{aligned}
V_m &= \text{minimum velocity, fps} \\
d &= \text{mean particle diameter, ft} \\
D &= \text{pipe diameter, ft} \\
\rho_m &= \text{mean mass density of the suspension, pcf} \\
\rho_s &= \text{particle density, pcf} \\
\mu_m &= \text{viscosity of the suspension, } \frac{\text{lb} \cdot \text{seconds}}{\text{ft}^2} \\
\rho &= \text{liquid mass density, pcf}
\end{aligned}
$$

The value of ρ_m may be determined using

$$\rho_m = X_v \rho_s + (1 - X_v)\rho \qquad (8)$$

where X_v is the volumetric fraction of the suspended solids. Ordinarily, minimum velocities are 2 and 3 fps for sanitary sewers and storm drains, respectively.

WATER DISTRIBUTION SYSTEMS

Water distribution systems are designed to satisfy the water requirements of the domestic, commercial, industrial, and firefighting sectors. The system should be capable of meeting the demands placed on it at all times and at satisfactory pressures. Pipe systems, pumping stations, storage facilities, fire hydrants, house service connections, meters, and other appurtenances are the main elements of the system [6].

5   GENERAL DESIGN CONSIDERATIONS

The design of water distribution systems involves considerations of hydraulic adequacy, structural adequacy, and economic efficiency. The general layout of the system is a function of the flow to be carried, the head available, the character of the conduit material, and limiting velocities.

Location

The routing of distribution systems is constrained by the availability of right-of-way and technical and economic considerations. A distribution system's beginning and end points are fixed by the source of supply and the location at which the water is to be delivered. Between these two locations, the most cost-effective route must be found. The choice of location is also a determinant of the type, or types, of conveyances to be used. Distribution systems built to grade require topography that allows cut-and-cover operations to be closely balanced. Pressurized pipes, on the other hand, can follow topography. Pumping, materials, and construction costs are related to topography.

In any conduit there must be sufficient hydraulic slope to obtain the required flow. Steep slopes generate high velocities with smaller conduit requirements. When sufficient fall is available, steep slopes are often economical. On the other hand, if head can be generated only by pumping or through construction of a dam, flatter slopes calling for larger conduits may be needed to reduce the cost of the lift. Some combination of lift and slope will yield the optimum economy. Usually some controlling feature establishes the elevation of the distribution system at a specified point. Examples of possible governing features are dam heights, tunnel locations, terminal reservoirs, and hilltops.

Sizing

The size and configuration of a distribution system usually vary along the route. For a given type of system, the size is usually determined on the basis of hydraulic, economic, and construction considerations. Occasionally, construction practices dictate a minimum size in excess of that required to handle the flow under the prevailing hydraulic conditions (available head). This condition is generally encountered for tunnels. Hydraulic factors that control the design are the head available and permissible velocities. Available heads are affected by reservoir drawdown and local pressure requirements. Limiting velocities are based on the character of the water to be transported and the need to protect transmission lines against excessive pressures that might develop through hydraulic surge. Where silt is transported with the water, minimum velocities of about 2.5 fps should be maintained. Maximum velocities must preclude pipe erosion or hydraulic surge problems and are ordinarily between 10 and 20 fps [7]. The usual range in velocities is from about 4 to 6 fps.

Where power generation is involved, pumping costs and/or the worth of power and conduit costs jointly determine the conduit size. For single gravity-flow pipelines, the size should be determined so that the available head is consumed by friction.

Strength

Pipelines and other conveyances must be designed to resist forces such as those resulting from water pressure within the conduit, hydraulic surge (transient internal pressure generated when the velocity of flow is rapidly reduced), external loads, forces at bends or changes in cross section, expansion and contraction, and flexural stresses [8, 9, 10].

Economics

Hydraulic head has economic value. It costs money to produce the head at the upstream end of a system, but the head can then be used to increase flow, to produce power, or for other purposes. A definite relationship always exists among system size, hydraulic gradient, and the value of head. In some cases, construction costs are related to the elevation of the hydraulic gradient. The elevation of the gradient also affects pumping costs and power production values, as does the slope of the hydraulic gradient. In long distribution systems composed of different types of conduits, a means of coordinating conduit types, choosing dam elevations, and selecting pump lifts or power drops is important. Dealing with this problem requires a joint application of hydraulic and economic principles [11, 12].

6   TYPES OF DISTRIBUTION SYSTEMS

Water distribution systems may include or be solely composed of open channels, pipelines, or tunnels. Factors that determine the type of distribution system include topography, head availability, climate, construction practices, economics, and the need to protect water quality.

Open Channels

Open channels are defined in various ways. Most generally, open channels are designed to convey water under conditions of atmospheric pressure. Given this design, the hydraulic gradient and free-water surface are coincident. If the channel is supported on or above the ground, it is also classified as a flume. Open channels may take on a variety of shapes and are sometimes covered with protective structures.

The choice of an open channel for conveyance is usually predicated on suitable topographic conditions that permit gravity flow with minimal excavation or fill. If the channel is unlined, the perviousness of the soil must be considered relative to seepage losses. Other important considerations are the potential for pollution and evaporative losses.

Open channels may be lined with concrete, bituminous materials, butyl rubber, vinyl, synthetic fabrics, or other products to reduce the resistance to flow, minimize seepage, and lower maintenance costs. Flumes are usually constructed of concrete, steel, or timber.

Pipelines

Pipelines are usually used where topographic conditions preclude the use of canals. Pipelines may be laid above or below ground or may be partly buried. Most water distribution pipes are made up of various combinations of asbestos–cement, ductile iron, high-density polyethylene (HDPE), polyvinyl chloride (PVC), and steel.

Pipelines may require gate valves, check valves, air-release valves, drains, surge-control equipment, expansion joints, insulation joints, manholes, and pumping stations. These appurtenances are provided to ensure safe and efficient operation, allow easy inspection, and facilitate maintenance. Gate valves are often spaced about 1200 ft apart so that the intervening section of line can be drained for inspection or repair and placed on either side of a check valve to permit its removal for inspection or repair. Check valves are normally located on the upstream side of pumping equipment and at the beginning of each rise in the pipeline to prevent backflow. Air-release valves are needed at the high points in the line to release trapped gases and to vent the line to prevent vacuum formation. Drains are located at low points to permit removal of sediment and allow the conduit to be emptied. Surge tanks or quick-opening valves provide relief from problems of hydraulic surge.

Tunnels

Where it is not practical or economical to lay a pipeline on the surface or provide an open trench for underground installation, a tunnel is an alternative choice. Tunnels are well suited to mountain or river crossings. They may be operated under pressure or act as open channels.

7   DISTRIBUTION SYSTEM COMPONENTS

A water distribution network is a collection of links connected at their endpoints, called *nodes* (refer to Figure 5). Links may include pipes, pumps, and valves. Nodes may be points of water withdrawal (demand nodes), locations where water is introduced to the network (source nodes), or locations of tanks or reservoirs (storage nodes). Flows may be stated as gallons per minute (gpm), cubic feet per second (cfs), million gallons per day (mgd), or liters per second (l/s).

Pipes   Pipes are used to convey water. The direction of flow is from the end at higher head (potential energy per pound of water) to that at a lower head. Pipes may contain check valves that restrict flow to a specific direction. Such valves can be made to open

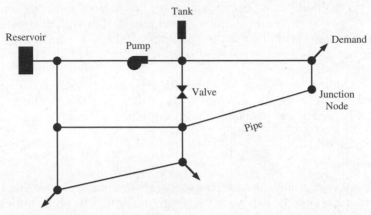

FIGURE 5   Network components.

or close at preset times, when tank levels fall below or above certain set points, or when nodal pressures fall below or above certain set points. Head lost to friction resulting from pipe flow can be expressed by the following type of equation:

$$h_L = Aq^B \tag{9}$$

In this equation, h_L is the head loss (length), A is a resistance coefficient, q is the flow in units of volume/time, and B is a flow exponent. The Hazen–Williams formula, the Darcy–Weisbach formula, and the Chézy–Manning formula can all be used to calculate friction head loss. The Hazen–Williams formula is the most commonly used, but it cannot be used for liquids other than water. The Darcy–Weisbach formula is the most theoretically correct, and it is suited to all liquids. The Chézy–Manning equation is generally used for problems of open channel flow. Table 3 gives expressions for the

TABLE 3   Pipe Head Loss Formulas for Full Flow (head loss in ft and flow rate in cfs)

Formula	Resistance Coefficient (A)	Flow Exponent (B)
Hazen–Williams	$4.727C^{-1.852}d^{-4.871}L$	1.852
Darcy–Weisbach	$0.0252f(\varepsilon, d, q)d^{-5}L$	2
Chézy–Manning	$4.66n^2d^{-5.33}L$	2

Notes: C = Hazen–Williams roughness coefficient
  ε = Darcy–Weisbach roughness coefficient (ft)
  f = friction factor (dependent on ε, d, and q)
  n = Manning roughness coefficient
  d = pipe diameter (ft)
  L = pipe length (ft)
  q = flow rate (cfs)
Source: Rossman [13].

resistance coefficient A, and values of the flow exponent B. The pipe roughness coefficients in these expressions must be determined empirically. Table 1 gives ranges of these coefficients generally encountered in practice. Note that as pipes age these coefficients can change significantly.

Junctions Junctions (also called nodes) are points where pipes come together and where water enters or leaves the network. Storage nodes (i.e., tanks and reservoirs) are special types of nodes where a free water surface exists and the hydraulic head is the elevation of water above sea level. To determine the total hydraulic head at a node, the elevation above sea level of all nodes must be specified. The magnitude of water withdrawals (demands) or inputs at nodes that are not storage nodes must be known over the time frame that the network is being analyzed.

Reservoirs Reservoirs are nodes that represent lakes, rivers, and groundwater aquifers. Because of their scale, reservoirs are often considered to represent an infinite source or sink of water to the distribution system. A major feature of a reservoir is its hydraulic head, which is the water surface elevation, providing that the reservoir is not under pressure. The hydraulic head may vary over time, however, and this must be taken into account when modeling water supply systems.

Tanks Tanks are storage nodes where the volume of water can vary with time. Tank properties include the bottom elevation where the water level is zero, the diameter or shape of the tank, the initial water level, and the minimum and maximum water levels within which the tank can operate. The change in water level of a storage tank can be calculated using the following equation:

$$\Delta y = (q/A)\Delta t \tag{10}$$

where

Δy = change in water level, ft
q = flow rate into $(+)$ or out of $(-)$ tank, cfs
A = cross-sectional area of the tank, ft^2
Δt = time interval, s

Emitters Emitters are nozzles or orifices that discharge to the atmosphere. The flow through these devices is a function of the pressure available at the node and is given by

$$q = Cp^\gamma \tag{11}$$

where

q = flow rate
C = a discharge coefficient
p = pressure
γ = pressure exponent

TABLE 4   Minor Head Loss Coefficients, K

Component	Loss Coefficient
Globe valve, fully open	10.0
Angle valve, fully open	5.0
Swing check valve, fully open	2.5
Gate valve, fully open	0.2
Short-radius elbow	0.9
Medium-radius elbow	0.8
Long-radius elbow	0.6
45° elbow	0.4
Closed return bend	2.2
Standard tee—flow through run	0.6
Standard tee—flow through branch	1.8
Square entrance	0.5
Exit	1.0

Source: Rossman [13].

For nozzles and sprinkler heads, γ equals 0.5. Manufacturers of emitters generally supply the value of the discharge coefficient in units of $gpm/psi^{0.5}$ (stated as the flow through the device at a 1 psi pressure drop). Emitters are used to model irrigation networks and sprinkler systems. They may also be used to estimate pipe leakage if a discharge coefficient and a pressure exponent can be estimated.

Minor Losses   Minor head losses are usually associated with turbulence that occurs at bends, junctions, meters, and valves. The importance of such losses depends on the nature of the pipe network and the degree of accuracy required in the analysis. Minor head losses may be accounted for by assigning a minor head loss coefficient to the appropriate fixture (see Table 4 for a list of such coefficients). The minor head loss is then calculated with the formula

$$h_L = K(v^2/2g) \tag{12}$$

where K is a minor head loss coefficient, v is flow velocity (length/time), and g is the acceleration of gravity (length/time^2).

Pumps   Pumps are used to increase the hydraulic head of water. A pump characteristic curve (Figure 6) describes the head imparted to a fluid as a function of its flow rate through the pump. Pump curves can be represented with a function of the form

$$h_G = h_o - aq^b \tag{13}$$

where h_G is the head gain imparted by the pump in ft, h_o is the shutoff head (head at no flow), a is a resistance coefficient, q is the flow through the pump, and b is a flow exponent. Flow through a pump is unidirectional and pumps must operate within the head

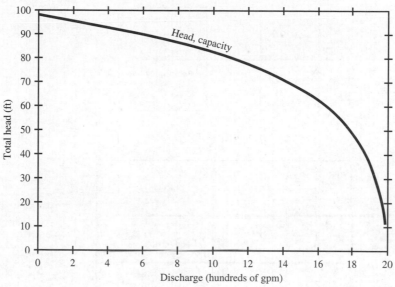

FIGURE 6   Typical pump curve.

and flow limits imposed by their characteristic curves. Pumps may be run at constant or variable speed. Pumps will be discussed further in Section 10.

Valves   Valves are links in pipelines that are used to regulate flow or pressure. There are numerous types of valves. Shutoff (gate) valves and check (nonreturn) valves completely open or close pipes. Pressure-reducing valves (PRVs) limit the pressure at a point in a pipe network. Pressure-sustaining valves (PSVs) maintain a set pressure at a specified location in a pipe network. Flow control valves (FCVs) limit the flow to a prescribed amount.

8   DISTRIBUTION SYSTEM CONFIGURATIONS

Water distribution systems may be classified as grid systems, branching systems, or a combination of the two. The configuration of the system is influenced by street patterns, topography, degree and type of development of the region to be served, and location of treatment and storage works. Figure 7 illustrates the basic types of distribution systems. Grid systems are usually preferred to branching systems, since they can supply a withdrawal point from at least two directions. Branching systems do not permit this type of circulation, because they have numerous terminals or dead ends. Grid and combination systems can both incorporate loop feeders, which can distribute water to a takeoff point from several directions. In locations where sharp changes in topography occur (hilly or mountainous regions) it is common practice to divide the distribution system into two or more service areas or zones. This precludes the difficulty of needing extremely high pressure in low-lying areas to maintain reasonable pressures at higher elevations. The usual practice is to interconnect the various systems, with the interconnections closed off by valves during normal operations.

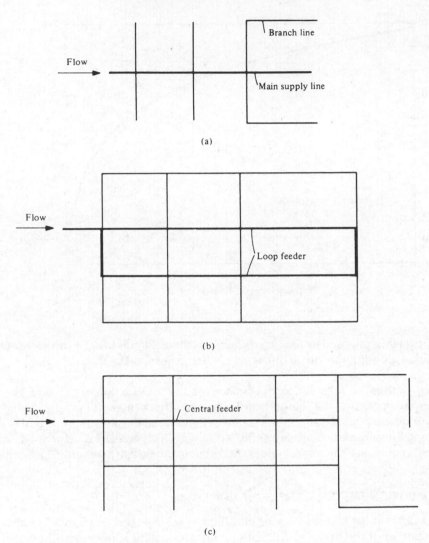

FIGURE 7 Types of water distribution systems: (a) Branching (b) Grid (c) Combination.

HYDRAULIC CONSIDERATIONS

Flows in a water conveyance system are analyzed through the application of basic principles of open-channel and closed-conduit hydraulics. We assume, in this text, that the reader has already been exposed to these concepts in courses in hydraulics or fluid mechanics.

Except for sludges, most flows may be treated hydraulically in the same way as clean water even though considerable quantities of suspended material are being carried. The Hazen–Williams and Manning formulas are used extensively in designing water conveyances. The Hazen–Williams formula is used primarily for pressure conduits, while the Manning equation has found its major application in open-channel problems. Both equations are applicable when normal temperatures prevail, a relatively high degree of turbulence is developed, and ordinary commercial materials are used [3, 6, 8, 13–15]. The Hazen–Williams equation is

$$V = 1.318CR^{0.633}S^{0.54} \text{ (English units)}$$
$$V = 0.85CR^{0.63}S^{0.54} \text{ (SI units)}$$

(14)

where

V = velocity of flow (ft/s or m/s)
C = a coefficient that is a function of the construction material and age of the pipe
R = hydraulic radius (cross-sectional area divided by the wetted perimeter) (ft or m)
S = slope of energy gradient in feet per foot of length or meters per meter of length

For circular conduits flowing full, the equation may be restated as

$$Q = 0.279CD^{2.63}S^{0.54}$$

(15)

where

Q = flow, mgd
D = pipe diameter, ft

and as

$$Q = 0.278CD^{2.63}S^{0.54}$$

where

Q = flow, m^3/s
D = pipe diameter, m

Some values of C for use in the Hazen–Williams formula are given in Table 1. A nomograph that facilitates the solution of this equation is given in Figure 8.

The Manning equation is stated in the form

$$V = 1.49R^{0.66}S^{0.5}/n$$

(16)

where

V = velocity of flow, fps
R = hydraulic radius, ft
S = slope of energy grade line
n = coefficient of roughness

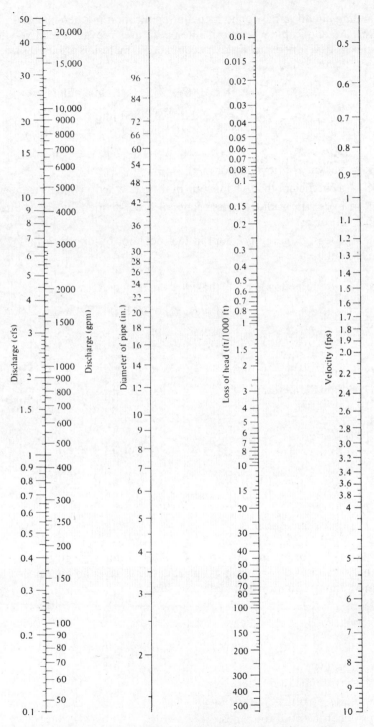

FIGURE 8   Nomograph for the Hazen–Williams formula with C = 100.

In metric units,

$$V = R^{0.66}S^{0.5}/n$$

where

V = velocity of flow, m/s

R = hydraulic radius, m

S = slope of energy grade line

n = coefficient of roughness

The equation is applicable as long as S does not materially exceed 0.10. In channels having no uniform roughness, an average value of n is selected. Where the cross-sectional roughness changes considerably, as in a channel with a paved center section and grassed outer sections, it is common practice to compute the flow for each section independently and sum these flows to obtain the total. For most purposes, n is considered a constant. It is actually a function of pipe diameter, however, and should be adjusted for pipe diameters exceeding several feet. As in the case of the Hazen–Williams equation, nomographs are available to permit rapid computation (see Figure 1). Values of n for use in Manning's equation are indicated in Table 1.

Head loss in pipelines results from pipe friction losses and from piping auxiliaries. Minor losses include those resulting from valves, fittings, bends, changes in cross section, and changes in flow characteristics at inlets and outlets. Over long lengths of pipeline, minor losses can usually be ignored in calculations of head loss because they contribute a relatively small proportion to the total losses. On the other hand, minor losses in short water transportation systems, such as those in water and wastewater treatment plants, should not be ignored because their proportion of the total head loss is significantly larger. Minor losses are usually expressed as a function of the velocity head in performing calculations, that is, $H_L = KV^2/2g$. Some values of the minor head loss coefficient K are given in Table 4 (see also 3, 6, 8–9, 13–15).

Head loss as a result of pipe friction can be computed by solving Eq. (14) or (16) for S and multiplying by the length of the pipeline. A slightly more direct method is to use the Darcy–Weisbach equation,

$$h_L = fLV^2/2Dg \tag{17}$$

where

h_L = head loss, ft

L = pipe length, ft

D = pipe diameter, ft

f = friction factor

V = flow velocity, fps

The friction factor is related to the Reynolds number and the relative roughness of the pipe. For conditions of complete turbulence, Figure 9 relates the friction factor to pipe geometry and characteristics.

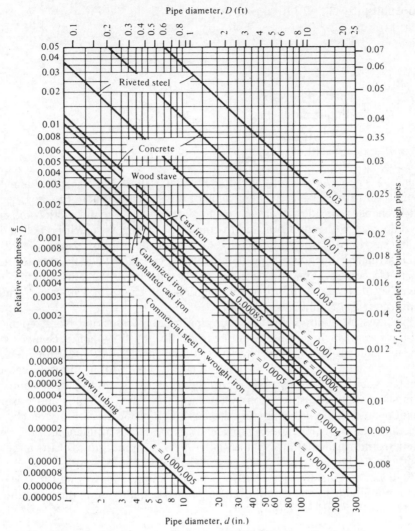

FIGURE 9 Relative roughness of pipe materials and friction factors for complete turbulence. *Source:* The Crane Company, Chicago, IL.

The Energy Equation

Consider flow in a straight pipe of uniform diameter. The energy equation for flow in a segment of length L between points 1 and 2 may be written as

$$Z_1 + \frac{P_1}{\gamma} + \frac{V_1^2}{2g} = Z_2 + \frac{P_2}{\gamma} + \frac{V_2^2}{2g} + H_L \tag{18}$$

where Z = elevation above an arbitrary datum (ft, m); p/γ = pressure head (ft, m); V = average velocity of flow (ft/sec, m/sec); and H_L = total head loss (energy loss) between the two cross sections.

Note that the terms of the energy equation are all in units of energy per unit weight (ft-lb/lb, kg-m/kg), which reduce to units of length (ft, m). If a pump were inserted into the pipeline, the quantity Hp would be added to the left-hand side of the equation to account for the additional energy head resulting from the action of the pump. If a turbine were inserted in the pipeline in place of the pump, the positive quantity Hp would be replaced by a negative quantity H, since a turbine converts the energy of flow into mechanical work, thereby consuming energy from the pipeflow instead of imparting energy to the flow as in the case of a pump.

Example 4

Consider that water is pumped 12 mi from a reservoir (Reservoir A) at elevation 100 ft to a second reservoir (Reservoir B) at elevation 220 ft. The pipeline connecting the reservoirs has a diameter of 48 in and is constructed of concrete with an absolute roughness of 0.003. If the flow is 28 mgd and the efficiency of the pumping station is 80%, what will be the monthly power bill if electricity costs 15 cents/kwh?

Solution:

1. Writing the energy equation between a point on the water surface of Reservoir A and a point on the water surface of Reservoir B, one obtains

$$Z_A + \frac{P_A}{W} + \frac{V_A^2}{2g} + H_p = Z_B + \frac{P_B}{W} + \frac{V_B^2}{2g} + H_L$$

2. Letting $Z_A = 0$, and noting that $P_A = P_B$ is equal to the atmospheric pressure and that $V_A = V_B = 0$ for a large reservoir, one can reduce the equation to

$$H_p = Z_B + H_L$$

where
H_p = head developed by the pump
H_L = total head lost between A and B, including pipe friction and minor losses
The following conversion factors are used in the calculations: mgd × 1.55 = cfs; and ft-lb × (3.766×10^{-7}) = kilowatt hours (kwh)

3. Using Figure 9, determine the value of f as 0.0182.
4. Using Eq. (17), find the pipe friction head loss. Assuming that the minor losses are negligible in this problem, this is equal to H_L:

$$H_L = f \frac{L}{D} \frac{V^2}{2g}$$

The velocity V must be determined before Eq. (15) can be solved:

$$V = Q/A = 28 \times 1.55/(\pi \times 4) = 3.45 \text{ ft/sec}$$

$$H_L = 0.0182 \times [(5280 \times 12)/4] \times ((3.45)^2/64.4) = 53.3 \text{ ft}$$

5. $H_p = (220 - 100) + 53.3 = 130 + 53.3 = 173.3$ ft-lb/lb (the energy imparted by the pump to the water).

6. The power requirement may be computed as

$$P = Q\gamma H_p$$
$$= 28 \times 1.55 \times 62.4 \times 177.3 = 469{,}324 \text{ ft-lb/s}$$

7. For 80% efficiency, the power requirement is

$$469{,}324/0.80 = 586{,}655 \text{ ft-lb/s}$$

8. $586{,}655 \times 3.766 \times 10^{-7} = 0.22 \text{ kwh/s}$
    The number of kilowatt-hours per 30-day month is then

$$0.22 \times 30 \times 86{,}400 = 570{,}240 \text{ kwh/month}$$

9. The monthly power cost is therefore $570{,}240 \times 0.15 = \$85{,}536$.

Flow in Branching Pipes

A common hydraulic problem is determining the direction and magnitude of flow in each pipe when several reservoirs are connected. The flow distribution will depend on the total head loss in each pipe, the diameter and length of the pipelines, and the number of connected facilities. A simple illustration is the classic *three-reservoir problem*, shown in Figure 10. Three reservoirs, *A, B*, and *C*, are connected by a system of pipelines that intersect at a single junction, *J*. Given the lengths and diameters of the pipes and the elevations of the three reservoirs, the problem is to determine the magnitude and direction of flow in each pipe.

It should be obvious that the flow will be out of Reservoir *A* and into Reservoir *C*, but it is not immediately evident whether the flow will be into or out of Reservoir *B*, because it is not known whether the pressure head at *J* is higher or lower than the water surface elevation at Reservoir *B*. This problem can be solved by making use of the continuity equation and the energy equation, which indicate that the flow into *J* equals the flow out of *J*, and the pressure head for all three pipes is the same at the point of intersection. Thus, by continuity,

$$Q_1 = Q_2 + Q_3 \text{ if the flow is into reservoir } B \tag{19a}$$

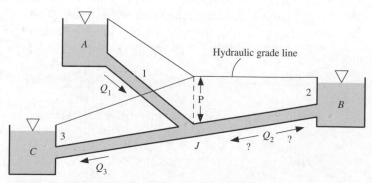

FIGURE 10   Branching-pipe system with single junction.

or

$$Q_1 + Q_2 = Q_3 \text{ if the flow is out of reservoir } B \qquad (19b)$$

and, by energy equivalence,

$$p_1/\gamma = p_2/\gamma = p_3/\gamma = P \qquad (20)$$

at J, where

Q = flow in each pipe (vol/time)

p/γ = pressure head in each pipe (height in units of length)

The solution is derived by choosing a trial height for P and solving for Q_1, Q_2, and Q_3 using the Manning equation, the Hazen–Williams equation, or the Darcy–Weisbach equation. The trial-and-error process is repeated until the continuity equation is satisfied.

An alternate, but more directly solved, branching-pipe problem is to find the elevation of one reservoir given all pipe lengths and diameters, the surface elevations of the other two reservoirs, and the flow either to or from one reservoir.

Flow in Pipes in Series

When a number of pipes of different diameters and lengths are connected in series, as depicted in Figure 11, the problem is either to determine the head loss given the flow, or to determine the flow given the head loss. The continuity equation allows us to state that the flow into and out of each pipe section must be the same, and the energy equation allows us to state that the head loss for the system is the sum of the head losses for each section of pipe. In other words, for the example shown in Figure 11,

$$Q = Q_1 = Q_2 = Q_3 \qquad (21)$$

and

$$H_L = H_{L1} + H_{L2} + H_{L3} \qquad (22)$$

For cases where the total head loss is given and the problem is to find the flow, the total head loss is written in terms of the dimensions of the head loss of each section, which for Figure 11 would be

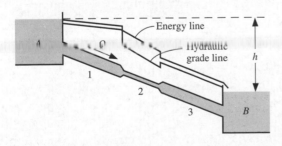

FIGURE 11 Flow in pipes in series.

$$H_L = [f_1(L_1/D_1)(V_1^2/2g) + \Sigma K(V_1^2/2g)]$$
$$+[f_2(L_2/D_2)(V_2^2/2g) + \Sigma(V_2^2/2g)] \qquad (23)$$
$$+[f_3(L_3/D_3)(V_3^2/2g) + \Sigma(V_3^2/2g)]$$

Minor losses are designated for each section as a function of velocity head, that is, $\Sigma K(V^2/2g)$. Since the flow is equivalent for each section, by continuity the velocity head for each section can be expressed as a function of the velocity head of any one section. For example, referring to Figure 11, we have

$$V_1^2/2g = V_2^2/2g(D_2/D_1)^4 \qquad (24)$$

and

$$V_1^2/2g = V_3^2/2g(D_3/D_1)^4 \qquad (25)$$

If a friction factor is assumed, the velocity of one pipe section can be found and used to calculate the flow, which would be the same for all pipe sections.

Example 5

Find the discharge from Reservoir A into Reservoir B in Figure 11 if three cast-iron pipes in series have diameters $D_1 = 15$ in., $D_2 = 10$ in., and $D_3 = 12$ in.; lengths $L_1 = 1500$ ft, $L_2 = 1350$ ft, and $L_3 = 2500$ ft; and a total head loss of 100 ft.

Solution:

1. Assuming $f = 0.01$ for all three pipes, and substituting the given values into the head loss equation given by Eq. (23), the objective is to determine V_1, V_2, and V_3.

    $$100 = 0.01[1500/(15/12)](V_1^2/2g) + 0.01[1350/(10/12)](V_2^2/2g)$$
    $$+ 0.01[2500/(12/12)](V_3^2/2g)$$

2. From Eqs. (24) and (25),

    $$V_1^2/2g = V_2^2/2g(10/15)^4 = 0.198(V_2^2/2g)$$
    $$V_3^2/2g = V_2^2/2g(10/12)^4 = 0.482(V_2^2/2g)$$

3. Substituting back into the head loss equation gives

    $$100 = V_2^2/2g[12(0.198) + 16.2 + 25(0.482)]$$
    $$V_2 = 14.5 \text{ ft/s}$$

4. Substituting V_2 back into the equations given in Step 2 yields

    $$V_1^2/2g = 0.198(14.5)^2/2g \qquad V_1 = 6.45 \text{ ft/s}$$
    $$V_3^2/2g = 0.482(14.5)^2/2g \qquad V_3 = 10 \text{ ft/s}$$

5. Since $Q = Q_1 = Q_2 = Q_3$, it follows that

    $$Q = Q_1 = V_1 A_1 = 6.459(\pi)(7.5/12)^2 = 7.9 \text{ cfs}$$

As a check, we have

$$Q = Q_2 = V_2 A_2 = 14.5(\pi)(5/12)^2 = 7.9 \text{ cfs}$$

$$Q = Q_3 = V_3 A_3 = 10(\pi)(6/12)^2 = 7.9 \text{ cfs}$$

Flow in Parallel Pipes

In the case of pipes connected in parallel, the problem is again either to determine the head loss and distribution of flow for the system given the total flow or to determine the total flow in the system given the head loss. For Figure 12, the continuity equation shows that the flow at the two junctions A and B is equivalent. In other words,

$$Q_A = Q_1 + Q_2 + Q_3 = Q_b \tag{26}$$

The head loss for the system can be shown by the energy equation to be equivalent to the head loss in each parallel pipe:

$$H_L = H_1 = H_2 = H_3 \tag{27}$$

Given the total flow, the head loss distribution may be determined by solving the Darcy–Weisbach head loss equation [Eq. (17)] for V for each pipe, producing

$$V = [2gH_L/f(L/D)]^{1/2}$$

and then substituting the preceding expression for V into $Q = VA$, that is,

$$Q = A[2gH_L/f(L/D)]^{1/2} \tag{28}$$

and writing Q as a function of the head loss and C, where C is constant for a given pipe $(C = A[2g/f(L/D))]^{1/2}$:

$$Q = C(H_L)^{1/2} \tag{29}$$

The flows for each pipe can then be summed and expressed as a function of the system head loss; for Figure 12, which has three pipes, this would be

$$Q = C_1(H_L)^{1/2} + C_2(H_L)^{1/2} + C_3(H_L)^{1/2}$$

From Eq. (26), this becomes

$$Q = (H_L)^{1/2}(C_1 + C_2 + C_3)$$

An alternate method of analysis for simple systems of pipes in parallel or series is the *equivalent-pipe method*. In this method, either a series of pipes or a system of parallel

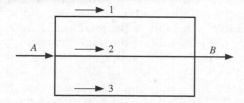

FIGURE 12   Flow in parallel pipes.

pipes is replaced with a pipe of equivalent head loss to simplify calculations. This method can also be used to simplify portions of complex pipe systems.

Equivalent Pipe Analysis

Hydraulic design of water distribution systems requires information on anticipated rates of water withdrawal, locations of withdrawals, and pressure gradients required for the system. The maximum daily rate of withdrawal plus fire protection and the maximum hourly rate of withdrawal should be investigated to determine which will govern the system design.

The spatial distribution of water use can be estimated using population densities and commercial and industrial use patterns that exist or are predicted for the region. When determining the peak hour for a feeder to an area consisting of residential, commercial, and industrial users, the predicted hydrograph for each type of user must be known. This will allow calculation of the specific hour in which the summation of the three component flows is greatest. Once the design demands have been determined, it is common practice to consider them to be concentrated at specified points on the feeder–main system.

Distribution systems are generally designed so that reasonably uniform pressures prevail [3, 6, 16]. Transmission mains may carry pressures up to 250 psi, but the need for pressures exceeding 150 psi is usually limited to those transmission mains serving pressure zones at higher elevations. The working pressure for residential areas is normally in the range of 40 to 60 psi. It should be noted that few plumbing fixtures will operate well at pressures less than about 20 psi. For urban water systems, the maximum design pressure that customers should experience is considered to fall within the range of 90–110 psi, while minimum design pressures (pressures at a customer's tap) are usually in the 40–50 psi range [6]. The maximum allowable velocity for pipelines is usually 5 fps.

The analysis of a distribution system is often simplified by first skeletonizing the system. This might involve replacing a series of pipes of varying diameter with one equivalent pipe or replacing a system of parallel pipes with an equivalent pipe. An "equivalent pipe" is one in which the loss of head for a specified flow is the same as the loss in head of the system it replaces. An example illustrates this method of analysis.

Example 6

Referring to the pipe system shown in Figure 13, replace (a) pipes BC and CD with an equivalent 12-in. pipe and (b) the system from B to D with an equivalent 20-in. pipe.

Solution:

1. Assume a discharge through BCD of 8 cfs. Using the Hazen–Williams formula [Eq. (14)], employ a spreadsheet to determine the parameters and head losses. The calculated values are shown in Table 5. The total head loss for pipe BC = 1.23 ft and that for pipe CD is 5.51 ft (see the right-hand column in the table). The total head loss between B and D is therefore 1.23 + 5.51 = 6.74 ft.

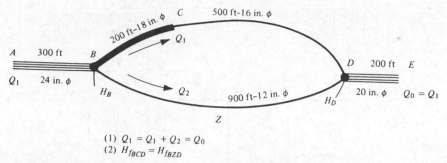

FIGURE 13 Example 6.

(1) $Q_1 = Q_1 + Q_2 = Q_0$
(2) $H_{f_{BCD}} = H_{f_{BZD}}$

TABLE 5 Spreadsheet Calculations for Example 6

Pipe Size (ft)	Length (ft)	Q (cfs)	Constant $1.318 \times C$	Area − A, $\pi d^{2/4}$	Perimeter, πd	RA/P	$R^{0.63}$	$S^{0.54}$	S	Total Head Loss
1.5	200	8	131.8	1.77	4.71	0.38	0.54	0.06	0.0061	1.23
1.33	500	8	131.8	1.39	4.18	0.33	0.50	0.09	0.0110	5.51
1	900	8	131.8	0.79	3.14	0.25	0.42	0.19	0.0441	39.71
1.67		9.69	131.8	2.19	5.25	0.42	0.58	0.06	0.0052	
1		6.931	131.8	0.79		0.25	0.42	0.1585	0.033	
1		2.761	131.8	0.79		0.25	0.42	0.0631	0.006	

Note: Lower part of table refers to Part 2 of the problem.

For a discharge of 8 cfs, the head loss S in ft/ft is found to be 0.0441. The equivalent length of 12-in. pipe is therefore

$$L = 6.74/0.0441 = 153.18 \text{ ft}$$

2. Assume a total head loss between B and D of 5.0 ft. For the 12-in. equivalent pipe this is 0.033 ft/ft (5/153.18). For the 900 ft of 12-in. pipe it is 0.006 ft/ft (5/900). Inserting these values in the Hazen–Williams formula reveals the flows to be 6.93 and 2.76 cfs, respectively. The total flow (the sum of the two) is thus 9.69 cfs at a head loss of 5 ft. For this discharge, a 20-in. pipe will have a head loss of 0.0052 ft/ft. The equivalent 20-in. pipe to replace the whole system will be

$$5/0.0052 = 961.5 \text{ ft long}$$

The analysis of this simple hydraulic system presents little difficulty. A slightly more complex system is shown in Figure 14. The method of equivalent pipes will fail to yield a solution in this case because there are crossover pipes (pipes that operate in more than one circuit) and a number of withdrawal points throughout the system. Solving this type of problem requires the use of network analysis techniques.

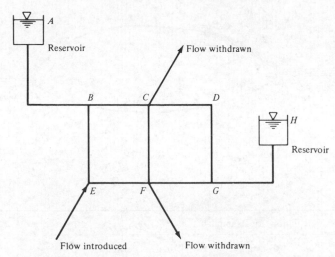

FIGURE 14　Pipe network showing pipe and fixed-grade nodes.

Pipe Networks

Most municipal water distribution systems are complex mazes containing pumps, storage elements, and pipelines of a variety of sizes. As pointed out in the preceding section, the ordinary methods of hydraulic analysis must be extended to take into account the looping characteristics of networks, changing reservoir levels, pumping, etc. Special techniques of network analysis come into play in analyzing water distribution systems. In these techniques, iterative solutions based on initial assumptions lead to either balancing flows in a system or balancing heads in a system. The underlying principles are those of preserving mass continuity and ensuring energy conservation.

Pipe networks are composed of a number of constant-diameter pipe sections containing pumps and fittings. The ends of each pipe section are called *nodes*. In Figure 14, the lettered points are nodes, which may be either fixed grade or junction type. *Junction nodes* are points where pipes meet and where flow may be introduced or withdrawn. *Fixed-grade nodes* are points where a constant grade is maintained. Connections to storage tanks or reservoirs or constant-pressure regions are examples (Figure 14). Networks are commonly divided into loops for computational purposes. Primary loops such as those shown in Figure 14 are closed pipe circuits in that the network has no other closed pipe circuits within them. Using this terminology, we may write

$$P = J + L + F - 1 \tag{30}$$

where

P = number of pipes
J = number of junction nodes
L = number of loops
F = number of fixed-grade nodes

This identity is directly related to the fundamental hydraulics equations that describe steady-state flow in a network. For Figure 14, $J = 6$, $L = 2$, $F = 2$, and thus the sum minus 1 is 9, the number of pipes in the complete network. Equations used to analyze steady-state pipe networks fall into two main categories—loop equations and node equations. The loop equations express mass conservation and energy conservation in terms of the discharge in a pipe section, while the node equations express mass continuity in terms of elevations or grades at junction nodes.

Many computer programs are available that can handle the analysis of flows in pipe systems of any configuration and with a variety of components such as storage tanks, pumps, check valves, pressure-regulating valves, and variable pressure water supplies [3, 6, 13, 17–28].

Loop Equations   Equation (30) is the basis for formulating a set of equations describing the hydraulic performance of a pipe network. In terms of unknown flows in the pipes, mass continuity and energy conservation equations can be written for the pipes and nodes. For each loop, an energy conservation equation can be written. A mass continuity equation can also be written for each node. For junction nodes, the inflow to the junction must be balanced by the outflow. This can be written

$$\Sigma Q_{in} - \Sigma Q_{out} = Q_e \text{(J equations)} \tag{31}$$

where Q_{in} is the inflow, Q_{out} is the outflow, and Q_e is the external flow into the system or the withdrawal from the system at the node. For the primary loops, energy conservation can be described by

$$\Sigma h_L = \Sigma E_p \text{ (L equations)} \tag{32}$$

where h_L is the pipe energy loss (minor losses included) and E_p is the energy introduced into the system by pumps. For loops having no pumps, the sum of the energy losses around the loop is zero. Note that a sign convention is used for loops. Clockwise flows might be considered positive and counterclockwise flows negative, for example.

Where there are F fixed-grade nodes, $F - 1$ independent energy conservation equations can be written for pipe paths between any two fixed-grade nodes. These equations take the form

$$\Delta E = \Sigma h_L - \Sigma E_p \quad (F - 1 \text{ equations}) \tag{33}$$

where ΔE is the difference in elevation (grade) between the two fixed-grade nodes. Any connected path between the two fixed-grade nodes can be selected by selecting a series of pipes so that the ending node of one path is the starting node for the next, etc. This procedure will produce the needed F 1 equations with no redundancy [17].

Equation (32) can be considered a special case of Eq. (33) where the difference in elevation (ΔE) is zero for a closed-loop path. It follows that the energy conservation equations for a pipe network can be expressed by $L + F - 1$ energy equations described by Eq. (33). The continuity and energy equations that describe the pipe network are P in number. They form a set of simultaneous nonlinear algebraic equations (loop equations) that describe steady-state flow conditions in a pipe network. To analyze an existing or proposed pipe network, the loop equations are solved to determine the flow in each pipe. To solve the loop equations, the terms in the energy equations must be expressed as functions of flow. Expressions for frictional losses in pipes, minor losses in fittings, and pump energy are needed.

Frictional losses in pipes are expressed as

$$h_{LP} = K_P Q^n \tag{34}$$

where K_P is a constant incorporating pipe length, diameter, and roughness, and n is an exponent. The values of K_P and n are generally determined by the selection of the Darcy–Weisbach, Hazen–Williams, or Manning equations for the expression of energy losses.

The minor losses in a section of pipe result from fittings, valves, meters, or other insertions that affect the flow. They are expressed as

$$h_{LM} = K_M Q^2 \tag{35}$$

where K_M is the minor loss constant, a function of the sum of the minor loss coefficients for all fittings in the length of pipe (ΣM) and the pipe diameter. It is given by

$$K_M = \sum M/2gA^2 \tag{36}$$

where A is the cross-sectional area of the pipe.

The term in the energy equations representing pumping energy can be expressed in several ways. A constant power input can be specified or a curve can be fitted to data obtained from pump operations. In any event, the relationship between pump energy E_P (head developed by the pump) and the flow Q can be represented by

$$E_P = P(Q) \tag{37}$$

If the pump operates at constant power, using the relationship for horsepower ($hp = Qwh/550$, where Q is the flow in cfs, w is the specific weight of water in pounds per ft^3, h is the head in feet, and 550 is a conversion factor) $P(Q)$ is given by $550\,hp/62.4Q$. Letting $Z = 550\,hp/62.4$, $P(Q)$ can be written, for constant power, as Z/Q.

Combining Equations (34–37), the energy relationships in terms of discharge become

$$\Delta E = \sum (K_P Q^n + K_M Q^2) - P(Q) \tag{38}$$

Equation (36) and the continuity equations [Eq. (31)] comprise the set of P simultaneous equations that must be solved in a loop analysis. There is no direct solution to these nonlinear algebraic relationships, but several algorithms for determining an answer are available. They will be discussed in subsequent sections.

Node Equations   Solving the loop equations begins generally with an assumption of flow rates in the pipe network. Computations proceed until adjustments in flows are considered to be within tolerable levels. When using node equations, adjustments are made in initial assumptions of head.

When considering nodes, the principal relationship used is the continuity equation [Eq. (31)]. The discharge in a section of pipe connecting nodes such as E and B (Figure 14) is expressed in terms of the grade (head) at junction node $A(H_a)$, the grade at junction node $B(H_b)$, and the resistance offered by the pipeline (K_{ab}). This can be expressed as

$$Q_{ab} = [(H_a - H_b)/K_{ab}]^{1/n} \qquad (39)$$

where it is assumed that the pipe section is free of pumps and the head loss is calculated as

$$h_L = KQ^n \qquad (40)$$

and K is determined as indicated for Eq. (34). Combine Eqs. (31) and (39):

$$\sum_{b=1}^{N}\left[\pm\left(\frac{H_a - H_b}{K_{ab}}\right)^{1/n} \right] = Q_e \qquad (41)$$

which expresses continuity at a given junction node where N pipes join. The sign of the term in the summation depends on the direction of flow into or out of the junction. A total of J junction node equations results. This basic set can be expanded to include pumps. For each pump encountered, junction nodes are specified at the pump inlet and outlet, locations b and c in Figure 15. Two additional equations are thus generated, one at the suction side and the other at the discharge side of the pump [17]. These equations involve the unknown heads (grades) on either side of the pump.

Following the notation of Figure 15, an equation using flow continuity in the suction and discharge lines can be written as

$$H_a - H_b = \frac{K_{ab}}{K_{cd}}(H_c - H_d) \qquad (42)$$

Another equation can be developed that relates the head change across the pump to the discharge in either the inlet or outlet pipe. Where the pump being considered is operating at constant power, the relationship in terms of the outlet line discharge, according to Eq. (37), is

$$H_c - H_b = P\left[\left(\frac{H_c - H_d}{K_{cd}}\right)^{1/n} \right] \qquad (43)$$

Equations (41) to (43) constitute the complete set of pipe network node equations. All of these equations are expressed in terms of the unknown grades at junction nodes and in terms of the suction and discharge grades at pumps within the system. This set of equations is also nonlinear, thus direct solution is impossible. Commonly used algorithms involving the node equations are discussed in later sections.

Algorithms for Solving Loop Equations

Several methods are widely used to solve the loop equations [17]. All use gradient methods to accommodate the nonlinear flow terms in Eq. (38). The gradient method

FIGURE 15   Pump notation for the node equation.

is derived from the first two terms of the Taylor series expansion. Any function $f(x)$ that is continuous (differentiable) can be approximated as follows:

$$f(x) \approx f(x_0) + f'(x_0)(x - x_0) \tag{44}$$

Examination of the right-hand side of Eq. (44) reveals that the approximation has reduced $f(x)$ to a linear form. However, if f is a function of more than one variable, Eq. (34) can be generalized as follows:

$$f[x(1), x(2), \dots] = f[x(1)_0, x(2)_0, \dots]$$

$$+ \frac{\partial f}{\partial x(1)}[x(1) - x(1)_0] + \frac{\partial f}{\partial x(2)}[x(2) - x(2)_0] + \cdots \tag{45}$$

in which the partial derivatives are evaluated at some $x(1) = x(1)_0, x(2) = x(2)_0$, etc.

The right-hand side of Eq. (38) represents the grade difference across a pipe carrying a discharge of Q. This can be stated as

$$f(Q) = K_P Q^n + K_M Q^2 - P(Q) \tag{46}$$

Substituting an estimated Q_i for Q and denoting $f(Q_i)$ by H_i, Eq. (46) becomes

$$H_i = f(Q_i) = K_P Q_i^n + K_M Q_i^2 - P(Q_i) \tag{47}$$

Differentiating Eq. (46) and setting $Q = Q_i$ gives the gradient of the function at $Q = Q_i$. Thus,

$$f'(Q_i) = n K_P Q_i^{n-1} + 2 K_M Q_i - P'(Q_i)$$

Denoting $f'(Q_i)$ by G_i,

$$G_i = n K_P Q_i^{n-1} + 2 K_M Q_i - P'(Q_i) \tag{48}$$

Both the function H_i and its gradient G_i evaluated at $Q = Q_i$ are used in algorithms for solving the loop equations.

Single-Path Adjustment (P) Method   This solution technique, first described by Hardy Cross [29], is the oldest and best known of all the loop methods. Originally, the method was restricted to closed-loop networks and provided only for line losses. A generalization of the procedure is described below [17, 30]:

1. An initial set of flow rates that satisfy continuity at each junction node is selected.
2. A flow adjustment factor is computed for each path $(L + F - 1)$ to satisfy the energy equation for that path. Continuity is maintained in this process.
3. Step 2 is repeated, building on improved solutions until the average correction factor is within an acceptable limit.

Equation (38) is used to compute the adjustment factor for a path using the gradient method to linearize the energy equations. Thus,

$$f(Q) = f(Q_i) + f'(Q_i)\Delta Q \tag{49}$$

in which $\Delta Q = Q - Q_i$, where Q_i is the estimated discharge. Applying Eq. (49) to Eq. (38) and solving for ΔQ gives

$$\Delta Q = \frac{\Delta E - \Sigma H_i}{\Sigma G_i} \qquad (50)$$

which is the flow adjustment factor to be applied to each pipe in the path. The numerator represents the imbalance in the energy relationship due to incorrect flow rates. The procedure reduces this to a negligible quantity. Flow adjustment is carried out for all L fundamental (closed) loops and $F - 1$ pseudoloops in the network.

The Hardy Cross method of network analysis permits the computation of rates of flow through a network and the resulting head losses in the system [29]. It is a relaxation method by which corrections are applied to assumed flows or assumed heads until an acceptable hydraulic balance of the system is achieved.

The Hardy Cross analysis is based on the principles that (1) in any system continuity must be preserved and (2) the pressure at any junction of pipes is single valued. The elements of the procedure can be explained with reference to the simple network of Figure 16. First, the system must be defined in terms of pipe size, length, and roughness. Then, for any inflow Q_1, the system can be balanced hydraulically only if $H_{fBCD} = H_{fBZD}$. This restriction limits the possibilities to only one value of Q_1 and Q_2 that will satisfy the conditions.

The procedure for deriving the basic equation for balancing heads by correcting assumed flows for the loop of Figure 16 [29] follows. First, find the required inflow Q_1. Then arbitrarily divide this flow into components Q_1 and Q_2. The only restriction on the selection of these values is that $Q_1 + Q_2 = Q_1$. You should, however, attempt to select realistic values. Since the procedure involves a number of trials, the amount of work involved will depend on the accuracy of the value originally selected. For example, in the network shown, BCD has a considerably larger diameter than BZD. It is logical to therefore assume that Q_1 will be larger than Q_2. The final solution to the problem will be the same regardless of the original choice, but much more rapid progress will result from reasonable initial assumptions.

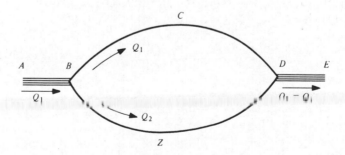

(1) $Q_1 = Q_1 + Q_2 = Q_0$
(2) $H_{fBCD} = H_{fBZD}$

FIGURE 16　Derivation of the Hardy Cross method.

After Q_1 and Q_2 have been chosen, H_{fBCD} and H_{fBZD} can be computed using the Hazen–Williams or some other pipe-flow formula. Remembering that the Hazen–Williams equation is of the form of Eq. (15),

$$Q = 0.279CD^{2.63}S^{0.54}$$

we may rewrite the equation as

$$Q = K_a S^{0.54} \tag{51}$$

where K_a is a constant when we are dealing only with a single pipe of specified size and material. Rearranging this equation and substituting H_f/L for S yields Eq. (34), or

$$H_f = KQ^n$$

where $n = 1.85$ in the Hazen–Williams equation. Equation (34) is convenient for expressing head loss as a function of flow in network analyses.

If the computed values of H_{fBCD} and H_{fBZD} are not equal (which is usually the case on the first trial), a correction must be applied to the initial values. Call this correction ΔQ. If, for example, $H_{fBCD} > H_{fBZD}$, then the new value for Q_1 will be $Q_1 - \Delta Q = Q_1'$ and the new value for Q_2 must be $Q_2 + \Delta Q = Q_2'$. The corresponding values of head loss will be H'_{fBCD} and H'_{fBZD}. If ΔQ is the true correction, then

$$H'_{fBCD} - H'_{fBZD} = 0 = K_1(Q_1 - \Delta Q)^n - K_2(Q_2 + \Delta Q)^n$$

The binomials may be expanded as follows:

$$K_1(Q_1^n - n\Delta Q Q_1^{n-1} + \cdots) - K_2(Q_2^n + n\Delta Q Q_2^{n-1} + \cdots) = 0$$

If ΔQ is small, the terms in the expansion involving ΔQ to powers greater than unity can be neglected. Therefore,

$$K_1 Q_1^n - n K_1 \Delta Q Q_1^{n-1} - K_2 Q_2^n - n K_2 \Delta Q Q_2^{n-1} = 0$$

Substituting H_{fBCD} for $K_1 Q_1^n$, H_{fBZD} for $K_2 Q_2^n$, and rewriting the terms KQ^{n-1} as $K(Q^n/Q)$ yields

$$H_{fBCD} - \Delta Q n K_1 \frac{Q_1^n}{Q_1} - H_{fBZD} - \Delta Q n K_2 \frac{Q_2^n}{Q_2} = 0$$

$$H_{fBCD} - H_{fBZD} = \Delta Q n \left(\frac{H_{fBCD}}{Q_1} + \frac{H_{fBZD}}{Q_2} \right)$$

and

$$\Delta Q = \frac{H_{fBCD} - H_{fBZD}}{n(H_{fBCD}/Q_1 + H_{fBZD}/Q_2)} \tag{52}$$

Expanding this expression to the more general case gives the following equation for the flow correction ΔQ:

$$\Delta Q = -\Sigma H / n\Sigma\left(\frac{H}{Q}\right) \tag{53}$$

Application of this equation involves an initial assumption of discharge and a sign convention for the flow. Either clockwise or counterclockwise flows may be considered positive, and the terms in the numerator will bear the appropriate sign. For example, if the counterclockwise direction is considered positive, all H values for counterclockwise flows will be positive and all H values for clockwise flows will be negative. The denominator, however, is the absolute sum without regard to sign convention. The correction ΔQ has a single direction for all pipes in the loop, and thus the sign convention must also be considered in applying the correction.

Example 7

Given the network, the inflow at A, and the outflows at B, C, and D in Figure 17, carry out a Hardy Cross analysis using a spreadsheet to find the flows in the individual pipes comprising the network. Assume that the Hazen–Williams coefficient C is 100.

Solution: The computational procedure is given in Table 6. The initial and final flows are also shown in Figure 17. In Table 6, Columns 1–4 are self-explanatory; Column 5 indicates the sign convention, the values used as multipliers for values that are sign-dependent; Column 6 gives the absolute values of Q for Trial 1 (these are the initial assumptions); Column 7 computes the values of head using Eq. (17) (these values are

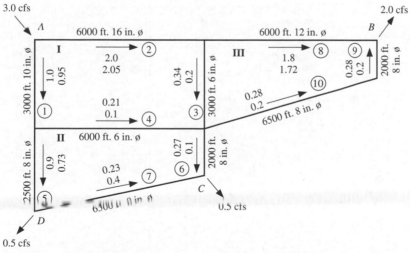

FIGURE 17   Pipe network analyzed by the Hardy Cross method. (The clockwise direction is considered positive. The flows are the initial assumed and final corrected values.)

TABLE 6 Spreadsheet Solution to Example 7

TRIAL 1

(1) Loop No.	(2) Pipe No.	(3) Pipe Diam. (in)	(4) Length (ft)	(5) Sign (− OR +)	(6) Q (cfs) ABS	(7) H (ft)	(8) (H/Q) ABS	(9) N(Sum(H/Q)) ABS	(10) Sum (H)	(11) Delta Q Loop	(12) Delta Q Pipe	(13) Q2	(14) Q2 ABS
1	1	10	3000	−1	1	−6.88	6.88				−0.00	−1.00	1
	2	16	6000	1	2	5.03	2.51				−0.00	2.00	2
	3	6	3000	1	0.2	4.22	21.06	99.65			−0.12	0.32	0.32
	4	6	6000	−1	0.1	−2.34	23.39		0.03	−0.00	0.17	−0.27	0.27
2	4	6	6000	1	0.1	2.34	23.39				0.17	0.27	0.27
	6	8	2000	1	0.1	0.19	1.92				0.17	0.27	0.27
	7	8	6500	−1	0.4	−8.11	20.28	113.09			0.17	−0.23	0.23
	5	8	2500	−1	0.9	−13.99	15.54		−19.57	0.17	0.17	−0.73	0.73
3	3	6	3000	−1	0.2	−4.22	21.06				−0.12	−0.32	0.32
	8	12	6000	1	1.6	16.80	9.33				−0.12	1.68	1.68
	9	8	2000	−1	0.2	−0.69	3.46	83.48			−0.12	−0.32	0.32
	10	8	6500	−1	0.2	−2.25	11.25		9.64	−0.12	−0.12	−0.32	0.32

TRIAL 2

(1) Loop No.	(2) Pipe No.	(3) Pipe Diam. (in)	(4) Length (ft)	(5) Sign (− OR +)	(6) Q2 (cfs) ABS	(7) H (ft)	(8) (H/Q) ABS	(9) N(Sum(H/Q)) ABS	(10) Sum (H)	(11) Delta Q Loop	(12) Delta Q Pipe	(13) Q3	(14) Q3 ABS
1	1	10	3000	−1	1	−6.88	6.88				0.04	−0.96	0.96
	2	16	6000	1	2	5.03	2.51				0.04	2.04	2.04
	3	6	3000	1	0.32	10.06	31.43	176.19			0.06	0.34	0.34
	4	6	6000	−1	0.27	−14.69	54.41		−6.48	0.04	0.01	−0.21	0.21
2	4	6	6000	1	0.27	14.69	54.41				0.01	0.21	0.21
	6	8	2000	1	0.27	1.21	4.47				−0.02	0.25	0.25
	7	8	6500	−1	0.23	−2.91	12.67	156.43			−0.02	−0.25	0.25
	5	8	2500	−1	0.73	−9.50	13.01		3.49	−0.02	−0.02	−0.75	0.75
3	3	6	3000	−1	0.32	−10.06	31.43				0.06	−0.34	0.34
	8	12	6000	1	1.68	14.79	8.80				0.02	1.70	1.7
	9	8	2000	−1	0.32	−1.65	5.16	115.02			0.02	−0.30	0.3
	10	8	6500	−1	0.32	−5.37	16.78		−2.29	0.02	0.02	−0.30	0.3

TRIAL 3

Loop No.	Pipe No.	Pipe Diam. (in)	Length (ft)	Sign (– OR +)	Q3 (cfs) ABS	H (ft)	(H/Q) ABS	N(Sum(H/Q)) ABS	Sum (H)	Delta Q Loop	Delta Q Pipe	Q4	Q4 ABS
1	1	10	3000	–1	0.96	–6.38	6.65				–0.01	–0.97	0.97
	2	16	6000	1	2.04	5.22	2.56				–0.01	2.03	2.03
	3	6	3000	1	0.34	11.25	33.09				0.02	0.31	0.31
	4	6	6000	–1	0.21	–9.23	43.95	159.55	0.86	–0.01	0.02	–0.24	0.24
2	4	6	6000	1	0.21	9.23	43.95				0.02	0.24	0.24
	6	8	2000	1	0.25	1.05	4.19				0.02	0.27	0.27
	7	8	6500	–1	0.25	–3.40	13.60				0.02	–0.23	0.23
	5	8	2500	–1	0.75	–9.96	13.31	138.83	–3.11	0.02	0.02	–0.73	0.73
3	3	6	3000	–1	0.34	–11.25	33.09				0.02	–0.31	0.31
	8	12	6000	1	1.7	15.11	8.89				0.02	1.72	1.72
	9	8	2000	–1	0.3	–1.47	4.89				0.02	–0.28	0.28
	10	8	6500	–1	0.3	–4.76	15.88	116.09	–2.37	0.02	0.02	–0.28	0.28

TRIAL 4

Loop No.	Pipe No.	Pipe Diam. (in)	Length (ft)	Sign (– OR +)	Q4 (cfs) ABS	H (ft)	(H/Q) ABS	N(Sum(H/Q)) ABS	Sum (H)	Delta Q Loop	Delta Q Pipe	Q5
1	1	10	3000	–1	0.97	–6.50	6.70				0.02	–0.95
	2	16	6000	1	2.03	5.17	2.55				0.02	2.05
	3	6	3000	1	0.31	9.48	30.60				0.02	0.34
	4	6	6000	–1	0.24	–11.81	49.23	164.79	–3.66	0.02	0.02	–0.21
2	4	6	6000	1	0.24	11.81	49.23				0.02	0.21
	6	8	2000	1	0.27	1.21	4.47				–0.00	0.27
	7	8	6500	–1	0.23	–2.91	12.67				–0.00	–0.23
	5	8	2500	–1	0.73	–9.50	13.01	146.84	0.61	–0.00	–0.00	–0.73
3	3	6	3000	–1	0.31	–9.48	30.60				0.02	–0.34
	8	12	6000	1	1.72	15.44	8.96				–0.00	1.72
	9	8	2000	–1	0.28	–1.29	4.61				–0.00	–0.28
	10	8	6500	–1	0.28	–4.19	14.96	109.44	0.47	–0.00	–0.00	–0.28

multiplied by the values in Column 5 so that they carry the appropriate sign); Column 8 displays the ratios of Column 7 to Column 6 values multiplied by the sign convention (Column 5; these are absolute values); Column 9 computes the denominator of Eq. (53) (absolute value); Column 10 is the sum of the values in Column 7 for each loop; Column 11 computes the ΔQ values for each loop using Eq. (53); Column 12 computes the ΔQ value for each pipe in the loop (it is the sum of all corrections that must be made if a pipe appears in more than one loop; Pipes 3 and 4 in the example appear in two loops, so a sign convention is needed); and Column 13 calculates the new value of Q for each pipe in the loop. Column 14 is the absolute value of Column 13. These values become the Column 6 values for the next iteration.

A similar procedure is to assume values of H and then balance the flows by correcting the assumed heads. The mechanics of the two methods are the same, and the applicable relationship,

$$\Delta H = -n\Sigma Q / \Sigma\left(\frac{Q}{H}\right) \tag{54}$$

can be derived in a manner similar to that for Eq. (53). The number of trials required for the satisfactory solution of any problem using Eq. (53) or (54) depends to a large extent on the accuracy of the initial set of assumed values and on the desired degree of accuracy of the results.

In using the Hardy Cross method to analyze large distribution systems, it is often useful to reduce the system to a skeleton network of main feeders [16]. Where the main feeder system has a very large capacity relative to that of the smaller mains, field observations indicate that this type of skeletonizing yields reasonable results. Where no well-defined feeder system is apparent, serious errors may result from skeletonizing. Figure 18 illustrates a skeletonized distribution network consisting of arterial mains only. Figure 19 shows how a portion of the distribution system of Figure 18 (that part lying within the dashed rectangle) looked before skeletonizing. A more complete discussion of such procedures is given by Reh [16]. The analysis of a large network may also be expedited by balancing portions of the system successively instead of analyzing the whole network simultaneously.

Normally, minor losses are neglected in network studies, but they can easily be introduced as equivalent lengths of pipe when it is felt that they should be included.

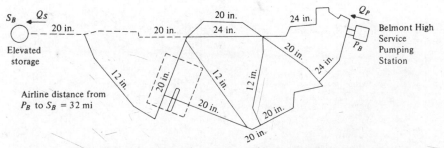

FIGURE 18   Arterial pipe network of the Belmont High Service District, Philadelphia. *Source:* Civil Engineering Department, University of Illinois, Urbana.

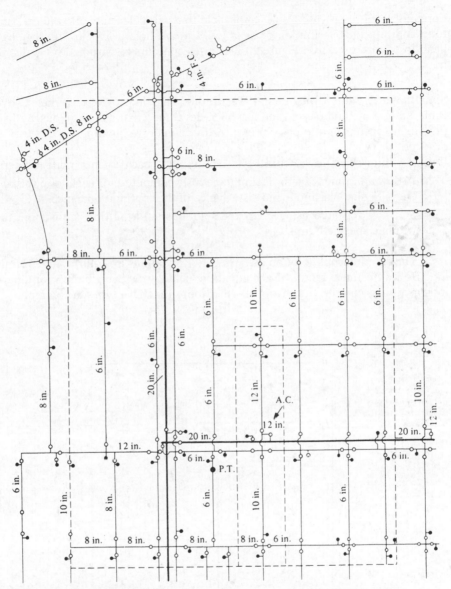

FIGURE 19 Intermediate grid sector, Belmont High Service District, Philadelphia.
Source: Civil Engineering Department, University of Illinois, Urbana.

Where C values are determined from field measurements, they invariably include a component due to the various minor losses encountered. McPherson gives a good discussion of local losses in water distribution networks [30].

The construction of pressure contours helps to isolate shortcomings in the hydraulic performance of distribution systems. Contours are often drawn with intervals of 1 to 5 ft of head loss but may have other intervals depending on local circumstances.

For a given set of operating rules applicable to a particular network, the pressure contours indicate the distribution of head loss and are helpful in showing regions where head losses are excessive. Figure 20 illustrates contours constructed for a distribution network.

Simultaneous Path Adjustment (SP) Method To improve convergence over the P methods, a method of solution has been developed that simultaneously adjusts the flowrate in each path of pipes represented by an energy equation [17]:

1. An initial set of flowrates satisfying continuity at each junction node is determined.
2. A flow adjustment factor is simultaneously computed for each loop to satisfy the energy equations and avoid disturbance of the continuity balance.
3. Step 2 is repeated using improved solutions until the flow adjustment factor is within a specified limit.

The simultaneous solution of $L + F - 1$ equations is required to determine the loop flow adjustment factors. Each equation includes the contribution for a particular loop as well as contributions from all other loops that have pipes in common.

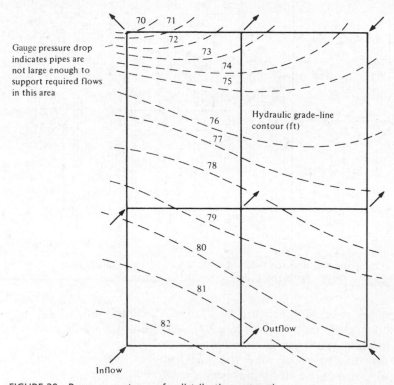

FIGURE 20   Pressure contours of a distribution network.

For loop j, the head change required to balance the energy equation is expressed in terms of the flow change in loop $j(\Delta Q_j)$ and the flow changes in adjacent loops (ΔQ_k); that is,

$$f(Q) = f(Q_i) + \frac{\partial f}{\partial Q}\Delta Q_j + \frac{f}{Q}\Delta Q_k$$

or

$$f(Q) = f(Q_i) + f'(Q_i)\Delta Q_j + f'(Q_i)\Delta Q_k \tag{55}$$

With the substitution $f(Q) = \Delta E, f(Q_i) = \Sigma H_i$, and $f'(Q) = \Sigma G_i$, Eq (55) becomes

$$\Delta E - \Sigma H_i = (\Sigma G_i)\Delta Q_j + \Sigma(G_iQ_k) \tag{56}$$

in which ΣH_i is the sum of the head changes for all pipes in loop j, $(\Sigma G_i) \times \Delta Q_j$ is the sum of all gradients for the same pipes times the flow change for loop j, and $\Sigma(G_i\Delta Q_k)$ is the sum of the gradients for pipes common to loops j and k multiplied by the flow change for loop k.

A set of simultaneous linear equations is thus formed in terms of flow adjustment factors for each loop representing an energy equation. The solution of these linear equations provides an improved solution for another trial until a specified convergence criterion is met.

Linear (L) Method   This procedure involves the solution of the basic hydraulic equations for a pipe network [17]. In the method, the energy equations are linearized using a gradient approximation. This is accomplished in terms of an approximate discharge Q_i as follows:

$$f(Q) = f(Q_i) + f'(Q_i)(Q - Q_i)$$

Introducing the expressions H_i and G_i, defined as before, the foregoing equation becomes

$$\sum G_iQ = \sum (G_iQ_i - H_i) + \Delta E \tag{57}$$

This relationship is employed to formulate $L + F - 1$ energy equations, which, together with the J continuity equations, form a set of P simultaneous linear equations in terms of the flow rate in each pipe. A significant advantage of this scheme is that an arbitrary set of initial flow rates, which need not satisfy continuity, can be used to start the iteration. Wood [17] has used a flow rate based on a mean flow velocity of 4 fps. Successive trials are carried out until the change in flow rate between successive trials becomes insignificant.

The use of the linear (L) method of analysis is illustrated by an example developed by Wood [17]. The calculations are given for one trial. The system analyzed is shown in Figure 21, which includes the necessary data and shows the numbers assigned to the pipe sections and junction nodes. The system includes a globe valve in Pipe 7 that imposes a noticeable minor loss. Other minor losses are neglected. A pump

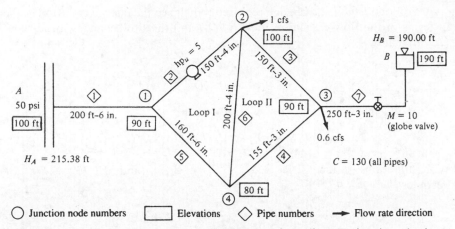

FIGURE 21   Wood's sample pipe system: ○, junction node numbers; □, elevations; ◇, pipe numbers; →, flow rate direction. *Source:* After D. T. Wood, "Algorithms for Pipe Network Analysis and Their Reliability." Res. Rep. No. 127, University of Kentucky, Water Resources Research Institute, Lexington, KY, 1981.

with constant power input is included in Pipe 2. The useful horsepower (hp) for this pump is given as 5. Thus, Eq. (37) becomes

$$E_P = P(Q) = Z/Q$$

and the pump constant $Z = 550 \, hp_u/62.4 = 44.07$ in the example. The pump terms used in the equations for H_i and G_i [Eqs. (47) and (48)] are

$$P(Q_i) = Z/Q_i \quad \text{and} \quad P'(Q_i) = -Z/Q_i^2$$

The Hazen–Williams equation is employed in the example for head loss calculations. Using that expression produces the pipeline constant,

$$K_P = \frac{4.73L}{C^{1.852}D^{4.87}}$$

where C is given in Table 1, L is the pipe length, and D is the pipe diameter. Formulas for computing the pipeline constant in English and metric units for both the Hazen–Williams and Darcy–Weisbach equations are given in Table 7.

Table 8 summarizes values of pipeline, minor loss, and pump constants for each pipe in the example system for a C value of 130.

In the example, four mass continuity equations for the four junction nodes and three energy equations are required. The energy equations include one for each of the two loops noted ($\Delta E = 0$) and one additional energy equation for pipes connecting the two fixed-grade nodes ($\Delta E = 25.38$ ft).

An arbitrary set of initial flow rates is defined to start the procedure. A flow rate based on a mean flow velocity of 4 fps is used for this purpose. The initial flow rates and corresponding values for G and H are shown in Table 9. Four continuity equations

TABLE 7 Formulas for Determining the Pipe Constant K_P

Equation Type	K_P	Units for			
		Q	L	D	H_f
Hazen–Williams	$\dfrac{4.73L}{C^{1.85}D^{4.87}}$	cfs	Ft	ft	ft
	$\dfrac{10.44L}{C^{1.85}D^{4.87}}$	gpm	Ft	in.	ft
	$\dfrac{10.70L}{C^{1.85}D^{4.87}}$	m^3/s	M	m	m
Darcy–Weisbach	$\dfrac{fL}{39.70D^5}$	cfs	Ft	ft	ft
	$\dfrac{fL}{32.15D^5}$	gpm	Ft	in.	ft
	$\dfrac{fL}{12.10D^5}$	m^3/s	M	m	m

TABLE 8 Pipe System Constants

Pipe No.	K_P	K_M	Z
1	3.36	0	0
2	18.18	0	44.1
3	73.78	0	0
4	76.24	0	0
5	2.69	0	0
6	24.23	0	0
7	122.97	64.44	0

TABLE 9 Values of Q_i, G_i, and H_i for the Linear Method

Pipe No.	Q_i	G_i	H_i
1	0.7854	5.072	2.151
2	0.3491	375.42	−123.66
3	0.1963	34.14	3.619
4	0.1963	25.279	0.710
5	0.7854	4.057	1.721
6	0.3491	18.308	3.451
7	0.1963	82.204	8.517

and three energy equations are to be solved simultaneously. The continuity equations [Eq. (31)] are

$$-Q_1 + Q_2 + Q_5 = 0 \qquad \text{(junction 1)}$$

$$-Q_2 + Q_3 - Q_6 = -1.0 \quad \text{(junction 2)}$$

$$-Q_3 - Q_4 + Q_7 = -0.6 \quad \text{(junction 3)}$$

$$Q_4 - Q_5 + Q_6 = 0 \qquad \text{(junction 4)}$$

The energy equations [Eq. (57)] are derived using the data in Table 9. Calculations on the right-hand side of these equations for the two loops and for the path AB between the two fixed-grade nodes are given in Table 10. The left-hand side of the equations is the sum of the products of the G_i and Q for each pipe in the loop or path. Notice that a sign convention must be used in accounting. The following are the resulting three energy equations:

$$5.072Q_1 + 375.42Q_2 + 34.14Q_3 + 82.204Q_7 = 292.63 \qquad \text{(path } AB\text{)}$$

$$375.42Q_2 - 4.057Q_5 - 18.308Q_6 = 250.304 \qquad \text{(loop I)}$$

$$34.14Q_3 - 35.278Q_4 + 18.308Q_6 = 2.837 \qquad \text{(loop II)}$$

The solutions of these equations (in cfs) are $Q_1 = 1.725, Q_2 = 0.705, Q_3 = 0.262,$ $Q_4 = 0.463, Q_5 = 1.020, Q_6 = 0.557,$ and $Q_7 = 0.125.$ These are used to formulate a second set of equations (only the energy equations change) and to obtain a second solution. The procedure continues until a specified convergence criterion is met. After five iterations, the final flows are found to be $Q_1 = 1.73, Q_2 = 1.37, Q_3 = 0.37,$ $Q_4 = 0.36, Q_5 = 0.36, Q_6 = 0.001,$ and $Q_7 = 0.131.$

TABLE 10　Calculations for Energy Equations for the Linear (L) Method

	Pipe No. and Sign	$G_i \times Q_i$	H_i	ΔE for Loop
Loop I	2+	$375.42 \times 0.3491 = +131.059$	+123.66	
	6−	$18.308 \times 0.3491 = -6.391$	+3.451	0
	5−	$4.057 \times 0.7854 = -3.186$	+1.721	
		$\Sigma\, G_iQ = \Sigma(G_iQ_i - H_i) + \Delta E = 121.482 + 128.832 + 0.0 = 250.31$		
Loop II	6+	$18.308 \times 0.3491 = +6.391$	−3.451	
	3+	$34.14 \times 0.1963 = +6.702$	−3.169	0
	4−	$35.278 \times 0.1963 = -6.925$	+3.740	
		$\Sigma\, G_iQ = \Sigma(G_iQ_i - H_i) + \Delta E = 6.168 - 3.330 + 0.0 = 2.838$		
Path AB	1+	$5.072 \times 0.7854 = +3.984$	−2.151	
	2+	$375.42 \times 0.3491 = +131.059$	+123.66	
	3+	$34.14 \times 0.1963 = +6.702$	−3.619	25.38
	7+	$82.204 \times 0.1963 = +16.137$	−8.517	
		$\Sigma\, G_iQ = \Sigma(G_iQ_i - H_i) + \Delta E = 157.882 + 109.373 + 25.38 = 292.635$		

Algorithms for Solving Node Equations

The two most widely used node methods are the single-node adjustment (N) method and the simultaneous node adjustment (SN) method [17]. The N method was originally described by Hardy Cross [29]:

1. A reasonable grade is assumed for each junction node in the system. The better the initial assumptions, the fewer the required trials.
2. A grade adjustment factor for each junction node that tends to satisfy continuity is computed.
3. Step 2 is repeated using improved solutions until a specified convergence criterion is met.

The grade adjustment factor is the change in grade at a particular node (ΔH) that will result in satisfying continuity and considering the grades at adjacent nodes fixed. For convenience, the required grade correction is expressed in terms of Q_i, the flow based on the grades at adjacent nodes before adjustment. With the gradient approximation,

$$f(Q) = f(Q_i) + f'(Q_i)\Delta Q$$

and substituting terms defined previously, we derive the flow correction

$$\Delta Q = \Sigma\left(\frac{1}{G_i}\right)\Delta H \tag{58}$$

where $\Delta H = H - H_i$, and the grade adjustment factor and ΔQ represent the flow corrections required to satisfy continuity at the nodes. From Eq. (31),

$$\Delta Q = \sum Q_i - Q_e \tag{59}$$

Thus, from Eqs. (58) and (59),

$$\Delta H = (\Sigma Q_i - Q_e)/\Sigma \frac{1}{G_i} \tag{60}$$

In Eq. (60), inflow is assumed positive. The numerator represents the unbalanced flow rate at the junction node [see also Eq. (54)].

The flow rate Q_i in a pipe section before adjustment is computed from

$$Q_i = (\Delta H_i/K)^{1/n}$$

in which ΔH_i is the grade change based on assumed initial values of grade.

When pumps are located in a pipeline, the following expression can be used to determine Q_i:

$$\Delta H_i = KQ_i^n - P(Q_i) \tag{61}$$

Equation (61) is solved using an approximation procedure. Adjustment of the grade for each junction node is made following each trial until a selected convergence criterion is satisfied [17]. The SN method is based on simultaneous solution of the basic network node equations. These equations must be linearized in terms of approximate values of grade (head). Details of the procedure are reported in [17].

Newton—Raphson Method   The Newton–Raphson method is a widely used numerical method for solving systems of nonlinear equations [3]. The method is applicable to problems that can be expressed in the form $F(H) = 0$, where the solution is the value of H that causes F to become zero. Applying the technique to a simple system where there is only one equation with one unknown illustrates the principle involved. Here, the derivative of F can be approximated as

$$\frac{dF}{dH} = \frac{F(H + \Delta H) - F(H)}{\Delta H} \tag{62}$$

With an initial assumption of H, the solution is obtained by determining the value of $H + \Delta H$ that forces F to zero. By setting $F(H + \Delta H)$ to zero, the solution for ΔH becomes

$$\Delta H = \frac{-F(H)}{dF/dH} \tag{63}$$

The value of H used in the next step of the iterative process then becomes $H + \Delta H$. Iterations continue until F closely approaches zero.

Analysis of the types of pipe networks encountered in practice usually means dealing with large numbers of equations and unknowns. The Newton–Raphson method can be applied to either the $N - 1$, ΔH equations [Eq. (33)] or the ΔQ equations exemplified by Eq. (49). For each node, a head equation of the form of Eq. (41) is written

$$F(H_b) = \sum_{b=1}^{N} \left[\pm \left(\frac{H_a - H_b}{K_{ab}} \right)^{1/n} \right] - Q = 0 \tag{64}$$

where

N = the number of pipes that join at a node
K = the pipeline constant
n = 1.85 for the Hazen — Williams equation
Q = the flow withdrawn at the node

The sign of the term in the summation depends on the direction of flow into or out of the junction. If $F(i)$ is the value of F at iteration i, it follows that

$$dF = F(i + 1) - F(i) \tag{65}$$

The same change can also be approximated as

$$dF = \frac{\partial F}{\partial H_1} \Delta H_1 + \frac{\partial F}{\partial H_2} \Delta H_2 + \cdots + \frac{\partial F}{\partial H_k} \Delta H_k \tag{66}$$

where ΔH is the change in H in the iteration from i to $i + 1$. The problem is one of iteratively determining the values of ΔH so that the end result is that $F(i + 1)$ becomes zero. The process involves setting Eq. (65) equal to Eq. (66). A system of k linear equations with k unknowns of the form ΔH results. These equations can be solved by various linear methods [3].

The solution is obtained by selecting initial values of H, calculating the partial derivatives of each F with respect to H, and solving the set of linear equations to find a new value of H. The process is repeated until all of the calculated F values are sufficiently close to zero. Note that the derivative of the terms in Eq. (64) is of the form

$$\frac{dF}{dH} = \pm \frac{(H_a - H_b)^{(1/n-1)}}{n(K_{ab})^{1/n}} \tag{67}$$

The following example illustrates the Newton–Raphson procedure.

Example 8

Given the simple pipe network of Figure 22, find the value of H_1 if $C = 100$ and $n = 1.85$.

Solution: Equations (64) and (67) are applied along with

$$H(i + 1) = H(i) - \frac{F}{dF/dH} \tag{68}$$

In this case, there arc only two pipes and only one equation must be solved for F, dF/dH, and $H(i + 1)$ at each iteration. Based on an initial assumption of 100 for H_1, the calculated values of F, dF/dH, and $H(i + 1)$ are displayed in Table 11. The first set of calculations follows:

1. Values of K_1 and K_2 are calculated by using the formula in Table 7 for the Hazen–Williams equation, where Q is in cfs and L and d are in ft:

$$K_1 = (4.73 \times 1000)/[(100)^{1.85}(0.5)^{4.87}]$$
$$= 275.95$$

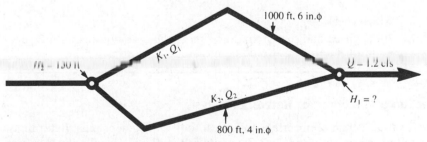

FIGURE 22   Network diagram for Example 8.

TABLE 11   Calculated Values of H, F, and dF/dH
             for Example 8

Iteration No.	H	F	dF/dH
1	100.00	−0.504	−0.0125
2	59.68	−0.097	−0.0084
3	48.13	−0.002	−0.0078
4	47.87		

In like manner, by substituting the appropriate values and solving, K_2 is found to be 167.78.

2. Assuming that $H_1 = 100$ and using Eq. (64) yields

$$F(H)_1 = \left(\frac{130 - 100}{275.95}\right)^{0.54} + \left(\frac{130 - 100}{167.78}\right)^{0.54} - 1.2 = -0.504$$

3. Using Eq. (67) gives

$$\left(\frac{dF}{dH}\right)_1 = \frac{-1}{1.85(275.95)^{0.54}(130 - 100)^{0.46}} +$$

$$\frac{-1}{1.85(167.78)^{0.54}(130 - 100)^{0.46}} = -0.0125$$

4. The new value of H is found from Eq. (68):

$$H_{i+1} = 100 - (-0.504/-0.0125)$$
$$= 59.68$$

5. The procedure is repeated, and the solutions are recorded in Table 11.

6. Noting that the sum of the Qs must equal 1.2 cfs, the equations for Q in pipes 1 and 2 are solved by using the head loss calculated to see if their sum is correct. From Eq. (39),

$$Q_1 = [(130 - 47.87)/275.95]^{0.54} = 0.52 \text{ cfs}$$

$$Q_2 = [(130 - 47.87)/167.78]^{0.54} = 0.68 \text{ cfs}$$

$$Q_1 + Q_2 = 0.52 + 0.68 = 1.2 \text{ cfs},$$

which checks.

7. If the check had shown that the sum of the Qs did not equal 1.2 very closely, additional iterations would be required.

Selection of a Method of Network Analysis

In order to select an appropriate analytical tool, an engineer must determine what is expected of the design or analysis. The network methods described in this chapter are all equipped to accommodate many features of pipe systems, but the methods are not all equal in their breadth, and they are not all equal in their ability to converge on a solution. Accordingly, engineers must know something about the virtues and deficiencies of these tools, as well as of any models they are interested in using.

Node equations are easy to formulate because they include only contributions from adjacent nodes. Loop equations require the identification of an appropriate set of energy equations, including terms for all pipes in the primary loops and for paths between fixed-grade nodes. Formulating this set of equations is considerably more difficult than formulating the node equations.

The procedures described in this chapter are iterative. Computation continues until a specified convergence criterion is met. The solutions are therefore approximate, although they can be very accurate. The ability of an algorithm to produce an acceptable solution is important, and the convergence problems associated with it must be understood.

A solution is considered satisfactory when all the basic equations are satisfied to a high degree of accuracy. Continuity is always exactly satisfied when loop equations are used. The loop algorithms satisfy the energy equations iteratively, and the degree to which heads are unbalanced for the energy equations is evidence of solution accuracy. For methods based on node equations, iterations are carried out to satisfy continuity at junction nodes and the imbalance in continuity is the indicator of solution accuracy.

For many years, shareware or proprietary software has been used to design most water distribution systems. GIS is often used in combination with these models to expedite design and to operate and maintain water distribution systems. The best sources for these models are the users' manuals and websites for the software. The most common models used to design water distribution systems are listed in Table 12. When selecting any sort of hydrologic or hydraulic model, consider the following features:

1. *The initial cost of the software and how many future licenses will be needed for the software.* It is also important to consider how often future software upgrades will be needed and how expensive they will be. The labor costs involved not only in creating these models but also in maintaining them should also be considered.
2. *The governing equations and assumptions used in the software.* The model specifications should be carefully reviewed and should meet or exceed industry standards for design. The model should also be reasonable to calibrate and verify and have a history of use on similar projects.
3. *The current and future uses of the software.* For example, many software packages now output information to both GIS and/or Computer Automated Design (CAD) software packages. Some models also provide optimization routines and special modules to expedite the design.
4. *The longevity and history of the company providing the software.* The company providing proprietary software should have a solid technical reputation and a reasonable chance of remaining in business for the entire time that that software will be used.
5. *Regulatory constraints related to the software.* The model should be acceptable to any regulatory agencies involved in the project.

TABLE 12 Common Models Used to Design Water Distribution Systems

Name of Model (Model Creator)	Website
EPANET (United States Environmental Protection Agency)	http://www.epa.gov/nrmrl/wswrd/dw/epanet.html
WaterGEMS (Bentley/Haestad Methods)	http://www.bentley.com/en-US/Products/WaterGEMS
WaterCAD (Bentley/Haestad Methods)	http://www.bentley.com/en-US/Products/WaterCAD
KY Pipe or Kentucky Pipe (KYPipe)	http://www.kypipe.com
H2ONET (MWH Soft)	http://www.mwhsoft.com/page/p_product/net/net_overview.htm

Regardless of the software used, the final quality of the model will depend heavily on the modeler(s) involved. As computers become faster and easier to use, modeling will become an increasingly important part of engineering design. Modeling should, however, only be undertaken by qualified engineers and analysts who understand the many factors involved. Since models will only be as good as the knowledge used to create them, it is important to become modelers and not merely model users.

PRESSURE CONSIDERATIONS

The performance of a distribution system can be based on the pressures available in the system for a specific rate of flow [16]. Pressures should be great enough to meet consumer and firefighting needs. At the same time, they should not be excessive, since the development of pressure head is an important cost consideration. In addition, higher pressures may cause leakage, which is associated with loss of treated water and higher costs. Costs of distribution systems are significant, and minimizing them must be a design objective.

For commercial areas, pressures in excess of 60 pounds per square inch gauge (psig) are usually required. Adequate pressures for residential areas usually range from 40 to 50 psig. In tower buildings it is often necessary to provide booster pumps to elevate the water to the upper floors. Storage tanks are usually provided at the highest level and water is distributed directly from them.

The capacity of the distribution system is determined on the basis of local water needs plus fire demands. Pipe sizes should be selected so that high velocities are avoided. Once the flow has been determined, pipe sizes can be selected by assuming velocities ranging from 3 to 5 fps. Where fire-fighting requirements are to be met, a minimum diameter of 6 in. is recommended. The National Board of Fire Underwriters recommends 8 in. as a minimum but permits 6-in. pipes in grid systems provided the length between connections does not exceed 600 ft.

9 GENERAL DESIGN SEQUENCE

The design of a water distribution system involves selecting a system of pipes and other components so that design flows can be carried with head losses that do not exceed those necessary for adequate operation of the system. Design flows should be based on estimated future water requirements, since distribution systems must provide service for many years (sometimes as long as 100 years). A typical sequence of evaluation, design, and layout operations follows [3, 6, 13–15, 31]:

1. Review maps, construction plans, billing records, planning studies, zoning regulations, population figures, water use studies, and any other data relevant to the system being analyzed. If the area in question has a geographic information system in place, this is often the best way to begin data collection.

2. For existing water systems, determine pipe ages, the roughness of pipe interiors, pipe lengths and diameters, and the locations of pipes and appurtenances. Water supply sources, pumping station locations and characteristics, and storage tank locations and volumes must also be determined.

3. Prepare a detailed map or begin building a GLS of the existing or proposed system.

4. Forecast population growth and distribution to the end of the design period (10 to 50 years). Project water use patterns (spatial and temporal) for domestic, industrial, and commercial uses to be served by the system. These estimates must also extend over the design life of the network. Water use estimates are based on population projections and anticipated trends in commercial and industrial activity.

5. Develop a computer model of the existing or proposed system. In analyzing a network, it is common to simplify the system by eliminating nonessential small lines, combining pipes using the equivalent-pipe method, and assuming water use to be concentrated at takeoff points (nodes). Almost always, shareware or commercially available models should be used due to the complexity of the analyses.

6. Use the computer model of the existing system to evaluate historical conditions. If observed data and model runs compare favorably, the model may be considered "calibrated." The model can then be presumed to be adequate for evaluating proposed modifications to, or extensions of, the existing system. Applying the model to the existing system will quickly identify areas of low pressure, pipelines having high head-loss characteristics, and overloaded parts of the network. Proposed replacements and extensions of the system can then be evaluated to see if they will resolve problems or meet new requirements.

7. Design a new or expanded water distribution system as follows:

    a. On a development plan of the area to be serviced, sketch the tentative location of all water mains that will be needed to supply the area. The completed drawing should differentiate between proposed feeder mains and smaller service mains. The various pipelines making up the system should be interconnected at intervals of 1200 ft or less. Looped feeder systems are desirable and should be used whenever possible. Two small feeder mains running parallel several blocks apart are preferable to a single large main with an equal or slightly larger capacity than the two mains combined.

    b. Using estimated values of the anticipated design flows, select appropriate pipe sizes by assuming velocities ranging from 3 to 5 fps.

    c. Mark the position of building service connections, fire hydrants, and valves. Service connections form the link between the distribution system and the individual consumer. Normally, the practice is one customer per service pipe. Figure 23 illustrates the details of a typical service connection for a private residence. Fire hydrants are located to provide complete protection to the area covered by the distribution system. Recommendations regarding average area per hydrant for various populations and required fire flow are given by the National Board of Fire Underwriters. Hydrants generally should not be farther apart than about 500 ft. Figure 24 illustrates a typical fire hydrant setting.

d. Apply projected water demands (including fire flow) to the network and calculate residual pressures.

e. Compare calculated pressures to standards. Identify areas of projected less-than-adequate service.

f. Check head losses in individual pipes to find excesses. These will usually occur in pipes where flow velocities are greater than 1.5 m/s (5 fps).

g. Add pipes or replace high-head-loss pipes with larger pipes. Run the model again and see if residual pressures under maximum future loads are adequate. If not, try other additions or changes until the system is adequate for anticipated future loads. The system must be able to handle maximum daily loads plus fire loads without decreasing residual pressures below minimum standards. The

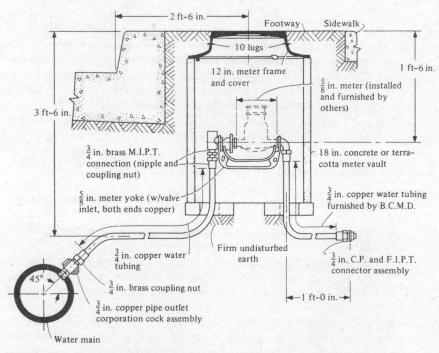

FIGURE 23   Typical installation of $^3/_4$-in. metered domestic service. *Source:* Baltimore County, MD, Department of Public Works.

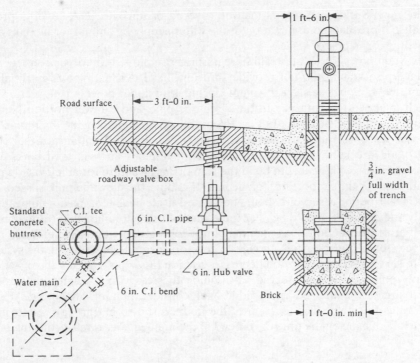

FIGURE 24   Typical fire hydrant setting. *Source:* Baltimore County, MD, Department of Public Works.

overall objective is to design a system that will meet projected water demands at the least cost while incorporating appropriate safety measures for looping or duplicate lines so that line breaks or other disturbances will not isolate users from a water supply. Note, however, the network analysis and resulting design will be no better than the assumptions made regarding water demands, pipe roughness, and so on.

8. Estimate construction costs for the proposed improvements.
9. Prepare a construction schedule for the identified improvements or new system that is consistent with the financial capabilities of the city.

10   DISTRIBUTION RESERVOIRS AND SERVICE STORAGE

Distribution reservoirs provide service storage to meet fluctuating demands often imposed on distribution systems, to accommodate firefighting and emergency requirements, and to equalize operating pressures. They may be elevated, partially buried, or below ground level.

The main categories are surface reservoirs, standpipes, and elevated tanks. Common practice is to line surface reservoirs with concrete, gunite, asphalt, or an asphaltic membrane. Surface reservoirs may be covered or uncovered. A cover is preferable because it prevents contamination of the water supply by animals or humans and prevents the formation of algae.

Standpipes or elevated tanks are normally employed where the construction of a surface reservoir would not provide sufficient head. A standpipe is essentially a tall cylindrical tank whose storage volume includes an upper portion (the useful storage), which is above the entrance to the discharge pipe, and a lower portion (supporting storage), which acts only to support the useful storage and provide the required head. For this reason, standpipes over 50 ft high are usually not economical. Steel, concrete, and wood are used in the construction of standpipes and elevated tanks. When it becomes more economical to build the supporting structure for an elevated tank than to provide for the supporting storage in a standpipe, the elevated tank is used.

Distribution reservoirs should be located strategically for maximum benefit. Normally, the reservoir should be near the center of use, but in large metropolitan areas a number of distribution reservoirs may be located at key points. Reservoirs providing service storage must be high enough to develop adequate pressures in the system they are to serve. A central location decreases friction losses by reducing the distance from supply point to the area served. Positioning the reservoir so that pressures may be approximately equalized is an additional consideration of importance. Figure 25 illustrates this point. The location of the tank, as shown in Part (a), results in a very large loss of head by the time the far end of the municipality is reached. Thus, pressures

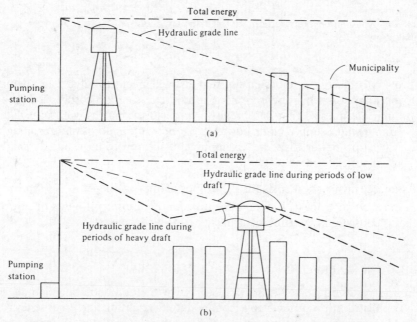

FIGURE 25   Pressure distribution as influenced by the location of a distribution reservoir.

too low will prevail at the far end or excessive pressures will be in evidence at the near end. In Part (b), pressures over the whole municipal area are more uniform for periods of both high and low demand. Note that during periods of high demand the tank is supplying flow in both directions (being emptied), whereas during periods of low demand the pump is supplying the tank and the municipality.

The amount of storage to be provided is a function of the capacity of the distribution network, the location of the service storage, and the use to which it is to be put. Water treatment plants are commonly operated at a uniform rate of flow such as the maximum daily rate. It is also desirable to operate pumping units at constant rates. Demands on the system in excess of these rates must therefore be met by operating storage. Requirements for firefighting purposes should be sufficient to provide fire flows for 10 to 12 hours in large communities and for 2 hours or longer in smaller ones. Emergency storage is provided to sustain the community's needs during periods when the inflow to the reservoir is shut off—for example, through a failure of the water supply works, failure of pumping equipment, or the need to take a supply line out of service for maintenance or repair. The length of time the supply system is expected to be out of service dictates the amount of emergency storage to be provided. Emergency storage sufficient to last for several days is desirable.

The amount of storage required for emergency and firefighting purposes is readily computed once the time period over which these flows are to be provided has been selected [32]. An emergency storage of three days for a community of 8000 having an average use rate of 150 gpcd is $3 \times 150 \times 8000 = 3.6$ mil gal. Given that a fire flow of 2750 gpm must be provided for 10 hours, this means a total firefighting storage of 1.65 mil gal. An additional equalizing or operating storage requirement would be added to the sum of these values. The determination of this volume is slightly more complex and needs further explanation.

To compute the required equalizing or operating storage, refer to a mass diagram or hydrograph indicating the hourly rate of water use. The procedure used in determining the needed storage volume is as follows:

1. Obtain a hydrograph of hourly demands for the maximum day. This may be obtained through a study of available records, by gauging the existing system during dry periods when lawn-sprinkling demands are high, or by using design criteria to predict a hydrograph for a future condition of development.
2. Tabulate the hourly demand data for the maximum day as shown in Table 13.
3. Find the required operating storage by using mass diagrams such as in Figures 26 and 27, the hydrograph of Figure 28, or the values tabulated in Column 6 of Table 13.

The required operating storage is found by using a mass diagram with the cumulative pumping curve plotted on it. Figure 26 illustrates this diagram for a uniform 24-hr pumping rate. Note that the total volume pumped in 24 hours must equal the total 24-hr demand, and thus the mass curve and cumulative pumping curve must be coincident at

TABLE 13 Hourly Demand for the Maximum Day

(1) Time	(2) Average Hourly Demand Rate (gpm)	(3) Hourly Demand (gal)	(4) Cumulative Demand (gal)	(5) Hourly Demand as a Percent of Average	(6) Average Hourly Demand Minus Hourly Demand: 286,250 − (3)	
					−	+
12 A.M.	0	0	0	0	—	—
1	2170	130,000	130,000	45.4		156,250
2	2100	126,000	256,000	44.1		160,250
3	2020	121,000	377,000	42.3		165,250
4	1970	118,000	495,000	41.3		168,250
5	1980	119,000	614,000	41.6		167,250
6	2080	125,000	739,000	43.2		161,250
7	3630	218,000	957,000	76.2		68,250
8	5190	312,000	1,269,000	108.9	25,750	
9	5620	337,000	1,606,000	117.8	50,750	
10	5900	354,000	1,960,000	123.6	67,750	
11	6040	363,000	2,323,000	126.7	76,750	
12 P.M.	6320	379,000	2,702,000	132.4	92,750	
1	6440	387,000	3,089,000	135.2	100,750	
2	6370	382,000	3,471,000	133.4	95,750	
3	6320	379,000	3,850,000	132.4	92,750	
4	6340	381,000	4,231,000	133.0	94,750	
5	6640	399,000	4,630,000	139.5	112,750	
6	7320	439,000	5,069,000	153.3	152,750	
7	9333	560,000	5,629,000	195.5	273,750	
8	8320	499,000	6,128,000	174.4	212,750	
9	5050	303,000	6,431,000	105.8	16,750	
10	2570	154,000	6,585,000	53.8		132,250
11	2470	148,000	6,733,000	51.7		138,250
12 A.M.	2290	137,000	6,870,000	47.9		149,250
Total		6,870,000			1,466,500	1,466,500

Average hourly demand $= \dfrac{6,870,000}{24} = 286,250$ gal

the origin and at the end of the day. Next, construct a tangent to the mass curve parallel to the pumping curve at Point A in the figure. Then draw a second parallel tangent to the mass curve at Point C and drop a vertical from C to an intersection with tangent AB at B. The required storage is equal to the magnitude of the ordinate CB measured on the vertical scale. In the example shown, the necessary storage volume is found to be 1.47 mil gal for a 24-hr pumping period.

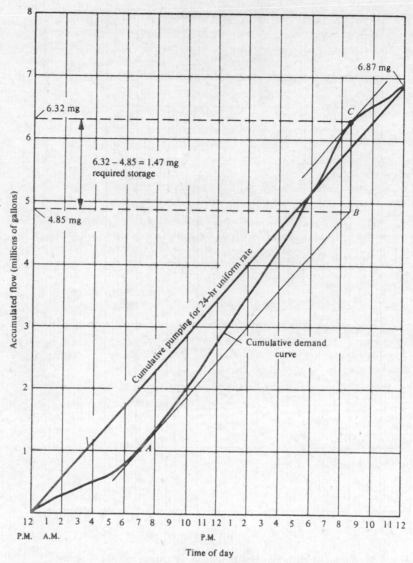

FIGURE 26   Operating storage for 24-hr pumping, determined by use of a mass diagram.

Note that the reservoir is full at *A*, is empty at *C*, is filling whenever the slope of the pump curve exceeds that of the cumulative demand curve, and is being drawn down when the rate of demand exceeds the rate of pumping.

It is often desirable to operate an equalizing reservoir so that pumping will take place at a uniform rate but for a period less than 24 hours. In small communities, for

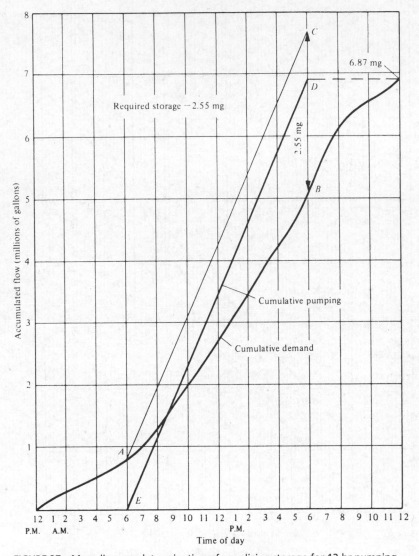

FIGURE 27   Mass diagram determination of equalizing storage for 12-hr pumping.

example, it is often advantageous to pump only during the normal working day. It may also be more economical to operate the pumping station at off-peak periods when electric power rates are low.

Figure 27 illustrates the operation of a storage reservoir where pumping occurs between 6 A.M. and 6 P.M. only. To find the required storage in this case, construct the cumulative pumping curve *ED* so that the total volume of 6.87 mil gal is pumped uniformly from 6 A.M. to 6 P.M. Then project point *E* vertically upward to an intersection with the cumulative demand curve at *A*. Construct line *AC* parallel to *ED*. Point *C* will

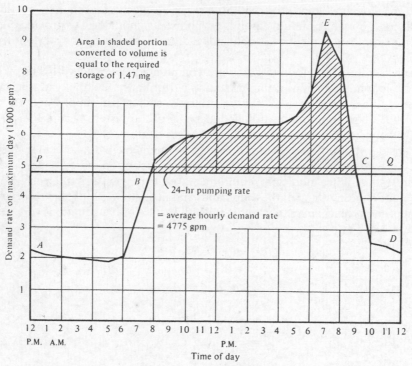

FIGURE 28   Graphical determination of equalizing storage.

be at the intersection of line AC with the vertical extended upward from 6 P.M. on the abscissa. The required storage equals the value of the ordinate CBD. Numerically, it is 2.55 mil gal and exceeds the storage requirement for 24-hr pumping. Another graphical solution to the storage problem may be obtained as outlined in Figure 28. The figure is a plot of the demand hydrograph for the maximum day. For uniform 24-hr pumping, the pumping rate will be equal to the mean hourly demand. This is shown as line PQ. The required storage is then obtained by planimetering or determining in some other manner the area between curve BEC and line PQ. Conversion of this area to units of volume yields the required storage of 1.47 mil gal. The required storage for 24-hr pumping may also be determined by summing either the plus or minus values of column 6 in Table 12.

Unless pumping follows the demand curve or demand hydrograph, storage will be required. Figure 26 shows that a maximum pumping rate of about 9400 gpm will be required with no storage, whereas if storage is provided, a maximum pumping rate of 4775 gpm (about 50% of that required with no storage) will suffice. This example illustrates the economics of providing operating storage.

Variable-rate pumping is normally not economical. In practice, it is common to provide storage and pumping facilities so that pumping at the average rate for the maximum day can be maintained. On days of less demand, some pumping units will stand idle. Another operational procedure is to provide enough storage for pumping at the average rate for the average day, with idle reserve capacity, and then to overload all available units on the maximum day. It is economically impractical to provide pumping and storage capacity to meet peak demands that are experienced for only a few hours every few years.

Analyses of distribution systems are commonly concerned with the pipe network, topographic conditions, pumping station performance, and the operating characteristics of the storage system. Where multiple sources of supply operate under variable-head conditions, the hydraulic balancing of the system becomes more complex. The simple system of Figure 29 illustrates this point.

Considering that the demand for water by the municipal load center fluctuates hourly, it is evident that there are essentially two modes of operation of the given distribution system. When municipal requirements are light, such as in the early morning, the pumping station will meet these demands and in addition supply the reservoir. The solution of the problem may then be found with the use of the equations

(1) $\quad Q_1 - Q_D = Q_2$

(2) $\quad Z_P + E_P = Z_{LC} + E_{R2} + H_{f1}$

(3) $\quad Z_{LC} + E_{R2} = Z_T + H_{f2}$

(2 + 3) $\quad H_{f1} + H_{f2} = E_P + Z_P - Z_T$

where

$\quad\quad Q_1 =$ flow from the pump

$\quad\quad Q_D =$ municipal demand

$\quad\quad Q_2 =$ flow to the tank

$Z_P, Z_{LC}, Z_T =$ elevation above the arbitrary datum

$\quad\quad\quad\quad\quad (Z_T =$ elevation of water surface in tank)

$\quad\quad E_P =$ energy produced by the pump

$\quad\quad E_{R2} =$ residual energy of the load center

$\quad\quad\quad\quad\quad$ (pressure head plus velocity head)

$H_{f1},$ etc. $=$ friction head losses

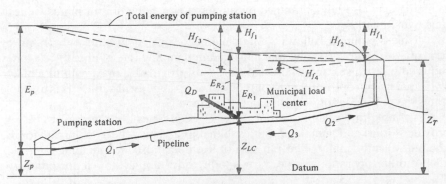

FIGURE 29   Modes of operation of a distribution system.

If Q_D, Z_P, Z_{LC}, and Z_T are specified, the equations may be solved by selecting values of E_{R2} and then solving for H_{f1} and H_{f2}. When a solution is reached so that Eq. $(2 + 3)$ is satisfied, Q_1 and Q_2 may be computed.

When demands are high, both the tank and the pump will supply the community. The direction of flow will then be reversed in the line from the tank to the pump and the applicable equations will be

1. $Q_1 + Q_3 = Q_D$
2. $Z_P + E_P = Z_{LC} + E_{R1} + H_{f3}$
3. $Z_{LC} + E_{R1} + H_{f4} = Z_T$

Again, an assumed value for E_R will be taken and trial solutions carried out until Eq. (1) is satisfied. Note that the foregoing illustration is a simple case, since Z_T has been specified. Actually, since Z_T fluctuates with time, it is necessary to have information on storage volume available versus water elevation in the tank so that at any specified condition of draft, the actual value for Z_T can be determined and used in the computations.

Water distribution systems generally are considered a composite of four basic constituents: the pipe network, the storage, the pump performance, and the pumping station and its suction source. These components must be integrated into a functioning system for various schedules of demand. A thorough analysis of each system must be made to ensure that it will operate satisfactorily under all anticipated combinations of demand and hydraulic component characteristics. The system may work well under one set of conditions but will not necessarily be operable under some other set. A comprehensive system balance requires an hourly simulation of performance for the expected operating schedule.

There are an infinite number of arrangements of the basic components in a distribution system, but the hydraulic analyses discussed in this chapter are applicable to all of them.

PUMPING

Pumps are important components of most water conveyance systems. The primary types of pumps are centrifugal and displacement. Airlift pumps, jet pumps, and hydraulic rams are also used in special applications. In water and sewage works, centrifugal pumps are most common. *Centrifugal pumps* have a rotating element (impeller) that imparts energy to the water. *Displacement pumps* are often of the reciprocating type, in which a piston draws water into a closed chamber and then expels it under pressure. Reciprocating pumps are widely used to handle sludge in sewage treatment works.

Electric power is the primary source of energy for pumping, but gasoline, steam, and diesel power are also used. Often, a standby engine powered by one of these other forms is included in primary pumping stations to operate in emergency situations when electric power fails.

11 PUMPING HEAD

The first step in selecting pumps is to determine the operating characteristics of the system in which they are to be used [33–36]. An important feature is the *total dynamic head* (TDH) against which the pump must operate. The TDH is composed of the difference in elevation between the pump centerline and the elevation to which the water

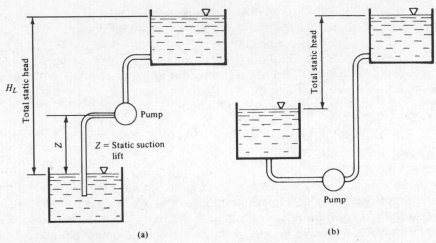

FIGURE 30   Total static head. (a) Intake below the pump centerline. (b) Intake above the pump center line.

is to be raised, the difference in elevation between the level of the suction pool and the pump centerline, the frictional losses encountered in the pump, pipe, valves and fittings, and the velocity head. Expressed in equation form, this becomes

$$\text{TDH} = H_L + H_F + H_V \tag{69}$$

where H_L is the total static head or elevation difference between the pumping source and the point of delivery, H_F is the total friction head loss, and H_V is the velocity head $V^2/2g$. Figure 30 illustrates the total static head.

12   POWER

For a known discharge and total pump lift, the theoretical horsepower (hp) is given by

$$\text{hp} = Q\gamma H/550 \tag{70}$$

where

Q = discharge, cfs
γ = specific weight of water
H = total dynamic head
550 = conversion from foot-pounds per second to horsepower

The actual horsepower required is obtained by dividing the theoretical horsepower by the efficiency of the pump and driving unit.

13   CAVITATION

Cavitation is the phenomenon of cavity formation or the formation and collapse of cavities [34]. Cavities develop when the absolute pressure in a liquid reaches the vapor pressure related to the liquid temperature. Under severe conditions, cavitation can result in the breakdown of pumping equipment. As the net positive suction head (NPSH) for a pump is reduced, a point is reached where cavitation becomes detrimental. This point is usually referred to as the *minimum net positive suction head* (NPSH_{min}) and is a function of the type of pump and the discharge through the pump. NPSH is calculated as

$$\text{NPSH} = \frac{V_1^2}{2g} + \frac{p_1}{\gamma} - \frac{p_v}{\gamma} \tag{71}$$

where V_1 is the velocity of flow at the center line of the inlet to the pump, p_1 is the pressure at the center line of the pump inlet, and p_v is the vapor pressure of the fluid. Referring to Figure 30(a) and writing the energy equation between the intake pool and the inlet to the pump, we have

$$\frac{p_a}{\gamma} = \frac{V^2}{2g} + \frac{p_1}{\gamma} + Z + h_L$$

or

$$\frac{p_a}{\gamma} - Z - h_L = \frac{V^2}{2g} + \frac{p_1}{\gamma}$$

where p_a is atmospheric pressure and h_L is the head loss in the intake.
Subtracting p_v/γ from both sides, we have

$$\frac{p_a}{\gamma} - Z - h_L - \frac{p_v}{\gamma} = \frac{V^2}{2g} + \frac{p_1}{\gamma} - \frac{p_v}{\gamma}$$

This may be written

$$\frac{p_a}{\gamma} - Z - h_L - \frac{p_v}{\gamma} = \text{NPSH}$$

The minimum value of the static lift is then determined as

$$Z_{min} = \frac{p_a - p_v}{\gamma} - \text{NPSH}_{min} - h_L \tag{72}$$

The required NPSH for any pump can be obtained from the manufacturer. This value can then be checked against the proposed installation using Eqs. (71) and (72) to ensure that the available NPSH is greater than the manufacturer's requirement.

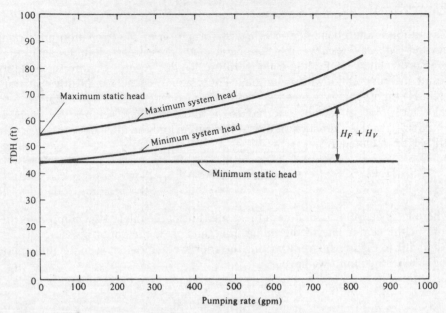

FIGURE 31   System head curves for a fluctuating static pumping head.

14   SYSTEM HEAD

The system head is represented by a plot of TDH versus discharge for the system being studied. Such plots are very useful in selecting pumping units [36]. It should be clear that the system head curve will vary with flow since H_F and H_V are both a function of discharge. In addition, the static head H_L may vary as a result of fluctuating water levels and similar factors, and it is often necessary to plot system head curves covering the range of variations in static head. Figure 31 illustrates typical system head curves for a fluctuating static water level.

15   PUMP CHARACTERISTICS

Each pump has its own characteristics relative to power requirements, efficiency, and head developed as a function of flow rate. These relationships are usually given as a set of pump characteristic curves for a specified speed. They are used in conjunction with system head curves to select correct pumping equipment for a particular installation. A set of characteristic curves is shown in Figure 32.

    At no flow, the head is known as the *shutoff head*. The pump head may rise slightly or fall from the shutoff value as discharge increases. Ultimately, however, the head for any centrifugal pump will fall with increase in flow. At maximum efficiency, the discharge is known as the *normal* or *rated discharge* of the pump. Varying the pump discharge by throttling will lower the efficiency of the unit. Changing the speed of the pump will cause the discharge to vary within a certain range without a loss of

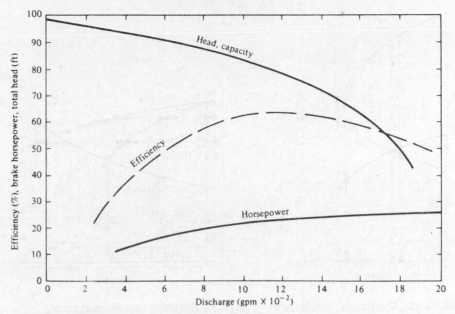

FIGURE 32   Typical pump characteristic curves.

efficiency. The most practical and efficient approach to a variable-flow problem is to provide two or more pumps in parallel so that the flow may be carried close to the units' peak efficiency.

The normal range of efficiencies for centrifugal pumps is between 50% and 85%, although efficiencies in excess of 90% have been reported. Pump efficiency usually increases with the size and capacity of the pump [35].

16   PUMP CURVES

Once the system head has been determined, the next step is to find a pump or pumps to deliver the required flows. This is done by plotting the system head curve on a sheet with the pump characteristic curves. The operating point is at the intersection of the system head curve and the pump head capacity curve. This gives the head and flow at which the pump will be operating. A pump should be selected so that the operating point is also as close as possible to peak efficiency. This procedure is shown in Figure 33.

Pumps may be connected in series or in parallel. For series operation at a given capacity, the total head equals the sum of the heads added by each pump. For parallel operation, the total discharge is multiplied by the number of pumps for a given head. It should be noted, however, that when two pumps are used in series or parallel, neither the head nor capacity for a given system head curve is doubled (Fig. 33).

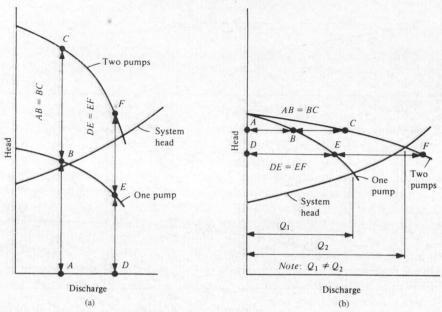

FIGURE 33   Characteristic curves for (a) Series. (b) Parallel pump operations of equal pumps.

Example 9

A proposed pumping station will have an ultimate capacity of 1200 gpm at a total head of 80 = ft. The present requirements are that the station deliver 750 gpm at a total head of 60 = ft. One pump will be required as a standby.

Solution: The system head curve is plotted as shown in Figure 34. Values for the curve are obtained as indicated in Sections 11 to 16.

Consider that three pumps will ultimately be needed (one as a standby). Determine the design flows as follows:

1. Two pumps at 1200 gpm at 80 ft of TDH.
2. One pump at 1200/2 = 600 gpm at 80 ft of TDH.
3. One pump must also be able to meet the requirements of 750 gpm at 60 ft of TDH.

From manufacturers' catalogs, two pumps *A* and *B* are found that will meet the specifications. The characteristic curves for each pump are shown in Figure 34. The intersection of the characteristic curves with the system head curve indicates that Pump *A* can deliver 750 gpm at a TDH of 60 ft, while Pump *B* can deliver 790 gpm at a TDH of 62 ft. A check of the efficiency curves for each pump indicates that Pump *B* will deliver the present flow at a much greater efficiency than Pump *A*. Therefore, select Pump *B*.

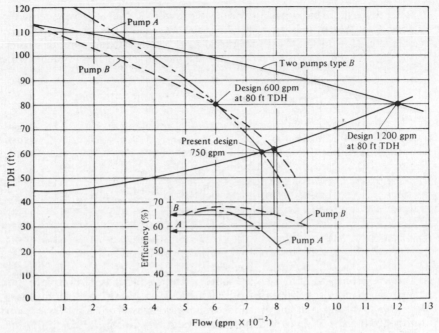

FIGURE 34 Solution to Example 9.

For the present, select two pumps of Type *B* and use one as a standby. For the future, add one more pump of Type *B*.

Operating characteristics for a wide range of pump sizes and speeds are available from pump manufacturers. Usually, special equipment manufactured to satisfy a customer's prescribed requirements must pass an acceptance test after it has been installed.

PROBLEMS

1 Given a V-shaped channel with a bottom slope of 0.001, a top width of 12 ft, and a depth of 6 ft, determine the velocity of flow. Find the discharge in cfs and m^3/s.

2 A trapezoidal channel measures 3 m across the top and 1 m across the bottom. The depth of flow is 1.5 m. For $s = 0.005$ and $n = 0.012$, determine the velocity and rate of flow.

3 Given an 18-in. concrete conduit with a roughness coefficient of $n = 0.013$, $s = 0.02$, and a discharge capacity of 15 cfs, what diameter pipe is required to triple the capacity?

4 Find the dimensions of a rectangular concrete channel to carry a flow of 150 m^3/s, with a bottom slope of 0.015 and a mean velocity of 10.2 m/s.

5 Determine the head loss in a 16-cm-diameter pipe with an average velocity of flow of 3.0 <1.0> m/s and a length of 40 m.

6 Find the discharge from a full-flowing cast-iron pipe with a 24-in. diameter and a slope of 0.004.

7 Refer to the figure below and assume that Reservoirs A, B, and C have water surface elevations of 150 ft, 90 ft, and 40 ft, respectively, and are connected by a system of concrete pipes
of lengths $L_1 = 2400$ ft, $L_2 = 1500$ ft, and $L_3 = 5500$ ft with respective diameters of 8, 12,
and 21 in. Find the discharge in each pipe and the elevation of the hydraulic gradient at P.

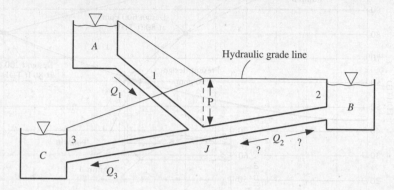

8 Three reservoirs—A, B, and C—are connected by a branching cast-iron pipe system. If the
pipe lengths are $L_1 = 3000$ ft, $L_2 = 2200$ ft, and $L_3 = 1600$ ft, the respective pipe diameters are 15, 10, and 18 in, and the surface water elevations of two of the three reservoirs are
$A = 125$ ft and $B = 55$ ft, find the surface water elevation of Reservoir C. Assume that
the flow to reservoir C is 15 cfs.

9 Solve Problem 8 by assuming that the flow in pipe 3 is from Reservoir C rather than to
Reservoir C.

10 Three riveted steel pipes are connected in series, with the flow through the system being
1.5 m³/s. Find the total head loss if the pipe diameters and lengths are $D_1 = 60$ cm,
$D_2 = 40$ cm, $D_3 = 54$ cm, $L_1 = 400$ m, $L_2 = 450$ m, and $L_3 = 750$ m. Assume the friction factor $f = 0.0125$.

11 Given the same lengths and diameters of the pipes in series as in Problem 10, determine
the total flow if the system head loss is 60 m.

12 Consider the pipe system in the figure. If the flow in BCD is 6 cfs, find (a) the flow in BED,
(b) the total flow, and (c) a length of 16-in pipe equivalent to the two parallel pipes.

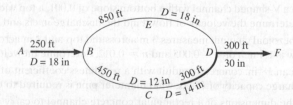

13 A flow of 1.3 m³/s is divided into three parallel pipes of diameters 30, 20, and 45 cm and
lengths of 30, 40, and 25 m, respectively. Find the head loss and distribution of flow.
Assume $f = 0.015$.

14 If a system of parallel pipes has diameters of 18, 8, and 21 in and lengths of 50, 95, and 60
ft, respectively, find the total flow in the system. Assume $f = 0.024$ and the total head loss
is 45 ft.

15 From the given layout, determine the length of an equivalent 24-cm pipe.

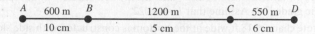

16 For the pipe layout in Problem 15, find the diameter of an equivalent 1000-m pipe.

17 For the pipe network shown, determine the direction and magnitude of flow in each pipe. Assume $C = 100$. Solve using a spreadsheet or another suitable method.

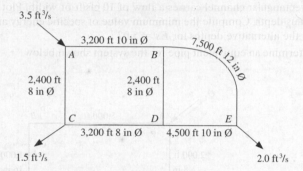

18 Solve Problem 17 if the flow at A is 4.0 cfs and that at E is 2.5 cfs.

19 Water is pumped 9 mi from a reservoir at elevation 100 ft to a second reservoir at elevation 210 ft. The pipeline connecting the reservoirs has a 54-in diameter. It is concrete and has an absolute roughness of 0.003. If the flow is 25 mgd and pumping station efficiency is 80%, what will be the monthly power bill if electricity costs 3 cents/kwh?

20 A reservoir at elevation 700 ft will supply a second reservoir at elevation 460 ft. The reservoirs are connected by 1300 ft of 24-in cast-iron pipe and 2000 ft of 20-in cast-iron pipe in series. What will be the discharge delivered from the upper reservoir to the lower one?

21 It is necessary to pump 6000 gpm of water from a reservoir at an elevation of 900 ft to a tank whose bottom is at an elevation of 1050 ft. The pumping unit is located at elevation 900 ft. The suction pipe is 24 in. in diameter and very short, so head losses may be neglected. The pipeline from the pump to the upper tank is 410 ft long and is 20 in. in diameter. Consider that minor losses in the line equal 2.5 ft of water. The maximum depth of water in the tank is 38 ft, and the supply lines are cast iron. Find the maximum lift of the pump and the horsepower required for pumping if the pump efficiency is 76%.

22 Rework Problem 21 if the water to be pumped is 7000 gpm and the elevation of the tank is 1000 ft.

23 If a flow of 5.0 cfs is to be carried by an 11,000-ft cast iron pipeline without incurring a head loss of 137 ft, what must the pipe diameter be?

24 Rework Problem 23 if the flow is 4.5 cfs and the head loss cannot exceed 120 ft.

25 A 48-in. water main carries 79 cfs and branches into two pipes at point A. The branching pipes are 36 and 20 in. in diameter and 2800 and 5000 ft long, respectively. These pipes rejoin at point B and again form a single 48-in. pipe. If the friction factor is 0.022 for the 36-in. pipe and 0.024 for the 20-in. pipe, what will the discharge be in each branch?

26 Water is pumped from a reservoir whose surface elevation is 1390 ft to a second reservoir whose surface elevation is 1475 ft. The connecting pipeline is 4500 ft long and 12 in. in diameter. If the pressure during pumping is 80 psi at a point midway on the pipe at elevation 1320 ft, find the rate of flow and the power exerted by the pumps. Also, plot the hydraulic grade line. Assume that $f = 0.022$.

27 A concrete channel 18 ft wide at the bottom is constructed with side slopes of 2.2 horizontal units to 1 vertical unit. The slope of the energy gradient is 1 in 1400 and the depth of flow is 4.0 ft. Find the velocity and the discharge.

28 A rectangular channel is to carry 200 cfs. The mean velocity must be greater than 2.5 fps. The channel bottom width should be about twice the channel depth. Find the channel cross section and the required channel slope.

29 A rectangular channel carries a flow of 10 cfs/ft of width. Plot a curve of specific energy versus depth. Compute the minimum value of specific energy and the critical depth. What are the alternative depths for $Es = 5.0$?

30 Determine an equivalent pipe for the system shown below.

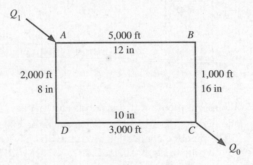

31 From the diagram below, compute (a) the total head loss from A to C, (b) P_a if $P_c = 25$ psi, and (c) the flow in each line.

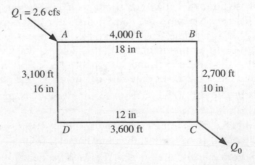

32 Given the pipe layout shown, determine the length of an equivalent 18-in. pipe.

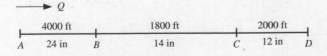

33 Given the following average hourly demand rates in gallons per minute, find the uniform 24-hr pumping rate and the required storage.

12 P.M.	0	12 A.M.	6300
1 A.M.	1900	1 P.M.	6500
2	1800	2	6460
3	1795	3	6430
4	1700	4	6500
5	1800	5	6700
6	1910	6	7119
7	3200	7	9000
8	5000	8	8690
9	5650	9	5220
10	6000	10	2200
11	6210	11	2100
		12 P.M.	2000

34 Solve Problem 33 if the period of pumping is from 6 A.M. to 6 P.M. only.

35 Determine the total dynamic head of a pumping system where the total static head is 50 ft, the total friction head loss is 5 ft, and the velocity head is 10 ft.

36 Calculate the horsepower requirements for the system described in Problem 35 if the flow is 25 cfs.

37 Plot the system head and the pump characteristic curves for the data given. At what point should the pump operate?

Total dynamic head (ft)	55	60	65	70	75	80	85	90
Flow (gal/min)	200	500	700	850	975	1075	1200	1300

Efficiency (%)	Horsepower (hp)	Total Head (ft)	Flow (gal/min)
22	8	95	225
37	12	93	400
49	17	90	600
57	20	87	800
63	22	84	1000
64	23	78	1200
62	24	72	1400
59	25	64	1600
54	26	49	1800

REFERENCES

[1] P. B. Bedient and W. C. Huber, *Hydrology and Floodplain Analysis* (Upper Saddle River, NJ: Prentice Hall, 2002).

[2] T. W. Sturm, *Open Channel Hydraulics* (New York, NY: McGraw-Hill, 2001).

[3] T. M. Walski, *Analysis of Water Distribution Systems* (New York: Van Nostrand Reinhold, 1984).

[4] G. M. Fair and J. C. Geyer, *Water Supply and Waste-Water Disposal* (New York: Wiley, 1954).

[5] K. E. Spells, *Trans. Inst. Chem. Engrs.* (London) 33 (1955).

[6] L. Cesario, *Modeling, Analysis, and Design of Water Distribution Systems* (Denver: American Water Works Association, 1995).

[7] N. Joukowsky, "Water Hammer" (translated by O. Simin), *Proc. Am. Water Works Assoc.* 24 (1904): 341–424.

[8] H. M. Morris, *Applied Hydraulics in Engineering* (New York: The Ronald Press, 1963).

[9] "Flow of Fluids Through Valves, Fittings, and Pipe," *Tech. Paper No. 410* (Chicago: Crane Co., 1957).

[10] G. E. Russell, *Hydraulics* (New York: Holt, Rinehart and Winston, 1957).

[11] J. M. Edmonston and E. E. Jackson, "The Feather River Project and the Establishment of the Optimum Hydraulic Grade Line for the Project Aqueduct," Metropolitan Water District of Southern California (Los Angeles; 1963).

[12] J. Hinds, "Economic Water Conduit Size," *Eng. News-Record* (January 1937).

[13] L. A. Rossman, "EPANET 2 Users Manual," Water Supply and Water Resources Division, National Risk Management Research Laboratory, Office of Research and Development, U.S. Environmental Protection Agency (Cincinnati, OH, September 2000).

[14] R. S. Gupta, *Hydrology and Hydraulic Systems* (Upper Saddle River, NJ: Prentice Hall, 1989).

[15] H. W. Gehm and J. I. Bregman, eds., *Handbook of Water Resources and Pollution Control* (New York: Van Nostrand Reinhold, 1976).

[16] C. W. Reh, "Hydraulics of Water Distribution Systems," *University of Illinois Engineering Experiment Station Circular No. 75* (February 1962).

[17] D. J. Wood, "Algorithms for Pipe Network Analysis and Their Reliability," Research Report No. 127 (Lexington, KY: University of Kentucky, Water Resources Research Institute, 1981).

[18] T. M. Walski, et al., "Battle of the Network Models: Epilogue," *J. Water Resources Planning Management*, 113, no. 2 (March 1987): 191–203.

[19] D. J. Wood and C. O. A. Charles, "Hydraulic Network Analysis Using Linear Theory," *Proc. Am. Soc. Civil Engrs., Hydraulics Div.* 98 (HY7) (July 1972).

[20] R. Epp and A. G. Fowler, "Efficient Code for Steady-State Flows in Networks," *J. Hydraulics Division* (New York: American Society of Civil Engineers, January 1970).

[21] T. M. Walski, "Sherlock Holmes Meets Hardy Cross or Model Calibration in Austin, Texas," *J. Am. Water Works Assoc.* (March 1990): 34–38.

[22] T. M. Walski, "Case Study: Pipe Network Calibration Issues," *J. Water Resources Planning Management* 112, no. 2 (April 1986): 238–249.

[23] D. J. Wood, "Pipe Network Analysis Programs: KYPIPE," Civil Engineering Software Center, University of Kentucky (Lexington, KY, 1987).

[24] A. L. Cesario, "Computer Modeling Programs: Tools for Model Operations," *J. AWWA*, 72, no. 9 (1980).

[25] G. C. Dandy, et al., "A Review of Pipe Network Optimization Techniques," in *Proc. Watercomp93, the 2nd Australian Conference on Technical Computing in the Water Industry* (Melbourne, Australia, March 30, 1993).

[26] R. W. Jeppson, *Analysis of Flow in Pipe Networks* (Ann Arbor, MI: Ann Arbor Science, 1976).

[27] L. D. Ormsbee, et al., "Network Modeling for Small Distribution Systems," *Proc. 1992 Computer Conference* (Nashville, TN, April 1992).

[28] T. M. Walski, et al., *Water Distribution System: Simulation and Sizing* (Chelsea, MI: Lewis Publishers, 1990).

[29] H. Cross, "Analysis of Flow in Networks of Conduits or Conductors," *University of Illinois Bull. No. 286* (November 1936).

[30] M. B. McPherson, "Generalized Distribution Network Head Loss Characteristics," *Proc. Am. Soc. Civil Engrs., J. Hydraulics Div.* 86 (HY1) (January 1960).

[31] E. L. Thackston, "Notes on Network Analysis," unpublished, Vanderbilt University (1982).

[32] J. E. Kiker, "Design Criteria for Water Distribution Storage," *Public Works* (March 1964).

[33] L. D. Benefield, et al., *Treatment Plant Hydraulics for Environmental Engineers* (Englewood Cliffs, NJ: Prentice-Hall, 1984).

[34] L. E. Ormsbee and T. M. Walski, "Identifying Efficient Pump Combinations," *J. Am. Water Works Assoc.* (January 1989): 30–34.

[35] R. M. Olson, *Engineering Fluid Mechanics*, 3rd ed. (New York: IEP, 1973).

[36] T. M. Walski and L. E. Ormsbee, "Developing System Head Curves for Water Distribution Planning," *J. Am. Water Works Assoc.* (July 1989): 63–66.

Wastewater Collection
and Stormwater Engineering

Wastewater Collection
and Stormwater Engineering

The collection and transportation of wastewater, stormwater, and other waste flows from residential, commercial, industrial, and rural sites pose different challenges from those encountered in developing water supply. Wastewater and stormwater flows both fluctuate rapidly based on a variety of manmade and natural variables. Additionally, both contain constituents that must be contained and treated to prevent harm to human health and the environment. Once treated, wastewater and stormwater play increasingly important roles as potential resources to meet current and future water supply challenges. This chapter will focus on wastewater collection and stormwater engineering.

DESIGN OF SANITARY SEWERS

Wastewater must be delivered to treatment locations as quickly as possible to prevent development of septic conditions and settling of solids. It is a universal principle of environmental engineering that waste discharges fluctuate over time. Wastewater conveyance systems must manage these fluctuating flows and handle the corrosive and hazardous constituents that are present in wastewater. These and other factors must be addressed when designing sanitary sewers.

The design of sanitary sewers involves (1) the appropriate application of the principles given in previous chapter to the estimation of design flows and (2) the application of hydraulic engineering principles to devise appropriate conveyances for transporting these flows [1, 2, 3]. Most sewers are designed to last 25 to 50 years. These conveyances must be capable of handling peak and minimum flows without allowing suspended solids to settle. In general, circular sanitary sewers are designed to flow at between one-half and full depth when carrying their design discharges. Ordinarily, they should not be designed to run full since some air space is desirable for ventilation

TABLE 1   Slopes Required to Maintain Velocities of 2 ft/sec[a]

Q (cfs)	Slope (ft/1000)
0.1	9.2
0.2	6.1
0.3	4.8
0.4	4.1
0.6	3.22
0.8	2.73
1.0	2.39
1.5	1.89
2.0	1.59
3.0	1.26
4.0	1.06

[a]For circular pipes where the flow is not less than 0.1% and not more than 95% of capacity [6].

and to suppress the generation of sulfide. Sewers at system extremities should be designed to flow about half full at peak flow. Large interceptor and trunk sewers are less subject to flow variations than are small collecting sewers, and greater depths of flow are justified for them. Gupta notes that pipes up to 16 in. (400 mm) in diameter are usually designed to flow half full, those between 16 and 35 in. (900 mm) are designed to flow two-thirds full, and larger pipes are usually designed to flow at three-quarters to full depth [2]. Once the flow that the sewer must carry has been determined, a pipe size and slope must be established. Since sewers are commonly located beneath roads and streets, their slopes are generally made to conform to street slopes. This practice also tends to minimize excavation costs. Where street slopes do not permit generating minimum carrying velocities (2 ft/s), sewer grades are set accordingly. Table 1 summarizes minimum slopes for a range of flow values. In cul-de-sacs and other short dead-end street sections, the designer will often find it impossible to meet minimum velocity requirements. Such pipes may require periodic flushing to scour accumulated solids.

1   HOUSE AND BUILDING CONNECTIONS

Connections from the main sewer to houses or other buildings are commonly constructed of vitrified clay, concrete, or asbestos cement pipe. Building connections are usually made on about a 2% grade with 6 inch or larger pipe. Grades less than 1% are to be avoided, as are extremely sharp grades.

2   COLLECTION SYSTEMS

Collection systems gather flows from individual buildings and transport the material to an interceptor or main lines. Local standards usually dictate the placement of these sewers, but they are commonly located under the street paving on one side of the storm drain, which is usually centered. The collection system should be capable of conveying the flow of the present and anticipated population of the area it is to serve. Design flows are the sum of the peak domestic, commercial, and industrial flows and infiltration. The collecting sewer must transport this design flow when flowing full. Grades requiring minimum excavation while meeting maximum and minimum restrictions on velocity are preferred. Manholes are normally located at changes in direction, grade, or pipe size or at intersections of collecting sewers. For 8-, 10-, or 12-in. sewers, manholes spaced no farther apart than about 400 ft permit inspection and cleaning when necessary. For larger sizes, the maximum spacing can be increased.

The minimum size pipe allowed by most codes is 8 in. Note that where changes in sewer direction occur and/or where flows combine, usually at manholes, head losses occur. When flow velocities are in the usual range for sewers, a drop of about 0.1 ft or 30 mm across a manhole is usually sufficient to account for such losses (Fig. 1). For

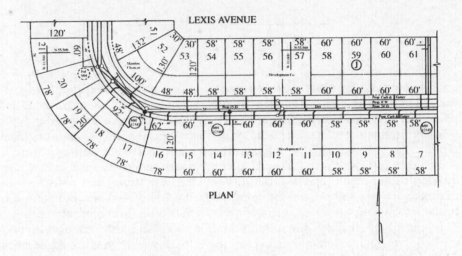

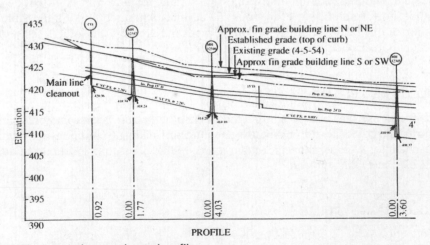

FIGURE 1   Typical sewer plan and profile.

large sewers, such as interceptors and trunks, head losses may require greater adjustments. At junctions where sewer size increases, common practice is to keep the crowns of the incoming and outgoing pipes, or the 0.8-in.-depth points of these pipes, at the same elevation. A typical plan and profile of a residential sewer are given in Figure 1.

3 INTERCEPTING SEWERS

Intercepting sewers (or interceptors) are expected to carry flows from the collector sewers in the drainage basin to the point of treatment or disposal of the wastewater. These sewers normally follow valleys or natural streambeds of the drainage area. When the sewer is built through underdeveloped areas, precautions should be taken to ensure the proper location of manholes for future connections. For 15- to 27-in. sewers, manholes are constructed at least every 600 ft; for larger sewers, increased spacing is common. Manholes or other transition structures are usually built at every change in pipe size, grade, or alignment. Horizontal or vertical curves are sometimes constructed for large sewers. Grades should be designed so that the criteria regarding maximum and minimum velocities are satisfied.

4 MATERIALS

Collecting and intercepting sewers are constructed of cast-iron pipe, concrete pipe, vitrified clay pipe, brick, plastic or PVC, and bituminized fiber pipe. Care should be exercised in designing the system so that permissible structural loadings are not exceeded for the material selected. Information on pipe loading is readily available from various pipe manufacturers.

5 SYSTEM LAYOUT

The first step in designing a sanitary sewer is to establish an overall system layout that includes a plan of the area to be sewered showing roads, streets, buildings, other utilities, topography, soil type, and the cellar or lowest floor elevation of all buildings to be drained. Where part of the drainage area to be served is undeveloped and proposed development plans are not yet available, care must be taken to provide adequate terminal manholes that can later be connected to the constructed system serving the area. If the proposed sewer connects to an existing one, an accurate location of the existing terminal manhole, giving invert elevation, size, and slope, is essential.

For the collection system just described, collecting sewers and the intercepting sewer or sewers should be tentatively laid out. When feasible, the sewer location should minimize the length required to provide service to the entire area. Length may be sacrificed if the shorter runs would require costlier excavation. Normally the sewer slope should follow the ground surface so that flows can follow the approximate path of the area's surface drainage. In some instances it may be necessary to lay the sewer slope in opposition to the surface slope or to pump wastes across a drainage divide. This situation can occur when a developer buys land lying in two adjacent drainage basins and, for economic or other reasons, must sewer the whole tract through only one basin.

Intercepting sewers or trunk lines are located to pass through the lowest point in the drainage area (the outlet) and to extend through the entire area to the drainage divide. Normally, these trunk lines follow major natural drainage ways and are located in a designated right-of-way or street. Land slopes on both sides should be toward the intercepting sewer. Lateral or collecting sewers are connected to the intercepting sewer and move upslope to the drainage divide. Collecting sewers should be located in all streets or rights-of-way within the area to provide service throughout the drainage basin. Figure 2 illustrates a typical sewer layout. Note that the interceptor sewer is located in the stream valley and collector sewers transport flows from the various tributary areas to the interceptor.

A general guideline for sewer system layout and design has been proposed by Thackston. Basic steps include the following [4]:

1. Obtain or develop a topographic map of the area to be served. This is usually done within a CAD or GIS system using the results of a survey effort.
2. Locate the drainage outlet. This is usually near the lowest point in the area and is often along a stream or drainage way.

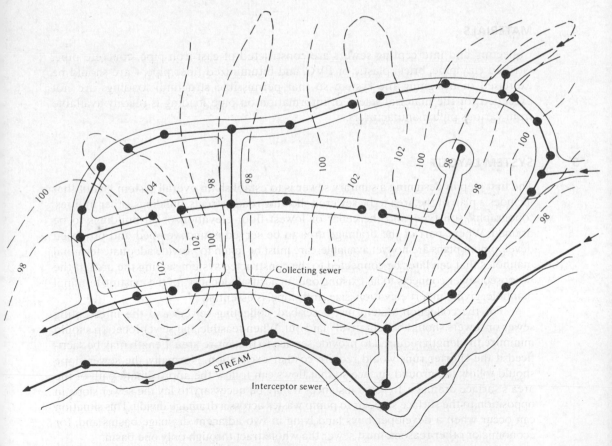

FIGURE 2   Typical layout for the design of a sewerage system.

3. Sketch in a preliminary pipe system to serve all of the contributors (Figure 2).

4. Locate pipes so that users or future users can readily connect. Pipes must also be located to provide access for maintenance. This is usually accomplished by placing them in streets or other rights-of-way.

5. As far as practical, allow sewers to follow natural drainage ways to minimize excavation and pumping requirements. Large trunk sewers are usually constructed in low-lying areas closely paralleling streams or channels. In general, pipes should cross contours at right angles.

6. Establish preliminary pipe sizes. Eight inches (usually the minimum allowable) can serve several hundred residences even at minimal grades.

7. Revise the layout to optimize flow-carrying capacity at minimum cost. Pipe lengths and sizes should be kept as small as possible, pipe slopes should be maximized within tolerances for velocity, excavation depth should be minimized, and the number of appurtenances should be kept as small as possible. Traditional hydraulic design procedures combined with the use of models and/or optimization techniques can be used as part of this process [6].

8. Try to avoid pumping across drainage boundaries. Pump stations are costly and add maintenance problems. Furthermore, energy costs for pumping can be significant. A balance must be achieved between excavating and pumping. While no hard-and-fast rule can be given, pumping should be considered only when excavations exceeding about 20 to 40 ft are contemplated.

6 HYDRAULIC DESIGN

The design of wastewater collection systems proceeds in a similar manner to hydraulic design procedures with some modifications to accommodate the unique chemical, biological, and physical properties of wastewater.

Systems Flowing Under Gravity

The hydraulic design of a sanitary sewer can be carried out systematically (see solution to Example 1). Pipes should carry peak design flows at velocities swift enough to prevent sedimentation, yet slow enough to prevent erosion. To minimize head losses at transitions and eliminate backwater effects, the hydraulic gradient must not change abruptly or slope in a direction adverse to the flow at changes in horizontal direction, pipe size, or quantity of flow. Sewers are usually designed to closely follow the grade of the ground surface or street paving under which they are laid. In addition, the depth of cover should be kept as close to the minimum (below the frost line) as possible. Sewer location must take into account the location of other subsurface utilities or structures. General practice is not to locate sewers in the same trench as water mains.

Pipe sizes are determined in the following manner. A profile of the proposed sewer route is drawn and the hydraulic gradient at the downstream end of the sewer noted (normally the elevation of the hydraulic gradient of the sewer being met). Where discharge is to a treatment plant or an open body of water, the hydraulic gradient is the elevation of the free water surface at this point. At the beginning elevation of the hydraulic gradient, a tentative gradient approximately following the ground surface is drawn upstream to the next point of control (usually a manhole). Exceptions to this occur when the surface slope is less than adequate to provide cleansing velocities, where obstructions preclude using this slope, or where adequate cover cannot be maintained. Using the tentative gradient slope, a pipe size is then selected that comes closest to carrying the design flow at the desired depth. Generally, it is not possible to find a standard size pipe that will carry the flow at the exact depth and gradient investigated. It is common practice then to select the next largest pipe size, modify the slope, or do both. The choice depends on a comparison of pipe-cost savings versus excavation cost and on local conditions, such as the placement of other utilities in the right-of-way. Regardless of velocity and pipe size calculations, pipe diameter is never decreased on downstream reaches because this can lead to sediment accumulation and blockage at the point of reduction.

Hydraulic computations using Manning's equation for full pipe flow are straightforward. Commonly, however, flow at less than full is encountered or desired in practice. In cases where pipes are not flowing full, relationships involving geometric properties (Table 2) and hydraulic elements of circular sections facilitate calculations. The use of these figures is illustrated in the following examples.

TABLE 2   Geometric Relationships for Circular Pipes

d/d_m	R/d_m	$AR^{2/3}/d_m^{8/3}$
0.01	0.0066	0.0000
0.05	0.0326	0.0015
0.10	0.0635	0.0065
0.15	0.0929	0.0152
0.20	0.1206	0.0273
0.25	0.1466	0.0427
0.30	0.1709	0.0610
0.35	0.1935	0.0820
0.40	0.2142	0.1050
0.45	0.2331	0.1298
0.50	0.2500	0.1558
0.55	0.2649	0.1825
0.60	0.2776	0.2092
0.65	0.2881	0.2358
0.70	0.2962	0.2608
0.75	0.3017	0.2840
0.80	0.3042	0.3045
0.85	0.3033	0.3212
0.90	0.2890	0.3324
0.95	0.2864	0.3349
1.00	0.2500	0.3117

d = actual depth of flow
d_m = full-flow depth
R = hydraulic radius
A = area of flow

Example 1

Find the peak hourly flow in mgd and m^3/s for an 800-acre urban area having the following features: domestic flows 90 gpcd, commercial flows 15 gpcd, infiltration 600 gpd/acre, and population density 20 persons per acre. Use a peak hour to average day ratio of 3.0.

Solution: Calculate the average daily flows for each contributor.

$$\text{Domestic: } 90 \times 20 \times 800 = 1.44 \text{ mgd}$$
$$\text{Commercial: } 15 \times 20 \times 800 = 0.24 \text{ mgd}$$
$$\text{Infiltration: } 600 \times 800 = 0.48 \text{ mgd}$$
$$\text{Total} = 1.44 + 0.24 + 0.48 = 2.16 \text{ mgd}$$

Using a peak hour to average day ratio of 3.0:

$$\text{Peak hourly flow} = 3.0 \times 2.16 = 6.48 \text{ mgd}$$
$$= 6.48 \times 0.044 = 0.29 \text{ m}^3/\text{s}$$

Example 2

A sewer system is to be designed for the urban area of Figure 3. Street elevations at manhole locations are shown on the figure. It has been determined that the population density is 40 persons per acre and that the sewage contribution per capita is 100 gpd. In addition, there is an infiltration component of 600 gallons per acre per day (gpad). Local regulations require that no sewers be less than 8 in. in diameter. Assume an *n* value of 0.013.

Solution: The design procedure follows a series of steps and the format of Tables 3 and 4.

1. Determine manhole locations. These are already indicated for the example in Figure 3, but in practice they are determined on the basis of changes in direction, junctions of pipes, and maximum lengths for various pipe sizes, as discussed earlier. Pipe lengths are tabulated in Column 3 of Table 3.

2. Determine street elevations at manhole locations. These are given in Figure 3, but they would be obtained from street profiles of the type shown in Figure 1.

3. Using the plan showing the location of manholes, determine the distance between them. In this example, the lengths are given in Column 3 of Table 3.

4. Calculate the street slopes between manholes. This is done by taking the differences in elevations between manholes and dividing them by the distances between the manholes. For example, the slope between M-6 and M-5 is

$$S = (112.19 - 109.23)/470 = 0.0063 \text{ ft/ft}$$

Calculated slopes are shown in Column 5 of Table 4.

Manhole	Street El.
1	101.3
2	104.18
3	105.33
4	107.25
5	109.23
6	112.19
7	116.6
8	112.04
9	115.04
10	117.46
11	113.77
12	110.29
13	115.8
14	111.92
15	108.58
16	116.37
17	112.57
18	108.89

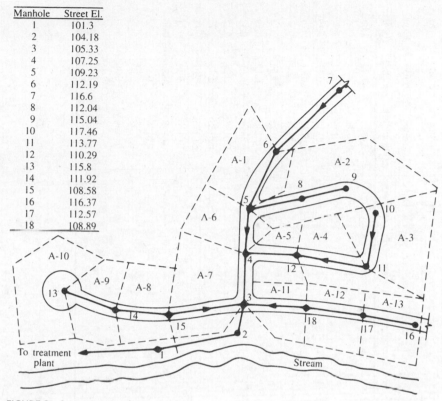

FIGURE 3 Sewer system for Example 2.

5. Determine the size of contributing areas to the sewer segments. This is done by using finished-grade topography and knowledge of the building connection schemes for contributing elements, such as houses, to the sewer segments. In this example, the contributing area boundaries are shown in Figure 3, and the area sizes in acres, both incremental and cumulative, are tabulated in Table 3, Columns 4–7.

6. Calculate the flow per contributing acre for each of the 13 areas. In this example, the per-acre flows are all the same, but they can be highly variable. They are calculated by using procedures described in Example 1. For this problem, the per-acre flows are calculated as follows:

    a. residential flow = (40 per acre) × (100 gpcd) = 4000 gpad
    b. infiltration = 600 gpad
       avg. daily flow = 4600 gpad
    c. assuming the design flow = 3 × avg. daily flow, peak flow = 3 × 4600 = 13,800 gpad

TABLE 3 Calculation of Sewage Flows for Example 2

(1)	(2)		(3)	(4)	(5)	(6)	(7)	(8)	(9)	(10)
	Manhole		Pipe Lgth.	Incr. Area	Cum. for Br.	Incr. Direct	Cum. Direct	Sewage	Flow	Flow
Pipe No.	From	To	(ft)	(acres)	(acres)	(acres)	(acres)	(mgd/acre)	(mgd)	(cfs)
1	7	6	630	—	—	—	87	0.0138	1.20	1.86
2	6	5	470	5.1	—	5.1	—	0.0138	—	—
—	6	5	—	—	—	—	92.1	0.0138	1.27	1.97
3	9	8	390	12.1	12.1	—	—	0.0138	0.17	0.26
4	8	5	385	—	—	—	—	0.0138	0.17	0.26
5	5	4	330	4.8	—	4.8	—	0.0138	—	—
—	5	4	—	—	—	—	109	0.0138	1.50	2.33
6	10	11	410	8.7	8.7	—	—	0.0138	0.12	0.19
7	11	12	400	6.3	15	—	—	0.0138	0.21	0.32
8	12	4	380	4.7	19.7	—	—	0.0138	0.27	0.42
9	4	3	370	—	—	—	128.7	0.0138	1.78	2.75
10	16	17	380	5	5	—	—	0.0138	0.07	0.11
11	17	18	400	4.9	9.9	—	—	0.0138	0.14	0.21
12	18	3	405	4.3	14.2	—	—	0.0138	0.20	0.30
13	13	14	400	13.1	13.1	—	—	0.0138	0.18	0.28
14	14	15	380	5.3	18.1	—	—	0.0138	0.25	0.39
15	15	3	411	9.7	28.1	—	—	0.0138	0.39	0.60
16	3	2	230	—	—	—	171	0.0138	2.36	3.66
17	2	1	600	—	—	—	171	0.0138	2.36	3.66

Column 4 = incremental area contributing to pipe.
Column 5 = cumulative area for branches entering collecting sewer.
Column 6 = incremental area contributing directly to collecting sewer.
Column 7 = cumulative area contributing to a sewer.
Column 8 = calculated contributing sewage flow in mgd/acre.
Column 9 = pipe flow in mgd ($0.0138 \times$ area).
Column 10 = values in Column 9 converted to cfs [(col.9) $\times$ 1.55].

TABLE 4 Calculation of Pipe Sizes and Velocities for Example 2

1	2		3	4	5	6	7	8	9	10	11	12	13	14	15	16
Pipe No.	Manhole To	From	Pipe Lgth. (ft)	Des. Flow (cfs)	Str. Sl. (ft/ft)	Min. Sl. (ft/ft)	Des. Sl. (ft/ft)	Pipe Size (cal.-in.)	Pipe Size (sel.-in.)	Pipe Flow Full	Q/Q-Full (cfs)	d/d-Max —	Flow-d (in.)	V-Full (fps)	V/V-Full —	V (fps)
1	6	7	630	1.86	0.0070	0.0027	0.007	10.04	12	2.98	0.62	0.58	6.96	3.80	1.05	3.99
2	5	6	470	—	—	—	—	—	—	—	—	—	—	—	—	—
—	5	6	—	1.97	0.0063	0.0016	0.0063	10.26	12	2.83	0.70	0.62	7.44	3.60	1.08	3.89
3	8	9	390	0.26	0.0077	0.0054	0.0077	—	8	1.06	0.25	0.35	2.8	3.04	0.82	2.49
4	5	8	385	0.26	0.0073	0.0054	0.0073	—	8	1.03	0.25	0.35	2.8	2.96	0.82	2.42
5	4	5	330	—	—	—	—	—	—	—	—	—	—	—	—	—
—	4	5	—	2.33	0.006	0.0015	0.006	10.93	12	2.76	0.84	0.7	8.4	3.52	1.12	3.94
6	11	10	410	0.19	0.009	0.0064	0.009	—	8	1.14	0.17	0.29	2.32	3.28	0.73	2.40
7	12	11	400	0.32	0.0087	0.0047	0.0087	—	8	1.13	0.28	0.36	2.88	3.23	0.83	2.68
8	4	12	380	0.42	0.008	0.0037	0.008	—	8	1.08	0.39	0.44	3.52	3.09	0.92	2.85
9	3	4	370	2.75	0.0052	0.0013	0.0052	11.63	15	4.66	0.59	0.55	8.25	3.80	1.04	3.95
10	17	16	380	0.11	0.01	0.0089	0.01	—	8	1.21	0.09	0.2	1.6	3.46	0.55	1.90
11	18	17	400	0.21	0.0092	0.006	0.0092	—	8	1.16	0.18	0.3	2.4	3.32	0.74	2.46
12	13	18	405	0.3	0.0088	0.006	0.0088	—	8	1.13	0.26	0.35	2.8	3.24	0.82	2.66
13	14	13	400	0.28	0.0097	0.005	0.0097	—	8	1.19	0.24	0.34	2.7	3.41	0.8	2.73
14	15	14	380	0.39	0.0088	0.0042	0.0088	—	8	1.13	0.34	0.41	3.28	3.24	0.89	2.89
15	3	15	411	0.6	0.0079	0.0032	0.0079	—	8	1.07	0.56	0.53	4.24	3.07	1.03	3.17
16	2	3	230	3.66	0.005	0.0013	0.005	12.94	15	4.57	0.80	0.68	10.2	3.73	1.11	4.14
17	1	2	600	3.66	0.0048	0.0013	0.0048	12.94	15	4.48	0.82	0.69	10.35	3.65	1.12	4.09

Column 5 = street slope; Column 7 = design slope, larger of values in Columns 5 and 6.
Column 6 = minimum slope from Table 3; Column 9 = closest standard pipe size.
Column 8 = full flow Q determined using Manning's equation; Column 9 = closest standard pipe size.
Column 10 = full flow in selected pipe size (Manning's equation); Column 11 = ratio of values in Columns 4 and 10.
Column 12 = value from Figure 2 for ratio of Column 11; Column 13 = value in Column 9 × value in Column 12.
Column 14 = Q/A for full pipe flow; Column 15 = ratio determined from Figure 2 for the d/d-max value of Column 12.
Column 16 = value in Column 14 × value in Column 15.

   d. converting to mgd, the design flow per acre is 0.0138 mgd/acre. This value appears in Column 8 of Table 3.

7. Calculate the sewage flows in pipes. This is done by multiplying the number of contributing acres by 0.0138 (the per-acre contribution). The flows in mgd and cfs are shown in Columns 9 and 10 of Table 3. Note that these calculations are performed by the spreadsheet used in the example. Spreadsheets are excellent tools for solving problems of this type.

8. Enter street slopes and minimum slopes for pipes in Table 4 (Column 7). Note that the minimum slopes are estimated from values in Table 1. The initial design slope, adjusted later if need be, is the street slope unless that slope is less than the minimum slope required or other conditions make it necessary to assign a different grade.

9. Calculate the pipe size required to handle the design flow under full-flow conditions. Calculations made in the spreadsheet use Manning's equation with $n = 0.013$. Computed diameters are given in Column 8 of Table 4. Note that a pipe size of 8 in. (the minimum allowable) is assigned to a number of pipes without calculating a diameter. The reasoning for that assignment is as follows. A look at the design flows of Column 4, Table 4, shows that many of them are small, less than 0.6 cfs. For these flows the minimum design slope is 0.0073. From Manning's nomograph, it can be seen that an 8-in. pipe at a slope of 0.0073 can carry a flow of about 1 cfs at a velocity of about 3 fps. Accordingly, it is clear that an 8-in. pipe will handle all flows up to 0.6 cfs for the slopes given. An 8-in. pipe is thus selected for these flows and tabulated in Column 9 of Table 4.

   The calculated pipe sizes (Column 8, Table 4) are modified to the next largest standard pipe size or to a size that accommodates the design flow at a desired depth. These selected sizes are entered in Column 9 of Table 4. Note that for the range of pipe sizes encountered in this problem, a desirable depth of flow is normally from about half to three-fourths full. Because of the low flows carried, many of the 8-in. pipes have design flow depths that are less than half the maximum depth. This cannot be avoided and does not create a problem as long as cleansing velocities are maintained.

10. Calculate full flows for selected pipe sizes (Column 10, Table 4). The design slope and a Manning's n of 0.013 are used.

11. Compute ratios of Q/Q_{full} (column 11, Table 4). Using these values and entering Figure 2, we determine d/dmax values and V/Vfull values and enter them in Columns 12 and 15 of Table 4. Multiplying the depth ratios by the full-flow depths for each pipe gives the flow depths for each pipe (Column 13, Table 4).

12. The full-flow velocity is calculated as Q/A (Column 14, Table 4). Multiplying the full-flow velocities by the velocity ratio gives the flow velocity for each pipe (Column 16, Table 4).

13. The calculated values of V are checked to see that they are at least 2 fps. All velocities agree except the velocity for Pipe 10, 1.9 fps, but this value is considered close enough. Had the calculated value been much less, the design slope would have to be modified.

Example 3

Given an invert elevation of 105.19 for the pipe leaving M-6 in Figure 3, calculate the invert elevations in and out of M-5 and M-4. Use the slopes and pipe lengths given in Example 2.

Solution: Calculations are as follows:

$$105.19 - (0.0063)(470) = 102.23 \text{ invert at entrance to M-5}$$
$$102.23 - 0.1 = 102.13 \text{ drop across M-5}$$
$$102.13 - (0.006)(330) = 100.15 \text{ invert at entrance to M-4}$$
$$100.15 - 0.25 = 99.9 \text{ invert out of M-4}$$

A drop across a manhole of 0.1 was applied where no change in pipe size occurred. At M-4, the upstream pipe is 12 in. and the downstream pipe is 15 in. In this case, a drop of $15 - 12 = 3$ in., or 0.25 ft, was used. The profile of Figure 1 illustrates this process.

Systems Flowing Under Pressure

Where pumping of sewage is required, force mains (pressure conduits) must be designed to carry the flows. The costs of pumping and associated equipment are important considerations. The hydraulics of these systems follows the principles already discussed. As in the case of open-channel sewers, pressure sewers must be able to transport sewage at velocities sufficient to avoid deposition and yet not so high as to create pipe erosion problems. Force mains are generally 8 in. in diameter or greater, but for small pumping stations smaller pipes may sometimes be acceptable. According to Metcalf and Eddy, the following C values for use in the Hazen–Williams equation for calculating friction losses in force mains are valid [7]:

100 for unlined cast-iron pipe

120 for cement-lined, cast-iron pipe, reinforced concrete pipe, asbestos–cement pipe, and plastic pipe

110 for steel pipe having bituminous or cement–mortar lining and exceeding 20 in. in diameter

Velocities encountered in force main operations are often in the range of 35 fps. In designing force mains, high points in lines should be avoided if possible. This eliminates the need for air relief valves. Good design practice dictates that the hydraulic gradient should lie above the line at all points during periods of minimum-flow pumping.

7   PROTECTION AGAINST FLOODWATERS

Because the volume of sanitary wastewater is extremely small compared with flood flows, it is important that sewers be constructed to prevent admittance of large surface-runoff volumes. This will preclude overloading treatment plants with the resultant reduction in the degree of treatment or, in some instances, the complete absence of treatment.

Where interceptor sewers are built along streambeds, manhole stacks frequently are raised above a design flood level, such as the 50-yr level. In addition, the manhole structures are waterproofed. Where stacks cannot be raised, watertight manhole covers are employed. Such measures as these keep surface drainage into the sewer at a minimum.

8   WASTEWATER PUMP STATIONS

It is often necessary to accumulate wastewater at a low point in the collection system and pump it to treatment works or to a continuation of the system at a higher elevation. Pumping stations consist primarily of a wet well, which intercepts incoming flows and permits equalization of pump loadings, and a bank of pumps that lifts the wastewater from the wet well. In most cases, centrifugal pumps are used and standby equipment is required for emergency purposes.

Pumping of sewage may be necessary in a number of circumstances. The area of concern may be lower in elevation than the nearest trunk sewer. It may also be that the area to be served lies outside the drainage area of the sewage treatment plant to be used. Such circumstances require pumping sewage flows across drainage divides. Excavation costs to construct gravity-flow systems may also be such that pumping is more economical than constructing a gravity sewer. In any event, circumstances and trade-offs will dictate the course of action to be followed. Additional details of pumping station designs may be found in *Wastewater Engineering* [7].

9   INFLOW/INFILTRATION AND EXFILTRATION

Because of the age of a system, unforeseen inflow and infiltration (I/I or I&I) and exfiltration may occur in sanitary sewers. Infiltration and exfiltration are both functions of the height of the groundwater table in the vicinity of the sewer, the type and tightness of sewer joints, and soil type. Exfiltration is undesirable since it may pollute groundwater, while infiltration reduces the capacity of the sewer to convey the waste flows for which it was designed. If the sewer is well above the groundwater table, infiltration will occur only during or after periods of precipitation, when water is percolating downward through the soil.

Inflow usually occurs in sewers that were designed when it was standard practice to connect wastewater and stormwater piping or when a third party has knowingly or unknowingly connected the two types of systems. These types of connections are highly undesirable because they produce overflows (commonly referred to as *sanitary sewer overflows* or *SSOs*). Sanitary sewer systems, pump stations, and treatment plants are now designed to account for I/I through the use of peak factors. Peak factors are highly dependent on soils, topography, and the age of the system and must be considered on a case-by-case basis.

STORMWATER MANAGEMENT

Up until the latter part of the twentieth century, stormwater management primarily focused on getting runoff away from populated areas as quickly as possible. This method of stormwater management has taken a significant toll on the environment and on our water supply. The environment has suffered from years of disruption of the natural hydrology, accelerated erosion, habitat loss, and declining water quality—all results of this incomplete stormwater management strategy. Today, the complexities of water supply, water quality, and ecological challenges have opened the door to broader alternatives for stormwater management. In fact, many engineers have started to recognize stormwater not only as an important part of our natural environment and ecology but also as a potential resource to meet our water supply needs while ensuring the health of the environment that we must protect. While the typical stormwater treatment system still consists of retention and detention ponds, many have started to use more localized and low-impact treatment techniques that provide more holistic ecological and aesthetic benefits. The rest of this chapter will discuss conventional and emerging stormwater management strategies.

10   RAINFALL

The hydrologic cycle forms the basis of our water supply. Water is indeed the keystone of our existence. For most stormwater managers, rainfall is the most common and always one of the most important parts of the hydrologic cycle that must be considered during a study or design. The manager must know what type and how much rainfall data should be used to solve a particular problem.

For most stormwater engineers, a critical consideration is the desired level of service for the system being designed. Should a stormwater system be designed to carry the maximum probable flow, or the 5%, the 1%, or some other chance discharge? Luckily, the return frequency is usually standardized in local or state rules. In fact, this information is usually available on the Internet or in a stormwater manual of some sort. Note, however, that there is no relationship between the expected life of the drainage works and the frequency of the design flow.

Table 5 shows, for example, that there is a 22% chance that the 100-yr storm will occur in any 25-yr period. This suggests that there is reason to question designing a structure for a life expectancy of 25 years and then using design flows expected on the

TABLE 5   Probability That an Event Having a Prescribed Recurrence Interval Will Be Equaled or Exceeded During a Specified Period

	Period (yr)					
T_R (yr)	1	5	10	25	50	100
1	1.0	1.0	1.0	1.0	1.0	1.0
2	0.5	0.97	0.999	1.0^a	1.0^a	1.0^a
5	0.2	0.67	0.89	0.996	1.0^a	1.0^a
10	0.1	0.41	0.65	0.93	0.995	1.0^a
50	0.02	0.10	0.18	0.40	0.64	0.87
100	0.01	0.05	0.10	0.22	0.40	0.63

[a]Values are approximate.

average of once in 25 years or less. If such an approach is taken, the chances are good that the structure will be damaged, destroyed, or at least overloaded before it has served its useful life.

Those who must select return frequencies must consider the potential threat to human life, property damage, and inconvenience that would result from various storm events. Statistics of historical events are always included in this analysis. Human life cannot be judged in terms of monetary values. If it is apparent that failure of a proposed drainage system would imperil human lives, the design should be revised accordingly. Property damage is an economic consideration and is generally one of the easier factors to consider numerically.

For some of the newer stormwater design strategies (such as Low-Impact Development or LID), it is necessary to model systems on an extended basis (usually referred to as *continuous simulation*). In these instances, actual rainfall data are used. When done correctly, continuous simulation is a more reliable form of modeling than modeling that uses design storms. Rainfall data selected for a continuous simulation should include historical droughts and floods of various sizes and durations, and should reflect a variety of conditions. Continuous simulation is usually conducted over many years. When possible, it is always preferable to calibrate a model, and many times it is convenient to gather rainfall data and information to calibrate against at the same time. These calibration data may include stage and flow information for a variety of areas.

11   RUNOFF

Another critical part of stormwater engineering is the management of runoff. Most simply, *runoff* is defined as stormwater that does not infiltrate into the ground. Normally, runoff becomes a concern as the quantity of runoff increases due to development and the construction of impervious surfaces such as roads, driveways, and buildings. Runoff is a critical concern from a water quantity and a water quality perspective. Issues associated with runoff are erosion, flooding, contamination of water supplies, and ecological damage [8]. As previously mentioned, the majority of water pollution now originates from nonpoint sources, with stormwater runoff being one of the most common sources of nonpoint source pollution in many parts of the United States.

Urban activities that disturb the natural environment are the greatest contributors after agriculture to nonpoint surface water pollution in the United States. With about 2000 hectares of U.S. rural land being converted daily to urban use, accelerated urbanization has led to increased nonpoint source pollution from urban runoff [9]. The primary sources of urban pollution are fertilizers from lawns and gardens, animal and bird feces, various fluids and heavy metals that originate with automobiles, street litter, herbicide and pesticide residues, and atmospheric fallout of air pollutants. In suburban areas, soil erosion and soil-adsorbed pollutants are also sources of nonpoint pollution. As runoff from precipitation travels over the land, wastes and residues are entrained by the flow and carried to receiving surface water bodies. These residues may contribute significant amounts of suspended solids, nitrates, phosphates, fecal coliforms, and toxic metals to receiving waters. Table 6 [9] summarizes the pollutant characteristics imparted to urban runoff by urban residues.

The magnitude of the pollution load transported by urban runoff to receiving water bodies is comparable to that of treated sewage or even untreated sewage in some cases. The highest concentration of pollutants in stormwater is measured during the initial stages of storm runoff, during which time the stormwater exhibits a so-called *first flush effect* by initially cleansing away the bulk of pollutants deposited during the preceding dry-weather period.

The concentration of pollutants in stormwater depends on whether runoff reaches the receiving water by overflow from combined sewers, flow from storm sewers or nonsewered overland flow, or municipal sewer overflow. A *combined sewer* is designed to receive both intercepted surface runoff and municipal sewage. *Combined sewer overflow* is the flow from a combined sewer in excess of the interceptor capacity that is discharged into a receiving body of water. A storm sewer carries intercepted surface runoff, street wash, and other wash waters or drainage, but excludes domestic sewage and industrial wastes. *Nonsewered urban runoff* is that part of the precipitation that runs off the surface of an urban drainage area and reaches a stream or other body of water without passing through a sewer system. It is about the same quality as water collected by a storm sewer. Stormwater can enter municipal sanitary sewers and, if infiltration of the sewer system is severe enough, may cause the municipal system to overflow [10].

The most significant characteristic of urban runoff is the suspended-solids content. On average, the suspended-solids concentration of combined sewer overflow is more than twice—and for surface runoff more than three times—the concentration of suspended solids in untreated sewage. For this reason, physical and chemical treatment of stormwater to remove suspended solids are usually the principal treatment methods employed.

The Biological Oxygen Demand (BOD_5) of combined sewer overflow and municipal sewer overflows are approximately equivalent—about half the concentration of

TABLE 6   Sources of Nonpoint Pollution from Urban Residential and Commercial Areas

Category	Parameters	Potential Sources
Bacteria	Total coliform, fecal coliform, fecal streptococci, other pathogens	Animals, birds, soil bacteria (humans)
Nutrients	Nitrogen, phosphorus	Lawn fertilizers, decomposing organic matter (leaves and grass clippings), street sweepings, atmospheric deposition
Biodegradable chemicals	BOD, COD, TOC	Leaves, grass clippings, animals, street litter, oil and grease
Organic chemicals	Pesticides, PCBs	Pest and weed control, packaging, leaking transformers, hydraulic and lubricating fluids
Inorganic chemicals	Suspended solids, dissolved solids, toxic metals, chloride	Erosion, dust and dirt on streets, atmospheric deposition, industrial pollution, traffic, deicing salts

untreated sewage. Surface runoff and storm sewer flow have about the same BOD_5 strength as secondary municipal effluent. The bacterial content of combined sewer overflow has been found to be typically one order of magnitude lower than that of untreated municipal sewage, whereas the bacterial content of surface runoff is two to four orders of magnitude lower than that of untreated sewage [10]. The bacterial concentrations in urban surface runoff, however, can be two to five orders of magnitude higher than those considered safe for water contact activities. Table 7 compares the quality of untreated and treated wastewater and urban runoff [10].

Many practicing engineers deal with runoff in urban areas in preparation for development and must deal with the water-quality issues discussed above in addition to the increased quantity of runoff that will be produced once the development takes place. The water quantity portion of urban drainage design focuses on determining the magnitude, distribution, and timing of rainfall and runoff events. Major storms are the basis for the design of drainage systems. In some cases, a knowledge of peak flow will suffice, but if storage or routing considerations are important, the volume and time distribution of flows must also be known. The latter requirement, time distribution, is especially important for water quality.

The quantity of runoff generated is related to the character of the rainfall event and the physical features of the area. Factors involved in rainfall–runoff relationships include precipitation type; rainfall intensity, duration, and areal distribution; storm direction; antecedent precipitation; initial soil moisture conditions; soil type; evaporation; transpiration; and the size, shape, slope, elevation, directional orientation, and land use characteristics of the drainage area. The design engineer should consider these and other relevant site conditions, in addition to regulations governing the design at the local, state, and federal level.

The design of effective urban drainage systems requires reliable estimates of the flows to be dealt with. Failures of drainage systems are more often the result of faulty estimates of flows than of structural inadequacies. Runoff may be generated by rainfall, snowmelt, or a combination of these factors. Maximum flows on urban areas usually result from high-intensity, short-duration storms, whereas floods on large drainage basins often result from a combination of rainfall and snowmelt.

TABLE 7   Generalized Quality Comparisons of Wastewaters[a]

Type	BOD_5 (mg/l)	Suspended Solids (mg/l)	Total Coliforms (mpn/100 ml)	Total Nitrogen (mg/l as n)	Total Phosphorus (mg/l as p)
Untreated municipal	200	200	5×10^7	40	10
Treated municipal					
Primary effluent	135	80	2×10^7	35	8
Secondary effluent	25	15	1×10^3	30	5
Combined sewage	115	410	5×10^6	11	4
Surface runoff	30	630	4×10^5	3	1

[a]Values based on flow-weighted means in individual test areas.

Source: Lager and Smith [10].

Procedures used to estimate runoff magnitude and frequency can be categorized as (1) empirical approaches, (2) statistical and probability methods, and (3) methods relating rainfall to runoff [11]. Historically, numerous empirical equations have been developed for predicting runoff. Most of these equations have been based on the correlation of only two or three variables and, at best, have given only rough approximations. Many are applicable only to specific localities—a fact that should be carefully considered before they are used. In most cases, the frequency of the computed flow is unknown. Formulas of this type are useful only when a more reliable means is unavailable.

Of the methods relating rainfall to runoff, the unit hydrograph method, the rational method, and various hydrologic models are widely used. As with all hydrologic methods and models, they should be employed only when appropriate and when all of the constraints involved are analyzed and understood. Local regulations for stormwater design must also be carefully considered when selecting a method and/or model for estimating runoff.

Unit Hydrograph Method

The *unit hydrograph method* (UHM) is widely used for estimating runoff magnitudes of various frequencies that may occur on a specific stream [11]. To use this approach it is necessary to have continuous records of runoff and precipitation for the drainage area under study. Infiltration capacity variations over time must also be determined. The UHM is limited to areas for which precipitation patterns do not vary markedly. For large drainage basins, hydrographs must be developed for subwatersheds and then synthesized into a single hydrograph at the critical location.

A unit hydrograph represents a runoff volume of 1 in. from a drainage area for a specified rainfall duration. A separate unit hydrograph is theoretically required for every possible rainfall length of interest. Ordinarily, however, variations of ±25% from any duration are considered acceptable. Unit hydrographs for short periods can be synthesized into hydrographs for longer durations, however.

Once a unit hydrograph has been derived for a drainage area and specified rainfall duration, the hydrograph for any other storm of equal duration can be obtained. The new hydrograph is developed by applying the unit hydrograph theorem, which states that the ordinates of all hydrographs resulting from equal unit time rains are proportional to the total direct runoff from that rain. The condition may be stated mathematically as

$$\frac{Q_s}{V_s} = \frac{Q_u}{1} \tag{1}$$

where

Q_s = magnitude of a hydrograph ordinate of direct runoff having a volume equal to V_s (in inches) at some instant of time after the start of runoff

Q_u = ordinate of the unit hydrograph having a volume of 1 in. at the same instant of time

Storms of reasonably uniform rainfall intensity, having a duration of about 25% of the drainage area lag time (the difference in time between the center of mass of the rainfall and the center of mass of the resulting runoff) and producing a total of 1 in. or more of runoff, are most suitable for deriving a unit hydrograph.

A unit hydrograph is developed by the following steps:

1. Analyze the stream flow hydrograph to permit separation of the surface runoff from the base flow. This can be accomplished by any one of several methods [12, 13].
2. Measure the total volume of surface runoff (direct runoff) from the storm producing the original hydrograph. The volume is equal to the area under the hydrograph after the base flow has been subtracted.
3. Divide the ordinates of the direct runoff hydrograph by the total direct runoff volume in inches. The resulting plot of these values versus time is a unit hydrograph for the basin.
4. Finally, determine the effective duration of the runoff-producing rain for the unit hydrograph. This can be estimated from the rainfall record.

These steps are used in deriving a unit hydrograph from an isolated storm. Other procedures are required for complex storms or for developing synthetic unit hydrographs when few data are available. In some cases, unit hydrographs may also be transposed from one basin to another [12]. The following example illustrates the derivation and application of a unit hydrograph.

Example 4

Using the hydrograph given in Figure 4, derive a unit hydrograph for the 3-mi^2 drainage area. From this unit hydrograph, derive a hydrograph of direct runoff for the rainfall sequence given (see Tables 8 and 9).

Solution:

1. Subtract the base flow to obtain the total direct runoff hydrograph. A number of procedures are reported in the literature, but a common method is to construct line AC beginning where the hydrograph begins an appreciable rise and ending where the recession curve intersects the base-flow curve. The important point is to be consistent in methodology from storm to storm.
2. Determine the duration of the effective rainfall (rainfall that actually produces surface runoff). The effective rainfall volume must be equivalent to the volume of direct surface runoff. Usually the unit time of the effective rainfall will be 1 day, 1 hr, 12 hr, or some other interval appropriate for the size of drainage area being studied. The unit storm duration should not exceed about 25% of the drainage area lag time. The effective portion of the storm for this example is given in Figure 4 together with its duration. The effective volume is 1.4 in.
3. Project the base length of the unit hydrograph down to the abscissa, giving the horizontal projection of the base-flow separation line AC. Unit hydrograph theory assumes that for all storms of equal duration, regardless of intensity, the period of surface runoff is the same.
4. Tabulate the ordinates of direct runoff at the peak rate of flow and at sufficient other positions to determine the hydrograph shape. Note that the

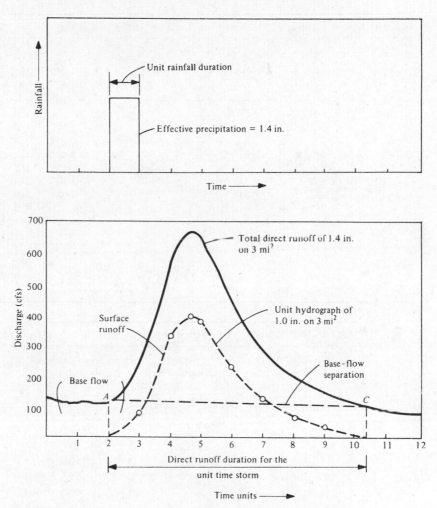

FIGURE 4   Derivation of a unit hydrograph from an isolated storm.

direct runoff ordinate is the ordinate above the base-flow separation line. See Table 8.

5.   Compute the ordinates of the unit hydrograph by using Eq. (1). In this example, the values are obtained by dividing the direct runoff ordinates by 1.4. Table 8 shows the computation of the unit hydrograph ordinates.

6.   Using the values from Table 8, plot the unit hydrograph as shown in Figure 4.

7.   Using the derived ordinates of the unit hydrograph, determine the ordinates of the hydrographs for each consecutive rainfall period as given in Table 9.

8.   Determine the synthesized hydrograph for unit storms 1–3 by plotting the three hydrographs and summing the ordinates. The procedure is indicated in Figure 5.

222

Wastewater Collection and Stormwater Engineering

TABLE 8   Determination of a Unit Hydrograph from an Isolated Storm

(1)	(2)	(3)	(4)	
Time Unit	Total Runoff (cfs)	Base Flow (cfs)	Total Direct Runoff: (2) − (3) (cfs)	Unit Hydrograph Ordinate: (4) ÷ 1.4 (cfs)
1	110	110	0	0
2	122	122	0	0
3	230	120	110	78.7
4	578	118	460	328
4.7	666	116	550	393
5	645	115	530	379
6	434	114	320	229
7	293	113	180	129
8	202	112	90	64.2
9	160	110	50	35.7
10	117	105	12	8.6
10.5	105	105	0	0
11	90	90	0	0
12	80	80	0	0

TABLE 9   Unit Hydrograph Application

Time Unit Sequence	Rain Unit Number	Effective Rainfall (in.)	Hydrograph Ordinates[a] for Rainfall Unit		
			1	2	3
1	1	0.7	55.1	—	—
2	2	1.7	229	134	—
2.7	3	1.2	275	—	—
3	—	—	265	558	94.3
3.7	—	—	—	668	—
4	—	—	161	664	393
4.7	—	—	—	—	472
5	—	—	90.5	389	455
6	—	—	44.9	219	275
7	—	—	25.0	109	155
8	—	—	6.0	60.7	77
9	—	—	—	14.6	42.8
10	—	—	—	—	10.3

[a]Values are obtained by multiplying effective rainfall values by unit hydrograph ordinates.

The unit hydrograph method provides the entire hydrograph resulting from a storm and offers advantages over procedures that only produce peak flows. It has the disadvantages of requiring both rainfall and runoff data for its derivation and of being limited in

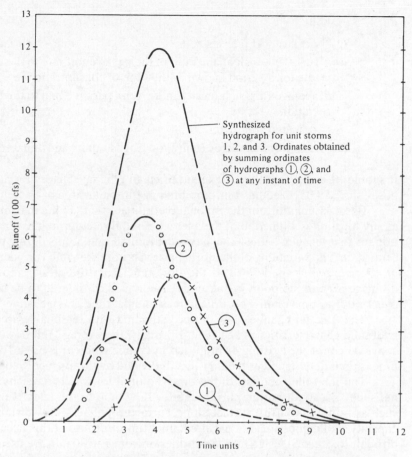

FIGURE 5   Synthesized hydrograph derived by the unit hydrograph method.

its application to a particular drainage basin. A number of refinements to the procedure may be found in the literature [12, 13, 14]. Procedures for producing synthetic unit hydrographs covering areas where adequate records are not available have also been derived [14].

Rational Method

The *rational method*, first proposed in 1889, is a widely used method for computing quantities of stormwater runoff from small areas [4]. The rational formula relates runoff to rainfall in the following manner:

$$Q = Kcia \qquad (2)$$

where

Q = peak runoff rate, cfs

c = runoff coefficient, the ratio of the peak runoff rate to the average rainfall rate for a period known as the time of concentration

i = average rainfall intensity, in./hr, for a period equal to the time of concentration

a = drainage area, acres

K = a conversion factor (unity for English units and 1/360 for metric units)

It should be noted that the assignment of cfs to Q is satisfactory for all practical purposes, since 1.008 cfs equals 1 in. of rainfall in 1 hr on an area of 1 acre ($K = 1$).

Basic assumptions of the rational method are that (1) the maximum runoff rate at any location is a function of the average rainfall rate during the time of concentration for that location and (2) the maximum rainfall rate occurs during the time of concentration. The variability of the storm pattern is not taken into consideration. The *time of concentration* t_c is defined as the flow time from the most remote point in the drainage area to the point in question. Usually it is considered to be composed of an overland flow time or, in most urban areas, an inlet time plus a channel flow time.

The time for channel flow can be estimated with reasonable accuracy from the hydraulic characteristics of the pipe. Normally, the average full-flow velocity of the conveyance for the existing or proposed hydraulic gradient is used. The channel flow time is then determined as the flow length divided by the average velocity.

The inlet time consists of the time required for water to reach a defined channel such as a street gutter, plus the gutter flow time to the inlet. Numerous factors, such as rainfall intensity, surface slope, surface roughness, flow distance, infiltration capacity, and depression storage affect inlet time. Because of this, accurate values are difficult to obtain. Design inlet flow times of from 5 to 30 min are used in practice. In highly developed areas with closely spaced inlets, inlet times of 5 to 15 min are common; for similar areas with flat slopes, periods of 10 to 15 min are common; and for very level areas with widely spaced inlets, inlet times of 20 to 30 min are frequently used [4].

Inlet times are also estimated by breaking the flow path into various components, such as grass, asphalt, and so on, then computing individual times for each surface and adding them. In theory this seems desirable, but in practice so many variables affect the flow that the reliability of computations of this type is questionable. The standard procedure is to use inlet times that have been found through experience to be applicable to the various types of urban areas.

An example method for estimating t_c, developed by Izzard for small experimental plots without developed channels, suggests the problems with using such approaches [15]:

$$t_c = \frac{41bL_o^{1/3}}{(ki)^{2/3}} \tag{3}$$

where

t_c = time of concentration, min

b = coefficient

L_o = overland flow length, ft

C = rational runoff coefficient (see Table 10)

i = rainfall intensity, in./hr, during time t_c

The equation is valid only for laminar flow conditions where the product iL_o is less than 500. The coefficient b is found using

$$b = \frac{0.0007i + C_r}{S_o^{1/3}} \tag{4}$$

TABLE 10   Typical C Coefficients for 5- to 10-yr Frequency Design

Description of Area	Runoff Coefficients
Business:	
Downtown areas	0.70–0.95
Neighborhood areas	0.50–0.70
Residential:	
Single-family areas	0.30–0.50
Multiunits, detached	0.40–0.60
Multiunits, attached	0.60–0.75
Residential (suburban)	0.25–0.40
Apartment dwelling areas	0.50–0.70
Industrial:	
Light areas	0.50–0.80
Heavy areas	0.60–0.90
Parks, cemeteries	0.10–0.25
Playgrounds	0.20–0.35
Railroad yard areas	0.20–0.40
Unimproved areas	0.10–0.30
Streets:	
Asphaltic	0.70–0.95
Concrete	0.80–0.95
Brick	0.70–0.85
Drives and walks	0.75–0.85
Roofs	0.75–0.95
Lawns, sandy soil:	
Flat, 2%	0.05–0.10
Average, 2–7%	0.10–0.15
Steep, 7%	0.15–0.20
Lawns, heavy soil:	
Flat, 2%	0.13–0.17
Average, 2–7%	0.18–0.22
Steep, 7%	0.25–0.35

TABLE 11   Izzard's Retardance Coefficient C_r

Surface	C_r
Smooth asphalt	0.007
Concrete paving	0.012
Tar and gravel paving	0.017
Closely clipped sod	0.046
Dense bluegrass turf	0.060

where

S_o = surface slope

C_r = coefficient of retardance

Values of C_r are given in Table 11. Note that the reliability of this equation is strongly influenced by the selection of parameters.

The *runoff coefficient* C_r is the component of the rational formula that requires the greatest exercise of judgment by the engineer. It is not amenable to exact determination, since it includes the influence of a number of variables, such as infiltration capacity, interception by vegetation, depression storage, and antecedent conditions. As used in the rational equation, the coefficient C represents a fixed ratio of runoff to rainfall, while in actuality it is not fixed and may vary for a specific drainage basin with time during a particular storm, from storm to storm, and with change in season. Fortunately, the closer the area comes to being impervious, the more reasonable the selection of C becomes. This is true because C approaches unity for highly impervious areas, and for these areas the nature of the surface is much less variable for changing seasonal, meteorological, or antecedent conditions. The rational method is thus best suited for use in urban areas with a high percentage of imperviousness.

There is no precise method for evaluating the runoff coefficient C, although some research has been directed toward that end [16]. Common engineering practice is to make use of average values of the coefficient for various types of land surface covers. Table 10 gives some values of the runoff coefficient. Figure 6 relates the rational C to imperviousness, soil type, and lawn slope. Most users of the rational method use information reported in similar tabular or graphical forms, using local conditions following their experience and practice.

To apply the rational method, use an average rainfall intensity i representing the design storm of a prescribed frequency for the time of concentration. The frequency chosen is largely a matter of economics. Frequencies of 1 to 10 yr are commonly used where residential areas are to be protected. For higher-value districts, 10- to 20-yr or higher return periods are commonly selected. Local conditions and practice normally dictate the criteria.

Once t_c and the rainfall frequency have been ascertained, the rainfall intensity i is usually obtained from a set of rainfall intensity–duration–frequency curves such as those shown in Figure 7. Entering the curves on the abscissa with the appropriate value of t_c and then projecting upward to an intersection with the desired frequency curve

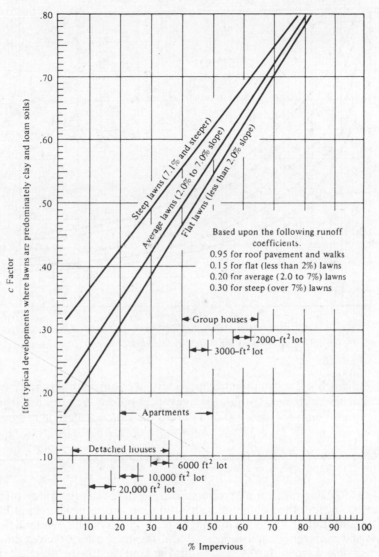

FIGURE 6 c factors for typical developments in clay soils. *Source:* Baltimore County, Maryland, Department of Public Works.

allows i to be found by projecting this intersection point horizontally to an intersection with the ordinate. If an adequate number of years of local rainfall records are available, curves similar to Figure 7 may be derived. Rainfall data compiled by the National Climatic Data Center, the Department of Commerce, the Department of Agriculture, and other government agencies may also be used.

Generally, the rational method should be used only on areas that are smaller than about 2 mi^2 (approximately 1280 acres) in size. Caution should be exercised for areas

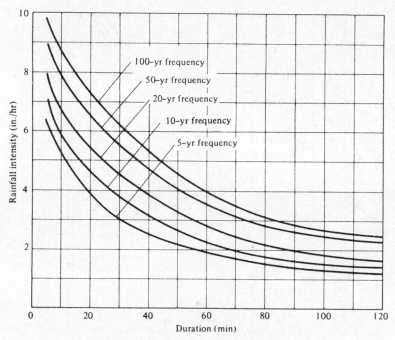

FIGURE 7   Typical intensity–duration–frequency curves.

larger than 100 acres. Most urban drainage areas served by storm drains become tributary to natural drainage channels or large conveyances before they reach 100 acres or
more in size, however, and for these tributary areas the rational method can be put to
reasonable use.

Example 5

Given the following data for a 25-year storm, estimate the peak rate of flow to a
culvert entrance. Consider the rainfall intensity–duration–frequency curves of Figure 7
applicable. The contributing upstream drainage area is 20 acres. The overland flow distance is 125 ft and the average land slope is 2.5%. The land use of the overland flow
portion of the drainage area is lawns, sandy soil. The land use for the drainage basin is
75% residential, multiple units, detached, and 25% lawns, sandy soil with an overall
average slope of about 2.7%. A channel leading to the culvert is 1550 ft long with a
slope of 0.016 ft/ft. Manning's n value for the grassed channel is 0.030. The channel is
trapezoidal with a bottom width of 3 ft and side slopes of 2 ft vertical to 1 ft horizontal.

Solution:

   1. Determine the rational C value.

       a. For the overland flow portion, using the data given and Table 10, C is
           found to be 0.15.

       b. For the residential portion, from Table 10, C is found to be 0.5.

The weighted average C value for the entire area is thus

$$C = (0.75 \times 0.5 + 0.25 \times 0.15)/1.0 = 0.41$$

where 0.75 and 0.25 are the percentages of residential and lawn areas and the denominator is the sum of them $= 1.0$

2. Calculate the time of concentration.

   a. For the overland flow area:

     Use the Federal Aviation Administration equation [17]

$$t_c = 1.8(1.1 - C)L^{0.5}/S^{0.333}$$

     where C = the rational coefficient (Table 10), L = overland flow length in ft, and S = surface slope in %.

$$t_c = 1.8(1.1 - 0.15)125^{0.5}/2.50^{0.333} = 14.09 \text{ min}$$

   b. For the main channel:

     From the channel geometry and assuming a depth of 2 ft, R is calculated to be 1.72 ft. Then, using Manning's equation,

$$V = (1.49/0.03)(1.72)^{0.666}(0.016)^{0.5} = 9.01 \text{ ft/s}$$
$$t_c = L/(V \times 60) = 1550/(9.01 \times 60) = 2.86 \text{ min}$$

     The total time of concentration is thus $14.09 + 2.86 = 16.95$, or 17 min.

3. Calculate the peak runoff for the 25-year storm.

   From Figure 7, using a time of concentration of 17 min and interpolating for the 25-year curve, the rainfall intensity is found to be 6.4 in./hr. Now the rational equation can be solved for Q:

$$Q = CiA = 0.41 \times 6.4 \times 20 = 52.48 \text{ cfs}$$

Modified Rational Method

The *modified rational method* provides for the development of a complete hydrograph [12, 18]. For this model, if the storm duration exceeds the time of concentration, the hydrograph rises to a peaking rate at the time of concentration, continues at a peaking rate until the storm event ceases, and then decreases to zero as excess rainfall is released from the drainage area. Numerous software packages are available to accommodate this approach. Figure 8 illustrates the shape of the rational method hydrograph for a rainfall intensity exceeding the time of concentration t_c. In this case, it is trapezoidal. If the rainfall duration is equal to t_c, the shape would be triangular.

Example 6

A watershed of 100 acres has a t_c of 30 min and a runoff coefficient of 0.6. Consider a storm having an average intensity of 2.5 in./hr and a duration of 50 min over the watershed. Use the modified rational method to develop a storm hydrograph.

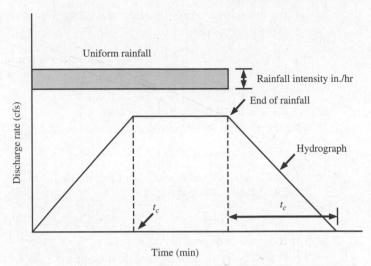

FIGURE 8   Rational method hydrograph for uniform rainfall intensity.

Solution:

1. At the time of concentration t_c, the discharge Q will be given by

$$Q = ciA = 0.6 \times 2.5 \times 100 = 150 \text{ cfs}$$

2. Between t_c and the end of the storm, the discharge will be 150 cfs.
3. At $t = 50$ minutes, rainfall ceases and the hydrograph recedes to zero over the t_c.

    The resulting hydrograph is given in Figure 9.

The previous discussion centered on developing a rational hydrograph for a storm having a uniform rainfall intensity. Since rainfall intensities are rarely uniform for very long periods, the rational hydrograph method has also been modified for use with continuous nonuniform rainstorm patterns [18].

For varying rainfall intensities over time, the peaking portion of the hydrograph begins when all portions of the watershed are contributing flow to the point under consideration. Before that time (the time of concentration), the hydrograph is defined by a rising limb. Once the storm event ceases, a recession limb lasts until all of the water being drained from the watershed reaches the point under consideration. Determining the rational hydrograph for time-varying intensities is based on the use of moving averages of rainfall intensities. The procedure is illustrated below for each of the three hydrograph components [18].

The Rising Limb. Before the time of concentration, when all portions of the watershed are contributing flow to the point under consideration, the rising portion of the hydrograph is characterized by increasing rates of flow. The area contributing

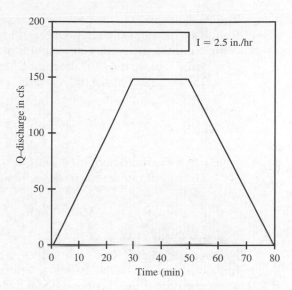

FIGURE 9 Rational method hydrograph for Example 6.

runoff at a time T, which is less than the time of concentration T_c, may be considered proportional to the ratio of T to T_c [18]. Accordingly, the contributing portion of the drainage area A is given by

$$A_c = A\frac{T}{T_c} \qquad (5)$$

where A_c is the contributing portion of area A. The average rainfall intensity for this segment of the hydrograph is given by

$$I_t = \frac{1}{T}\sum_{T=0}^{T} P_t \qquad \text{for } T_c \geq T \geq 0 \qquad (6)$$

where

I_t = the average rainfall intensity at time T

P_t = the cumulative precipitation to time T

The runoff rate for the rising segment of the hydrograph is given by

$$Q_t = KCA_cI_t = KCA\frac{T}{T_c}I_t \qquad \text{for } T_c \geq T \geq 0 \qquad (7)$$

where

Q_t = runoff at time T

K = a unit conversion factor that is 1 for English units and 1/360 for metric units

C = the rational runoff coefficient

The Peak Segment. The peaking portion of the hydrograph occurs during the period from T_c until rainfall ceases. During this period, all portions of the watershed are contributing to the outflow at the point of interest. The average rainfall intensity for a period of T_c before time T is determined using a moving average.

The average rainfall intensity for this period is determined by the following equation:

$$I_t = \frac{1}{T_c} \sum_{t=T-T_c}^{T} P_t \qquad \text{for } T_d \geq T \geq T_c \qquad (8)$$

where T_d is the time that rainfall ends.

The runoff rate for the peak segment of the hydrograph is given by

$$Q_t = KCAI_t \qquad \text{for } T_d \geq T \geq T_c \qquad (9)$$

The Recession Limb. At the time that rainfall ceases, the recession portion of the hydrograph begins. Recession curves are often represented by exponential decay functions, but for small basins a linear approximation may be made. Such an approximation is used for the rational hydrograph.

$$Q_t = Q_{T_d}\left[1 - \frac{T - T_d}{T_c}\right] \text{ for } T_d \leq T \leq (T_d + T_c) \qquad (10)$$

and

$$Q_{T_d} = KCAI_{T_d}$$

where Q_{T_d} = the rate of flow at the time T_d that rainfall ceases.

Example 7

A 50-min rainstorm occurs on a 9-acre urban area having a runoff coefficient of 0.65. The time of concentration has been calculated as 20 min. Incremental rainfall depths for the storm are given in Table 12. Using a spreadsheet, calculate the runoff from the storm at 5-minute intervals. Plot the resulting hydrograph.

Solution: The solution is obtained through the use of Eqs. (5) to (10). They are inserted in the spreadsheet shown in Table 12. Example computations for one point on each of the rising, peak, and falling components of the hydrograph illustrate those made by the spreadsheet.

1. Calculation for rising limb ordinate at $T = 20$ min. Using Eq. (6), I_{20} is computed as

$$I_{20} = (60/20) \times (0.1 + 0.22 + 0.33 + 0.57) = 3.6 \text{ in./hr}$$

The value 60 min/hr converts the result to in./hr

Using Eq. (5), A_c is determined as

$$A_c = 9 \times (20/20) = 9 \text{ acres}$$

TABLE 12   Modified Rational Method Data and Solution to Example 7

Time (min)	Incremental Rainfall Depth (in.)	$\Sigma\ P(t)$ (in.)	$\Sigma\ P(t)$ from $T - T_c$ to T	Average Rainfall Intensity $(1 - $ in./hr$)$	Runoff Rate $(Q - $ cfs$)$
0	0.0	0.0	0.0	0.0	0.0
5	0.1	0.1		1.2	1.8
10	0.22	0.32		1.92	5.6
15	0.31	0.63		2.52	11.1
20	0.57	1.2		3.6	21.1
25	0.63		1.73	5.19	30.4
30	0.5		2.01	6.03	35.3
35	0.29		1.99	5.97	34.9
40	0.18		1.6	4.8	28.1
45	0.1		1.07	3.21	18.8
50	0.06		0.63	1.89	11.1
55	0.0			0.0	8.3
60	0.0			0.0	5.5
65	0.0			0.0	2.8
70	0.0			0.0	0.0

Using Eq. (7), the flow at $T = 20$ minutes is computed as

$$Q_{20} = 0.65 \times 9 \times 3.6 = 21.1 \text{ cfs}$$

2. Calculation for peaking ordinate at $T = 40$ min. Using Eq. (8), I_{40} is computed as

$$I_{40} = (60/20) \times (0.62 + 0.5 + 0.29 + 0.18) = 4.8 \text{ in./hr}$$

Using Eq. (9), the flow at $T = 40$ minutes is computed as

$$Q_{40} = 0.65 \times 9 \times 4.8 = 28.1 \text{ cfs}$$

3. Calculation for recession ordinate at $T = 60$ min. Using Eq. (10), Q_{60} is computed as

$$Q_{60} = Q_{50} \times (1 - (60 - 50)/20) = 5.5 \text{ cfs}$$

Figure 10 is a plot of the hydrograph ordinates given in the last column of Table 12.

Given both the quantity and quality characteristics discussed in this section, it is easy to see why the collection and treatment of stormwater are so critical. For the safety of humans and the environment alike, it is critical to first collect runoff and then treat stormwater responsibly. The remainder of this chapter will focus on the design involved in the collection and treatment of stormwater.

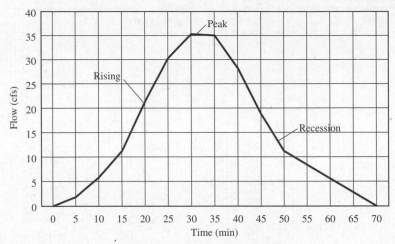

FIGURE 10   Rational method hydrograph for Example 7.

12   COLLECTION AND CONVEYANCE

Storm collection and conveyance systems may be closed conduit, open conduit, or some combination of the two. In most urban areas the smaller drains frequently are closed conduits, and, as the system moves downstream, open channels are often employed. Because quantities of stormwater runoff are usually quite large when contrasted with flows in sanitary sewers, the pipes needed to carry them are also large and thus important from the standpoint of utilities placement. Common practice is to build storm drains under the centerline of the street and offset water mains to one side and sanitary sewers to the other.

To produce a workable system layout, a map of the area is needed showing contours, streets, buildings, other utilities, natural drainage ways, and areas for future development. Storm drains are generally located under streets or in designated drainage rights-of-way. The entire area to be served must be considered. Many times, GIS or CAD programs provide a convenient way to view and design the system. For larger stormwater systems, hydrologic and hydraulic models are employed. These models will be discussed in more detail at the end of this chapter.

The first step in laying out the drainage system is to tentatively locate the inlet structures. Once this has been done, a skeleton pipe system connecting the inlets is drawn, along with the locations of all proposed manholes, branches, special bend or junction structures, and the outfall.

Customarily, a manhole or junction structure will be required at all changes in grade, pipe size, direction of flow, and quantity of flow. Figure 11 illustrates the details of a typical manhole. Note that today most of these structures are precast, although nonstandard structures can be manufactured if needed. Storm drains are usually not built smaller than 12 in. in diameter, as smaller diameter pipes tend to clog readily with debris. Maximum manhole spacing for pipes 27 in. and under should not exceed about 600 ft. No maximum spacing is prescribed for larger pipes. The normal requirements for locating these structures should provide access to the drain for inspection, cleaning, or maintenance. As with all stormwater design, the local requirements should be reviewed before any design begins. Many times, typical details for structures will be provided by local or state agencies.

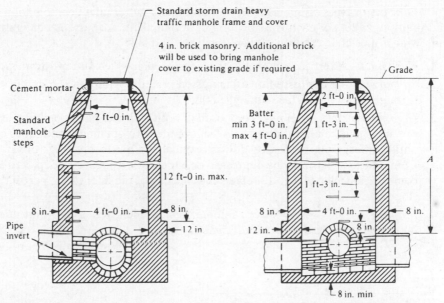

FIGURE 11   Typical storm drainage manhole details. *Source*: Baltimore County, Maryland, Department of Public Works.

13   STORM INLETS

Stormwater inlet capacity is an important consideration. Regardless of the adequacy of the underground drainage system, proper drainage cannot result unless stormwater is efficiently collected and introduced into it. Knowing the ability of stormwater inlets to accept incoming flows has important implications: Inadequate inlet capacity can result in street flooding, inefficient use of the storm drainage system, and blocking of inlets by debris. Street grade, cross slope, and depression geometry affect the hydraulic efficiency of stormwater inlets, and the inlet type must be chosen accordingly. No specific inlet type can be considered best for all conditions. Ideally, a simple opening across the flow path would be the most effective type of inlet structure, but construction of this type would be impractical and unsafe. The opening must be covered with a grate or located in the curb. Unfortunately, grates obstruct the flow of water and often collect debris, while curb openings are not in the direct path of flow. Thus, compromises are required.

Increasing the street cross slope will increase the depth of flow of the gutter, and gutter depressions will concentrate flows at the inlet. Then curb and gutter openings can be combined. These and other measures can be taken to increase inlet capacities, although some of them are not compatible with high-volume traffic.

Numerous inlet designs are in evidence, most of which have been developed from the practical experience of engineers or by rule-of-thumb procedures. The hydraulic capacity of many of these designs is unknown, and estimates of it are often in error. However, laboratory studies of inlet capacities have produced efficient designs and improved our understanding of inlet behavior [19].

Four major types of inlets are in use: curb inlets, gutter inlets, combination inlets, and multiple inlets. For each classification of design, there are various configurations. Following is a brief description of the basic types of inlets:

1. *Curb inlet*—A vertical opening in the curb through which gutter flow passes.
2. *Gutter inlet*—A depressed or undepressed grated opening in the gutter section through which the surface drainage falls.
3. *Combination inlet*—An inlet composed of both curb and gutter openings. Gutter openings may be placed directly in front of the curb opening (contiguous combination inlet) or upstream or downstream of the gutter opening (offset inlet). Combination inlets may be depressed or undepressed. Figure 12 depicts a typical combination inlet. Figure 13 relates the capacity of the inlet to the percent gutter slope.
4. *Multiple inlets*—Closely spaced interconnected inlets acting as a unit. Identical inlets end to end are called *double inlets*.

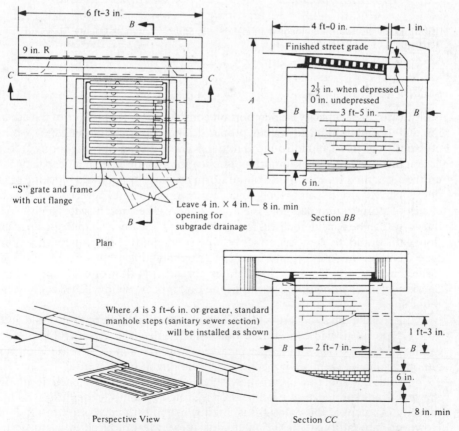

FIGURE 12   Baltimore type *S* combination inlet. *Source*: Baltimore County, Maryland, Department of Public Works.

The selection of an inlet type for a specific location should be based on the exercise of engineering judgment relative to the importance of limiting clogging, traffic hazards, risks, and cost. In general, consistent with vehicle safety and driver comfort, street cross slopes as steep as practical should be used. Inlets should be located and designed so that there will be a 5- to 10% bypass in gutter flow. This significantly increases inlet capacity. But the amount of bypass flow should not be so great as to inconvenience pedestrians or vehicular traffic. On streets where parking is permitted or where vehicles are not expected to travel near the curb, contiguous combination curb-and-gutter inlets with longitudinal grate bars could be used, or if clogging is not a problem, depressed gutter inlets could be used. Where clogging is likely, use depressed curb inlets for low gutter flows; for large flows use depressed combination inlets with the curb openings upstream. On streets having slopes in excess of 5%, where traffic passes close to the

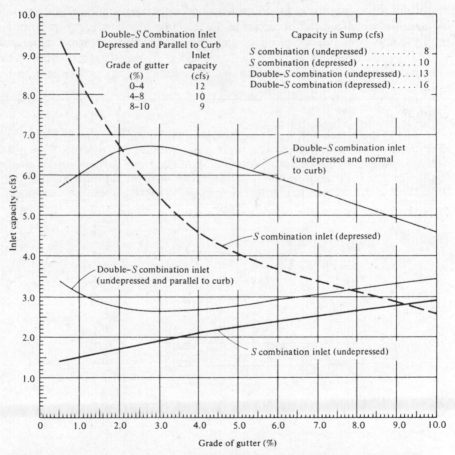

FIGURE 13   Inlet capacity curves for type *S* combination inlets. The inlet capacities have been reduced by 20% for the estimated effects of debris partially clogging the inlet (on slopes). The capacities are based on standard $7\frac{3}{16}$-in. curb and gutter and 1–18 average crown slope for a distance of about 5 ft from the face of the curve. *Source*: Baltimore County, Maryland, Department of Public Works.

curb, use deflector inlets if road dirt will not pack in the grooves. For flat slopes or where dirt is a problem, use undepressed gutter inlets or combination inlets with longitudinal bars only. For streets having flat grades or sumps (lows), pitch the grade toward the inlet on both ends. This will provide a sump at the inlet. For true sump locations, use curb openings or combination inlets. The total open area, not the size and arrangement of bars, is important because the inlet will act as an orifice. Normally, sump inlets should be overdesigned because of the unique clogging problems that develop in depressed areas.

Inlets should be constructed in all sumps and at all street intersections where the quantity of flow is significant or where nuisance conditions warrant such construction. Inlets are required at intermediate points along streets where the curb and gutter capacity would be exceeded without them. Inlet capacities should be equal to or greater than design flows. Figure 13 shows a relationship between inlet capacity and gutter slope. This relationship must be taken into account when selecting inlet configurations for specific locations.

Rapid and efficient removal of surface runoff from streets and highways is important for safety. Street grade, crown slope, inlet type, grade design, and tolerable bypass flow are all important factors in the selection of inlet structures. Knowledge of the hydraulic performance of inlets is essential for effective storm drainage designs.

The basic hydraulic and hydrologic principles discussed in this chapter are applicable to the design of urban drainage systems. The following examples illustrate their use.

Example 8

Given the sketch of the urban drainage area shown in Figure 14, use the standard rational method to determine the pipe sizes required for the pipes from M1–M2, M2–M3, and M3 to the outfall. Assume a Manning's n of 0.013, a runoff coefficient c for all areas = 0.60, the pipe lengths and slopes shown on Table 13, and the IDF curve for a 10-year storm given in Figure 7. Solve using a spreadsheet.

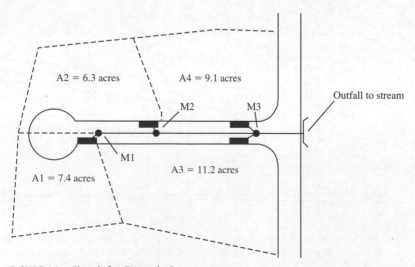

FIGURE 14   Sketch for Example 8.

TABLE 13 Spreadsheet Solution for Example 8

Pipe Section	Drainage Area	Area (acres)	Flow Time (min.) Inlet	Flow Time (min.) Pipe	Flow Time (min.) Total	Rainfall Intensity (i-in./hr)	c	Q (cfs)	Pipe Length ft	Slope ft/ft	Calculated Diameter ft	Diameter Selection (ft)	Diameter Selection (in.)	Velocity	Flow Time (min)
$M_1 - M_2$	A_1	7.4	5	—	5	7	0.6	31.08	450	0.012	2.18	2.33	28	7.29	1.03
$M_2 - M_3$	$A_1 + A_2$	13.7	5	1.03	6.03	6.7	0.6	55.07	700	0.025	2.35	2.5	30	11.22	1.04
$M_3 -$ Out	A_1 to A_4	34		1.04	7.07	6.4	0.6	130.56	200	0.025	3.25	3.67	44	12.34	0.27

Solution: Enter the given data on the spreadsheet (Table 13). Then enter formulas for calculating Q, pipe diameter, flow velocity, pipe flow time, and total flow time to manhole moving downstream to the outfall. To get pipe diameter D, solve Manning's equation for D. Then determine the velocity V using the relationship $V = Q/A$, and the flow time can be determined using the relationship $T = L/V$.

The solution is shown in Table 13. Note that calculated diameters are converted to diameters used based on standard pipe sizes.

Example 9

Design a storm drainage system for the Mextex drainage area shown in Figure 15. Note that the eight subareas are tributary to individual stormwater inlets. Assume that a 10-yr frequency rainfall satisfies local design requirements. Assume clay soil to be predominant and that average lawn slopes prevail.

Solution:

1. Prepare a drainage area map showing drainage limits, streets, impervious areas, and direction of surface flow.
2. Divide the drainage area into subareas tributary to the proposed stormwater inlets (Figure 15).
3. Compute the acreage and imperviousness of each area.

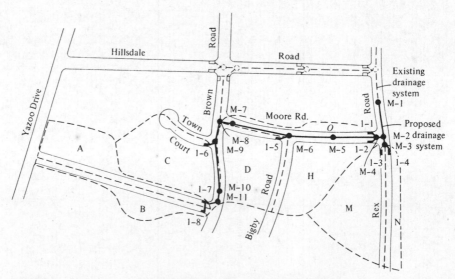

FIGURE 15   Plan view of the Mextex storm drainage system. Drainage areas: A, 1.93; B, 1.34; C, 3.19; D, 2.66; H, 2.25; M, 2.75; N, 1.27; O, 0.40.

TABLE 14 Required Storm Water Inlet Capacities for Example 9

(1) Inlet	(2) Area Designation	(3) Area (acres)	(4) Percent Impervious	(5) C	(6) Rainfall Intensity	Q: (3) × (5) × (6) (cfs)
I-1	O	0.40	49	0.57	7.0	1.59
I-2	H	2.25	20	0.35	7.0	5.52
I-3	M	2.75	26	0.40	7.0	7.70
I-4	N	1.27	26	0.40	7.0	3.55
I-5	D	2.66	26	0.40	7.0	7.43
I-6	C	3.19	24	0.38	7.0	8.48
I-7	A	1.93	23	0.37	7.0	4.99
I-8	B	1.34	29	0.42	7.0	3.93

4. Calculate the required capacity of each inlet, using the rational method. Assume a 5-min inlet time to be appropriate and compute inlet flows for a rainfall intensity of 7.0 in./hr. This is obtained by using the 10-yr frequency curve in Figure 7 with a 5-min concentration time. Appropriate c values are obtained from Figure 6 by entering the graph with the calculated percentage imperviousness (the percent of the inlet area covered by streets, sidewalks, drives, roofs, etc.), projecting up to the average lawn-slope curve, and reading c on the ordinate. Computations for the inlet flows are tabulated in Table 14.

5. Select the type of inlets required to drain the flows given in Table 14. The choice will be based on knowledge of the street slopes and their relation to inlet capacities. Inlet capacity curves such as those given in Figure 13 should be used. For this example, no selections will be made, but the reader should recognize that this is the next logical step — and an important one.

6. Beginning at the upstream end of the system and moving downstream, compute the discharge to be carried by each successive length of pipe. Calculations are summarized in Table 15. Note that at each downstream location where a flow is introduced a new time of concentration must be determined as well as new values for c and drainage area size. As the upstream inlet areas are combined to produce a larger tributary area at a design point, a revised c value representing this composite area must be determined. This is generally done by taking a weighted average of the individual c values of the components of the combined area. For example, for computing the flow to be carried by the pipe from M-9 to M-8, the tributary area is A + B + C = 6.46 acres, and the composite value of c is determined as

$$c = \frac{\Sigma c_i a_i}{\Sigma a_i} = \frac{0.37 \times 1.93 + 0.42 \times 1.34 + 0.38 \times 3.19}{6.46} = 0.38$$

At the design location, the value of t_c will be equal to the inlet time at I-8 plus the pipe flow time from I-8 to M-9 (see Table 15), which must be known to determine the rainfall intensity to be used in computing the runoff from composite area A + B + C.

TABLE 15 Computation of Design Pipe Flows for the Storm Drainage System of Example 9

Pipe Section	Tributary Area	Area (acres)	Flow Time (min)			Rainfall Intensity i	c	Q (cfs)	Slope (%)	Pipe		
			Inlet	Pipe	Total					Size (in.)	Full-Flow Velocity (fps)	Length (ft)
I-8-I-7	B	1.34	5	0.10	5	7.0	0.42	3.93	1.0	15	5.2	30
I-7-M-11	A + B	3.27	5	0.13	5.10	7.0	0.39	8.93	1.0	18	5.9	46
M-11-M-10	A + B	3.27	—	0.24	5.23	—	0.39	8.93	1.0	18	5.9	85
M-10-M-9	A + B	3.27	—	0.37	5.47	—	0.39	8.93	2.0	18	8.1	178
I-6-M-9	C	3.19	5	—	5	7.0	0.38	8.48	1.0	18	5.9	40
M-9-M-8	A + B + C	6.46	—	0.21	5.80	6.9	0.38	16.90	1.8	21	8.5	110
M-8-M-7	A + B + C	6.46	—	0.11	6.01	—	0.38	16.90	1.8	21	8.5	57
M-7-M-6	A + B + C	6.46	—	0.47	6.12	—	0.38	16.90	1.6	21	8.1	230
I-5-M-6	D	2.66	5	—	5	7.0	0.40	7.43	2.0	15	7.4	19
M-6-M-5	A + B + C + D	9.12	—	0.38	6.59	6.8	0.39	24.20	2.0	24	10.0	230
M-5-M-4	A + B + C + D	9.12	—	0.42	6.97	—	0.39	24.20	1.9	24	9.8	247
I-1-M-4	O	0.40	5	—	5	7.0	0.57	1.59	3.0	15	9.0	19
I-2-M-4	H	2.25	5	—	5	7.0	0.35	5.52	3.0	15	9.0	17
M-4-M-2	A + B + C + D + O + H	11.77	—	0.05	7.39	6.6	0.39	30.3	1.5	27	9.4	29
I-3-M-3	M	2.75	5	—	5	7.0	0.40	7.70	2.0	15	7.4	15
I-4-M-3	N	1.27	5	—	5	7.0	0.40	3.55	2.0	15	7.4	20
M-3-M-2	M + N	4.02	—	—	5	7.0	0.40	11.30	1.8	18	7.8	37
M-2-M-1	A + B + C + D + O + H + M + N	15.79	—	—	7.44	6.6	0.39	40.6	1.4	30	9.8	176

7. Using the computed discharge values, select tentative pipe sizes for the approximate slopes given in Column 10 of Table 15. Once the pipe sizes are known, flow velocities between input locations can be determined. Normally, velocities are approximated by computing the full-flow velocities for maximum discharge at the specified grade. These velocities are used to compute channel flow time for estimating the time of concentration. If, upon completing the hydraulic design, enough change has been made in any concentration time to alter the design discharge, new values of flow should be computed. Generally, this will not be the case.

8. Using the pipe sizes selected in Step 7, draw a profile of the proposed drainage system. Begin the profile at the point farthest downstream, which can be an outfall into a natural channel, an artificial channel, or, as in the case of the example, an existing drain. In constructing the profile, be certain that the pipes have at least the minimum required cover. Normally, 1.5 to 2 ft is sufficient. Pipe slopes should conform to the surface slope wherever possible. Indicate the change in invert elevation at all manholes. In this example, where there is no change in pipe size through the manhole, a drop of 0.2 ft will be used. Where the size decreases upstream through a manhole, the upstream invert will be set above the downstream invert a distance equal to the difference in the two diameters. In this way, the pipe crowns are kept at the same elevation. A portion of the profile of the drainage system in the example is given in Figure 16.

9. Compute the position of the hydraulic gradient along the profile of the pipe. If the gradient lies less than 1.5 ft below the ground surface, it must be lowered to preclude the possibility of surcharge during the design flow. Note that the value of 1.5 ft is arbitrarily chosen here. In practice, local standards indicate the limiting value. Hydraulic gradients may be lowered by increasing pipe

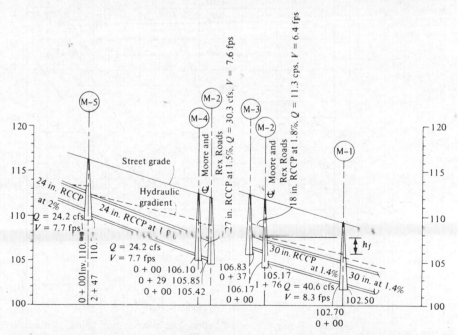

FIGURE 16 Profile of part of the Mextex storm drain showing the hydraulic gradient.

sizes, decreasing head losses at structures, designing special transitions, lowering the system below ground, or a combination of these means.

Computations for a portion of the hydraulic gradient of the example are carried out in the following manner. Pipe head losses are determined by applying Manning's equation, assuming $n = 0.013$ in this example. Head losses in the structures are determined by using the relationships defined in Figures 17 and 18. These curves were developed for

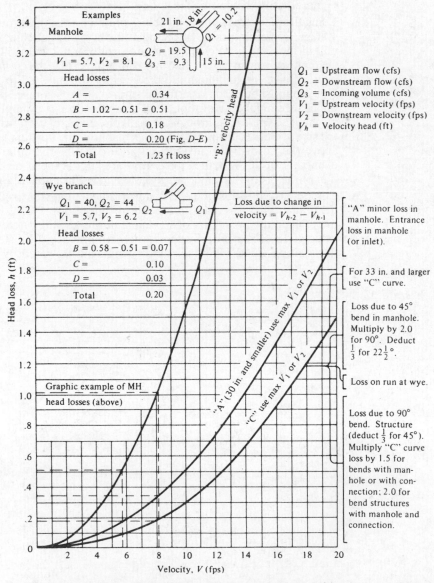

FIGURE 17 Types *A*, *B*, and *C* head losses in structures. *Source:* Baltimore County, Maryland, Department of Public Works.

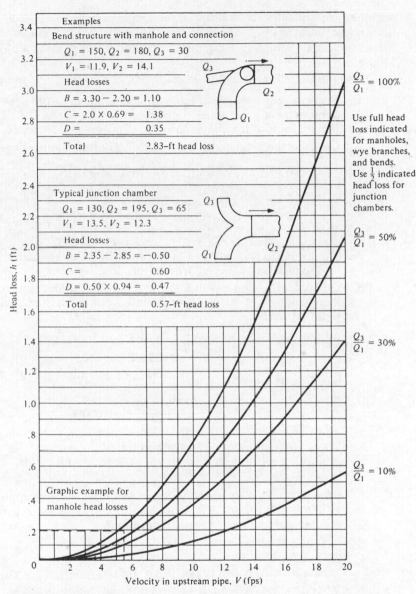

Examples

Bend structure with manhole and connection

$Q_1 = 150, Q_2 = 180, Q_3 = 30$

$V_1 = 11.9, V_2 = 14.1$

Head losses

$B = 3.30 - 2.20 = 1.10$

$C = 2.0 \times 0.69 = 1.38$

$D = \quad\quad\quad\quad 0.35$

Total   2.83-ft head loss

$\dfrac{Q_3}{Q_1} = 100\%$

Use full head loss indicated for manholes, wye branches, and bends. Use $\frac{1}{2}$ indicated head loss for junction chambers.

Typical junction chamber

$Q_1 = 130, Q_2 = 195, Q_3 = 65$

$V_1 = 13.5, V_2 = 12.3$

Head losses

$B = 2.35 - 2.85 = -0.50$

$C = \quad\quad\quad\quad 0.60$

$D = 0.50 \times 0.94 = 0.47$

Total   0.57-ft head loss

$\dfrac{Q_3}{Q_1} = 50\%$

$\dfrac{Q_3}{Q_1} = 30\%$

$\dfrac{Q_3}{Q_1} = 10\%$

Graphic example for manhole head losses

Head loss, h (ft)

Velocity in upstream pipe, V (fps)

FIGURE 18   Type *D* head loss in structures. *Source:* Baltimore County, Maryland, Department of Public Works.

surcharged pipes entering rectangular structures but may be applied to wye branches, manholes, and junction chambers [20]. The *A* curve is used to find entrance and exit losses; the *B* curve is used to evaluate the head loss due to an increased velocity in the downstream direction. This loss is designated as the difference between the head losses found for the downstream and upstream pipes $(V_{h-2} - V_{h-1})$ In cases where the greatest velocity occurs upstream, the difference will be negative and may be applied to offset other losses in the structure. The C loss results from a change in direction in a manhole, wye branch, or bend structure. The D loss is related to the impact of secondary flows entering the structure. Examples of the use of these curves are shown in Figures 17 and 18.

Computations for the hydraulic gradient shown in Figure 16 are as follows:

1. Begin at the elevation of the hydraulic gradient at the upstream end of the existing 30-in. reinforced concrete culvert pipe (RCCP). This elevation is 105.50. The existing hydraulic gradient is shown in Figure 16.
2. Compute the head losses in manhole M-1 using Figures 17 and 18.

A loss = 0.36 ft (V = 8.3 fps = Q/A)
B loss = 0; no change in velocity, $V_1 = V_2$
C loss = 0; no change in direction
D loss = 0; no secondary flow
    total = 0.36 ft

The hydraulic gradient rises in the manhole to an elevation of 105.50 + 0.36 = 105.86 ft, as plotted in M-1 in Figure 16.

3. Compute the head loss due to friction in the 30-in. drain from M-1 to M-2. Assume that n = 0.013. Using Manning's equation, the head loss per linear foot of drain is

$$S = \frac{(nV)^2}{2.21R^{4/3}}$$

and from M-1 to M-2,

$$S = \frac{(0.013 \times 8.3)^2}{2.21 \times 0.534} = 0.00986$$

The total frictional head loss is therefore

$$hf = S \times L = 0.00986 \times 176 = 1.73 \text{ ft}$$

Elevation of the hydraulic gradient at the downstream end of M-2 is thus 105.86 + 1.73 = 107.59 ft. This elevation is plotted in Figure 16, where the hydraulic gradient in this reach is drawn in.

4. Compute the head losses in M-2.

A = 0.36 (V = 8.3 fps)
B = 1.07 − 0.90 = 0.17 (V_2 = 8.3, V_1 = 7.6 = Q/A for 27-in. drain)
C = 0.20 × 2.0 (multiply by 2 for 90° bend in manhole−
    see Figure 17) = 0.40
D = 0.22 for Q_3/Q_1 = 11.3/30.3 = 37%

The total head loss in M-2 equals 1.15 ft and the elevation of the hydraulic gradient in M-2 is therefore 107.59 + 1.15 = 108.74 ft.

5. Compute the friction head loss in the section of pipe from M-2 to M-3.

$$S = \frac{(0.013 \times 6.4)^2}{2.21 \times 0.272} = 0.0113$$

$$hf = 0.0113 \times 37 = 0.42 \text{ ft}$$

The elevation of the hydraulic gradient at the downstream end of M-3 is therefore $108.74 + 0.42 = 109.16$ ft. Plot this point on the profile and draw the gradient from M-2 to M-3.

The hydraulic gradient in the above example was computed under the assumption of uniform flow. In closed-conduit systems, if the pipes are flowing full or the system is surcharged (the usual design flow conditions), the method will produce good results. When open conduits are used, or in partial-flow systems, the hydraulic gradient can be determined by computing surface profiles.

14   STABLE CHANNEL DESIGN

Many stormwater conveyance systems are open channels and/or discharge to natural channels. In both cases, the stormwater engineer must ensure that erosive velocities do not occur. Whether the channel is natural or manmade, the same general principles for stable channel design apply. In the past, many streams or channels were lined with manmade materials or even concrete. This type of design has caused significant environmental and ecological damage in many natural bodies of water and can even be related to property damage and increased downstream flooding. The use of these manmade materials usually increases velocities in these channels, and they also greatly reduce or eliminate critical habitat for various species. Engineers also often straighten open channels or natural bodies of water, either as a side effect of a poor hydraulic design or intentionally as part of construction plans. All of these practices alter the hydrology and ecology of the project site and of offsite areas and may result in some unintended consequences for humans and the environment alike. This section will briefly cover stable channel design but the reader is encouraged to consult other references [21, 22] for a more in-depth treatment of this and related topics.

Good stable channel design is sometimes more art than science, as are many types of sustainable stormwater management. This is perhaps why many engineers still revert to the standard practices of rip rap, concrete, or filter point mat. Regardless of the materials that will be used to line or restore channels, the same equations apply and velocities must be checked to ensure that adverse impacts will not occur. Additionally, the use of biological materials in channel design or restoration may involve experts in biology, ecology, botany, and soils—or even specific experts in this area (called *fluvial geomorphologists*). It sometimes seems like a daunting task for the design engineer to consult these experts. However, the hydrologic and ecological results can make this extra cost and effort worthwhile.

A good stable channel design would generally follow these steps:

1. The design engineer should find out as much as possible about historical site conditions. This includes hydrology, soils, ecology, land use (previous and current), geology, and the regulations that will apply to the site. This is the also the time to assemble an interdisciplinary team and visit the site. The engineer must get qualified professionals involved to ensure that the future design will be permittable and implementable in all aspects.

2. The project team should carefully collect site data. This work may include water quality and biological sampling, wetlands evaluations, species surveys, and soils and geotechnical investigations.

3. The team should design a preliminary layout for the project. This would involve a simple site layout so that the team members can work on their individual parts of the project in consultation with one another. At this time, it is often helpful to discuss the preliminary design with the regulatory agency that will have jurisdiction over the project.

4. The engineer will need to carefully analyze the project's impacts to site hydrology and hydraulics. This may be done in collaboration with fluvial geomorphologists, geologists, soil scientists, and wetland experts. Usually a hydraulic and/or hydraulic model would be used for a project of reasonable complexity. Current and proposed curvature of the system and impacts of the system's sediment budget should also be considered in addition to the traditional considerations for water quantity and quality.

5. The team needs to iterate to arrive at a design that meets all interdisciplinary objectives. Often a hydraulic design will not provide adequate habitat and iterations are necessary to effectively coordinate between the hydraulics experts and ecologists.

6. The project team should complete applicable permit applications, respond to final inquires from permitting agencies, and complete a final evaluation to ensure constructability—as well as future ease of monitoring and maintenance. An experienced construction expert should examine the plans to check for potential construction issues and to ensure that the site will be accessible for future maintenance.

7. The project team and owners of the system should complete and implement a maintenance and monitoring plan. More will be said about operations and maintenance of stormwater projects throughout this chapter.

It is also important to note that armoring a channel or stream at one location without considering impacts to the remainder of the system is not sound engineering. Channels and streams are dynamic living systems and the entire range of biological, hydraulic, hydrologic, and erosive conditions must be considered.

15   BEST MANAGEMENT PRACTICES

Planning and engineering professionals have adopted the term *best management practices* (BMPs) to represent a wide variety of structural and nonstructural alternatives for addressing the water quality and quantity concerns related to stormwater [23]. Table 16 compares structural and nonstructural stormwater BMPs. As the table shows, however, the success of such measures in controlling nonpoint source pollution depends very much on educational programs and passage of legislation or ordinances to encourage or force the public to comply with the intended BMPs [12, 22].

Although Table 16 shows that a large variety of BMPs is available, most engineers routinely only design a few types of structural BMPs, with the most common

TABLE 16   A Brief Summary of Common Urban Stormwater BMPs

BMP Type	Major Category	Examples of Individual BMPs
Nonstructural	Planning	Integrated Water Management, Watershed Management, Site Planning, Erosion Control Plans, Stormwater Master Plans
	Inspection	Erosion and Sediment Control, Stormwater System Construction Inspections, Stormwater System Operations Inspections
	Public Education	School Curricula, Stakeholder/Public Involvement Groups, Developer Education, Public Events, Public Education Campaigns
	Compliance/Enforcement	Permitting, Fines, Various Orders or Decrees, Civil and/or Criminal Prosecution
	Operations, Monitoring, and Maintenance	Monitoring Plans, Operations and Maintenance Plans, Asset Management via GIS, Checklists
	Other Miscellaneous Nonpoint Source Controls	Street Sweeping, Litter Campaigns, Street, Stream, and Beach Cleanup Campaigns, Recycling, Reduced Use of Deicing Materials
Structural	Ponds	Detention and Retention Ponds
	Low Impact Development[a]	Wetlands, Bioretention, Biofiltration, Green Roofs, Pervious Pavements, Reduced Grading, Reduced Soil Compaction
	Gross Pollutant Removal Devices	Baffle Boxes and Hydrodynamic Separators
	Erosion Control Measures	Natural and Manmade Matting, Vegetation, Various Polymers, Rip Rap, Sodding, Seeding, Check Dams
	Retrofits	Pond and Wetland Improvements, Channel Stabilization, Installation of Baffle Boxes into Existing Stormsewer Systems, Removal of Septic Tanks

[a]LID makes use of a variety of both nonstructural and structural measures.

being retention and detention ponds (see the following sections). A number of local, county, and state governments throughout the United States have also implemented significant stormwater programs that include a variety of structural and nonstructural measures in addition to stormwater models and GIS of varying complexities. Since nonpoint source pollution is heavily linked to the behavior of individuals, many of these programs involve public education. The menu of stormwater BMPs continues to expand. Two of the most important concepts, sustainability and low impact development (LID), have continued to evolve and most likely represent the future of stormwater management. Both sustainability and LID will be discussed further in Section 18.

The importance of operations and maintenance of stormwater systems constructed in accordance with BMPs must also be mentioned. Just as one would not construct a water or wastewater treatment plant and then leave it to operate with no monitoring or maintenance, one should apply the same type of considerations to stormwater BMPs. Although BMPs are used to construct systems many stormwater every year, only a small majority receive the maintenance they need. Unfortunately, lack of maintenance will eventually cause the structures to fail.

The traditional stormwater conveyance systems required less maintenance than the newer ones that involve a variety of manmade and natural materials. Increased development and complexity of BMPs have increased the loads on berms, dams, tanks, and reservoirs. These stormwater systems must be maintained to ensure that they remain safe and do not fail. In fact, experts have reported that failed stormwater systems can lead to water quality conditions that are worse than if the system were never constructed at all. The capacity for dedicated operations and maintenance of each BMP should be considered on a case-by-case basis before design is undertaken. More information on this topic can be found in the references at the end of this chapter or in many hardcopy or Internet-based stormwater management publications.

16   DETENTION POND DESIGN

As previously mentioned, the most common types of structural treatment systems for stormwater are various types of ponds. A *detention pond* is defined as a pond that discharges to surface water, whereas a *retention pond* is defined as a pond that discharges to groundwater via infiltration. Both types of ponds should be designed to consider both the quantity and quality of the runoff they receive, as well as the potential adverse impacts to downstream bodies of water. Some other specific considerations for the stormwater engineer engaged in pond design include the following:

1. The quality of the groundwater and soils data must be high. Incorrect data in either capacity can cause a pond to fail.

2. Pond side slopes should be stable and should ensure the safety of the public. All applicable local and state regulations should be reviewed before designing a pond. Stormwater manuals often specify a maximum side slope for ponds.

3. Whenever possible, it is desirable to mimic nature and design ponds with plan views that are irregular and more natural looking.

4. The pond should be stabilized with some form of natural materials and/or native vegetation. Usually, some form of sod or seed is used. Again, the stabilizing agents should comply with local requirements, be native to the area, and require minimal maintenance. A qualified biologist, botanist, or landscape architect should design the layout of all vegetated areas.

5. Erosion protection should be designed at all pond outlets and emergency overflows. Again, the form of erosion protection should be designed to meet local requirements while agreeing with conditions at the project site.

6. Future maintenance of the pond should be an integral part of the design process. This may include some consideration for loadings from heavy equipment as well as lighter maintenance (such as mowing and removal of nuisance vegetation).

While ponds are often the most common form of stormwater treatment, many other types of BMPs exist. Section 18 will focus on more holistic stormwater management techniques.

A typical detention pond is shown in Figure 19. Detention pond design and analysis are founded on storage–discharge relationships and closely resemble typical storage routing techniques. If in Figure 19 Q_i represents the inflow to the pond, Q represents the outflow, and S represents storage in the pond, then a continuity equation of the form

$$Q_i - Q = dS/dt \qquad (11)$$

can be written, where dS/dt is the rate of change of storage with respect to time. If one considers that storage increments can be calculated as the product of mean surface area of the pond at a specified depth and the depth increment, then

$$\frac{dS}{dt} = A(h)\frac{dh}{dt} \qquad (12)$$

where $A(h)$ is a relationship equating pond surface area A to a reference depth (or elevation) and dh/dt is the rate of change of depth with respect to time. Depth–area relationships for ponds can be obtained by developing contours for the pond (usually from CAD or GIS) and then relating the surface areas contained within these contours to the elevations associated with them. Incremental volumes can be determined by using average end-area or other formulas. Often, a relationship of the form

$$A = Kh^m \qquad (13)$$

can be derived relating surface area to depth. In Eq. (13) A is the surface area, K and m are constants for the site, and h is the depth of water in the reservoir above a reference point such as the elevation of the centerline of the outlet [1, 24]. Where the

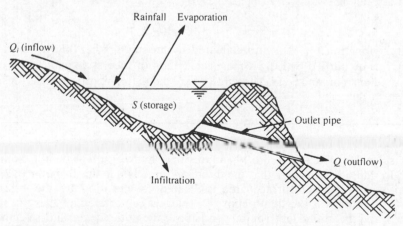

FIGURE 19   A detention basin configuration.

outlet is a pipe, as shown in Figure 19, the outflow can be calculated using the orifice equation

$$Q = C_d A_o (2gh)^{0.5} \tag{14}$$

where Q is the outflow, C_d is a discharge coefficient, A_o is the orifice area, g is the acceleration due to gravity, and h is the elevation above the orifice. Discharge coefficients for submerged pipes behaving as orifices range from about 0.62 to 1.0, depending on whether they are sharp edged or well rounded [25].

If we insert Eqs. (14) and (12) in Eq. (11), the result is

$$Q_i = C_d A_o (2gh)^{0.5} = A(h) \frac{dh}{dt} \tag{15}$$

Solving for dh/dt, we get

$$\frac{dh}{dt} = \frac{Q_i - C_d A_o (2gh)^{0.5}}{A(h)} \tag{16}$$

which is the governing differential equation for depth as a function of time. Specifying the right side of Eq. (16) as $f(h, t)$, then

$$dh/dt = f(h, t) \tag{17}$$

This equation can be solved numerically in several ways. The Euler method is described here and is applied to the example that follows. The procedure is simple but coarse [24, 27].

If a time step of Δt is assumed, the derivative in Eq. (17) can be approximated as

$$\frac{dh}{dt} = \frac{h(t + \Delta t) - h(t)}{\Delta t} \tag{18}$$

The equation can be solved for $h(t + \Delta t)$ as follows:

$$h(t + \Delta t) = h(t) + \Delta t f(h, t) \tag{19}$$

Note that the function $h(t)$ is always evaluated at time step t rather than at step $t + \Delta t$. Since $f(h, t)$ is quantified by Eq. (16), the calculation of successive values of h can be accomplished in an organized and straightforward manner. The procedure is illustrated in Example (10).

Example 10

Consider the sketch of Figure 19 and the input hydrograph given in Column 1 of Table 17. In addition, consider that the discharge pipe is 8 in. in diameter (0.203 m), that C_d is 0.9, the pond surface area is related to elevation by the expression $A = 400h^{0.7}$ (where h is the depth above the culvert centerline and A is the surface area in m^2), and the initial depth in the pond above the outlet centerline is 0.5 m.

TABLE 17 Spreadsheet Detention Pond Analysis

(1) Time (hr)	(2) Q-In. (cms)	(3) h(t) (m)	(4) Q-Out (cms)	(5) A-Surf (sq. m)	(6) dh/dt (m/s)	(7) h(t + dt) (m)
0	0	0.5	0.09141	246.2289	−0.00037	0.165882
0.25	0.18	0.16634	0.052724	113.9614	0.001117	1.17149
0.5	0.36	1.17206	0.139954	447.018	0.000492	1.615088
0.75	0.54	1.615474	0.164309	559.59	0.000671	2.219706
1	0.72	2.220068	0.192617	699.063	0.000754	2.899041
1.25	0.9	2.89938	0.220122	842.7012	0.000807	3.625486
1.5	1.1	3.625808	0.246158	985.4699	0.000866	4.405597
1.75	0.99	4.405905	0.271349	1129.496	0.000636	4.978537
2	0.88	4.978833	0.288453	1230.408	0.000481	5.411529
2.25	0.77	5.411818	0.300734	1304.368	0.00036	5.735607
2.5	0.66	5.735891	0.309607	1358.566	0.000258	5.968013
2.75	0.55	5.968294	0.315817	1396.867	0.000168	6.119178
3	0.44	6.119456	0.319792	1421.54	8.46E-05	6.195562
3.25	0.33	6.19584	0.321781	1433.937	5.73E-06	6.200998
3.5	0.22	6.201274	0.321923	1434.817	−7.1E-05	6.137343
3.75	0.11	6.137619	0.320266	1424.492	−0.00015	6.004772
4	0	6.00505	0.316788	1402.884	−0.00023	5.801819
4.25	0	5.802097	0.311389	1369.523	−0.00023	5.597464
4.5	0	5.597744	0.305856	1335.578	−0.00023	5.391638
4.75	0	5.39192	0.300181	1301.009	−0.00023	5.184264
5	0	5.184549	0.294352	1265.778	−0.00023	4.975257
5.25	0	4.975544	0.288357	1229.839	−0.00023	4.764523
5.5	0	4.764812	0.282185	1193.142	−0.00024	4.551957
5.75	0	4.552249	0.275819	1155.628	−0.00024	4.337442
6	0	4.337736	0.269242	1117.234	−0.00024	4.120845
6.25	0	4.121142	0.262434	1077.885	−0.00024	3.902018
6.5	0	3.902319	0.255371	1037.495	−0.00025	3.680791
6.75	0	3.681094	0.248027	995.9644	−0.00025	3.456965
7	0	3.457272	0.240369	953.1768	−0.00025	3.230313
7.25	0	3.230624	0.232356	908.9929	−0.00026	3.000567
7.5	0	3.000882	0.223942	863.2453	−0.00026	2.767405
7.75	0	2.767725	0.215066	815.7293	−0.00026	2.530441
8	0	2.530766	0.205654	766.1898	−0.00027	2.289196
8.25	0	2.289527	0.195607	714.3023	−0.00027	2.043068
8.5	0	2.043406	0.184794	659.6419	−0.00028	1.791277

(1) Time sequence
(2) Inflow data
(3) Head above outlet centerline (meters)
(4) Outflow calculated using orifice equation
(5) Surface area of pond calculated using power relationship
(6) $dh/dt = $ (inflow−outflow)/(surface area)
(7) $h(t + dt) = h(t) + dt[f(h, t)]$

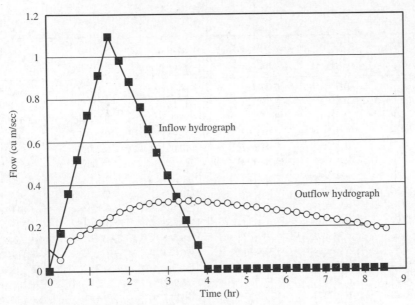

FIGURE 20   Detention pond hydrographs.

Solution: A spreadsheet analysis is suggested. For ease of calculations, we calculate the product of $C_d A_o$ to be 0.02918. Substituting this value, the numerical value of the product $2g = 2 \times (9.8 \text{ m/s}) = 19.6$, and the relationship for h in Eq. (16), we get

$$\frac{dh}{dt} = \frac{Q_i t - 0.02918(19.6h)^{0.5}}{400h^{0.7}}$$

With this relationship, a solution for successive values of h, at quarter-hour (900 sec) time steps, can be carried out as illustrated in Table 17. In the table the values in Columns 1 and 2 are given, as is the initial value of depth (0.5 m) in Column 3. Column headings are described in the table footnotes and follow the terminology of Eqs. (11) to (19). The calculated outflow hydrograph is plotted in Figure 20, along with the inflow hydrograph. It is easy to see from the plot that the inflow rates are significantly attenuated by the detention structure. Note that the drop in outflow at Time Step 1 occurs because there was no inflow at $t = 0$ and there was already a positive head on the outlet of 0.5 m at the start of inflow. Accordingly, the system was draining at that time.

   Once the spreadsheet is set up, it is easy to test selected inflow sequences and reservoir and outlet dimensions. From there, it is possible to determine the flow attenuation and modify the aforementioned parameters if the amount of attenuation is unacceptable.

17   RETENTION POND DESIGN

It is easy to see why the design of retention ponds is more complex, since retention ponds discharge via infiltration and the equations of groundwater must be involved. Many engineers now use the wide variety of pond design models available to analyze groundwater mounding when a retention pond must be designed. The same general principles apply to this type of modeling as with all types of hydrologic and hydraulic modeling. The general approach to modeling will be covered further in Section 19.

18   SUSTAINABILITY AND LOW-IMPACT DEVELOPMENT

Sustainability and low-impact design have become specialties within many engineering disciplines and most recently both concepts have crept into the media and public consciousness. Stormwater engineers have worked on sustainability and low-impact development for many years and have learned numerous lessons. The stormwater paradigm has solidly shifted away from the drainage solutions of the past and the emerging stormwater philosophy is based on working more in harmony with hydrology and ecology. In fact, this general philosophy pervades much of water resources engineering and is the subject of much research and debate.

As with many terms in water resources, the term *sustainability* has different definitions. Most simply, it describes systems that meet the needs of humans both today and in the future. However, many include in this definition environmental and ecological sustainability. Regardless of the definition, most agree that sustainability includes a definite concern for the future and for ensuring adequate resources for our descendants [28]. Sustainability will remain the subject of much research and debate within the stormwater management community for the foreseeable future.

Low-impact development (LID), sustainable urban design, or water sensitive urban design are synonyms used to describe another important subdiscipline within the stormwater management community. All three terms refer to approaches that are based on mimicking hydrologic conditions before development took place through a variety of techniques that store, infiltrate, evaporate, and detain stormwater. In the United States, Prince George's County in Maryland was one of the first to start experimenting with LID in the late 1990s. Prince George's County summarizes the primary objectives of LID as [29] follows:

- Minimizing impacts on hydrology that normally result from development. Techniques to reduce impacts include reducing imperviousness, ensuring ecological conservation, maintaining natural drainage, reducing use of pipes, and minimizing clearing and grading. Many times, there is also a focus on minimizing soil compaction.
- Storing and treating stormwater in dispersed locations throughout the project site. LID emphasizes the use of multiple decentralized facilities, which differs from the traditional approach of constructing a large storage facility in a central downstream location.
- Maintaining predevelopment times of concentration.
- Educating the public to keep the LID measures in place and to generally reduce nonpoint source pollution.

Many proponents consider LID to be more aesthetically pleasing than traditional stormwater treatment techniques (such as large ponds) because of the increased use of native vegetation and decentralized storage. Some LID measures include bioretention, wetlands, grass swales, permeable pavements, and vegetated rooftops (also called *green roofs*). Generally, LID requires a more diverse project team than traditional stormwater design and should include ecologists, soil scientists, hydrologists, and public education experts. The EPA reported that constructing LID projects is less expensive than constructing traditional stormwater facilities, although the cost of maintenance is higher than traditional stormwater management [30]. Since many LID measures are constructed on private property, public education is critical to ensuring that the facilities are maintained and that the LID measures are ultimately successful in mimicking predevelopment hydrology. Prince George's County, Maryland summarized the LID approach [29]:

- Site planning is used to minimize impervious surfaces and maintain predevelopment hydrology.
- The hydrologic analysis involves both standard and specialized computational techniques to analyze the hydrology of the site. Although traditional design techniques are used (such as time of concentration), the engineer employing LID must be familiar with a wide variety of modeling methodologies. Currently, there is much debate about the best ways to model LID but there is a general consensus that continuous simulation should be used to model most LID projects. At the conclusion of the hydrologic analysis, specific LID measures are discussed.
- Integrated Management Practices (IMPs), the specific LID measures that will be used to accomplish the goals identified during the hydrologic analysis, are carefully evaluated and prioritized.
- Erosion and sediment control are carefully analyzed and implemented to ensure that the site will not be adversely affected.
- Public outreach is used to ensure that the LID approach will be understood and embraced by the new property owners.

In the near future it is likely that conventional stormwater controls will remain popular. However, LID will likely become more and more popular as the constraints of both types of stormwater management are better understood and documented. The Internet is a good source of further information on sustainability and LID.

19   HYDROLOGIC AND HYDRAULIC MODELING

Although the two previous chapters have primarily focused on manual techniques for hydrologic and hydraulic analysis, most stormwater engineers routinely involve some form of hydrologic and hydraulic modeling in their design process. These models vary greatly in their sizes, complexity, capabilities, and uses, but they offer speed and convenience unavailable to engineers a generation ago. However, with this new speed and convenience comes a higher level of individual responsibility. Engineers must learn to use these models responsibly and that requires a firm understanding of the concepts in this text and beyond as well as a large body of knowledge about the models themselves. A model will only be as accurate as the data used to parameterize it and, more importantly, as the modeler who is in charge of this process.

Before selecting a model, an engineer should carefully review the user's manual and any related documentation, as well as independent tests and critiques of the model. Training is widely available for the most common hydrologic and hydraulic models and is an excellent resource for the engineer involved in dedicated stormwater management. Once a model is selected, it should be carefully parameterized and documented. Like any engineering work, the model should also be carefully checked as part of an independent quality-control process.

The previous chapters have briefly covered many of the methods and equations used in hydrologic and hydraulic models. However, modeling is a critical specialty within water resource and water supply and usually specialized training and education are required to truly master the more complex models. Regardless of the model involved, a few basic tenets usually apply:

1. The model should be carefully selected. This topic was discussed in previous chapter.

2. The modelers should have a solid foundation in the governing assumptions and equations used in the model.

3. The model should be parameterized efficiently and correctly.

4. The model parameterization should be carefully documented and checked by an experienced modeler.

5. The model should be carefully checked, calibrated, and verified whenever possible. In general, the review should be conducted by an independent reviewer with experience in the specific model.

6. If necessary, the modeler and review team should test the sensitivity of various key variables (also called a *sensitivity analysis*) [25].

7. Production runs should be carefully labeled and run in batches whenever possible.

8. Model results should be well documented in a final memorandum or report.

9. Final model files should be carefully archived in their electronic formats. This is critical for models that will be maintained over time but it also is usually necessary to meet the requirements for legal documentation. Hardcopy documentation should also be archived.

It is also important to note that, as new versions or modeling techniques arise, a dedicated modeler should make an effort to read documentation and experiment with the new technologies. As with all of the other engineering disciplines, being a good modeler requires a lifetime of dedication.

PROBLEMS

1 Research stormwater BMPs for agriculture. Provide a list of both structural and nonstructural BMPs that are used to mitigate nonpoint source pollution from agricultural land use.

2 Using the Internet, classify the following models as hydrologic, hydraulic, or both: HEC-HMS, HEC-RAS, SWMM, TR-55, and FLDWAV. Provide a brief description of each model and how the model should be used.

3 Wastewater flows in a rectangular concrete channel 5.0 ft wide and 4.0 ft deep. The design flow is 25 cfs. Find the critical velocity. Also find the slope of the channel if the flow velocity is to be 2.5 fps.

4 A 16-in. sanitary sewer pipe flowing full is expected to carry 5.5 cfs. The n value is 0.011. The minimum flow is $1/12$ that of the maximum. Find the depth and velocity at minimum flow.

5 Domestic wastewater from an area of 350 acres is to be carried by a circular pipe at a velocity not less than 2.5 fps. Manning's $n = 0.013$. The population density is 16 persons per acre. Find the maximum hourly and minimum hourly flows. Determine the pipe size required to handle these flows and the required slope.

6 Water flows in a rectangular concrete channel 9.5 ft wide and 9 ft deep. The channel invert has a slope of 0.10% and the applicable n value is 0.013. The flow carried by the channel is 189 cfs. At an intersection of this channel with a canal, the depth of flow is 7.1 ft. Find the distance upstream to a point where normal depth prevails. Plot the surface profile.

7 A 54-in. sewer ($n = 0.013$) laid on a 0.17% grade carries a flow of 18.5 mgd. At a junction with a second sewer, the sewage depth is 36 in. above the invert. Plot the surface profile back to the point of uniform depth.

8 Determine the minimum velocity and gradient required to transport $3/16$-in. gravel through a 42-in.-diameter pipe, given $n = 0.013$ and $K = 0.05$.

9 Given the following 25-yr record of 24-hr maximum annual stream flows (cfs), plot on log-probability paper (or in a spreadsheet program) these values versus the percent of years during which runoff was equal to or less than the indicated value. Find the peak flow expected on the average of (a) once every 5 yr, (b) once every 15 yr.

220	196	89	53	47
200	129	76	50	38
218	142	62	52	36
199	127	67	49	32
180	118	54	47	28

10 Given the following unit storm, storm pattern, and unit hydrograph determine the composite hydrograph.

Unit storm = 1 unit of rainfall for 1 unit of time

Actual storm	(time units)	1	2	3	4
Pattern	(rainfall units)	1	43	56	4

Unit hydrograph: triangular with base length of 4 time units, time of rise of 1 time unit, and maximum ordinate of $1/2$ rainfall unit height.

11 Given a unit rainfall duration of 1 time unit, an effective precipitation of 1.5 in., and the following hydrograph and storm sequence determine (a) the unit hydrograph and (b) the hydrograph for the given storm sequence.

Storm Sequence

Time units	1	2	3	4
Precipitation (in.)	0.4	1.2	1.7	0.9
		1.1	1.8	

Hydrograph

Time units	1	2	3	4	4.5	5	6
Flow (cfs)	101	96	218	512	610	580	460
Time units	7	8	9	10	11	12	13
Flow (cfs)	320	200	180	100	86	60	50

12 Repeat Problem 11, using the following storm sequence:

Time units	1	2	3	4
Precipitation (in.)	0.5	1.1	1.8	0.8

13 Determine the discharge of a trapezoidal channel having a brick bottom and grassy sides with the following dimensions: depth—5 ft, bottom width—12 ft, top width—16 ft. Assume $S = 0.001$.

14 Assuming that the local stormwater manual states that the velocity in grassy channels cannot exceed 2 fps, can the channel designed in Problem 13 be considered stable?

15 Determine the discharge of a rectangular channel built of concrete with the following dimensions: depth—6 ft, bottom width—10 ft. Assume $S = 0.0015$.

16 Given the following data for a 50-year storm, estimate the peak rate of flow to a culvert entrance. Consider the rainfall intensity–duration–frequency curves of Figure 7 applicable. The contributing upstream drainage area is 45 acres. The overland flow distance is 180 ft and the average land slope is 2.5%. The land use of the overland flow portion of the drainage area is lawns, sandy soil. The land use for the drainage basin is 75% residential, single-family units and 25% lawns, sandy soil with an overall average slope of about 2.7%. A channel leading to the culvert is 1900 ft long with a slope of 0.012 ft/ft. The grassed channel is trapezoidal with a bottom width of 5 ft and side slopes of 2 ft vertical to 1 ft horizontal.

17 Given the following data for a 10-year storm, estimate the peak rate of flow to a culvert entrance. Consider the rainfall intensity–duration–frequency curves of Figure 7 applicable. The contributing upstream drainage area is 20 acres. The overland flow distance is 125 ft and the average land slope is 2.5%. The land use of the overland flow portion of the drainage area is lawns, sandy soil. The land use for the drainage basin is 75% residential, multiple units, detached, and 25% lawns, sandy soil with an overall average slope of about 2.7%. A channel leading to the culvert is 2000 ft long with a slope of 0.016 ft/ft. The Manning's n value for the grassed channel is 0.030. The channel is trapezoidal with a bottom width of 3 ft and side slopes of 2 ft vertical to 1 ft horizontal.

18 Rework solved Example 8 for the drainage areas as follows: A1 = 6.5 acres, A2 = 5.4 acres, A3 = 8 acres, and A4 = 9 acres.

19 Rework solved Example 8 for the following pipe slopes: M1 − M2 = 0.025 ft/ft, M2 − M3 = 0.035 ft/ft, and M3 to outfall = 0.04 ft/ft.

20 Rework solved Example 8, using the areas in Problem 18 above and the slopes in Problem 19.

21 Compute, by the rational method, the design flows for the pipes shown in the accompanying sketch: I-1 to M-4, M-4 to M-3, M-3 to M-2, M-2 to M-1, and M-1 to outfall. A-1 = 2.1 acres, c_1 = 0.5; A-2 = 3.0 acres, c_2 = 0.4; A-3 = 4.1 acres, c_3 = 0.7. Pipe flow times are I-1 to M-3, 1 min, and M-3 to M-1, 1.5 min.

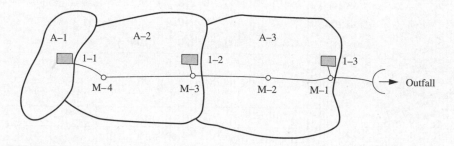

22 A watershed of 90 acres has a t_c of 25 min and a runoff coefficient of 0.6. Consider that a rainstorm having an average intensity of 2.0 in./hr and a duration of 40 min occurs over the watershed. Use the modified rational method to develop a storm hydrograph.

23 A 45-min rainstorm occurs on a 9-acre urban area having a runoff coefficient of 0.7. The time of concentration has been calculated as 20 min. Incremental rainfall depths for the storm are given in the table below. Using a spreadsheet, calculate the runoff from the storm at 5-minute intervals. Plot the resulting hydrograph.

Time (min)	Incremental Rainfall Depth (in.)
0	0
5	0.1
10	0.18
15	0.29
20	0.6
25	0.64
30	0.51
35	0.3
40	0.17
45	0.07
50	0
55	0
60	0
65	0
70	0

24 Given the data below, design a section of sanitary sewer to carry these flows at a minimum velocity of 2.5 fps. Assume that the minimum depth of the sewer below the street must be 8.5 ft and that an *n* value of 0.013 is applicable. Make a plan and profile drawing. (*Note:* The invert into Manhole F must be 937 ft. Assume an invert drop of 0.2 ft across each manhole.)

Manholes	Distance Between Manholes (ft)	Flow (gpm)	Street Elevations at Manholes (ft)
A to B	180	1200	A—978
B to C	300	1450	B—972
C to D	450	2200	C—964
D to E	300	2500	D—958
E to F	400	3000	E—954
			F—949

25 For an inlet area of 2.5 acres having an imperviousness of 0.50 and a clay soil, find the peak rate of runoff for the 5-, 10-, and 20-yr storms.

26 Using the manhole spacing–elevation data given in Problem 21 and the data below, design a storm drainage system such that Manhole A is at the upper end of the drainage area and Manhole F is replaced by an outfall to a stream. The outfall invert elevation is equal to 940.3 ft. Design for the 5-yr storm.

Inflow Point	Incremental Area Contributing to Inflow Point (acres)	Imperviousness of Areas (%)
A to B	3.0	41
B to C	2.7	50
C to D	5.3	55
D to E	3.6	45
Total area = 14.6 acres		

27 Given the following storm pattern, unit storm, and unit hydrograph determine the composite hydrograph.

Unit storm = 1 in. effective rainfall in 1 hr

Actual Storm Pattern	Time	Volume of Effective Rainfall (in.)
	1:00	2
	2:00	2.5
	3:00	7
	4:00	3

Unit hydrograph (triangular) with base length = 5 hr, time to peak flow = 1.5 hr, and maximum ordinate = 0.4 in./hr.

28 Using the derived unit hydrograph from Example 4, calculate the storm hydrograph for the following rainstorm pattern: time unit 1, rainfall = 1 in.; time unit 2, rainfall = 3 in.; time unit 3, rainfall = 2 in. Assume the storm data are effective rainfall.

29 The following hydrograph was measured on a creek for a storm that produced 1.9 in. of rainfall in 2 hr. Losses due to depression storage, infiltration, and interception amounted to 0.4 in.

	Time from Beginning of Storm (hr)	Discharge (ft^3/s)
Storm begins	0	73
	6	75
	12	900
	18	3400
	24	4350
	30	2900
	36	1450
	42	600
	48	450
	54	375
	60	250
	66	180
	72	135

A spillway design storm is 10 in. of effective rainfall in 8 hr. Estimate the inflow hydrograph for the design storm.

30 The ordinates of a 2-hr unit hydrograph are given in the following table. Derive a 4-hr unit hydrograph from the 2-hr unit hydrograph by (a) the lagging method and (b) the S-hydrograph method.

Time Unit	2-hr Unit Hydrograph Ordinates
0	0
1	200
2	400
3	300
4	200
5	100
6	0

31 Find the peak hourly flow in mgd and m³/s for a 1500-acre urban area having the following features: domestic flows 100 gpcd, commercial flows 15 gpcd, infiltration 650 gpd/acre, and population density 20 persons per acre.

32 A sewer with a flow of 11 cfs enters Manhole 2. The distance downstream to Manhole 3 is 450 ft. The finished street surface elevation at Manhole 2 is 165.0 ft; at Manhole 3 it is 162.8 ft. Note that the crown of the pipe must be at least 6 ft below the street surface at each manhole. For a Manning's $n = 0.013$, find the required standard size pipe to carry the flow under (a) full flow and (b) one-half full flow. The flow velocity must be at least 2 ft/s and must not exceed 10 ft/s.

33 A sewer system is to be designed for the urban area of Figure 3. Street elevations at manhole locations are shown on the figure. It has been determined that the population density is 50 persons per acre and that the sewage contribution per capita is 100 gpd. In addition, there is an infiltration component of 658 gpad. Local regulations require that no sewers be less than 8 in. in diameter. Assume an n value of 0.013.

34 Given an invert elevation of 105.1 for the pipe leaving M-6 in Figure 3 and using the pipe sizes determined in Problem 29, calculate the invert elevations in and out of M-5 and M-4 if the street elevation at M-5 is 108.95 ft and at M-4 is 106.82 ft.

35 Solve Problem 33 if the population density is 45 persons per acre and the infiltration component is 625 gpad.

36 Find the peak hourly flow in mgd and m³/s for a 700-acre urban area having the following features: domestic flows 100 gpcd, commercial flows 18 gpcd, infiltration 650 gpd/acre, and population density of 25 persons per acre.

37 A sewer with a flow of 8 cfs enters Manhole 2. The distance downstream to Manhole 3 is 380 ft. The finished street surface elevation at Manhole 2 is 135.0 ft; at Manhole 3 it is 133.9 ft. Note that the crown of the pipe must be at least 6 ft below the street surface at each manhole. For a Manning's $n = 0.013$, find the required standard size pipe to carry the flow under (a) full flow and (b) one-half full flow. The flow velocity must be at least 2 ft/s and must not exceed 10 ft/s.

38 Modify the data given in Example 10 so that the initial depth is 0.6 m and the outlet pipe is 10 in. in diameter. Use a spreadsheet to solve the problem.

39 Solve Problem 38 if the inflows given are all increased by 10%.

REFERENCES

[1] G. M. Fair and J. C. Geyer, *Water Supply and Waste-Water Disposal* (New York: Wiley, 1954).

[2] R. S. Gupta, *Hydrology and Hydraulic Systems* (Upper Saddle River, NJ: Prentice Hall, 1989).

[3] H. W. Gehm and J. L. Bregman, eds. *Handbook of Water Resources and Pollution Control* (New York: Van Nostrand Reinhold, 1976).

[4] E. L. Thackston, "Notes on Sewer System Design," unpublished, Vanderbilt University, 1982.

[5] W. Viessman, Jr. and C. Welty, *Water Management: Technology and Institutions* (New York: Harper & Row, 1985).

[6] Metcalf and Eddy, Inc., *Wastewater Engineering* (New York: McGraw-Hill, 1972).

[7] http://www.epa.gov/owow/nps/qa.html

[8] V. Novotny and G. Chesters, *Handbook of Nonpoint Pollution: Sources and Management* (New York: Van Nostrand Reinhold, 1981).

[9] J. A. Lager and W. G. Smith, *Urban Stormwater Management and Technology: An Assessment*, U.S. EPA Rep. No. EPA-670/2-74-040 (Washington, DC, 1975).

[10] L. K. Sherman, "Streamflow from Rainfall by the Unit Hydrograph Method," *Eng. News-Record* 108 (1932): 501–505.

[11] W. Viessman, Jr. and G. L. Lewis, *Introduction to Hydrology*, 5th ed. (Upper Saddle River, NJ: Prentice Hall, 2003).

[12] R. K. Linsley, Jr., M. A. Kohler, and J. L. H. Paulhus, *Applied Hydrology* (New York: McGraw-Hill, 1949), 387–411, 444–464.

[13] B. S. Barnes, "Consistency in Unitgraphs," *Proc. Am. Soc. Civil Engrs., J. Hydraulics Div.* 85 (August 1959): 39–61.

[14] C. F. Izzard, "Hydraulics of Runoff from Developed Surfaces," *Proc. Highway Res. Bd.* 26 (1946): 129–150.

[15] J. C. Schaake, *Report No. XI of the Storm Drainage Research Project* (Baltimore: The Johns Hopkins University, Department of Sanitary Engineering, September 1963).

[16] Federal Aviation Administration, "Circular on Airport Drainage," Report A/C 050-5320-5B (Washington, DC, 1970).

[17] J. C. Y. Guo, *Urban Storm Water Design*, Water Resources Publications, LLC (Highlands Ranch, CO, 2003).

[18] *The Design of Storm Water Inlets* (Baltimore: The Johns Hopkins University, Department of Sanitary Engineering and Water Resources, June 1956).

[19] *Baltimore County Department of Public Works Design Manual* (Towson, MD: Baltimore County Department of Public Works, 1998).

[20] T. W. Sturm, *Open Channel Hydraulics* (New York, NY: McGraw-Hill, 2001).

[21] Watershed Management Institute, Inc., "Final Project Report: Ecological Effects of Stormwater and Stormwater Control on Small Streams," Cooperative Agreement CX824446 (Washington, DC, 1970).

[22] J. A. Lager, et al., *Urban Stormwater Management and Technology, Update and Users Guide*, U.S. EPA Rep. No. EPA-600/8-77-014 (Washington, DC, 1977).

[23] Watershed Management Institute, Inc., "Operations, Maintenance, & Management of Stormwater Management Systems," (Ingleside, Maryland and Crawfordville, Maryland, August 1997).

[24] P. B. Bedient and W. C. Huber, *Hydrology and Floodplain Analysis* (Upper Saddle River, NJ: Prentice Hall, 2002).

[25] R. L. Daugherty, J. G. Franzini, and E. J. Finnemore, *Fluid Mechanics with Engineering Applications* (New York: McGraw-Hill, 1985).

[26] R. W. Hornbeck, *Numerical Methods* (Upper Saddle River, NJ: Prentice Hall, 1982).

[27] Task Committee on Sustainability Criteria, Water Resources Planning and Management Division, American Society of Civil Engineers and the Working Group of UNESCO/IHP IV Project M-4.3, *Sustainability Criteria for Water Resources Systems* (Reston, VA: American Society of Civil Engineers, 1998).

[28] Prince George's County, Maryland, "Low-Impact Development Design Strategies: An Integrated Design Approach," Department of Environmental Resources Programs and Planning Division (Largo, Maryland, June 1999).

[29] U.S. Environmental Protection Agency, "Low Impact Development (LID): A Literature Review," EPA 841-B-00-005, Office of Water (Washington, DC, October 2000).

Water Quality

MICROBIOLOGICAL QUALITY

A variety of pathogens are present in domestic wastewater, with the kinds and concentrations relating to the health of the contributing community. Although conventional wastewater treatment reduces pathogens, even after chlorination the effluent still contains persistent pathogens. (For unrestricted water reuse, filtration after chemical coagulation and disinfection for an extended time are necessary to remove all pathogens.) Thus, surface waters downstream from wastewater discharges may contain pathogens, and water treatment must remove these pathogens. Since testing water samples for pathogens is not practical, nonpathogenic fecal coliform bacteria are used as indicators for the potential presence of pathogens. The following sections discuss waterborne diseases and coliform bacteria as indicator organisms.

1 WATERBORNE DISEASES

Many human diseases are transmitted by consumption of or even contact with water contaminated by the feces of an infected person. In addition, some pathogens may reinfect people who inhale dust or aerosol droplets, and a few (notably hookworm) can penetrate through the skin. Some of these communicable diseases are endemic in form; that is, they are constantly present in a particular region or country. The four major groups of pathogens are viruses, bacteria, protozoa, and helminths (worms).

Pathogens Excreted in Human Feces

Viruses are obligate, intracellular parasites that replicate only in living hosts' cells. They are composed of only complex organic compounds and lack the metabolic systems for self-reproduction. Enteric viruses range in size (20–100 nm, about $\frac{1}{50}$ the size of bacterial cells), and require electron microscopy for viewing. Human feces contain over 130 serotypes of enteric viruses. Of those, the groups listed in Table 1 are most likely to be transmitted by water. Persons infected by ingesting these viruses do not

Water Quality

TABLE 1 Typical Pathogens Excreted in Human Feces

Pathogen Group and Name	Associated Diseases	Category for Transmissibility[a]
Virus:		
Adenoviruses	Respiratory, eye infections	I
Caliciviruses	Diarrhea	I
Enteroviruses		
Polioviruses	Aseptic meningitis, poliomyelitis	I
Echoviruses	Aseptic meningitis, diarrhea, respiratory infections	I
Coxsackie viruses	Aseptic meningitis, herpangina, myocarditis	I
Hepatitis A virus	Infectious hepatitis	I
Rotaviruses	Gastroenteritis	I
Other viruses	Gastroenteritis, diarrhea	I
Bacterium:		
Campylobacter	Gastroenteritis	II
Legionella pneumophila	Pneumonia	II
Salmonella typhi	Typhoid fever	II
Salmonella paratyphi	Paratyphoid fever	II
Other salmonellae	Gastroenteritis	II
Shigella spp.	Bacillary dysentery	II
Vibrio cholerae	Cholera	II
Other vibrios	Diarrhea	II
Yersinia enterocolitica	Gastroenteritis	II
Protozoan:		
Giardia lamblia	Diarrhea	I
Crytosporidium spp.	Diarrhea	I
Entamoeba histolytica	Amoebic dysentery	I
Helminth:		
Ancylostoma duodenale (Hookworm)	Hookworm	III
Ascaris lumbricoides (Roundworm)	Ascariasis	III
Hymenolepis nana (Dwarf tapeworm)	Hymenolepiasis	I
Necator americanus (Hookworm)	Hookworm	III
Strongyloides stercoralis (Threadworm)	Strongyloidiasis	III
Trichuris trichiura (Whipworm)	Trichuriasis	III

[a] I = Nonlatent, low infective dose
II = Nonlatent, medium to high infective dose, moderately persistent
III = Latent and persistent

Source: Adapted from R.G. Feachem, D.J. Bradley, H. Garelick, and D. D. Mara, *Sanitation and Disease, Health Aspects of Excreta and Wastewater Management; World Bank Studies in Water Supply and Sanitation 3* (Chichester: Wiley, 1983), and G. Bitton, *Wastewater Microbiology* (Wiley, 1994)

always become ill, but disease is a possibility in persons infected with any of the enteric viruses, particularly the hepatitis A virus. Several diseases involving the central nervous system, and more rarely the skin and heart, are caused by enteroviruses. Waterborne outbreaks of infectious hepatitis have occurred, but the most common route of transmission is by person-to-person contact. Infectious hepatitis may cause diarrhea and jaundice, and result in liver damage. Human beings are the reservoir for all of the enteric viruses.

Bacteria are microscopic single-celled organisms that use soluble food and are capable of self-reproduction without sunlight. Their approximate range in size is 0.5–5 μm (500–5000 nm). The feces of healthy persons contain 1 to 1000 million of each of the following groups of bacteria per gram: enterobacteria, enterococci, lactobacilli, clostridia, bacteroides, bifidobacteria, and eubacteria. *Escherichia coli*, the common fecal coliform, is in the enterobacteria group. For many bacterial infections of the intestines, the major symptom is diarrhea. The most serious bacterial waterborne diseases are typhoid fever, paratyphoid fever, dysentery, and cholera. Typhoid and paratyphoid result in high fever and infection of the spleen, gastrointestinal tract, and blood. Dysentery causes diarrhea, bloody stools, and sometimes fever. Cholera symptoms are diarrhea, vomiting, and dehydration. While all of these diseases are debilitating and can cause death if untreated, their transmission can be controlled by effective treatment, disinfection and proper disposal of wastewater, and effective treatment and disinfection of water supplies.

Protozoa infecting humans are intestinal parasites that replicate in the host and exist in two forms. Trophozoites live attached to the intestinal wall where they actively feed and reproduce. At some time during the life of a trophozoite, it releases and floats through the intestines while making a morphological transformation into a cyst, or oocyst, for protection against the harsh environment outside of the host. This cyst form is infectious for other persons by the fecal–oral route of transmission. The cysts are 5–15 μm in size, significantly larger than intestinal bacteria. The most common protozoal diseases are diarrhea and dysentery (Table 1). *Entamoeba histolytica* causes amoebic dysentery that is severely debilitating to the human host. *Giardia lamblia* causes the less severe gastrointestinal infection of giardiasis, resulting in diarrhea, nausea, vomiting, and fatigue. *Cryptosporidium* species cause diarrhea with variable severity. While many infected persons have mild, nonspecific symptoms, others have prolonged diarrhea with accompanying weight loss. In persons with immunodeficiency syndrome, serious diarrhea can cause life-threatening illness. Both humans and animals can serve as sources of both of these infectious protozoans.

Helminths are intestinal worms that (except for *Strongyloides*) do not multiply in the human host. Therefore, the worm burden in an infected person is directly related to the number of infective eggs ingested. The worm burden is also related to the severity of the infected person's disease symptoms. Eggs are excreted in the host's feces. Of the helminths listed in Table 1, most can be transmitted by ingestion of contaminated water or food after a latent period of several days. Hookworms live in the soil and, after molting, can infect humans by penetrating their skin. A heavy worm infection produces symptoms like anemia, digestive disorder, abdominal pain, and debility. Helminth eggs are commonly 40–60 μm in length and denser than water.

Human carriers exist for all enteric diseases. Thus, in communities where a disease is endemic, some of the healthy persons excrete pathogens in feces. In some infections, the carrier condition may cease along with symptoms of the illness, but in others it may persist for months, years, or a lifetime. The carrier condition exists for most bacterial and viral infections, including the dreaded diseases of cholera and infectious hepatitis. The asymptomatic carriers of *Entamoeba histolytica* and *Giardia lamblia* are primarily responsible for continued transmission of these intestinal protozoa. In light helminthic infections, the human host may have only minor symptoms of illness while passing eggs in feces for more than a year.

Factors Affecting Transmission of Diseases

The transmission of waterborne diseases is influenced by latency, persistence, and infective dose of the pathogens. *Latency* is the period of time between excretion of a pathogen and its becoming infective to a new host. No excreted viruses, bacteria, or protozoa have a latent period. Among the helminths, only a few have eggs or larvae passed in feces that are immediately infectious to humans. The majority of helminths require a distinct latent period either for eggs to develop to the infectious stage or to pass through an intermediate form to complete their life cycles. For example, *Ascaris lumbricoides* has a latency of 10 days and hookworms have a latency of about 7 days. *Persistence* is measured by the length of time that a pathogen remains viable in the environment outside a human host. Persistent microorganisms can follow a long route—for example, through a wastewater treatment system—and still infect persons located remotely from the original host. In general, persistence increases from bacteria, the least persistent, to protozoa, to viruses, to helminths, whose persistence is measured in months. *Infective dose* is the number of organisms that must be ingested to result in disease. Usually, the minimum infective doses for viruses and protozoa are low and less than for bacteria, while a single helminth egg or larva can infect. Median infective dose is the dose required to infect half of those persons exposed [1].

The transmission characteristics of pathogens can be categorized based on latency, persistence, and infective dose, as shown in the right column of Table 1. Category I infections have a low median infective dose (less than 100) and are infective immediately upon excretion. These infections are transmitted person to person where personal and domestic hygiene are poor. Therefore, control of these diseases requires improvements in personal cleanliness and environmental sanitation, including food preparation, water supply, and wastewater disposal. Category II infections include all bacterial diseases having a medium to high median infective dose (greater than 10,000) and are less likely to be transmitted by person-to-person contact than category I infections. Control measures include those given for category I; for category II, wastewater collection, treatment, and reuse are of greater importance, particularly if personal hygiene and living standards are high enough to reduce person-to-person transmission. Category III contains soil-transmitted helminths that are both latent and persistent. Their transmission is less related to personal cleanliness since these helminth eggs are not immediately infective to human beings. Most relevant is the cleanliness of vegetables grown in fields exposed to human excreta by reuse of wastewater for irrigation and sludge for fertilization. Effective wastewater treatment is necessary to remove helminth eggs, and sludge stabilization is necessary to inactivate the removed eggs.

Waterborne Diseases in the United States

Waterborne disease outbreaks are not a major cause of illness in the United States. The number of outbreaks reported during the 35-year period of 1946–1980 was 672, and they affected more than 150,000 persons [2]. Based on a served population of 150 million, this is only an average illness rate of 4400 persons throughout the country or about 1 per 34,000 persons per year. During the 15-year period of 1981–1996, 156 outbreaks occurred in the 54,000 community water systems for an average of 1.9 per 10,000 systems per year, and 148 outbreaks occurred in 150,000 noncommunity systems for an average of 0.7 per 10,000 systems per year [3]. The cases of illness from the outbreaks of all water systems during the period 1981–1996 was approximately 500,000 persons, which is extraordinarily high because of outbreaks of waterborne crytosporidiosis and giardiasis in large systems in 1993 and 1994. In the eight-year period from 1997 to 2004 there were 117 waterborne disease outbreaks associated with drinking water, causing about 7900 illnesses and 13 deaths.

The causative agent was determined in half of the waterborne disease outbreaks reported prior to 1997 and in 67% of the outbreaks from 1997 to 2004. The most common identified bacterial diseases were gastroenteritis (salmonellosis) and dysentery (shigellosis). Gastroenteritis is an inflammation of the membrane lining the stomach and intestines, and dysentery is diarrhea with bloody stools and sometimes fever. The most serious viral disease identified as waterborne is infectious hepatitis, resulting in loss of appetite, fatigue, nausea, and pain. The most characteristic feature of the disease is a yellow color that appears in the white of the eyes and skin, hence the common name jaundice. None of the outbreaks of waterborne infectious hepatitis have occurred in municipal water systems. For 1991 and 1992, 34 disease outbreaks associated with drinking water were reported, affecting an estimated 17,000 persons [4]. Five of the 34 were in community systems and the remaining 29 in campgrounds, resorts, recreation areas, restaurants, and private systems. Of the 11 outbreaks for which an etiologic agent was determined, a protozoal parasite (*Giardia lamblia* or *Cryptosporidium*) was identified in seven. The remaining 4 were hepatitis A, *Shigella sonnei*, or chemicals. For 1993 and 1994, 30 outbreaks associated with drinking water were reported, affecting an estimated 405,000 persons [5]. This unusually large number of affected persons was the result of 403,000 cases of gastrointestinal illness in a large city resulting from *Cryptosporidium parvum* in the lake-water source. Oocysts were identified in both the raw and treated waters. Failure of adequate chemical coagulation and filtration was primarily attributed to inadequate operation, even though the treated water met all existing state and federal water quality standards in effect at that time. Of the 25 outbreaks for which an etiologic agent was determined, 10 were caused by *Giardia lamblia* or *Cryptosporidium parvum*, 8 were caused by chemical poisoning, 3 by *Campylobacter jejuni*, 2 by *Shigella* spp., and 1 each by *Vibrio cholerae* and *Salmonella*. Eight of the outbreaks occurred in community systems and the remainder in private homes, resorts, and other noncommunity establishments.

Giardiasis is a common waterborne protozoal disease characterized by diarrhea that usually lasts one week or more and that may be accompanied by abdominal cramps, bloating, flatulence, fatigue, and weight loss. A unique feature of giardiasis is transmission to humans through beavers serving as amplifying hosts. In mountainous regions, beavers have been infected by upstream contamination with human excreta containing *G. lamblia*. After being infected, they return millions of cysts to the water for every one ingested, amplifying the number of *Giardia* cysts in clear mountain streams. Outbreaks of disease have occurred in downstream resorts and towns where the water supplies withdrawn from these streams were not properly treated to remove the cysts.

Cryptosporidiosis is mild to profuse and watery diarrhea for which no effective remedial treatment is known. Depending on the immune competency and health status of a sick person, *Cryptosporidium* can produce a continuum of deviations from normal diarrhea disease and require hospitalization. *Cryptosporidium* oocysts have been found in surface waters contaminated by runoff containing cattle and sheep feces; hence, waterborne disease in humans has been attributed to infected livestock. As with *Giardia* cysts, oocysts are persistent in nature and much more resistant to chlorination than are bacteria and viruses. Removal of oocysts in water treatment requires effective chemical coagulation and granular-media filtration. As an aside, these two parasitic diseases are also readily transmitted by contaminated food, resulting in traveler's diarrhea, and many reported cases are from person-to-person transmission, e.g., among diapered children and workers at day-care centers.

Although all of these waterborne gastrointestinal diseases can stress sensitive individuals, they are not like the dreaded bacterial diseases of cholera and typhoid that resulted in hundreds of deaths per year in the United States during the early years of the twentieth century. "During the 35-year period of 1946–1980 the rate (of deaths resulting from waterborne disease outbreaks) has been reduced to one death per year." [2] If the deaths of 50 to 100 persons in 1993 and 1994 from waterborne outbreaks of cryptosporidiosis and giardiasis are included, the rate of deaths during the 55-year period of 1946–2000 is only two deaths per year for the average population over that period of approximately 200 million.

2   COLIFORM BACTERIA AS INDICATOR ORGANISMS

Public water supplies, reclaimed waters, and wastewater effluents are not tested for pathogens to determine microbiological quality. Laboratory analyses for pathogens are difficult to perform and quantitatively unreliable, and for some pathogenic microorganisms, they are impossible to perform. Therefore, the microbial quality is based on testing for an indicator organism, i.e., a microorganism whose presence is evidence that the water has been polluted with feces of humans or other warm-blooded animals, and may therefore contain pathogens.

The coliform group of bacteria reside in the human intestinal tract and are excreted in large numbers in feces, averaging about 50 million coliforms per gram. Untreated domestic wastewater generally contains more than 3 million coliforms per 100 ml. Pathogenic microorganisms causing enteric diseases in humans originate from fecal discharges of diseased persons. Consequently, water contaminated by fecal pollution is identified as being potentially dangerous by the presence of coliform bacteria. Hence, coliform bacteria are indicator organisms of fecal contamination and the possible presence of pathogens. Nevertheless, some genera of the coliform group of bacteria found in water and soil are not of fecal origin but grow and reproduce on organic matter outside the intestines of humans and animals. These coliforms indicate neither fecal contamination nor the possible presence of pathogens. In laboratory testing, the term *total coliforms* refers to coliform bacteria from feces, soil, or other origin, and *fecal coliforms* refers to coliform bacteria from human or warm-blooded animal feces. Tests for total coliforms (see section 12), fecal coliforms, and *Escherichia coli* are within the capability of the majority of water microbiology laboratories. The procedures are well established and laboratory equipment and supplies are readily available from vendors. Occasionally, false positives result from inadvertent contamination of a water sample during collection. Also interference from *Klebsiella* organisms, which respond as coliform bacteria in testing, gives a false indication of contamination caused by presence of biological organic carbon in distribution piping. Approximately 15% of *Klebsiella* are thermotolerant and can result in a false positive test for the presence of fecal coliforms [6]. Testing drinking water for *Escherichia coli* (*E. coli*) by the presence–absence test is recommended as the preferred and most specific indicator of microbiological drinking water quality. Sterile reagents and apparatus for the Colilert® technique are available, making the test for *E. coli* easy to perform.

The reliability of coliform bacteria to indicate the presence of pathogens in water depends on the persistence of the pathogens relative to coliforms. For pathogenic bacteria, the die-off rate is greater than for coliforms outside the intestinal tract of humans. Thus, exposure in the water environment reduces the number of pathogenic bacteria relative to coliform bacteria. Viruses, protozoan cysts, and helminth eggs are more persistent than coliform bacteria. For example, the threshold chlorine residual effective as a bactericide may not inactivate enteric viruses, is ineffective in killing protozoan cysts, and cannot harm helminth eggs. In contrast, filtration through natural sand aquifers for a sufficient distance, or granular media in a treatment plant after chemical coagulation, can entrap cysts and eggs because of their relatively large size while allowing viruses to be carried through, suspended in the water. In surface water treatment, coliforms are a reliable indicator of the safety of the processed water for human consumption, provided the treatment includes chemical coagulation and filtration to remove cysts, eggs, and suspended matter and effective disinfection of the clear water to inactivate viruses and kill bacteria. In a similar manner, coliforms can be used as an indication of water quality for reuse of reclaimed wastewater, provided the treatment processes physically remove the persistent protozoal cysts and helminth eggs.

E. coli O157 : H7, which is pathogenic to humans, is an antibiotic-resistant mutant strain found in the feces of infected cattle. The primary transmission is through contaminated ground beef, raw milk, unpasteurized fruit juices, and through person-to-person transmission. The only documented U.S. waterborne outbreak of *E. coli* O157 : H7 (with 243 case patients and four deaths) occurred in 1987 in a community with a population of 2090 [7]. Contamination of the water was attributed to wastewater entering distribution piping during repair of water-main breaks.

Drinking Water Standards

The Safe Drinking Water Act (SDWA), initially enacted in 1974, authorizes the EPA to establish comprehensive national regulations to ensure the drinking water quality of public water systems [8]. The following are the three categories of public water systems.

A community water system serves at least 25 people at their primary residences (or at least 15 primary residences). Examples are a municipality, mobile home park, and homeowner subdivision. A nontransient–noncommunity water system regularly serves at least 25 of the same people for at least six months per year but not at their primary residences. Examples are schools, commercial facilities, or manufacturing plants that have their own water systems. A transient–noncommunity water system serves 25 or more people for at least 60 days per year but not the same people or not on a regular basis. Examples are highway rest areas, recreation areas, gas stations, and motels that have their own water available for employees and the public.

The Total Coliform Rule in the SDWA specifies a maximum contaminant level goal (MCLG) of zero for total coliforms, fecal coliforms, and *E. coli*. The Surface Water Treatment Rule specifies an MCLG of zero for *Giardia lamblia*, *Cryptosporidium* species, enteric viruses, and *Legionella*. (MCLG is a nonenforceable, health-based goal set at a level with an adequate margin of safety to ensure no adverse effect on human health.)

The maximum contaminant level (MCL) for coliforms allows for a limited number of positive samples because of inadvertent contamination, but not for fecal coliforms and *E. coli*. (The MCL is an enforceable standard set as close to the MCLG as feasible using best available treatment technology and taking cost and analytical capability into consideration.) Coliform bacteria are common in the natural environment—for example, on dirty water faucets, on the hands of the person collecting the water sample, and in dust and soil. Even with careful sampling procedures, an occasional water sample is likely to test positive for coliform bacteria of nonfecal origin. When a positive test occurs, multiple repeat samples are required to identify whether the contamination is actual or inadvertent, and the positive sample is tested further to determine if the coliforms are fecal coliforms.

The number of water samples tested for monitoring a public water supply is based on the population served on a sliding scale. For example, for a population up to 1000, one sample per month is required; for a population of 100,000, 100 samples per month are required; for a population of 1,000,000, 300 samples per month are required. For a population under 33,000, only one sample may test positive per month for total coliforms for no violation and, above 33,000, no more than 5.0% may test positive. Violation of this MCL requires public notification and an evaluation to determine the source of contamination and risk of contamination with pathogens.

The Safe Drinking Water Act rules also specify the disinfection treatment of public water supplies in addition to the coliform MCL of the water in the distribution system. The regulations on treatment technique are to ensure removal of pathogens more persistent than coliform bacteria during treatment. Strictly speaking, the coliform standard for drinking water applies only after proper treatment and disinfection of water supplies.

Wastewater Effluent Standards

Conventional treatment removes 99–99.9% of pathogenic microorganisms in the raw wastewater; however, the effluent still contains significant concentrations of excreted viruses, bacteria, protozoan cysts, and helminth eggs. The kinds of pathogens in the wastewater depend on the health of the contributing human population. If discharged to recreational waters, effluents are generally disinfected at chlorine dosages in the range of 8–15 mg/l with a minimum contact time of 30 minutes at peak hourly flow. Satisfactory effluent disinfection is normally defined by an average fecal coliform count of 200 per 100 ml or less. This is a reduction from about 1,000,000 per 100 ml in the biologically treated and settled effluent. The safety of disposing of chlorinated effluent by dilution in surface water is based on the argument that this reduction eliminates the great majority of bacterial pathogens and inactivates large numbers of viruses. In fact, viruses and bacteria may be harbored and protected in suspended organic matter (allowable suspended solids in a secondary effluent is 30 mg/l), and protozoan cysts and helminth eggs are resistant to chlorination.

Adequate disinfection for unrestricted reuse of wastewater effluents requires removal or inactivation of all pathogens. The processes following biological treatment are tertiary filtration to physically remove helminth eggs, protozoan cysts, and suspended solids, and disinfection to inactivate viruses and bacteria. The tertiary scheme may be conventional coagulation–sedimentation–filtration or direct filtration without sedimentation or filter screens and membrane filtration. The subsequent disinfection most commonly requires rapid mixing of the chlorine followed by a long contact time (usually about 2 hr) in a tank simulating plug flow. The common effluent standard for unrestricted reuse for irrigation is 2.2 fecal coliforms per 100 ml and a turbidity of less than 2 NTU (nephelometric turbidity unit).

3 MONITORING DRINKING WATER FOR PATHOGENS

Laboratory tests for pathogenic bacteria, viruses, and protozoans are difficult to perform and generally not quantitatively reproducible. Most utilities have neither qualified personnel nor laboratories equipped to monitor for pathogens. Some large utilities with surface water sources test for *Cryptosporidium* oocysts and *Giardia* cysts at a frequency of a few samples per month. Since pathogens are most likely to enter a distribution system because of a treatment malfunction on an intermittent rather than continuous basis, conducting limited monitoring provides little value as a means of protecting public health. In the case of groundwater, the most likely pathogens are selected species of enteric viruses for which tests are impractical and, for some viruses, impossible to perform. The available methods for detection and identification of human pathogens do not produce credible data for making public health decisions.

"Past experience and data have shown that pathogen monitoring does not and cannot confirm the absolute presence or absence of infectious microorganisms in drinking water. With public health protection at stake, one obvious solution lies in treatment process optimization coupled with source water protection and infrastructure integrity practices." [9]

Testing for Enteric Viruses

Viruses of particular importance in drinking water and reclaimed water are those that infect the gastrointestinal tract of humans and are excreted with feces of infected persons. Testing for these viruses requires extraction, concentration, and identification [3]. The two-stage process of extraction is by pumping a large volume of water, several hundred liters, through an adsorptive filter to increase the probability of virus detection since virus levels are likely to be low. The different techniques used to concentrate the eluate from the filter are microporous filters, chemical adsorption–precipitation, and dialysis. During extraction and concentration, only a portion of the viruses present in the original sample is likely captured. Therefore, to determine the precision of separation, the test procedure must be conducted on samples to which known suspensions of one or more test virus types have been added to a water sample to establish recovery efficiency.

Assay and identification of viruses in sample concentrates rely on viruses as obligate intracellular parasites to multiply in and destroy their host cells. The two major host cell systems are mammalian cell cultures of primate origin and whole animals such as sucking mice. No single universal host system exists for all enteric viruses. A measured portion of virus concentrate is spread on the surface of a cell tissue. Following incubation, the monolayer of host cells is microscopically examined to count the number of plaques. (A *plaque* is a clear area produced by viral destruction of the cells.) Virus concentration in the water sample is expressed as the number of plaque-forming units (PFUs) per liter. Further examination is required to identify the virus type creating a plaque. Precise identification involves recovering viruses from an individual plaque and inoculating them into different cell cultures and assay in mice. Virus assay and identification require a trained virologist working in a specially equipped virology laboratory facility.

Testing for *Giardia* Cysts

The procedure consists of filtration of the water, extraction from the filter material, extract concentration, and microscopic examination by immunofluorescence detection [3]. A large volume of water, several hundred liters, is pumped through a filter with a 1 μm nominal porosity. The *Giardia* cyst is oval, 8 to 18 μm long and 5 to 15 μm wide, and contains two to four nuclei and distinctive axonemes. The retained particles and cysts are eluted, the filter extract is concentrated by centrifugation, and the cysts are separated by flotation. A portion is placed on a membrane filter and stained with an indirect fluorescent antibody and examined using epifluorescent microscopy. Because slide examination requires subjective judgment, extraneous organisms may be misidentified as *Giardia* cysts. As a result, greater confidence should be given to counts of cysts in which appropriate internal structures have been identified rather than counts including empty organisms.

Testing for *Cryptosporidium* Oocysts

The procedure is similar to that of *Giardia* cysts and includes filtration of a large volume of water for extraction, removal of particles and oocysts from the filter, concentration by centrifugation, separation of oocysts from debris, and staining with a fluorescent antibody for microscopic identification. Nevertheless, *Cryptosporidium* oocysts are more difficult to separate because they are less than half the size of *Giardia* cysts and more difficult to distinguish from similarly shaped organisms. The *Cryptosporidium* oocyst is spherical, 4–6 μm in size, and contains four sporozoites.

Case histories reveal that boil-water advisories had been unnecessarily issued in two major cities, resulting in false public health concerns and anxiety among the residents [9]. In one case, the suspected contamination was based on "observed" oocysts in treated water in the distribution pipe network, although no cases of human disease were apparent. In another, algae were misidentified as oocysts in both raw and treated water. Laboratories conducting tests for *Cryptosporidium* oocysts must be audited and approved for quality assurance.

CHEMICAL QUALITY OF DRINKING WATER

The primary drinking water standards, which are approval limits for health, are specified for inorganic chemicals, organic chemicals, radionuclides, and turbidity. Secondary standards that recommend limits for aesthetics include inorganic chemicals, dissolved salts, corrosivity, color, and odor. Risk assessment is the process applied in developing standards for toxic chemicals.

4   ASSESSMENT OF CHEMICAL QUALITY

Treated drinking water can contain trace amounts of toxic chemicals often so low in concentration that predicting an observable effect on human health is difficult. Reliable information on the toxicity to humans of most chemicals is difficult to obtain, since it must usually be based on uncontrolled accidental or occupational exposures. Therefore, data from long-term animal studies are applied to evaluate chronic exposure and carcinogenic risk to humans.

Risk Assessment

Risk assessment is the scientific evaluation of toxic chemicals, human exposure, and adverse health effects. Identification of a hazard results from exploratory studies on laboratory animals or case reports of actual human exposure. Based on the inference of toxicity, dose–response relationships are determined on laboratory animals between specific quantities of the substance and associated physical responses, such as growth of tumors, birth defects, or neurologic deficits. Then follows an evaluation of exposure and assessment. The purpose is to describe the magnitude and duration of exposure to human populations both in the past and anticipated in the future. Finally, a quantitative estimate of risk to humans is predicted from the expected exposure levels by applying a dose–response model. If human exposure data are not available, which is often the case, the quantitative estimate is a hypothetical risk based on dose–response data from studies of laboratory animals.

Risk assessment has been used extensively for estimating the risk of developing cancer [10] and is now being applied to assess risks to development, reproduction, and neurologic functioning. Development effects include embryo and fetal death, growth retardation, and malfunctions. Developmental toxicity studies are very complex, and applying results to risk assessment remains problematic. Also highly complex is reproductive toxicity affecting any event from germ cell formation and sexual functioning in the parents through sexual maturation of the offspring. Neurotoxicity in humans ranges from cognitive, sensory, and motor impairments to immune system deficits. Numerous chemicals, including many pesticides, are known neurotoxins.

EPA maintains a database of potential human health effects from various substances in the environment called the Integrated Risk Information System (IRIS).

Chronic Noncarcinogenic Toxicity

For noncarcinogens and nonmutagens, human exposure should be less than the threshold level causing chronic disease. The acceptable daily intake (ADI) of a noncarcinogenic chemical is defined as the dose anticipated to be without lifetime risk to humans when taken daily, expressed in milligrams of chemical per kilogram of body weight per day. It is an empirically derived value determined by combining exposure knowledge and uncertainty concerning the relative risk of a chemical.

The ADI is based on toxicity data from chronic (long-term) feeding studies of laboratory animals to identify the highest no-observed-adverse-effect level (NOAEL) and the lowest-observed-adverse-effect level (LOAEL). The dosage of a toxin given to laboratory animals is assumed to be physiologically equivalent to humans on the basis of body weight. (Typical weights are 0.3 kg for a rat, 10 kg for a dog, and 70 kg for an adult human.) In other words, the intake per unit body weight of a rat or dog is equated to the intake per unit body weight of a human. After determining the NOAEL or LOAEL in animals, an uncertainty factor (safety factor) is applied to reduce the allowable human intake to account for uncertainties involved in extrapolating from animals to humans. The EPA determines the no-effect level, known as the reference dose (RfD), for chronic or lifetime exposure without significant risk to humans, including adults or sensitive subgroups such as infants, children, pregnant women, the elderly, and immunodeficient persons. Human and/or animal toxicology data are used to calculate the RfD, which is expressed in milligrams per kilogram of body weight per day, as follows:

$$RfD = \frac{NOAEL \text{ or } LOAEL}{\text{uncertainty factor}} \tag{1}$$

The uncertainty factors used in calculating acceptable daily intakes for establishing drinking water standards are a factor of 10 when chronic human exposure data are available and are supported by chronic oral toxicity data in animal species; a factor of 100 when good chronic oral toxicity data are available in some animal species but not in humans; and a factor of 1000 when chronic animal toxicity data are limited [11].

Using the RfD, the drinking water equivalent level (DWEL) is calculated as follows:

$$DWEL \text{ (mg/l)} = \frac{RfD \times \text{body weight (kg)}}{\text{drinking water consumption (l/d)}} \tag{2}$$

The DWEL represents a lifetime exposure with no adverse health effects assuming only exposure from drinking water. For regulatory purposes, a body weight of 70 kg and drinking water consumption rate of 2 l/d are assumed for adults, and a body weight of 10 kg and consumption of 1 l/d are assumed for infants. These values are applied to

Eq. (2). The DWEL is used with a relative source contribution (RSC) factor to establish the MCLG:

$$MCLG = DWEL \times RSC \qquad (3)$$

The RSC, which is the fraction of the total contribution of water to the contaminant intake, accounts for intake by other means such as food, beverages and air.

For example, consider the element cadmium, which is used in electroplating, batteries, and electronic equipment. By oral dose, it causes renal dysfunction, hypertension, and anemia. The NOAEL for rats was established as 0.75 mg/kg·d. From Eqs. (1) and (2) with an uncertainty factor of 1000, the DWEL equals 0.026 mg/l. Then, assuming 20% of the intake apportioned to water (RSC = 0.2), the allowable concentration becomes 0.005 mg/l or 5 μg/l [12].

Carcinogenic Toxicity

The development of cancer appears to have three distinct stages: initiation, promotion, and progression. Each stage is influenced by such factors as age, heredity, diet, metabolic activity, and exposure to carcinogenic chemicals. The most widely used tests for carcinogen evaluation are long-term animal bioassays.

The hazard of ingesting a chemical assessed as a confirmed or suspected carcinogen can be evaluated in terms of dose-related risk. The two major problems in assessing risk are (1) extrapolation from observed risks in relatively high exposure levels used in laboratory animal studies to the low levels of exposure in humans and (2) extrapolation of the estimated risk from laboratory animals to humans. The assessment based on high-dose animal bioassay to low-dose human exposure further suffers from a lack of basic knowledge concerning the disease process in animals and humans and the total lack of data regarding potential synergistic and antagonistic reactions of chemicals.

The estimate of risk from results of animal bioassays is made by first converting the laboratory animal dose to the physiologically equivalent human dose. One method of conversion is on the basis of relative skin areas of test animals and the human body. This is justified from the observation that effects of acute toxicity in humans on a dose per unit of body surface area are in the same range as those in experimental animals [10]. The linearized multistage mathematical model, based on the one-hit theory of cancer initiation, is generally used for low-dose risk estimation [10]. Although its application cannot be proved or disproved by current scientific data, it is considered the best available model that yields an estimate of risk representing a plausible upper limit. The actual risk is not likely to be higher than the risk predicted by this model.

For example, consider the insecticide lindane, which is related to tumorigenic effects observed in laboratory mice and neurologic impairment in humans. The risk estimate in humans at a concentration in drinking water of 1.0 μg/l and daily consumption of 1 l/d is between 3.3×10^{-6} and 8.1×10^{-6} [10]. (Most experts agree that current technologies for assessing cancer and neurotoxicity risk cannot generate a single precise estimate of human risk, and risks are best expressed in terms of ranges or confidence intervals.) The upper 95% confidence estimate of risk at the same chemical dose is from 5.6×10^{-6} to 13×10^{-6}. These risk estimates are expressed as the probability of cancer after a lifetime consumption of 1 liter of water per day containing 1.0 μg/l of chemical. The MCL for lindane is 0.0002 mg/l. With 2.0 l/d water consumption at an MCL of 0.2 μg/l, the numerical risks decrease to 0.4 of the values for 1.0 l/d and 1.0 μg/l. They become 1.3×10^{-6} to 3.2×10^{-6} and 2.2×10^{-6} to 5.2×10^{-6}. The average value of 3.0×10^{-6} means that exposure to lindane at 0.2 μg/l over a 70-yr lifetime would be expected to produce one excess case of cancer for every 340,000 persons exposed.

5 CHEMICAL CONTAMINANTS

The chemicals listed in Table 2 are currently regulated in drinking water by the EPA. Retaining the chemicals on this list and/or the associated maximum contaminant levels depends on the results of ongoing risk assessments. A chemical may be deleted when future studies lack convincing evidence of risk to human health, or the use of the chemical may be banned, resulting in significantly reduced presence in water. On the other hand, new chemicals may be added, resulting from additional risk assessments. In the future, drinking water standards are likely to be flexible, with continuous adjustments to keep up with the changing chemical environment. Current U.S. standards are listed on the EPA web site www.epa.gov/safewater. Individual state standards may be more stringent than the EPA standards.

TABLE 2 Chemical Drinking Water Standards, Maximum Contaminant Levels in Milligrams per Liter

Inorganic Chemicals

Antimony	0.006	Fluoride[b]	4.0
Arsenic	0.01	Lead	TT[a]
Barium	2.	Mercury (inorganic)	0.002
Beryllium	0.004	Nitrate (as N)	10.
Cadmium	0.005	Nitrite (as N)	1.
Chromium (total)	0.1	Nitrate + Nitrite (as N)	10.
Copper	TT[a]	Selenium	0.05
Cyanide	0.2	Thallium	0.002

Asbestos 7 million fibers/liter (longer than 10 μm)

Volatile Organic Chemicals

Benzene	0.005	Ethylbenzene	0.7
Carbon tetrachloride	0.005	Monochlorobenzene	0.1
Chlorobenzene	0.1	Styrene	0.1
Dichloromethane	0.005	Tetrachloroethylene	0.005
p-Dichlorobenzene	0.075	Toluene	1.
o-Dichlorobenzene	0.6	1,2,4-Trichlorobenzene	0.07
1,2-Dichloroethane	0.005	1,1,1-Trichloroethane	0.2
1,1-Dichloroethylene	0.007	1,1,2-Trichloroethane	0.005
cis-1,2-Dichloroethylene	0.07	Trichloroethylene	0.005
trans-1,2-Dichloroethylene	0.1	Vinyl chloride	0.002
Dichloromethane	0.005	Xylenes (total)	10.
1,2-Dichloropropane	0.005		

(continued)

TABLE 2 Continued

Synthetic Organic Chemicals

Acrylamide	TT[a]	Heptachlor	0.0004
Alachlor	0.002	Heptachlor epoxide	0.0002
Atrazine	0.003	Hexachlorobenzene	0.001
Carbofuran	0.04	Hexachlorocyclopentadiene	0.05
Chlordane	0.002	Lindane	0.0002
Dalapon	0.2	Methoxychlor	0.04
Di(2-ethylhexyl)adipate	0.4	Oxamyl (Vydate)	0.2
Dibromochloropropane	0.0002	PAHs [benzo(a)pyrene]	0.0002
Diethylhexyl phthalate	0.006	Pentachlorophenol	0.001
Dinoseb	0.007	Picloram	0.5
Diquat	0.02	Polychlorinated biphenyls	0.0005
Endothall	0.1	Simazine	0.004
Endrin	0.002	2,3,7,8 TCDD (Dioxin)	0.00000003 (3×10^{-8})
Epichlorohydrin	TT[a]	Toxaphene	0.003
Ethylene dibromide	0.00005	2,4-D	0.07
Glyphosate	0.7	2,4,5-TP (Silvex)	0.05

Disinfection By-Products

Bromate	0.01
Chlorite	1.0
Five haloacetic acids (HAA5)	0.060
Total trihalomethanes (TTHM)	0.080

Radionuclides

Beta particle and photon radioactivity	4 mrem/yr
Gross alpha particle activity	15 pCi/l
Radium-226 + Radium-228	5 pCi/l
Uranium	0.03 mg/l

Turbidity

Turbidity[c]	0.3 NTU

[a]Treatment technique (TT) requires modification or improvement of water processing to reduce the contaminant concentration.
[b]Many states require public notification at least annually of fluoride in excess of 2.0 mg/l to warn consumers of potential dental fluorosis.
[c]Turbidity is a performance standard in filtration treatment of surface waters to ensure removal of *Giardia lamblia* cysts and *Cryptosporidium* spp. oocysts.

The MCL is an enforceable standard for protection of human health. Monitoring requirements are established for each contaminant on a prescribed schedule of routine sampling and check sampling to confirm the results if an MCL is exceeded. The frequency of sampling varies from every three years for chemicals in groundwater to every three months for selected chemicals in treated surface waters. Testing is performed in an approved laboratory by specified methods.

Generally, the MCLG for a carcinogenic chemical is zero. Treatment techniques rather than an MCL are specified for selected chemicals, for example, acrylamide and epichlorohydrin. These chemicals are used during water treatment in flocculants to decrease turbidity. The treatment technique requirements limit the concentration of these chemicals in polymers and their application in water treatment.

The regulation of specific MCLs depends on the kind of water system. All of the standards are applicable to community systems and nontransient-noncommunity systems that supply water to the same people for a long period of time, e.g., schools and factories. Transient-noncommunity systems that serve different people for a short time (e.g., campgrounds, parks, and highway rest stops) are required to meet only the MCLs of those contaminants with health effects caused by short-term exposure.

Inorganic Chemicals

The sources of trace metals are associated with the natural processes of chemical weathering and soil leaching and with human activities such as mining and manufacturing. Corrosion in distribution piping and customers' plumbing can also add trace metals to tap water.

Antimony, arsenic, barium, beryllium, cadmium, chromium, mercury, nickel, selenium, and thallium are toxic metals affecting the internal organs of the human body. *Antimony* is a trace metal used as a constituent of alloys and is rare in natural waters. Ingestion affects the blood, decreasing longevity. *Arsenic* is widely distributed in waters at low concentrations, with instances of higher concentrations in groundwater, and is also found in trace amounts in food. It has acute toxic effects and has been linked to cancer of a variety of human organs. *Barium*, one of the alkaline earth metals, occurs naturally in low concentrations in most surface waters and in many treated waters. *Beryllium* is not likely to be found in natural waters in greater than trace amounts because beryllium oxides and hydroxides are relatively insoluble. Soluble beryllium sulfate is transported in the bloodstream to bone, where it induces bone cancer in animals. *Cadmium* can be introduced into surface waters in amounts significant to human health by improper disposal of industrial wastewaters. Nevertheless, the major sources are food, cigarette smoke, and air pollution; hence, the MCL is set so that less than 10% of the total intake is expected to be from drinking water. The health effects of cadmium can be acute, resulting from overexposure at a high concentration, or chronic, caused by accumulation in the liver and renal cortex. *Copper* is commonly found in drinking water. Trace amounts below 20 µg/l can derive from weathering rock, but the principal sources in house water supplies are from corrosion of copper service pipes and brass plumbing fixtures. As an essential element in human nutrition, copper intake is safe and adequate at 1.5 to 3 mg/day. As an indicator of corrosivity, copper has a no-action level of 1.3 mg/l in first-flush samples from household plumbing.

Chromium can exist in water in several valence states. The content in natural waters is extremely low because it is held in rocks in essentially insoluble trivalent forms. Acute systemic poisoning can result from high exposures to hexavalent chromium; trivalent chromium is relatively innocuous. *Mercury* is a scarce element in nature and has been banned for most applications with environmental exposure, such as mercurial fungicides. The biological magnification of mercury in freshwater food fish is the most significant route by which mercury endangers human health. The mercury becomes available in the food chain through the transformation of inorganic mercury to organic methylmercury by microorganisms present in the sediments of lakes and rivers. Toxicity via the oral route is related mainly to methylmercury compounds rather than to inorganic mercury salts or metallic mercury. Symptoms of methylmercury poisoning include mental disturbance, ataxia, and impairment of speech, hearing, vision, and movement. *Selenium* is a trace metal naturally occurring in soils derived from some sedimentary rocks. Surface streams and groundwater in seleniferous regions contain variable concentrations. Cattle grazing on seleniferous vegetation may suffer from "blind staggers." Effects on human health have not been clearly established—a low-selenium diet is beneficial, whereas high doses can produce undesirable physical manifestations.

Lead exposure occurs through air, soil, dust, paint, food, and drinking water. Lead toxicity affects the red blood cells, nervous system, and kidneys, with young children, infants, and fetuses being most vulnerable. Depending on local conditions, the contribution of lead from drinking water can be a minor or major exposure for children. Lead is not a natural contaminant in surface waters or groundwater and is rarely found in source water. It is a corrosion by-product from high lead solder joints in copper piping, old lead-pipe goosenecks connecting the service lines to the water main, and old brass fixtures. Lead pipe and brass fixtures with high lead content are not installed today, and lead-free solder has replaced the old 50% lead–50% tin solder for joining water piping. Since dissolution of lead requires an extended contact time, lead is most likely to be present in tap water that has been in the service connection piping and plumbing overnight. Therefore, the first-flush sample concentration, collected after water remains stagnant in piping for at least 6 hr, is the highest expected, and if it is less than 0.015 mg/l, no corrective action is required.

Fluoride is commonly found in trace amounts in most soil and rock. Groundwater usually contains fluoride ions dissolved from geologic formations while surface waters generally contain smaller amounts, under 0.3 mg/l, except when contaminated by industrial wastes. EPA has set the MCL for fluoride at 4 mg/L to protect from bone disease. A secondary standard of 2 mg/L has been set to prevent dental disease of fluorosis, also referred to as mottling (a discoloration of teeth in children). On the other hand, an absence or low concentration of fluoride in drinking water results in a high incidence of dental caries in children's teeth. The optimum fluoride concentration in drinking water protects teeth from decay without causing noticeable fluorosis. Food is another source of fluoride in the diet; however, as a contributor of fluorides, many studies have shown that the average dietary intake from food is a constant amount throughout the United States. Hence, the dental effect of fluoride results primarily from the concentration in the public water supply. Since water consumption is influenced by climate, the recommended optimum concentrations listed in Table 3 are based on the annual average of the maximum daily air temperatures. Cities with water supplies deficient in natural fluoride have successfully provided supplemental fluoridation to optimum levels to reduce the rate of dental decay in children [13].

Nitrate is the common form of inorganic nitrogen found in water solution. In agricultural regions, heavy fertilizer application results in unused nitrate migrating down into the groundwater. As a result, groundwater withdrawn by private and public wells is likely to have measurable concentrations of nitrate, and in the same regions well waters in many rural communities can exceed the recommended limit of 10 mg/l

TABLE 3   Recommended Optimum Concentrations of Fluoride
           Based on the Annual Average of the Maximum Daily
           Air Temperatures

Temperature Range (°F)	Recommended Optimum (mg/l)
53.7 and below	1.2
53.8 to 58.3	1.1
58.4 to 63.8	1.0
63.9 to 70.6	0.9
70.7 to 79.2	0.8
79.3 to 90.5	0.7

of nitrate-nitrogen. Surface waters can be contaminated by nitrogen from both discharge of municipal wastewater and drainage from agricultural lands. The health hazard of ingesting excessive nitrate in water is infant methemoglobinemia. In the intestine of an infant, nitrate can be reduced to nitrite that is absorbed into the blood and interferes with oxygen transfer, resulting in cyanosis and giving the baby a blue color. Infants under the age of three months are particularly susceptible. Incidents of infant methemoglobinemia are extremely rare since most mothers in regions of known high-nitrate drinking water use either bottled water or a liquid formula requiring no dilution. Healthy adults are able to consume large quantities of nitrate in drinking water without adverse effects. The principal sources of nitrate in the average adult diet are saliva and vegetables, amounting to about 130 mg/day [10]. Justified by epidemiological evidence on the occurrence of methemoglobinemia in infants, the standard of 10 mg/l is the maximum contaminant level for water with no observed adverse health effects.

Organic Chemicals

The EPA groups organic chemicals into three categories, depending on the evidence of carcinogenicity. Category I chemicals are probable human carcinogens, based on human or animal risk assessment, and are assigned MCLGs of zero. Category II chemicals are not regulated as human carcinogens, but the MCLGs are lower than MCLs based on inconclusive evidence of carcinogenicity. Category III chemicals causing chronic disease without evidence of carcinogenicity are given MCLs based on the acceptable daily intake.

The MCLs of chemicals are set as close to the MCLGs as feasible, including the feasibility of laboratory testing. Gas chromatography has high sensitivity and reliability in detecting concentrations down to a few micrograms per liter; therefore, for many carcinogenic and highly toxic chemicals the MCLs are set at the lowest level of quantitative measurement achievable in a good laboratory. For example, several of the volatile organic chemicals considered carcinogens have MCLGs of zero and MCLs of 0.005 mg/l, which is the practical quantitative level of measurement.

Volatile organic chemicals (VOCs) are produced in large quantities for use in industrial, commercial, agricultural, and household activities. The adverse health effects of VOCs include cancer and chronic effects on the liver, kidneys, and nervous system. Because of their volatility, air stripping is a proposed method of removal from water. Volatility also reduces their concentrations in surface waters. Groundwater contamination is more common because VOCs have little affinity for soils and are diminished only by dispersion and diffusion, which is often limited. Those most frequently detected in contaminated groundwaters are trichloroethylene, a degreasing solvent in metal industries and a common ingredient in household cleaning products; tetrachloroethylene, a dry-cleaning solvent and chemical intermediate in producing other compounds; carbon tetrachloride, used in the manufacture of fluorocarbons for refrigerants and solvents; 1,1,1-trichloroethane, a metal cleaner; benzene, used for making plastics, rubber, and synthetic organic chemicals and also a component of gasoline; and vinyl chloride, used in the manufacture of plastics and polyvinyl chloride resins.

Many of the synthetic organic chemicals (SOCs) listed in Table 2 are pesticides, including *insecticides* and *herbicides*. Pesticides may be present in surface waters receiving runoff from either agricultural or urban areas where these chemicals are applied. Groundwaters can be contaminated by pesticides, manufacturing wastewaters, spillage, or infiltration or rainfall runoff and irrigation water. Alachlor, aldicarb, atrazine, carbofuran, ethylene dibromide, and dibromochloropropane have been detected in drinking waters. Most pesticides can be absorbed into the human body through the lungs, skin, and gastrointestinal tract. From acute exposure, the symptoms in humans are dizziness, blurred vision, nausea, and abdominal pain. Chronic exposure of laboratory animals indicates possible neurologic and kidney effects and, for some pesticides, cancer.

Pharmaceutical chemicals, hormones, insect repellants and steroids have been found in wastewater effluents as well as surface water and groundwater. Although standards have not yet been established for these contaminants, there is growing concern regarding their increasing occurrence and health effects.

Disinfection By-Products and Disinfectants

Over 500 disinfection by-products (DBPs) have been reported to occur as a result of disinfection [14]. Disinfection is arguably the most important water treatment process because it is the major barrier to pathogenic microorganisms and the waterborne diseases that they cause. Nevertheless, many DBPs have been associated with cancer and other adverse health effects and accordingly have received much attention in the regulatory and water treatment professional community. The DBPs that are currently regulated by the EPA are shown in Table 2, although this list may be expanded in the future. Four trihalomethanes (THMs) and five haloacetic acids (HAA5) are regulated as groups. THMs and HAA5 are produced by the reaction of natural organic matter (NOM), largely the result of the decay of vegetation, with the disinfectant chlorine and to a much lesser extent with chloramine disinfectants. If the water contains bromide ion, it will be oxidized to bromine by chlorine and then will also form THMs and HAA5.

Monitoring requirements for THMs and HAA5 differ from typical monitoring requirements for other water contaminants because the DBP formation reactions continue throughout the potable water distribution system. A utility must use sampling sites that are typically high in THMs and HAA5 as determined by a detailed evaluation of the distribution system. Running annual averages are calculated from quarterly sampling at each sampling site, and these averages must all meet the respective MCLs to demonstrate compliance (Table 2).

Bromate ion is a DBP formed when the naturally occurring bromide ion reacts with ozone, a disinfectant that has seen increasing use in recent years because it is a better disinfectant than chlorine and does not form THMs or HAA5. Chlorite is a chemical that is used in the preparation of chlorine dioxide, another effective disinfectant that does not produce THMs or HAA5. Chlorine dioxide reactions and decay in the distribution system produce chlorite, and unreacted chlorite from chlorine dioxide generation can also contribute to the total chlorite concentration.

The disinfectants chlorine, chlorine dioxide, and the chloramines are also regulated because high levels over long periods have been shown to damage kidneys and blood. Since these disinfectants are intentionally added to the water their limits are referred to as maximum residual disinfectant levels (MRDLs). The MRDL for chlorine and the chloramines is 4.0 mg/l and for chlorine dioxide is 0.8 mg/L.

Radionuclides

Radioactive elements decay by emitting alpha, beta, or gamma radiation caused by transformation of the nuclei to lower energy states. An alpha particle is the helium nucleus (two protons + two neutrons); e.g., radon-222 decays to polonium-218 and emits helium-4. A beta particle (β^-) is an electron emitted from the nucleus as a result of neutron decay; e.g., radium-228 decays to actinium-228 and emits β^-. In these processes, the loss of the helium nucleus emitted as an alpha particle or the electron ejected as a beta particle changes the parent atom into a different element. A gamma ray is a form of electromagnetic radiation; other forms are light, infrared and ultraviolet radiations, and X-rays. Gamma decay involves only energy loss and does not create a different element. Alpha, beta, and gamma radiations have different energies and masses, thus producing different effects on matter and therefore different effects on the human organs that are irradiated.

The ability to penetrate matter varies among nuclear radiations. Most alpha particles are stopped by a single thickness of paper, while most gamma rays pass through the human body, as do X-rays. Since alpha particles are stopped by short penetrations, more energy is deposited and does more damage per unit volume of matter receiving radiation.

MCLs for radionuclides are shown in Table 2. Note that the uranium MCL is written in terms of a mass concentration (mg/L) as are the MCLs for other contaminants in the table. The other radionuclide limits are written either in terms of the amount of radioactivity per liter of water (pCi/L) or in terms of the effect of radioactivity on the body per liter of water (mrem/L). The nuclei of radionuclides disintegrate at a particular rate, depending on the particular radionuclide, producing radiation in the form of alpha and beta particles and gamma rays. This radiation is measured in terms of the number of disintegrations per time, and a picoCurie (pCi) is equal to 2.22 disintegrations per minute, the rate of decay of one gram of radium. When radiation is absorbed by human tissue, the tissue may be damaged. The amount of radiation absorbed per kilogram of matter is the radiation absorbed dose (RAD). But different types of radiation produce different biological effects in the body. The relative biological effectiveness factor (RBE) accounts for these differences. For example, beta particles may have an RBE of 1, whereas the more damaging alpha particles may have an RBE of 10. The actual RBE depends upon the type and extent of radiation and the tissue in which it is absorbed. The product of absorbed radiation dose (RAD) and the effectiveness of that dose (RBE) gives the effective radiation dose measured in REM. Doses of equal REM are expected to produce the same effect in the body. Although current regulations are given in pCi/L and mrem/L, the SI units for radioactivity and human effects are becquerels per liter (Bq/L) and sieverts/L (Sv/L), respectively. One Bq = 27 pCi, and 1 Sv = 100 rem.

Radioactivity in drinking water can be from natural or artificial radionuclides. Radium-226 is usually found in groundwater as a result of geologic conditions. Radioactivity from radium is widespread in surface waters because of fallout from testing of nuclear weapons. In some localities this radioactivity could be increased by small releases from nuclear power plants and industrial users of radioactive materials. The average amount of background radiation from cosmic rays and terrestrial sources is about 100 mrem/yr [15]. Only a small portion of this unavoidable background radiation comes from drinking water containing radionuclides.

The natural background of radiation can be estimated to cause 4.5–45 fatal cases of cancer per year per million people, depending on the risk model used to make the calculation. Less than 1% of this is attributed to radionuclides in drinking water [10].

A new EPA regulation for radon in drinking water was proposed in 1999, but its promulgation has been delayed. Radon is a radioactive gas (by release of an alpha particle) that is a product of the decay of radium, so when radium in present in the ground, radon is usually present in the soil and groundwater. As a soil gas, radon can migrate upwards and into homes, and this inhalation hazard can be the most significant exposure to radon. The major hazard associated with radon in water is its release into the air, e.g. in a shower, and then inhalation of the gaseous radon. The proposed regulation for radon is 300 pCi/L, but a higher alternate MCL is also proposed in connection with a multimedia mitigation (MMM) program whereby air concentrations of radon will also be addressed and reduced.

Turbidity

Insoluble particulates impede the passage of light through water by scattering and absorbing the rays. This interference of light passage is referred to as turbidity. The turbidity standard is a suspension of silica of specified particle size selected so that a 1.0-mg/l suspension measures as 1.0 nephelometric turbidity unit (NTU). The common method of measurement uses a photoelectric detector and nephelometry to measure the intensity of scattered light. In surface water filtration for treatment of drinking water, turbidity in the filtered water must be equal to or less than 0.3 NTU in at least 95% of the measurements taken each month and must be less than 1.0 NTU at any one sampling event. Measurements are often performed directly in pipes and channels and at a minimum of every 4 hr.

TABLE 4   Recommended Secondary Contaminant Standards for Aesthetics of Drinking Water

Aluminum	0.05 to 0.2 mg/l	Manganese	0.05 mg/l
Chloride	250 mg/l	Odor	3 threshold odor numbers
Color	15 color units	pH	6.5 to 8.5
Copper	1.0 mg/l	Silver	0.1 mg/l
Corrosivity	noncorrosive	Sulfate	250 mg/l
Fluoride	2 mg/l	Total dissolved solids	500 mg/l
Foaming agents	0.5 mg/l	Zinc	5 mg/l
Iron	0.3 mg/l		

Secondary Standards

Standards for aesthetics, listed in Table 4, are recommended limits for characteristics that render the water less desirable for use. They are not related to health hazards and are nonenforceable by the EPA.

Excessive color, foaming, or odor cause customers to question the safety of drinking water and result in complaints from users. Aluminum contributes to color in water, copper has a metallic taste and causes blue-green stain, and zinc has a metallic taste. Excessive dietary intake of silver causes skin discoloration and graying of the white of the eye. Excessive fluoride causes tooth discoloration (see discussion of fluoride under *Inorganic Chemicals*. Chloride or sulfate ion concentrations greater than 250 mg/l, or dissolved solid concentrations greater than 500 mg/l, can have taste and laxative properties. Sodium sulfate and magnesium sulfate are laxatives, with the common names of Glauber salt and Epsom salt, respectively. The laxative effect may be noticed by travelers or new consumers drinking waters high in sulfates; however, most persons become acclimated in a relatively short time. Excessive dissolved salts can also affect the taste of coffee and tea brewed with the water. For persons on a sodium-restricted diet, which is usually 2000 mg of sodium per day, the recommended maximum concentration in their drinking water is 100 mg/l [10]. For a severely restricted diet of 500 mg of sodium per day, the recommended maximum concentration is 20 mg/l of sodium ion.

Iron and manganese above 0.3 mg/l and 0.05 mg/l, respectively, are objectionable because of brown stains imparted to laundry and porcelain and the bittersweet taste of iron. A noncorrosive water with an alkaline pH is desirable to reduce the probability of pipe corrosion contributing iron and other trace metals to the water by dissolution from water mains and plumbing.

QUALITY CRITERIA FOR SURFACE WATERS

The Clean Water Act authorizes the EPA to direct and define natural water pollution control programs [16]. The objective is to maintain the chemical, physical, and biological quality of surface waters, seawater, and groundwater by placing ecological considerations and protection of human health ahead of economic concerns. In 1972, many of the nation's waters were polluted; thus, the initial goals were to reduce discharge of pollutants and achieve an interim water quality to protect fish, shellfish, and wildlife and achieve a water quality for fishing and swimming wherever attainable. Congressional policy was to recognize and preserve the states' primary responsibility to meet these goals. In the original act, the two principal policies were to research, study, and establish water quality standards for surface waters and to prohibit the discharge of toxic pollutants in toxic amounts.

An important amendment to the act was the National Pollutant Discharge Elimination System (NPDES) permit program. Technology-based effluent limits and water quality–based limits backed by surface water quality standards were defined for treatment plants discharging pollutants through a pipe or conveyance. For compliance, the owner of the treatment plant is required to monitor and record discharge data and report any violations. For enforcement, a willful or negligent violator, or one making a false statement or representation regarding a discharge, can be fined and is also subject to possible imprisonment.

The NPDES program for wastewater treatment plants has changed significantly and expanded since its initiation. Specific changes are in the areas of effluent standards, water quality–based permitting, controls of toxic substances, industrial wastewater pretreatment program, new performance standards, inspection and monitoring provisions, and seawater discharge criteria. In addition, several other programs have been incorporated into the NPDES permit system, including the control of combined sewer overflows; use and disposal of waste sludge by regulating management practices and acceptable levels of toxic substances in sludge; and watershed protection strategy to integrate the NPDES to support states' basin management.

6   WATER QUALITY STANDARDS

States are required to develop water quality standards, on a site-specific basis, for all of their surface waters. These should

- Include provisions for restoring and maintaining the chemical, physical, and biological integrity of water supplies.
- Provide, where attainable, water quality for protection and propagation of fish, shellfish, and wildlife and recreation in and on the water ("fishable/swimmable")
- Consider the use and value of waters for public water supplies, propagation of fish and wildlife, recreation, agriculture and industrial purposes, and navigation.

The water quality standards must meet the requirements of the Clean Water Act [16] and water standards regulations [17, 18].

Water quality standards are composed of use classifications, quality criteria, and an antidegradation policy. The classification system is based on expected beneficial water uses including drinking water supplies, recreation, and propagation of fish and wildlife. More specific uses may be designated. Designated uses should support a "fishable/swimmable" classification unless an attainability analysis shows that only subcategories of this designation that require less stringent criteria can be applied.

The second part of standards is the water quality criteria necessary to support the designated uses, which may be both numeric values and narrative statements. The latest criteria that have been developed are best accessed through the EPA web site, www.epa.gov/waterscience/criteria. The aquatic life criteria consist of

- a critical maximum concentration (CMC) – highest concentration to which aquatic life can be exposed briefly without unacceptable effect.
- a criteria continuous concentration (CCC) – highest concentration to which aquatic life can be exposed indefinitely.
- duration over which the concentration of a constituent is averaged for comparison to the CMC and the CCC.
- maximum frequency the CMC and the CCC may be exceeded.

Narrative statements can supplement numeric values or can be the basis for limiting pollutants where no numeric criteria exist. Examples are "free from toxic substances in toxic amounts" and "free of objectionable color, odor, taste, or turbidity."

An antidegradation policy provides three tiers of protection from degradation of water quality:

- Protects existing uses.
- Protects the level of water quality necessary to support propagation of fish, shellfish, and wildlife and recreation in waters that are currently of higher quality than required to support these uses. Before water quality can be lowered, an antidegradation review must be undertaken.
- Protects the quality of outstanding national resources, such as waters of state and national parks, wildlife refuges, and waters of recreational or ecological significance.

Total Maximum Daily Load (TMDL)

The Clean Water Act also requires states to develop lists of impaired waters that do not meet the water quality standards that the states have established. A total maximum daily load (TMDL) for each pollutant of concern must be established for all these waters. A TMDL is the maximum amount of a pollutant that a water body can receive and still meet the water quality standards that the state has set. The TMDL will include a wasteload allocation (WLA) for each point source of contamination, such as a wastewater treatment plant discharge, and a load allocation (LA) for each nonpoint source as well as a margin of safety (MOS) as shown in Equation 4 and Figure 1a.

$$\Sigma \, WLA + \Sigma \, LA + MOS = TMDL \qquad (4)$$

TMDLs can be specified in mass per time units, such as pounds per day, toxicity units, or other measures, such as percent reduction. The TMDL concept is shown in Figure 1b where a water quality standard of 2 mg/l of ammonia as nitrogen and a stream flow of 30 mgd give a TMDL of 500 lbs/day. With a given nonpoint source load allocation for agricultural runoff of 75 lbs/day and a margin of safety of 50 lbs/day, the wasteload allocation for the treatment plant is determined to be 375 lbs/day which would be written into the operating permit for the wastewater treatment plant. The discharge permit for the treatment plant would be written so that this wasteload allocation would not be exceeded.

a) margin of safety = 50 lb/day

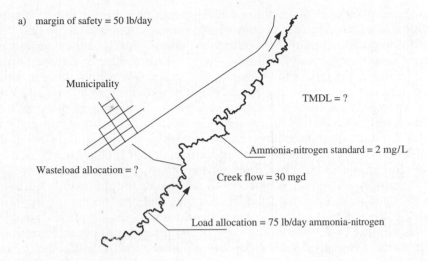

Municipality

TMDL = ?

Ammonia-nitrogen standard = 2 mg/L

Wasteload allocation = ?

Creek flow = 30 mgd

Load allocation = 75 lb/day ammonia-nitrogen

b) $\text{TMDL} = \dfrac{2 \text{ mg}}{\text{L}} \times \dfrac{30 \text{ MG}}{\text{d}} \times \dfrac{8.34 \; {}^{\text{lb}}\!\big/_{\text{MG}}}{{}^{\text{mg}}\!\big/_{\text{L}}} = 500 \; {}^{\text{lb}}\!\big/_{\text{d}}$

$\text{WLA} = \text{TMDL} - \text{LA} - \text{MOS} = 500 - 75 - 50 = 375 \; {}^{\text{lb}}\!\big/_{\text{d}}$

FIGURE 1   Total Maximum Daily Load. a. Contributing components.
b. Example of TMDL calculation.

7   POLLUTION EFFECTS ON AQUATIC LIFE

A normal, healthy stream or lake has a balance of plant and animal life represented by great species diversity. Pollution disrupts this balance, resulting in a reduction in the variety of individuals and dominance of the surviving organisms. Complete absence of species normally associated with a particular habitat reveals extreme degradation. Of course, biological diversity and population counts are meaningful only if existing communities in a polluted environment are compared with those normally present in that particular habitat. Fish are good indicators of water quality, and no perennial river can be considered in satisfactory condition unless a variety of fish can survive in it.

Being an end product of the aquatic food chain, fish reflect both satisfactory water quality and a suitable habitat for food supply, shelter, and breeding sites. Even though depletion of dissolved oxygen is commonly blamed, poisons appear to cause the most damage to plant and animal life in surface waters. The effects of toxic substances are frequently magnified by environmental conditions; for example, temperature has a direct influence on morbidity. At a given concentration of a toxic substance, a rise of 10°C generally halves the survival time of fish; poisons therefore become more lethal in rivers during the summer. Many toxic substances become more lethal with decreasing dissolved oxygen content. Also, the rate of oxygen consumption of fish is altered by the presence of poisons, and the resistance of the fish to low oxygen levels can be impaired. The pH of water within the allowable range of 6.5–9 can influence some poisons. The dissolved salt content can also influence toxicity, particularly the presence of calcium, which reduces the adverse effect of some heavy metals. For example, cadmium, copper, lead, nickel, and zinc decrease in toxicity with increased hardness in the water.

Poisonous effects on fish also relate to the character of the watercourse, species of fish, and season of the year. During the winter fish are much more resistant because of the cold water. The rapid rise of temperature in spring and hot periods in summer create critical times when fish are susceptible to unfavorable conditions and likely to die. During spawning even slight pollution can cause damage to salmon and trout.

Acute toxic effects (24–16-hr exposure) have been studied for most toxic pollutants. In contrast, few data are available on chronic toxicity. Applying a safety factor to the median lethal concentration can result in a criterion that is either too conservative or unsafe for long-term exposure. Chronic effects often occur in the species population rather than in the individual. If eggs fail to develop or the sperm does not remain viable, the species is eliminated from an ecosystem because of reproductive failure. Physiologic stress can make a species less competitive, resulting in a gradual population decline or absence from an area. The same phenomenon could occur if a crustacean that serves as a vital food during the larval period of a fish's life is eliminated. Finally, biological accumulation of certain toxic substances can result in acute effects in fish that are the ultimate consumers in the aquatic food chain. A notable example is the bioaccumulation of mercury in fish which has led to numerous fish consumption health warnings across the U.S. [19]

8   CONVENTIONAL WATER POLLUTANTS

The common water pollutants are biodegradable organic matter (typically characterized by biochemical oxygen demand (BOD), suspended solids, fecal coliforms, pH, ammonia nitrogen, phosphorus, oil and grease, and chlorine residual. For these pollutants the EPA has developed water quality criteria consisting of numerical limits; their rationale is based on bioassays of aquatic organisms [18]. Toxicity tests (bioassays) are the best method for determining safe concentrations of conventional pollutants to aquatic organisms. Test species, usually fish, are exposed to various concentrations of a pollutant in water for a specified time span of 96 hr or less in laboratory tanks. The median lethal concentration (LC_{50}) is the level that kills 50% of the test organisms. The maximum allowable toxic concentration in surface waters is usually between 0.1 and 0.01 of the LC_{50} value. The uncertainty factor of 10–100 is to account for long-term exposure and other constituents already present in the river water creating additional physiologic stresses. These criteria may be modified to take into account the variability of local waters in establishing state standards.

Water quality standards associate particular numerical limits with the designated beneficial uses for specific surface waters, thus recognizing that use and criteria are interdependent. Local conditions commonly considered are natural background levels of pollutants and other constituents such as hardness, the presence or absence of sensitive aquatic species, characteristics of the biological community, temperature and weather, flow characteristics, and synergistic or antagonistic effects of combinations of pollutants. In general, EPA criteria are considered conservative estimates of pollutant concentrations that can be safely tolerated by a general ecosystem, whereas state standards address site-specific pollution problems.

The *dissolved-oxygen* standard establishes lower limits to protect propagation of fish and other aquatic life, enhance recreation and reduce the possibility of odors resulting from decomposition of organic matter, and maintain a suitable quality of water for treatment. The primary pollutant associated with depletion of dissolved oxygen is carbonaceous BOD. In addition, sedimentation of suspended solids can cause a buildup of decomposing organic matter in sediments, and dissolved ammonia can contribute to oxygen depletion by nitrification. Fish vary in their oxygen requirements according to species, age, activity, temperature, and nutritional state. EPA water-quality criteria are written with respect to cold-water or warm-water fish and to whether the fish are in early life stages (up to 30 days) or not. The criteria are also given in terms of 1, 7, and 30-day mean concentrations. The 30-day mean concentrations are 6.5 mg/L and 5.5 mg/L for cold-water and warm-water fish, respectively. Requirements for fish in early life stages are higher.

Suspended solids interfere with the transmission of light and can settle out of suspension, covering a streambed or lake bottom. Turbid water interferes with recreational use and aesthetic enjoyment. Excess suspended solids adversely affect fish by reducing their growth rate and resistance to disease, preventing the successful development of fish eggs and larvae, and reducing the amount of food available. Solids covering the bottom damage invertebrate populations and fill gravel spawning beds. The EPA criterion states that solids should not reduce the depth of the compensation point (penetration of sunlight) for photosynthetic activity by more than 10% from the seasonally established norm for aquatic life [18].

Oil and grease contaminants include a wide variety of organic compounds having different physical, chemical, and toxicological properties. Common sources are petroleum derivatives and fats from vegetable oil and meat processing. Domestic water supplies need to be virtually free from oil and grease, particularly from the tastes and odors that emanate from petroleum products. Surface waters should be free of floating fats and oils. Based on EPA criteria, individual petrochemicals should not exceed 0.01 of the median lethal concentration that kills 50% (LC_{50}) of a specific aquatic species during an exposure period of 96 hr [18].

E. coli and enterococci bacteria indicate the possible presence of pathogenic organisms. The correlation between these bacteria and human pathogens in natural waters is not absolute since these bacteria can originate from the feces of both humans and other warm-blooded animals. Therefore, the significance of testing in pollution surveys depends on a knowledge of the river basin and probable source of the observed *E. coli* or enterococci. The EPA criterion for *E. coli* bacteria in freshwater is a geometric mean of 126 per 100 ml, based on a minimum of five samples taken over a 30-day period; if enterococci bacteria are used, the geometric mean should not exceed 33/100 ml. Since shellfish may be eaten without being cooked, the strictest coliform criterion applies to shellfish cultivation and harvesting; accordingly, the EPA criterion states that the mean fecal coliform concentration should not exceed 14 per 100 ml, with not more than 10% of the samples exceeding 43 per 100 ml [18].

Residual chlorine resulting from disinfection of wastewater effluents is very toxic to fish. When chlorine is added to wastewater, chloramines are formed by reacting with ammonia. These can be eliminated in wastewater effluents by the addition of a reducing agent such as sulfur dioxide. EPA water quality criteria for total chlorine residuals are a CMC of 19 μg/l and a CCC of 11 μg/l [18].

Un-ionized ammonia is toxic to fish and other aquatic animals. When ammonia dissolves in water, a portion reacts with the water to form ammonium ions (NH_4^+) with the balance remaining as un-ionized ammonia (NH_3). The percentage of the total ammonia concentration that is un-ionized increases with increasing pH and increasing temperature, and decreases with decreasing ionic strength. The EPA criteria for total ammonia–nitrogen are calculated with respect to pH, temperature and the type of species [20]. For example, the CMCs for total ammonia–nitrogen when salmonid fish are present are 24.1 mg/L and 5.62 mg/L at pH levels of 7.0 and 8.0, respectively (note no temperature dependence for the CMC). The total ammonia–nitrogen CCC values at 20°C are 4.15 mg/L and 1.71 mg/L at pH levels of 7.0 and 8.0, respectively, for waters with fish in early life stages present. These CMC values decrease as the temperature increases.

Concern over ammonia criteria results from the high concentration of ammonia nitrogen in treated effluents from municipal wastewater plants. After biological treatment without nitrification, an average domestic wastewater contains 24 mg/l of ammonia nitrogen. Ammonia can be converted to nitrate to reduce the effluent concentration by additional aeration in biological treatment. This nitrification process, usually a second stage of aeration, adds significant cost to wastewater treatment.

The *pH of surface waters* is specified for protection of fish life and to control undesirable chemical reactions, such as the dissolution of metal ions in acidic waters. Many substances increase in toxicity with changes in pH. For example, the ammonium ion is shifted to the poisonous form of un-ionized ammonia as the pH of water rises above neutrality. The EPA criteria for pH are 6.5–9.0 for freshwater aquatic life, 6.5–8.5 for marine aquatic life, and 5–9 for domestic water supplies [18].

Phosphate phosphorus (P) is a key nutrient stimulating excessive plant growth— both weeds and algae—in lakes, estuaries, and slow-moving rivers. Cultural eutrophication is the accelerated fertilization of surface waters arising from phosphate pollution associated with discharge of wastewaters and agricultural drainage. Since phosphate removal is feasible by chemical precipitation in wastewater treatment, effluent permits for municipal and industrial discharges to lakes, or streams that flow into lakes, commonly limit the concentration to 1.0 mg/l or less of phosphate phosphorus; that is equivalent to about 85% or more removal from domestic wastewater. For lakes in the northern United States to be free of algal nuisances, the generally accepted upper concentration limit in impounded water when completely mixed in the spring of the year is 0.01 mg/l of orthophosphate as P. EPA criteria are specific to selected ecoregions of the United States, so the actual water quality criteria vary according to regional water supply character. For example, the limit for total phosphorus in the Florida Everglades is 0.01 mg/L as P.

Discharges of conventional pollutants from wastewater treatment plants are controlled through the National Pollutant Discharge Elimination System (NPDES) permit program. Technology-based effluent limits of BOD, suspended solids, oil and grease, fecal coliforms, and pH define secondary treatment. As a general guideline, an adequate dilution ratio for secondary effluent discharged to flowing water is 20 to 1 or greater. Water quality–based effluent limits are set to ensure water quality standards are not exceeded in the receiving water. These may reduce the limits for secondary treatment where flow in the receiving watercourse does not provide adequate dilution. Water quality standards may also require limits on phosphorus to reduce eutrophication or limit un-ionized ammonia and residual chlorine to reduce toxicity.

9   TOXIC WATER POLLUTANTS

Numerous organic chemicals and several inorganic ions, mostly heavy metals, are classified as toxic water pollutants. To qualify as a priority toxin, a substance must be an environmental hazard and known to be present in polluted waters. Toxicity to fish and wildlife may be related to either acute or chronic effects on the organisms themselves or to humans by bioaccumulation in food fish. Persistence in the environment (including mobility and degradability) and treatability are also important factors. Currently, the EPA list of priority toxic pollutants consists of 120 substances. While some are well-documented toxic substances, others have limited data supporting their hazard in the environment.

The majority of the toxic pollutants can be categorized into 10 groups. *Halogenated aliphatics* are used in fire extinguishers, refrigerants, propellants, pesticides, and solvents. Health effects include damage to the central nervous system and liver. *Phenols* are industrial compounds used primarily in production of synthetic polymers, pigments, and pesticides and occur naturally in fossil fuels. They impart objectionable taste and odor at very low concentrations, taint fish flesh, and vary in toxicity depending on chlorination of the phenolic molecule. *Monocyclic aromatics* (excluding phenols and phthalates) are used in the manufacture of chemicals, explosives, dyes, fungicides, and herbicides. These compounds are central nervous system depressants and can damage the liver and kidneys. *Ethers* are solvents for polymer plastics. They are suspected carcinogens and aquatic toxins. *Nitrosamines*, used in production of organic chemicals and rubber, are suggested carcinogens. *Phthalate esters* are used in production of polyvinylchloride and thermoplastics. They are an aquatic toxin and can be biomagnified. *Polycyclic aromatic hydrocarbons* are in pesticides, herbicides, and petroleum products. *Pesticides* of concern are those that biomagnify in the food chain and are persistent in nature; chlorinated hydrocarbons are common in this group of pesticides. Aldrin, dieldrin, and chlordane applications are already restricted by the EPA. *Polychlorinated biphenyls* (PCBs) were banned from production in 1979. They are readily assimilated by the aquatic environment and still persist in sediments and fish; PCBs were used in electric capacitors and transformers, paints, plastics, insecticides, and other industrial products. *Heavy metals* vary in toxicity and some, such as mercury, are subject to biomagnification.

The general goal of wastewater treatment in the NPDES permit program is to reduce the discharge of toxic pollutants to an insignificant level by enforcing an industrial wastewater pretreatment program. Toxicity reduction evaluation of a treatment plant is the first step. For municipal plants, the objectives are to evaluate operation and performance to identify and correct treatment deficiencies causing effluent toxicity;

identify the toxic substances in the effluent; trace the toxic pollutants to their sources in the wastewater collection system; and implement appropriate remedial measures to reduce effluent toxicity.

Chemical Evaluation of Effluent

Gross toxicity of a wastewater effluent is evidenced in the receiving watercourse by a reduction in species diversity. Presence of a poison disrupts the normal balance of plant and animal life, which is represented by a great variety of individuals. Complete absence of species normally associated with a particular aquatic habitat is evidence of severe degradation. Obviously, a fish kill is evidence of extreme acute toxicity from the discharge of a lethal quantity of a poison. Periodic upset of the biological process in wastewater treatment is an indication that industrial toxic chemicals are being discharged to the sewer collection system and passing through the treatment plant. If the evidence of toxicity is less dramatic, the presence of toxic chemicals in a wastewater effluent may be unnoticed.

The chemical-specific approach, if toxicity is indicated by the whole effluent toxicity (WET) test, is to test effluent samples for selected toxic chemicals. This can be very costly unless the toxic chemicals likely to be present can be reduced to a reasonable number. Initial tests should be for those substances related to wastes from industries served by the sewer system. After the toxic pollutants have been quantitatively identified, the NPDES permit is modified to ensure protection of aquatic life in accordance with appropriate criteria. Remedial measures must be taken by industrial pretreatment and improved municipal treatment to meet the revised effluent standards. Mandatory monitoring for toxic chemicals in the effluent is established by the NPDES discharge permit. Potential deficiencies of this analytical approach through chemical analyses are the possible presence of undetected toxic chemicals and combinations of synergistic toxic pollutants.

Effluent Biological Toxicity Testing

Biological testing by the WET method defined by the EPA is required under their NPDES permit for selected municipal treatment plants [21, 22]. This bioassay to determine toxicity is performed by exposing selected aquatic organisms to wastewater effluent in a controlled laboratory environment. In the static short-term WET test, effluent and uncontaminated water are placed in separate laboratory containers. Test organisms are added to both containers and then monitored for toxic effects in a controlled laboratory environment.

The containers are borosilicate glass or disposable polystyrene ranging in volume from 250 ml to 1000 ml, depending on the size of the test organism [23]. During the test period the dissolved oxygen concentration should be near saturation, and temperature should be held at 25°C for warm-water species (12°C for cold-water species). The pH is checked periodically. The effluent is a 24-hr composite filtered through a sieve to remove suspended solids. During effluent preparation, aeration should be limited to prevent loss of volatile organic compounds. The common warm-water test organisms are fathead minnow (*Pimephales promelas*), daphnid *(Ceriodaphnia dubia)*, and a green alga *(Selenastrum capricornutum)*. The fathead minnow, a popular bait fish, feeds primarily on algae, and grows to an average length of 50 mm with a life span of less than 3 yr. Daphnids are invertebrates that feed on algae, grow to a maximum of 4–6 mm, and have a life span of 40–60 days. Some states have developed culturing and testing methods for indigenous species.

The test result is expressed in terms of mortality after a 24-hr exposure. A 25% reduction in survival is defined as the threshold of biological significance indicating probable impairment of the receiving water. The WET test measures the aggregate toxic effect of a mixture of unknown toxic pollutants in the effluent. When significant toxicity is indicated by biological testing, a chemical evaluation of the effluent is required. This can be very costly unless toxic substances likely to be present can be reduced to a reasonable number. A release inventory of toxic pollutants from industries contributing wastewater to the sewer system is the best way to identify possible toxic substances and their sources. A proper pretreatment program for an industry requires sampling, flow measurement, laboratory testing, and reporting. After toxic pollutants have been quantitatively identified, remedial measures to reduce or eliminate effluent toxicity can be taken by additional industrial pretreatment and improved municipal wastewater treatment.

Impairment in the receiving water and effluent toxicity are related to dilution of the effluent within the receiving water. Therefore, a more definitive toxicity test is to set up a series of laboratory containers at increasing effluent dilution, such as 100%, 50%, 25%, 12.5%, and 6.25% of the effluent concentration (a geometric series). The objective is to estimate the safe, or no-observed-effect level, that will permit normal propagation of aquatic life in the receiving water. This range of effluent dilution is to encompass the recorded one-in-10-year, seven-consecutive-day low flow in the receiving water relative to the effluent flow. The average low flow over a seven-consecutive-day period that is likely to occur once every 10 years is usually the flow in a river or stream established for the maximum allowable concentration of pollutants set by surface water standards. The dilution water used in laboratory testing is from the receiving stream above the outfall pipe or from the edge of the mixing zone. It is filtered through a plankton net to remove indigenous organisms that may attack or be confused with the test organisms. As an alternate, the dilution water may be a moderately hard mineral water.

These tests may be conducted for either acute 24-hr toxicity or chronic toxicity monitored up to seven days. In chronic testing, food is supplied to the organism cultures, for example, flake fish food or brine shrimp for fathead minnows. Also, chronic tests may be static-renewal tests where test organisms are transferred every 24 hr to a fresh solution of the same concentration of wastewater. Based on the results, the no-observed-effect concentration is determined for effluent in the diluted test samples. This can be compared against the ratio of wastewater diluted with the seven-consecutive-day, one-in-10-year low flow.

SELECTED POLLUTION PARAMETERS

Total solids, suspended solids, BOD, chemical oxygen demand (COD), and coliform bacteria are common parameters used in water and wastewater engineering. Knowledge of testing procedures is essential to understand the meaning of these terms. For a detailed description of testing procedures for these and other substances, refer to *Standard Methods for the Examination of Water and Wastewater* [24].

10   TOTAL AND SUSPENDED SOLIDS

The term *total solids* refers to the residue left in a drying dish after evaporation of a sample of water or wastewater and subsequent drying in an oven (Figure 2). After a measured volume is placed in a porcelain dish, the water is evaporated from the dish on a steam bath. The dish is then transferred to an oven and dried to a constant weight at 103°–105°C. The total residue is equal to the difference between the cooled weight of the dish and the original weight of the empty dish. The concentration of total solids is the weight of dry solids divided by the volume of the sample, usually expressed in mg/l.

Total volatile solids are determined by igniting the dry solids at 550° ± 50°C in an electric muffle furnace. The residue remaining after burning is referred to as fixed solids, and the loss of weight on ignition is reported as volatile solids. The concentration of total volatile solids is the weight of dry solids minus the weight of fixed solids divided by the volume of the original liquid sample. Volatile solids content also can be expressed as a percentage of the dry solids in the sample.

The term *total suspended solids* refers to the nonfilterable residue that is retained on a glass-fiber disk after filtration of a sample of water or wastewater (Figure 3). A measured portion of a sample is drawn through a glass-fiber filter, retained in a funnel, by applying a vacuum to the suction flask under the filter. The filter with damp suspended solids adhering to the surface is transferred from the filtration apparatus to an aluminum or stainless steel dish as a support. After drying at 103°–105°C in an oven, the filter with the dry suspended solids is weighed. The weight of suspended solids is equal to the difference between this weight and the original weight of the clean filter. The concentration of total suspended solids is the weight of the dry solids divided by the volume of the sample and is usually expressed in milligrams per liter.

Volatile suspended solids are determined by igniting the dry solids at 550° ± 50°C after placing the filter disk in a porcelain dish. The concentration of volatile suspended solids is the weight of dry solids minus the weight of fixed solids divided by the volume of the original liquid sample.

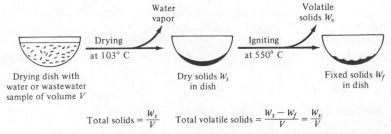

$$\text{Total solids} = \frac{W_s}{V} \qquad \text{Total volatile solids} = \frac{W_s - W_f}{V} = \frac{W_v}{V}$$

FIGURE 2   Diagram of laboratory procedure to determine total solids and total volatile solids concentrations of a water or wastewater sample.

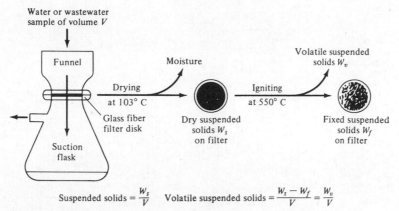

$$\text{Suspended solids} = \frac{W_s}{V} \qquad \text{Volatile suspended solids} = \frac{W_s - W_f}{V} = \frac{W_v}{V}$$

FIGURE 3   Diagram of laboratory procedure to determine the total suspended-solids and volatile suspended-solids concentrations of a water or wastewater sample.

Dissolved solids are the solids that pass through the glass-fiber filter and are calculated from total and suspended solids analyses. Total dissolved solids equals total solids minus total suspended solids. Volatile dissolved solids equals total volatile solids minus volatile suspended solids.

11   BIOCHEMICAL AND CHEMICAL OXYGEN DEMANDS

Biochemical Oxygen Demand

Biochemical oxygen demand (BOD) is the quantity of oxygen used by microorganisms in the aerobic stabilization of wastewaters and polluted waters. The standard 5-day BOD value is commonly used to define the strength of municipal wastewaters, to evaluate the efficiency of treatment by measuring oxygen demand remaining in the effluent, and to determine the amount of organic pollution in surface waters.

Laboratory analyses of wastewaters and polluted waters are conducted using 300-ml BOD bottles incubated at a temperature of 20°C. The preparation of BOD tests is diagrammed in Figure 4. To measure the BOD of a wastewater sample, a measured portion is placed in the BOD bottle, seed microorganisms are added if needed, and the bottle is filled with aerated dilution water containing phosphate buffer and inorganic nutrients. The amount of wastewater added to a 300-ml bottle depends on the estimated strength. For example, typical amounts are 5.0 ml for untreated wastewater in the BOD range of 120–420 mg/l and 50 ml for effluents with 12–42 mg/l. Unchlorinated municipal wastewaters and unchlorinated effluents have adequate microbial populations without seeding. Industrial wastewaters and dechlorinated effluents require a prepared seed, usually aged domestic wastewater, to perform the biological reactions. While the waste-water provides the organic matter, the dilution water provides the dissolved oxygen for aerobic decomposition. For a polluted surface water, the sample is adjusted to 20°C and aerated to increase the dissolved oxygen to near saturation. The sample, or a portion

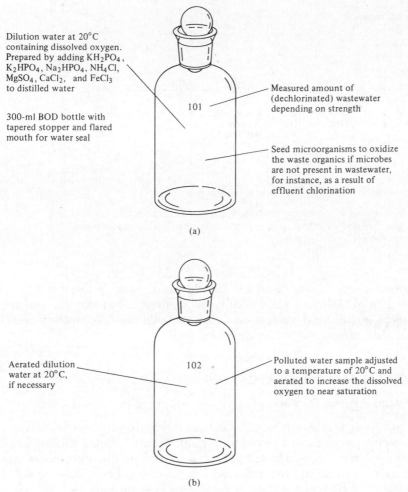

Dilution water at 20°C
containing dissolved oxygen.
Prepared by adding KH_2PO_4,
K_2HPO_4, Na_2HPO_4, NH_4Cl,
$MgSO_4$, $CaCl_2$, and $FeCl_3$
to distilled water

300-ml BOD bottle with
tapered stopper and flared
mouth for water seal

101

Measured amount of
(dechlorinated) wastewater
depending on strength

Seed microorganisms to oxidize
the waste organics if microbes
are not present in wastewater,
for instance, as a result of
effluent chlorination

(a)

Aerated dilution
water at 20°C,
if necessary

102

Polluted water sample adjusted
to a temperature of 20°C and
aerated to increase the dissolved
oxygen to near saturation

(b)

FIGURE 4   Preparation of biochemical oxygen demand (BOD) tests on
(a) wastewater sample, (b) polluted surface water.

of the sample mixed with dilution water, is then placed in the BOD bottle. A 50%
mixture of sample and dilution waters is suitable for a polluted-water BOD in the
range of 4–14 mg/l.

The biochemical oxygen demand exerted by diluted wastewater progresses
approximately by first-order kinetics as shown in Figure 5. The initial depletion of dissolved oxygen is the result of carbonaceous oxygen demand resulting from organic
matter degradation:

$$\text{Dissolved oxygen + organic matter} \xrightarrow[\text{and protozoans}]{\text{bacteria}} \text{carbon dioxide + biological growths} \qquad (5)$$

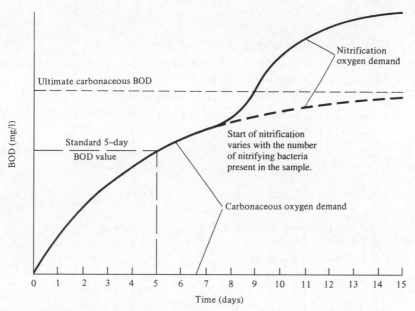

FIGURE 5   Hypothetical biochemical oxygen demand reaction curve showing
the carbonaceous and nitrification reactions.

If present in sufficient numbers, nitrifying bacteria exert a secondary oxygen demand
by oxidation of ammonia:

Dissolved oxygen + ammonia nitrogen

$$\xrightarrow[\text{bacteria}]{\text{nitrifying}} \text{nitrate nitrogen} + \text{bacterial growth} \tag{6}$$

Nitrification often lags several days behind the start of carbonaceous oxygen demand.
The carbonaceous oxygen demand curve can be expressed mathematically as

$$\text{BOD}_t = L(1 - 10^{-kt}) \tag{7}$$

where

BOD_t = biochemical oxygen demand at time t, mg/l
L = ultimate BOD, mg/l
k = deoxygenation rate constant, day^{-1}
t = time, days

The equation for calculating BOD from a seeded laboratory test is

$$\text{BOD} = \frac{(D_1 - D_2) - (B_1 - B_2)f}{P} \tag{8}$$

where

$$BOD = \text{biochemical oxygen demand, mg/l}$$

D_1 = dissolved oxygen (DO) of diluted seeded wastewater immediately after preparation, mg/l

D_2 = DO of wastewater after incubation, mg/l

B_1 = DO of diluted seed sample immediately after preparation, mg/l

B_2 = DO of seed sample after incubation, mg/l

f = ratio of seed volume in seeded wastewater test to seed volume in BOD test on seed

P = decimal fraction of wastewater sample used

$$= \frac{\text{volume of wastewater}}{\text{volume of dilution water plus wastewater}}$$

If the sample is unseeded, the relationship is

$$BOD = \frac{D_1 - D_2}{P} \tag{9}$$

The standard value is the BOD exerted during the first five days of incubation. At least 2 mg/l of DO should be used during the test period and at least 1 mg/l of DO should remain at the end of the test period for meaningful results.

Example 1

BOD tests were conducted on composited samples of a raw wastewater and a treated wastewater after chlorination.

1. The BOD tests for the raw wastewater were set up by pipetting 5.0 ml into each 300-ml bottle. For one pair of bottles, the test results were as follows: The initial dissolved oxygen (DO) was 8.4 mg/l, and after five days of incubation at 20°C the final DO was 3.7 mg/l. Calculate the BOD_5 and estimate the 20-day BOD value assuming a k of 0.10 day^{-1}. Assume no BOD is associated with the dilution water ($B_1 = B_2$)

2. The treated wastewater sample was dechlorinated prior to conducting a seeded test. The BOD bottles were set up with 50.0 ml of treated wastewater and 0.5 ml of raw wastewater for seed added to each bottle. For one pair of bottles, the test results were as follows: The initial DO was 7.6 mg/l, and the final DO was 2.9 mg/l. Calculate the BOD.

Solution:

1. Using Eq. (9)

$$BOD_5 = \frac{8.4 - 3.7}{5.0/300} = 282 \text{ mg/l}$$

Using Eq. (7)

$$L = \frac{282}{1 - 10^{-0.1 \times 5.0}} = 412 \text{ mg/l}$$

$$BOD_{20} = 412(1 - 10^{-0.1 \times 20}) = 408 \text{ mg/l}$$

2. Using Eq. (8)

$$BOD = \frac{(7.6 - 2.9) - (8.4 - 3.7)(0.5/5.0)}{50/300} = 25 \text{ mg/l}$$

Chemical Oxygen Demand

The *chemical oxygen demand* (COD) of wastewater or polluted water is a measure of the oxygen equivalent of the organic matter susceptible to oxidation by a strong chemical oxidant. The organic matter destroyed by the mixture of chromic and sulfuric acids is converted to CO_2 and water. The test procedure is to add measured quantities of standard potassium dichromate, sulfuric acid reagent containing silver sulfate, and a measured volume of sample into a flask. After attaching a condenser on top, reflux (vaporize and condense) this mixture for 2 hr. The oxidation of organic matter converts dichromate to trivalent chromium.

$$\text{Organic matter} + Cr_2O_7^{2-} + H^+ \xrightarrow[Ag^+]{\text{heat}} CO_2 + H_2O + 2Cr^{3+} \tag{10}$$

After cooling, washing down the condenser, and diluting the mixture with distilled water, measure the excess dichromate remaining in the mixture by titration with standardized ferrous ammonium sulfate. A blank sample of distilled water is carried through the same COD testing procedure as the wastewater sample. The purpose of testing a blank is to compensate for any error that can result because of the presence of extraneous organic matter in the reagents. COD is calculated from the following equation:

$$COD = \frac{(a - b)[\text{molarity of Fe }(NH_4)_2\,(SO_4)_2]8000}{V} \tag{11}$$

where

COD = chemical oxygen demand, mg/l

a = amount of ferrous ammonium sulfate titrant added to blank, ml

b = amount of titrant added to sample, ml

V = volume of sample, ml

8000 = multiplier to express COD in mg/l of oxygen

Applications of BOD and COD Testing

BOD is the most common parameter for defining the strengths of untreated and treated municipal and biodegradable industrial wastewaters. The oxygen requirement and tank sizing for aerobic treatment processes are based on BOD loadings. BOD is also used in quantifying the quality of an effluent from a treatment plant; the maximum allowable BOD is specified in the wastewater discharge permit. Since oxygen depletion in surface waters results from aquatic microorganisms exerting oxygen demand, the BOD test is a key measurement in the evaluation of water pollution by biodegradable wastes.

Commonly, COD is used to define the strength of industrial wastewaters that either are not readily biodegradable or contain compounds that inhibit biological activity. Frequently, laboratory wastewater treatability studies are based on COD testing rather than on BOD analyses. The COD test has the advantages of rapid analysis and reproducible results. The BOD test requires incubation for five days, and the results of multiple analyses on an industrial wastewater sample often show considerable scatter. Also, COD testing is becoming more popular in all applications of oxygen demand analyses as a result of simplified laboratory techniques.

The relationship between BOD and COD concentrations must be defined for each individual wastewater. Ideally, for a wastewater composed of biodegradable organic substances, the COD concentration approximates the ultimate carbonaceous BOD value. Yet this simple relationship is rarely substantiated in testing of municipal wastewaters. Many organic compounds can be oxidized chemically that are only partly biodegradable.

12   COLIFORM BACTERIA

The coliform group of bacteria is defined as aerobic and facultative anaerobic, nonspore-forming, Gram's-stain negative rods that ferment lactose with gas production within 48 hr of incubation at 35°C.

Fermentation Tube Technique

The basic coliform analysis, diagrammed in Figure 6, is the test for total coliforms based on gas production during the fermentation of lauryl tryptose broth, which contains beef extract, peptone (protein derivatives), and lactose (milk sugar). Ten-milliliter portions of a water or wastewater sample are transferred using sterile pipettes into prepared fermentation tubes containing inverted glass vials. The inoculated tubes are placed in a warm-air incubator at 35° ± 0.5°C for 48 hr. Growth with the production of gas, identified by the presence of a bubble in the inverted vial, is a positive test, indicating that coliform bacteria may be present. A negative reaction, either no growth or growth without gas, excludes the coliform group.

The common test for fecal coliforms is a second-phase confirmatory test following growth of coliforms in the presumptive total coliform test. A minute portion of the broth from a positive test, or a positive colony from a membrane filter, is transferred aseptically on a sterile wire loop to a fermentation tube of an EC medium containing

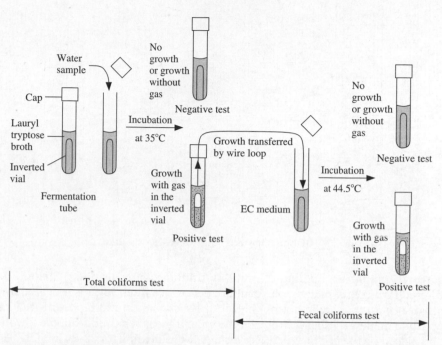

FIGURE 6 Diagram of the basic test for total coliforms and second-phase confirmatory test for thermotolerant fecal coliforms.

tryptose, lactose, bile salts, and chemical buffers. The glass tube has a removable cap and an inverted vial at the bottom of the tube in the broth, as illustrated in Figure 6. A positive test is growth with gas after 22–26 hr at 44.5°C. Gas production is evidence that coliforms have converted the lactose sugar to lactic acid, thus lowering the pH and releasing gas. If no gas appears in the inverted vial, the test is negative and no fecal coliform bacteria were present in the presumptive total coliform test.

Membrane Filter Technique

The membrane filter test for coliform testing, diagrammed in Figure 7, consists of drawing a measured volume of water through a filter membrane with small enough openings to take out bacteria, and then placing the filter on a growth medium in a culture dish. This technique assumes that each bacterium retained by the filter grows and forms a small visible colony. The number of coliforms present in a filtered sample is determined by counting the number of typical colonies and expressing this value in terms of number per 100 ml of water.

The apparatus to perform membrane filter coliform testing includes a filtration unit, sterile filter membranes, sterile absorbent pads, culture dishes, nutrient media, and forceps. The forceps for handling the filters are sterilized before each use. Rapid decontamination of filter units between successive filtrations can be accomplished using an ultraviolet sterilizer with exposure to radiation for 2 min. The filter membranes with pore openings of 0.45 μm are in 2-in.-diameter disks with a grid printed on the

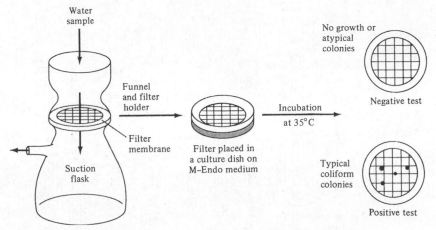

FIGURE 7   Diagram of membrane filter technique for coliform testing.

surface for ease in counting colonies. In drinking water testing, a 100-ml sample is filtered through the membrane. A culture dish with a fitted cover is prepared by placing an absorbent pad in the bottom half of the dish and saturating it with 1.0–2.0 ml of M-Endo medium. Using the forceps, the membrane is removed from the filtration unit and placed on the pad in the culture dish. After incubation for 22–24 hr at 35° ± 0.5°C, the cover is removed from the dish and the membrane examined for growth. Typical coliform colonies are a pink to dark-red color with a green metallic surface sheen. Absence of bacterial growth on the membrane is a negative test. Occasionally, atypical colonies occur as light-colored growth without dark centers or a green sheen.

Presence–Absence Technique

The presence–absence (P–A) test can determine if coliform bacteria or *E. coli* are present in a water sample without indicating the number of coliforms in a positive result. This test is intended for use in routine monitoring of drinking water immediately after treatment and in the distribution system pipe network. This test is based on the concept that the MCL for coliform bacteria is zero.

The drinking water to be tested is collected in a sterile bottle containing 15–30 mg of sodium thiosulfate, which is sufficient to neutralize and stop the disinfecting action of 10 mg/l of chlorine. The test procedure starts by vigorously shaking the sample bottle to suspend the bacteria and the particulate matter. The lid of the P–A culture bottle is aseptically removed to add 100 ml of the water sample and to add the contents of one packet of Colilert® reagent. The reagent contains bacterial nutrients and two special compounds (ONPG, O-Nitrophenyl-β-d-galactopyranoside, and MUG, 4-Methylumbelliferyl-β-d-glucuronide) that indicate the growth and presence of coliform bacteria and *E. coli*. (Colilert® is based on IDEXX's patented Defined Substrate Technology®.)

The culture bottle is incubated for 24 hr at 35°C. Growth of coliform bacteria in the Colilert® uses the enzyme β-galactosidase to metabolize ONPG and change the color of the sample from clear to yellow. If a yellow color does not appear, the test is negative and no coliforms were present in the water sample. *E. coli* uses the enzyme β-galactosidase to metabolize MUG and create fluorescence under 365-nanometer ultraviolet light. (Fluorescence is the emission of radiation as visible light resulting from the absorption of radiation from another source.) If the yellow-colored broth glows fluorescent with a bluish color, the test is positive for *E. coli*. Absence of a blue color is a negative test.

PROBLEMS

1 Define the meaning of the term *pathogen* and give the names of pathogen groups. What determines the kinds and concentrations of pathogens in wastewater? Define the meaning of fecal–oral route in the transmission of diseases.

2 Compare the latency, persistence, and infective dose of *Ascaris* and *Salmonella*.

3 Discuss the significance of the carrier condition in transmission of enteric diseases. What major waterborne diseases in the United States are commonly spread by carriers? How are these diseases amplified by animals?

4 Historically in the United States, the prevalent infectious diseases have been typhoid, cholera, and dysentery. How have these diseases been virtually eliminated? Currently, the prevalent infectious diseases are *giardiasis* and *cryptosporidiois*, causing diarrhea that can be life-threatening for persons with immunodeficiency syndrome. What actions are being taken to reduce the probability of waterborne transmission of these diseases? (Refer to Section 1.)

5 What are the symptoms produced by the two pathogenic protozoa that are found world-wide? What is the common mode of *transmission* and in what environments is transmission most likely to occur?

6 Why can coliform bacteria be used as indicators of drinking water quality? Discuss the limitations of coliforms as an indicator. Why is a positive test for fecal coliforms in a public water supply considered more serious than a positive test for total coliforms?

7 What are the significant differences between *E. coli* and *E. coli* O157:H7?

8 What is the definition of a community water system? What is the difference between a nontransient–noncommunity water system and a transient–noncommunity system?

9 Outline the three phases in testing for enteric viruses in relatively unpolluted water. Since extraction and concentration capture only a portion of the viruses in a water sample, how is the precision of separation determined? When is testing for enteric viruses recommended?

10 In one statement, what is the general process in testing for *Giardia* cysts and *Cryptosporidium* oocysts? If the water sample is only 10 liters for testing natural stream water for *Cryptosporidium* oocysts, why is the accuracy for detection and enumeration of oocysts likely to be low? Why must laboratories conducting tests for *Cryptosporidium* oocysts be audited and approved for quality assurance?

11 Based on laboratory animal studies, a synthetic organic chemical has an estimated cancer risk of 1×10^{-6} after a lifetime consumption of 1 l/d of water containing 1.0 μg/l of chemical. If the MCL is 0.005 mg/l and consumption is 2 l/d, what is the calculated risk and the number of excess cases of cancer expected among persons exposed?

12 Discuss the health risk of finding lead in drinking water.

13 What is the health risk of excess nitrate ion in drinking water?

14 What are the most frequently detected VOCs in contaminated groundwater? What pesticide SOCs have been detected in drinking water?

15 List the regulated disinfection by-products. What is their source in drinking water?

16 Compare the federal (EPA) primary drinking water standards to the standards in your locale. Compare both the constituents regulated and the MCLs of the constituents. (Current standards are available on the EPA and state web sites.)

17 Why are iron and manganese included in secondary standards for aesthetics in drinking water?

18 What are the objectives of the Clean Water Act?

19 What does the acronym NPDES refer to? List several aspects of this permit program. How is the NPDES program monitored?

20 If a river with a seasonal low flow of 200 cfs has a water quality standard for phosphate of 0.02 mg/L as P, find the TMDL for P. Diffuse agricultural runoff contributes 10 lbs of P per day. If the margin of safety is set at 4 lbs of P per day, what would be the maximum waste-load allocation of P from a wastewater treatment plant discharging to the river? Ignore all other point and nonpoint sources.

21 List the types of load applications and wasteload applications that may be used in developing a TMDL. What other information is required?

22 What are the technology-based standards for secondary (biological) treatment for all municipal wastewater treatment plants? (Refer to Section 8.) When are water quality–based standards necessary for a wastewater discharge?

23 What are the major steps in performing the whole effluent toxicity (WET) test?

24 What is the procedure following a negative effluent biological toxicity test that indicates probable impairment of the receiving water?

25 The following data are from total solids and total volatile solids tests on a wastewater sample. Calculate the total and volatile solids concentrations in milligrams per liter.

   Weight of empty dish = 68.942 g
   Weight of dish plus dry solids = 69.049 g
   Weight of dish plus ignited solids = 69.003 g
   Volume of wastewater sample = 100 ml

26 Listed below are total solids and suspended-solids data on an industrial wastewater sample. Calculate the total and volatile solids, suspended solids, and dissolved solids.

   Total solids data
   Weight of empty dish = 85.337 g
   Weight of dish plus dry solids = 69.049 g
   Weight of dish plus ignited solids = 85.375 g
   Volume of wastewater sample = 85 ml

Suspended solids data

Weight of glass-fiber filter disk = 0.1400 g

Weight of disk plus dry solids = 0.1530 g

Weight of disk plus ignited solids = 0.1426 g

Volume of wastewater filtered = 200 ml

27 An unseeded BOD test is conducted on a polluted surface water sample by adding 100 ml to a 300-ml BOD bottle and filling with dilution water. The initial dissolved oxygen measured 8.2 mg/l, and the final concentration after five days of incubation at 20°C measured 2.9 mg/l. Calculate the BOD.

28 A BOD test was conducted on the unchlorinated effluent of a municipal treatment plant. The wastewater portion added to a 300-ml BOD bottle was 30 ml, and the dissolved oxygen values listed below were measured using a dissolved-oxygen probe. Plot a BOD-versus-time curve and determine the five-day BOD value.

Time (days)	DO (mg/l)	Time (day)	DO (mg/l)
0	8.7	6.0	4.9
2.0	6.7	10.0	3.9
4.0	5.7	14.0	0.7

29 A BOD test was conducted on a raw domestic wastewater sample. The wastewater portion added to each 300-ml test bottle was 8.0 ml. The dissolved-oxygen values and incubation periods are listed below. Plot a BOD-versus-time curve and determine the 5-day BOD value.

Bottle Number	Initial DO (mg/l)	Incubation Period (days)	Final DO (mg/l)	DO Drop (mg/l)	Calculated BOD (mg/l)
1	8.4	0	8.4		
2	8.4	0	8.4		
3	8.4	1.0	6.2		
4	8.4	1.0	5.9		
5	8.4	2.0	5.2		
6	8.4	2.0	5.2		
7	8.4	3.0	4.4		
8	8.4	3.0	4.6		
9	8.4	5.0	3.8		
10	8.4	5.0	3.5		

30 A seeded BOD analysis was conducted on a food-processing wastewater sample. Ten-milliliter portions were used in preparing the 300-ml bottles to determine the dissolved-oxygen demand of the aged, settled wastewater seed. The seeded sample BOD bottles contained 2.7 ml of food-processing wastewater and 1.0 ml of seed wastewater. The results of this series of test bottles are listed below. Calculate the wastewater BOD values and plot a BOD–time curve. What is the five-day BOD?

Time (days)	Seed Tests B_1 (mg/l)	B_2 (mg/l)	Sample Tests D_1 (mg/l)	D_2 (mg/l)
0	7.8	—	8.1	—
1.0	7.8	6.9	8.1	5.6
2.0	7.8	6.6	8.1	4.3
3.0	7.8	6.3	8.1	3.6
4.0	7.8	5.8	8.1	3.0
5.0	7.8	5.7	8.1	2.5
6.0	7.8	5.3	8.1	2.0
7.0	7.8	5.4	8.1	1.8

31 In laboratory testing for coliform bacteria, what techniques can be performed to enumerate total coliforms in treated wastewater effluent or drinking water? What test can be used to determine the presence of *E. coli* in drinking water?

REFERENCES

[1] R. G. Feachem, D. J. Bradley, H. Garelick, and D. D. Mara, *Sanitation and Disease, Health Aspects of Excreta and Wastewater Management: World Bank Studies in Water Supply and Sanitation 3* (Chichester: Wiley, 1983).

[2] E. C. Lippy and S. C. Waltrip, "Waterborne Disease Outbreaks, 1946–1980: A Thirty-Five-Year Perspective," *J. Am. Water Works Assoc.* 76, no. 2 (1984): 60–67.

[3] *Waterborne Pathogens*, AWWA M48 (Denver, CO: Am. Water Works Assoc., 1999).

[4] A. C. Moore, et al., "Waterborne Disease in the United States, 1991 and 1992," *J. Am. Water Works Assoc.* 86, no. 2 (1994): 87–99.

[5] M. H. Kramer, et al., "Waterborne Disease: 1993 and 1994," *J. Am. Water Works Assoc.* 88, no. 3 (1996): 66–80.

[6] S. C. Edberg, M. J. Allen, and D. B. Smith, *Comparison of the Colilert Method and Standard Fecal Coliform Methods*, AWWA Research Foundation (Denver, CO: *J. Am. Water Works Assoc.,* 1994.)

[7] D. L. Swerdlow, et al., "A Waterborne Outbreak in Missouri of *Escherichia coli* O157: H7 Associated with Bloody Diarrhea and Death," *Annals of Internal Medicine* 117, no. 10 (1992): 812–819.

[8] F. W. Pontius and S. W. Clark, "Drinking Water Quality Standards, Regulations, and Goals," in *Water Quality & Treatment*, 5th ed. (New York: McGraw-Hill/Am. Water Works Assoc., 1999).

[9] M. J. Martin, J. L. Clancy, and E. W. Rice, "The Plain, Hard Truth About Pathogen Monitoring," *J. Am. Water Works Assoc.* 92, no. 9 (2000): 64–76.

[10] *Drinking Water and Health*, Vol. 1, National Academy of Sciences (Washington, DC: National Academy Press, 1977).

[11] *Drinking Water and Health*, Vol. 3, National Academy of Sciences (Washington, DC: National Academy Press, 1980).

[12] *Drinking Water and Health*, Vol. 4, National Academy of Sciences (Washington, DC: National Academy Press, 1982).

[13] D. F. Striffler, W. O. Young, and B. A. Bart, "The Prevention and Control of Dental Caries: Fluoridation," in *Dentistry, Dental Practice, and the Community* (Philadelphia: Saunders, 1983), 155–199.

[14] H.S. Weinberg, S.W. Krasner, S.D. Richardson, and A.D. Thurston, Jr., "The Occurrence of Disinfection Byproducts of Health Concern in Drinking Water: Results of a Nationwide DBP Occurrence Study," EPA-600-R-02-068 (2002).

[15] "Radioactivity in Drinking Water," Environmental Protection Agency, Office of Drinking Water, EPA-570/9-81-002 (January 1981).

[16] "The Federal Water Pollution Control Act, as amended through Public Law 107-303," EPA web site: www.epa.gov (2002)

[17] *Water Quality Standards Handbook*, 2nd ed., Environmental Protection Agency, Office of Water, EPA-823-B-94-005a (1994).

[18] "Quality Criteria for Water," Environmental Protection Agency Office of Water Regulations and Standards, EPA-440/5-86-001 (1986).

[19] F. M. Morel, A. M. Kraepiel, and M. Amyot, "The Chemical Cycle and Bioaccumulation of Mercury," *Annual Review of Ecology and Systematics*, 29 (1998), 543–566.

[20] "1999 Update of Ambient Water Quality Criteria for Ammonia," EPA-822-R-99-014 (1999).

[21] *Short-Term Methods for Estimating the Chronic Toxicity of Effluents and Receiving Water to Freshwater Organisms*, 3rd ed., Environmental Protection Agency, Research and Development, EPA-600-4-91-002 (July 1994).

[22] *Evaluating Whole Effluent Toxicity Testing as an Indicator of Instream Biological Conditions* (Alexandria, VA: Water Environment Federation, Water Environment Research Foundation, 1999).

[23] "Methods of Measuring the Acute Toxicity of Effluents to Freshwater and Marine Organisms," 3rd ed., Environmental Protection Agency, Environmental Monitoring and Support Laboratory, EPA-600/4-85-013 (March 1985).

[24] *Standard Methods for the Examination of Water and Wastewater.* (Washington, DC: Am. Public Health Assoc., 1998).

[25] M. J. Hammer and M. J. Hammer, Jr., *Water and Wastewater Technology*, 5th ed. (Upper Saddle River, NJ: Prentice Hall, 2004).

Systems for Treating Wastewater and Water

Systems for Treating Wastewater and Water

OVERVIEW

In Chapters 10 through 13 the design of physical, chemical, biological, and sludge treatment processes will be discussed in detail. In this chapter water and wastewater treatment plants will be described as a collection of these processes, each process having particular functions to improve the quality of the water or wastewater. The intention in this approach is to give the readers an understanding of the overall systems so that they will have a better appreciation of the individual process functions and their relationship to one another.

WASTEWATER TREATMENT SYSTEMS

The purpose of municipal wastewater treatment is to prevent pollution of the receiving waters or to reclaim the water for reuse. Characteristics of a municipal wastewater depend to a considerable extent on the type of sewer collection system and industrial wastewaters entering the sewers. The degree of treatment required is determined by the intended uses of the receiving waters or, in the case of reclamation, the reuse application. Pollution of flowing waters and eutrophication of impounded waters are particularly troublesome in water use for water supplies and recreation.

1 PURPOSE OF WASTEWATER TREATMENT

Wastewaters from households and industries are collected in a sewer system and transported to the treatment plant. The treated effluent is commonly disposed of by dilution in rivers, lakes, and estuaries. Disposal to the ocean is through a submerged outfall sewer extending into deep water. Three common reuse applications are agricultural irrigation, urban landscape irrigation, and groundwater recharge.

Water quality criteria have been established by the Clean Water Act for receiving waters to define the degree of treatment required for disposal of treated wastewater by dilution to protect prescribed beneficial uses. Effluent standards prescribe the required quality of the discharge from each treatment plant. The minimum extent of processing is secondary treatment, i.e., treatment to address BOD, suspended solids, oil and grease, fecal coliform bacteria and pH. Some cities and industries are required to install tertiary or advanced wastewater treatment processes for removal of pollutants that are resistant to conventional treatment, e.g., removal of phosphorus to retard eutrophication of receiving lakes. Stream classification documents, published by each state as required by federal law, categorize surface waters according to their most beneficial present or future use (i.e., for drinking water supplies, body-contact recreation, etc.). These publications also incorporate water quality standards that establish maximum allowable pollutant concentrations for a given watercourse under defined flow conditions and TMDLs for impaired waters.

Effluent standards under the National Pollutant Discharge Elimination System (NPDES) are used for regulatory purposes to achieve compliance with these water quality standards. Technology-based effluent limits define the minimum level of effluent quality that must be attained by secondary treatment of municipal wastewater without regard to the quality of the receiving waters, but the extent of treatment may need to exceed these minimum levels to protect a given water body.

Acceptable secondary effluent is defined in terms of biochemical oxygen demand, suspended solids, oil and grease, fecal coliform bacteria, and pH. The arithmetic mean of BOD and suspended-solids concentrations for effluent samples collected in a period of 30 consecutive days must not exceed 30 mg/l; and, during any seven-consecutive-day period, the average must not exceed 45 mg/l. Furthermore, removal efficiencies shall not be less than 85% (i.e., if an influent concentration is less than 200 mg/l, the effluent cannot exceed 15% of this value). For concentrations of oil and grease, the arithmetic mean must exceed neither 10 mg/l for any period of 30 days nor 20 mg/l for any period of seven days. Where specified in a discharge permit, the geometric mean of fecal coliform counts for effluent samples collected in a period of 30 consecutive days must not exceed 200 per 100 ml; and the geometric mean of fecal coliform bacteria for any seven-consecutive-day period must not exceed 400 per 100 ml. The effluent values for pH shall remain within the limits 6.0–9.0. These effluent limits for biological treatment require a well-designed plant that is properly operated. Moderately loaded activated-sludge processes, biological towers, and two-stage trickling-filter plants are capable of achieving this degree of treatment. However, some designs that were popular in the past are not efficient enough, such as single-stage trickling-filter plants and high-rate activated-sludge systems. Stabilization ponds are often permitted to discharge suspended-solids concentrations of 50–70 mg/l, since these suspended solids are algae with little or no raw organic matter. Disinfection for control of bacterial populations may not be required if no threat to public health exists.

Refractory contaminants, both inorganic and organic materials, are pollutants resistant to or totally unaffected by conventional treatment processes. The mineral quality of wastewater depends largely on the character of the municipal water supply, but during water use numerous substances are added such as common salt (sodium chloride) and other dissolved solids. Phosphates, which occur in low concentrations in most natural waters, are increased during municipal use of water. Phosphorus and nitrogen removals in secondary treatment are only about 30%, depending on the types of processes and concentrations in the raw wastewater. Eutrophication of lakes and reservoirs, induced by disposal of treated wastewater, can be retarded by employing advanced treatment processes to remove phosphorus. Organic nitrogenous compounds decompose to ammonia and to a variable extent oxidize to nitrate in biological treatment. While nitrification of ammonia nitrogen is feasible by additional aeration of the wastewater, denitrification (conversion to nitrogen gas) requires special processes that are costly. Aside from disposal of treated wastewater, no ready solution exists for removing nutrients from runoff, either from natural land or cultivated fields.

A primary goal of the Clean Water Act is to prohibit the discharge of toxic pollutants in toxic quantities. Wastewaters from industries discharging to a municipal sewer system can contain toxic metal ions and hazardous organic chemicals. Toxic substances interfere with the operation of biological treatment processes, and many are refractory, passing through in the plant effluent to contaminate the receiving water. Under their NPDES permit, municipalities are required to establish regulations for pretreatment of wastewaters from industries at the industrial sites to remove toxic substances. To ensure removal, industrial wastewaters entering the sewer system are monitored by the municipality, and the effluent from the municipal treatment plant is tested for biological toxicity.

2 SELECTION OF TREATMENT PROCESSES

Conventional wastewater treatment consists of preliminary processes (pumping, screening, and grit removal), primary settling to remove heavy solids and floatable materials, and secondary biological aeration to metabolize and flocculate colloidal and dissolved organics (Figure 1). Waste sludge drawn from these unit operations is thickened and processed for ultimate disposal.

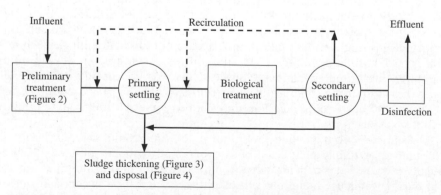

FIGURE 1   Schematic diagram of conventional wastewater treatment.

Preliminary Treatment Units

The following preliminary processes are used in municipal wastewater treatment: coarse screening (bar racks), medium screening, shredding of solids, flow measuring, pumping, grit removal, and preaeration. Although not common in pretreatment, flotation, flocculation, and chemical treatment are sometimes dictated by the industrial pollutants in the municipal wastewater. Flotation is used to remove fine suspensions, grease, and fats and is performed either in a separate unit or in a preaeration tank also used for grit removal. If adequate pretreatment is provided by petroleum industries and meat-processing plants, flotation units are not required at a municipal facility. Flocculation with or without chemical additions may be practiced on high-strength municipal wastewaters to provide increased primary removal and prevent excessive loads on the secondary treatment processes. Chlorination of raw wastewater is sometimes used for odor control and to improve settling characteristics of the solids.

The arrangement of preliminary treatment units varies depending on raw wastewater characteristics, subsequent treatment processes, and the preliminary steps employed. A few general rules always apply in arrangement of units. Screens are used to protect pumps and prevent solids from fouling grit-removal units and flumes. In small plants a Parshall flume is normally placed ahead of constant-speed lift pumps, but may be located after them in large plants or where variable-speed pumps are used. Grit removal should be placed ahead of the pumps when heavy loads are anticipated, although the grit chamber follows the lift pumps in most separate sanitary wastewater plants. Three possible arrangements for preliminary units are shown in Figure 2.

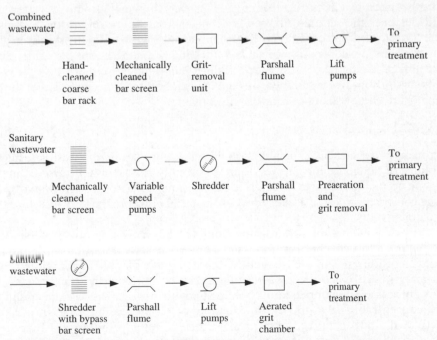

FIGURE 2   Possible arrangements of preliminary treatment units in municipal wastewater processes.

Primary Treatment Units

Primary treatment is sedimentation. In common usage, the term usually includes the preliminary treatment processes. Sedimentation of raw wastewater is usually practiced in all large municipal plants and must precede trickling (biological) filtration. Completely mixed activated-sludge processes can be used to treat unsettled raw wastewater; however, this method is generally used in smaller treatment plants because of the costs involved in sludge disposal and operation.

Secondary Treatment Units

Primary sedimentation removes 30%–50% of the suspended solids in raw municipal wastewater. Remaining organic matter is extracted in biological secondary treatment to the allowable effluent residual using activated-sludge processes or trickling filters. In the activated-sludge method, wastewater is fed continuously into an aerated tank, where microorganisms degrade the organics. The resulting microbial floc (activated sludge) is settled from the aerated mixed liquor under quiescent conditions in a final clarifier and returned to the aeration tank (Figure 1). The plant effluent is clear supernatant from secondary settling. Advantages of suspended-growth aeration are high-BOD removals, ability to treat high-strength wastewater, and adaptability for future use in plant conversion to advanced treatment. On the other hand, a high degree of operational control is needed, shock loads may upset the stability of the biological process, and sustained hydraulic or organic overloading results in process failure.

Trickling filters have stone or, more commonly in current practice, plastic media to support microbial films. These slime growths extract organics from the wastewater as it trickles over the surfaces. Oxygen is supplied from air moving through voids in the media. Excessive biological growth washes out and is collected in the secondary clarifier. In northern climates, two-stage shallow trickling filters are needed to achieve efficient treatment. Biological towers (deep trickling filters) may be either single- or two-stage systems. Advantages of filtration are ease of operation and capacity to accept shock loads and overloading without causing complete failure.

Sludge Disposal

Primary and secondary sedimentation processes concentrate the waste organics into a volume of sludge significantly less than the quantity of wastewater treated. But disposal of the accumulated waste sludge is a major economic factor in wastewater treatment. The construction cost of a sludge processing facility is approximately one-third that of a treatment plant.

Flow schemes for withdrawing, holding, and thickening raw waste sludge from sedimentation tanks are illustrated in Figure 3. The settled solids from clarification of trickling-filter effluent are frequently returned to the plant head for removal with the primary sludge (Figure 3a). Raw settlings may be stored in the primary tank bottom until processed or pumped into a holding tank for storage. The withdrawn sludge may be concentrated in a gravity thickener prior to processing. In Figure 3b, waste-activated sludge is mixed with primary residue after withdrawal. Alternatives for processing and disposal of raw sludge are shown in Figure 4. Common methods are

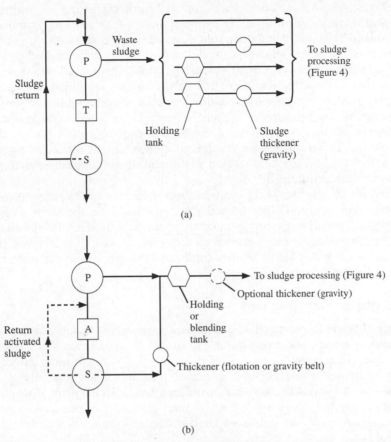

(a)

(b)

FIGURE 3 Flow schemes for withdrawal, holding, and thickening of waste sludge. P, primary settling; T, trickling filtration; A, activated-sludge aeration; S, secondary settling. (a) trickling filter
plant; (b) activated sludge plant.

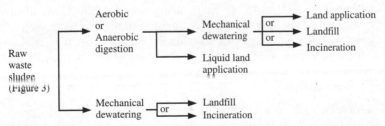

FIGURE 4 Common methods for processing and disposal of raw waste sludge.

anaerobic digestion and mechanical dewatering by belt filter pressing or centrifugation. Conventional methods of disposal are application as a fertilizer/soil conditioner on agricultural land and landfill in a dedicated disposal site or codisposal with municipal solid waste. In small plants, anaerobically digested sludge may be applied on agricultural land by surface spreading or subsurface injection. Dewatered raw sludge must be covered by soil the same day if applied on the surface or buried. Therefore, the common methods are codisposal in a municipal solid waste landfill or disposal in a dedicated disposal site. Incineration, although significantly higher in cost, is sometimes the only acceptable method of sludge disposal in large urban areas. Waste-activated sludge from a plant without primary sedimentation is usually stabilized by aerobic digestion and spread on the land surface as a liquid or mechanically dewatered for application on agricultural land.

All possible sludge disposal processes for a municipal treatment plant must be given careful consideration. The method selected should be the most economical process, with due regard to environmental conditions. Attention must be given to such factors as trucking sludge through residential areas, future use of landfill areas, groundwater pollution, air pollution, regulatory considerations, other potential public health hazards, and aesthetics.

Advanced Wastewater Treatment

Phosphorus removal is practiced in processing wastewaters that are discharged to receiving waters subject to eutrophication, including lakes, reservoirs, and slow-moving rivers acting as impoundments. Since nitrogen removal is much more difficult and costly, it is rarely performed, although nitrification to reduce the ammonia content is sometimes done to control the oxygen demand and toxicity of the plant effluent. Water reclamation is achieved in varying degrees by many plants depending on the local environmental concerns; however, only a few large-scale plants are reclaiming water to near original quality.

Size of Municipality

Operational management and control and the necessity for sludge handling dictate the selection of wastewater treatment processes for small communities. Methods that do not require sludge disposal (stabilization ponds) or only occasional sludge withdrawals (extended aeration) are preferable for small villages and subdivisions. Towns large enough to employ a part-time operator frequently use systems that require more operational control and maintenance (e.g., oxidation ditch plants). Cities with trickling-filter and activated-sludge treatment plants employ several workers.

Layout of Treatment Plants

The flow diagram for a two-stage trickling-filter plant is given in Figure 5, and an aerial view is shown in Figure 6. For optimum removal of organic matter, trickling-filter recirculation and humus return are controlled to maintain a constant hydraulic loading rate. Humus washed off the filter media collects in the intermediate and final clarifiers. Underflow from these clarifiers to the influent pumping station is controlled to return

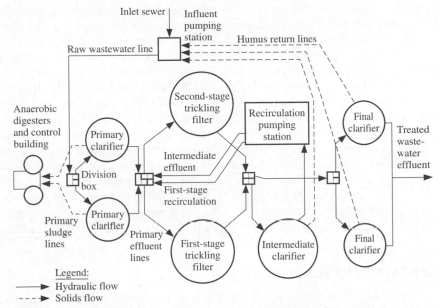

FIGURE 5   Plant layout for a two-stage trickling-filter plant, Sidney, NE. Average design flow of 1.0 mgd with 210 mg/l of BOD and 230 mg/l of suspended solids and maximum wet-weather flow of 2.4 mgd. *Source:* HDR Engineering, Inc.

FIGURE 6   Aerial view of two-stage filter plant shown in Figure 5. Note domes on trickling filters to prevent ice formation. *Source:* HDR Engineering, Inc.

more flow at night when raw wastewater inflow is reduced. Primary sludge containing raw organics and filter humus is withdrawn from the bottom of the clarifiers and pumped into the first-stage anaerobic digester for stabilization. The second-stage digester is for storage and thickening of the digested sludge and collection of methane gas under a floating-dome cover for use as a fuel. The digested sludge is dewatered to a cake on drying beds. The liquid sludge can also be composted with wood chips.

The sequence of wastewater treatment units in the activated-sludge plant is diagrammed in Figure 7. Cascade aeration increases the dissolved-oxygen level in the effluent to the river, and effluent pumping conveys the effluent to irrigation. Fine-bubble diffusers in the aeration tanks provide high-efficiency oxygen transfer for suspended-growth biological treatment. Primary sludge is pumped through a grinder and blended with waste-activated sludge after it is thickened by dissolved-air flotation. The mixed sludges are stabilized by anaerobic digestion and then pumped into a storage tank. After concentrating from approximately 2% to 7% on gravity belt thickeners, the biosolids are applied to agricultural land as a fertilizer/soil conditioner.

WATER TREATMENT SYSTEMS

The purpose of a municipal water supply system is to provide potable water that is chemically and microbiologically safe for human consumption and has adequate quality for industrial users. For domestic uses, water should be free from unpleasant tastes and odors, and improved for human health (i.e., by fluoridation). Since the quality of public supplies is based primarily on drinking water standards, the special temperature and other needs of some industries are not always met by public supplies. Boiler feedwater, water used in food processing, and process water in the manufacture of textiles and paper have special quality tolerances that may require additional treatment of the municipal water at the industrial site.

3   WATER SOURCES

Typical water sources for municipal supplies are deep wells, shallow wells, rivers, natural lakes, and impounding reservoirs. No two sources of supply are alike, and the same origin may produce water of varying quality at different times. Water treatment processes selected must consider the raw water quality and differences in quality for each particular water source.

Municipal water quality factors of temperature, appearance, taste and odor, absence of pathogens, and chemical balance are most easily and frequently satisfied by a deep-well source. Furthermore, the treatment processes employed are simplest because of the relatively uniform quality of such origin. Excessive concentrations of iron, manganese, and hardness habitually exist in well waters. Some deep-well supplies may contain hydrogen sulfide; others may have excessive concentrations of chloride, sulfate, and carbonate. Hydrogen sulfide can be removed by air stripping or oxidation processes.. Calcium and magnesium can be removed by precipitation softening, ion exchange or membrane processes. Concentrations of naturally occurring contaminants that exceed the primary drinking water regulations, such as arsenic and fluoride,

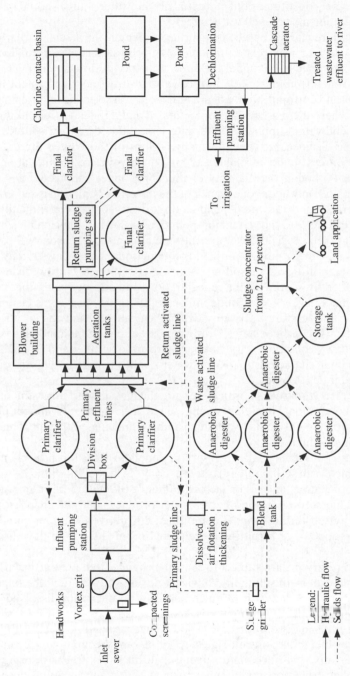

FIGURE 7 Plant layout for a completely mixed activated-sludge wastewater treatment plant, Big Dry Creek Water Reclamation Facility, Westminster, CO. *Source:* HDR Engineering, Inc.

require either advanced levels of treatment or abandonment of the well water supply; accordingly, mineral constituents of a potential groundwater source should be carefully examined in selecting a deep-well water supply.

Shallow wells recharged by a nearby surface water may have quality characteristics similar to deep wells or may relate more closely to the surface water quality. Shallow wells that are determined to be "under the direct influence of surface water" are required by the Surface Water Treatment Rule to receive water treatment equivalent to surface waters. Pollution and eutrophication are major concerns in selecting and treating surface water supplies. Where these are highly contaminated and difficult to treat, municipalities seek either groundwater supplies or alternate less polluted surface sources within a feasible pumping distance. However, in many regions of the United States, adequate groundwater resources are not available and high-quality surface supplies are not within economic reach. Although the majority of municipal water supply systems are from underground origins, only about one-fourth of the nation's population is served by these sources. In general, larger cities are dependent on surface supplies. Water quality in rivers depends on the character of the watershed; pollution caused by municipalities, industries, and agricultural practices; river development such as dams; the season of the year; and climatic conditions. During spring runoff and other periods of high flows, river water may be muddy and high in taste- and odor-producing compounds. During drought flows, pollutants are often present in higher concentrations and odorous conditions can occur. During late summer, algal blooms frequently create turbidity as well as taste and odor problems. River temperature variations depend on latitude and the location of the stream headwaters. In northern states, river water is warm in the summer and cold in the winter. Water quality conditions vary from one stream to another and, in addition, each has its own peculiar characteristics. River water quality is usually deteriorating if the watershed is under development.

Water supplies from rivers normally require the most extensive treatment facilities and the greatest operational flexibility of any source. A river water treatment plant must be capable of handling day-to-day variations and the anticipated quality changes likely to occur within its useful life.

The quality of water in a lake or reservoir depends on the physical, chemical, and biological characteristics (limnology) of the body. Size, depth, climate, watershed, degree of eutrophication, and other factors influence the nature of an impoundment. The relatively quiescent retention of river water produces marked changes in quality brought about by self-purification. Common benefits derived from impounding river water include reduction of turbidity and elimination of the day-to-day variations in quality.

Lakes and reservoirs are subject to seasonal changes that are particularly notice-able in eutrophic waters. In summer and winter during stratification, the hypolimnion (unmixed bottom water layer) in a eutrophic lake may contain dissolved iron and manganese and taste and odor compounds. The decrease of oxygen by bacterial activity on the bottom results in dissolution of iron and manganese and production of hydrogen sulfide and other metabolic intermediates. Algal blooms frequently occur in the epil-imnion (warmer mixed surface water layer) of fertile lakes in early spring and late summer. Cyanobacteria (more commonly known as blue-green algae) produce difficult-to-remove tastes and odors and cyanotoxins. Normally, the best quality of water is found near mid-depth, below the epilimnion and above the bottom. The intake for a fertile lake or reservoir should preferably be built so that water can be drawn from a variety of selected depths. Lakes that stratify experience spring and fall overturns, which occur when the temperature profile is nearly uniform and wind action stirs the lake from top to bottom. If the bottom water has become anaerobic during stratification, water drawn from all depths during the overturn will contain taste- and odor-producing compounds. The limnology of a lake or reservoir and the present and future level of eutrophication should be thoroughly understood before beginning the design of intake structures or treatment systems.

The concept of multiple barriers is important for water treatment systems. The use of several barriers is effective in preventing pathogens and contaminants from reaching water customers. The first barrier is source protection. For a surface water source, land and water use on the watershed should be controlled and wastewater contamination from human and animal sources minimized. For a groundwater source, a wellhead protection program should be adopted to prevent surface contamination from entering the aquifer and proper design and construction of wells should be implemented to prevent surface water from entering the bore holes. The most important barrier for a surface supply is water treatment, commonly consisting of chemical coagulation, sedimentation, and filtration. Treatment facilities for well water vary with the quality of the groundwater, and may involve softening, iron and manganese removal, or no treatment. The third barrier is disinfection of the treated water and an adequate protective disinfectant residual maintained in the distribution system. As the final barrier, the distribution system mains and storage reservoirs are properly maintained and operated at a high enough pressure to prevent infiltration of groundwater and other subsurface contamination from entering the system. Enforcement of a cross-connection-control program is essential to prevent backflow of contaminated water through service connections from industries, hospitals, and other institutions handling hazardous substances and into the water supply.

4   SELECTION OF WATER TREATMENT PROCESSES

Current pretreatment processes in municipal water treatment are screening, presedimentation or desilting, chemical addition, and aeration. Screening is practiced in pretreating surface waters. Presedimentation is regularly used to remove suspended matter from river water. Chemical treatment, in advance of in-plant coagulation, is most frequently applied to improve presedimentation, to pretreat hard-to-remove substances such as taste and odor compounds and color, and to reduce high bacterial concentrations. Conventional chemicals used in presedimentation are polymers and alum. Aeration is customarily the first step in treatment for the removal of iron and manganese from well waters and is a standard way to remove dissolved gases such as hydrogen sulfide and carbon dioxide.

Treatment processes used in water plants depend on the raw water source and quality of finished water desired. The specific chemicals selected for treatment are based on their effectiveness to perform the desired reaction and cost. For example, activated carbon, chlorine, chlorine dioxide, and potassium permanganate are all used for taste and odor control. While chlorination is least expensive, it can create undesired disinfection byproducts; accordingly, activated carbon is often the most effective treatment chemical. In surface water treatment plants, equipment for feeding two or three taste- and odor-removal chemicals is usually provided, so the operator can select the most effective and economic chemical applications. There is no fixed rule for color removal applicable to all waters. Coagulation with adequate pretreatment and applying oxidizing chemicals or activated carbon may provide satisfactory removal. Bench-scale testing is often used to select the best chemical coagulant and dosage.

Perhaps the most important consideration in designing water treatment processes is to provide operational flexibility. The operator should have the means to change the dose and point of application of certain chemicals. For example, chlorine feedlines are normally provided for pre-, intermediate-, and postchlorination. Multiple chemical feeders and storage tanks should be supplied so that various chemicals can be employed in the treatment process. Regulatory agencies can add new contaminants to the list of regulated chemicals, lower the maximum contaminant level (MCL) of currently regulated contaminants, add requirements for new or enhanced treatment techniques, or promulgate other regulations in the Safe Drinking Water Act. The flow in rivers may change due to construction of dams, channel improvements, or upstream water use. The quality of water changes due to human alteration and occupation of the watershed. Concentrations of pollutants from disposal of municipal and industrial wastewaters and agricultural land runoff may increase. Lakes can become more eutrophic. Although all these future changes may be difficult, if not impossible, to predict, they must be carefully considered in water treatment design, and providing treatment flexibility will help ensure the continued production of high quality water.

5   TYPES OF WATER TREATMENT SYSTEMS

A few examples of water treatment process plants are shown in Figures 8 through 12. Each plant uses different processes to address particular problems with the raw water sources. Iron and manganese removal is the primary purpose for treatment of groundwater by the scheme shown in Figure 8.

The treatment scheme of groundwater shown in Figure 9 is partial softening and iron and manganese removal. An aerial view of this treatment plant is shown in Figure 10, with the major treatment units labeled.

The treatment plant with the flow diagram in Figure 11 was originally constructed for processing lake water by alum coagulation, flocculation, sedimentation, and sand filtration. Since then the lake water source has become increasingly eutrophic, and additional facilities for taste and odor control have been provided. Activated carbon, chlorine dioxide, and various auxiliary chemicals for improved chemical treatment are now available to the operator during critical periods of poorer raw water quality. During most of the year the finished water is very palatable, but tastes and odors cannot be completely removed during spring and fall lake overturns.

The river water–processing scheme shown in Figure 12 is a very complex, flexible treatment system for a turbid and polluted stream with highly variable quality. Operation of this plant is varied from day to day and from season to season depending on the raw water quality.

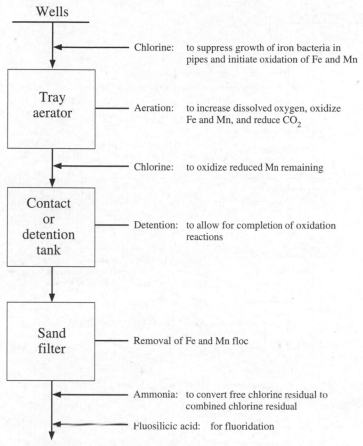

FIGURE 8 Iron and manganese removal plant using aeration and chlorine for oxidation.

6   WATER-PROCESSING RESIDUALS

Water-processing residuals consist of sludge removed from sedimentation basins that follow chemical coagulation, precipitation softening, and filter backwashing processes, as well as water containing high concentrations of dissolved solids from ion exchange and membrane processes. Water quality regulations require proper disposal of these wastes to minimize environmental degradation. The method of eliminating residues is unique to each water utility because of the individuality of each treatment scheme and differing characteristics of the waste products generated. These residuals are relatively nonputrescible and high in mineral content. Figure 13 is a generalized scheme of alternatives for disposing of water-processing sludges. Filter wash water is a very dilute waste discharged for only a few minutes once or twice a day for each filter bed. Therefore, a holding tank is necessary for flow equalization (i.e., to accept the intermittent peak

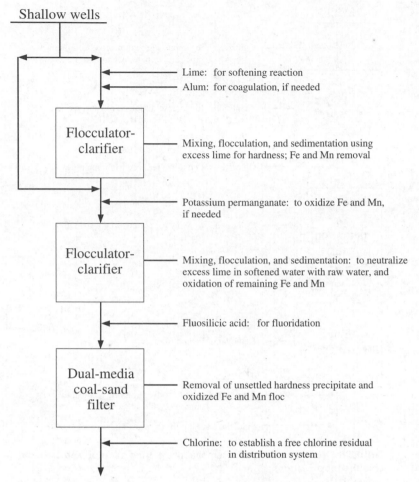

FIGURE 9   Plant using split treatment for partial softening and iron and manganese removal.

discharges and release a relatively uniform effluent flow). Backwash water is settled in a clarifier-thickener with the overflow recycled to the plant influent; the more concentrated solids are withdrawn for further processing. Waste sludge from sedimentation basins may also be concentrated further in a clarifier-thickener.

Disposal alternatives for gravity-thickened sludges are diagrammed in Figure 14. In some municipalities, slurries can be drained into a sanitary sewer for processing with the municipal wastewater. Air drying is accomplished either in lagoons or on sand-drying beds. Ponding is a popular method for dewatering, thickening, and temporary storage of waste solids. Where suitable land area is available, this technique is both inexpensive and efficient when compared to other methods. Drying beds are more costly and applicable only to small water plants. Centrifugation and pressure filtration are the two most

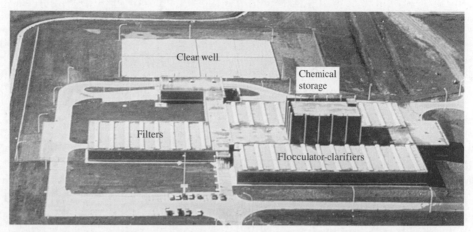

FIGURE 10   Aerial view of a water treatment plant. The flow diagram for this water utility is given in Figure 9. Note: the clearwell stores water after filtration and provides contact time for chlorine disinfection. *Source:* Metropolitan Utilities District, Omaha, NE.

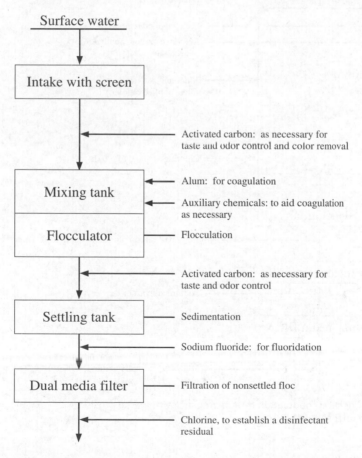

FIGURE 11   Chemical coagulation and partial-softening treatment plant with provisions for handling high turbidity, tastes and odors, and color.

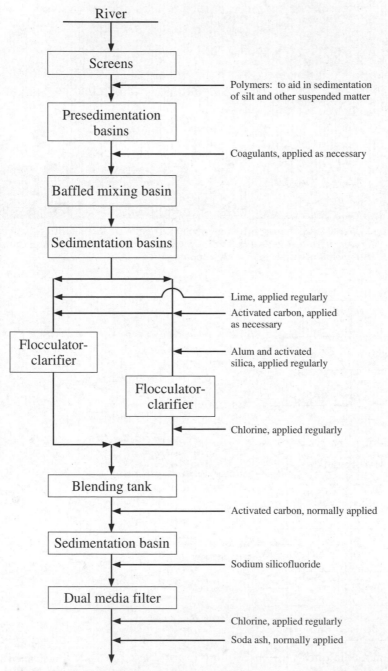

FIGURE 12   Chemical coagulation treatment plant with special provisions for taste and odor control.

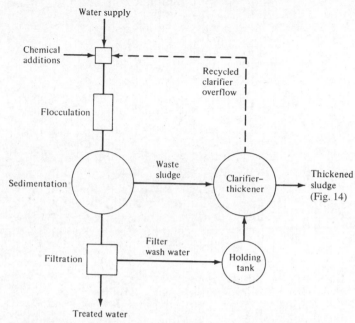

FIGURE 13   General flow scheme for withdrawal and gravity thickening of water-processing wastes.

successful mechanical dewatering processes. Residuals from air drying and concentrated cake from dewatering can be disposed of by codisposal in a municipal solid-waste landfill, burial in a dedicated landfill, or spreading on agricultural land if beneficial for the soil.

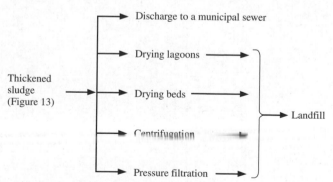

FIGURE 14   Common methods for dewatering and disposal of water-processing sludges.

Physical Treatment Processes

Physical Treatment Processes

FLOW-MEASURING DEVICES

Measurement of flow is essential for operation, process control, and record keeping of water and wastewater treatment plants.

1   MEASUREMENT OF WATER FLOW

The flow of water through pipes under pressure can be measured by mechanical or differential head meters, such as a venturi meter, flow nozzle, or orifice meter. The drop in piezometric head between the undisturbed flow and the constriction in a differential head meter is a function of the flowrate. A venturi meter (Figure 1), although more expensive than a nozzle or orifice meter, is preferred because of its lower head loss.

Piping changes upstream from a venturi meter produce nonuniform flow, causing inaccuracies in metering. In general, a straight length of pipe equal to 10–20 pipe diameters is recommended to minimize error from flow disturbances created by pipe fittings.

Flow in a venturi meter can be calculated using the equation

$$Q = CA_2\left[2g\left(\frac{P_1 - P_2}{w}\right)\right]^{0.5} \tag{1}$$

where

$$
\begin{aligned}
Q &= \text{flow, cfs} \\
C &= \text{discharge coefficient, commonly in the range of } 0.90\text{--}0.98 \\
A_2 &= \text{cross-sectional area of throat, ft}^2 \\
g &= \text{acceleration of gravity, ft/s}^2 \\
P_1 - P_2 &= \text{differential pressure, lb/ft}^2 \\
w &= \text{specific weight of water, lb/ft}^3
\end{aligned}
$$

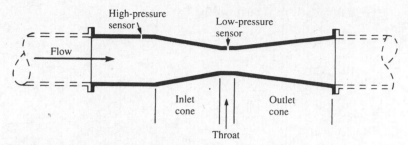

FIGURE 1 Venturi meter for measuring flow in a pipeline by differential pressure between inlet and throat.

2   MEASUREMENT OF WASTEWATER FLOW

The flow of wastewater through an open channel can be measured by a weir or a venturi type flume, such as the Parshall flume [1] (Figure 2). Parshall flumes have the advantages of lower head loss than a weir and smooth hydraulic flow preventing deposition of solids.

Under free-flowing (unsubmerged) conditions, the Parshall flume is a critical-depth meter that establishes a mathematical relationship between the stage h and

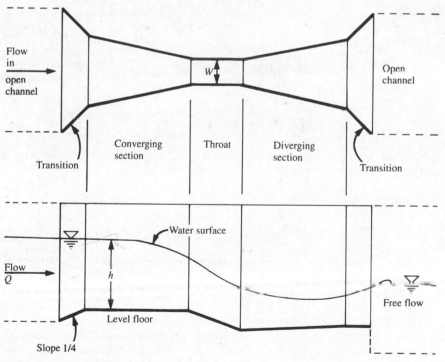

FIGURE 2 Parshall flume for measuring flow in an open channel by measuring the free-flowing upper head h.

discharge Q. For a flume with a throat width of at least 1 ft, but less than 8 ft, flow can be calculated as

$$Q = 4Wh^{1.522W^{0.026}}$$ (2)

where

Q = flow, cfs
W = throat width, ft
h = upper head, ft

Example 1

What is the calculated water flow through a venturi meter with $5\frac{1}{16}$ in. throat diameter when the measured pressure differential is 160 in. H_2O? Assume $C = 0.95$ and a water temperature of 50° F.

Solution: Substituting in Eq. (1), we obtain

$$Q = 0.95 \times \frac{\pi\left(\dfrac{5\,^{1}/_{16}\text{ in}}{12\text{ in}/\text{ft}}\right)^2}{4} \left(2 \times 32.2\frac{\text{ft}}{\text{s}^2}\,\frac{160\text{ in} \times 62.4\dfrac{\text{lb}}{\text{ft}^3}}{12\dfrac{\text{in}}{\text{ft}} \times 62.4\dfrac{\text{lb}}{\text{ft}^3}}\right)^{0.5}$$

$$= 3.9\text{ cfs} = 1750\text{ gpm}$$

Example 2

What is the calculated wastewater flow through a Parshall flume with a throat width of 2.0 ft at the maximum free-flow head of 2.5 ft?

Solution: By Eq. (2),

$$Q = 4 \times 2.0 \times 2.5^{1.522 \times 2.0^{0.026}}$$
$$= 33.1\text{ cfs} = 21.4\text{ mgd}$$

SCREENING DEVICES

River water and wastewater in sewers frequently contain suspended and floating debris varying in size from logs to small rags. These solids can clog and damage pumps or impede the hydraulic flow in open channels and pipes. Screening is the first step in treating water or wastewater containing large solids.

3   WATER-INTAKE SCREENS

River-water intakes are commonly located in a protected area along the shore to minimize collection of floating debris. Lake water is withdrawn below the surface to preclude interference from floating materials.

Coarse screens of vertical steel bars having openings of 1–3 in. are employed to exclude large materials. The clear openings should have sufficient total area so that the velocity through them is less than 3 fps to prevent pulling through stringy solids. These screens are available with mechanical rakes to clear accumulated material from the bars. A coarse screen can be installed ahead of a finer one used to remove leaves, twigs, small fish, and so on. Traveling screens, as shown in Figure 3a, are mechanically cleaned fine screens with openings of $\frac{1}{8}$ to $\frac{3}{8}$ in. The screen sections rotate upward and are cleaned with water sprays when they get to the head enclosure.

(a)   (b)

FIGURE 3   (a) Traveling water-intake screen. *Source:* U.S. Filter/Envirex. (b) Mechanically cleaned bar screen for wastewater treatment. *Source:* U.S. Filter/Envirex.

4   SCREENS IN WASTEWATER TREATMENT

Coarse screens (bar racks) constructed of steel bars with clear openings not exceeding 2.5 in. are normally used to protect wastewater lift pumps. (Centrifugal pumps used for wastewater works, in sizes larger than 100 gpm, are capable of passing spheres at least 3 in. in diameter.) To facilitate cleaning, the bars are usually set in a channel inclined 22°–45° to the horizontal.

Mechanically cleaned medium screens (Figure 3b) with clear bar openings of $^5/_8$–$1\,^3/_4$ in. are commonly used instead of a manually cleaned coarse screen. The maximum velocity through the openings should not exceed 2.5 fps.

Collected screenings are generally hauled away for disposal by land burial or incineration, although they can be shredded in a grinder and returned to the wastewater flow for removal in sedimentation.

Fine screens with openings as small as $^1/_{32}$ inch have been used in wastewater treatment, but because of their high head loss and high installation and operation cost, they are rarely employed in handling municipal wastewater. Fine screens are used to take out suspended and settleable solids in pretreating certain industrial waste streams. Typical applications are the removal of coarse solids from cannery and packing-house wastewaters. Self-cleaning filter screens with 1-mm openings are used prior to spray irrigation and membrane filtration.

5   SHREDDING DEVICES

A comminutor or grinder cuts solids to about $^1/_4$–$^3/_4$ in. in size. Comminutors are installed directly in the wastewater flow channel and provided with a bypass so that the channel containing the unit can be isolated and drained for machine maintenance. In small waste treatment plants, a comminutor may be installed without being preceded by a screen. The bypass channel around a comminutor contains a hand-cleaned medium screen.

MIXING AND FLOCCULATION

Chemical reactors in water treatment and biological aeration basins are mixed to produce the desired reactions and to keep the solids produced by the process in suspension. Rapid mixers are used to blend chemicals into the water. Flocculation mixers provide gentle mixing to promote agglomeration of particles into large flocs that can be removed from suspension by subsequent sedimentation. Mixing results from dissipating power in water. Mixing intensity is most often quantified by the root mean square velocity gradient, given by the equation

$$G = \left(\frac{P}{\mu V}\right)^{1/2} \tag{3}$$

where

$$G = \text{root mean square velocity gradient, } s^{-1} \; (s^{-1})$$
$$P = \text{power input to water, ft} \cdot \text{lb/s} \; (N \cdot m/s)$$
$$\mu = \text{absolute viscosity, lb} \cdot s/ft^2 \; (N \cdot s/m^2 \text{ or kg/m} \cdot s)$$
$$V = \text{volume, ft}^3 \; (m^3)$$

For flow-through systems, the volume of the tank or pipe containing the water can be computed by the equation

$$V = Q \times t_R \tag{4}$$

where t_R is the theoretical mean residence time.

G represents an average intensity over the entire mixed volume, so it is important to ensure that the mixing is distributed throughout this volume. One way to help distribute the mixing for mechanical mixers is to use a suitable ratio of the impeller diameter (D) to the effective tank diameter. The effective tank diameter, T_e, for square or rectangular tanks is given by

$$T_e = 1.13\sqrt{L_L \times L_W} \tag{5}$$

where L_L and L_W are the tank length and width respectively. Appropriate values of T_e will be given in subsequent sections that will describe the different types of mixing.

6   RAPID MIXING

A rapid mixer provides dispersion of chemicals into water so that blending occurs typically between 10 and 30 seconds. Most common is mechanical mixing using a vertical-shaft impeller in a tank with stator baffles, as illustrated in Figure 4. The

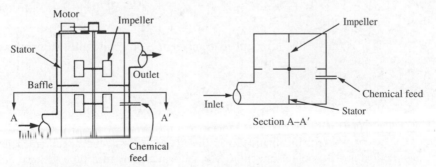

FIGURE 4   Impeller-type mechanical rapid mixer for dispersion of chemicals into water.

stator baffles reduce the rotational flow of vortexing about the impeller shaft which hinders mixing and reduces the effective impeller power usage. The turbulent flow pattern in mixing is a function of the tank size and shape; number, shape, and size of impellers; kind and location of stator baffles; and power input. Recommended guidelines for designing a mechanical rapid mixer are the following: a square vessel is superior in performance to a cylindrical vessel; stator baffles are advantageous; a flat-bladed impeller performs better than a fan or propeller impeller; and chemicals introduced at the agitator blade level enhance coagulation [2]. G values for mechanical mixers in rapid mixing usually range from 300 to 1000 s^{-1} and D/T_e values range from 0.25 to 0.40.

Example 3

Chemical addition in a 25-mgd water treatment plant will be performed in two parallel mixing basins with mechanical mixers. The mixing intensity as measured by the root mean velocity gradient should be a minimum of $750\ s^{-1}$, and the mean residence time should be 15 s at the design flow. Find the volume of the tanks and the power required for the mixers. The water temperature varies between 15 and 20°C annually. Assume the mechanical mixer is 70% efficient in transferring power to the water.

Solution: Since there is an inverse relationship between viscosity and the velocity gradient (Eq. 3), 15°C will be selected as the design temperature. From the table in the appendix for water at 15°C, $\mu = 1.139 \times 10^{-3}$ kg/m·s. The flow will be split between the two parallel tanks so the tank volume can be calculated from Equation 4:

$$V_{\text{each tank}} = Q \times t_R = \frac{25 \times 10^6\ \text{gal}}{2\ \text{tanks}\ \text{d}} \times \frac{\text{m}^3}{264\ \text{gal}} \times 15\ \text{s} \times \frac{\text{d}}{86400\ \text{s}} = 8.22\ \text{m}^3$$

The required power input to the water is calculated from a rearrangement of Eq. 3.

$$P = G^2 \mu V = \frac{750^2}{\text{s}^2} \times \frac{1.139 \times 10^{-3}\ \text{N} \cdot \text{s}}{\text{m}^2} \times 8.22\ \text{m}^3 = 5270 \frac{\text{N} \cdot \text{m}}{\text{s}} = 5.27\ \text{kW}$$

Since the mixer is only 70% efficient in transferring power to the water, the mixer power should be

$$P_{\text{mixer}} = \frac{P_{\text{water}}}{\text{eff.}} = \frac{5.27\ \text{kW}}{0.70} = 7.52\ \text{kW} = 10.0\ \text{hp}$$

Other methods of rapid mixing include hydraulic action, e.g., injection of chemical into the inlet of a centrifugal pump, jet injection into the water flow in a pipe (Figure 5a), and mechanical or static in-line blending. The static mixing elements, shown in Figure 5b, are inserted into a pipe immediately after the point of chemical injection for blending. The kind of mixer configuration selected depends on whether the blending is for dispersion, reaction, or gas–water contact.

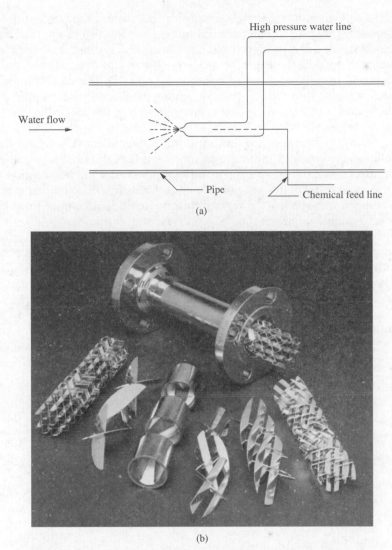

High pressure water line

Water flow

Pipe

Chemical feed line

(a)

(b)

FIGURE 5   (a) Jet injection mixer (b) Static mixing elements that are inserted into a pipe for in-line blending of chemicals. *Source:* Koch-Glitsch, Inc.

7   FLOCCULATION

Flocculation is agitation of chemically treated water to induce particle growth from very small suspended particles to larger heavier flocs that settle out by gravity. Chemical coagulation and flocculation are the principal mechanisms in removing turbidity from water. Floc growth is dependent on the physical action induced by agitation causing particle collisions and agglomeration. On the other hand if the mixing is too intense, the fragile flocs may be sheared into smaller fragments, defeating the purpose of the process.

The common mechanical mixing devices in water treatment are paddle (reel) flocculators (Figure 6a), and vertical-turbine mixers (Figure 6b). The paddle flocculator consists of a shaft with protruding steel arms that support wooden, plastic, or steel blades. The paddle shafts can be located transverse to or parallel to the flow, although transverse installation is more common (Figure 6c). The paddle units slowly rotate, usually at 1–10 rpm, causing collision among the floc particles that are held in suspension by the gentle agitation. The result is growth of the suspended particles from colloids to settleable floc.

The importance of the root mean velocity gradient (G) in flocculation has been challenged in research literature [3]; however, G is still used as a guide for mixing in flocculation. Optimum G values and durations exist for flocculation and are often determined by laboratory or pilot studies. G values can be modified in the plant if variable speed drives are used for the mixers. Below a minimum time, no flocculation occurs, and increasing the time beyond maximum floc formation does not significantly improve flocculation. Based on experience, flocculation tanks with a minimum of three compartments in series reduce the time required for flocculation. In general, the minimum and maximum values of G for mechanical mixers to promote satisfactory growth of floc are 10 and 75 s^{-1}, respectively, with an optimum range in water treatment with paddle flocculators of 30–60 s^{-1} [4]. In tapered flocculation mixing in each of the compartments is varied from higher G values to lower G values to handle the flocs more gently as they grow in size.

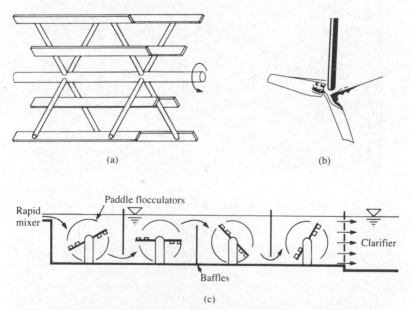

(a)

(b)

(c)

FIGURE 6   The common mixing devices for flocculation in water treatment are (a) the paddle flocculator and (b) the axial mixer. (c) A typical flocculation tank arrangement—horizontal shaft paddles in a series of compartments separated by baffles to direct water flow through the paddle flocculators. Water flows to the clarifier through a ported wall.

The power dissipated in water by a paddle flocculator can be calculated as

$$P = \frac{C_d A \rho [v_p(1 - k)]^3}{2} \tag{6}$$

where

P = power dissipated, ft · lb/s (N · m/s)
C_d = coefficient of drag; 1.8 for flat plates
A = area of paddles, ft^2 (m^2)
ρ = density of water, lb · s^2/ft^4 (kg/m^3)
v_p = velocity of paddle, ft/s (m/s)
k = ratio of the rotational velocity of the water to the velocity of the paddle, normally 0.25–0.50, with 0.3 being a common value

For a paddle flocculator,

$$v_p = 2\pi r N \tag{7}$$

where

v_p = velocity of paddle blade, ft/s (m/s)
r = distance from shaft to center of paddle, ft (m)
N = rotational speed, rev/s (rev/s)

Then for a flocculation tank with n symmetrical paddle arms with blades at radii $r_1, r_2 \ldots r_j$ rotating at N rev/s, the power dissipated is

$$P = \frac{n}{2} C_d A_i \rho (1 - k)^3 (2\pi N)^3 \sum_1^j r_i^3 \tag{8}$$

where

A_i = area of each paddle blade, ft^2 (m^2)

With regard to flocculation, the following recommendations are presented in the *Recommended Standards for Water Works, Great Lakes Upper Mississippi River Board of State Sanitary Engineers* [5]:

1. Inlet and outlet design shall prevent short-circuiting and destruction of floc.
2. The flow-through velocity shall be not less than 0.5 ft/min nor greater than 1.5 ft/min with a detention time for floc formation of at least 30 min.
3. Agitators shall be driven by variable-speed drives with the peripheral speed of paddles ranging from 0.5 ft/s to 3.0 ft/s.
4. Flocculation and sedimentation basins shall be as close together as possible. The velocity of flocculated water through pipes or conduits to settling basins shall be

not less than 0.5 ft/s nor greater than 1.5 ft/s. Allowances must be made to minimize turbulence at bends and changes in direction.

A preferred method to move water into a sedimentation basin from a flocculator is through a ported wall (Figure 6c), a wall containing numerous holes to allow the water with large flocs to enter the sedimentation basin without a high degree of turbulence that would tend to shear the flocs.

For vertical turbine flocculators the D/T_e values should be 0.3 to 0.45.

Example 4

A 25-mgd water treatment plant has a flocculation tank 64 ft long and 100 ft wide with a water depth of 16 ft. The four horizontal shafts of paddle flocculators are in compartments separated by baffles (Figure 6c). All the paddle units have four arms with two blades (Figure 6a), with radii of 3.0 and 6.0 ft measured from the shaft to the center of the 0.80-ft-wide boards. The total length of the paddle boards across the tank is 90 ft. Assume a ratio of water velocity to paddle velocity of 0.3, rotational speed of 3 rev/min, C_d equal to 1.8, and water temperature of 50°F. Calculate the velocity gradient.

Solution: From a table in the appendix for water at 50°F, $\rho = 1.936 \text{ lb} \cdot \text{s/ft}^4$, and $\mu = 2.735 \times 10^{-5} \text{ lb} \cdot \text{s/ft}^2$. The number of paddle arms = 4 stages × 4 arms/stage. Then, using equation 8,

$$P = \frac{4 \times 4}{2} \times 1.8(0.80 \text{ ft} \times 90 \text{ ft})1.936\frac{\text{lb} \cdot \text{s}^2}{\text{ft}^4}(1 - 0.3)^3\left(2 \times \pi \times 3\frac{\text{rev}}{\text{min}} \times \frac{\text{min}}{60 \text{ s}}\right)^3$$
$$[(3.0 \text{ ft})^3 + (6.0 \text{ ft})^3]$$

$$= 5187 \text{ ft} \cdot \text{lb/s}$$

$$G = \left(\frac{5187\dfrac{\text{ft} \cdot \text{lb}}{\text{s}}}{2.735 \times 10^{-5}\dfrac{\text{lb} \cdot \text{s}}{\text{ft}^2} \times 16 \text{ ft} \times 64 \text{ ft} \times 100 \text{ ft}}\right)^{1/2} = 43 \text{ s}^{-1}$$

SEDIMENTATION

Sedimentation (clarification) is the removal of solid particles from suspension by gravity. In water treatment, the common application of sedimentation is after chemical treatment to remove flocculated impurities and precipitates. In wastewater processing, sedimentation is used to reduce suspended solids in the influent wastewater and to remove settleable solids after biological treatment.

Design of clarifiers is based on empirical data from the performance of full-scale sedimentation tanks. Mathematical relationships to predict settling of suspensions in actual treatment processes have not been successful in design, and the application of data from laboratory settling column tests has met with only limited success. For these reasons, design criteria are derived from operation of clarifiers settling similar kinds of waters and wastewaters.

8   FUNDAMENTALS OF SEDIMENTATION

Settling of nonflocculent particles in dilute suspension, as defined by classical settling theory of discrete particles, has no direct application in water and wastewater sedimentation. It is, however, the basis for the hypothetical relationship between settling velocity and overflow rate. Figure 7 illustrates an ideal rectangular clarifier with an inlet zone for transition of influent flow to uniform horizontal flow, a sedimentation zone where the particles settle out of suspension by gravity, an outlet zone for transition of uniform flow in the sedimentation zone to rising flow for discharge, and a sludge zone where the settled particles collect. All influent discrete particles with a settling velocity equal to or greater than V_0 (the critical settling velocity) settle to the sludge zone and are removed. Particles with settling velocities of V_i, less than V_0, are removed only if they enter the basin within a vertical distance from the sludge zone of $H_i = V_i t_R$, where t_R is the flow-through or detention time. The velocity V_0 is defined as the overflow rate (gpd/ft^2), or as the surface settling rate (ft/s), and is calculated as

$$V_0 = \frac{Q}{A} \tag{9}$$

where

$\qquad V_0$ = overflow rate, gpd/ft^2 (m^3/m$^2 \cdot$ d)

$\qquad Q$ = average daily flow, gpd (m^3/d)

$\qquad A$ = surface area of the clarifier, ft^2 (m^2)

Overflow rate is an important design criterion in the sizing of sedimentation tanks. A second criterion specified in design is liquid depth in the tank. In addition to overflow rate and depth, performance of a sedimentation tank is affected by many other factors, such as nonideal inlet and outlet conditions, presence of sludge removal equipment, and currents causing nonuniform flow and disturbance of settled sludge on the bottom.

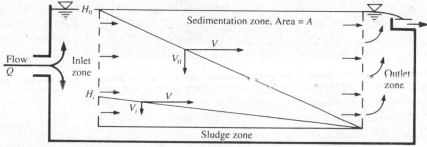

FIGURE 7 An ideal rectangular clarifier settling discrete particles with an overflow rate of $V_0 = Q/A$.

Settling of flocculent particles results in coalescence during sedimentation, with the particles growing into larger flocs as they descend. Flocculation is caused by differences in settling velocities of particles, resulting in heavy particles overtaking and coalescing with slower ones and velocity gradients within the water producing collisions among particles. The beneficial results are smaller particles growing into faster-settling floc and flocculation sweeping smaller and slower particles from suspension. The opportunity for contact among settling solids increases with depth. As a result, removal of suspended solids depends on water depth as well as overflow rate and detention time. Flocculent settling is common in clarifying both chemical and biological suspensions.

Zone settling occurs when flocculent particles in high concentration settle as a mass with a well-defined, clear interface between the surface of the settling particles and the clarified water above. Because of crowding of the particles, upward velocity of the displaced water acts to reduce settling velocity. This hindered settling reduces the differences in settling velocities of different-sized particles and increases the sweeping action of flocculation. The suspension settles as a blanket without interparticle movement; individual particles of all sizes move downward at the same velocity. Deceleration of settling occurs as hindered settling changes to *compression settling*. This occurs when subsiding particles accumulate at the bottom of the tank. Compaction slowly continues from the weight of supported particles above. Hindered settling is usually negligible in water treatment sedimentation and in clarifying of raw wastewaters, because the particles in suspension are dispersed in low concentration. Zone settling does take place in clarifying biological activated sludge in wastewater treatment. Gravity thickening in both water and wastewater sludges exhibits zone settling with hindered settling in the upper layer and compression in the bottom layer.

9   TYPES OF CLARIFIERS

Figure 8 illustrates several types of clarifiers, showing the direction of flow through the tanks. In a long rectangular clarifier, the influent is spread across the end of the tank by a baffle structure that dissipates energy to reduce the velocity of the entering water and uniformly distributes the flow. The effluent overflows V-notch weirs mounted along the edges of discharge channels that convey the water out of the tank. To reduce vertical velocities as the water rises up to the discharge channels, the total effluent weir length is several times greater than the width of the tank. Rectangular clarifiers in water treatment often have long "finger" channels extending into the tank (Figure 8a). In contrast, sedimentation tanks in wastewater treatment require scum collectors; therefore, the effluent channels are placed across the width of the tank close to the discharge end (Figure 8b). Sludge is removed by flat scrapers attached to continuous chains that are supported and driven by sprocket wheels mounted on the inside walls of the tank. Rather than submerged chain-and-sprocket mechanisms, in warm climates without snow or ice the scrapers can be hung in the water from an overhead bridge that spans the width of the tank. The wheels of the bridge roll on steel rails mounted on the side walls of the clarifier. Sludge can also be siphoned from the bottom of the tank from traveling overhead bridge structures.

In a circular clarifier, the influent enters through a vertical riser pipe with outlet ports discharging behind a circular inlet well. This baffle dissipates energy and directs

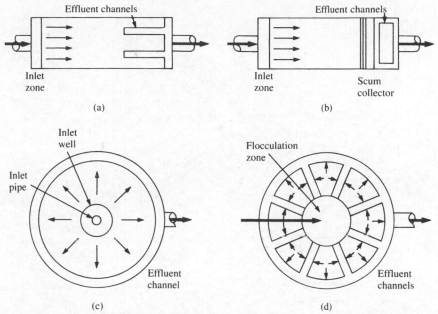

FIGURE 8 Diagrams of various clarifier shapes shown with flow patterns. (a) Rectangular clarifier with horizontal flow to effluent "finger" channels extending into the tank from the outlet end. (b) Rectangular clarifier with a scum collector and effluent channels located at the outlet end. (c) Circular clarifier with central feed well and radial flow to a peripheral effluent channel. (d) Circular flocculator–clarifier with water flowing up to radial effluent channels in the settling zone surrounding the submerged hood of the flocculation zone.

the flow downward and radially out from the center (Figure 8c). The effluent channel may be attached to the outside wall with only a single peripheral weir, or the channel may be located inboard, supported from the outside wall with brackets so that water can overflow weirs located on both sides of the channel. Sludge is scraped toward a central hopper by blades attached to arms that rotate around the center of the tank. The drive is a sealed turntable, with gear and pinion running in oil, supported by a bridge or pier. Circular clarifiers are more common in wastewater treatment. In wastewater sedimentation, a circular shallow scum baffle is placed in front of the weir channel to prevent the overflow of floating solids, and a rotating skimmer pushes the scum into a hopper that discharges to a scum tank outside the clarifier.

Figure 8d diagrams the plan view of a flocculator–clarifier that is illustrated in Figure 9. The flocculation zone is under a conical cone-shaped hood that extends to near the bottom of the tank. As the water flows out from under the hood, it rises vertically to radial effluent channels. This kind of settling tank, common in water softening, is also referred to as an upflow clarifier or a reactor–clarifier.

Several parameters are used in sizing clarifiers. The most common is overflow rate, which is the flow rate divided by the total surface area of the tank [Eq. (9)]. Of equal significance is the side-water depth, which is the depth of water in the tank

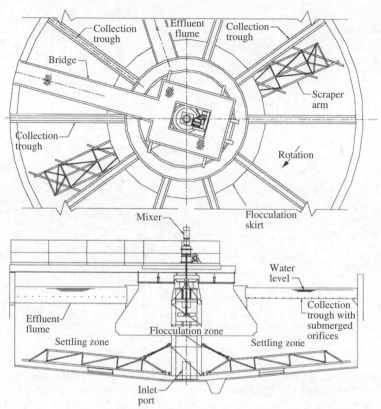

FIGURE 9   Flocculator–clarifier provides mixing, flocculation, and sedimentation in a compartmented concentric circular tank. *Source:* Walker
Process Equipment, Division of McNish Corp.

excluding the sludge zone. Freeboard (the distance between the water surface and the
top of the tank) should be a minimum of 1 ft under peak flow conditions to avoid water
overflow from the effects of wind currents and wave action in the tank. Detention time,
which is the volume divided by the average flow, although less important as a design
parameter, is often specified to ensure greater water depth at the design overflow rate.
Solids loading rates, expressed as the maximum allowable weight of solids per unit area
of tank bottom per day, apply only to gravity sludge thickening and final clarifiers of
wastewater aeration systems carrying a high concentration of biological solids.

Conservative overflow rate and sufficient depth are important to compensate for
hydraulic instability caused by temperature gradients, inlet energy dissipation, outlet
currents, equipment movement, and wind effects. Warm influent to a sedimentation
tank containing cooler water can lead to short-circuiting, with the warm water rising to
the surface and reaching the effluent channels in a fraction of the theoretical detention
time. Similarly, cold water flowing into a tank containing warm water can sink, flow
along the bottom, and short-circuit up to the effluent channels. When the inflow and
water in the tank are the same temperature, a density current is often caused by the

TABLE 1   Design Criteria for Drinking Water Sedimentation Facilities[a]

Design Parameter	Rectangular and Circular Sedimentation Basins	Reactor–Clarifiers (Solids Contact Units)
overflow rate (gpd/ft^2)	500 – 1400	700 – 1400 1500 – 2500 (softening)[b]
depth (ft)	10 - 16	
weir loading (gpd/ft)	18,000 – 24,000	12,000 – 15,000 24,000 – 30,000 (softening)
horizontal velocity (ft/min)	1 – 4	
detention time (hours)	1.5 – 4	
length to width ratio	≥ 5	
length to depth ratio	≥ 15	

[a]includes criteria from references
[4], [5], and [6]
[b]for precipitative softening processes

higher turbidity of the influent. The particles entering are heavier than the clarified water, so they descend and move under the water surface toward the discharge end.

Inlet energy dissipation is important to slow down and distribute the water at the tank entrance. This is particularly critical if the water enters the inlet zone from a pipe conveying the flocculated water at the higher velocity necessary to keep the solids in suspension in the pipeline. Outlet currents are reduced by proper design of the effluent weirs and channels. In preference to flow plates, V-notch weirs provide better lateral distribution of overflow when leveling is not perfect. Channels require sufficient length and adequate spacing to reduce the approach velocity of overflow. Weir length can be designed by applying the criteria in Table 1 for weir loading (the flow per unit length of weir). Movement of sludge collection mechanisms through the sludge is slow to prevent resuspension of solids. Finally, wind can have a significant effect on large open sedimentation tanks by creating a surface current that moves the upper layer of water downwind.

10   SEDIMENTATION IN WATER TREATMENT

Sedimentation Tanks

Surface water containing high turbidity (e.g., from a muddy river) may require sedimentation prior to chemical treatment. Presedimentation basins can have hopper bottoms or be equipped with continuous mechanical sludge-removal apparatus. The minimum recommended detention period for presedimentation is 3 hr, although in many cases this is not adequate to settle out fine suspensions that occur at certain times of the year. Chemical feed equipment for coagulation is frequently provided ahead of presedimentation basins for periods when the raw water is too turbid to clarify adequately by plain sedimentation.

Sedimentation following flocculation depends on the settling characteristics of the floc formed in the coagulation process. Typical ranges of overflow rates, detention times, and other sedimentation design parameters are given in Table 1.

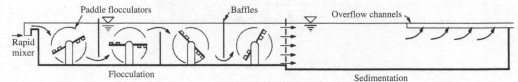

FIGURE 10   Rapid mixer, flocculation basin, and rectangular sedimentation tank in series.

Plan-view diagrams of clarifiers used in water treatment are sketched in Figure 8. Although circular clarifiers are sometimes used, rectangular tanks are more common in new designs. Figure 10 shows the arrangement of rapid mixing, flocculation, and sedimentation. Water enters at the right side of the figure where it receives a dose of coagulant in the rapid mixing tank and then flows directly into the flocculators, where the floc is developed. The treated water then enters the sedimentation tank through a ported wall, traverses the tank and flows into effluent channels over V-notch weirs.

Solids Contact Units

Where quality of the water supply does not vary greatly, such as that from a well supply, flocculator–clarifiers (solids contact units) are an efficient method of chemical treatment. One such unit, shown in Figure 9, combines the processes of mixing, flocculation, and sedimentation in a single-compartmented tank. Raw water and added chemicals are mixed with the slurry of previously precipitated solids to promote growth of larger crystals and agglomerated clusters that settle more readily.

The *Recommended Standards for Water Works* [5] states that flocculator–clarifiers are generally acceptable for combined softening and clarification where water characteristics, especially temperature, do not fluctuate rapidly, flow rates are uniform, and operation is continuous. Before such units are considered as clarifiers without softening, specific approval of the reviewing authority shall be obtained. Clarifiers should be designed for the maximum daily flow and should be adjustable to changes in flow that are less than the design rate and for changes in water characteristics. Design criteria are shown in Table 1.

Sludge

The volume of sludge removed from clarifiers in water treatment plus the quantity of backwash water from cleaning granular-media filters is generally from 4% to 6% of the processed water. The exact amount of wastewater produced depends on the chemical treatment processes employed, the type of sludge collection apparatus, and the kind of filter backwash equipment.

Example 5

Four rectangular clarifiers in parallel, each 200 ft long and 40 ft wide with a water depth of 12 ft, are used to settle a total flow of 20.0 mgd after a flocculation process. Calculate the overflow rate, detention time, and horizontal velocity. Also determine the length of effluent weir required to meet a specification of 20,000 gpd/ft.

Solution: For each sedimentation tank,

$$Q = 20 \text{ mgd}/4 = 5 \text{ mgd}$$

$$\text{overflow rate} = \frac{Q}{A} = \frac{5 \times 10^6 \, \text{gal}/\text{d}}{200 \text{ ft} \times 40 \text{ ft}} = 625 \, \text{gpd}/\text{ft}^2$$

$$V = 200 \text{ ft} \times 40 \text{ ft} \times 12 \text{ ft} = 96,000 \text{ ft}^3$$

$$t_0 = \frac{96,000 \text{ ft}^3 \times 7.48 \, \text{gal}/\text{ft}^3 \times 24 \, \text{hr}/\text{d}}{5 \times 10^6 \, \text{gal}/\text{d}} = 3.45 \text{ hr}$$

$$\text{horizontal velocity} = \frac{Q}{\text{cross-sectional area}}$$

$$= \frac{5 \times 10^6 \, \text{gal}/\text{d}}{40 \text{ ft} \times 12 \text{ ft} \times 7.48 \, \text{gal}/\text{ft}^3 \times 1440 \, \text{min}/\text{d}} = 0.97 \text{ fpm}$$

Note: the horizontal velocity can also be calculated by

$$\frac{L}{t_0} = \frac{200 \text{ ft}}{3.45 \text{ hr} \times 60 \, \text{min}/\text{hr}} = 0.97 \text{ fpm}$$

$$\text{weir length} = \frac{5 \times 10^6 \text{ gpd}}{20,000 \, \text{gpd}/\text{ft}} = 250 \text{ ft}$$

11   SEDIMENTATION IN WASTEWATER TREATMENT

Clarifiers used to settle raw wastewater are referred to as *primary tanks*. Sedimentation tanks used between trickling filters in a two-stage secondary treatment system are called *intermediate clarifiers*. *Final clarifiers* are settling tanks following secondary aerobic treatment units. Design criteria for wastewater sedimentation tanks are provided in Table 2.

TABLE 2   Design Criteria for Wastewater Sedimentation Facilities[a]

Design Parameter	Primary	Final (Trickling Filter)	Final (Activated Sludge)
overflow rate (gpd/ft^2)	600–1000	800–1200	400–800
	1500 peak[b]	1200–2500 peak	1000–1600 peak
depth (ft)	10–16	10–15	12–20
weir loading (gpd/ft)	10,000–20,000	10,000–15,000	10,000–20,000
		30,000 peak	30,000 peak
detention time (hours)	1.5–2.5		2–3
solids loading			20–40
(lb/ft$^2 \cdot$ d)			35–50 peak

[a]includes criteria from references [7], [8], [9], and [10]
[b]peak hourly flow

Figure 11 shows a typical primary settling tank. Wastewater enters at the center behind a stilling baffle and travels down and outward toward effluent weirs located on the periphery of the tank. The inlet line usually terminates near the surface, but the wastewater must travel down behind the stilling baffle before entering the actual settling zone. A stilling well reduces the velocity and imparts a downward motion to the solids, which drop to the tank floor.

(a)

(b)

FIGURE 11   Typical primary settling tank for wastewater treatment. (a) Circular settling tank with an inboard weir trough. (b) Stilling well and sludge-collecting mechanism in a circular clarifier. *Source:* Walker Process Equipment, Division of McNish Corp.

Final settling tanks for activated-sludge processes are sized to account for zone settling of a flocculent suspension. Design detention times, overflow rates, and weir loadings are selected to minimize the problems with solids loadings, density currents, inlet hydraulic turbulence, and occasional poor sludge settleability. Compared to other wastewater sedimentation tanks, activated-sludge final clarifiers are deeper to accommodate the greater depth of hindered solids settling, have a lower overflow rate to reduce carryover of buoyant biological floc, and have inboard weir channels to reduce the approach velocity of the effluent. Typical design criteria are shown in Table 2. Clarifiers with shallow water depths or high overflow rates may be limited to lower allowable solids loading rates.

The BOD removal from raw domestic wastewater in primary settling is generally 30%–40%, with the commonly assumed design BOD removal being 35% and suspended-solids removal being 50%. Of course, the effectiveness of plain sedimentation depends on the characteristics of the wastewater as well as clarifier design. If a municipal wastewater contains an unusual amount of soluble organic matter from industrial wastes, the BOD removal could be less than 30%; conversely, if industrial wastes contribute settleable solids, the BOD removal could be greater than 40%.

Design of a clarifier, the hydraulic loading, and wastewater characteristics influence the density of the accumulated sludge withdrawn from a clarifier [8]. With proper design and operation, the sludge gravity thickens in the bottom of the tank. Hydraulic disturbances usually result in a more dilute sludge, in addition to reduced BOD and suspended-solids removal from the wastewater. Retaining the sludge solids too long can increase biological activity and expansion of the settled sludge blanket in both primary and final tanks. The higher the wastewater temperature, the greater the biological gas production and thinning of the settled sludge. In primary sedimentation, return of waste-activated sludge to the head of a plant can cause detrimental microbiological activity in the settled raw sludge, leading to foul odors, floating sludge, and thinning of the withdrawn sludge. Shortening the retention time of the sludge in the tank by more frequent withdrawal can help, but the best arrangement is separate disposal of the waste-activated sludge. In final sedimentation of activated sludge, retention of the settled sludge for too long can lead to floating solids and thinning of the sludge. The best solution is to use a scraper mechanism with uptake pipes spaced along the arm to remove the solids from the entire floor of the tank rather than plowing them to a central hopper prior to withdrawal.

The clarifier in Figure 12 is designed as a final clarifier for an activated-sludge secondary. The liquid flow pattern is the same as that of a primary clarifier, but the sludge collection system is unique. Suction pipes are attached to and spaced along a V-plow-scraper mechanism rotated by a turntable above the liquid surface. The discharge elevation of the suction riser pipes in the sight well is lower than the water surface in the tank so that sludge is forced up and out of the uptake pipes by water pressure.

Rapid uniform withdrawal of sludge across the entire bottom of an activated-sludge final clarifier has two distinct advantages. The retention time of solids that settle near the tank's periphery is not greater than those that land near the center; thus, aging of the biological floc and subsequent floating solids due to gas production are eliminated. With a scraper collector, the residence time of settled solids depends directly on the radial distance from the sludge hopper. The second advantage is that the direction

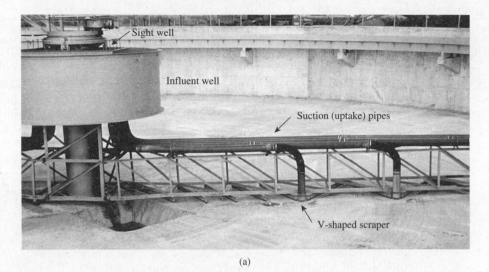

(a)

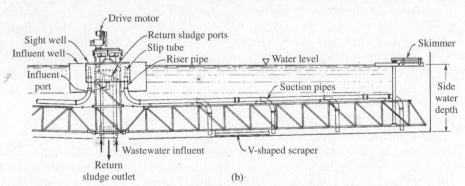

(b)

FIGURE 12   Final clarifier designed for use with activated-sludge processes. Return sludge
is withdrawn through suction (uptake) pipes located along the collector arm for rapid return
to the aeration tank. Sludge flowing from each pipe can be observed in the sight well.
Source: Walker Process Equipment, Division of McNish Corporation.

of activated-sludge return flow is essentially perpendicular to the tank bottom, rather
than horizontal toward a centrally located sludge hopper. Downward flow through a
sludge blanket enhances gravity settling of the floc and increases sludge density. This is
an important factor when one considers that the return flow may be as great as one-
half of the influent flow.

Zone settling occurs in gravity separation of flocculent biological suspensions
from activated-sludge aeration in wastewater treatment and flocculent chemical suspensions from coagulated water. Figure 13 is a schematic diagram of the circular
final clarifier in Figure 12. The influent, a flocculent suspension, enters in the center
from the biological aeration tank, and clear effluent overflows the outlet weir around
the periphery of the tank. In this continuous-flow system, zone settling is represented
by the clear supernatant and the hindered settling layer beneath. Compression of

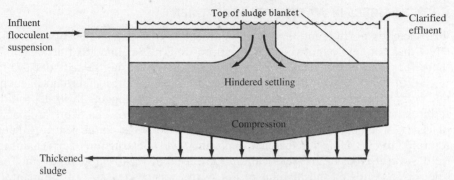

FIGURE 13 A schematic diagram of zone settling in the activated-sludge final clarifier illustrated in Figure 12.

solids occurs near the bottom of the tank. Thickened sludge is continuously withdrawn from the tank bottom by uptake pipes and returned to the aeration tank.

Example 6

Determine the dimensions for two rectangular primary clarifiers to settle 3400 m^3/d of domestic wastewater based on the following criteria: an overflow rate of 32 $m^3/m^2 \cdot d$, a side-water depth of 2.4 m, weir loading of 125–250 $m^3/m \cdot d$, and a length/width ratio in the range of 3/1 to 5/1. Calculate the detention time and estimate the BOD removal efficiency after sizing the tanks.

Solution:

$$\text{surface area of each tank} = \frac{3400 \text{ m}^3/\text{d}}{2 \times 32 \text{ m}^3/\text{m}^2 \cdot \text{d}} = 53.1 \text{ m}^2$$

The appropriate width for a standard-sized sludge-removal mechanism is 4.0 m. Therefore, the tank length is 53.1/4.0 = 13.3 m, and the length/width ratio is 13.3/4.0 = 3.3/1, which is within the desired range of 3/1–5/1.

$$\text{detention time} = \frac{2 \times 53.1 \text{ m}^2 \times 2.4 \text{ m} \times 24 \text{ hr/d}}{3400 \text{ m}^3/\text{d}} = 1.8 \text{ hr}$$

$$\text{maximum weir length} = \frac{3400 \text{ m}^3/\text{d}}{125 \text{ m}^3/\text{m}^2 \cdot \text{d}} = 27.2 \text{ m}$$

$$\text{minimum weir length} = \frac{3400 \text{ m}^3/\text{d}}{250 \text{ m}^3/\text{m}^2 \cdot \text{d}} = 13.6 \text{ m}$$

Consider one inboard effluent channel and an end weir across the width of each tank. For this arrangement,

$$\text{weir loading} = \frac{3400 \text{ m}^3/\text{d}}{2 \times 3 \times 4 \text{ m}} = 140 \text{ m}^3/\text{m} \cdot \text{d (OK)}$$

The BOD removal efficiency for an overflow rate of 32 $m^3/m^2 \cdot d$ = 800 gpd/ft^2/day is assumed to be 35%.

12   GRIT CHAMBERS IN WASTEWATER TREATMENT

Grit includes gravel, sand, and heavy particulate matter such as corn kernels, bone chips, and coffee grounds. For design purposes, grit is defined as fine sand, 0.2-mm-diameter particles with a specific gravity of 2.65 and a settling velocity of 0.075 fps.

Grit removal in municipal wastewater treatment protects mechanical equipment and pumps from abnormal abrasive wear, prevents pipe clogging by its deposition, and reduces accumulation in settling tanks and digesters. Grit chambers are commonly placed between lift pumps and primary settling tanks. Wear on the centrifugal pumps is tolerated to obtain the convenience of ground-level construction of grit chambers.

Several types of grit-removal units are used in wastewater treatment. The kind selected depends on the amount of grit in the wastewater, size of the plant, convenience of operation and maintenance, and costs of installation and operation. Standard types are channel-shaped settling tanks, aerated tanks of various shapes with hopper bottoms, clarifier-type tanks with mechanical scraper arms, and cyclone grit separators with screw-type grit washers.

Historically popular but rarely in use today, the channel-type grit chamber is a long, narrow, shallow settling channel with a proportional weir placed in the discharge end. The weir opening is shaped to keep the horizontal velocity relatively constant with varying depths of flow. To prevent scouring of the precipitated grit, the horizontal velocity is controlled at approximately 1 fps.

Square and rectangular hopper-bottom tanks with the inlet and effluent weir on opposite sides of the tank are generally used in small plants. These units are often mixed by diffused aeration to keep the organic solids in suspension while the grit settles out. Design of an aerated hopper-bottom grit tank is based on a detention time of approximately 1 min at peak hourly flow. Settled substances are removed from the hopper bottom by pumping, screw conveyor, bucket elevator, or, if possible, gravity flow.

Clarifier-type tanks are generally square, with influent and effluent weirs on opposite sides. A centrally driven collector arm scrapes the settled grit into an end hopper. The grit is then elevated into a receptacle with a chain and bucket, or screw conveyor. The clarifier may be a shallow tank or a deeper aerated chamber.

Grit taken from these kinds of grit chambers is sometimes relatively high in organic content. A counterflow grit washer that functions like a screw conveyor can be used to wash the grit and return waste organics to the plant influent. Alternatively, a special centrifugal pump can lift the slurry from a grit sump to a centrifugal cyclone. The cyclone separates the grit from the organic material and discharges it to a classifier for washing and draining. Wash water and washed-out organics from the cyclone and classifier return to the wastewater.

Preaeration of raw wastewater prior to primary sedimentation is practiced to restore freshness, scrub out entrained gases, and improve subsequent settling. The process is similar to flocculation if the detention time is not less than 45 min without chemical addition, or about 30 min with chemicals. Normally, the purpose of preaeration is freshening wastewater, not flocculation, and little or no BOD reduction occurs. The detention time in preaeration basins is generally less than 20 min. Air supplied for proper agitation ranges from 0.05 to 0.20 ft^3/gal of applied wastewater.

Processes of grit removal and preaeration can be performed in the same basin—a hopper-bottom or clarifier-type tank provided with grit-removal and washing equipment. Aeration mixing improves grit separation while freshening the wastewater.

Example 7

Design wastewater flows for a treatment plant are an average daily flow of 280 gpm and a peak hourly rate of 450 gpm. Estimate tank volumes and dimensions for the following grit-removal units: (1) a hopper-bottom tank with grit washer and (2) a clarifier-type unit for grit removal and preaeration.

Solution:

1. Design criteria for a hopper-bottom grit-removal tank:

    detention time $= 1$ min at peak flow

    volume of tank required $= 450 \times 1.0 = 450$ gal $= 60$ ft^3

2. Design criteria for a preaeration basin with grit removal:

    detention time $= 20$ min

    volume of basin required $= 280 \times 20 = 5600$ gal $= 750$ ft^3

    Use a 12×12 ft basin 6 ft deep + freeboard. Provide a revolving clarifier mechanism, a separate grit washer, and diffused aeration along one side of the tank.

FILTRATION

Filtration is used to separate nonsettleable solids from water and wastewater by passing it through a porous medium. The most common system is filtration through a layered bed of granular media, usually a coarse anthracite coal underlain by a finer sand.

13   GRAVITY GRANULAR-MEDIA FILTRATION

Gravity filtration through beds of granular media is the most common method of removing colloidal impurities in water processing and tertiary treatment of wastewater.

The mechanisms involved in removing suspended solids in a granular-media filter are complex, consisting of interception, straining, flocculation, and sedimentation, as shown schematically in Figure 14. Initially, surface straining and interstitial removal results in accumulation of deposits in the upper portion of the filter media. Because of the reduction in pore area, the velocity of water through the remaining voids increases, shearing off pieces of captured floc and carrying impurities deeper into the filter bed. The effective zone of removal passes deeper and deeper into the filter. Turbulence and the resulting increased particle contact within the pores promotes flocculation, resulting in trapping of the larger floc particles. Eventually, clean bed depth is

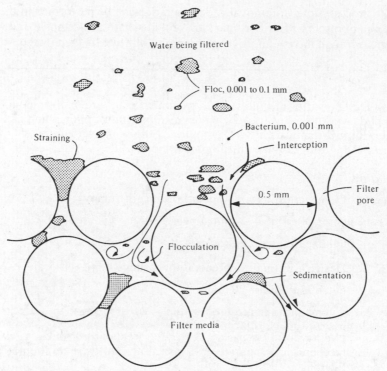

FIGURE 14   Schematic diagram illustrating straining, flocculation, interception, and sedimentation actions in a granular-media filter.

no longer available and breakthrough occurs, carrying solids out in the underflow and
causing termination of the filter run. It is important to terminate the filter run before
breakthrough occurs and to clean the filter before it is returned to service. This means
that more than one filter needs to be provided in any filtration process so that water
can continuously be processed through the plant. While one filter is being cleaned in a
process called "backwashing," the remaining filters process the plant flow, and accordingly, their flow rates proportionally increase. Four filters are usually considered to be
the minimum number for proper plant operation to avoid excessive filtration rates
during the backwashing of one filter.

Microscopic particulate matter in raw water that has not been chemically treated
will pass through the relatively larger pores of a filter bed. On the other hand, suspended solids fed to a filter with excess coagulant carryover from chemical treatment
produces clogging of the bed pores at the surface. Optimum filtration occurs when
impurities in the water and coagulant concentration cause "in-depth" filtration. The
impurities neither pass through the bed nor are all strained out on the surface, but a
significant amount of flocculated solids are removed throughout the entire depth of
the filter.

Granular-media filtration of surface water for removal of *Giardia* cysts using field-
scale pilot filters and testing at full-scale treatment plants has demonstrated the

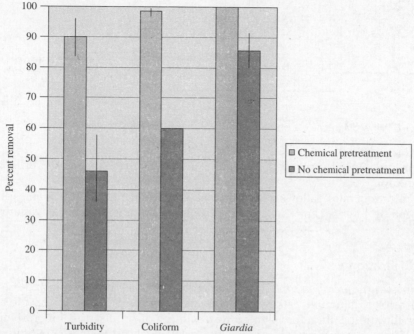

FIGURE 15 Comparison of turbidity, coliform, and *Giardia* removal efficiencies by filtration with and without chemical pretreatment.

necessity of proper chemical pretreatment for effective removal of microscopic particles (Figure 15) [11]. Even a lapse in chemical feed for a short time allows a higher proportion of particles, including cysts, to pass through the filter. The best indicators of proper chemical pretreatment for removal of *Giardia* cysts and other microscopic particles are the percentage reduction in turbidity and the concentration of turbidity in the filtered water. The survey of full-scale treatment plants processing waters from mountain streams containing *Giardia* cysts verified the importance of proper chemical pretreatment. *Giardia* cysts were found in the finished waters of those plants with either no chemical pretreatment or improper coagulation. In filtering these low-turbidity waters (less than 1 NTU), effective chemical pretreatment is determined by either a finished water turbidity of less than 0.1 NTU or the absence of microscopic particles [11].

Traditional Filtration

A typical scheme for processing surface supplies to drinking water quality, shown in Figure 16, consists of flocculation with a chemical coagulant and sedimentation prior to filtration. Under the force of gravity, often by a combination of positive head and suction from underneath, water passes downward through the media that collect the floc and particles. When the media become filled or solids break through, a filter bed is cleaned by backwashing where upward flow fluidizes the media and conveys away the impurities that have accumulated in the bed. Destruction of bacteria

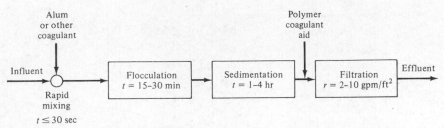

FIGURE 16　Flow diagram for a traditional surface water treatment system.

and viruses depends on satisfactory turbidity control to enhance the efficiency of chlorination.

Filtration rates following flocculation and sedimentation are in the range of $2-10 \text{ gpm/ft}^2$ $(1.4-6.8 \text{ l/m}^2 \cdot \text{s})$; 5 gpm/ft^2 $(3.4 \text{ l/m}^2 \cdot \text{s})$ is normally the maximum design rate.

Direct Filtration

The process of *direct filtration*, diagrammed in Figure 17, does not include sedimentation prior to filtration; rather, particles and flocs are removed in the filter alone. Direct filtration is therefore limited to treatment of waters with low turbidity and color. When suitable, direct filtration allows substantial cost savings in treatment plant construction because large and costly sedimentation tanks are not required. *Contact flocculation*, sometimes referred to as in-line filtration and less commonly in use, eliminates the flocculation as well as the sedimentation process. Some flocculation occurs in the filter itself [12]. Successful advances in direct filtration are attributed to the development of coarse-to-fine multimedia filters with greater capacity for "in-depth" filtration, improved backwashing systems using mechanical or air agitation to aid cleaning of the media, and the availability of better polymer coagulants.

Surface waters with low turbidity and color are most suitable for processing by direct filtration. Based on experiences cited in the literature, waters with less than 40 units of color, turbidity consistently below 5 units, iron and manganese concentrations of less than 0.3 and 0.05 mg/l, respectively, and algal counts below 2000/ml can be successfully processed [13]. Operational problems in direct filtration are expected when

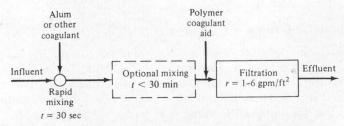

FIGURE 17　Flow diagram for direct filtration of a surface water supply or tertiary treatment of wastewater.

color exceeds 40 units or turbidity is greater than 15 units on a continuous basis. Potential problems can often be alleviated during a short period of time by application of additional polymer as a filtration aid. Tertiary filtration of wastewaters containing 20–30 mg/l of suspended solids following biological treatment can be reduced to less than 5 mg/l by direct filtration. For inactivation of viruses and a high degree of bacterial disinfection, filtration of chemically conditioned wastewater often precedes disinfection.

The feasibility of filtration without prior flocculation and sedimentation relies on a comprehensive review of water quality data. The incidence of high turbidities caused by runoff from storms and blooms of algae must be evaluated. Often, pilot testing is valuable in determining efficiency of direct filtration compared to conventional treatment, design of filter media, and selection of chemical conditioning.

Filtration rates in direct filtration are usually $1-6$ gpm/ft^2 $(0.7-4.1$ l/m$^2\cdot$s$)$, somewhat lower than the rates following traditional pretreatment.

14   DESCRIPTION OF A TYPICAL GRAVITY FILTER SYSTEM

A cutaway view of a gravity filter is shown in Figure 18. During filtration, the water enters above the filter media through an inlet flume. After passing downward through the granular media (depth of 24–30 in.) and the supporting gravel bed, it is collected in

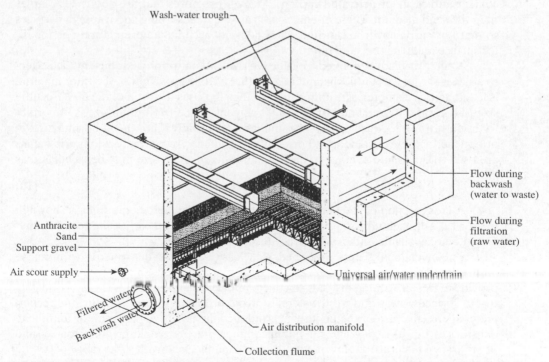

FIGURE 18   Cutaway view of a gravity-filter box with water and air piping, wash-water troughs, and dual-media filter supported on a plastic block underdrain. *Source:* The F. B. Leopold Company, Inc.

the underdrain system and discharged through the underdrain pipe. To backwash the dirty filter, the water level is lowered to near the surface of the granular bed, and the media are scoured by either upward flow of air alone or by upward flow of air and water concurrently. Wash water entering the underdrain is distributed under the media and flows upward hydraulically, expanding the media and conveying out impurities. The turbid wash water is collected in the wash-water troughs that discharge to the outlet flume.

Filter Media

Broadly speaking, filter media should be (1) coarse enough to retain large quantities of floc, (2) sufficiently fine to prevent passage of suspended solids, (3) deep enough to allow relatively long filter runs, and (4) graded to permit backwash cleaning. These attributes are not all compatible. For example, a very fine sand retains floc, which also tends to shorten the filter run, while for a coarse sand the opposite would be true. Typically dual-media beds of anthracite, or sometimes activated carbon, overlying sand are used so that high rates of filtration can be obtained.

A sand filter bed with a relatively uniform grain size can provide effective filtration throughout its depth. If the grain size gradation is too great, effective filtering is confined to the upper few inches of sand. This results because the finest sand grains accumulate on the top of the bed during stratification after backwashing. The problem of surface plugging of sand filters led to the development of dual-media filters. The coarser anthracite or activated carbon top layer has pores that are about 20% larger than the sand medium. These openings are capable of adsorbing and trapping particles so that floc carried over in clarified water does not accumulate prematurely on the filter surface and plug the sand filter.

A filter medium is defined by effective size and uniformity coefficient. The effective size is the 10-percentile diameter (d_{10}); that is, 10% by weight of the filter material is less than this diameter. The uniformity coefficient (U) is the ratio of the 60-percentile size (d_{60}) to the 10-percentile size. The 90-percentile size (d_{90}) grain size is important to the filtration backwash process. Granular media usually follow a log-normal distribution (the log of the diameter is normally distributed). Accordingly, geometric means are used to determine average grain sizes, and the d_{90} grain size may be calculated as

$$d_{90} = d_{10} U^{1.67} \tag{10}$$

A cross-section of the anthracite coal and sand in a dual media filter is shown in Figure 19. Although uniformity coefficients of 1.7 are acceptable, smaller coefficients 1.4 – 1.5 are available and provide a better filtration process.

Unconventional filters described by Cleasby [14] are dual media with coarse anthracite having an effective size of about 1.5 mm and a low uniformity coefficient to provide a greater volume of voids to collect impurities and extend filter runs of highly turbid surface waters and wastewaters. To avoid problems in backwashing, the recommended effective size of the underlying sand medium is 0.75 to 0.90 mm for anthracite densities of 1.45 to 1.65. While still not in common practice, single-medium coarse-sand or anthracite filters are gaining popularity. For example, sand with a size range of 0.9–1.5 mm and about 1.0 m depth has been used in surface water treatment plants. These filters are scoured with concurrent air and water at nonfluidizing velocity followed by a brief

Anthracite (coal):
Specific gravity 1.4–1.6
Effective size 0.9–1.1 mm
Uniformity coefficient < 1.7

Sand:
Specific gravity 2.65
Effective size 0.45–0.55 mm
Uniformity coefficient < 1.7

Coarse sand

Layers of fine to
coarse gravel

Underdrain

FIGURE 19   Cross section of the media in a coal–sand dual-media filter and supporting gravel layer showing typical grain sizes, specific gravities, effective sizes, and uniformity coefficients.

wash at high velocity with water alone. Triple-media filters comprising anthracite, sand, and garnet layers have been used for many years in the United States. Both dual- and triple-media filters are substantially better than the conventional sand filter in providing longer filter runs with a corresponding reduction in required backwash water. In a comparison of these two filters, however, the benefit of adding a third layer has not been well demonstrated [14].

As will be shown in the section on backwashing and fluidization, a correct match of dual or triple media is important to the proper operation of the filter. If not properly matched, the backwash velocity required to fluidize the coarse grains of one of the media may cause the fine grains of the other media to be washed out of the filter and lost in the backwashing process.

Underdrain Systems

The purposes of the underdrain of a filter are to support the filter media, collect the filtered water, and distribute the water for backwashing and air for scouring. Layers of gravel have been used as the top portion of the underdrain system, but porous plates or nozzles that keep media out of the clear well and adequately distribute backwash water and air have been used in many recent filter installations. The number and depths of the gravel layers, both to prevent loss of the media during filtration and to contribute to uniform distribution of backwash water, depend on the size of openings in the underdrain. Large openings require a deep gravel layer, and hence a deeper filter box, but have reduced head loss during backwashing. Smaller openings, such as the slots in nozzles, require only the finer gravel layers but have

362   Physical Treatment Processes

TABLE 3   Common Filter Underdrain Systems

Kind of Underdrain	Features
Pipe laterals with orifices	Deep gravel layer
	Medium head loss
	No air scouring
Pipe laterals with nozzles	Shallow gravel layer
	High head loss
	Air scouring
Vitrified tile block	Shallow gravel layer
	Medium head loss
	No air scouring
Plastic dual-lateral block	Deep gravel layer
	Low head loss
	Concurrent air-and-water scouring
	or air scouring
Plastic nozzles	Shallow or no gravel layer
	High head loss
	Air scouring

higher head loss. When gravel is used, it is graded from fine (about 1/16 in.) in the top layer, through several layers, to coarse (about $2\frac{1}{2}$ in.) in the bottom layer. The underdrain systems of pipe laterals with orifices and vitrified tile blocks allow only water backwash; some underdrains permit separate air scour and water backwash; and others are designed for concurrent air-and-water scour and water backwash. Table 3 lists some of the common filter underdrain systems. Vitrified tile, plastic block, and nozzles are manufactured, proprietary systems. Pipe lateral underdrains can be fabricated on site. The quality of water or wastewater being filtered, type of filter media, backwash, and scouring system desired, and cost are factors that influence underdrain design [15].

The earliest underdrain was composed of pipe laterals with orifices composed of perforated pipes surrounded and overlain by graded gravel layers. If the pipe laterals were fitted with nozzles, the gravel layer could be shallower and air scouring could be used. Vitrified tile blocks have upper and lower laterals with orifices. Wash water enters the lower lateral, flows up through orifices into the upper lateral, and flows upward again through a second set of orifices for uniform distribution under the gravel layer. The disadvantage is the inability to use air scouring or air-and-water backwash. The plastic block shown in Figures 18 and 20 has a dual-parallel lateral design for distribution of either air scouring and water backwash or concurrent air-and-water scouring and water backwash. The underdrain illustrated in Figure 21 consists of plastic nozzles without a gravel layer. Each nozzle is constructed of wedge-shaped segments assembled with stainless steel bolts to form media-retaining slots that are tapered larger in the direction of filtering water. For air scouring before water backwash, the nozzles have 6-in.-long plastic tubes that extend into the collecting well. Air is applied through the air holes that are sized to maintain a 3.5-in. cushion to ensure equal nozzle pressure and uniform air distribution.

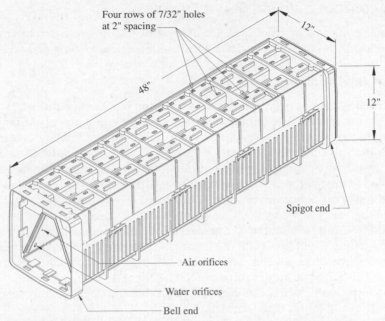

Four rows of 7/32" holes
at 2" spacing

12"

12"

48"

Spigot end

Air orifices

Water orifices

Bell end

FIGURE 20　High-density polyethylene underdrain block with dual-parallel lateral design for either air scour followed by a water backwashing or concurrent air-and-water scouring and water backwashing. *Source:* The F. B. Leopold Company, Inc.

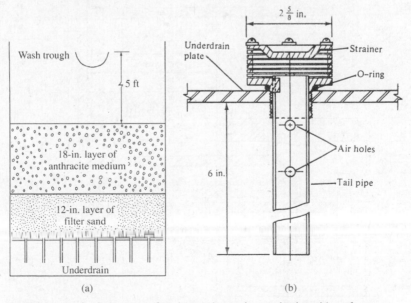

Wash trough

5 ft

18-in. layer of
anthracite medium

12-in. layer of
filter sand

Underdrain

(a)

$2\frac{5}{8}$ in.

Underdrain
plate

Strainer

O-ring

6 in.

Air holes

Tail pipe

(b)

FIGURE 21　Underdrain system for air scouring and water backwashing of a granular-media filter. (a) Cross section of the filter. (b) Detail of the air-water nozzle. *Source:* General Filter Co., Ames, IA.

15   FLOW CONTROL THROUGH GRAVITY FILTERS

Depending on the design, the operation of a gravity filter can be controlled by the following methods: rate of discharge, constant level, influent flow splitting, and declining rate.

Rate-of-Flow Control

Traditional systems for control of gravity filtration regulate the rate of discharge from the filter underdrain. The influent enters each filter below the operating water level and is essentially unrestricted. A step-by-step description of the flow control operation follows the valve numbering illustrated in Figure 22. Initially, valves 1 and 4 are open and 2, 3, and 5 are closed, permitting filtration to proceed. Flow from the settling basin is applied to the filter, and water passes through the bed into the clear well. When head loss becomes excessive, valves 1 and 4 are closed (3 remains closed), and 2 and 5 are opened to permit backwashing. Clean wash water flows into the filter underdrain system, where it is distributed upward through the filter media. Dirty wash water is collected by troughs and flows into the flume connected to a drain. At the beginning of a filter run, some filtered water can be wasted to flush out the wash water remaining in the bed. This initial wasting is accomplished by opening valve 3 when valve 1 is opened to start filtration (2, 4, and 5 are shut). Then valve 4 is opened while valve 3 is being closed. The sequence is then repeated.

       The piezometric diagrams in Figure 23 illustrate the approximate hydraulic profiles through a gravity filter system operated by rate-of-flow control. During filtration the

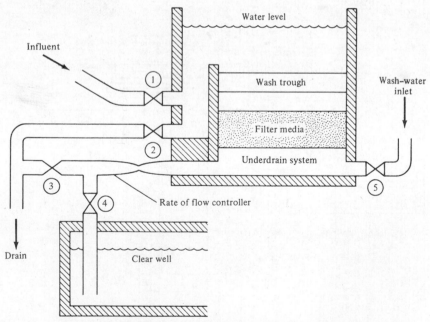

FIGURE 22   Diagram illustrating the operation of a traditional gravity filter system by control of the rate of flow.

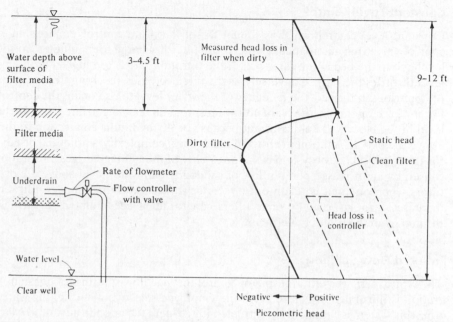

FIGURE 23   Piezometric head diagrams through a gravity filter system operated by control of the rate of flow.

depth of water above the surface of the filter media is 3–4.5 ft (0.9–1.4 m). The filter effluent pipe is trapped in the clear well to provide a connection to water above the media and to prevent backflow of air to the bottom of the filters. The total head available for filtration is equal to the difference between the elevation of the water surface above the media and the water level in the clear well, commonly 9–12 ft (2.7–3.7 m). A rate-of-flow controller (a valve controlled by a flowmeter) in the filter effluent pipe regulates the rate of flow through a clean bed. As the pores of the filter media fill, the head loss in the bed increases and the valve automatically opens wider to maintain constant flow. The flow controller valve is wide open when the measured head loss through the filter media is 8–10 ft (2.4–3.0 m) and the bed is cleaned by backwashing. A control console for each filter unit is provided with a head-loss gauge, flowmeter, and rate controller.

Note in Figure 23 that the pressure in the media can drop below atmospheric pressure (negative head). This negative head permits the release of dissolved gases, which tend to fill the pores of the filter, causing air binding. Air binding reduces the effective volume of the filter, increases the head loss, and reduces the rate of filtration.

The advantage of rate-of-flow control is that the design procedures are well established. The main disadvantages are the high construction and maintenance costs of this relatively complex control system. Also, manual or automatic control of plant influent is necessary to equal the outflow and to maintain constant water levels above the filter beds.

Constant-Level Control

Constant-level control, which is similar to constant-rate control, employs an effluent control valve that automatically adjusts the filter discharge to maintain a preset water level above the bed in the filter box. If the filtration rate is too high, a dropping water level throttles the valve. Conversely, as the rate decreases, resulting from accumulation of impurities in the bed, the tendency of the water level to rise opens the control valve. For uniform operation, the plant inflow must remain unchanged and the effluent water level in the clear well held constant because of the hydraulic connection to the water above the bed. In addition to cost and mechanical complexity, a potential disadvantage for this type of control system is the possibility of momentary surges in filtration rates caused by an increased plant inflow or sudden rise in water level above the operating filters when one unit is taken out of service for backwashing. Sudden filtration rate increases through partially dirty filters can result in accumulated impurities being flushed from the bed in the effluent.

Influent Flow Splitting

The typical arrangement of filtration control through flow splitting for constant-rate filtration is illustrated in Figure 24. While employed selectively in drinking water filtration, this system is commonly constructed for effluent filtration in advanced wastewater processing.

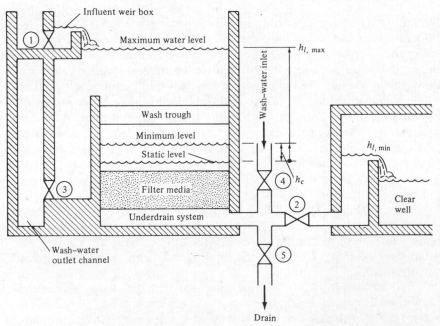

FIGURE 24   Typical arrangement of flow control by influent flow splitting for constant-rate filtration.

Plant inflow is split equally to all operating filters through an influent weir box (1) at each unit, passes through the media to the underdrain, and then passes into the clear well through valve 2. At minimum operating water level, the applied water is conveyed over the bed through the wash troughs and overflows into the water overlying the bed without disturbing the media. Head loss through the clean filter is h_c (Fig. 24). After the troughs are submerged, the influent weir discharges directly into the water above the bed. To prevent accidental dewatering of the filter media, the underflow passes over an effluent weir located above the surface of the bed to enter the clear well. This arrangement eliminates the possibility of creating a negative head in the filter since the hydraulic pressure for filtration is generated only by the depth of water above static level. Constant-rate filtration is achieved without rate-of-flow controllers if the total plant inflow remains constant. Furthermore, effluent flowmeters are not necessary on the filters because the flow per filter is approximately the total plant inflow divided by the number of units in operation. As impurities fill the media, the water level above the bed rises to maintain the constant filtration rate. Thus, the head loss is apparent by the depth of water above the filter bed, which can be read by either a simple staff gauge or an automatic water-level recorder. When the water level reaches the maximum operating level, the filter is backwashed.

The sequence for cleaning the bed is started by closing influent valve 1 and opening valve 3 to the wash-water outlet channel, thus draining out the water overlying the bed and lowering the level to the wash troughs. After valve 2 to the clear well has been closed, wash-water valve 4 can be opened, allowing wash water to flush impurities out of the fluidized bed. The clean media are allowed to restratify in quiescent water before closing and opening appropriate valves to restore filtration. The initial filtered water, if contaminated, can be wasted to a drain by opening valve 5. When one unit is taken out of service for backwashing, the water level gradually rises above the remaining beds until sufficient head is achieved to filter the higher flow received. Filtration rates increase slowly and smoothly with minimal effect on the filtered water quality.

The flow-splitting filtration system reduces the need for the piping and hydraulic controls required by traditional rate-of-flow control systems. The only disadvantage is the additional 5–6 ft (1.5–1.8 m) required in the depth of filter boxes to provide available head above the bed for filtration. On the other hand, eliminating the suction head under the bed removes the possibility of a negative pressure in the media with the consequent release of dissolved gases.

Declining-Rate Filtration

As illustrated in Figure 25, the cross-sectional view of a declining-rate filter appears similar to that of an influent flow-splitting unit. The principal differences are the location and type of influent arrangement and the provision of less available head loss.

Inflow enters a filter through valve 1 below the low-water level from a common channel (or large influent pipe) supplying a series of filters. It passes through the filter media, underdrain, and valve 2 into the clear well. Because of the common supply, the depth of water over all filters in the group being served is the same at any time. The filtration rate of any one unit depends on the head loss through that bed; consequently, the cleanest filter accepts the greatest flow and the dirtiest the least. As the rates of filtration

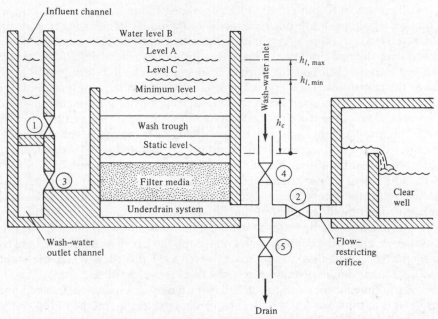

FIGURE 25   Typical arrangement of a declining-rate filtration system.

through some beds decrease, inflow is automatically redistributed to the cleaner beds to compensate for the capacity lost by the dirtier filters. During redistribution of flow, filtration rates shift gradually among the interconnected units as the water level rises slowly, providing the needed additional hydraulic head to maintain a constant overall quantity of water being processed. Eventually, the operating water level reaches the maximum elevation and the dirtiest filter is backwashed to increase its rate of filtration. After this unit returns to service, the flow to all filters redistributes at a lower operating water level.

The general behavior of declining-rate filters is depicted in Figure 26 [16]. The upper curve gives the rate of filtration for filter 1 starting at 6 gpm/ft^2 and slowly declining to 3 gpm/ft^2, which represents the time from starting as a clean bed to backwash. In the lower diagram, the solid line shows the water level gradually rising above all filters as their head losses increase, resulting from accumulation of impurities in the granular media. At point A the dirtiest bed (2) is backwashed and the three remaining filters receive additional flow to compensate for this unit being removed from service for cleaning. Overall filtration capacity is retained by the automatic increase in rates through the operating filters forced by the rise in water level from point A to point B. After the clean filter 2 is returned to operation, the common water level drops to level C.

The vertical distance from the horizontal axis of Figure 26 to the water level line is the elevation of water above the effluent weir, which is the total head loss through any filter. The dashed lines apply to filter 1 starting as a clean bed to the time of backwash. Measuring upward from the horizontal axis, the vertical distances between the lines represent head losses in the underdrains and piping, clean media,

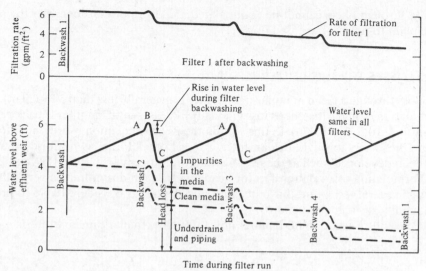

FIGURE 26   Diagrams for declining-rate filtration showing the filtration rate, water level, and head losses for one filter run in a plant having four filters. *Source:* From J. L. Cleasby, "Declining-Rate Filtration," *J. Am. Water Works Assoc.* 73, no. 9 (1981): 485.

and head loss caused by the accumulation of impurities in the media. The latter increases as the bed becomes dirtier, and the losses in the clean media and underdrain system decrease relative to the loss caused by solids removal as the rate of filtration through filter 1 decreases. Backwashing of filters 2–4 causes the temporary rises in all of the curves.

Design considerations unique to a declining-rate filtration system are predicting water-level variations, preventing excessive rates through clean filters, and the influence of inflow variation on filtration hydraulics. Cleasby and DiBernardo [17] discuss the hydraulic considerations in declining-rate filtration in detail, including sample calculations to predict water-level variations and head losses necessary for design. The minimum water level with a head loss of h_c in Figure 25 results only if all beds are clean. The other water levels, labeled A–C in Figure 25, correspond to the labeled points in Figure 26. The maximum level B results when one filter is out of service for backwashing. The range between levels C and A is the normal operating zone of head loss during the time period between backwashing of filters. The recommendation for preventing an excessive filtration rate through a clean filter is to insert a flow-restricting device in the pipeline leading from the filter underdrain to the clear well. This could be an orifice, a fixed-position valve, or a two-position valve.

Advantages attributed to declining-rate filtration compared with traditional systems are that effluent quality is improved, head loss is lower for an equal length of filter run, smooth transitions in filtration rate changes are attained, negative pressure cannot occur in the bed, flowmeters and effluent control equipment are not needed, and construction and maintenance costs are lower. The disadvantages are that a greater depth is required in filter boxes, a high-water-level alarm is desirable, and, since the rate through filters cannot be manipulated, the operator must consider the ability of the plant to process increased flows [17].

16　HEAD LOSSES THROUGH FILTER MEDIA

Head loss through a clean granular-media filter is generally less than 3 ft (0.9 m). With accumulation of impurities, head loss gradually increases until the filter is backwashed, usually at 8–10 ft (2.4–3.0 m). In this section the Kozeny equation is presented for calculating head loss through a clean filter. Several other formulas not discussed here have been developed, such as those of Carman and Kozeny [18], Rose [19], and Ergun [20]. Formulation of a relationship for head loss through dirty filters is very difficult; although several techniques have been proposed, none is considered able to provide substantially accurate predictions.

Poiseuille's equation for laminar flow through a circular capillary tube is

$$\frac{h}{l} = \frac{32\nu V}{gD^2} \tag{11}$$

where

$$h/l = \text{head loss per unit length, ft H}_2\text{O/ft (m/m)}$$
$$\nu = \text{kinematic viscosity } (\mu/\rho), \text{ ft}^2\text{/s (m}^2\text{/s)}$$
$$V = \text{mean velocity of flow, ft/s (m/s)}$$
$$g = \text{acceleration of gravity, ft/s}^2 \text{ (m/s}^2)$$
$$D = \text{capillary tube diameter, ft (m)}$$

Granular media can be idealized as a bundle of capillary tubes representing the pore passages of the bed. The hydraulic radius for such an ideal bed is equal to the volume of the pores divided by the wetted internal surface area of the tubular passages. For a unit volume of the bed, the pore volume is the porosity and the wetted surface area is the fraction of the bed occupied by solids $(1 - \varepsilon)$ multiplied by the surface area per unit volume of spherical solid. Therefore,

$$\text{hydraulic radius} = \frac{\varepsilon}{(1 - \varepsilon)\dfrac{\pi d^2}{\pi d^3/6}} = \frac{\varepsilon d}{6(1 - \varepsilon)} \tag{12}$$

where

$$\varepsilon = \text{porosity of the stationary filter bed, dimensionless}$$
$$d = \text{diameter of spherical grains, ft (m)}$$

Replacing the 6 with S (the shape factor), substituting a constant times the square of the hydraulic radius for D^2 in Poiseuille's equation, and recognizing that the actual pore velocity is the superficial velocity divided by the porosity yields the Kozeny equation [21] for the rate of head loss for water flow through a clean granular medium:

$$\frac{h}{l} = \frac{Jv(1 - \varepsilon)^2 V S^2}{g\varepsilon^3 d^2} \tag{13}$$

where

h/l = head loss per unit depth of filter bed, ft H_2O/ft(m/m)

J = constant, approximately 6 for filtration in the laminar flow region, dimensionless

v = kinematic viscosity (μ/ρ), ft²/s (m²/s)

g = acceleration of gravity, ft/s² (m/s²)

ε = porosity of the stationary filter bed, dimensionless

V = superficial (approach) velocity of water above the bed, volumetric flow rate divided by the overall bed cross-sectional area, ft/s(m/s)

S = shape factor ranging from 6.0 for spherical grains to 7.5 for angular grains, dimensionless

d = mean grain diameter, ft (m)

Equation (13) can be easily applied to determine head loss in a homogeneous granular-media bed. Filter beds in water and wastewater, however, are usually graded beds stratified as a result of backwashing with the coarsest grains on the bottom and finest on top. The grain-size distribution in a bed is defined by a sieve analysis. Table 4 lists the U.S. sieve series by the sieve designation number (the approximate number of meshes per inch) and the size of openings. For practical purposes, the thicknesses of substantially uniform layers in a stratified bed can be assumed to be proportional to the weights of the portions separated by the sieves. Hence, the total head loss is the sum of the head losses calculated by the Kozeny equation for successive layers based on the weight gradation from a sieve analysis of the filter material. Fair and Hatch [22] developed this concept and proposed the following equation for calculating head loss through each layer of a clean stratified filter bed:

$$\frac{h}{l} = \frac{36kv(1 - \varepsilon)^2 V}{g\varepsilon^3 \psi^2} \sum_{i=1}^{n} \frac{P_i}{d_i^2} \tag{14}$$

TABLE 4   U.S. Sieve Series

Sieve Designation Number	Size of Opening (mm)	Sieve Designation Number	Size of Opening (mm)
200	0.074	20	0.84
140	0.105	18	1.00
100	0.149	16	1.19
70	0.210	12	1.68
50	0.297	8	2.38
40	0.42	6	3.36
30	0.59	4	4.76

where

k = constant equal to 5.0, dimensionless

ψ = sphericity of grains, ratio of surface area of equal volume spheres to the actual surface area of grains, dimensionless

P_i = fraction of total weight of filter grains in any layer i, dimensionless

d_i = geometric mean diameter of grains in layer i, ft (m)

Based on tests, Fair and Hatch [22] used a value for k of 5.0 as opposed to Kozeny's J of 6. The geometric mean grain diameter d_i (the square root of the product of the upper and lower grain sizes) can be computed from either the upper and lower sieve size of any layer i or taken from the gradation curve of a grain size analysis. P_i is the percentage by weight of filter grains trapped between adjacent sieves. The $6/\psi$ is the same as the shape factor S. Values of ψ for filter sand are generally in the range of 0.8–0.7, rounded to angular, and for anthracite media from 0.7 to 0.4, angular to jagged.

Example 8 illustrates the application of Eq. (14).

Example 8

Calculate the head loss through a clean sand filter with a gradation defined by the sieve analysis given in Table 5 at a filtration rate of $2.7 \text{ l/m}^2 \cdot \text{s}$ (0.0027 m/s). The bed has a depth of 0.70 m with a porosity of 0.45 and the grains of sand have a sphericity of 0.75. Assume a water temperature of 10° C.

Solution: From Table 5, the computed value is

$$\sum \frac{P_i}{d_i^2} = 2.34 \text{ mm}^{-2} = 2.34 \times 10^6 \text{ m}^{-2}$$

Appendix Table 9 gives v at 10° C as $1.306 \times 10^{-6} \text{ m}^2/\text{s}$.

TABLE 5   Sieve Analysis and Computation of Head Loss for Example 8

Sieve Designation Number	Size of Opening S (mm)	Geometric Mean Diameter $(S_1 \times S_2)^{0.5}$ (mm)	Fraction of Sand Retained	$\frac{P_i}{d_i^2}$ (mm)$^{-2}$
12	1.68			
16	1.19	1.41	0.02	0.01
20	0.84	1.00	0.25	0.25
30	0.59	0.70	0.47	0.96
40	0.42	0.50	0.24	0.96
50	0.297	0.35	0.02	0.16
Total			1.00	2.34

Substituting into Eq. (14),

$$\frac{h}{l} = \frac{36 \times 5.0 \times 1.306 \times 10^{-6} \text{ m}^2/\text{s} \times (1 - 0.45)^2 \, 0.0027 \text{ m/s} \times 2.34 \times 10^6 \text{ m}^{-2}}{9.807 \text{ m/s}^2 (0.45)^3 (0.75)^2}$$

$$= 0.89 \text{ m/m}$$

head loss through clean filter $= 0.70 \text{ m} \times 0.89 \text{ m/m} = 0.62 \text{ m}.$

17 BACKWASHING AND MEDIA FLUIDIZATION

As each filter accumulates solids in the pores of the media, the head loss through the media increases, and solids are driven deeper into the media as a result of the increased pore velocities. The filter run is terminated and backwashing begins when the first of two limiting conditions occurs: (1) a breakthrough of turbidity occurs in the filter effluent or (2) the head loss in the filter reaches the maximum available head for the desired flow rate. Effluent turbidity and head loss as a function of filter production volume are shown in Figure 27. These indicate that the filter run should cease and the filter backwashed at turbidity

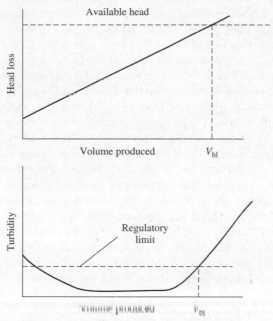

FIGURE 27   Head loss and effluent turbidity as a function of filter run time showing the production volume when reaching the available head loss (V_{hl}) and the production volume at turbidity breakthrough (V_{bt}).

breakthrough even though the available head loss has not been reached. Of course, for a given filter, the available head loss may be attained before turbidity breakthrough. Low head loss build-up and consequently a large production volume prior to reaching the available head loss is meaningless if turbidity breakthrough is reached much sooner, and vice versa. Optimum design will maximize production volume by having turbidity breakthrough and reaching available head loss occur at the same time of the filter run.

Under average operating conditions, granular-media filters are backwashed with previously filtered water about once in 24 hr at a rate of 15 to 24 gpm/ft^2 (0.010 to 0.016 m/s) for a period of 5–10 min, gradually increasing the backwash flow up to the desired backwash rate and then gradually decreasing the flow so as to allow the media to properly restratify as it settles in the bed. Immediately after the filter bed is backwashed, floc particles may not effectively attach to the filter media, causing high turbidity counts in the effluent. In this case the filter is conditioned by either directing filter water to waste until flocs begin to coat the media or by adding a polymer to help the flocs attach to the media. This step in filtration is called ripening and may last 5 to 30 min. A bed may be out of operation for 10 to 40 min to complete the cleaning and ripening process. The amount of water used in backwashing varies from 2% to 4% of the filtered water. During backwashing the bed of filter media is expanded hydraulically from between 15% and 50%, and the released impurities are conveyed in the wash water to the wash troughs.

Problems in backwashing of dual-media filters can result if the cleaning action is limited to wash-water fluidization. Nonuniform expansion and poor scouring can result in mud balls (small masses of media and floc that bind together) dropping through the coarser coal media and lodging on top of the sand layer. The common methods of cleaning dual-media filters are either air scouring or air-and-water scouring prior to water backwash, or surface washing during backwash. For separate air scouring, the water level is lowered below the wash-water troughs to near the surface of the media and only air is introduced to mix and scour the media. Wash water is then used to fluidize the bed and purge contaminants. For air-and-water scouring, the wash cycle also begins by draining off the water above the filter. After backwash flow has started, at about one-quarter of the fluidizing rate, air is supplied and the simultaneous flow of air and water scours the bed as the wash-water level rises in the filter box. When the water surface approaches the bottom of the wash troughs, air injection is terminated and the backwash rate increases to the desired fluidization velocity to carry the impurities out of the expanded bed. Surface washing is achieved by spraying previously filtered water through nozzles, either fixed or rotating, a few inches above the unexpanded filter bed, during backwashing to increase the level of particle agitation.

The granular media are thoroughly mixed in the agitated, turbulent flow of an expanded bed during backwashing. When the upward flow of wash water is stopped, the suspended grains settle down to form a stratified bed with the finest grains of each medium on top. In a mixed-media bed the medium of lowest density settles on top, that is, the anthracite layer above the sand bed.

Fluidization

Fluidization is defined as upward flow through a granular bed at sufficient velocity to suspend the grains in the water. During the process of fluidization, the upward flow overcomes the gravitational force on the grains, and the energy loss is due to fluid motion. The viscous energy loss is proportional to the velocity of flow, and the kinetic energy loss is proportional to the square of the velocity.

The pressure loss through a fixed bed is a linear function of flow rate at low superficial velocities when flow is laminar. As the flow rate increases further, the resistance of the grains to wash-water flow increases until this resistance equals the gravitational force, and the grains are suspended in the water. Any further increase in upward velocity results in additional expansion of the bed while maintaining a constant pressure drop equal to the buoyant weight of the media. The characteristics of an ideal fluidized bed and departures from the ideal case because of real conditions are shown in Figure 28 [23].

The frictional drag of grains suspended in upward flowing water is counterbalanced exactly by the pull of gravity. Therefore, the pressure drop after fluidization is equal to the buoyant weight of the grains, which can be calculated as

$$\Delta p = h\rho g = l(\rho_s - \rho)g(1 - \varepsilon) \qquad (15)$$

where

Δp = pressure drop after fluidization, lb (N)

h = head loss (as a water column height), ft (m)

l = height of expanded bed, ft (m)

ρ = mass density of wash water, lb $\cdot$ s^2/ft^4 (kg/m^3)

ρ_s = mass density of solid grains, lb $\cdot$ s^2/ft^4 (kg/m^3)

ε = porosity of expanded bed, dimensionless

g = acceleration of gravity, ft/s^2 (m/s^2)

Since the quantity of filter medium remains the same whether the bed is stationary or fluidized, the volume of grains initially can be equated to the volume of grains after expansion.

$$l(1 - \varepsilon) = l_0(1 - \varepsilon_0) \qquad (16)$$

where

l_0 = height of stationary bed

ε_0 = porosity of stationary clean bed

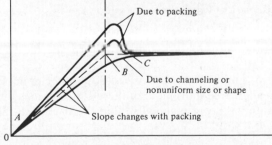

Superficial velocity V

FIGURE 28   Characteristics of a fluidized bed of granular media. Solid curves: real bed; dashed lines: ideal bed. *Source:* From J. L. Cleasby and K. Fan, "Predicting Fluidization and Expansion of Filter Media," *J. Env. Eng. Div., Proc. Am. Soc. Civil Engrs.* 107 (EE3) (1981): 459.

Minimum Fluidizing Velocity

The superficial water velocity required for the onset of fluidization is defined by point B in Figure 28 for an ideal bed composed of unisized spherical particles. For a graded bed, the minimum fluidizing velocity is not the same for all the grains. Therefore, the change from a stationary to an expanded bed occurs gradually, with complete fluidization at a higher superficial velocity indicated by point C. Further increase in flow causes the concentration of particles to decrease and the porosity to approach 1. Ideally, the superficial velocity equals the unhindered terminal settling velocity of a single particle. It can be measured by experimentation in a laboratory using a filter column. At gradually increasing superficial velocities, head losses through the expanding bed are measured and plotted in a form similar to Figure 28. The minimum fluidizing velocity is at the point where the curve becomes horizontal and subsequent head loss measurements remain constant.

The minimum fluidizing velocity can also be calculated from relationships substantiated by experimental observations. One rational approach equates the head loss determined by the Ergun equation [20] to the head loss using Eq. (15) at the point of incipient fluidization. For nonspherical particles, Wen and Yu [24] modified this relationship to account for sphericity and stationary bed porosity. The following equations resulted:

$$Ga = \frac{d_{eq}^3 \rho (\rho_s - \rho) g}{\mu^2} \tag{17}$$

$$Re_{mf} = [(33.7)^2 + 0.0408 \, Ga]^{0.5} - 33.7 \tag{18}$$

$$Re_{mf} = \frac{d_{eq} V_{mf} \rho}{\mu} \tag{19}$$

where

Re_{mf} = Reynolds number, dimensionless

Ga = Galileo number, dimensionless

d_{eq} = grain diameter of a sphere of equal volume, ft(m)

V_{mf} = minimum fluidizing velocity (superficial velocity at the point of minimum fluidization), gpm/ft^2 or ft/s (m/s)

μ = absolute (dynamic) viscosity of water, lb $\cdot$ s/ft^2 (kg/m $\cdot$ s)

ρ = mass density of water, lb $\cdot$ s^2/ft^4 (kg/m^3)

ρ_s = mass density of water, lb $\cdot$ s^2/ft^4 (kg/m^3)

In order to fluidize all the media, the d_{90} grain size is used for d_{eq} (90% of the grains by weight are smaller). Furthermore, to allow free movement of these coarse grains during backwashing, a 30% margin of safety is recommended so that the backwash rate becomes $1.3 V_{mf}$ [23].

In designing backwashing systems, the engineer should provide the operator with the flexibility to vary the rate of backwash based on the plant operational experience. Accordingly, the $1.3V_{mf}$ backwash velocity is a target, but backwash head, piping, and appurtenances should be designed to provide higher, and perhaps lower, backwashing flows, as required.

Example 9

Calculate the recommended minimum backwash rate for a sand filter with a d_{90} sieve opening equal to 1.00 mm (0.001 m). This grain diameter designation means that 90% of the filter sand by weight passed through a U.S. sieve number 18, which has an opening size of 1.00 mm. The water temperature is 25° C and the density of the sand is 2.65 g/cm^3 (2650 kg/m^3).

Solution: Calculate the Galileo number using Equation (17):

$$Ga = \frac{(0.001 \text{ m})^3 \times 997 \text{ }^{kg}/_{m^3} \times \left[(2650 - 997)^{kg}/_{m^3} \right] \times 9.81 \text{ }^{m}/_{s^2}}{(0.89 \times 10^{-3 \text{ }kg}/_{m \cdot s})^2} = 20{,}410$$

Using Ga calculate the Reynolds number at minimum fluidization with Equation (18):

$$Re_{mf} = [(33.7)^2 + 0.0408 \times 20410]^{0.5} - 33.7 = 10.67$$

Calculate the minimum fluidization velocity with Equation (19):

$$V_{mf} = \frac{10.67 \times (0.89 \times 10^{-3 \text{ }kg}/_{m \cdot s})}{0.001 \text{ m} \times 997 \text{ }^{kg}/_{m^3}}$$

$$V_{mf} = 0.0095 \text{ m/s} = 9.5 \text{ mm/s} = 9.5 \text{ l/m}^2 \cdot s = 14 \text{ gpm/ft}^2$$

With addition of a 30% margin of safety, the recommended backwash rate is $1.3 \times 9.5 = 12 \text{ l/m}^2 \cdot s = 18 \text{ gpm/ft}^2$.

Backwash velocities for various media sizes and specific gravities as calculated from equations 17 – 19 with the backwash velocity equal to $1.3 \times V_{mf}$ are shown in Figure 29 for water at 20°C. This figure can be used to properly match media for fluidization in backwashing as illustrated in Example 10. Similar figures can be developed at other water temperatures, or reasonable estimations of backwash velocities can be calculated by using Figure 29 and modifying the velocities with values from Table 6. Note that required backwash velocities increase as the temperature increases, so the highest expected water temperature should be used for the minimum backwash velocity in design.

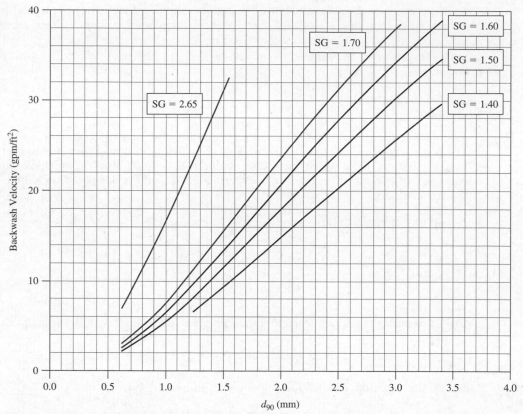

FIGURE 29 Backwash velocities 1.3 $\times$ V_{mf} as a function of d_{90} for media with various specific gravities (S.G.) 1 gpm/ft^2 = 0.0407 m/min

TABLE 6 Temperature Correction Factors for Modifying Backwash Velocities at 20°C from Figure 29 for Other Water Temperatures

Temperature (°C)	Multiply Backwash Velocity from Figure 29 by
10	0.82
15	0.91
25	1.09
30	1.16

Example 10

Calculate the backwash velocity for a dual-media filter of sand (S.G. = 2.65) and coal (S.G. = 1.6) and select the sand and coal effective size and uniformity coefficient. The water temperature range is 20 – 25 °C.

Solution: From Figure 19 choose a sand effective size and uniformity coefficient.

$$d_{10} = 0.5 \text{ mm}$$
$$U_{\text{sand}} = 1.5$$

Calculate the d_{90} for the sand layer using Eq. (10):

$$d_{90} = 0.5 \text{ mm} \times (1.5)^{1.67} = 0.98 \text{ mm}$$

Enter Figure 29 at d_{90} of 0.98 mm and read upward to the plot for S.G. = 2.65. Then read left to determine the required backwash velocity (16.0 gpm/ft^2). Since the same backwash velocity is applied to both sand and coal, read right from the same intersection to the plot for the coal S.G. (1.6 in this case) and then read down from that intersection to read the d_{90} for coal to be 1.7 mm. Select a uniformity coefficient for the coal. A value of 1.4 will help ensure good filter operation although this selection will have a higher cost than larger values of U. Calculate the d_{10} for coal using Eq. (10).

$$d_{10} = 1.7 \text{ mm} \times (1.4)^{-1.67} = 0.97 \text{ mm}$$

Since the minimum backwash velocity should be designed at the maximum temperature, use the temperature correction factor in Table 6.

$$V_{\text{backwash } 25°C} = 16.0 \text{ gpm/ft}^2 \times 1.09 = 17.4 \text{ gpm/ft}^2$$

Note: this is the target value. Good design will provide for higher velocities through elevated storage or pumping and allow the operator to control the backwash to suit the temperature and particular plant conditions.

---

18 PRESSURE FILTERS

Pressure filters have the granular media and underdrains contained in a steel tank. Water is pumped through the filter under pressure, and the media are washed by reversing flow through the bed, flushing out the impurities. Filtration rates are comparable to gravity filters; however, the maximum head loss can be significantly greater since it is a function of the input pump pressure rather than static water levels. Pressure filters are commonly installed in small municipal softening and iron-removal plants, in industrial water treatment processes, and for tertiary filtration of effluent from small wastewater plants.

19 MEMBRANE FILTRATION

Although membrane filtration for particulate removal is a physical unit process, membranes are also used to remove dissolved constituents from water in desalination and softening processes.

PROBLEMS

1 A venturi water meter with a throat of 6.0 in. registers a pressure head difference of 128 in. of water between the inlet and throat. Calculate the quantity of flow through the meter using a discharge coefficient of 0.93.

2 Calculate the upper head in a Parshall flume with a throat width of 1.5 ft for a flow of 5.56 cfs.

3 The recommended minimum and maximum measurements for a Parshall flume have been experimentally determined. For a throat width of 1.5 ft, the minimum head is 0.10 ft and the maximum is 2.5 ft. Calculate the flow rates for these heads.

4 A wastewater bar screen is constructed with 0.25-in.-wide bars spaced 2 in. apart center to center. If the approach velocity in the channel is 2.0 fps, what is the velocity through the screen openings?

5 A rapid mix tank, equipped with mechanical mixers, will be used to mix the coagulant, alum, into water at 10°C in 10 seconds with a root mean velocity gradient of 800 s^{-1} for a flow of 10 mgd. Find the power of the mixer motor assuming it operates at 70% efficiency.

6 Find the mixing intensity as measured by the root mean velocity gradient in water at 15°C that will be produced by a 5 kw mixer operating at 75% efficiency in a basin with a volume of 10 m^3.

7 A rapid mix basin has an operating volume of 400 ft^3 and uses a mechanical mixer operating at 80% efficiency. Plot the velocity gradient generated as a function of temperature between 10°C and 25°C.

8 A flocculation basin equipped with revolving paddles is 60 ft long (the direction of flow), 45 ft wide, and 14 ft deep and treats 10 mgd. The power input to provide paddle-blade velocities of 1.0 and 1.4 fps for the inner and outer blades, respectively, is 930 ft · lb/s. Calculate the detention time, horizontal flow-through velocity, and G (the mean velocity gradient) for a water temperature of 50°F.

9 A surface water treatment plant designed to process 70,000 m^3/d at a water temperature of 10° C has a four-compartment flocculation tank with a total length of 25 m, width of 12 m, and water depth of 5.0 m. The paddle flocculator in each of the four chambers between baffles has 4 blades, each 25 cm wide and 11.5 m long with the center line of the paddles at a radius of 1.8 m. Assume the velocity of the water is 30% of the paddle velocity and the drag coefficient is 1.8. At a rotational speed of 2.0 rpm, calculate the velocity gradient.

10 A surface water treatment plant is being designed to process 50 mgd. The preliminary size of the flocculation tank is 96.0 ft long, with a series of six baffled compartments to create an over–under flow pattern. The tank width is 96.0 ft, and the water depth is 14.5 ft. Each of the six compartments has a horizontal shaft supporting six paddle flocculators with four arms on which to attach blades; the total number of units in the tank is 36. Up to five blades, each 15 ft by 0.5 ft, can be attached on each arm at radii of 6.5 ft, 5.5 ft, 4.5 ft, 3.5 ft, and 2.5 ft from the center line of the shaft to the center of the blades. The maximum rotation of the flocculators, driven by variable-speed drives, can provide a velocity of 2.5 fps at a radius of 6.5 ft (center of the outer blade). What is the minimum number of blades needed on the flocculators for a velocity gradient of 60 fps/ft? Assume a ratio of water velocity to paddle velocity of 0.3, C_d equal to 1.8, and a water temperature of 50°F.

11 The settling velocity of alum floc is approximately 0.0014 fps in water at 10°C. Calculate the equivalent overflow rate in gpd/ft^2. What is the minimum detention time in hours to settle out alum floc in an ideal basin with a depth of 10 ft?

12 A treatment plant has straight-line processing with rapid mix chambers, flocculation tanks, and settling tanks sized according to the minimum values specified by *GLUMRB* and Table 1. If the volume of the flocculation tanks is 100,000 gal, compute the design capacity of the plant. What are the total volumes of the rapid mix and sedimentation tanks?

13 Each half of a treatment plant, with a longitudinal cross-section as illustrated in Figure 10, has the following sized units: rapid mixing chamber with a volume of 855 ft^3; flocculation tank 140 ft wide, 58 ft long, and 14.5 ft of water depth; and sedimentation tank 140 ft wide, 280 ft long, and 17.0 ft of water depth. The length of the effluent weir along four weir channels and along the end of the tank is 1260 ft. Calculate the major parameters used in sizing these units based on a design flow of 40.0 mgd for each half of the plant. Compare the calculated values for the sedimentation tank to those in Table 1.

14 Two rectangular clarifiers, each 30 ft long, 15 ft wide, and 10 ft deep, settle 0.40 mgd following alum coagulation. The effluent channels have a total weir length of 60 ft. Calculate the detention time, horizontal velocity of flow, and rate of flow over the outlet weir. Compare the calculated values to those in Table 1.

15 Lime precipitation of raw wastewater is one method for removing phosphorus. Circular primary clarifiers with aerated flocculation wells as illustrated in Figure 30 were installed at a wastewater treatment plant for phosphorus precipitation and enhanced suspended-solids removal. The maximum hourly flow rate for each tank was 1.1 mgd. The lime dosage of 300 mg/l of CaO in a slurry was applied to the influent prior to entering the flocculation well. For this peak hydraulic loading, calculate the detention time based on the entire tank volume, flocculation time based on the volume of the flocculation well, overflow rate, and weir loading. Compare these values with the values for flocculator–clarifiers given in Table 1.

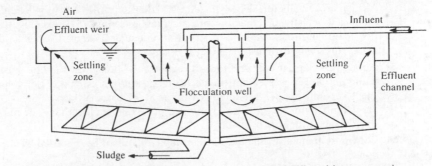

FIGURE 30   Illustration for Problem 15. A circular primary clarifier with an aerated flocculation well that receives the wastewater after the addition of lime in a rapid-mix tank. The key dimensions are diameter of the tank 40 ft, diameter of the flocculation well 20 ft, side-water depth 10 ft, and submergence of flocculation well 6.0 ft.

Now, consider that the performance of the clarifiers was very poor. The overflow was continuously milky, carrying out approximately one-third of the applied lime. Subsequent recarbonation was not adequate to neutralize the pH below the range of 8.5–9.5; consequently, calcium carbonate precipitated in the following equalization tank and RBC tanks. The sludge production was significantly less than the anticipated quantity. Why was the operation of the clarifiers unsatisfactory? (Read the discussion of flocculator–clarifiers and examine Figure 9.)

16 A wastewater treatment plant has two primary clarifiers, each 20 m in diameter with a 2-m side-water depth. The effluent weirs are inboard channels set on a diameter of 18 m. For a flow of 12,000 m³/d, calculate the overflow rate, detention time, and weir loading.

17 Calculate the diameter and depth of a circular sedimentation basin for a design flow of 3800 m³/d based on an overflow rate of 0.00024 m/s and a detention time of 3 hr.

18 Two final clarifiers following activated-sludge processing have diameters of 60 ft and side-water depths of 11 ft. The effluent weirs are inboard channels set on a mean diameter of 55 ft. For a total flow of 3.4 mgd, calculate the overflow rate, detention time, and weir loading.

19 A rectangular sedimentation basin will have a flow of 1.0 mgd using a 2:1 length/width ratio, an overflow rate of 0.00077 fps, and a detention time of 3.0 hr. What will the dimensions of the basin be?

20 Calculate the overflow rate and detention time in a primary clarifier with a diameter of 24 m and water depth of 2.3 m for a flow of 10,000 m^3/d.

21 A wastewater treatment plant has two rectangular primary settling tanks, each 40 ft long, 12 ft wide, and 7 ft deep. The effluent weir length in each tank is 45 ft. The average daily wastewater flow is 387,000 gal. Calculate the overflow rate and effluent weir loading. What is the estimated BOD removal?

22 How does the final clarifier for use with biological aeration illustrated in Figure 12 differ from the primary clarifier in Figure 11? Why are these differences important in gravity separation of suspended solids? (Refer to Figure 13, zone settling.) The proposed renovation of a wastewater treatment plant is considering construction of activated-sludge aeration tanks to replace existing trickling filters and keeping the existing final clarifiers in service. If you were reviewing this proposal, what would you recommend?

23 List the recommended design criteria for final clarifiers for an activated-sludge process with a design capacity of 20 mgd. Assuming four identical circular clarifiers, calculate the surface area, diameter, side-water depth, detention time, and weir loading based on an inboard weir channel. If the flow into each tank is 6.5 mgd (5.0 mgd plus 30% recirculation flow) and the suspended-solids concentration equals 2500 mg/l, calculate the solids loading. Is this solids loading satisfactory?

24 An aerated clarifier-type unit for grit removal and preaeration is 12 ft square with an 8-ft liquid depth. The wastewater flow is 0.80 mgd with an estimated grit volume of 3 ft^3/mil gal. A separate hopper-bottomed grit storage tank has a usable volume of 3 yd^3. Compute the detention time in the aerated unit and the estimated length of time required to fill the storage tank with grit.

25 Why must granular-media filtration in water treatment be preceded by chemical coagulation?

26 What are the limitations in applying direct filtration in water processing?

27 What is the major advantage of a dual-media coal-sand filter compared with a conventional sand filter?

28 Of the underdrains discussed, which kinds can use air scouring, air-and-water scouring, and no air scouring for filter backwashing?

29 In a gravity filter, how can the head loss gauge record a 9-ft loss when the water depth above the filter media surface is only 3.5 ft?

30 Refer to Figure 23. Assume the water depth above the surface of the filter media is 4 ft, the filter media is 2 ft deep, and the measured head loss as diagrammed in the dirty filter is 8 ft. This traditional flow-control system, by regulating the discharge from the underdrain, was installed at a treatment plant where the influent was cold water transported in a pipeline from a mountain reservoir at a higher elevation. Being delivered under pressure, the influent contained dissolved gases released during processing by depressurization and warming of the water. The dissolved gases came out of solution under the negative piezometric head in the filter media and formed tiny bubbles. This "air binding" (Section 15) increased the head loss and, at the start of backwashing, disturbed the underdrain media by eruption of the accumulated gas bubbles. A plant expansion is being proposed. What change in design of the filtration system would you recommend to reduce the problem of air binding?

31 What are the principal similarities and differences between declining-rate filtration and influent flow-splitting filtration?

32 Calculate the initial head loss through a filter with 18 in. of uniform sand having a porosity of 0.42 and a grain diameter of 1.6×10^{-3} ft. Assume spherical particles and a water temperature of 50°F. The filtration rate is 2.5 gpm/ft^2. Use the Kozeny equation.

33 Calculate the initial head loss through a dual-media filter consisting of a 12-in. layer of uniform anthracite with a grain diameter of 2.0 mm and a 24-in. layer of uniform sand with a grain diameter of 1.0 mm at a filtration rate of 4.0 gpm/ft^2. The porosity of both media is 0.40, the shape factor for the anthracite is 7.5, and the shape factor for the sand is 6.0. Assume a water temperature of 60°F.

34 Calculate the initial head loss through a dual-media filter consisting of a 0.30-m layer of uniform anthracite with a grain diameter of 1.0 mm and a 0.30-m layer of uniform sand with a grain diameter of 0.50 mm at a filtration rate of 2.7 l/m$^2 \cdot$ s. The porosity of both media is 0.42, the shape factor for the anthracite is 7.5, and the shape factor for the sand is 6.0. Assume a water temperature of 10°C.

35 Calculate the head loss through a clean sand filter with a gradation as given by the sieve analysis below. The filtration rate is 2.7 l/m$^2 \cdot$ s, and the water temperature is 10° C. The filter depth is 0.70 m with a porosity of 0.45, and the sand grains have a sphericity of 0.75.

Sieve designation number	12	16	20	30	40	50
Fraction of sand retained	0	0.05	0.22	0.51	0.20	0.02

36 Calculate the recommended minimum backwash rate for a sand filter with a d_{90} sieve opening equal to 0.84 mm. (Ninety percent of the filter sand by weight passed through a sieve number 20.) The water temperature is 10°C and the density of the sand is 2650 kg/m^3.

37 Calculate the recommended minimum backwash rate for a single-medium, coarse-sand filter for tertiary filtration of reclaimed water at a temperature of 20°C. The grain diameter of a sphere of equal volume is 1.2 mm, density of the sand is 2650 kg/m^3, filter depth is 1.0 m, and porosity is 0.40. Also calculate the pressure drop through the filter during fluidization.

38 A dual-media filter consists of a 0.50-m layer of anthracite and 0.30-m layer of sand. The anthracite medium has a specific gravity of 1.67, porosity of 0.50, and a d_{90} grain size of 1.50 mm. The sand medium has a specific gravity of 2.65, a porosity of 0.40, and a d_{90} grain size of 0.90 mm. The water temperature is 20°C. (a) Calculate the recommended minimum backwash rate for the filter. (b) Calculate the pressure drop through the filter during fluidization. Use equations 17 – 19 for this problem.

39 Calculate the fluidization velocity of water at 20°C that will expand filter sand with an effective size of 0.6 mm, a uniformity coefficient of 1.4, and a specific gravity of 2.65. Also find the effective size of anthracite coal with a uniformity coefficient of 1.4 that will be used with the sand in a dual media filter.

40 Redraw Figure 29 for a temperature of 10°C using equations 17 – 19.

REFERENCES

[1] L. D. Benefield and J. F. Judkins, Jr., *Treatment Plant Hydraulics for Environmental Engineers* (Upper Saddle River, NJ: Prentice Hall, 1984).

[2] A. Amirtharajah, "Design of Rapid Mix Units," in *Water Treatment Plant Design*, R. Sanks, ed. (Ann Arbor, MI: Ann Arbor Science, 1978), 131–147.

[3] M. Han and D. F. Lawler, "The (Relative) Insignificance of G in Flocculation," *Journal of the American Water Works Association* 84, no. 10 (October 1992): 79–91.

[4] American Water Works Association and American Society of Civil Engineers, *Water Treatment Plant Design* 4th ed., (New York, NY: McGraw Hill, 2005).

[5] *Recommended Standards for Water Works, Great Lakes Upper Mississippi River Board of State Sanitary Engineers* (Albany, NY: Health Research Inc., 2003).

[6] MWH, *Water Treatment: Principles and Design,* revised by J. Crittenden, R. Trussell, D. Hand, K. Howe, and G. Tchobanoglous (Hoboken, NJ: Wiley, 2005).

[7] *Recommended Standards for Wastewater Facilities, Great Lakes Upper Mississippi River Board of State Public Health & Environmental Managers* (Albany, NY: Health Research Inc., 2004).

[8] "Design Manual, Dewatering Municipal Wastewater Sludges," U.S. Environmental Protection Agency, Office of Research and Development, Center for Environmental Research Information, EPA/625/1-87/014 (September 1987).

[9] Metcalf and Eddy, Inc., *Wastewater Engineering, Treatment and Reuse,* 4th ed., revised by G. Tchobanoglous, F. Burton, and H. Stensel (New York, NY: McGraw Hill, 2003).

[10] Water Environment Association, *Wastewater Treatment Plant Design*, P. A. Vesilind, ed. (Alexandria, VA, 2003).

[11] D. W. Hendricks, et al., *Filtration of Giardia Cysts and Other Particles Under Treatment Plant Conditions* (Denver: Am. Water Works Assoc. Research Foundation, 1988).

[12] J. L. Cleasby and G. S. Logsdon, "Granular Bed and Precoat Filtration," in *Water Quality and Treatment* (New York: McGraw Hill, 1999).

[13] Committee Report, "The Status of Direct Filtration," *J. Am. Water Works Assoc.* 72, no. 7 (1980): 405–411.

[14] J. L. Cleasby, "Unconventional Filtration Rates, Media, and Backwashing Techniques," in *Innovations in the Water and Wastewater Fields*, E. A. Glysson, et al., eds. (Boston: Butterworths, 1985), 1–23.

[15] R. D. G. Monk, "Design Options for Water Filtration," *J. Am. Water Works Assoc.* 79, no. 9 (1987): 93–106.

[16] J. L. Cleasby, "Declining-Rate Filtration," *J. Am. Water Works Assoc.* 73, no. 9 (1981): 484–489.

[17] J. L. Cleasby and L. DiBernardo, "Hydraulic Considerations in Declining-Rate Filtration," *J. Env. Eng. Div., Proc. Am. Soc. Civil Engrs.* 106(EE6) (1980): 1043–1055.

[18] L. G. Rich, *Unit Operations of Sanitary Engineering* (New York: Wiley, 1961), 137–146.

[19] H. E. Rose, "On the Resistance Coefficient-Reynolds Number Relationship for Fluid Flow through a Bed of Granular Material," *Proc. Inst. Mech. Engrs.* 153 (1945): 154–168; 160 (1949): 492–511.

[20] S. Ergun, "Fluid Flow through Packed Columns," *Chem. Eng. Progress* 48, no. 2 (1952): 89–94.

[21] T. R. Camp, "Theory of Water Filtration," *J. San. Eng. Div., Proc. Am. Soc. Civil Engrs.* 90(SA4) (1964): 1–30.

[22] G. M. Fair and L. P. Hatch, "Fundamental Factors Governing the Streamline Flow of Water through Sand," *J. Am. Water Works Assoc.* 25, no. 11 (1933): 1551–1565.

[23] J. L. Cleasby and K. Fan, "Predicting Fluidization and Expansion of Filter Media," *J. Env. Eng. Div., Proc. Am. Soc. Civil Engrs.* 107(EE3) (1981): 455–471.

[24] C. Y. Wen and Y. H. Yu, "Mechanics of Fluidization," *Chem. Eng. Progress Symposium Series* 62 (1966): 100–111.

Chemical Treatment Processes

CHEMICAL CONSIDERATIONS

The purpose of these initial sections is to refresh students on selected fundamental concepts, including definitions, compounds, units of expression, the bicarbonate–carbonate system, chemical equilibria, and process kinetics. Basic chemistry is also presented as introductory material for each specific unit process discussed in the chapter. These brief comments are not intended to replace formal chemistry courses prerequisite to water and wastewater engineering.

1 INORGANIC CHEMICALS AND COMPOUNDS

Definitions

Chemical elements and their atomic weights are given in Table 7 in the Appendix. *Atomic weight* is the weight of an element relative to that of carbon-12, which has an atomic weight of 12. *Valence* is the combining power of an element relative to that of the hydrogen atom, which has an assigned value of 1. Thus, an element with a valence of 2+ can replace two hydrogen atoms in a compound or, in the case of a 2− valence, can react with two hydrogen atoms. Equivalent or combining weight of an element is equal to its atomic weight divided by the valence. For example, the equivalent weight of calcium (Ca^{2+}) equals 40.0 g divided by 2, or 20.0 g.

The *molecular weight* of a compound equals the sum of the atomic weights of the combining elements and is conventionally expressed in grams. A *mole* is the mass of a substance in grams that is equal to its molecular weight. *Equivalent weight* is the molecular weight divided by the number of positive or negative electrical charges resulting from dissolution of the compound. Consider sulfuric acid (H_2SO_4), which has a molecular weight of 98.1 g. *Ionization* releases two H^+ ions and one SO_4^{2-} ion; therefore, the equivalent weight of sulfuric acid is 98.1 divided by 2, or 49.0 g.

Chemicals Applied in Treatment

The common inorganic compounds used in water and wastewater processing are listed in Table 1. Given are the name, formula, common usage, molecular weight, and equivalent weight when appropriate. Common names and purity of commercial-grade chemicals are presented in the sections dealing with specific chemical treatment processes.

TABLE 1   Common Chemicals in Water and Wastewater Processing

Name	Formula	Common Application	Molecular Weight	Equivalent Weight
Activated carbon	C	Taste and odor control	12.0	n.a.[a]
Aluminum sulfate	$Al_2(SO_4)_3 \cdot 14.3\ H_2O$	Coagulation	600	100
Ammonia	NH_3	Chloramine disinfection	17.0	n.a.
Ammonium sulfate (alum)	$(NH_4)_2SO_4$	Coagulation	132	66.1
Calcium hydroxide	$Ca(OH)_2$	Softening, pH adjustment	74.1	37.0
Calcium hypochlorite	$Ca(ClO)_2 \cdot 2\ H_2O$	Disinfection, oxidation	179	n.a.
Calcium oxide (quicklime)	CaO	Softening, pH adjustment	56.1	28.0
Carbon dioxide	CO_2	Recarbonation	44.0	22.0
Chlorine	Cl_2	Disinfection, oxidation	71.0	n.a.
Chlorine dioxide	ClO_2	Taste and odor control	67.0	n.a.
Copper sulfate	$CuSO_4$	Algae control	160	79.8
Ferric chloride	$FeCl_3$	Coagulation	162	54.1
Ferric sulfate	$Fe_2(SO_4)_3$	Coagulation	400	66.7
Ferrous sulfate	$FeSO_4 \cdot 7\ H_2O$	Coagulation	278	139
Fluosilicic acid	H_2SiF_6	Fluoridation	144	n.a.
Magnesium hydroxide	$Mg(OH)_2$	Defluoridation	58.3	29.2
Oxygen	O_2	Aeration	32.0	16.0
Ozone	O_3	Disinfection, oxidation	48	n.a.
Potassium permanganate	$KMnO_4$	Oxidation	158	n.a.
Sodium aluminate	$NaAlO_2$	Coagulation	82.0	n.a.
Sodium bicarbonate	$NaHCO_3$	pH adjustment	84.0	84.0
Sodium carbonate (soda ash)	Na_2CO_3	Softening	106	53.0
Sodium chloride	$NaCl$	Ion exchanger regeneration	58.4	58.4
Sodium fluoride	NaF	Fluoridation	42.0	n.a.
Sodium fluosilicate	Na_2SiF_6	Fluoridation	188	n.a.
Sodium hexametaphosphate	$(NaPO_3)_n$	Corrosion control	n.a.	n.a.
Sodium hydroxide	$NaOH$	pH adjustment	40.0	40.0
Sodium hypochlorite	$NaClO$	Disinfection	74.4	n.a
Sodium silicate	Na_4SiO_4	Coagulation aid	184	n.a.
Sodium thiosulfate	$Na_2S_2O_3$	Dechlorination	158	n.a.
Sulfur dioxide	SO_2	Dechlorination	64.1	n.a.
Sulfuric acid	H_2SO_4	pH adjustment	98.1	49.0

[a]Not applicable.

Moles and Chemical Reactions

Chemical reactions are written interms of the number of moles of reactants and products. For example, in the reaction

$$H_2S + 4\,Cl_2 + 4\,H_2O \rightarrow SO_4^{2-} + 8\,Cl^- + 10\,H^+ \tag{1}$$

4 moles of chlorine are required to oxidize 1 mole of hydrogen sulfide (an odor-causing chemical found in groundwater and wastewater) to the sulfate ion. These quantitative relationships between the reactants and products (called stoichiometry) can be used to calculate the amounts of chemical needed or the amounts of products produced in chemical reactions.

Example 1

Calculate the mass of chlorine required to oxidize 2.5 mg of hydrogen sulfide to sulfate.

Solution:

Molecular weight of $H_2S = 2 \times 1 + 32 = 34$

Then convert the mass of H_2S to moles:

$$\frac{2.5 \times 10^{-3}\,g}{34\,^{g}/_{mole}} = 7.35 \times 10^{-5}\,moles$$

Molecular weight of chlorine $= 71$

Then find the mass of chlorine required:

$$71\frac{g}{mole\ Cl_2} \times 4\frac{moles\ Cl_2}{mole\ H_2S} \times 7.35 \times 10^{-5}\,moles\ H_2S =$$

$$2.09 \times 10^{-2}\,g = 20.9\,mg\ Cl_2$$

Expressing Concentrations and Doses

The concentration of ions or chemicals in solution is normally expressed as mass of the element or compound per volume of water, such as milligrams per liter of water, abbreviated as mg/l. Occasionally, concentration is expressed as mass of the substance per mass of water, such as the term *parts per million* (ppm). If the density of the solution or suspension is not affected by the substance(s) dissolved or suspended in water, 1 mg/l is equivalent to 1 ppm. Since the percent difference between the concentrations expressed as mg/l and ppm is less than 0.1% at 1000 mg/l, the terms are usually considered equivalent. Chemical dosages may be expressed in units of pounds per million gallons or rarely as grains per gallon. To convert milligrams per liter to pounds per million gallons, multiply by 8.34.

$$\frac{1.0\,mg}{liter} \times \frac{g}{1000\,mg} \times \frac{lb}{453.6\,g} \times \frac{3.785\,liters}{gal} \times \frac{10^6\,gal}{million\,gal} = 8.34\,^{lb}/_{million\ gal}$$

One pound contains 7000 grains, and 1.0 grain per gallon (gpg) equals 17.1 mg/l.

Elemental concentrations expressed in units of mg/l can usually be interpreted to mean that the solution contains the stated number of milligrams of that particular element. For example, water containing 1.0 mg/l of fluoride means that there is 1.0 mg of F ion by weight per liter. However, in some cases, the concentration given in milligrams of weight does not relate to the specific element whose concentration is being expressed. For example, hardness, which is a measure of the calcium ion and magnesium ion content of water, is given in weight units of calcium carbonate. This facilitates treating hardness as a single value rather than two concentrations expressed in different weight units, one for Ca^{2+} and the other for Mg^{2+}. The alkalinity of a water may consist of one or more of the following ionic forms: OH^-, CO_3^{2-}, and HCO_3^-. For commonality, the concentrations of these various ions are given in mg/l as $CaCO_3$. According to *Standard Methods* [1], all nitrogen compounds—ammonia, nitrate, and organic nitrogen—may be expressed in units of mg/l as nitrogen and phosphates are given in mg/l as phosphorus.

The term *milliequivalents per liter* (meq/l) expresses the concentration of a dissolved substance in terms of its electrical charge or its combination in reaction. Milliequivalents are calculated from the mass of the substance divided by its equivalent weight as shown in Eq. (2).

$$\text{milliequivalents (meq)} = \frac{\text{mass in mg}}{\text{equivalent weight}} \tag{2}$$

An important equivalent concentration in water treatment is the expression *mg/l as CaCO₃*. To convert a mg/l concentration to a mg/l as $CaCO_3$, first convert mg/l to meq/l and then use the factor 50 mg $CaCO_3$ per meq as illustrated in Example 2. Molar concentrations (moles/L) are expressed in brackets in this text (e.g., the molar concentration of chlorine would be $[Cl_2]$).

Milliequivalents-per-Liter Bar Graph

Results of a water analysis are normally expressed in milligrams per liter and reported in tabular form. For better visualization of the chemical composition, these data can be expressed in milliequivalents per liter to permit graphical presentation, as illustrated in Figure 1. The top row of the bar graph consists of major cations arranged in the order of calcium, magnesium, sodium, and potassium. Anions in the bottom row are aligned in the sequence of carbonate (if present), bicarbonate, sulfate, and chloride. To maintain the electroneutrality of water, the sum of the positive milliequivalents per liter must equal the sum of the negative values for a water sample in equilibrium. Large differences between the sum of positive and negative milliequivalents in a water quality report indicate that there may be an error in the analysis. These milliequivalent graphs are useful in evaluating a water for lime–soda ash softening discussed later in this chapter.

Table 2 lists basic data for selected elements, ions, and compounds. Included are equivalent weights for calculating milliequivalents per liter for use in bar graph presentations and chemical equations.

TABLE 2   Data on Selected Elements, Ions, and Compounds

Name	Symbol or Formula	Atomic or Molecular Weight	Equivalent Weight
Elements			
Aluminum	Al^{3+}	27.0	9.0
Calcium	Ca^{2+}	40.1	20.0
Carbon	C	12.0	
Chloride	Cl	35.5	35.5
Hydrogen	H^+	1.0	1.0
Magnesium	Mg^{2+}	24.3	12.2
Manganese	Mn^{2+}	54.9	27.5
Nitrogen	N	14.0	
Oxygen	O	16.0	
Phosphorus	P	31.0	
Sodium	Na^+	23.0	23.0
Ions			
Ammonium	NH_4^+	18.0	18.0
Bicarbonate	HCO_3^-	61.0	61.0
Carbonate	CO_3^{2-}	60.0	30.0
Hydroxyl	OH^-	17.0	17.0
Hypochlorite	OCl^-	51.5	51.5
Nitrate	NO_3^-	62.0	62.0
Orthophosphate	PO_4^{3-}	95.0	31.7
Sulfate	SO_4^{2-}	96.0	48.0
Compounds			
Aluminum hydroxide	$Al(OH)_3$	78.0	26.0
Calcium bicarbonate	$Ca(HCO_3)_2$	162	81.0
Calcium carbonate	$CaCO_3$	100	50.0
Calcium sulfate	$CaSO_4$	136	68.0
Carbon dioxide	CO_2	44.0	22.0
Ferric hydroxide	$Fe(OH)_3$	107	35.6
Hydrochloric acid	HCl	36.5	36.5
Magnesium carbonate	$MgCO_3$	84.3	42.1
Magnesium hydroxide	$Mg(OH)_2$	58.3	29.1
Magnesium sulfate	$MgSO_4$	120	60.1
Sodium sulfate	Na_2SO_4	142	71.0

Example 2

The results of a water analysis are calcium 40.0 mg/l, magnesium 10.0 mg/l, sodium 11.7 mg/l, potassium 7.0 mg/l, bicarbonate 110 mg/l, sulfate 67.2 mg/l, and chloride 11.0 mg/l. Draw a milliequivalents-per-liter bar graph and express the hardness and alkalinity in units of mg/l as $CaCO_3$. Assume the hydrogen and hydroxide ion concentrations are negligible.

Solution: Use Eq. (2) and the data in Table 3 to develop the bar graph shown in Figure 2.

Hardness is the sum of the Ca^{2+} and Mg^{2+} concentrations expressed in mg/l as $CaCO_3$, and alkalinity equals the sum of the bicarbonate, carbonate, and hydroxide content. Thus,

$$hardness = 2.82 \text{ meq/l} \times 50 \frac{\text{mg of CaCO}_3}{\text{meq}} = 141 \text{ mg/l}$$

$$alkalinity = 1.80 \times 50 \frac{\text{mg of CaCO}_3}{\text{meq}} = 90 \text{ mg/l}$$

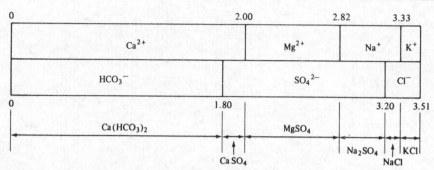

FIGURE 1   Milliequivalents-per-liter bar graph for water analysis in example 2.

TABLE 3   Water Analysis Data for Example 2

Component	mg/l	Equivalent Weight	meq/l
Ca^{2+}	40.0	20.0	2.00
Mg^{2+}	10.0	12.2	0.82
Na^+	11.7	23.0	0.51
K^+	7.0	39.1	0.18
		Total cations =	3.51
HCO^{3-}	110.0	61.0	1.80
SO_4^{2-}	67.2	48.0	1.40
Cl^-	11.0	35.5	0.31
		Total anions =	3.51

2   CHEMICAL EQUILIBRIA

Many chemical reactions are reversible to some degree, and the concentrations of reactants and products determine the final state of equilibrium. For the general reaction expressed by Eq. (3), increase in either A or B shifts the equilibrium to the right, whereas a larger concentration of either C or D drives it to the left. A reaction in true equilibrium can be expressed by an equilibrium expression, Eq. (4):

$$a\text{A} + b\text{B} \leftrightarrow c\text{C} + d\text{D} \tag{3}$$

$$\frac{\{\text{C}\}^c \{\text{D}\}^d}{\{\text{A}\}^a \{\text{B}\}^b} = \text{K} \tag{4}$$

where

A, B = reactants
C, D = products
{ } = activity of the chemical
K = equilibrium constant

The activity of a chemical in dilute solution is approximated well by its molar concentration. So in this text and often in the field of water and wastewater treatment, molar concentrations will be used in place of activities in equilibrium expressions as shown in Eq. (5).

$$\frac{[C]^c [D]^d}{[A]^a [B]^b} = K \tag{5}$$

Strong acids and bases in dilute solutions approach 100% ionization (high values of K), while weak acids and bases are poorly ionized (low values of K). The degree of ionization of the latter is expressed by the equilibrium expression. For example, Eqs. (6–9) are, for carbonic acid,

$$H_2CO_3 \leftrightarrow H^+ + HCO_3^- \tag{6}$$

$$\frac{[H^+][HCO_3^-]}{[H_2CO_3]} = K_1 = 4.45 \times 10^{-7} \text{ at } 25°C \tag{7}$$

$$HCO_3^- \leftrightarrow H^+ + CO_3^{2-} \tag{8}$$

$$\frac{[H^+][CO_3^{2-}]}{[HCO_3^-]} = K_2 = 4.69 \times 10^{-11} \text{ at } 25°C \tag{9}$$

The foregoing characterizes homogeneous chemical equilibria where all reactants and products occur in the same physical state. Heterogeneous equilibrium exists between a substance that is in two or more physical states. For example, at greater than pH 10, solid calcium carbonate in water reaches a stability with the calcium and carbonate ions in solution,

$$CaCO_{3(s)} \leftrightarrow Ca^{2+} + CO_3^{2-} \tag{10}$$

By definition the activity of a solid in equilibrium with a solution is 1. So in the equilibrium expression

$$\frac{\{Ca^{2+}\}\{CO_3^{2-}\}}{\{CaCO_{3(s)}\}} = K \tag{11}$$

$\{CaCO_{3(s)}\} = 1$. Using molar concentrations to approximate activities and using K_s (the solubility product) to represent the equilibrium constant for dissolution of a solid gives

$$K_{sp} = [Ca^{2+}][CO_3^{2-}] = 4.6 \times 10^{-9} \text{ at } 25°C \tag{12}$$

If the product of the ionic molar concentrations is less than the solubility-product constant, the solution is unsaturated, and if a solid phase is present, it will tend to dissolve. Conversely, a supersaturated solution contains an $[A^+][B^-]$ value greater than K_{sp}. In this case, solids form and precipitation progresses until the ionic concentrations are reduced to a point where they are equal to those of a saturated solution.

Other ions in solution affect the solubility of a substance by either the common-ion effect or the secondary-salt effect. The common-ion effect is a repression of solubility of a substance in the presence of an excess of one of the solubility-product ions. For example, in pure water the solubility of $CaCO_3$ is about 13 mg/l, whereas in a solution containing 60 mg/l of carbonate ion, the solubility is only 0.5 mg/l. The secondary-salt effect is the increase in solubility of slightly soluble salts when other salts in solution do not have an ion in common with the slightly soluble substance. For example, $CaCO_3$ is several times more soluble in seawater than in fresh water.

3   HYDROGEN ION CONCENTRATION

The hydrogen ion activity (i.e., intensity of the acidic or basic condition of a solution) is expressed by the term pH, which is defined as

$$pH = \log \frac{1}{\{H^+\}} \tag{13}$$

Again, in dilute solutions the activity is approximated well by the molar concentration, so the pH is often expressed

$$pH = \log \frac{1}{[H^+]} \tag{14}$$

Water dissociates to only a slight degree, yielding hydrogen ions and hydroxyl ions (Eq. 15) with an equilibrium constant (K) of 10^{-14}. Since the activity of water is defined to be 1.0 in most contexts, using the molar concentration of hydrogen ions and hydroxide ions to approximate their activities gives the equilibrium expression in Equation 16.

$$H_2O \longleftrightarrow H^+ + OH^- \tag{15}$$

$$K = 10^{-14} = [H^+][OH^-] \text{ at } 25°C \tag{16}$$

Pure water dissociates to give the same number of hydrogen and hydroxide ions, 10^{-7} M, so the pH of a pure water solution is 7.0. Note the inverse relationship between hydrogen and hydroxide ions. When an acid is added to water, the reaction in Eq. (15) reacts from right to left to reestablish equilibrium and satisfy Eq. (16). The hydrogen ion concentration increases, resulting in a lower pH value. Similarly when a base such as NaOH is added to water, $[OH^-]$ increases, $[H^+]$ decreases, and the pH correspondingly increases. The pH scale is acidic from 0 to 7 and basic from 7 to 14.

The chemical equilibrium of water can be shifted by changing the hydrogen ion activity in solution. Thus pH adjustment is used to optimize coagulation, softening, and disinfection reactions, and for corrosion control. In wastewater treatment, pH must be maintained in a range favorable for biological activity.

4 ALKALINITY AND pH RELATIONSHIPS

Alkalinity is a measure of water's capacity to neutralize acids. It is determined in the laboratory by titrating a water sample with a standardized sulfuric acid solution. Any base will contribute to alkalinity, but the most commonly found bases are bicarbonates, carbonates, and hydroxides. Bicarbonates represent the major form since they originate naturally from reactions of carbon dioxide in water and reactions of acids with carbonate minerals and predominate in waters and wastewaters near neutrality as determined by Eqs. (9) and (16).

Below pH 4.5, no alkalinity exists. Between pH 4.5 and 8.3, the balance shown in Eq. (6) shifts to the right, creating HCO_3^- ions. As the pH rises above 8.3, the bicarbonates are converted to carbonate ions as shown in Eq. (8). Hydroxide ions usually become a significant form of alkalinity above a pH of 9.5. Figure 2 shows the relationship between carbon dioxide and the three forms of alkalinity with respect to pH calculated for water having a total alkalinity of 100 mg at 25°C. Temperature, total alkalinity, and the presence of other ionic species influence alkalinity–pH relationships; nevertheless, Figure 2 is a realistic representation of most natural waters.

Substances that offer resistance to change in pH as acids or bases are added to a solution are referred to as *buffers*. Since the pH falls between 6 and 9 for most natural waters and wastewaters, the primary buffer is the bicarbonate–carbonate system. When acid is added, a portion of the H^+ ions is combined with HCO_3^- to form un-ionized

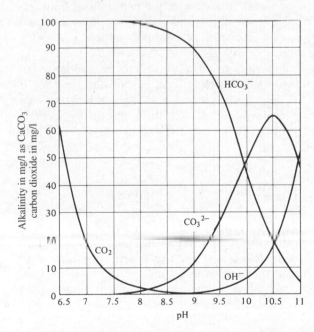

FIGURE 2 Carbon dioxide and various forms of alkalinity relative to pH in water at 25°C. Total alkalinity is 100 mg/l as $CaCO_3$.

H_2CO_3; only the H^+ remaining free affect pH. If a base is added, the OH^- ions react with free H^+, increasing the pH. However, some of the latter are replaced by a shift of HCO_3^- to CO_3^{2-}, attenuating the change in hydrogen ion concentration and therefore pH. Both chemical reactions and biological processes depend on this natural buffering action to control pH changes. Sodium carbonate or calcium hydroxide can be added if naturally existing alkalinity is insufficient, such as in the coagulation of water where the chemicals added react with water to produce hydrogen ions which then decrease alkalinity by Eqs. (6) and (8) as these equations proceed from right to left.

Precipitation softening is better understood by referring to the pH–alkalinity relationship illustrated in Figure 2. Calcium and magnesium ions are soluble when associated with bicarbonate anions. But, if the pH of a hard water is increased, insoluble precipitates of $CaCO_3$ and $Mg(OH)_2$ are formed. This is accomplished in water treatment by adding lime to raise the pH level. At a value of about 10, hydroxyl ions convert a sufficient amount of bicarbonate to carbonate to allow the formation of calcium carbonate precipitate as follows:

$$\underset{\substack{\text{bicarbonate} \\ \text{hardness}}}{Ca(HCO_3)_2} + \underset{\substack{\text{lime} \\ \text{slurry}}}{Ca(OH)_2} \longrightarrow \underset{\substack{\text{solid} \\ \text{precipitate}}}{2CaCO_3 \downarrow} + 2H_2O \tag{17}$$

Precipitation of $Mg(OH)_2$ is usually carried out at or above a pH of 11.0 where a sufficient concentration of OH^- is present.

5   WAYS OF SHIFTING CHEMICAL EQUILIBRIA

Chemical reactions in water and wastewater treatment rely on shifting of homogeneous or heterogeneous equilibria to achieve the desired results. The most common methods for completing reactions are by formation of insoluble substances, weakly ionized compounds, gaseous end products, and oxidation and reduction.

The best example of shifting equilibrium to form precipitates is lime–soda ash softening. Calcium is removed from solution by adding lime, as shown in Eq. (17). If insufficient alkalinity is available to complete this reaction, sodium carbonate (soda ash) is also applied. However, magnesium hardness must be removed by forming $Mg(OH)_2$ since $MgCO_3$ is relatively soluble. This is effected by addition of excess lime to increase the value of $[Mg^{2+}][OH^-]^2$ above the solubility product of magnesium hydroxide, which equals 9×10^{-12}.

$$MgCO_3 + Ca(OH)_2 \xrightarrow{\text{excess } OH^-} CaCO_3 \downarrow + Mg(OH)_2 \downarrow \tag{18}$$

Oxidation and reduction reactions typically go to completion (reaction proceeds to the right with almost no back reaction to the left.) An example is the oxidation of hydrogen sulfide by chlorine as shown in Eq. (1). In this reaction each atom of sulfur in hydrogen sulfide loses 8 electrons (is oxidized) in reacting with chlorine to form sulfate, while each atom of chlorine gains one electron (is reduced) to form the chlorine ion. Sulfate ion will not combine with chloride ion in the reverse reaction.

6   CHEMICAL KINETICS

Chemical reactions are classified on the basis of stoichiometry, which defines the number of moles of a substance entering into a reaction and the number of moles of products, and process kinetics that describe the rate of reaction. The types discussed in this section are irreversible reactions occurring in one phase where the reactants are distributed uniformly throughout the liquid. Heterogeneous processes involve the presence of a solid-phase, such as adsorption onto a granular medium. In irreversible reactions, the stoichiometric combination of reactants leads to their complete depletion and conversion to products. Many reactions in water and wastewater, particularly oxidation–reduction and precipitation reactions, are sufficiently irreversible to allow this assumption for purposes of kinetic interpretation of experimental data. The type of reactor containing a reaction influences the degree of completion; therefore, process kinetics must also incorporate the hydrodynamic behavior of reactors discussed in Sections 9 and 10.

Reaction Rates

Zero-Order Reactions These reactions proceed at a rate independent of the concentration of any reactant or product. Consider conversion of a single reactant to a single product, represented as

$$A \text{ (reactant)} \rightarrow P \text{ (product)}$$

If C represents the concentration of A at any time t, the disappearance of A is expressed as

$$\frac{dC}{dt} = -k \tag{19}$$

where

$\dfrac{dC}{dt}$ = rate of change in concentration of A with time

k = reaction-rate constant

The negative sign in front of k means that the concentration of A decreases with time. Integrating Eq. (19) and rearranging yields

$$C = C_0 - kt \tag{20}$$

where

C = concentration of A at any time t

C_0 = initial concentration of A

and C_0 becomes the constant of integration if we let $C = C_0$ when $t = 0$.

A plot of a zero-order reaction is shown in Figure 3a by the straight line with a constant slope equal to $-k$.

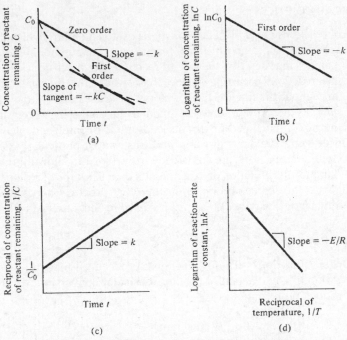

FIGURE 3   Diagrams illustrating reaction rates for irreversible homogeneous reactions occurring in one phase. (a) Arithmetic graphs of a
zero-order reaction as a solid line and first-order reaction as a dashed
line. (b) Semilogarithmic plot of a first-order reaction. (c) Plot of a
second-order process. (d) Diagram showing the effect of temperature on
reaction-rate plotting ln k versus $1/T$ based on the Arrhenius equations
[Eqs. (26) and (27)].

First-Order Reactions   These reactions proceed at a rate directly proportional to the
concentration of one reactant. Again consider conversion of a single reactant to a
single product:

$$A(\text{reactant}) \longrightarrow P(\text{product})$$

If C represents the concentration of A at any time t, the disappearance of A is
expressed

$$\frac{dC}{dt} = -kC \tag{21}$$

Integrating Eq. (21) and letting $C = C_0$ at $t = 0$ gives

$$\ln\frac{C_0}{C} = kt \quad \text{or} \quad \log\frac{C_0}{C} = \frac{kt}{2.30} \quad \text{or} \quad C = C_0\,e^{-kt} \tag{22}$$

Plotting a first-order reaction on arithmetic paper results in a curve, as shown by
the dashed line in Figure 3a, with the slope of a tangent at any point equal to $-kC$.

With passage of time from the start of the reaction, the rate decreases with the decreasing concentration of A remaining; this is reflected by the reduction in tangent slopes along the curve. First-order reactions can be linearized by graphing on semi-logarithmic paper, as illustrated in Figure 3b.

Second-Order Reactions These reactions proceed at a rate proportional to the second power of a single reactant being converted to a single product,

$$A \text{ (reactant)} \rightarrow P \text{ (product)}$$

The rate of disappearance of A is described by the rate equation

$$\frac{dC}{dt} = -kC^2 \tag{23}$$

The integrated form for a second-order reaction is

$$\frac{1}{C} - \frac{1}{C_0} = kt \quad \text{or} \quad C = \frac{C_0}{1 + ktC_0} \tag{24}$$

A plot of Eq. (24) is shown in Figure 3c. On arithmetic paper, the reciprocal of the concentration of reactant remaining versus time plot is a straight line with a slope equal to k.

Effect of Temperature on Reaction Rate

The rates of simple chemical reactions accelerate with increasing temperature of the liquid in a reactor, provided the higher temperature does not alter a reactant or catalyst. In 1889 Arrhenius examined the available data on the effect of temperature on the rates of chemical reactions and proposed the following equation:

$$\frac{d(\ln k)}{dT} = \frac{E}{RT^2} \tag{25}$$

where

k = reaction rate constant
T = absolute temperature, K
E = a constant characteristic of the reaction called activation energy, J/mole
R = ideal gas constant (8.314 J/K/mole)

Integration of this equation between T_1 and T_2, corresponding to reaction-rate constants k_1 and k_2, respectively, gives the relationship

$$\ln \frac{k_2}{k_1} = \frac{E(T_2 - T_1)}{RT_1T_2} \tag{26}$$

If experimental data are available, then E/R can be determined from the slope of a plot of $\ln k$ versus $1/T$ (Figure 3d). In turn, the activation energy E for the reaction can be calculated by

$$E = -slope \times R \tag{27}$$

Eq. (26) may be rearranged to give

$$\frac{k_2}{k_1} = \left(e^{E/RT_1T_2}\right)^{T_2-T_1} \tag{28}$$

For water and wastewater reactions near ambient temperature, the quantity E/RT_1T_2 located on the right side of Eq. (28) can be assumed constant for practical temperature ranges. Replacing the term in brackets with a temperature coefficient Θ yields

$$\frac{k_2}{k_1} = \Theta^{T_2-T_1} \tag{29}$$

which is commonly used to adjust the value of a rate constant for a temperature change. Equation (29) is applied to both chemical and biological processes, although in some cases linearity may be limited to a narrow temperature range. A common value for the temperature coefficient is 1.072, which doubles the reaction-rate constant with a 10°C temperature rise.

Reaction order and the reaction rate constant for a particular reaction are determined by collecting experimental data and performing the graphical and mathematical analyses described in this section. Reaction order should not be determined from the reaction stoichiometry.

REACTIONS IN CONTINUOUS-FLOW SYSTEMS—REAL AND IDEAL REACTORS

Chemical and biological reactions are performed in tanks that are often referred to as reactors in process engineering. These include rapid mixing tanks, flocculators, and disinfection contact basins in water treatment, and activated sludge and disinfection contact basins in wastewater treatment. Reaction-rate orders and rate constants are based on batch reactor analyses typically performed in a lab setting, in which the reactants are added to a stirred container and the change in concentrations is measured with respect to time. Most reactors in water and wastewater treatment occur in continuous flow reactors. In a continuous-flow reactor, the extent of a reaction depends on how the hydrodynamic characteristics of the reactor affect reaction time. For steady-state conditions of uniform flow and reactant concentrations, mass balance analyses are used both to determine the hydrodynamic characteristics of the reactor and, when combined with the kinetics of the chemical or biological reaction, to calculate the changes that occur between the influent and effluent of a reactor. Mathematical expressions can be derived for process reactions to predict the degree of reaction completion in a particular system or to compute the volume of the reactor needed for a specific degree of reaction completion.

7 MASS BALANCE ANALYSIS

A schematic reactor diagram is shown in Figure 4. Water flows into a reactor with volume V with a flow rate of Q_{in} and a concentration of a chemical C_0 and leaves the reactor with a flow Q_{out} and chemical concentration C. We may account for changes in the mass of the chemical in the reactor with a mass balance. The rate of mass accumulation in the reactor is equal to the rate of mass flowing in minus the rate of mass flowing out plus the rate of mass generation.

$$(\text{Accumulation}) = (\text{In}) - (\text{Out}) + (\text{Generation}) \tag{30}$$

An equation can be written in mathematical form for a reactor of constant volume (V) as

$$\frac{d(CV)}{dt} = Q_{in}C_0 - (QC)_{out} + V\frac{dC}{dt} \tag{31}$$

where

C = mass concentration of the chemical within the reactor

t = time

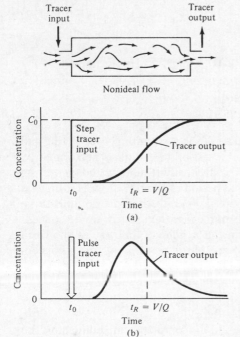

FIGURE 4   Output tracer distribution curves for flow through a nonideal reactor in response to (a) a continuous tracer input; (b) a pulse tracer input.

When we use the mass balance to characterize the hydrodynamic behavior of reactors with an unsteady-state unreactive tracer analysis, the generation term is zero because the tracer is neither generated or destroyed. When we analyze the destruction of a chemical or microorganism in a steady-state flow reactor, the accumulation term is zero (steady state means no change with time) and the rate equation from reactor kinetics is used in the generation term. In the following discussion the flow rate of water is considered to be constant into and out of the reactor; therefore there is no accumulation, generation, or loss of water itself.

8   RESIDENCE TIME DISTRIBUTION

The hydrodynamic character of a process reactor is defined by the residence time distribution of individual particles of the liquid flowing through the tank. Clearly there are not distinct "parcels" or "particles" of water that are kept separate from others throughout the reactor; however, one can think of these "particles" as one bacterium or chemical molecule traveling through the reactor with the water. Since routes through the reactor differ in travel times, the effluent age or residence time (how long the particle, molecule or bacterium spends in the reactor) may be different for each. This residence time variability can be expressed as a distribution that is shown in Figure 4b for a nonideal (real) reactor. Residence times extend from less than to greater than the theoretical detention time, also known as the hydraulic residence time (HRT), which is defined as

$$t_R = \frac{V}{Q} \tag{32}$$

where

t_R = theoretical mean residence time
V = volume of the reactor
Q = rate of flow through the reactor

This variability in residence times is the result of short-circuiting, backmixing and dispersion within the reactor. Evaluation of an actual process tank is performed by introducing a nonreactive tracer to the influent during steady-state flow and measuring the concentration in the output over an extended period of time. If the tracer input is suddenly initiated and then held at a constant application rate, the tracer output curve of concentration in the effluent slowly rises and approaches the influent tracer concentration C_0 at a time interval greater than the mean residence time t_R, as shown in Figure 4a. Applying a pulse input of dye solution results in an effluent tracer concentration curve as shown in Figure 4b.

9   IDEAL REACTORS

Common ideal reactors are the plug-flow reactor and the completely mixed reactor. The residence time distributions of these units can be expressed in mathematical equations. Although real process tanks never precisely follow these flow patterns, many designs approximate ideal conditions with negligible error. Laboratory analyses of biological and chemical processes are often conducted using small tanks that are considered ideal reactors.

Plug-Flow Reactor

The ideal plug-flow reactor is a tube with all portions of liquid entering and discharging in the same sequence with no mixing in the direction of flow. The residence time of each particle is equal to the mean residence time t_R, as illustrated in Figure 5. If a tracer with concentration C_0 is applied to the input, at time t_R the output contains the tracer at the same concentration. A pulse input is observed as a pulse in the output after time t_R. Turbulent flow in pipes is usually considered to be plug flow. Actual treatment units that approach plug flow are long rectangular tanks used as chlorine contact chambers and in the conventional activated-sludge process. Increasing the length to width ratio of any reactor will increase its plug-flow character.

If the hydrodynamic behavior of a reactor has been characterized as plug flow, chemical or biological conversion in the reactor under steady-state conditions may be determined by mass balance analysis around a differential volume (dV) of the reactor as shown in Figure 5 with the reaction rate expression included in the generation term:

$$0 = QC - Q(C + dC) + \text{reaction rate} \times dV \tag{33}$$

For a first order reaction, substituting the rate expression of Eq. (21) into 33 gives

$$0 = QdC - Q(C + dC) + -kCdV \tag{34}$$

which simplifies to

$$Q\frac{dC}{C} = -kdV \tag{35}$$

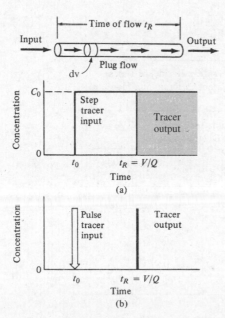

FIGURE 5 Output residence time distributions for an ideal plug-flow reactor in response to (a) a continuous input; (b) a pulse input.

Integrating between the limits from C_0 to C and from 0 to V, and using Eq. (32) gives

$$C = C_0\, e^{-kt_R} \tag{36}$$

Note the similarity of Eqs. (22) and (36). Since the water flows through an ideal plug-flow reactor without mixing in the direction of flow, each portion of entering water can be visualized as a batch reactor that travels through the flow reactor for the time t_R. The horizontal time scales in Figure 5 represent time of passage, or travel distance along the reactor at a known velocity of flow. The plug-flow chemical reaction equations relating mean hydraulic detention time to reaction-rate constants for irreversible zero-, first-, and second-order reactions are given in Table 4. These were derived by substituting the reaction rates in Eqs. (19), (21), and (23), respectively, into Eq. (33) and solving as above.

Completely Mixed Reactor

In complete contrast to the plug-flow reactor, a completely mixed reactor uniformly and continuously redistributes its contents. Water and chemicals entering are dispersed immediately throughout the tank and leave in proportion to their concentration in the mixing liquid. Figure 6a is the residence time distribution for a step tracer input of concentration C_0. For an unreactive tracer the generation term is zero, and the mass balance becomes

$$V\frac{dC}{dt} = QC_0 - QC \tag{37}$$

Rearranging and integrating between the limits of 0 and C and 0 and t, and using Eq. (32) gives

$$C = C_0(1 - e^{-t/t_R}) \tag{38}$$

TABLE 4 Mean Hydraulic Detention Times (Mean Residence Times) for Irreversible Reactions of Different Order in Plug-Flow and Completely Mixed Reactors

	Equations for Mean Hydraulic Detention Times	
Reaction Order	Ideal Plug-Flow	Ideal Completely Mixed Flow
0	$\frac{1}{k}(C_0 - C)$	$\frac{1}{k}(C_0 - C)$
1	$\frac{1}{k}\left[\ln\left(\frac{C_0}{C}\right)\right]$	$\frac{1}{k}\left(\frac{C_0}{C} - 1\right)$
2	$\frac{1}{kC_0}\left(\frac{C_0}{C} - 1\right)$	$\frac{1}{kC_o}\left(\frac{C_0}{C} - 1\right)$

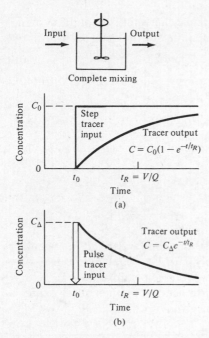

FIGURE 6   Output residence time distributions for an ideal completely mixed reactor in response to (a) a continuous input; (b) a pulse input.

The solution to Eq. 37 is possible because the concentration of the tracer in a completely mixed reactor is identical at all points, and it is the same as the concentration in the effluent.

Figure 6b is the residence time distribution for a pulse input of tracer. The concentration of tracer in the effluent with passage of time under constant Q is derived from Eq. (37) recognizing that after the pulse is introduced, the inlet concentration C_0 is zero, and therefore the input term $QC_0 = 0$ for all t (the pulse of tracer is washed out with the influent water).

$$C = C_\Delta \, e^{-t/t_R} \tag{39}$$

where

$$C_\Delta = \frac{\text{mass of pulse tracer}}{\text{volume of reactor}}$$

Treatment processes that closely simulate this ideal reactor are chemical mixing tanks and completely mixed activated-sludge basins. Studies of wastewater treatability and the evaluation of biological kinetics are commonly performed in laboratory containers that are completely mixed reactors.

If the hydrodynamic behavior of a reactor has been characterized as completely mixed flow, chemical or biological conversion in the reactor under steady-state conditions may be determined with a mass balance analysis around the reactor. Again, the concentrations of reactants and products are uniform throughout the mixing liquid, and the effluent has identical concentrations of reactants and products. Considering both the rate of reaction within the reactor, the hydraulic characteristics of the system, and the fact that the accumulation term is zero for steady state, the mass balance is

$$0 = QC_0 - QC - V(\text{rate of reaction}) \tag{40}$$

For a first order reaction, substituting the rate expression of Eq. (21) into (40) gives

$$0 = QC_0 - QC - V(kC) \tag{41}$$

Rearranging Eq. (41) and using Eq. (32) for t_R gives the effluent concentration (C) for a completely mixed reactor and first-order kinetics:

$$C = \frac{C_0}{1 + kt_R} \tag{42}$$

where k = the first order reaction rate constant (same units as t_R)

The equations for zero- and second-order reactions can be derived in a similar manner substituting Eqs. (19), and (23), respectively, into Eq. (40). Table 4 lists the equations for mean hydraulic residence times of ideal completely mixed-flow reactors based on irreversible zero-, first-, and second-order reactions. Mathematical expressions for more complex chemical process kinetics are given by others [2, 3].

Example 3

An organic contaminant has been shown to decay in a chemical oxidation process by irreversible first-order kinetics with a rate constant of 5 hr^{-1}. If the treatment goal is to decrease the contaminant concentration from 200 μg/l to 20 μg/l, and the flow rate is 10 mgd, find the required volume of the reactor if the reactor used is (a) plug flow or (b) completely mixed.

Solution: For a plug-flow reactor,

$$t_R = \frac{1}{k}\ln\left(\frac{C_0}{C}\right) = \frac{1\ \text{hr}}{5}\ln\left(\frac{200}{20}\right) = 0.46\ \text{hr}$$

$$V = Q \times t_R = \frac{10 \times 10^6\ \text{gal}}{\text{d}} \times 0.46\ \text{h} \times \frac{\text{d}}{24\ \text{h}} = 192{,}000\ \text{gal}$$

For a completely mixed reactor,

$$t_R = \frac{1}{k}\left(\frac{C_0}{C} - 1\right) = \frac{1\ \text{hr}}{5}\left(\frac{200}{20} - 1\right) = 1.8\ \text{hr}$$

$$V = Q \times t_R = \frac{10 \times 10^6\ \text{gal}}{\text{d}} \times 1.8\ \text{h} \times \frac{\text{d}}{24\ \text{h}} = 750{,}000\ \text{gal}$$

This example points out the superior efficiency of the plug flow reactor. Any real reactor would have an active volume somewhere between these two calculated volumes for the same effluent concentration.

---

10   REAL REACTORS

The plug-flow (no mixing) and completely mixed flow reactors are ideal models. All real reactors fall somewhere between these idealities. For all positive order reactions, plug-flow reactors will yield the greatest extent of reaction (lowest C/C_0 value) compared with any other reactor with equal t_R, while completely mixed flow reactors will yield the lowest extent of reaction (highest C/C_0 value) compared with any other reactor of equal t_R. All other real reactors will yield C/C_0 values that are between those of a plug-flow and a completely mixed flow reactor of equal t_R. Accordingly, when evaluating real reactors for positive order reactions, using the plug-flow and completely mixed flow analysis discussed above with the same t_R will give a best case and worst case prediction of the extent of treatment.

Real reactors can be evaluated with models; one of the most popular models is the completely-mixed-reactors-in-series model (tanks in series). The first task is to fit the model to the data obtained in an unsteady-state tracer analysis for the real reactor, and the second task is to use the model to predict the extent of reaction (extent of treatment) in the real reactor under steady-state flow.

Tracer Analysis

Tracer analysis consists of introducing either a pulse or step concentration of unreactive tracer in the influent of a reactor at time = 0 and monitoring the effluent (output) concentration as a function of time. An example is shown in Figure 4. After dye is injected at the inlet of the tank, output samples are collected at time intervals from $^1/_2$ min to several minutes, with the greatest frequency during discharge of the dye peak. Both the mean and the variance of the output data may be calculated from these data. For large extents of dispersion, which are common in tracer studies of actual processing tanks, the residence time curves are often positively skewed. This is evidenced by an elongated curve where the concentration of tracer gradually approaches zero.

The mean of the tracer output distribution is given by

$$\bar{t} = \frac{\displaystyle\int_0^\infty tC\, dt}{\displaystyle\int_0^\infty C\, dt} \simeq \frac{\sum tC\,\Delta t}{\sum C\,\Delta t} \tag{43}$$

and the variance is given by

$$\sigma^2 = \frac{\displaystyle\int_0^\infty (t - \bar{t})^2\, C\, dt}{\displaystyle\int_0^\infty C\, dt} \simeq \frac{\sum t^2 C\,\Delta t}{\sum C\,\Delta t} - \bar{t}^2 \tag{44}$$

where

$\bar{t}$ = the mean residence time

σ^2 = variance

C = tracer concentration at time t

t = time

Δt_i = time interval between t_{i-1} and t_i

Note that $\bar{t}$ should equal t_R if the full volume of the reactor is being used. When dead zones exist in the reactor, the effective volume will be less than the full volume, and $\bar{t}$ will be less than t_R.

The values of $\bar{t}$ and σ^2 are used to determine the characteristic parameters of the completely mixed reactors in series model. The above analysis applies only to a pulse tracer input.

Completely Mixed Reactors in Series

Combining completely mixed reactors in series, as shown in Figure 7, is conceivable in a water or wastewater treatment scenario, but the model is more often used to evaluate the hydrodynamic behavior and to predict treatment efficiencies of real reactors. This is because plug-flow reactors can be thought of as an infinite number of completely mixed reactors in series. Consider the n equal-sized ideal completely mixed

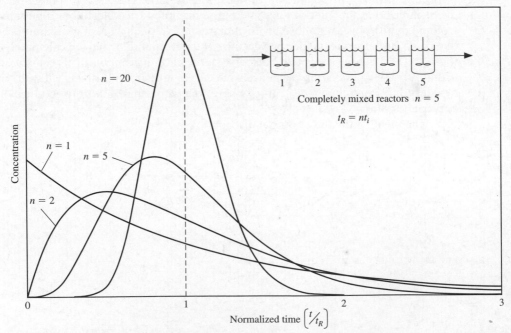

FIGURE 7   Output residence time distributions for ideal completely mixed reactors in series in response to a pulse tracer input.

reactors each with a mean residence time of t_i in Figure 7 that simulate a real reactor with a mean residence time of t_R such that

$$t_R = \bar{t} = n\, t_i \tag{45}$$

Figure 7 shows the output residence time distributions of the real reactor in response to a pulse tracer input as a function of normalized time (t/t_R). Each curve represents a different number of reactors in series, while the sum of their individual mean residence times remains constant at t_R. Note that as the number of ideal reactors used to simulate the real reactor increases, the curves become more peaked and tend to approach the pulse tracer output for a plug-flow reactor $(n = \infty)$. By selecting an appropriate number of tanks in series, you can calibrate the model to simulate the behavior of the real reactor, that is, to match the tracer output data. For example, observe the similarity in the shapes of the curves in Figure 4b and the distribution for an $n = 5$ in Figure 7.

The number of reactors in series that would best fit the pulse tracer output data for a real reactor can be determined from $\bar{t}$ and σ^2.

$$n = \frac{(\bar{t})^2}{\sigma^2} \tag{46}$$

For the last tank in a series of n, the residence time distribution can be calculated using the generalized equation

$$C_n = C_\Delta \frac{n\left(\frac{nt}{t}\right)^{n-1}}{(n-1)!} e^{-\frac{nt}{t}} \tag{47}$$

where

$\ \ \ \ C_n = $ effluent tracer concentration from reactor n (real reactor effluent)

$\ \ \ \ C_\Delta = $ mass of pulse tracer divided by the volume of the real reactor

$$= \frac{1}{\bar{t}} \int_0^\infty C\, dt$$

$\ \ \ \ n = $ number of reactors in series

$\ \ \ \ t = $ time elapsed since tracer input

$\ \ \ \ \bar{t} = $ sum of mean residence times of n ideal reactors

$\ \ \ \ \ \ \ = $ mean residence time of the real reactor

Substituting $n = 1$ into Eq. (47) yields Eq. (39). Note when the value of n is not an integer, $(n-1)!$ can be evaluated by

$$(n-1)! = \Gamma(n) \tag{48}$$

where

$\ \ \ \ \Gamma(n) = $ the gamma function of n

or approximated by

$$(n-1)! \cong e^{-n} n^n \sqrt{\frac{2\pi}{n}} \tag{49}$$

When the number of reactors in series (n) has been determined, extents of reaction in the reactor may be predicted. For irreversible first-order reactions the steady-state effluent concentration is given by

$$C = \left(\frac{1}{1 + k\frac{\bar{t}}{n}} \right)^n \tag{50}$$

where

$\bar{t}$ = mean residence time of the reactor = $n \times t_i$

Equations to predict effluent concentrations for other reaction orders can be found elsewhere [2, 4].

Example 4

A chlorine contact basin is used in a disinfection process at a wastewater treatment plant with a peak flow of 10 mgd. Chlorine decays in the wastewater by irreversible first-order kinetics with a reaction rate constant of 0.02 min^{-1}. Conservative (unreactive) tracer data for a pulse input is given in Table 5 below.

a. Find the mean residence time and variance from the tracer data.
b. Find the number of tanks in series that can be used to model the reactor based on the tracer data and compare the model distribution to the data.
c. Find the concentration of chlorine at the influent of the basin that would be required to ensure a disinfection residual of 0.5 mg/L at the effluent at peak flow.

Solution: The computation procedure is illustrated in Table 5.

a. The mean residence time is calculated using Eq. (43):

$$\bar{t} \simeq \frac{\Sigma Ct\,\Delta t}{\Sigma C\,\Delta t} = \frac{31952}{979} = 32.6 \text{ min}$$

The variance of the distribution is calculated using Eq. (44):

$$\sigma^2 \simeq \frac{\Sigma t^2 C\,\Delta t}{\Sigma C\,\Delta t} - \bar{t}^2 = \frac{1137863}{979} - (32.6)^2 = 96.9 \text{ min}^2$$

TABLE 5 Tracer Data and Computations for Example 4

t min	C mg/L	Δt min	$\dfrac{(C_i + C_{i-1})}{2}\Delta t$	$\dfrac{(Ct)_i + (Ct)_{i-1}}{2}\Delta t$	$\dfrac{(Ct^2)_i + (Ct^2)_{i-1}}{2}\Delta t$
0	0.0				
5	0.0	5	0	0	0
10	0.7	5	1.75	18	175
15	6.0	5	16.75	243	3550
20	18.0	5	60	1125	21375
22	31.0	2	49	1042	22204
24	34.4	2	65.4	1508	34818
26	37.0	2	71.4	1788	44826
28	39.1	2	76.1	2057	55666
30	42.0	2	81.1	2355	68454
32	39.0	2	81	2508	77736
34	36.0	2	75	2472	81552
40	25.0	6	183	6672	244848
45	17.0	5	105	4413	186063
50	7.0	5	60	2788	129813
55	4.0	5	27.5	1425	74000
60	2.0	5	15	850	48250
65	0.8	5	7	430	26450
70	0.2	5	2.5	165	10900
75	0.1	5	0.75	54	3856
80	0.1	5	0.4	31	2366
85	0.0	5	0.15	12	960
90	0.0	5	0	0	0
		Σ	979	31952	1137863

b. The number of reactors in series that will model the real reactor is calculated with Eq. (46):

$$n = \frac{(\bar{t})^2}{\sigma^2} = \frac{(32.6)^2}{96.9} = 11.0$$

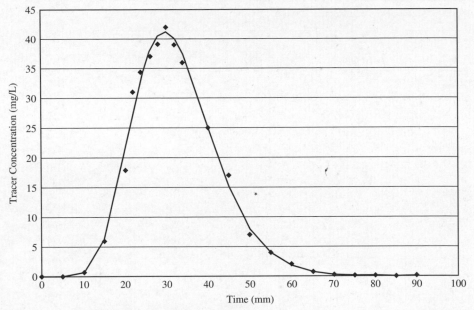

FIGURE 8   Tracer data and model curve for Example 4.

The predicted effluent for a pulse input to a completely mixed reactor in series model is given by Eq. (47) and is shown with the actual data in Figure 8. Note the curve fits well; therefore, the model will give a good estimate of the extent of steady-state reaction in part (c).

c. The extent of the reaction is determined from Eq. (50):

$$\frac{C}{C_0} = \left(\frac{1}{1 + k\dfrac{\bar{t}}{n}} \right)^n = \left(\frac{1}{1 + \dfrac{0.08}{\min} \times \dfrac{32.6 \ \min}{11}} \right)^{11} = 0.096$$

and $C_0 = \dfrac{0.5 \text{ mg/l}}{.096} = 5.2 \text{ mg/l}$

Cumulative Residence Time Distribution Functions

In the foregoing analysis, a pulse of tracer was used at the input of the reactor and a tracer distribution function was generated. A modification and integration of this curve will lead to a cumulative distribution function showing the fraction of water that exits the reactor before a time t. Another way to generate the same cumulative distribution function is simply to use a step input of tracer and monitor the effluent concentration. The resulting curve is shown in Figure 4a. This type of curve is important for the analysis of disinfection systems and will be discussed in more detail in Section 29.

COAGULATION

Coagulation is the process of adding chemicals to surface waters to collect small partic-ulate matter and natural organic matter into clusters that can be removed from solution by subsequent sedimentation and filtration through granular media. Although this clar-ification process improves the aesthetic character of the water by decreasing turbidity and natural color, the primary purpose of clarification is to remove substances that interfere with the disinfection of drinking water, to reduce the number of pathogenic protozoa such as *Cryptosporidium*, and to reduce the amount of disinfection byproducts that are formed in the disinfection process.

11   COLLOIDAL DISPERSIONS

Colloidal dispersions in water consist of discrete particles held in suspension by their extremely small size (1–200 nm), state of hydration (chemical combination with water), and surface electric charge. The size of colloids and their surface charge are the most significant properties responsible for their stability. With larger particles, the ratio of surface area to mass is low, and mass effects, such as sedimentation by gravity forces, predominate. For colloids, the ratio of surface area to mass is high, and surface phe-nomena, such as electrostatic repulsion and hydration, become important. Clays are the most common colloids that are removed in water treatment systems.

The concept of *zeta potential* is derived from the diffuse double-layer theory applied to hydrophobic colloids (Figure 9). A fixed covering of positive ions is attracted to the negatively charged particle by electrostatic attraction. This stationary zone of positive ions is referred to as the *Stern layer* and is surrounded by a movable, diffuse layer of counterions. The concentration of these positive ions in the diffuse zone decreases as it extends into the surrounding bulk of electroneutral solution. Zeta potential is the magnitude of the charge at the surface of shear. The boundary surface between the fixed ion layer and the solution serves as a shear plane when the particle undergoes movement relative to the solution. The zeta potential magnitude can be estimated from electrophoretic measurement of particle mobility in an electric field.

A colloidal suspension is defined as stable when the dispersion shows little or no tendency to aggregate (Figure 10a). The repulsive force of the charged double layer dis-perses particles and prevents aggregation; thus, particles with a high zeta potential pro-duce a stable colloidal suspension. Factors tending to destabilize a sol are van der Waals forces of attraction and colloid movement including Brownian motion. *Van der Waals forces* are the molecular cohesive forces of attraction that increase in intensity as parti-cles approach each other. These forces are negligible when the particles are slightly sepa-rated but become dominant when particles contact. *Brownian motion* is the random motion of colloids caused by their bombardment by molecules of the dispersion medium. This movement has a destabilizing effect on a sol because aggregation may result.

Destabilization of hydrophobic colloids can be accomplished by double layer com-pression, charge neutralization, enmeshment, and interparticle bridging. Adding elec-trolytes to the solution (Figure 10b) can destablize colloids by *double layer compression*. Counterions of the electrolyte suppress the double-layer charge of the col-loids sufficiently to permit particles to contact because the van der Waals attractive

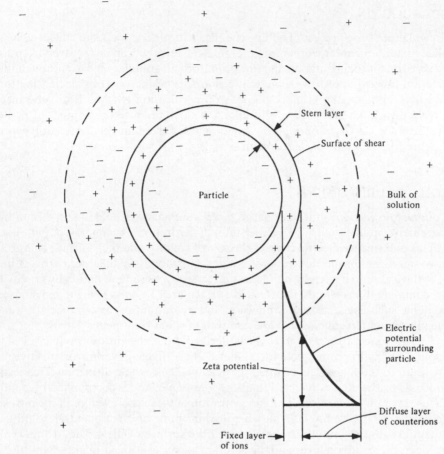

FIGURE 9   Derivation of the zeta potential in diffuse double-layer theory.

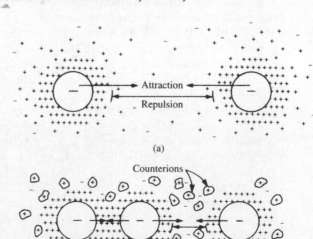

FIGURE 10   Schematic representations of coagulation and bridging of colloids. (a) A stable suspension of particles where forces of repulsion exceed the forces of attraction. (b) Destabilization and coagulation caused by counterions of a coagulant suppressing the double-layer charges.

forces overcome the electrostatic repulsive forces and aggregation results. The concentration of electrolytes such as sodium chloride that are required to sufficiently compress the double-layer is not practical in water treatment since these salts would degrade the quality of the water and are difficult to remove. In the *charge neutralization* mechanism charged species adsorb to (attach to the surface of) the colloid and reduce the surface charge (Figure 11a). Trivalent metals such as aluminum and iron hydrolyze in water to produce hydroxo complexes that carry positive charge and have an affinity to attach to negatively charged colloids, thereby reducing the overall colloidal charge and resulting in aggregation. At particular pH conditions and high enough aluminum or iron concentrations the metals will precipitate as $Al(OH)_{3(s)}$ or $Fe(OH)_{3(s)}$ respectively. Colloids then tend to adsorb to these solids and become enmeshed in the resulting solid (Figure 11b). This enmeshment mechanism is often called *sweep floc* coagulation. Interparticle bridging is the adsorption of colloids to a relatively large molecule, such as an organic polymer, to destabilize and aggregate the colloidal suspension. The long polymer molecule attaches to absorbent surfaces of colloidal particles by chemical or physical interactions, resulting in aggregation (Figure 11c).

In contrast to the electrostatic nature of hydrophobic colloids, the stability of hydrophilic colloids is related to their state of hydration (i.e., their marked affinity for water). Chemical coagulation does not materially affect the degree of hydration of colloids. Therefore, hydrophilic colloids are extremely difficult to coagulate, and heavy doses of coagulant salts, often 10–20 times the amount used in conventional water treatment, are needed for destabilization.

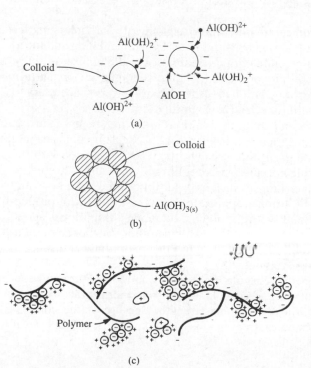

FIGURE 11   Coagulation mechanisms: (a) charge neutralization, (b) sweep floc, (c) agglomeration of destabilized particles by attachment of coagulant ions and bridging of polymers.

12   NATURAL ORGANIC MATTER

Natural organic matter (NOM) is present in all surface waters and to a lesser extent in groundwater, although some groundwater sources in Florida with high NOM concentrations are notable exceptions. NOM can be created by the activity of algae in the water or leached from soils in the watershed or groundwater. Although NOM can be in particulate form, often adsorbing to clays and other particles on the water, it most commonly occurs in soluble form. The molecules of soluble NOM have no definite chemical makeup and can be very large with molecular weights ranging from several hundred to tens of thousands. NOM typically carries negative charge as a result of the ionization of portions of the molecules which increases their solubility in water. Although NOM causes natural color in water, its primary impact is in the production of potentially harmful byproducts (DBPs) in the process of disinfection, particularly when chlorine is used as the disinfectant. Accordingly, NOM as measured by total organic carbon (TOC) in water is a major target of the clarification process; in fact, coagulation to target both turbidity and NOM removal, as required by EPA regulations, is referred to as *enhanced coagulation*.

13   COAGULATION PROCESS

Two basic mechanisms have been defined in destabilizing a colloidal suspension to produce floc for subsequent solids-separation processes: *Coagulation* reduces the net electrical repulsive forces at particle surfaces by adding coagulant chemicals, whereas *flocculation* is agglomeration of the destabilized particles by chemical joining and bridging. Both of these processes involve physical processes of mixing and chemical processes.

The primary purpose of chemical treatment is to agglomerate particulate matter and colloids into floc that can be separated from the water by sedimentation and filtration. In water treatment, coagulation and flocculation are used to destabilize turbidity, color, odor-producing compounds, pathogens, and other contaminants in surface waters. In wastewater reclamation, coagulation precedes tertiary filtration necessary to clarify a biologically treated effluent for effective chemical disinfection.

The common unit operations and chemical additions in the treatment of surface waters for a potable supply are diagrammed in Figure 12. Coagulant chemicals are added by rapid mixing, and a coagulant aid, usually a polymer, is blended into the destabilized water prior to or during flocculation. After filtration, the turbidity must be equal to or less than 0.3 NTU to ensure satisfactory removal of protozoan cysts and subsequent disinfection. Activated carbon is applied to adsorb taste- and odor-producing compounds and both natural and synthetic organic compounds. Fluoride is added to achieve an optimum concentration as a public health measure. Chemical treatment varies with the season of the year, and, for river waters, operational flexibility is required to handle the day-to-day variations.

The removal of contaminants by coagulation depends on their nature and concentration, the use of both coagulants and coagulant aids, and other characteristics of the water, including pH, temperature, and ionic strength. Because of the complex nature of coagulation reactions, chemical treatment is based on empirical data derived from laboratory and field studies.

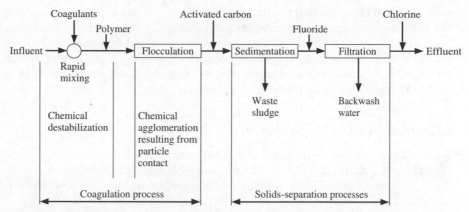

FIGURE 12 Schematic diagram of the coagulation process as a part of the scheme for treating surface water for a potable supply.

The *jar test* is widely used to simulate a full-scale coagulation–flocculation process to determine optimum chemical dosages. The apparatus consists of six agitator paddles coupled to operate at the same rotational speed, which can be varied from 10 to 300 rpm. The laboratory containers are 1- to 2-liter beakers or square jars. The general procedure for conducting a jar test is as follows:

1. Fill six 1- or 2-liter beakers with a measured amount of the water to be treated.
2. Add the coagulant and/or other chemicals to each sample.
3. Flash-mix the samples by agitating at maximum speed (300 rpm) for 30 seconds or less.
4. Flocculate the samples at a stirring rate of 20–100 rpm for 10–30 min. Record the time of floc appearance for each beaker. Tapered flocculation may be used by starting at a high rate and tapering to lower rates.
5. Stop the agitation and record the nature of the floc, clarity of supernatant, and settling characteristics of the floc.

Experiments can be conducted to evaluate the effectiveness of different coagulants and optimum dosage for destabilization, optimum pH, effectiveness of various coagulant aids and best dosage for floc formation, and the most effective sequence of chemical applications [5]. Ordinarily, a full-scale plant provides better results than the laboratory jar test for the same chemical dosages.

14   COAGULANTS

The most widely used coagulants for water and wastewater treatment are aluminum and iron salts. The most common coagulant is aluminum sulfate. Iron coagulants are effective over a wider pH range and are generally more effective at removing NOM from water, but they usually cost more. For some waters, cationic polymers are effective as a primary coagulant, but polymers are more commonly applied as coagulant aids. The final choice of coagulants and chemical aids is based on being able to achieve the contaminant removals and low turbidity desired in the filtered water at least cost.

The following paragraphs discuss various coagulants and present the theoretical chemical reactions. These traditional coagulation reactions yield only approximate results. The molecular and equivalent weights of chemical compounds listed in Tables 1 and 2 are useful in solving numerical problems.

Aluminum Sulfate (Filter Alum)

Aluminum sulfate is the standard coagulant used in water treatment. A formula used for filter alum is $Al_2(SO_4)_3 \cdot 14.3\ H_2O$ with a molecular weight of 600. The material is commonly shipped and fed in a dry granular form, although it is available as a powder or liquid alum syrup.

Aluminum sulfate reacts with natural alkalinity in water to form soluble aluminum hydroxo complexes [Eq. (51)] or aluminum hydroxide floc [Eq. (52)].

$$Al_2(SO_4)_3 \cdot 14.3H_2O + 2H_2O \rightarrow 2Al(OH)^{2+} + 2H^+ + 3SO_4^{2-} + 14.3H_2O \qquad (51)$$

$Al(OH)^{2+}$ is one of many different hydroxo complexes that can be formed. Note the production of H^+ which will tend to depress the pH. This is an important consideration in coagulation because the types of hydrolysis products formed depend on the pH. Addition of base to control the pH shift may be required. Polyaluminum chloride (PACl) is a preformed mixture of soluble aluminum hydroxo complexes that have been shown in some cases to be superior to alum in the coagulation process. If sufficient alum is added and the pH is adjusted in the range of 6 to 8, aluminum hydroxide precipitate is formed for the sweep floc coagulation mechanism.

$$Al_2(SO_4)_3 \cdot 14.3\ H_2O + 6\ H_2O \rightarrow 2\ Al(OH)_3\downarrow + 3\ SO_4^{2-} + 6\ H^+ + 14.3\ H_2O \qquad (52)$$

From Eq. (52) each mg/l of alum decreases water alkalinity by 0.50 mg/l (as $CaCO_3$).

Lime or soda ash is typically added to provide the necessary alkalinity and control the pH of the coagulation process.

$$Al_2(SO_4)_3 \cdot 14.3H_2O + 3Ca(OH)_2 \rightarrow 2Al(OH)_3\downarrow + 3CaSO_4 + 14.3H_2O \qquad (53)$$

$$Al_2(SO_4)_3 \cdot 14.3H_2O + 3Na_2CO_3 + 6H_2O$$
$$\rightarrow 2Al(OH)_3\downarrow + 3Na_2SO_4 + 3CO_2 + 17.3H_2O \qquad (54)$$

Lime, which is more popular, is less expensive than soda ash.

The dosage of alum used in water treatment is in the range of 5–50 mg/l. The effective pH range for alum coagulation is 5.5–8.0. The lower pH range is used for enhanced coagulation.

Ferric Salts

Ferric sulfate and ferric chloride are available as coagulants under a variety of trade names. The reactions of these salts with natural alkalinity and with lime are similar to those for aluminum sulfate.

$$2FeCl_3 + 3Ca(HCO_3)_2 \rightarrow 2Fe(OH)_3\downarrow + 3CaCl_2 + 6CO_2 \qquad (55)$$

$$2FeCl_3 + 3Ca(OH)_2 \rightarrow 2Fe(OH)_3\downarrow + 3CaCl_2 \qquad (56)$$

Advantages of the ferric coagulants are that (1) coagulation is possible over a wider pH range, generally pH 4–9 for most waters; (2) the floc settles better than alum floc and (3) they are more effective in the removal of NOM, taste, and odor compounds.

Ferric sulfate is available in crystalline form and may be fed using dry or liquid feeders. Ferric sulfate, although not as aggressive as ferric chloride, must be handled by corrosive-resistant equipment.

Ferric chloride is supplied in either crystalline or liquid form. Ferric chloride is frequently used in wastewater treatment (e.g., as a waste-sludge-conditioning chemical in combination with lime prior to mechanical dewatering).

Polymers

Synthetic polymers are water-soluble high-molecular-weight organic compounds that have multiple electrical charges along a molecular chain of carbon atoms. If the ionizable groups have a positive charge, the compound is referred to as a cationic polymer. If ionizable groups have a negative charge, it is an anionic polymer. If no charges are exhibited or if the net charge is zero, it is a nonionic polymer.

Cationic polymers can be effective for coagulation, without hydrolyzing metals, by producing destabilization through charge neutralization and interparticle bridging. Because polymers do not affect pH, they are advantageous for coagulating low-alkalinity waters. Another potential advantage of polymers relative to metal salts is reduced sludge production. Dosages of cationic polymers for coagulation are commonly 0.5–1.5 mg/l, which is much less than the dosages of metal coagulants.

In water and wastewater coagulation, anionic and nonionic polymers are effective coagulant aids. After destabilizing the colloidal suspension by hydrolyzing metals such as alum, polymers promote larger and tougher floc by a bridging mechanism (Figure 11c). Generally, nonionic polymers are more effective in water containing higher concentrations of divalent cations (i.e., Ca^{2+} and Mg^{2+}). Common dosages are 0.1–0.5 mg/l to aid alum coagulation. The combination of polymer and alum can reduce the alum dosage that would be required without the polymer. Since a wide selection of proprietary polymers is available, the brand name of the selected polymer should be determined and verified by laboratory and full-scale testing to ensure it is the best aid at least cost. The effectiveness of a polymer also depends on the point of application. The mixing must be adequate for complete blending but not so turbulent as to hinder particle bridging.

In wastewater treatment, polymers can be applied in activated-sludge processing after aeration to remedy overflow of biological floc from the final clarifier, usually as a result of plant overloading or poor settleability of filamentous growths and poorly agglomerated floc. Polymers are the flocculating chemicals in the agglomeration of organic solids to release bound water for sludge thickening on a gravity belt and for dewatering by a belt press or centrifuge.

Feed control of polymer coagulants must be precise since the effective dosage has a narrow band; overdosing results in restabilization of the colloidal particles.

Acids and Alkalies

Acids and alkalies are added to water to adjust the pH for optimum coagulation. Typical acids used to lower the pH are sulfuric and phosphoric. Alkalies used to raise the pH are lime, sodium hydroxide, and soda ash. Hydrated lime, with about 70% available CaO, is suitable for dry feeding but costs more than quicklime, which is 90% CaO. The latter must be slaked (combined with water) and fed as a lime slurry. Sodium hydroxide is purchased and fed as a concentrated solution.

Example 5

A surface water is coagulated with a dosage of 30 mg/l of aluminum sulfate as alum and an equivalent dosage of lime to neutralize the hydrogen ions produced in the hydrolysis of aluminum. (a) How many pounds of alum are needed per mil gal of water treated? (b) How many pounds of quicklime are required, assuming a purity of 70% CaO? (c) How many pounds of $Al(OH)_3$ sludge are produced per mil gal of water treated?

Solution: Converting the dosage of alum from mg/l to lb/mil gal, one obtains

$$30\frac{mg}{l} \times 8.34\frac{lb/mil\ gal}{mg/l} = 250\ lb/mil\ gal$$

By Eq. (53) and molecular weights from Tables 1 and 2, one mole of alum reacts with 3 moles of lime to produce 2 moles of aluminum hydroxide.

$$\frac{30\ mg\ alum}{600 \times 10^3\ mg/mole} = 5 \times 10^{-5}\ moles\ of\ alum\ reacted$$

$$5 \times 10^{-5}\ moles\ alum \times \frac{3\ moles\ Ca(OH)_2}{mole\ alum} = 1.5 \times 10^{-4}\ moles\ Ca(OH)_2$$

and $CaO + H_2O \rightarrow Ca(OH)_2$, so 1.5×10^{-4} moles of CaO are required

$$1.5 \times 10^{-4}\ moles\ CaO \times \frac{56 \times 10^3\ mg\ CaO}{mole} \times \frac{mg\ CaO}{0.7\ mg\ pure\ CaO} \times$$

$$\frac{8.34\ lb/mil\ gal}{mg/l} = 100\ lb\ CaO/mil\ gal$$

$$5 \times 10^{-5} \text{ moles alum} \times \frac{2 \text{ moles Al(OH)}_3}{\text{mole alum}} \times \frac{78 \times 10^3 \text{ mg Al(OH)}_3}{\text{mole}} \times$$

$$\frac{8.34 \text{ lb/mil gal}}{\text{mg/l}} = 65 \text{ lb Al(OH)}_3/\text{mil gal}$$

WATER SOFTENING

Hardness in water is caused by the ions of calcium and magnesium. Although ions of iron, manganese, strontium, and aluminum also produce hardness, they are not present in significant quantities in natural waters.

A single criterion for maximum hardness in public water supplies is not possible. Water hardness is largely the result of geological formations of the water source. Public acceptance of hardness varies from community to community, consumer sensitivity being related to the degree of hardness to which the consumer is accustomed.

Hardness of more than 300–500 mg/l as $CaCO_3$ is considered excessive for a public water supply and results in high soap consumption as well as objectionable scale in plumbing fixtures and pipes. Many consumers object to water harder than 150 mg/l, a moderate figure being 60–120 mg/l. The magnesium hardness should be less than 40 mg/l to prevent magnesium hydroxide scale in household water heaters.

15   CHEMISTRY OF THE LIME–SODA ASH PROCESS

The lime–soda water-softening process uses lime, $Ca(OH)_2$, and soda ash, Na_2CO_3, to precipitate hardness from solution. Carbon dioxide and carbonate hardness (calcium and magnesium bicarbonate) are complexed by lime. Noncarbonate hardness (calcium and magnesium sulfates or chlorides) requires the addition of soda ash for precipitation.

The following are chemical reactions in lime–soda ash treatment:
Reaction with CO_2 and precipitation of Ca^{2+} from lime.

$$CO_2 + Ca(OH)_2 = CaCO_3\downarrow + H_2O \tag{57}$$

Precipitation of bicarbonate Ca^{2+} and Ca^{2+} from lime.

$$Ca^{2+} + 2HCO_3^- + Ca(OH)_2 = 2CaCO_3\downarrow + 2H_2O \tag{58}$$

Conversion of HCO_3^- to CO_3^{2-} and precipitation of Ca^{2+} from lime.

$$Mg^{2+} + 2\,HCO_3^- + Ca(OH)_2 = CaCO_3\downarrow + Mg^{2+} + CO_3^{2-} + 2\,H_2O \tag{59}$$

Precipitation of carbonate Mg^{2+} and Ca^{2+} from lime.

$$Mg^{2+} + CO_3^{2-} + Ca(OH)_2 = Mg(OH)_2\downarrow + CaCO_3\downarrow \tag{60}$$

Precipitation of noncarbonate Mg^{2+}, leaving Ca^{2+} from lime in solution.

$$Mg^{2+} + SO_4^{2-} + Ca(OH)_2 = Mg(OH)_2\downarrow + Ca^{2+} + SO_4^{2-} \tag{61a}$$

$$Mg^{2+} + 2\,Cl^- + Ca(OH)_2 = Mg(OH)_2\downarrow + Ca^{2+} + 2\,Cl^- \tag{61b}$$

Precipitation of noncarbonate Ca^{2+} by addition of soda ash.

$$Ca^{2+} + Na_2CO_3 = CaCO_3\downarrow + 2\,Na^+ \tag{62}$$

These equations give all the reactions taking place in softening water containing both carbonate and noncarbonate hardness, by additions of both lime and soda ash. The carbon dioxide in Eq. (57) is not hardness as such, but it consumes lime and must therefore be considered in calculating the amount required. Equations (58–60) demonstrate removal of carbonate hardness by lime. Note that only 1 mole of lime is needed for each mole of calcium hardness, whereas 2 moles are required for each mole of magnesium hardness [Eqs. (58) and (59)]. Equation (61) shows the removal of magnesium noncarbonate hardness by lime. No softening results from this reaction because 1 mole of calcium noncarbonate hardness is formed for each mole of magnesium salt present. Equation (62) is for removal of noncarbonate calcium originally present in the water and also that formed as stated in Eq. (61).

Precipitation softening cannot produce water completely free of hardness because of the solubility of calcium carbonate and magnesium hydroxide. Furthermore, completion of the chemical reactions is limited by physical considerations, such as adequate mixing and limited detention time in settling basins. Therefore, the minimum practical limits of precipitation softening are 30 mg/l of Ca^{2+} and 10 mg/l of Mg^{2+}, both expressed as $CaCO_3$. Hardness levels of 80–100 mg/l are generally considered acceptable for a public water supply, but the magnesium content should not exceed 40 mg/l as $CaCO_3$ in a softened municipal water.

It may seem counterproductive to add a compound containing calcium to remove calcium from water, but calcium hydroxide is by far the cheapest form of hydroxide which elevates the pH so that bicarbonate is converted to carbonate to cause $CaCO_3$ precipitation, and which provides sufficient hydroxide ions to cause $Mg(OH)_2$ precipitation. Sodium hydroxide is more expensive and will leave sodium ion in solution. High sodium concentrations have been associated with hypertension. By using $Ca(OH)_2$ the total dissolved solids may be significantly reduced; hardness is taken out of solution, and the lime added is also removed. When soda ash is applied, sodium ions remain in the finished water; however, noncarbonate hardness requiring the addition of soda ash is generally a small portion of the total hardness. Lime also precipitates the soluble iron and manganese often found in groundwater. In processing surface waters, excess lime treatment provides disinfection and aids in coagulation for removal of turbidity.

16 PROCESS VARIATIONS IN LIME–SODA ASH SOFTENING

Three different basic schemes are used to provide a finished water with the desired hardness: excess-lime treatment, selective calcium removal, and split treatment.

Excess-Lime Treatment

Carbonate hardness associated with the calcium ion can be effectively removed to the practical limit of $CaCO_3$ solubility by stoichiometric additions of lime [Eq. (58)]. Precipitation of the magnesium ions [Eqs. (60) and (61)] calls for a surplus of approximately 35 mg/l of CaO (1.25 meq/l) above stoichiometric requirements. The practice of excess-lime treatment reduces the total hardness to about 40 mg/l (i.e., 30 mg/l of $CaCO_3$ and 10 mg/l of magnesium hardness).

After excess-lime treatment, the water is scale forming and must be neutralized to remove caustic alkalinity. Recarbonation and soda ash are regularly used to stabilize the water. Carbon dioxide neutralizes excess lime as follows:

$$Ca(OH)_2 + CO_2 = CaCO_3\downarrow + H_2O \tag{63}$$

This reaction precipitates calcium hardness and reduces the pH from near 11 to about 10.2. Further recarbonation of the clarified water converts a portion of the remaining carbonate ions to bicarbonate by the reaction

$$CaCO_3 + CO_2 + H_2O = Ca(HCO_3)_2 \tag{64}$$

The final pH is in the range 9.5–8.5, depending on the desired carbonate-to-bicarbonate ratio (Figure 2).

Carbon dioxide may be provided either from commercial liquid carbon dioxide or by the combustion of methane or other carbon fuel sources. The ease of storing bulk quantities of carbon dioxide and feeding it reduces equipment and operating costs compared to on-site gas generation. The equipment required for generating carbon dioxide gas consists of a furnace to burn the fuel (coke, coal, gas, or oil), a scrubber to remove soot and other impurities from the gas, and a compressor for forcing the gas into the water.

A two-stage system is preferred for excess-lime treatment as diagrammed in Figure 13. Lime is applied in first-stage mixing and sedimentation to precipitate both calcium and magnesium. Then carbon dioxide is applied to neutralize the excess lime [Eq. (63)], and soda ash is added to reduce noncarbonate hardness. Solids formed in these reactions are removed by secondary settling and subsequent filtration. Recarbonation immediately ahead of the filters may be used to prevent scaling of the media [Eq. (64)].

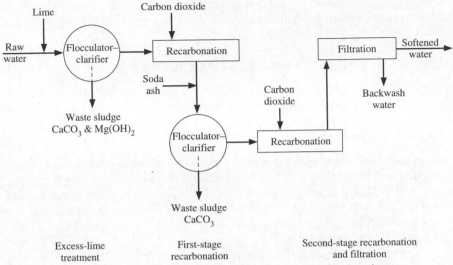

FIGURE 13 Schematic flow diagram for a two-stage excess-lime softening plant.

Example 6

Water defined by the following analysis is to be softened by excess-lime treatment in a two-stage system (Figure 13):

$$CO_2 = 8.8 \text{ mg/l as } CO_2 \quad Alk(HCO_3^-) = 115 \text{ mg/l as } CaCO_3$$
$$Ca^{2+} = 70 \text{ mg/l} \qquad\qquad SO_4^{2-} = 96 \text{ mg/l}$$
$$Mg^{2+} = 9.7 \text{ mg/l} \qquad\qquad Cl^- = 10.6 \text{ mg/l}$$
$$Na^+ = 6.9 \text{ mg/l}$$

The practical limits of removal can be assumed to be 30 mg/l of $CaCO_3$ and 10 mg/l of $Mg(OH)_2$, expressed as $CaCO_3$. Sketch a meq/l bar graph and list the hypothetical combinations of chemical compounds in the raw water. Calculate the quantity of softening chemicals required in pounds per million gallons of water treated and the theoretical quantity of carbon dioxide needed to provide a finished water with one-half of the alkalinity converted to bicarbonate ion. Draw a bar graph for the softened water after recarbonation and filtration.

Solution:

Component	mg/l	Equivalent Weight	meq/l
CO_2	8.8	22.0	0.40
Ca^{2+}	70	20.0	3.50
Mg^{2+}	9.7	12.2	0.80
Na^+	6.9	23.0	0.30
Alk	115	50.0	2.30
SO_4^{2-}	96	48.0	2.00
Cl^-	10.6	35.5	0.30

The meq/l bar graph of the raw water is shown in Figure 14a, and the hypothetical combinations are listed.

$$\text{lime required} = \text{stoichiometric quantity} + \text{excess lime}$$
$$= 3.5 \times 28 + 35 = 133 \text{ mg/l of CaO} = 1100 \text{ lb/mil gal}$$
$$\text{soda ash required} = 2.0 \times 53 = 106 \text{ mg/l of Na}_2\text{CO}_3 = 900 \text{ lb/mil gal}$$

Component	meq/l	Lime	Soda Ash
CO_2	0.4	0.4	0
$Ca(HCO_3)_2$	2.3	2.3	0
$CaSO_4$	1.2	0	1.2
$MgSO_4$	0.8	0.8	0.8
		3.5	2.0

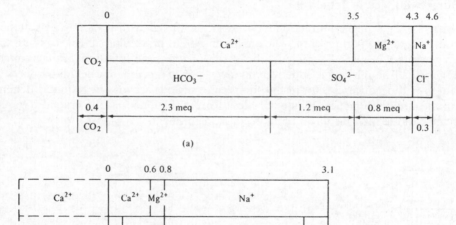

(a)

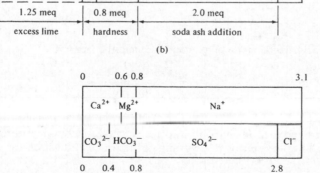

(b)

(c)

FIGURE 14   Milliequivalent bar graphs for Example 6. (a) Bar graph and hypothetical chemical combinations in the raw water. (b) Bar graph of the water after lime and soda ash additions and settling but before recarbonation. (c) Bar graph of the water after two-stage recarbonation and final filtration.

A hypothetical bar graph for the water after addition of softening chemicals and first-stage sedimentation is shown in Figure 14b. The dashed box is the excess-lime addition, 35 mg/l of CaO = 1.25 meq/l. The 0.6 meq/l of Ca^{2+} (30 mg/l as $CaCO_3$) and 0.20 meq/l of Mg^{2+} (10 mg/l as $CaCO_3$) are the practical limits of hardness reduction. The 2.0 meq/l of Na_2SO_4 results from the addition of soda ash. Alkalinity consists of 0.20 meq/l of OH^- associated with $Mg(OH)_2$ and 0.60 meq/l of CO_3^{2-} related to $CaCO_3$.

Recarbonation converts the excess hydroxyl ion to carbonate ion; using the relationship in Eq. (63) and using 22.0 as the equivalent weight of carbon dioxide provides $(1.25 + 0.2)22.0 = 31.9$ mg/l of CO_2. After second-stage processing, final recarbonation converts half the remaining alkalinity to bicarbonate ion by Eq. (64), giving $0.5 \times 0.8 \times 22.0 = 8.8$ mg/l of CO_2. Therefore the total carbon dioxide reacted is $(31.9 + 8.8)8.34 = 340$ lb/mil gal of CO_2.

The bar graph of the finished water is shown in Figure 14c.

Selective Calcium Removal

Waters with a magnesium hardness of less than 40 mg/l as $CaCO_3$ can be softened by removing only a portion of the calcium hardness. The processing scheme can be a single-stage system of mixing, sedimentation, recarbonation, and filtration, as diagrammed in Figure 15. Enough lime is added to the raw water to precipitate calcium hardness without providing any excess for magnesium removal. Soda ash may be required, depending on the amount of noncarbonate hardness. Recarbonation is usually practiced to reduce scaling of the filter media and produce a stable effluent.

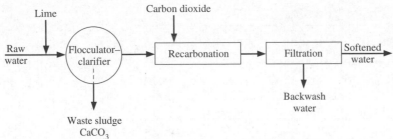

FIGURE 15   Schematic flow diagram for a single-stage calcium-carbonate softening plant.

Example 7

Determine the chemical dosages needed for selective calcium softening of the water described in Example 6. Draw a bar graph of the processed water.

Solution: The hypothetical combinations of concern in calcium precipitation are CO_2, $Ca(HCO_3)_2$, and $CaSO_4$ (Figure 14a).

Component	meq/l	Lime	Soda Ash
CO_2	0.4	0.4	0
$Ca(HCO_3)_2$	2.3	2.3	0
$CaSO_4$	1.2	0	12
		2.7	12

lime required = 2.7 × 28 = 76 mg/l of CaO = 630 lb/mil gal
soda ash required = 1.2 × 53 = 64 mg/l of $Na_2\,CO_3$ = 530 lb/mil gal

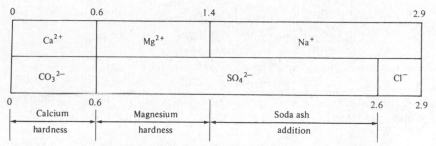

FIGURE 16   Bar graph of the softened water after selective calcium removal.

Final hardness is all the Mg^{2+} in the raw water plus the practical limit of $CaCO_3$ removal (30 mg/l or 0.60 meq/l), (0.8 + 0.6)50 = 70 mg/l as $CaCO_3$. The bar graph of the softened water is shown in Figure 16. Recarbonation would be desirable to stabilize the water by converting a portion of the carbonate alkalinity to bicarbonate.

Split Treatment

Split treatment consists of treating a portion of the raw water by excess lime and then neutralizing the excess lime in the treated flow with the remaining portion of raw water. When split treatment is used, any desired hardness level above 40 mg/l is attainable. Since hardness levels of 80–100 mg/l are generally considered acceptable, split treatment can result in considerable chemical savings. Recarbonation is not customarily required.

Split treatment is particularly advantageous on well waters. In softening surface waters, where taste, odor, and color may be problems, two stages of processing for the total flow are usually preferred over split treatment.

The flow pattern of a typical two-stage split-treatment plant is shown in Figure 17. If X is the ratio of the bypassed flow to the total quantity Q, then bypassed flow is XQ, and that through the first stage is $Q - XQ$ or $(1 - X)Q$. The magnesium content leaving the first stage (designated Mg_1) will be less than 10 mg/l (as $CaCO_3$). Magnesium in the bypass will be the same as that in the raw water (designated as Mg_r). Permissible magnesium in

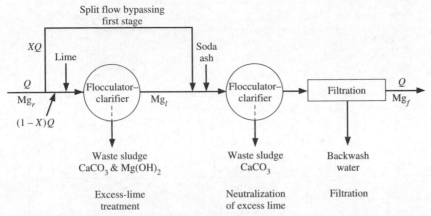

FIGURE 17   Schematic flow diagram for a spilt-treatment softening plant.

finished water (designated Mg_f) is about 50 mg/l as $CaCO_3$. The bypass flow fraction can be calculated for any desired level of magnesium by using the formula

$$X = \frac{Mg_f - Mg_1}{Mg_r - Mg_1}$$ (65)

The bypass flow is usually 30%–50%, depending on the limiting concentration of about 50 mg/l magnesium hardness in the finished water, with a total hardness of 80–100 mg/l.

The first stage in split treatment is excess-lime treatment to precipitate both calcium carbonate and magnesium hydroxide (Figure 17). However, soda ash is not applied until the combined lime-treated flow $(1 - X)Q$ and bypassed flow XQ enter the second stage. In second-stage flocculation and sedimentation, the excess lime in the treated flow reacts with the carbon dioxide and calcium bicarbonate to precipitate as calcium carbonate with no precipitation of magnesium hydroxide. Blending of these two flows neutralizes the pH and eliminates the need for recarbonation. Suspended solids in the overflow of the flocculator–clarifier are removed by filtration.

Split-treatment calculations are illustrated in Examples 8 and 9. The solution in Example 8 is theoretically precise and calculations are in the same sequence as the treatment processes. Refer to the bar graphs in Figure 18 in order from top to bottom: (a) the raw water and bypassed water, (b) settled overflow from first-stage lime treatment, (c) combined bar graphs of treated and bypass flows entering the second stage, (d) after reaction of excess lime in the combined flows and removal of calcium carbonate precipitate, and (e) finished water after second-stage treatment with soda ash and final granular-media filtration.

The solution in Example 9 is a somewhat simplified method of calculations for split treatment of the same raw water as in Example 8. Although the results are approximately the same, the process is not theoretically correct. The calculated chemical dosages

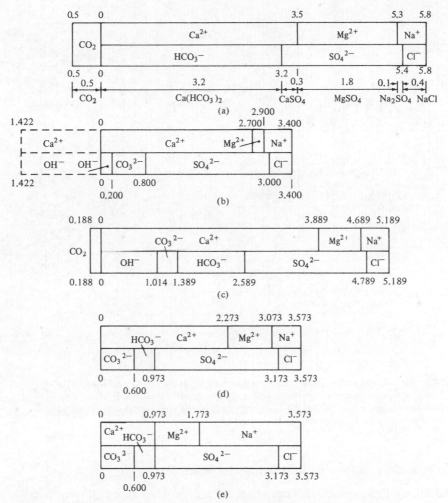

FIGURE 18   Milliequivalent bar graphs for Example 8. (a) Bar graph and hypothetical chemical combinations in the raw water. (b) Bar graph of the water after first-
stage treatment with lime. (c) Unreacted combination of the first-stage effluent times
0.625 plus the bypassed flow times 0.375. (d) Hypothetical graph after reaction of the
excess lime in the combined flows. (e) Bar graph of finished water after second-stage
treatment with soda ash, sedimentation, and final filtration.

for the first stage are identical to those for separate excess-lime treatment. The bar graphs
in Figure 19 summarize the results: (a) the raw water and bypassed water as in Figure 18,
(b) the first stage after excess-lime treatment, with additions of both lime and soda ash,
and (c) the finished water after combining the treated and bypassed flows. This bar graph
differs only slightly from the bar graph of finished water in Example 8.

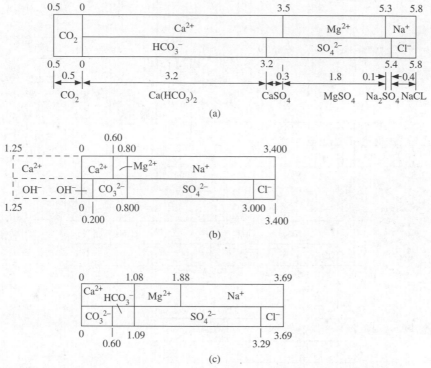

FIGURE 19   Milliequivalent bar graphs for Example 9. (a) Bar graph and hypothetical chemical combinations in the raw water. (b) Bar graph of the water after
excess-lime–soda ash softening. (c) Bar graph of finished water after second-stage
blending, sedimentation, and final filtration.

Coagulation, Softening, and Enhanced Softening

Addition of a coagulant or a coagulant aid may result in more efficient removal of the
hardness precipitates formed in lime–soda softening. Alum is the prevalent coagulant
although ferric salts and polymers are also used. Hard waters that also contain natural
organic matter (NOM) may require treatment not only to soften the water but also to
reduce the NOM concentration and thereby avoid disinfection byproduct formation
during the disinfection process.

This process is referred to as *enhanced softening*. NOM removal is improved
by elevating the pH to 10.8 or greater (usually with excess lime), delaying carbonate
addition for several minutes, and delaying the sludge recycling which will cause
smaller calcium carbonate particles to form [6]. These practices may have an
adverse effect on softening efficiency, and precipitation of $Mg(OH)_2$ may adversely
affect the removal of the solid precipitates, so jar testing is recommended prior to
process modification.

Example 8

Consider the split-treatment softening of water described by the following analysis. Criteria for the finished water are a maximum permissible magnesium hardness of 40 mg/l as $CaCO_3$ and calcium hardness in the range 40–60 mg/l.

$$CO_2 = 0.5 \text{ meq/l} \qquad HCO_3^- = 3.2 \text{ meq/l}$$

$$Ca^{2+} = 3.5 \text{ meq/l} \qquad SO_4^{2-} = 2.2 \text{ meq/l}$$

$$Mg^{2+} = 1.8 \text{ meq/l} \qquad Cl^- = 0.4 \text{ meq/l}$$

$$Na^+ = 0.5 \text{ meq/l}$$

Solution: Solving for the fraction of bypassed flow using Eq. (65) gives

$$X = \frac{40 - 10}{(1.8)(50) - 10} = \frac{30}{80} = 0.375$$

The first-stage flow is therefore

$$1 - X = 1 - 0.375 = 0.625$$

The lime and soda ash required for treatment are as follows:

		Lime		
Component	meq/l	First-Stage Flow	Bypassed Flow	Soda Ash
CO_2	0.5	$0.625 \times 0.5 = 0.313$	$0.375 \times 0.5 = 0.188$	0
$Ca(HCO_3)_2$	3.2	$0.625 \times 3.2 = 2.000$	$0.375 \times 3.2 = 1.200$	0
$CaSO_4$	0.3	0	0	0.3
$MgSO_4$	1.8	$0.625 \times 1.0 = \underline{0.625}$	$\underline{0}$	$\underline{1.0}$
		2.938	1.388	1.300

The lime dose for $MgSO_4$ is for only 1.0 meq/l of the 1.8 meq/l, since 0.8 meq/l of Mg (40 mg/l of magnesium hardness) is the allowable concentration in the finished water. The lime addition to the first stage is

$$2.938 + 1.388 = 4.326 \text{ meq/l} = 121 \text{ mg/l of } CaO$$

The soda ash addition to the second stage is

$$1.300 \text{ meq/l} = 69 \text{ mg/l of } Na_2CO_3$$

The hypothetical bar graphs of the water at various stages of treatment are shown in Figure 18. The first bar graph showing the hypothetical combinations is for the raw water. All of the lime is applied to this water in the first stage. Since only $0.625Q$ of the influent is treated, the lime addition relative to the full bar graph is the actual amount of 4.326 meq/l divided by 0.625 to equal 6.922 meq/l. Reacting with this applied lime are 0.5 meq/l of CO_2 [Eq. (57)], 3.2 of $Ca(HCO_3)_2$ [Eq. (58)], and 1.8 of $MgSO_4$ [Eq. (61a)]. The excess lime remaining after these reactions equals $6.922 - (0.50 + 3.20 + 1.80) = 1.422$ meq/l, which is greater than the required minimum of 1.25 meq/l for $Mg(OH)_2$ precipitation. The 0.3 meq/l of $CaSO_4$ does not react, and the 1.8 meq/l of $MgSO_4$ is converted to $CaSO_4$ [Eq. (61a)]. The practical limits of removal are assumed to be 0.60 meq/l of $CaCO_3$ and 0.20 meq/l of $Mg(OH)_2$. Figure 18b is a bar graph for the settled effluent from the first stage.

The next step is the reaction between the first-stage effluent and the untreated bypassed flow. Figure 18c is a bar graph of the combined flow without considering any reactions. It was drawn by adding Figure 18a times 0.375 to Figure 18b times 0.625. The 1.014 meq/l of $Ca(OH)_2$ reacts with the CO_2 and $Ca(HCO_3)_2$ to form $CaCO_3$, which precipitates, leaving 0.60 meq/l of $CaCO_3$ in solution. Figure 18d is a hypothetical bar graph after reaction of the excess lime in the first-stage effluent with the CO_2 and $Ca(HCO_3)_2$ in the bypassed flow.

In the second stage, 1.30 meq/l of soda ash (Na_2CO_3) is added and reacts with 1.30 meq/l of $CaSO_4$ to precipitate 1.30 meq/l of $CaCO_3$ in accordance with Eq. (62a). The net effect in the bar graph is the replacement of 1.30 meq/l of Ca with Na. The finished water after sedimentation and filtration is graphed in Figure 18e.

The finished water has the following calculated alkalinity and hardness values:

$$\text{alkalinity} = 0.973 \times 50 = 49 \text{ mg/l}$$
$$\text{calcium hardness} = 0.973 \times 50 = 49 \text{ mg/l}$$
$$\text{magnesium hardness} = 0.800 \times 50 = 40 \text{ mg/l}$$
$$\text{total hardness} = 49 + 40 = 89 \text{ mg/l}$$

Example 9

This is an alternate solution to the split-treatment softening of the water described in Example 8. Although less precise, these calculations result in similar answers.

Solution: From Example 8, $X = 0.375$ and $(1 - X) = 0.625$.

From the meq/l bar graph of the raw water in Figure 19, the hypothetical combinations are $Ca(HCO_3)_2$, $CaSO_4$, and $MgSO_4$. Calcium hardness = $3.5 \times 50 = 175$ mg/l as $CaCO_3$, and magnesium hardness = $1.8 \times 50 = 90$ mg/l.

The lime and soda ash for excess-lime softening are as follows.

Component	meq/l	Applicable Equation	Lime meq/l	Soda Ash meq/l
CO_2	0.5	(57)	0.50	
$Ca(HCO_3)_2$	3.2	(58)	3.20	
$CaSO_4$	0.3	(62)		0.30
$MgSO_4$	1.8	(61a)&(62)	1.80	1.80
			5.50	2.10

Flow passing through the first stage is processed as excess-lime treatment. However, the chemical additions are reduced by multiplying by 0.625, since this is the fraction of raw water being treated.

$$lime\ required = stoichiometric\ quantity + excess\ lime$$
$$= 0.625[(5.50 \times 28) + 35] = 118\ mg/l\ of\ CaO$$
$$soda\ ash\ required = 0.625(2.10 \times 53) = 69\ mg/l\ of\ Na_2CO_3$$

Figure 19a is the bar graph of the bypassed flow, and Figure 19b is the bar graph of the water after first-stage excess-lime treatment. These two are blended in the second stage, where excess lime reacts with the untreated water. The amount of excess hydroxide ion in the mixed flows is equal to

$$0.625(1.25 + 0.20) = 0.906\ meq/l\ of\ OH^-$$

The other components of interest in the blended water are

$$CO_2 = 0.375 \times 0.50 = 0.188\ meq/l$$
$$Ca(HCO_3)_2 = 0.375 \times 3.20 = 1.20\ meq/l$$

First, the carbon dioxide is eliminated by the excess lime:

$$0.906 - 0.188 = 0.718\ meq/l\ of\ OH^-\ remaining$$

Then, the balance of the hydroxide ion reacts with calcium bicarbonate, reducing it to

$$1.20 - 0.718 = 0.48\ meq/l\ Ca(HCO_3)_2$$

Final calcium hardness equals this remainder plus the limit of calcium carbonate removal:

$$0.48 + 0.60 = 1.08\ meq/l = 54\ mg/l\ as\ CaCO_3$$

and magnesium hardness in the finished water is

$$0.375 \times 1.80 + 0.625 \times 0.20 = 0.80\ meq/l$$
$$= 40\ mg/l\ as\ CaCO_3$$

for a total hardness of 94 mg/l.

The sulfate ion and chloride ion concentrations are unchanged from the raw water, 2.20 meq/l and 0.40 meq/l, respectively. The carbonate ion concentration is at the practical limit of $CaCO_3$ removal equal to 0.60 meq/l.

Figure 19c is the bar graph of the finished water after second-state sedimentation and filtration.

17   OTHER METHODS OF WATER SOFTENING

Although precipitative softening is currently the most popular method of softening water in large-scale water treatment plants, ion exchange and membrane systems are also available. Ion exchange treatment is the most popular method of softening water for individual household systems and is often used to soften small water supplies because of the ease of operation; however, ion exchange softening increases the concentration of sodium in the treated water, and waste products from the process can pose pollution problems. Sodium has been associated with hypertension, and although food is the primary source of sodium in most diets, some states have primary drinking water standards that restrict the concentration in drinking water. Selected membrane processes are also used to soften water and their use is increasing. Both membrane and ion exchange processes will be discussed in more detail in sections 38 and 43, respectively.

IRON AND MANGANESE REMOVAL

Iron and manganese in concentrations greater than 0.3 mg/l of iron and 0.05 mg/l of manganese stain plumbing fixtures and laundered clothes. Although discoloration from precipitates is the most serious problem associated with water supplies having excessive iron and manganese, foul tastes and odors can be produced by growth of iron bacteria in water distribution mains. These filamentous bacteria, using reduced iron as an energy source, precipitate it, causing pipe encrustations. Decay of the accumulated bacterial slimes creates offensive tastes and odors.

Dissolved iron and manganese are often found in groundwater from wells located in shale, sandstone, and alluvial deposits. Impounded surface water supplies may also have troubles with iron and manganese. An anaerobic hypolimnion (stagnant bottom-water layer) in a reservoir dissolves precipitated iron and manganese from the bottom muds, and during periods of overturn these minerals are dispersed throughout the entire depth.

18   CHEMISTRY OF IRON AND MANGANESE

Iron (II) (Fe^{2+}) and manganese (II) (Mn^{2+}) are chemically reduced, soluble forms that exist in a reducing environment (one characterized by an absence of dissolved oxygen and low pH). These conditions exist in groundwater and anaerobic reservoir water. When water is pumped from underground or an anaerobic hypolimnion, carbon dioxide and hydrogen sulfide are released, raising the pH. In addition, the water is exposed to air, creating an oxidizing environment. The reduced iron and manganese start transforming to their stable, oxidized, insoluble forms of iron (III) (Fe^{3+}) and manganese (IV) (Mn^{4+}).

The rate of oxidation of iron and manganese depends on the type and concentration of the oxidizing agent, pH, alkalinity, organic content, and presence of catalysts [7].

Oxygen, chlorine, and potassium permanganate are the most frequent oxidizing agents. The natural reaction by oxygen is enhanced in water treatment by using spray nozzles or waterfall-type aerators. Chlorine and potassium permanganate ($KMnO_4$) are the chemicals commonly used in iron- and manganese-removal plants. Oxidation reactions using potassium permanganate are

$$3Fe^{2+} + MnO_4^- \rightarrow 3Fe^{3+} + MnO_2 \tag{66}$$

$$3Mn^{2+} + 2MnO_4^- \rightarrow 5MnO_2 \tag{67}$$

Rates of oxidation of the ions depend on the pH and bicarbonate ion concentration. The pH for oxidation of iron should be 7.5 or higher; manganese oxidizes readily at pH 9.5 or higher. Natural organic matter (NOM) can create complexes with iron (II) and manganese (II) ions, holding them in the soluble state at higher pH levels. If a large concentration of organic matter is present, iron can be held in solution at pH levels of up to 9.5.

Manganese oxides act as catalysts that increase the rate of manganese oxidation. Tray aerators frequently contain coke or stone contact beds through which the water percolates. These media develop and support a catalytic coating of manganese oxides. After chemical-oxidation pretreatment to remove manganese, the grains of sand in a filter bed become coated with manganese oxide. When a new sand filter is initially put into operation, reduced soluble manganese (II) can pass through until the filter is "conditioned" by coating the sand grains with catalytic manganese (IV) oxides from removal of manganese in the water.

19 PREVENTIVE TREATMENT

When an industry or a city is confronted with the problem of iron and manganese in the water supply, solutions are difficult and usually costly. Treatment of the water supply is the only permanent answer. Control and preventive measures can be employed with expectation of reasonable success.

Phosphate chemicals may be effective in sequestering iron and manganese in well water supplies [6]. The sequestering chemical is added directly into the groundwater pumped from the well prior to any unintentional aeration. When applied at the proper dosage, before oxidation of the iron and manganese occurs, polyphosphates tend to hold the metals in solution and suspension, preventing destabilization and thus stopping agglomeration of the individual tiny particles of iron and manganese oxides. The concept is that the sequestered metals will pass through the distribution system without creating discolored water. Nevertheless, oxidized particles often settle out and collect in water mains at times when the velocities of flow in the pipes are low and in storage reservoirs during quiescent periods. Then, when the velocities of flow increase and when water in storage is agitated, these particles are resuspended in the water at much higher concentrations than in the raw water. The scouring and mixing flows can be caused by the dramatic increase in water consumption (e.g., because of lawn watering in the spring of the year), operation of well or booster pumps in the distribution system that have not been used for several weeks or months, and sudden withdrawals of water from hydrants.

Growth of iron bacteria also aggravates the adverse effects of iron and manganese. Some of the iron bacteria are autotrophs that oxidize soluble iron (II) to insoluble iron (III) for energy and use carbon dioxide as a carbon source. Filamentous *Crenothrix* grow in sheaths impregnated with ferric hydroxide that form reddish-colored slimes (biofilms). *Crenothrix* infestations in distribution systems are often widespread, since these bacteria produce and release vast numbers of spores that can be carried throughout the pipe network. *Leptothrix*, a member of the genus *Sphaerotilus*, grow on iron (II) and organic matter. Their growth may be accompanied by a musty odor, which changes to a foul odor upon their death. Also associated with decay of the biofilm growth, sulfate-reducing bacteria can release hydrogen sulfide, giving the water a rotten-egg odor. Manganese oxidation is also attributed to several species of iron bacteria.

No easy or inexpensive way exists for controlling the chemical and bacterial oxidation of iron and manganese. Periodic flushing of small distribution pipes can be effective in removing accumulations of oxide particles; however, elimination of iron bacteria is generally impossible. Heavy chlorination of isolated sections of water mains followed by flushing may be effective for a limited time. If chlorine is continuously added for disinfection, the rate of oxidation of iron and manganese is increased and the problem of colored water is likely to become more severe. The only permanent solution is treatment to remove iron and manganese from the raw water before it is distributed in the pipe network.

20   IRON AND MANGANESE REMOVAL PROCESSES

Aeration–Filtration

The simplest form of oxidation treatment uses plain aeration. The units most commonly employed are the tray type, where a vertical riser pipe distributes the water on top of a series of trays, from which it then drips and spatters down through a stack of three or four of them. Soluble iron is readily oxidized by the following reaction:

$$2Fe(HCO_3)_2 + 0.5O_2 + H_2O \rightarrow 2Fe(OH)_3 + 4CO_2 \qquad (68)$$

Manganese cannot be oxidized as easily as iron, and aeration alone is generally not effective. If, however, the pH is increased to 8.5 or higher (by the addition of lime, soda ash, or caustic soda), and if aeration is accompanied by contact with coke beds coated with oxides in the aerator, catalytic oxidation of the manganese occurs.

Plants that employ the aeration–filtration process use an intermediate basin to provide sufficient contact time for the oxidation process to occur. The oxidized iron and manganese is then removed by a granular-media filter.

Aeration–Chemical Oxidation–Sedimentation–Filtration

This sequence of processes is the usual method for removing iron and manganese from well water without softening treatment. Contact tray aeration is designed to displace dissolved gases (i.e., carbon dioxide) and initiate oxidation of the reduced iron and manganese.

Chlorine, potassium permanganate, ozone, or chlorine dioxide can chemically oxidize both iron and manganese. When chlorine is utilized, a free available chlorine residual is maintained throughout the treatment process. The rate of manganese (II) oxidation by chlorine depends on the pH, the chlorine dosage, mixing conditions, and other factors.

Potassium permanganate oxidation is many times faster than chlorine for the oxidation of manganese. Also, the rate of reaction is relatively independent of the hydrogen ion concentration within a pH range of 5–9.

Filtration following chemical oxidation is very important. Practice has shown that filters pass oxidized manganese unless grains of the media are coated with manganese oxides serving as a catalyst. This covering develops naturally during filtration of manganese-bearing water.

Ozone oxidizes manganese faster than other oxidants, but if the dosage is too high, it may convert the manganese to permanganate and thereby cause the water to turn pink (the color of a permanganate solution).

Example 10

A well water supply contains 3.2 mg/l of iron and 0.8 mg/l of manganese at pH 7.8. Estimate the dosage of potassium permanganate required for iron and manganese oxidation.

Solution: Using molecular weights and the stoichiometry from Eqs. (66) and (67):

For iron

$$\frac{3.2(mg/l)Fe}{56(mg/mmole)Fe} \times \frac{1(mmole)KMnO_4}{3(mmole)Fe} \times \frac{158(mg)KMnO_4}{(mmole)KMnO_4} = 3.01 \ mg/l \ KMnO_4$$

For manganese

$$\frac{0.8(mg/l)Mn}{55(mg/mmole)Mn} \times \frac{2(mmole)KMnO_4}{3(mmole)Mn} \times \frac{158(mg)KMnO_4}{(mmole)KMnO_4} = 1.53 \ mg/l \ KMnO_4$$

The total requirement is then

$$3.01 + 1.53 = 4.54 \ mg/l \ of \ KMnO_4$$

Water Softening

Lime–soda ash softening will also remove iron and manganese. If split treatment is employed, potassium permanganate can oxidize the iron and manganese in water, bypassing the first-stage excess-lime treatment. Lime–soda ash softening should be given careful consideration as a possible process for treating hard water requiring iron and manganese elimination.

Lime treatment has been used to remove organically bound iron and manganese from surface water. The process scheme aeration–coagulation–lime treatment–sedimentation–filtration can treat surface waters containing color, turbidity, and organically bound iron and manganese.

Greensand Filtration

The mineral glauconite, commonly known as greensand, can be used in pressure filters with either continuous or periodic addition of permanganate to remove both iron and manganese. Oxides on the surface of the greensand can oxidize both iron and manganese. Permanganate oxidizes the iron and manganese and regenerates the greensand.

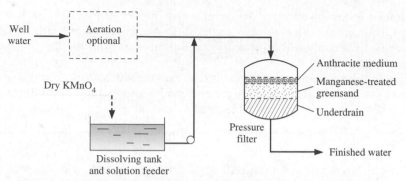

FIGURE 20   Schematic flow diagram for removal of iron and manganese from groundwater by the manganese-zeolite process using a dual-media pressure filter with manganese-treated greensand.

Manganese leakage and waste of excess permanganate to regenerate the greensand have been substantially overcome by continuously supplying a feed of potassium permanganate solution ahead of a dual-media filter of anthracite and manganese zeolite. Figure 20 is a schematic flow diagram of a continuous-flow system ahead of a pressure filter. The anthracite filter media remove most insolubles, thereby reducing the problem of plugging the greensand. A continuous feed of permanganate reduces the frequency of greensand regeneration. When the permanganate feed is less than the reduced iron and manganese in the water, excess iron and manganese are oxidized by the greensand. If a surplus is applied, it regenerates the greensand.

DISINFECTION AND BY-PRODUCT FORMATION

While chlorine is the common chemical used for disinfection of water and wastewater, it is increasingly being replaced by alternative disinfectants and oxidants such as ozone, chlorine dioxide, and ultraviolet radiation, particularly for drinking water applications. The technology shift to alternative disinfectants has been driven by their lower potential to form disinfection by-products (DBPs) and, for some, their greater disinfection efficiency. On the other hand, alternative disinfectants are typically more costly and have other disadvantages that will be discussed in the following sections. Nevertheless, chlorine is still one of the most used and important chemicals in water and wastewater treatment and, accordingly, will be addressed first.

21   CHLORINE AND CHLORAMINES

Chlorine gas is soluble in water (7160 mg/l at 20°C and 1 atm) and hydrolyzes rapidly to form the disinfectant and oxidant hypochlorous acid (HOCl), a hydrogen ion, and the chloride ion, which has no disinfection potential:

$$Cl_2 + H_2O \rightarrow HOCl + H^+ + Cl^- \tag{69}$$

Hydrolysis goes virtually to completion at pH values and concentrations normally experienced in water treatment and waste treatment operations.

Hypochlorous acid is a weak acid and partially ionizes according to Eq. (70) with an equilibrium constant defined in Eq. (71):

$$HOCl \leftrightarrow H^+ + OCl^- \tag{70}$$

$$\frac{[H^+][OCl^-]}{[HOCl]} = K = 10^{-7.6} \text{ at } 25°C \tag{71}$$

Figure 21 shows the relationship between HOCl and OCl⁻ at various pH levels and two temperatures. Both HOCl and OCl⁻ are capable of oxidation and disinfection, although HOCl is a more effective disinfectant – almost 80 times better for inactivating some species of bacteria.

Chlorine reacts with ammonia in water to form chloramines as follows:

$$HOCl + NH_3 \rightarrow H_2O + NH_2Cl \quad \text{(monochloramine)} \tag{72}$$

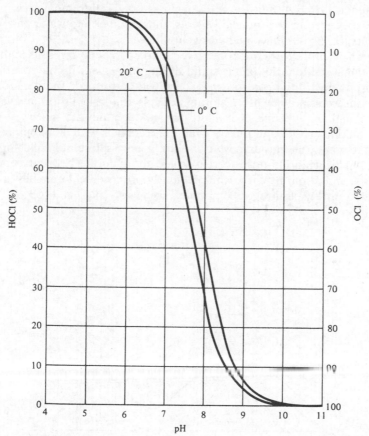

FIGURE 21   Effect of pH on the portions of hypochlorous acid (HOCl) and hypochlorite ion (OCl⁻) present in water.

$$HOCl + NH_2Cl \rightarrow H_2O + NHCl_2 \quad \text{(dichloramine)} \tag{73}$$

$$HOCl + NHCl_2 \rightarrow H_2O + NCl_3 \quad \text{(trichloramine)} \tag{74}$$

The chloramines formed depend on the pH of the water, the chlorine to ammonia concentration ratio, and the temperature. In the pH range 4.5–8.5, monochloramine and dichloramine are formed. At room temperature, monochloramine exists alone above pH 8.5 and dichloramine occurs alone at pH 4.5. Below pH 4.4, trichloramine is produced.

Free available residual chlorine is that residual chlorine existing in water as hypochlorous acid or hypochlorite ion. *Combined available residual chlorine* is that residual existing in chemical combination with ammonia (chloramines) or organic nitrogen compounds. *Chlorine demand* is the difference between the amount added to a water and the quantity of free and combined available chlorine remaining at the end of a specified contact period.

When chlorine is added to water containing reducing agents and ammonia, residuals develop that yield a curve similar to that in Figure 22. Chlorine reacts first with reducing agents present and develops no measurable residual, as shown by the portion of the curve extending from *A* to *B*. The chlorine dosage at *B* is the amount required to meet the demand exerted by the reducing agents (those common to water and wastewater include nitrites, ferrous ions, and hydrogen sulfide).

The addition of chlorine in excess of that required up to point *B* results in the formation of chloramines. Monochloramines and dichloramines are usually considered together because there is little control over which will be formed. The quantities of each are determined primarily by pH. Chloramines thus established show an available chlorine residual and are effective as disinfectants although they are much less effective than free chlorine (HOCl and OCl$^-$). Chlorine combines with ammonia to form chloramines up to point *C* in the curve which occurs at a mass dose ratio of chlorine to nitrogen of 5. As the chlorine dose increases and the chlorine residual decreases between points *C* and *D* on the curve, the previously produced chloramines are oxidized to produce a variety of nitrogen compounds such as N_2, N_2O and NO_3^-.

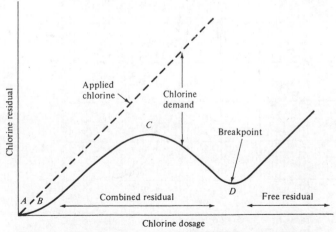

FIGURE 22   Chlorine residual curve for breakpoint chlorination.

Once most of the chloramines are oxidized at point D, additional chlorine applied to the water creates an equal residual, as indicated by the rising curve at point D. Point D is generally referred to as the *breakpoint;* beyond it, all added residual is free available chlorine. Some resistant chloramines can still be present beyond D, but their relative importance is small.

Chloramination is often practiced in water treatment, particularly to maintain a residual in the distribution system after some other disinfectant (chlorine, ozone, or chlorine dioxide) is used as the primary disinfectant. When used in this manner, the chlorine to ammonia mass dose ratio is usually between 3 and 4. Exceeding point C on the breakpoint curve is avoided because undesirable tastes and odors are produced, and the residual is more difficult to control.

Hypochlorites (salts of hypochlorous acid) may be used for chlorination at small installations such as swimming pools and in emergencies. Since hypochlorites are more expensive, liquid chlorine is applied in most water treatment plants in the United States. Calcium hypochlorite, $Ca(OCl)_2$, is available commercially in granular and powdered forms that contain about 70% available chlorine. Sodium hypochlorite ($NaOCl$) is handled in liquid form at concentrations between 5% and 15% available chlorine. These salts in water solution yield the hypochlorite ion directly which then may protonate to form HOCl depending on the pH of water as equilibrium is established [Eq. (71)].

Feeding of chlorine involves controlled dissolution of the gas into a carrier water supply for delivery to the point of application and blending with the water or wastewater being chlorinated. Direct feed of chlorine gas into a pipe or channel is not practiced for safety reasons (the danger is pipes leaking gas outside the controlled environment of the chlorine room). Figure 23 is a schematic diagram of a vacuum chlorinator and ejector

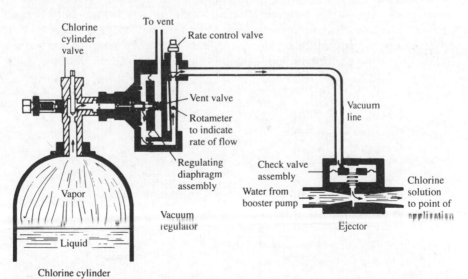

FIGURE 23   Gas chlorinator with a vacuum regulator mounted on a cylinder and an ejector to dissolve the chlorine in water for conveying a strong solution to the point of application. *Source:* Severn Trent Services, Capitol Controls.

suitable for a small system. Chlorine is shipped as a liquid in pressurized steel cylinders ranging in size from 100 1b to 1 ton. As gas is released, the liquid vaporizes, yielding about 450 volumes of gas per volume of liquid. To start the flow of gas from the cylinder, water under pressure is pumped at high velocity through the ejector throat to draw a vacuum on the regulator. The safety features of the regulator are that the gas cannot be released except under vacuum, and the regulator case is vented to release the gas outside the room if the diaphragm leaks. The rate of flow is controlled by the rate-control valve on the regulator, and the flow can be observed by the rotameter. The ejector dissolves the gas in water, and this concentrated solution is piped to the water being treated. Moist chlorine gas is extremely corrosive, so piping and dosing equipment are nonmetallic or a special alloy. The yellow-green chlorine gas is poisonous, causing respiratory and eye irritation at very low concentrations and physiologic damage at high doses. Chlorine feeding rooms and storage areas must be kept cool and ventilated.

A manual-control chlorinator, as illustrated in Figure 23, is appropriate for a small treatment plant or well water supply discharging water at a nearly constant rate of flow. For large facilities, controlling the chlorine rate of feed based on water flow rate or chlorine residual is important for reliable performance and economical operation. The automatic proportional-control system illustrated in Figure 24 adjusts the feed rate to maintain a constant preset dosage for all rates of flow. The chlorine feeder is responsive to signals from both the flowmeter transmitter and the chlorine residual analyzer. In this manner rate-of-flow measurement is the primary feed regulator, and residual monitoring trims the dosage. At some installations, it may be satisfactory to proportion feed to flow and thus apply a constant preset dosage without residual monitoring. However, this type of regulator is only satisfactory where chlorine demand and flow are reasonably constant and an operator is available to make adjustments as necessary.

Because gaseous chlorine represents a health hazard, transportation through communities and storage onsite at water and wastewater treatment plants has recently received careful consideration with regard to safety and safeguards against terrorism. In some cases water treatment plants have abandoned chlorine gas as a chlorine source in favor of onsite electrolytic generation of chlorine from sodium chloride.

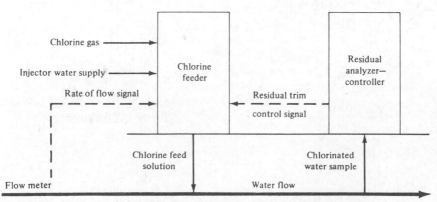

FIGURE 24   Automatic proportional-control system for feeding to a constant preestablished chlorine residual.

22   CHLORINE DIOXIDE

Chlorine dioxide has had limited application in the United States as a water disinfectant and has been used for taste and odor control. Because chlorine dioxide is explosive, it cannot be stored; rather, it is manufactured onsite by mixing solutions of sodium chlorite and chlorine in controlled proportions, as shown by Eq. (75):

$$2NaClO_2 + Cl_2 \longrightarrow 2ClO_2 + 2NaCl \qquad (75)$$

Maintaining the pH in the reactor at about 3.5 optimizes the production of ClO_2 with minimum residuals of unreacted chlorine or chlorite. A mineral acid such as HCl or H_2SO_4 can be added to reduce the pH in the reactor if necessary. Under good control, chlorine dioxide yields of greater than 95% are expected with solution concentrations between 500 and 2000 mg/l [8].

Disinfection using chlorine dioxide has several advantages. It is a strong bactericide and viricide over a wide pH range and forms a residual capable of persisting in the distribution system. Equally important in treatment of surface waters, chlorine dioxide reacts with neither nitrogenous compounds to form chloramines nor humic acids to form regulated DBPs. The greatest potential disadvantage is creation of chlorate and chlorite residuals, which are toxic. For this reason, chlorite is regulated as a DBP in the primary drinking water standards at 1.0 mg/l, and chlorine dioxide's maximum residual disinfectant level leaving the treatment plant is 0.8 mg/l. Chlorate is unregulated at this printing. Additionally, the high cost of sodium chlorite makes ClO_2 disinfection more expensive than chlorination.

23   OZONE

Ozone is a strong oxidizing gas that reacts with most organic and many inorganic molecules. It is more reactive than chlorine and chlorine dioxide. The reactions are rapid in inactivating microorganisms, oxidizing iron, manganese, sulfide, and nitrite, and slower in oxidizing organic compounds like humic and fulvic substances, pesticides, and volatile organic compounds. Unlike chlorine, ozone does not react with water to produce disinfecting species but decomposes in water to produce oxygen and the potent oxidant, the hydroxyl free radical. The half-life of ozone in water is approximately 10–30 min and shorter above pH 8; therefore, it must be generated onsite.

An ozonation system consists of (1) air preparation or oxygen feed, (2) electric power supply, (3) ozone generation, (4) ozone contacting, and (5) ozone contactor exhaust gas destruction. Ambient air is dried to prevent fouling of the ozone production tubes and to reduce corrosion. A common system uses desiccant dryers in conjunction with compression and refrigerant dryers. The voltage or frequency of the electrical supply is varied to control the rate of ozone production, which requires a specialized power source normally supplied by the generator manufacturer. Generators for water treatment usually employ a corona discharge cell. The cell consists of two electrodes separated by a discharge gap and a dielectric material across which high-voltage potentials are maintained. As the air or oxygen flows between the electrodes, ozone is produced. If ambient air is used, the concentration of ozone is 1%–4% by weight. This is an adequate concentration to dissolve enough ozone to attain the concentration–contact time necessary in water processing. When pure oxygen is used, the concentration of ozone is 6–16% by weight. The common ozone contactor has two or three compartments in series with porous diffusers under a 16-ft water column, as sketched in Figure 25. The water flows downward in each compartment counter to the rising fine bubbles of ozonated air. The covered tank increases the partial pressure of ozone and collects the head gases for disposal. Ozone in the exhaust gas must be destroyed or removed by recycling prior to venting, since the concentration of ozone exceeds air quality standards. When the ozone is generated from air, reducing ozone by the process of thermal–catalytic destruction is less expensive than recirculating the exhaust gas through the air preparation system.

Use of ozone in drinking water treatment has been increasing in response to the need to balance pathogen inactivation with DBP control. Ozone reacts rapidly with natural organic matter (NOM), producing smaller organic compounds such as aldehydes, carboxylic acids, and ketones. Although the total carbon concentration of the NOM is not substantially reduced under nominal ozone doses, the biodegradability of the resulting organic carbon is increased. This biodegradable organic matter (BOM), measured as biodegradable dissolved organic carbon (BDOC) or assimilable organic carbon (AOC), can cause problems of bacterial regrowth in the distribution system, production of tastes and odors, and increased residual disinfectant demand. To address this problem, granular media filters can be operated in a biologically active state (i.e., microbial growth is encouraged in the filter to biodegrade the organics so they are not released to the distribution system) [9].

In addition to modifying the NOM in water, ozone will also oxidize the naturally occurring bromide ion (Br^-) to bromate (BrO_3^-), a DBP that is regulated at 10 μg/l. Once formed, bromate is difficult to remove from water, so careful consideration must be given to the formation potential of this DBP.

Since ozone does not produce a disinfecting residual, chlorine or chloramines are used to maintain a disinfectant residual in distribution systems. Although ozone has generally shown to decrease the potential of a water to form THMs and HAAs after chlorination and chloramination, in some instances an increase in these DBPs has been found [10].

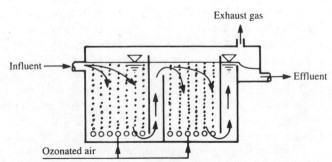

FIGURE 25 Two-compartment ozone contactor with porous diffusers.

24   ULTRAVIOLET RADIATION

Ultraviolet (UV) radiation, increasingly used in wastewater disinfection applications since the 1990s, is gaining popularity in potable water as a primary disinfectant, particularly because it is very effective at inactivating *Cryptosporidium* oocysts which are resistant to chemical disinfection. UV rays have wavelengths from 100 to 400 nm as shown in Figure 26 and are produced by a variety of lamps as shown in Table 6. UV radiation is absorbed by and damages the nucleic acids in DNA and RNA of microorganisms which prevents their replication. The nucleic acids absorb primarily in the UV range which is shown in Figure 27 along with the relative energy outputs and wavelengths for the major lamp types. Note that the low pressure lamps produce less energy but provide this energy in the peak absorbance area for the microorganisms' nucleic acids. Although many microorganisms have enzymes that enable them to repair the damaged nucleic acids, higher UV doses and residual chemical disinfectants are expected to inhibit the repair and maintain inactivation.

The UV dose for inactivation of microorganisms is directly related to radiation intensity and time of exposure, so that high-intensity UV energy over a short period of time is as effective as lower-intensity UV energy at a proportionally longer period of time. The dose of UV radiation is, therefore, measured by the product of the power that is incident on the microorganism and the time of exposure. Typical dose units are mJ/cm^2. EPA has adopted a method of dose measurement for potable water disinfection that

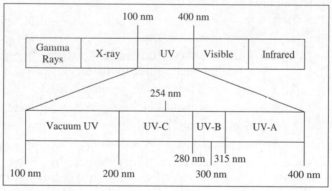

FIGURE 26   UV light in the electromagnetic spectrum

TABLE 6   Characteristics for UV Lamps Used in Water and Wastewater Disinfection

Characteristic	Low Pressure	Low Pressure High Output	Medium Pressure
germicidal UV light	254 nm	254 nm	200 – 300 nm
operating temperature°C	40	60 – 100	600 – 900
germicidal UV output (W/cm of arc)	0.2	0.5 – 3.5	5 – 30
arc length (cm)	10 – 150	10 – 150	5 – 120
lifetime (hrs)	8000 – 10,000	8000 – 12,000	4000 – 8000
relative number of lamps needed for a given dose	high	intermediate	low

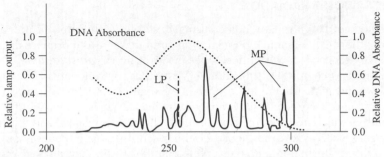

FIGURE 27   UV lamp energy output for low-pressure (LP) and medium-pressure (MP) lamps and the absorbance spectra for DNA.

requires calibration with an easily measured test organism and elements of the particular UV disinfection system being calibrated, including the lamps and the vessel that
contains the lamps. A typical equation that may fit the data is shown in Eq. (76) [11].
The units of the variables are typical but will depend on the values used in the calibration procedure.

$$\text{RED} = 10^a \times (\text{UVA})^b \times (S/S_0)^c \times (1/Q)^d \times (B)^e \qquad (76)$$

where

$$
\begin{aligned}
\text{RED} &= \text{Reduction Equivalent Dose} - \text{the calculated dose for a particular} \\
&\quad \text{level of inactivation} \\
\text{UVA} &= \text{ultraviolet absorbance at 254 nm } (\text{cm}^{-1}) - \text{measures the amount} \\
&\quad \text{of radiation absorbed by the water} \\
S &= \text{measured UV sensor value } (\text{mw/cm}^2) \\
S_0 &= \text{UV intensity at 100\% lamp power } (\text{mw/cm}^2) \\
Q &= \text{flow rate(mgd)} \\
B &= \text{number of banks of lamps} \\
a, b, c, d, e &= \text{model coefficients determined by fitting calibration data to} \\
&\quad \text{the model equation by multiple regression analysis}
\end{aligned}
$$

In potable water systems certain levels of disinfection or inactivation are
required and specified in EPA rules for viruses and protozoa (these levels also ensure
the bacteria will be inactivated). These levels and required doses of chemical disinfectants and UV radiation are discussed in the section on the disinfection of potable
water. The RED values determined from Equation 76 need to be adjusted to
account for variability in the calibration methods and for the test organism by using a
validation factor (VF). To determine whether compliance with the regulation is being
achieved, the RED is divided by the VF to give the validated dose and is compared
with the required dose:

$$\text{Validated dose} = \frac{\text{RED}}{\text{VF}} \geq \text{Required Dose} \quad \Rightarrow \quad \text{satisfies requirement} \qquad (77a)$$

$$\text{Validated dose} = \frac{\text{RED}}{\text{VF}} < \text{Required Dose} \quad \Rightarrow \quad \text{requirement not met} \qquad (77b)$$

Eq. (76) indicates that an increase in the absorbance of UV light by constituents in the water (such as NOM which also absorbs UV at 254 nm) will result in a decrease in the UV dose to the microorganism. An increase in flow rate has a similar effect because water will spend less time in contact with radiation at higher flow rates.

Potable water systems typically have low turbidity and suspended solids after filtration where UV disinfection is usually applied, but wastewater systems, which usually are not filtered, have higher levels of suspended solids. The concentration and size of suspended solids in the wastewater are particularly important because bacteria and viruses contained within the clusters are shielded from the UV radiation. In contrast, chemical water quality parameters like pH, temperature, alkalinity, and total organic carbon do not influence the effectiveness of UV disinfection. Nevertheless, chemical and biological films reduce transmittance and cause problems with keeping the lamp sleeves clean. UV systems can be cleaned off-line with chemical cleaning systems and are cleaned on-line with automatic chemical wipers.

A microprocessor control system in the UV disinfection unit adjusts UV intensity in response to changes in water or wastewater quality and rate of flow to conserve energy and extend lamp life. The ballasts enclosed in the tops of the frames operate at multiple power settings between 60% and 100%. The system control can also turn frames of lamps on and off in relation to the water flow. The dose pacing program is based on flow signal, UV transmittance value, and lamp age.

Because UV radiation has no residual disinfecting power once the water leaves the reactor, chemical disinfectants are used to maintain a disinfectant residual in potable water systems. Although UV radiation is very effective against protozoa and bacteria, it is less effective in virus inactivation, particularly the adenovirus. Chemical disinfectants may be used in conjunction with UV to achieve the required disinfection for viruses. Wastewater effluents do not require residual disinfectant unless reuse is planned. Wastewater effluents discharging directly to receiving waters should not contain residual disinfectants; accordingly, UV radiation has this particular advantage for disinfecting wastewaters.

Example 11

A manufacturer of a UV disinfection unit had the unit evaluated by an independent testing facility that provided the following model for calculating the required dose for 99% inactivation of a challenge microorganism:

$$\text{RED} = 10^{-0.83} \times (\text{UVA})^{-2.52} \times (S/S_0)^{0.17} \times (1/Q)^{0.41} \times (n)^{0.85}$$

A nonpathogenic microorganism with a greater resistance to UV than *Cryptosporidium* was used in the validation testing procedure. Based on this difference in UV resistance, and the uncertainty of the model, the validation factor (VF) was 2.2 for calculating a 99% inactivation of *Cryptosporidium*. Find the validated dose for a flow rate of 5 mgd, S/S_0 of 0.75, an ultraviolet absorbance at 254 nm of 0.150 cm^{-1}, and two banks of lamps. Compare this value with the required dose of 5.8 mJ/cm^2 for 99% inactivation of *Cryptosporidium*.

Solution: The RED is computed from Eq. (76):

$$\text{RED} = 10^{-0.83} \times (0.15)^{-2.52} \times (0.75)^{0.17} \times (\tfrac{1}{5})^{0.41} \times (2)^{0.85} = 15.2 \text{ mJ/cm}^2$$

The validated dose is then calculated by Eq. (77):

$$\text{Validated dose} = \frac{15.2 \dfrac{\text{mJ}}{\text{cm}^2}}{2.2} = 6.9 \frac{\text{mJ}}{\text{cm}^2}$$

Since the validated dose is higher than the required dose of 5.8 mJ/cm^2, the requirement is met. Note that if one bank was used the requirement would not have been met.

---

25   DISINFECTION BY-PRODUCTS

The balance between adequate inactivation of pathogenic microorganisms and limited production of by-products that have adverse health effects is a major challenge in water and wastewater treatment. Chlorination inactivates pathogenic microorganisms and oxidizes many organic molecules to carbon dioxide. In the treatment of surface waters and groundwaters containing NOM, however, it also produces chlorinated by-products and incompletely oxidized compounds that are risks to human health. Studies involving chlorination of humic and fulvic acids, main components of NOM that can be isolated from waters, have improved the understanding of by-product formation during disinfection of water supplies. Many of the specific chemical structures have been characterized and vary with chlorine-to-carbon (Cl/C) ratio, pH, time of reaction, and other factors [11]. The principal by-products at high Cl/C molar ratios of 3:1 or 4:1 are trihalomethanes (THMs) and haloacetic acids (HAAs).

An extensive study on the occurrence of disinfection by-products in 35 water treatment plants processing surface waters revealed that trihalomethanes (mainly chloroform, bromodichloromethane, and dibromochloromethane) accounted for about 50% of the total by-products on a weight basis [12]. Five haloacetic acids were the next most significant fraction, accounting for about 25%, and aldehydes accounted for about 7%. Of the remaining by-products, none was present in a significant concentration. The median total trihalomethane concentration was 39 μg/l, and the median haloacetic acids concentration was 19 μg/l [12].

Although chlorine reactions with NOM account for most of the DBPs that have been identified, other alternative disinfectants also may cause DBPs that have adverse effects on water quality and health. As discussed above, ozone may cause the formation of bromate and other organic compounds that are not currently regulated. Chlorine dioxide causes chlorite formation, and the use of chloramines has been linked to the formation of significant HAAs (although substantially less than with chlorine), cyanogen chloride, and nitrosodimethylamine (NDMA), a potent carcinogen [13].

26   CONTROL OF DISINFECTION BY-PRODUCTS

Disinfection by-product concentrations can be controlled by four general methods:

1. Remove the precursor, the organic or inorganic compound that reacts with the disinfectant to produce DBPs.
2. Change the disinfectant or lower the disinfection dose so that smaller amounts of DBPs are produced.
3. Change the water quality or treatment characteristics such as pH, ammonia concentration, or reaction time, because these characteristics may affect the extent of DBP formation.
4. Remove the DBP once it is formed.

Precursor Removal

NOM precursors can be partially removed by chemical coagulation and flocculation followed by sedimentation and/or filtration. This process is designed to remove turbidity and when optimized to also address DBP precursor removal is called enhanced coagulation. The DBP rule (see next section) requires either enhanced coagulation or enhanced softening to remove specific amounts of NOM as measured by total organic carbon (TOC) for selected source waters. Enhanced coagulation has been shown to remove greater than 50% of NOM precursors although the removal efficiency varies with the type of water being treated, and removal efficiencies may be lower [14]. Removing NOM precursor early in the treatment process lowers the disinfectant demand and allows for lower disinfectant doses after coagulation. NOM may also be removed by activated carbon, ion exchange, and membrane processes which will be discussed in more detail later in this chapter.

Alternative Disinfectants

Ozone, chlorine dioxide, chloramines, and UV radiation produce lower levels of organic DBPs than chlorine, as discussed previously, although ozone may produce bromate and chlorine dioxide may produce chlorite. If chlorine is used, applying the dosage either before or after filtration, after NOM precursor has been lowered by enhanced coagulation, will lower the chlorine demand and, therefore, the required dose.

Water Quality and Treatment Adjustments

Formation of THMs increases with increasing pH, while HAAs increase with decreasing pH. Bromate formation in ozonation decreases with decreasing pH. Addition of ammonia prior to or after chlorination converts chlorine to chloramines. Limiting the disinfectant contact time will decrease the formation of DBPs, but will also decrease disinfection effectiveness.

DBP Removal

DBP removal is not a common control strategy, because disinfectant residuals must be maintained in drinking water distribution systems, and some NOM remains even after effective coagulation to react with these disinfectant residuals. Activated carbon has the potential to remove organic DBPs and chlorite. Air stripping can remove volatile organic DBPs such as chloroform, but is less effective against the less volatile bromoform and other more hydrophilic organics such as aldehydes and HAAs.

27   DISINFECTION/DISINFECTION BY-PRODUCTS RULE

The conflicting requirements to provide effective disinfection and to reduce adverse health effects of disinfection by-products led to the Disinfection/Disinfection By-Products (D/DBP) rule. The stage 1 D/DBP rule and the Enhanced Surface Water Treatment Rule were promulgated in 1998 to address these requirements. These rules were updated in 2006 with the promulgation of the Stage 2 D/DBP Rule and the Long-term 2 Enhanced Surface Water Treatment Rule to reduce potential health risks from DBPs and the disinfectants themselves while strengthening protection against microbial contaminants. Under the two D/DBP rules, public water systems are required to limit the concentration of DBPs at the far reaches of the distribution system, and maintain a chlorine residual in the distribution system. The rule also dictates detailed regulations on sampling and monitoring for compliance of by-product concentrations in the distribution system.

Hundreds of DBPs have been identified but only a few are regulated. Accordingly, to ensure that nonregulated NOM-related DBPs are minimized, water treatment plants that treat surface water or ground water under the direct influence of surface water (referred to as subpart H waters in EPA regulations) with conventional clarification systems must also achieve prescribed reductions of NOM, as measured by total organic carbon (TOC), depending on source water quality. These required reductions by enhanced coagulation or enhanced softening are shown in Table 7 [15]. Required TOC reductions are waived for waters with low TOC ($<$2 mg/l) either before or after treatment, and for waters with low values of other measures of DBP formation potential, because these waters are not likely to form high concentrations of any organic DBP.

DISINFECTION OF POTABLE WATER

Coliform and fecal coliform concentrations are used as surrogate parameters to demonstrate the presence or absence of pathogenic bacteria and other pathogens that have equal or greater sensitivity to disinfection as the coliforms. As discussed in

TABLE 7   Required Percent Removal of TOC by Enhanced Coagulation and Enhanced Softening for Surface Water and Waters Under the Direct Influence of Surface Waters and Using Conventional Treatment

Source Water TOC (mg/l)	Source water alkalinity (mg/l as $CaCO_3$)		
	0–60	60–120	>120
>2.0 to 4.0	35	25	15
>4.0 to 8.0	45	35	25
>8.0	50	40	30

Previous chapter, some pathogens such as protozoa and viruses have less sensitivity to disinfection than coliforms. The EPA has established maximum contaminant level goals of zero for *Giardia lamblia, Cryptosporidium* species, enteric viruses, and *Legionella* for public water supplies. Since routine tests cannot be used to determine the presence of these microorganisms, treatment techniques have been established to ensure their removal and inactivation during water processing. Furthermore, because *G. lamblia* cysts, *Cryptosporidium* oocysts, and viruses represent the most persistent pathogens, treatment for their removal ensures the absence of other pathogens. Although some water supplies may not contain significant numbers of these pathogens, demonstrating their absence by water quality monitoring is not feasible and cannot be used in lieu of applying the specified treatment techniques. The three categories of water supplies are (1) surface water open to the atmosphere and subject to surface runoff, (2) groundwater under the direct influence of surface water (i.e., containing algae, insects, or other macroorganisms, or experiencing significant and relatively rapid shifts in water characteristics), and (3) groundwater.

28   CONCEPT OF THE $C \cdot t$ PRODUCT

Chemical inactivation of a specific species of microorganism is a function of disinfectant concentration and contact time. Other important factors are the kind of disinfectant, temperature, pH, viability of the microorganisms, and presence of suspended organic matter.

The rate equation for the inactivation of microorganisms, the Chick–Watson Law, can be written

$$\frac{dN}{dt} = -k'C^n N \tag{78}$$

where

k' = reaction rate constant dependent on the type of microorganism, the type of disinfectant, and temperature

n = a constant for a particular microorganism and type of disinfectant

C = disinfectant concentration

t = time

If the concentration of the disinfectant is assumed to be constant over time, Eq. (78) may be integrated to give

$$\log\frac{N_0}{N} = \frac{k'}{2.3}C^n t \tag{79}$$

where

N = concentration of microorganisms at time t

N_0 = concentration of microorganisms at time $t = 0$

The ratio, N_0/N, is the inactivation ratio and represents the degree of inactivation. If 90% of the microorganisms are inactivated, the log of the inactivation ratio would be 1, or there would be 1 log of inactivation. If the inactivation was 99%, it would be 2 logs of inactivation; 99.9% would give 3 logs of inactivation and so on. Eq. (79) may be rearranged to give

$$\frac{2.3 \log\left(\dfrac{N_0}{N}\right)}{k'} = C^n t \tag{80}$$

The left-hand side of Eq. (80) is constant for a selected inactivation ratio, temperature, microorganism, and constant concentration of chemical disinfectant.

To apply this equation, results of several individual experiments with different disinfectant concentrations under identical conditions to achieve a particular inactivation ratio are plotted as the log t versus the log C. This plot produces a straight line with a slope of n. Experimental results have yielded values of n of approximately 1.0 for many microorganisms and disinfectants; however, the inactivation of *Giardia lamblia* cysts with chlorine is a notable exception. The above equations underscore an important concept in disinfection: disinfection efficiency is a function of concentration and time. If the concentration of a disinfectant is lowered, more contact time must be provided to achieve the same inactivation ratio. If the value of n is 1.0, both time and concentration have equal weight in the disinfection process.

EPA requires 3-log (99.9%) inactivation of *Giardia lamblia*, 4-log (99.99%) inactivation of viruses and 2-log (99%) inactivation of *Cryptosporidium* for water systems using surface water or ground water under the direct influence of surface water that have low concentrations of these microorganisms in their source water. Higher levels of inactivation are required as the source water pathogen concentrations increase. Credit is given for systems with properly operating filtration systems that remove turbidity. For systems with low concentrations of *Cryptosporidium* in the source water no additional treatment is required beyond conventional rapid rate filtration, direct filtration, slow sand filtration or diatomaceous earth filtration. Filtration credit awarded toward meeting the $C \cdot t$ requirements for *Giardia* and viruses is shown in Table 8. For filtration to be

TABLE 8   Typical Removal Credits and Inactivation Requirements for Various Treatment Technologies

Process	Typical log removal credits		Resulting disinfection log inactivation requirements	
	Giardia	Viruses	*Giardia*	Viruses
Conventional (rapid rate) filtration	2.5	2.0	0.5	2.0
Direct filtration	2.0	1.0	1.0	3.0
Slow sand filtration	2.0	2.0	1.0	2.0
Diatomaceous earth filtration	2.0	1.0	1.0	3.0
Membranes	*	*	*	*
Unfiltered	0	0	3	4

* Systems must demonstrate to the state by pilot study or other means that the alternative filtration technology provides the required log removal and inactivation.

considered effective in pathogen removal, the turbidity in the combined filtered water must be equal to or less than 0.3 NTU in at least 95% of the measurements taken each month. The combined filtered water must not exceed 1 NTU. For filtration systems serving more than 10,000 people, turbidity must be monitored in the filtered water from each individual filter in order to identify poor performance so corrective action can be taken. In systems serving fewer than 10,000 people, turbidity in the combined filtered water must be measured at least every 4 hr.

EPA has developed and published tables based on this $C \cdot t$ concept for *Giardia lamblia*, viruses, and *Cryptosporidium* [16, 17, 18, 19]. Tables 9 and 10 provide selected representative data from the EPA tables. The tables in the EPA references provide $C \cdot t$ values for partial inactivation (0.5-log, 1-log, 2-log, etc.); however, accurate estimates may be obtained by dividing the $C \cdot t$ values in Tables 9, 10, and 11 by an appropriate factor. For example, to obtain the $C \cdot t$ value for 2-log inactivation of viruses, divide the 4-log $C \cdot t$ value by 2 (4/2), and to obtain a 0.5 log inactivation of *Giardia* divide the 3-log $C \cdot t$ value by 6 (3/0.5). Note that in Table 9 the $C \cdot t$ value is a function of pH, temperature and the chlorine concentration. The increase in $C \cdot t$ values with increasing pH is the result of a shift from hypochlorous acid to the less effective hypochlorite ion as

TABLE 9 $C \cdot t$ Values for 3-log Inactivation of *Giardia* Cysts with Chlorine at 10 and 20°C, given in mg/l · min

Chlorine concentration (mg/l)	10°C			20°C		
	pH = 6.0	pH = 7.0	pH = 8.0	pH = 6.0	pH = 7.0	pH = 8.0
≤0.4	73	104	149	36	52	74
0.6	75	107	153	38	54	77
0.8	78	110	158	39	55	79
1.0	79	112	162	39	56	81
1.2	80	114	166	40	57	83

TABLE 10 $C \cdot t$ Values for 3-log Inactivation of *Giardia* Cysts, 4-log Inactivation of Viruses, and 2-log Inactivation of *Cryptosporidium* with Alternative Disinfectants at 10 and 20°C, given in mg/l · min

Disinfectant	*Giardia* 3-log		Viruses 4-log		*Cryptosporidium* 2-log	
	10°C	20°C	10°C	20°C	10°C	20°C
Ozone	1.43	0.72	1.0	0.52	20	7.8
Chlorine dioxide*	23	15	25.1	12.5	553	233
Chloramines*	1850	1100	1491	746	N/A	N/A
Chlorine	**	**	6.0*	3.0*	N/A	N/A

*For pH values between 6 and 9.
**pH dependent; see Table 9
N/A-Not applicable; free chlorine and chloramines are not effective against *Cryptosporidium*.

TABLE 11   UV Dose Table for *Cryptosporidium, Giardia lamblia,* and Virus Inactivation Credit

Log credit	*Cryptosporidium* mJ/cm^2	*Giardia lamblia* mJ/cm^2	virus mJ/cm^2
0.5	1.6	1.5	39
1.0	2.5	2.1	58
1.5	3.9	3.0	79
2.0	5.8	5.2	100
2.5	8.5	7.7	121
3.0	12	11	143
3.5	15	15	163
4.0	22	22	186

pH increases. Increases in temperature increase the rate of the inactivation reaction; accordingly, the $C \cdot t$ values decrease. Note also the $C \cdot t$ values for various disinfectants at a common temperature; disinfection efficiency in decreasing order is ozone, chlorine dioxide, chlorine, and chloramines.

$C \cdot t$ for UV Radiation

For disinfection with UV radiation, the appropriate value to use for disinfection effectiveness is the radiation dose measured in units of mJ/cm^2, which includes both the power of the UV radiation and the time of exposure. UV dosage values for inactivation of important pathogens are shown in Table 11 [19]. Note that viruses control the dosage and therefore size of the UV system, but the required UV dosage is low for *Cryptosporidium,* which is difficult to inactivate with chemical disinfectants. Since UV must be followed with some type of chemical to provide a disinfectant residual in the distribution system, the chemical disinfectant may be able to provide some if not all of the required credit for virus inactivation.

29   SURFACE WATER DISINFECTION

The various EPA Surface Water Treatment Rules shown in Table 12 require both filtration treatment techniques and adequate disinfection for surface water and groundwater under the direct influence of surface water unless the source water meets stringent water quality criteria. The fecal coliform concentration in the raw water must be equal to or less than 20 per 100 ml, or total coliform concentration must be equal to or less than 100 per 100 ml, in at least 90% of the samples tested. The turbidity level cannot exceed 5 NTU except for an unexpected event, but the number of events cannot exceed two in the preceding 12 months. A comprehensive watershed control program is mandated to minimize the potential for contamination by *Giardia, Cryptosporidium,* and viruses, and a defined water quality monitoring schedule must be instituted.

TABLE 12 Surface Water Treatment Rules, Federal Register Citations, and Dates of Promulgation

Rule	Federal Register Citation	Date of Promulgation
Surface Water Treatment Rule (SWTR)	54 FR 27486	June 1989
Interim Enhanced Surface Water Treatment Rule (IESWTR)	63 FR 69478	December 1998
Long term 1 Enhanced Surface Water Treatment Rule (LT1ESWTR)	67 FR 1812	January 2002
Long term 2 Enhanced Surface Water Treatment Rule (LT2ESWTR)	71 FR 654	January 2006

The primary disinfection requirements with respect to *Cryptosporidium*, *Giardia*, and viruses have been discussed in the previous section. In addition, the free-plus-combined chlorine residual in the water entering the distribution system cannot be less than 0.2 mg/l for more than 4 hr, and the chlorine residual in the distribution system must be detectable in at least 95% of the samples tested each month. Where the residual is undetectable, a measurement of heterotrophic bacteria by a plate count equal to or less than 500 per ml is deemed to be equivalent to a detectable chlorine residual.

The procedure for calculating the $C \cdot t$ for a treatment system is described in EPA guidance [17]. The $C \cdot t$ is the sum of the calculated $C \cdot t$ values before the water arrives at the first customer, with C being the disinfectant residual measured at the end of each disinfectant segment, in milligrams per liter, and t being the calculated contact time of the segment, in minutes. As discussed in Section 8 and 10, real reactors, such as contact basins for disinfection, have residence time distributions. If the mean residence time were used to calculate the contact time, a substantial portion of the water spending less time in the basin would not receive adequate disinfection. To help ensure that all of the water is properly treated, EPA requires the use of t_{10} determined under peak hourly flow conditions for $C \cdot t$ calculations. Ten percent of the water entering a reactor spends less than t_{10} in the reactor. This t_{10} can be determined for basins with tracer analysis. The response of a step tracer input can be easily used by normalizing the effluent (response) concentration (dividing it by the input concentration) as shown in Figure 28a. The t_{10} is the time needed for the C/C_0 concentration to reach 0.10 (i.e., the time for 10% of the

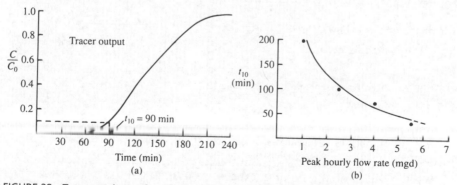

FIGURE 28 Tracer analyses of a chlorine contact tank to determine t_{10} times at peak hourly flow for calculating $C \cdot t$ values. (a) Normalized tracer output for a test applying a continuous tracer input. (b) A plot of the t_{10} times for four tracer tests at different flow rates to draw a curve to determine t for calculating $C \cdot t$ values.

tracer to pass through the basin). Figure 28b is a plot of t_{10} times versus flow rate that can be used to determine t for daily $C \cdot t$ calculations. Flow in pipes is assumed to be plug flow where t_{10} equals the mean residence time (hydraulic residence time).

The successive segments of disinfection are additive, and the required inactivation must be attained at a peak flow prior to the water reaching the first customer. The disinfectant concentration used in each disinfection segment is the disinfectant residual at the end of the segment. This is a conservative calculation method, since the disinfectant tends to decay during any process segment, so that the concentration at the end of the segment will be the lowest concentration.

Example 12

A conventional surface water plant with coagulation, flocculation, sedimentation, and filtration produces a filtered water with a turbidity less than 0.3 NTU, pH 8, and temperature 10°C on a day when the peak hourly flow is 2.0 mgd. After filtration, the water is chlorinated in a baffled storage tank and then pumped to the first customer in one mile of 12-inch diameter pipe as shown in Figure 29. The residual chlorine concentration at the end of the storage tank is 0.6 mg/l and at the end of the pipeline is 0.2 mg/l. The effluent response to a step input of tracer in a tracer analysis of the storage tank is given in Table 13.

a. Determine whether the required $C \cdot t$ value has been met.
b. If the water system wanted to use a chloramine disinfectant in the pipeline to control DBP formation, and maintained a 0.4 mg/l concentration at the first customer, would the $C \cdot t$ requirements be met?
c. An ozone disinfection system is being considered in place of the chlorination and storage tank. What contact time would be required in the ozone contact tank if the ozone residual at the end of the tank was 0.2 mg/l and the $C \cdot t$ requirements are to be met before the pipeline?

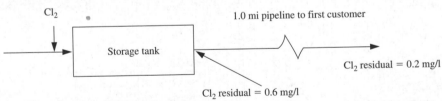

FIGURE 29 Disinfection schematic for Example 12.

TABLE 13 Effluent Response to a 2 mg/l Tracer Input for the Baffled Storage Tank

tracer (mg/l)	0	0.02	0.05	0.08	0.13	0.18	0.24	0.31	0.38	0.46	0.54	0.62
time (min)		10	15	20	25	30	35	40	45	50	55	60	65

Solution:

a. The tracer concentration data are normalized by dividing each effluent response value by the step input concentration of 2 mg/l and are plotted as shown in Figure 30. The t_{10} value for the storage tank is read from Figure 30 at $C/C_0 = 0.10$ as 37 min. Since the conventional filtration system is operating properly 2.5-log credits are allowed for *Giardia* and 2-log credits are allowed for viruses (Table 8). The required disinfection for *Giardia* is therefore 0.5 log of inactivation and for viruses is 2.0 logs of inactivation. Table 9 gives the $C \cdot t$ requirement for 3-logs of *Giardia* at 10°C, chlorine concentration of 0.6 mg/l, and pH of 8.0 as 153 mg/l $\cdot$ min. For 0.5 logs of inactivation the value $C \cdot t$ requirement would be 153/6 = 25.5 mg/l $\cdot$ min. The actual $C \cdot t$ for the storage tank is

$$(C \cdot t)_{\text{storage}} = 0.6\,{}^{\text{mg}}\!/_{\text{l}} \times 37\ \text{min} = 22.2\,{}^{\text{mg}}\!/_{\text{l}} \cdot \text{min}$$

The t_{10} in the pipeline is equal to the hydraulic residence time (for plug flow that is assumed) and is calculated from the flow and pipe volume as follows:

$$\text{Volume} = \text{area} \times \text{length} = \frac{\pi}{4}(1)^2\ \text{ft}^2 \times 5280\ \text{ft} \times 7.48\frac{\text{gal}}{\text{ft}^3} = 31{,}020\ \text{gal}$$

$$\text{Contact time} = t_{10} = \frac{V}{Q} = \frac{31020\ \text{gal} \times 1440\dfrac{\text{min}}{\text{d}}}{2 \times 10^6 \dfrac{\text{gal}}{\text{d}}} = 22.3\ \text{min}$$

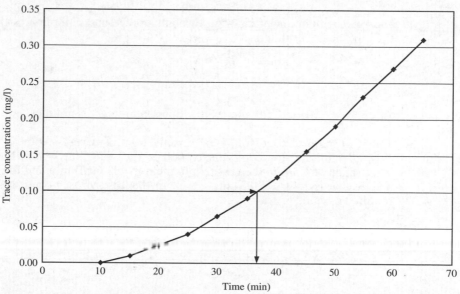

FIGURE 30   Normalized effluent response from a step input of tracer to the storage tank in Example 12.

The $C \cdot t$ for the pipeline is

$$(C \cdot t)_{pipeline} = 0.2 \frac{mg}{l} \times 22.3 \text{ min} = 4.5 \frac{mg}{l} \cdot min$$

but the chlorine residual of 0.2 mg/l requires a different $C \cdot t$ value. From Table 10 this value is 149/6 = 24.8 mg/l · min.

    The combination of storage and pipeline disinfection can be calculated as follows.

$$\frac{(C \cdot t)_{actual}}{(C \cdot t)_{required}} = \left(\frac{22.3}{25.5}\right)_{storage} + \left(\frac{4.5}{24.8}\right)_{pipeline} = 1.05$$

since $\dfrac{(C \cdot t)_{actual}}{(C \cdot t)_{required}} > 1.0$, the disinfection requirement for *Giardia* is met.

    The $C \cdot t$ requirement for 4-log inactivation of viruses is 6.0 mg/l · min. The 2-log requirement is 6.0/2 = 3.0 mg/l · min. This requirement is easily satisfied.

b. If chloramine was used in the pipeline instead of chlorine, and the residual at the end of the pipeline (at the first customer) was 0.4 mg/l, the applicable $C \cdot t$ requirement for 4-log virus inactivation from Table 10 is 1491 mg/l · min; therefore, for 2-log inactivation is 1491/2 = 746 mg/l · min. Note that the required chloramine $C \cdot t$ is greater for viruses than for Giardia (1850/6). The actual $C \cdot t$ is

$$(C \cdot t)_{pipeline} = 0.4 \frac{mg}{l} \times 22.3 \text{ min} = 8.9 \frac{mg}{l} \cdot min$$

and the combination of chlorine through storage and chloramines through the pipeline is calculated as

$$\frac{(C \cdot t)_{actual}}{(C \cdot t)_{required}} = \left(\frac{22.2}{25.5}\right)_{storage} + \left(\frac{8.9}{746}\right)_{pipeline} = 0.88$$

Since $\dfrac{(C \cdot t)_{actual}}{(C \cdot t)_{required}} < 1.0$, the disinfection requirement is not met.

c. The $C \cdot t$ requirement for 4-log inactivation of viruses with ozone is 1.0 mg/l · min, and for 2-log inactivation is 1.0/2 = 0.5 mg/l · min. For 3-log inactivation of *Giardia* the $C \cdot t$ requirement is 1.43 mg/l · min and for 0.5-log inactivation is 1.43/6 = 0.24 mg/l · min. In this case viruses control and the required t_{10} value is

$$t_{10} = \frac{C \cdot t}{C} = \frac{0.5}{0.2} = 2.5 \text{ min}$$

---

30   GROUNDWATER DISINFECTION

The primary pathogens of concern in the contamination of groundwater are fecal viruses, since large pathogens such as *Giardia* cysts and *Cryptosporidium* oocysts are removed by natural filtration through the vadose zone and aquifer. Testing for the presence of pathogenic viruses at low concentrations and identifying their species involve complex and difficult procedures. Furthermore, no indicative biological organism or substance has been identified to reliably confirm or deny the presence of enteric viruses. Thus, direct monitoring of well water to indicate the presence of enteric viruses (without concurrent coliform bacteria) is not feasible. The Centers for Disease Control and Prevention (CDC), during the 6-year period 1986–1992, reported 110 outbreaks of illness from consuming drinking water from a groundwater source. Only one of these 110 outbreaks was attributed to untreated groundwater in a community supply; the remainder were caused from contamination entering the distribution system [20]. Although outbreaks in transient and noncommunity systems may be underreported, outbreaks in community systems under closer surveillance are more likely to be reported to the CDC.

The 1986 Amendments to the Safe Drinking Water Act required disinfection for all public water supply systems; however, implementing this requirement would have imposed great challenges for 147,000 ground water systems nationwide. Therefore, in 1996, Congress amended the Safe Drinking Water Act (SDWA) to require that EPA take a targeted risk-based approach to require public groundwater supplies that are at the greatest risk of contamination to take action to protect public health. Data indicate that only a small percentage of groundwater systems are contaminated with pathogenic microorganisms, so in promulgating the Groundwater Rule in 2006, the EPA sought to specifically address these high-risk systems [21]. The basic components of the rule are as follows:

- Periodic sanitary surveys of groundwater systems that require the evaluation of eight critical elements and the identification of significant deficiencies. The critical elements are the water source; the distribution system; the finished water storage; the pumps, pump facilities and controls; monitoring reporting and data verification; system management and operation; and operator compliance with state requirements.
- Triggered source water monitoring when a system that does not provide 4-log virus inactivation identifies a positive sample during its routine coliform monitoring (in compliance with the Total Coliform Rule) and additional monitoring for high-risk systems identified by the state.
- Implementation of corrective actions by groundwater systems with a significant deficiency or evidence of source water fecal contamination to reduce the risk of contamination. Such corrective actions would include one or more of the following corrective action options:
  1. Correct all significant deficiencies (e.g., repairs to well pads and sanitary seals, repairs to piping tanks and treatment equipment, control of cross-connections)
  2. Provide an alternate source of water (e.g., new well, connection to another PWS)
  3. Eliminate the source of contamination (e.g., remove point sources, relocate pipelines and waste disposal, redirect drainage or run-off, provide or fix existing fencing or housing of the wellhead)
  4. Provide treatment that reliably achieves at least 4-log treatment of viruses (using inactivation, removal, or a state-approved combination of 4-log virus inactivation and removal).

• Compliance monitoring for systems that are sufficiently disinfecting drinking water to ensure that the treatment is effective at removing pathogens.

Example 13

Positive total colifom samples in the distribution system of a public water supply from groundwater has caused a utility to provide a 4-log (99.99%) virus reduction. Sketch a plan for a continuous-flow chlorine contact tank housed in a building for a water temperature of 10°C and a well capacity of 400 gpm.

Solution: From Table 10, the $C \cdot t$ for a 4-log reduction at 10°C equals 6 (mg/l) · min. Based on a tolerable chlorine residual of 0.5 mg/l in the drinking water,

$$\text{contact time} = 6/0.5 = 12 \text{ min}$$

A continuous-flow chlorine contact tank requires a much greater detention time because of short-circuiting and backmixing and the requirement that no more than 10% of the water can receive less than the required contact time of 12 min. Using a long and narrow chlorine contact channel with a length to width ratio of at least 40 to 1, the t_{10} time required for design is assumed to be three times greater than the theoretical detention time. Therefore,

$$\text{design detention time} = 3 \times 12 = 36 \text{ min}$$

and

$$\text{design water volume} = 400 \times 36 = 14{,}400 \text{ gal}$$
$$= 1925 \text{ ft}^3$$

A plan-view sketch of the disinfection building is shown in Figure 31. The channel is constructed as a serpentine open channel. Using a channel width of 3.5 ft and length of 157 ft, the liquid volume is 1924 ft^3 and the length-to-width ratio equals 45 to 1.

The treatment building is sized at 32 ft by 50 ft for a channel folded 4 times, chlorination equipment, inlet chamber with a vertical riser pipe from the well, outlet chamber for a vertical-turbine pump to discharge disinfected water to the distribution system, pump controls, laboratory bench, and storage area for supplies and tools. Water must be retained in the channel at all times to supply upon demand. The building must be secure and have heating, lighting, ventilation, and utilities.

The best protection against contamination of water in a distribution system is to prevent backflow by installing backflow preventers in high-risk service connections (e.g., hospitals and mortuaries) and enforcing a plumbing code for all residential, commercial, and industrial buildings. In case of an unprotected system outlet, back-siphonage is prevented by maintaining adequate pressure in the supply mains to prevent reversal of flow. The risk of backflow is remote in a properly designed and operated water distribution system. A chlorine residual is not a substitute for a well-maintained system with backflow protection.

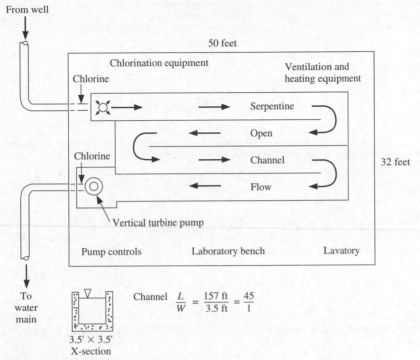

FIGURE 31 Plan-view sketch for Example 13 of a disinfection building with a continuous flow chlorine contact tank to disinfect groundwater pumped from a drinking water well with a capacity of 400 gpm.

DISINFECTION OF WASTEWATER

The degree of wastewater disinfection depends on the uses of the receiving watercourse or direct reuse of the wastewater. In general, conventionally treated wastewater discharged to recreational bodies of water with adequate dilution is given only plain chlorination. Reclaiming water for reuse involving human contact or protection of sensitive aquatic organisms for a food source (e.g., shellfish) requires filtration prior to chemical disinfection.

31   CONVENTIONAL EFFLUENT DISINFECTION

The kinds and numbers of pathogens in wastewater depend on the health of the contributing population. Although the concentrations of fecal microorganisms are reduced progressively by each stage in wastewater treatment, the effluent still contains a remnant of those contributed to the wastewater in human excreta. The removal of microorganisms by conventional treatment processes is summarized in Table 14 [22]. Helminth eggs are most likely to be removed by primary sedimentation because of their large size. In contrast, bacteria and protozoa removals are generally greater in

TABLE 14   Removal of Microorganisms in Conventional Wastewater Treatment

Kind of Microorganism	Primary Sedimentation (%)	Trickling Filtration (%)	Activated Sludge (%)	Postchlorination (%)
Bacteria	0–90	0–99	0–99	99–99.99
Viruses	0–90	0–90	0–90	—
Protozoa	0–90	0–99	0–90	—
Helminths	0–99	0–90	0–90	0

Source: Adapted from R.G. Feachem, et al., *Sanitation and Disease, Health Aspects of Excreta and Wastewater Management* (Chichester: Wiley, 1983).

trickling filtration. Apparently they adhere to the fixed-film biological growths coating the filter media. Removals in the activated-sludge processing rank low because of the variability in operational control. If the suspended biological floc under aeration settle out of suspension, removals of all the kinds of microorganisms can be as high as 99%. When the activated-sludge floc are carried out in the effluent, removals of microorganisms are greatly reduced. Even though sedimentation and biological treatment are able to remove 99% to 99.9% of microorganisms, the effluent still can contain significant concentrations of fecal viruses, bacteria, protozoal cysts, and helminth eggs.

Chlorination   Wastewater effluents can be chlorinated to inactivate pathogens in an attempt to protect public health where discharges enter surface waters used for body-contact recreation or as municipal water supplies. Disinfection is accomplished by rapid mixing of the chlorine solution with the wastewater followed by contact with the chloramines formed when the chlorine reacts with ammonia present in the wastewater [Eqs. (72) and (73)]. Acceptable disinfection is defined by the reduction of fecal coliforms to either less than 1000 per 100 ml or less than 200 per 100 ml, depending on the state standard. Some standards are more stringent and require pretreatment by granular-media filtration. The requirement for effluent disinfection may also be seasonal, depending on recreational water use. Since biologically treated wastewater contains approximately 1,000,000 coliforms per 100 ml, oxidative reduction of fecal coliforms from this large number to 200–1000 per 100 ml destroys most bacteria (Table 14). Nevertheless, viruses and protozoan cysts are more resistant to chlorination than are bacteria, and helminth eggs are unharmed. Furthermore, the presence of suspended solids inhibits disinfection by harboring viruses within floc material, shielding them from the action of the chlorine.

     An efficient chlorination system provides initial contact of the chlorine solution with the wastewater during mixing, followed by contact time with chloramines in a plug-flow tank for a minimum of 30 min at the peak hourly flow. Rapid blending can be accomplished by applying the chlorine into a pressure pipe conveying turbulent flow or into a channel immediately upstream from a mechanical mixer. Figure 32 illustrates the importance of longitudinal baffling in a chlorine contact tank to provide a long narrow flow stream to approach plug flow. Cross baffling with a wider flow stream creates

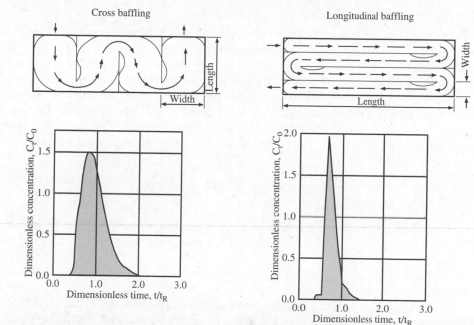

FIGURE 32 Plan views of chlorine contact tanks with cross baffling and longitudinal baffling for serpentine flow and corresponding output residence time distributions in response to pulse tracer inputs in field analyses of full-scale tanks.

short-circuiting of flow through the center with stagnant corners and excessive dispersion resulting from intermixing and backmixing. The tracer response curves are normalized residence time distributions in response to a pulse input of dye. The *y*-axis is dimensionless concentration C_t/C_0 (effluent concentration/influent concentration) and the *x*-axis is dimensionless time t/t_R (time elapsed since tracer input/theoretical residence time). The curve for cross baffling exhibits an intermediate or a large amount of dispersion, while the curve for longitudinal baffling exhibits a small amount of dispersion, much closer to the desired plug flow and therefore more efficient in the disinfection process.

Control of chlorine dosage is extremely important for proper operation. A well-designed unit provides adequate disinfection of a secondary effluent with a dosage of 8–15 mg/l. Automatic residual monitoring and feedback control is necessary to prevent either inadequate disinfection or excessive chlorination resulting in discharge of an effluent toxic to aquatic life. To protect receiving streams, some regulatory agencies have specified maximum chlorine residuals in undiluted effluents of 0.1–0.5 mg/l. Dechlorination may be required to detoxify a discharge after chlorination. This is usually done by adding sulfur dioxide or sodium bisulfite in aqueous solution at the discharge end of the chlorination tank. The oxidation–reduction reaction [Eq. (81a)] between the chloramine residual and the sulfur dioxide is very rapid. Any excess sulfur dioxide applied reduces dissolved oxygen [Eq. (81b)].

$$NH_2Cl + SO_2 + 2H_2O = NH_4^+ + SO_4^{2-} + Cl^- + 2H^+ \qquad (81a)$$

$$2SO_2 + O_2 + 2H_2O = 2SO_4^{2-} + 4H^+ \qquad (81b)$$

Alternative Disinfectants

With the increased use of UV radiation and the introduction of new UV lamps and systems, the costs of the disinfection process have declined considerably and the effectiveness has increased. Since there is no residual to UV radiation, there is correspondingly no residual toxicity in the receiving water. At doses that exceed typical disinfection doses and with addition of hydrogen peroxide, UV radiation can decrease the concentrations of some organic chemicals such as NDMA. Although ozone and chlorine dioxide are primarily used in drinking water disinfection, their use in wastewater systems is gaining favor, despite the increased cost, as a result of their increased disinfection effectiveness.

32   TERTIARY EFFLUENT DISINFECTION

The inability of gravity sedimentation to remove small suspended solids following biological aeration is a major limitation of conventional treatment. Tertiary granular-media filtration preceded by chemical coagulation can be used for effluent clarification to remove tiny particles, like helminth eggs, and colloidal solids that interfere with the disinfecting action of chlorine.

Tertiary treatment and disinfection processes are similar to those applied in surface water treatment for potable supplies: (1) rapid mixing of chemicals, flocculation, sedimentation, and granular-media filtration or (2) direct filtration after chemical mixing without sedimentation. The flocculation–sedimentation–filtration system is recommended for tertiary treatment of a conventional biologically treated effluent with BOD and suspended solids of 30 mg/l. For direct filtration, the biologically treated wastewater must be of consistently higher quality, which can be achieved only by extended aeration in an activated-sludge process. The state of California regulatory guideline for direct filtration is a settled wastewater turbidity of less than 5 NTU.

The effluent chlorination system following filtration must be properly designed and operated to ensure effective disinfection. Rapid mixing is used to blend the chlorine solution with the filtered wastewater, and chlorine contact is by plug flow through the tank with a minimum of short-circuiting and backmixing in a long narrow channel. Common design specifications are a theoretical detention time of at least 2.0 hr and an actual modal contact time of at least 1.5 hr. A chlorine residual in the range of 5–10 mg/l is maintained by automatic residual monitoring and feedback control. This provides a chloramine $C \cdot t$ in the range of 360–720 mg/l · min based on a t_{10} equal to 60% of the theoretical detention time. If dechlorination of the effluent is necessary, a solution of sulfur dioxide can be added at the discharge end of the chlorination tank.

TASTE AND ODOR

Surface waters contain tastes and odors associated with decaying organic matter, biological growths, and chemicals originating from industrial waste discharges. Land drainage from snowmelt and spring rains contains pollutants that are difficult to remove, especially at the low water temperatures that occur in northern climates. During the summer, lake and reservoir supplies may be plagued by blooms of algae that impart compounds producing fishy, grassy, or other foul odors. Actinomycetes are moldlike bacteria that create an earthy odor. Well waters may contain dissolved gases, such as hydrogen sulfide, and inorganic salts or metal ions that flavor the water. Tastes in groundwater can be identified, but defining specific odor-bearing substances in surface waters is usually an impossible task. Therefore, the best practical treatment for each water supply is determined by experiment and experience.

33   CONTROL OF TASTE AND ODOR

Water treatment plant designs should allow maximum flexibility of operations for control of tastes and odors. Problems may vary considerably during different seasons of the year, and future adverse changes in water quality of a supply are difficult to predict. Breakpoint chlorination and treatment with activated carbon are common control techniques for surface water supplies, while aeration is applied most frequently in groundwater processing. Preventive measures, such as selection of a source with the best water quality, should be given primary consideration. Regulatory controls should be used to reduce contaminants from waste discharges that enter surface and underground waters. Algal blooms may be suppressed in reservoirs by regular application of copper sulfate or approved herbicide.

Oxidative Methods

Chlorine dioxide, potassium permanganate, and ozone are strong oxidants capable of destroying many odorous compounds. These chemicals rather than heavy chlorination are favored since they do not form significant by-products. Occasionally, a combination of chemicals can be used to achieve maximum control.

Powdered Activated Carbon

Adsorption on activated carbon is the most effective means of taste and odor removal. It is primarily a surface phenomenon; that is, one substance is attracted to the surface of another. The larger the surface area of an adsorbent, the greater is its power. Carbon for water treatment is rated in terms of square meters of surface area per gram. One gram of activated carbon may have an estimated pore surface area of 500 to 1500 square meters. Besides controlling tastes and odors, powdered carbon aids in sludge stabilization, improved floc formation, and reduction in non-odor-causing organics.

Carbon is fed to water either as a dry powder or as a wet slurry. The latter has the advantage of being cleaner to handle and assures complete effectiveness by thoroughly wetting the carbon. Although granular carbon adsorption beds are used extensively to purify product water in the food and beverage industries, their application in municipal water processing is often limited by economic considerations.

Activated carbon can be introduced at any stage of water processing ahead of filtration. Although adsorption is nearly instantaneous, a contact time of 15 min or more is desirable before sedimentation or filtration. The best point of application is generally determined by trial and error based on previous experience. Carbon is often fed during flocculation or just prior to filtration. Since carbon adsorbs chlorine, these two chemicals should not be applied simultaneously or in close sequence.

Air Stripping

Air stripping is effective for removing dissolved gases and highly volatile odorous compounds. Air stripping as a first step in processing well water may achieve any of the following: removal of hydrogen sulfide, reduction of dissolved carbon dioxide, and addition of dissolved oxygen for oxidation of iron and manganese. Air stripping is rarely effective in processing surface waters, since the odor-producing substances are generally nonvolatile.

FLUORIDATION

The incidence of dental caries relative to the concentration of fluoride in drinking water is well established [23]. Low levels of fluoride result in increasing incidence of caries, while excessive fluoride results in mottled tooth enamel. At the optimum concentration for the local climate, consumers realize maximum reduction in tooth decay with no esthetically significant dental fluorosis. Recommended limits given in Table 15 are based on air temperature, since this influences the amount of water ingested by people. Medical studies have also indicated that fluoride benefits older persons by reducing the prevalence of osteoporosis and hardening of the arteries. Most public water supplies add fluoride ion to achieve an optimum level as a public health measure.

34   FLUORIDATION

The fluoride compounds most commonly applied in water treatment are sodium fluoride, sodium silicofluoride, and fluosilicic acid (Table 16). Sodium silicofluoride is commercially available in various gradations for application by dry feeders. Sodium fluoride is also popular, particularly the crystalline type where manual handling is involved. Fluosilicic acid is a strong corrosive acid that must be handled with care. It is preferred in waterworks where it can be applied by liquid feeders without prior dilution.

TABLE 15 Recommended Fluoride Limits for Public Drinking Water Supplies

Annual Average of Maximum Daily Air Temperatures Based on Temperature Data Obtained for a Minimum of 5 Yr (°F)	Fluoride Ion Concentrations (mg/I)		
	Recommended Limits		
	Lower	Optimum	Upper
50.0–53.7	0.9	1.2	1.7
53.8–58.3	0.8	1.1	1.5
58.4–63.8	0.8	1.0	1.3
63.9–70.6	0.7	0.9	1.2
70.7–79.2	0.7	0.8	1.0
79.3–90.5	0.6	0.7	0.8

Source: National Primary Drinking Water Regulations, U.S. Environmental Protection Agency.

TABLE 16   Common Chemicals Used in the Fluoridation of Drinking Water

	Sodium Fluoride	Sodium Silicofluoride	Fluosilicic Acid
Formula	NaF	Na_2SiF_6	H_2SiF_6
Fluoride ion (%)	45	61	79
Molecular weight	42	188	144
Commercial purity (%)	90–98	98–99	22–30
Commercial form	Powder or crystal	Powder or fine crystal	Liquid

Design of a fluoridation system varies with size and type of water facility, chemical selection, and availability of operating personnel. Small utilities often choose liquid feeders to apply solutions of NaF or Na_2SiF_6 that are prepared in batches. The solution tank may be placed on a platform scale for the convenience of weighing during preparation and feed. Saturator tanks containing a bed of sodium fluoride crystals yield a solution of about 4.0% (18,000 mg/l of F). Larger water plants use either gravimetric dry feeders to apply chemicals or solution feeders to inject full-strength H_2SiF_6 directly from the shipping drum. Automatic control systems use flow meters and recorders to adjust feed rate.

Application of fluoride is best in a channel or water main coming from the filters, or directly to the clear well. If it is applied prior to filtration, some of the fluoride could be lost due to reactions with other chemicals, such as coagulation with heavy alum doses or lime softening. If no treatment plant exists, fluoride can be injected into mains carrying water to the distribution system. This may be a single point or several separate fluoride feeding installations where wells supply water at different points in the piping network.

Example 14

The fluoride ion concentration in a water supply is increased from 0.30 mg/l to 1.00 mg/l by applying 98% pure sodium silicofluoride. How many pounds of chemical are required per million gallons of water?

Solution: From Table 16, Na_2SiF_6 is 61% F.

$$\text{dosage} = \frac{(1.00 - 0.30) \times 8.34}{0.98 \times 0.61} = 9.77 \text{ lb/mil gal}$$

CORROSION AND CORROSION CONTROL

Internal corrosion of piping and valves is a serious problem in many water distribution systems. A national survey of the chemical composition of water in 130 systems throughout the United States revealed that 17% had highly corrosive water and approximately 50% more had moderately aggressive water [24]. In addition to causing economic losses, corrosive waters have the potential to degrade water quality by the dissolution of metals from the distribution system and household plumbing.

35   ELECTROCHEMICAL MECHANISM OF IRON CORROSION

The primary mechanism in metal dissolution is a chemical process accompanied by the passage of an electric current. In water containing oxygen, the following complementary electrode process is capable of absorbing electrons and therefore acting as a cathode.

$$O_2 + 2\,H_2O + 4e^- \longrightarrow 4\,OH^- \tag{82}$$

As shown in Figure 33, the principal reaction at the lower potential, the anode, is dissolution of the iron-releasing iron ions into solution. These are oxidized in the presence of hydroxide ions and dissolved oxygen to form ferric oxides that are only slightly soluble. Thus, rather than the ferrous ions being carried away in the water, leaving a clean surface, as in the case of corrosion in deoxygenated water, the iron oxides collect around the anode. Nodules created by this precipitation reduce the diffusion of oxygen and strengthen the anodic character of the surface covered by the oxide nodules. The result is pitting and the ultimate perforation of the pipe wall by corrosive action.

Corrosion is generally considered to be limited by formation of protective films that coat interior pipe surfaces [25]. In potable water systems the carbonate–carbon dioxide equilibrium can be shifted and controlled by chemical treatment to deposit and maintain a calcium carbonate film. The mechanically applied cement lining in new ductile iron pipe is preserved by this chemical stabilization. After water has been slightly oversaturated with calcium carbonate, polyphosphates are applied at a dosage

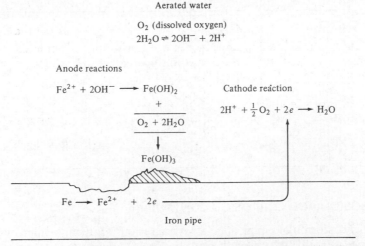

FIGURE 33   Electrochemical mechanism for corrosion of iron exposed to aerated water. Metal dissolution is the result of iron oxidation at the anode coupled with reduction of oxygen at the cathode.

of about 2 mg/l to inhibit crystal nucleation. Then, the protective carbonate scale does not dissolve and the excess calcium ions cannot precipitate.

The primary chemical characteristics of water quality that influence corrosion of iron pipe are pH, alkalinity, and bicarbonate–carbonate buffer capacity [26]. In the pH range of 7 to 9, dissolution of iron and precipitation of nodules of iron hydroxides generally increase with increasing pH. Increased alkalinity generally lowers dissolution of iron, and higher buffer capacity attenuates pH changes from corrosion reactions at anodic and cathodic areas. As illustrated in the chemical reactions in Figure 33, dissolved oxygen is an important electron acceptor in the dissolution of iron and in the precipitation of iron hydroxide. Scale is actually composed of many heterogeneous compounds, including calcite ($CaCO_3$, a protective scale), siderite ($FeCO_3$), and green rust (iron compounds containing both ferrous and ferric iron plus other anions). Other parameters potentially contributing to corrosion include age of pipe, biological activity, chlorine residual, water temperature, and chloride concentration.

Iron corrosion is a very complex process highly variable among different water distribution pipe networks. None of the mathematical corrosion indexes can either universally indicate or resolve corrosion problems. The Langelier index (also referred to as the Saturation Index, SI) has been improperly applied as a cure-all method for solving corrosion problems since it was first proposed in 1936 [26]. Although successful sometimes, it is not a universal method for controlling corrosion. Another method, the Larson index, has provided mixed results. Phosphate inhibitors are added for corrosion control, for sequestering soluble iron to reduce "red water," and for protective $CaCO_3$ scale formation. Along with a comprehensive list of references on iron pipe corrosion, McNeill and Edwards [26] provide a summary of key factors that utilities must evaluate in order to mitigate iron corrosion problems.

36 CORROSION OF LEAD PIPE AND SOLDER

Lead in excess of 5 μg/l in raw water sources is rare. In tap water, it is a corrosion by-product from customer service lines, household piping, and plumbing fixtures. The sources are solder containing 50% lead and 50% tin joining copper pipes (which is no longer being used), old lead goosenecks that were used to connect the service line to the water main, and brass fixtures containing 3%–8% lead. The highest lead concentration is in water that has been in contact with the service line and plumbing for several hours, while the content in flowing water is undetectable. Therefore, first-flush sampling is recommended in monitoring for compliance with the allowable limit of 15 μg/l at the customer's tap. Aging of copper plumbing reduces the dissolution of lead from solder to a level below 15 μg/l, usually after 5 years. Chemical characteristics that increase dissolution of lead are low alkalinity, acidic pH, and high temperature. Recommended methods of controlling excessive lead concentrations are corrosion-control treatment and replacement of long lead service lines.

Lead corrosion control is complicated because of the many interdependent reactions that occur in the formation of protective films on lead surfaces. The effect of pH on lead solubility is very strong [27]. Based on this, one recommendation to reduce lead corrosion has been to increase the pH to 8.0 or above. Nevertheless, dissolution in actual service lines is often lower than the theoretically predicted concentration because of protective coatings and other factors. The formation of an effective film of lead carbonates (e.g., $PbCO_3$) depends on pH and alkalinity, which has resulted in a second recommendation of chemical addition for supplementing alkalinity. But because the relationship is complex, increasing the carbonate content (except in very low alkalinity waters) can be complicated by the precipitation of calcium carbonate. Although $CaCO_3$ deposition is accepted practice to reduce iron corrosion, the adequacy of protection from lead leaching has been questioned by the argument that sloughing off of the deposit or incomplete coating of the pipe could result in periodic dissolution of lead in high concentrations. Despite this, in well waters high in calcium and alkalinity, service lines with lead goosenecks and copper lines joined with lead solder have shown negligible lead content in first-flush samples.

The use of phosphate compounds (orthophosphates and polyphosphates) as a remedial measure to reduce lead levels is controversial. Recent experimental studies concluded that polyphosphates cannot be recommended for lead corrosion control [28]. Orthophosphates reduced soluble lead in most cases by about 70%, except in new pipes, where lead release was observed to be comparable to that of the same system in the absence of orthophosphate addition. Dosing with hexametaphosphate generally increased soluble lead release over a range of water qualities. Polyphosphate cannot be recommended for lead corrosion control without extensive testing that provides evidence contradicting this research [28].

Verifying the effectiveness of a lead corrosion control program is time-consuming and complicated by changing conditions. The most likely measures are adjustment of pH or supplementing alkalinity, or some combination of these. The only way to measure the success of corrective treatment is to monitor changes in lead concentrations in selected first-flush tap waters. Because formation of protective films is a slow process, changing field conditions can occur that are independent of the treatment. For example, the most significance source of lead at the tap is lead-based solder in copper service lines [29]. Aging of the solder rapidly decreases lead dissolution. In fact, the most important measure to control lead in drinking water has been to require the use of lead-free solder and plumbing fixtures in public water supplies.

37   CORROSION OF SEWER PIPES

Corrosion in sewers is the destruction of pipe materials by chemical action. Sewer corrosion can result from biological production of sulfuric acid and is caused by strong industrial wastes unless they are neutralized prior to disposal. Most municipal sewer ordinances prohibit industrial wastes having a pH less than 5.5 or higher than 9.0 or having other corrosive effects.

Crown corrosion in sanitary sewers is most prevalent in warm climates where the pipes are laid on flat grades or where the sulfur content of the wastewater is high. Biological activity in wastewater in a sewer creates anaerobic conditions, producing hydrogen sulfide. Condensation moisture on the crown and walls of the sewer pipe absorbs hydrogen sulfide and oxygen from the atmosphere in the sewer. The sulfur-oxidizing bacteria *Thiobacillus* form sulfuric acid in the moisture of condensation:

$$H_2S + O_2 \xrightarrow{\textit{Thiobacillus}} H_2SO_4$$

In concrete sewers, sulfuric acid reacts with lime to form calcium sulfate, which lacks structural strength. If the concrete is sufficiently weakened, the pipe can collapse under heavy loads.

The best protection for sanitary sewers is a corrosion-resistant pipe material such as vitrified clay or plastic. In large sewers, where size and economics dictate concrete pipe, sacrificial concrete can be placed in the crown of the pipe. Crown corrosion can be retarded by ventilation or by chlorinating the wastewater to control hydrogen sulfide generation. Recent advances for the protection of concrete pipe include the development of synthetic coatings and linings.

MEMBRANE TREATMENT PROCESSES

The use of membranes in the treatment of water and wastewater has increased dramatically since 1990 and will continue to grow in the future as membrane manufacturing technology advances and as capital and operational costs of membranes decreases. The application of different membrane systems is based on pore size for removal of contaminants. Water and wastewater treatment membranes are manufactured with different pore sizes, and therefore are selected based on the contaminants that they are designed to remove. Figure 34 shows the removal range for the membranes and the size of selected species that they may remove. Selection of a membrane process is determined by the desired treatment, such as turbidity reduction, disinfection, removal of organic compounds, softening, desalination, or specific ion removal (e.g., arsenic or nitrate). The cost of membrane treatment increases with the decreasing size of the contaminants to be removed. The major factors in operating costs are pretreatment and posttreatment for membrane separation and operating pressure to force water through the membrane. Membrane types, their operating pressures, and their applications are shown in Table 17.

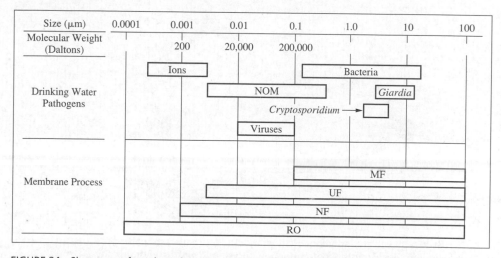

FIGURE 34   Size ranges for selected species and nominal pore sizes of membranes.

TABLE 17   Membrane Types, Operating Pressures, and Applications

Membrane Type	Operating Pressure (psi)	Applications
Microfiltration	vacuum −3 to −7	removal of bacteria and protozoa
	pressure 3 to 35	removal of bacteria and protozoa
Ultrafiltration	5 to 50	removal of bacteria, protozoa, viruses, NOM
Nanofiltration	50 to 150	softening, Ca^{2+} and Mg^{2+} removal, NOM removal
Reverse Osmosis (brackish water)	150 to 600	desalination
Reverse Osmosis (seawater)	800 to 1500	desalination

38   MEMBRANE FILTRATION

These membranes for water and wastewater applications are usually hollow fibers bundled into a pressure vessel with one end potted with an epoxy resin. In the ultrafiltration module shown in Figure 35, the feedwater flows inside the fibers and the filtrate is collected from inside the pressure vessel by a central core tube. Concentrate is collected from the ends of the hollow fibers and discharged to waste. The hollow-fiber membranes are available in two inside diameters, 0.8 mm and 1.2 mm for higher turbidity feedwater. Filtrate flow is 10–50 gpm. In the backwash mode, filtrate flows in reverse from the central core tube inside the pressure vessel through fibers to flush out the contaminants to waste. The water backwash cycle is every 15–90 min for 30–60 sec at 35 psi. Chemical enhanced backwash frequency is a minimum of one or two times per day for a duration of 1–10 min.

Flow from inside to outside through the hollow fiber can be either "dead end" or "cross-flow." In a dead end system all flow moves through the membrane and particulates

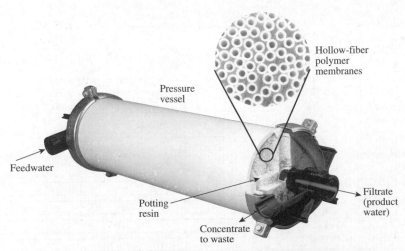

FIGURE 35   Ultrafiltration hollow-fiber module for removal of pathogens, including *Giardia* cysts, *Cryptosporidium* oocysts and viruses, and turbidity-producing particles. *Source:* Hydranautics, a Nitto Denko Corp.

are strained and left inside. In cross-flow mode high flow rates move through the inside of the fiber and only a small fraction of the flow is transmitted through the membrane. The high flows inside the membrane are recycled back through the system and tend to keep the membrane surface free from potential clogging with particulates.

Microfiltration and ultrafiltration systems can also be constructed with hollow-fiber membranes that filter water from outside-in, transverse flow from the pressure vessel through the walls to the inside of the membranes. In transverse-flow systems, contaminants in the feedwater build up on the outside of the hollow-fiber membrane surface and clean filtrate flows out of the inside. The advantage is the lower pressure drop for a given flow and number of fibers because of the greater surface area on the outside of the fibers than on the inside. The transmembrane pressure (pressure difference from the feed side to the product side of the membrane) increases as the contaminant load increases, and a set point air-water backwash is automatically initiated. Pulses of compressed air from inside a hollow-fiber membrane dislodge contaminants from the outside of the membrane surface. The contaminants are then carried out of the pressure vessel with either feedwater or filtrate as backwash water. Using air in the backwash sequence keeps fibers from coming together to impede cleaning. Other advantages demonstrated by the transverse-flow system are up to 95% recovery of feedwater and a significant reduction in the quantity of backwash-water production by using air–water backwash.

. Microfiltration and ultrafiltration may play large roles in filtration of drinking water in the future. The Long-term 2 Enhanced Surface Water Treatment Rule allows high log inactivation credit for these membranes after testing and with continued monitoring and evaluation [30].

Example 15 [31]

Until 1997, the public water supply for Marquette, Michigan, was water taken from Lake Superior and then chlorinated. The lack of processing, other than chlorination, did not meet the Surface Water Treatment Rule (Section 29), which states that filtration is required unless the water supplier can demonstrate its drainage basin is fully controlled and the raw water quality meets stringent criteria. Under this rule, filtration was required even though the raw water turbidity averaged between 0.2 and 0.3 NTU (with a historical maximum of 5–6 NTU) from an intake on a rock bottom at a depth of 60 ft and 3000 ft from the shoreline. The recommendation for compliance was to construct a direct filtration plant. The serious problem for the city was limited building space at the existing pumping station on the shore of the lake. Also, the site was surrounded by private residences and a museum, and the ground surface was bedrock.

Solution: Direct filtration was not a viable option. Microfiltration was recommended because it could, along with chlorination, meet the required $C \cdot t$ (disinfectant concentration time of contact), only minimal amounts of chemicals are required, and better water quality can be produced compared with direct filtration.

Two manufacturers provided microfiltration equipment for a 6-month testing period to demonstrate the effectiveness of microfiltration during critical coldwater months. System A was microfiltration using an outside-in flow path (transverse-flow) and air–water backwash. System B was microfiltration using an inside-out flow path and water backwash. The pilot study monitored filtrate water quality by particle counts in the critical range of *Giardia* cysts and *Cryptosporidium* oocysts, turbidity, transmembrane pressure, and general operating parameters, such as backwash production and cleaning frequency. Results of the particle removal in the range of 2–10 μm in *log base 10* was 3.3 for system A and 3.8 for system B, and the turbidity was consistently in the range of 0.03–0.05 NTU for both systems. Both pilot units provided excellent filtrate water quality. Nevertheless, the air–water backwash of system A was more effective in cleaning the hollow fibers, and more effective in controlling transmembrane pressure. For systems A and B, the backwash production in percentage of filtered water were 8% and 40%, respectively, and the average cleaning frequencies expressed in days were 22 d and 2.4 d. Because of these considerations, system A was selected.

The full-scale microfiltration plant was designed with the following parameters: maximum membrane flux rate of 125 $l/m^2 \cdot h$, based on demonstrated pilot rates; average daily flow of 11,000 m^3/d (2.8 mgd); 8 frames with 90 modules per frame for a total of inside membrane area of 10,800 m^2 (116,000 ft^2) with one frame out of service; plant-rated flow of 26,000 m^3/d (7.0 mgd) with one frame out of service, which is a flux rate of 100 $l/m^2 \cdot h$; and maximum backwash design of 3000 m^3/d (0.80 mgd).

Self-cleaning strainers (screens) were installed as pretreatment for microfiltration. Air–water backwash is discharged without treatment to Marquette Harbor under a NPDES (National Pollutant Discharge Elimination System) permit. Backwash from chemical cleaning of the membranes (sodium hydroxide and surfactant) is neutralized with acid before discharge to the sanitary sewer. The filtered water is chlorinated as it flows into the ground-level storage reservoir and rechlorinated as it is pumped into the distribution system. All operations are highly automated using computer-based control software.

---

39   REVERSE OSMOSIS AND NANOFILTRATION

Reverse osmosis (RO) is the most common process for reducing the salinity of brackish groundwater and desalting seawater. Nanofiltration (NF) membranes allow the passage of monovalent ions but reject divalent ions—hence their application in water softening. Both RO and NF membranes reject NOM to a high degree, so they will remove almost all of the potential to form THMs and HAAs once the product is chlorinated. They do not, however, have high THM or HAA removal efficiency if these DBPs enter in the feed stream. In both processes water under pressure is forced through a membrane against the natural osmotic pressure to accomplish separation of water from a solution of dissolved salts. The process of osmosis is illustrated in Figure 36, where a thin membrane separates waters with different salt concentrations. In direct osmosis, water naturally flows from the side of lower salt concentration through the membrane to the solution of higher concentration, attempting to equalize the salt content; the membrane allows water flow while blocking the passage of salt ions. If pressure is applied to the side of higher salt content, this flow of water can be prevented at a pressure termed the *osmotic pressure* of the salt solution. In reverse osmosis, the water is forced by high pressure from a salt solution through the membrane into fresh water, separating desalted water from the saline solution. The rates of flow through nanofiltration

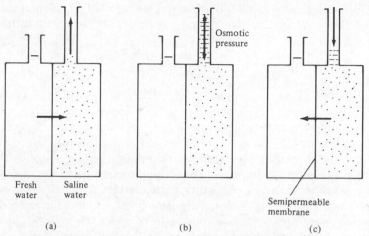

Fresh   Saline
water   water

Semipermeable
membrane

(a)   (b)   (c)

FIGURE 36   Illustrations describing the process of reverse osmosis to
remove dissolved salts from water. (a) Direct osmosis. (b) Osmotic equilibrium.
(c) Reverse osmosis.

and reverse-osmosis membranes are directly proportional to the effective pressure
(i.e., to the difference between the applied and osmotic pressures).

$$F_w = k_w (\Delta P - \Delta \pi) \qquad (83)$$

where

F_w = the water flux (flow divided by membrane area),
      gal/(ft^2 d) or liters/(m^2 s)

k_w = water permeation coefficient, gal/(ft^2 d psi) or liters/(m^2 s bar)

ΔP = transmembrane pressure (pressure difference across membrane from
      the feed to the permeate side), psi or bar

$\Delta \pi$ = transmembrane osmotic pressure, psi or bar

The osmotic pressure can be estimated for salt solutions as 1.0 psi for each 100 mg/l of
TDS. Seawater, which has a TDS of about 35,000 mg/l, would therefore have an
osmotic pressure of about 350 psi. This pressure must be overcome by the mechanical
pressure of the system pumps before any product water would be produced.

Solutes, such as cations, ions, and organic molecules are either rejected due to
their size or diffuse much more slowly through the membrane. Their individual fluxes
can be determined with the appropriate permeation coefficients that are a function of
the membrane and the solute.

$$F_s = k_s (\Delta C) \qquad (84)$$

where

F_s = mass flux of solute through the membrane(mg/m^2 s)

k_s = solute permeation coefficient (liters/m^2 s)

ΔC = transmembrane concentration of the solute (mg/l)

Since the product or permeate consists of the water and solute flux, the permeate concentration (C_p) can be calculated using appropriate units and conversion factors.

$$C_p = \frac{F_s}{F_w} \tag{85}$$

The two common membrane materials are cellulose acetate (CA) and polyamide (PA) and their derivatives. CA type membranes can tolerate some oxidant exposure (0.5 mg/l of chlorine), operate in a pH range of 4 to 8, and tolerate some biological fouling. PA type membranes tolerate a wider pH range, but are less tolerant to oxidants (they can tolerate weak oxidants such as low chloramine concentrations). PA type membranes usually require less pressure to produce the same flow rates as CA membranes, so their use is becoming more popular, particularly where high salt concentrations in the feed water lead to high osmotic pressure. By assembling the membranes in modular units, a large membrane surface area can be compacted into a cylindrical pressure vessel fitted with an inlet for the saline feedwater and outlets for the product water (permeate) and reject brine.

A *spiral-wound module* (Figure 37) is made up of large membrane sheets covering both sides of a flat sheet of porous backing material that collects the permeate (product water). The membranes are sealed on the two long edges and one end to form an envelope enclosing the permeate collector. The other end of the membrane envelope is sealed to a perforated tube, which receives and carries away the permeate from the collectors. Several of these membrane envelopes, with mesh spacers in between for brine flow, are rolled up to form a spiral-type module. Feed water enters the end of the module through the voids between the membrane envelopes provided by the spacers. Under high pressure, water is forced from the feed-concentrate in the spacer voids through the membranes and conveyed by the enclosed porous permeate collectors to the perforated tube in the center of the module. Concentrate (also referred to as brine) discharges from the spacer voids at the outlet end of the module.

A *hollow-fiber module* is a pressure vessel containing a very large number of microfiber membranes densely packed in a U-bundle with their openings secured in an

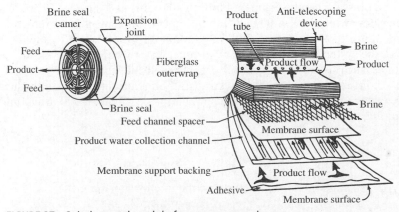

FIGURE 37   Spiral-wound module for reverse osmosis.

end block of the module. The hollow fibers have an outside diameter of 85–100 μm and an inside diameter of 42 μm. Because of their small diameter and thick wall, these tubes can withstand the high reverse-osmosis pressure required to force water from the surrounding concentrate into the hollow cores of the fibers. The process flow is shown in Figure 38. Saline water enters the module through a central perforated feed tube and flows radially through the fiber bundle toward the outer shell of the cylinder. Under high pressure, water enters the hollow fibers and exits from their open ends at the discharge end of the module. Reject concentrate arriving at the outer shell of the cylinder is collected by a flow screen and conveyed from the module.

NF and RO process performance may be characterized by two major parameters, recovery and rejection, shown schematically in Figure 39. Recovery is the fraction or percentage of feed flow that is converted to permeate (useful product). The remainder of the flow becomes the concentrate as indicated in the mass balance below.

$$Q_f = Q_p + Q_c \tag{86}$$

and

$$Y = \frac{Q_p}{Q_f} \quad \text{or} \quad Y = \frac{Q_p}{Q_f} \times 100 \tag{87}$$

where

Q_f, Q_p, and Q_c are the feed, permeate and concentrate flow rates, respectively, gal/d or L/s

Y = recovery expressed as a fraction or as a percent.

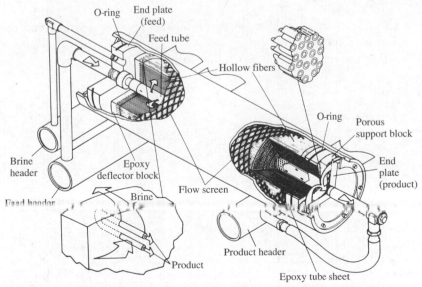

FIGURE 38   Hollow-fiber module for reverse osmosis. *Source:* Permasep Products, E. I. du Pont de Nemours & Co.

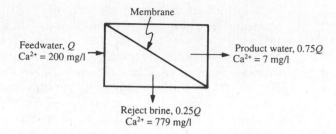

FIGURE 39 Schematic diagram of a reverse-osmosis module illustrating the concentration of calcium ion in the reject brine relative to the feedwater and product water for 75% recovery.

Recoveries for individual membrane modules are low, on the order of 10%, but they are typically assembled in series within pressure vessels and then arranged in arrays to improve recovery as shown in Figure 40. Recoveries for NF range from 75 to 90%, while RO systems treating brackish water operate with recoveries between 70 to 85% and RO desalination systems operate between 30 and 50%.

The rejection determines the amount of solute that will be rejected by the membrane and therefore remain in the concentrate and correspondingly, the amount of solute that will be allowed to diffuse through the membrane and become part of the permeate. A mass balance can be written on each of the individual solutes because each will have its own rejection for a particular membrane as determined by its k_s.

$$Q_f C_f = Q_p C_p + Q_c C_c \qquad (88)$$

and

$$R = \frac{C_f - C_p}{C_f} \quad \text{or} \quad R = \frac{C_f - C_p}{C_f} \times 100 \qquad (89)$$

where

$C_f, C_p,$ and C_c are the feed, permeate and concentrate concentrations, respectively, mg/l

R = the rejection expressed as a fraction or a percent.

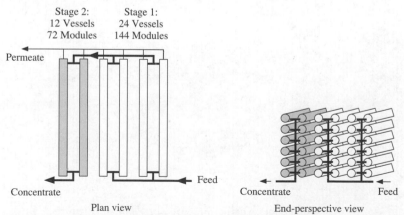

FIGURE 40 Staged arrays used for reverse osmosis and nanofiltration systems to improve recovery.

Rejections are sometimes written in terms of the average concentration of the feed and concentrate since the feed becomes the concentrate as water moves through the membrane unit on the same side of the membrane. The concentration of solute in the permeate is a function of the water flux, which is dependent on the osmotic pressure and therefore the concentration of solute on the feed-concentrate side of the membrane, as well as the solute flux, which is dependent on the transmembrane concentration difference. Thus, the rejection for one solute and membrane may vary from the start of the system to the final membrane module. Rejections can be very high (95+%) for most solutes except gases and small organic molecules for RO membranes. NF membranes have lower rejections for monovalent ions but high rejections for multivalent ions.

Combining equations 86 through 89 produces the following equation for C_c, with Y and R expressed as fractions:

$$C_c = \frac{[1 - Y(1 - R)]C_f}{1 - Y} \tag{90}$$

The concentrate concentration is important with respect to fouling and scaling which must be considered in both the design and operation of an NF or RO system. If the solubility of salts are exceeded there is a potential for precipitation on the membrane surface. In some cases, as with calcium carbonate, pH adjustment with an acid dosage to the feed can control the precipitation. With other compounds such as calcium sulfate and silica, polymeric antiscalants are needed to control scaling. Fouling can be caused by the accumulation of natural organic matter on the membrane surface, and periodic off-line cleaning of the membranes is needed.

Example 16

A low-pressure RO membrane system treating a brackish groundwater is operating at 80% recovery. The rejection for both calcium and sulfate is 95%. The feed water contains 100 mg/l of calcium and 200 mg/l of sulfate, and the K_{sp} for $CaSO_4$ is 2.5×10^{-5}. Find the concentration of calcium and sulfate in the concentrate and determine if the solubility of $CaSO_4$ is exceeded.

Solution: Calculate the concentration factor using Eq. (90) which applies to both ions since their rejection is the same.

$$\frac{C_c}{C_f} = \frac{[1 - Y(1 - R)]}{1 - Y} = \frac{[1 - 0.75(1 - 0.95)]}{1 - 0.75} = 3.85$$

The concentration of both the calcium and sulfate will be increased by the factor 3.85 and will become

$$[Ca^{2+}] = 3.85 \times \frac{100 \text{ mg/l}}{40,000 \text{ mg/mole}} = 9.6 \times 10^{-3} \text{ mole/l}$$

$$[SO_4^{2-}] = 3.85 \times \frac{200 \text{ mg/l}}{96,000 \text{ mg/mole}} = 8.0 \times 10^{-3} \text{ mole/l}$$

and the ion product is

$$[Ca^{2+}] \times [SO_4^{2+}] = 7.7 \times 10^{-5}$$

The ion product exceeds the solubility product; therefore, precipitation on the membrane is possible. An antiscalant should be used in the feed to control the potential scaling.

The feedwater must be clear and low in chemical ions that can cause scale (e.g., calcium). In groundwater, silt and iron oxides are the two common contaminants resulting from poor well construction. If the gravel pack and screen are not properly designed and placed, fine sand and silt from the aquifer can be carried out in the well water. Since many groundwaters are aggressive, the well casing, pump column, and transmission piping must be constructed of noncorrosive materials to prevent formation of rust particles. To protect membranes from damaging solids that may enter in the feed stream, a cartridge filter, typically 5 μm, is placed in the feed stream just prior to the membrane.

Permeates from NF and RO processes are highly corrosive, with low pH and high concentration of carbon dioxide. Low pH results from acidification to control scale, and the high carbon dioxide concentration is formed from bicarbonate when the pH is lowered. Carbon dioxide and other gases and volatiles are transmitted by the membranes. The three methods of stabilization are degasification (decarbonation), addition of lime or soda ash for neutralization and increase in alkalinity, and blending with raw water. Degasification can be performed in a packed column with the water sprayed in at the top and percolating through the media against a countercurrent of air. Carbon dioxide is reduced to less than 10 mg/l and the pH raised to near neutrality. Addition of lime slurry $[Ca(OH)_2]$ neutralizes the carbon dioxide, increases the calcium concentration, and raises the pH. Soda ash (Na_2CO_3) addition increases alkalinity and raises the pH. It also adds sodium ion, which is undesirable both for corrosion control and for consumption in drinking water by persons with hypertension (high blood pressure). Nevertheless, soda ash is often applied in small systems because it is much easier to feed; a solution of soda ash is a clear liquid, whereas lime is a milky slurry. Blending permeate (after degasification, if performed) with raw water is often an economical method of partial or, in some cases, complete stabilization. The blending ratio depends on the chemical characteristics of the two waters. Since the fluoride ion content is reduced in desalting, supplemental fluoridation of the stabilized water to the optimum level is recommended. Residual disinfectants are also added to the permeate at the end of the process.

Concentrate disposal must be considered in RO and NF designs and can limit the use of membranes when disposal becomes either too costly or is prohibited by regulatory agencies. Options for disposal include discharge to surface water, land application, deep well injection, evaporation ponds, and discharge to wastewater treatment systems.

This limited discussion and the calculations in Examples 16 and 17 are only an overview of reverse osmosis. The presentation by Ko and Guy [32] on brackish and seawater desalting expands the topics of membranes, modules, pretreatment, and design and operation. In the same book, Ridgway [33] reports the results of research studies on biological fouling of membrane surfaces. The EPA Guidance Manual [30] is also an excellent source of membrane information and is available for download from the EPA web site.

Example 17

A reverse-osmosis plant treats warm brackish groundwater with total dissolved solids of 2600–2700 mg/l and pH 6.8–7.2. Since the well water is free of silt, iron, and manganese and low in silica, no granular-media filtration is required. The first step in pretreatment is to cool the water in a heat exchanger to 35°C, when necessary, for longer membrane life. Next, the water is acidified to pH 5.8 with 150 mg/l of sulfuric acid to prevent $CaCO_3$ scale formation, and 10 mg/l of hexametaphosphate are added to prevent $CaSO_4$ formation. Cartridge filters remove particles down to 5 microns in size; the average life of the replaceable filter elements is 12 weeks. To force the pre-treated water through the membranes, a high-pressure pump at each reverse-osmosis unit increases the pressure to 370 psi. Each unit has 13 modules, with 9 in the first stage and 4 in the second stage. The feedwater applied to the first stage produces 50% permeate and 50% brine. The first-stage brine is applied to the second stage to again produce 50% permeate and 50% brine, which is rejected. Therefore, the total recovery of product water is 75% of the feedwater, and the reject brine is 25%. The product water is stripped to remove carbon dioxide in packed countercurrent columns, raising the pH from 5.8 to about 7.0. It is then stabilized by adding approximately 10 mg/l of soda ash to raise the pH to 8.2–8.5. The fluoride ion concentration is increased from 0.2 mg/l to the optimum of 0.8 mg/l by adding fluosilicic acid. The finished water has a total dissolved-solids concentration of 250–350 mg/l, alkalinity of 80–100 mg/l, and calcium ion concentration of approximately 7 mg/l.

Trace the chemical changes that occur in the water during treatment. The milliequivalents-per-liter bar graph of the untreated groundwater is shown in Figure 41a.

Solution: Adding 150 mg/l of sulfuric acid for acidification to a pH of 5.8 converts bicarbonate ion to carbon dioxide and increases the sulfate ion content as shown in Figure 41b.

If the water recovery is 75%, the concentrations of ions in the reject brine are about four times the concentrations in the acidified feedwater. Therefore, the contents are calcium ion 860 mg/l (0.0215 moles/l), sulfate ion 2270 mg/l (0.0236 moles/l), alkalinity 228 mg/l (4.56 meq/l), total dissolved solids 10,200 mg/l, and ionic strength 0.226. The scaling potential of $CaCO_3$ can be estimated by calculating the Langelier saturation index by using the following equation:

$$SI = pH - pH_s = pH - [(pK_2' - pK_s') + pCa^{2+} + pAlk] \qquad (91)$$

where

pH = measured pH of the water

pH_s = pH at $CaCO_3$ saturation (equilibrium)

pK_2', pK_s' = constants based on ionic strength and temperature

pCa^{2+} = negative logarithm of the calcium ion concentration, moles/liter

$pAlk$ = negative logarithm of the total alkalinity, equivalents/liter

$$SI = 5.8 - [2.1 + p(1/0.0215) + p(1000/4.56)]$$
$$= -0.3 \text{ (non-scale-forming water)}$$

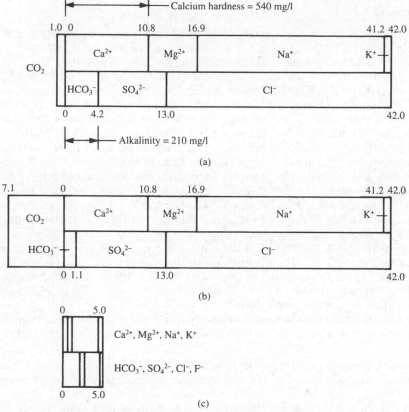

FIGURE 41   Milliequivalents-per-liter bar graphs for Example 14.
(a) Untreated groundwater with a total dissolved-solids concentration of 2600 mg/l.
(b) Feedwater after acidification to pH 5.8. (c) Product water after post treatment
with a total dissolved-solids concentration of 350 mg/l.

The $pK_2' - pK_s'$ value for ionic strength is less than 0.020 and total dissolved solids are less than 800 mg/l. The value of 2.10 used in the above calculation was taken from a Langelier diagram in [34] for a total dissolved-solids content of 10,200 mg/l.

The potential for $CaSO_4$ scale is estimated by calculating the product of the ionic molar concentrations of the calcium and sulfate ions and comparing the result to the solubility-product constant. For the acidified brine,

$$[Ca^{2+}][SO_4^{2-}] = 0.0215 \times 0.0236 = 0.51 \times 10^{-3}$$

The estimated K_{sp} for a brine after addition of sodium hexametaphosphate is 1.0×10^{-3}; hence, this brine is unsaturated and non-scale-forming.

Figure 41c is the approximate bar graph of the finished water with a total dissolved-solids concentration of 350 mg/l after carbon dioxide stripping, soda ash addition, and fluoridation.

VOLATILE ORGANIC CHEMICAL REMOVAL

The two processes for removal of volatile organic chemicals (VOCs) are stripping by aeration and granular activated carbon (GAC) adsorption. Because of their volatility, these chemicals are rarely found in surface waters. However, VOCs are stable in groundwaters contaminated by leaching of chemicals from industrial discharges, improper chemical use, and spillage. The maximum contaminant levels for VOCs are in the range of 2–10,000 μg/l, with a most common value of 5 μg/l. Because of these extremely low allowable concentrations, air stripping in a countercurrent packed tower is the only aeration method satisfactory for drinking water treatment. In cold climates the process may not be feasible because of low volatility and consequent poor removal at low temperatures and the possibility of ice formation on the tower packing. The most costly process of GAC adsorption may replace air stripping or be applied as a second stage following partial removal by aeration.

40   DESIGN OF AIR-STRIPPING TOWERS

The water is sprayed on the top of the packing and passes down through the column while air is blown countercurrent up through the tower. The packing can be random or stacked lightweight plastic media. As the water spreads over the surfaces of the packing, a large area of water is exposed for mass transfer to the flow of air. The VOCs can move freely toward equilibrium between liquid and gas phases. For air stripping very dilute solutions, this equilibrium can be expressed by Henry's law as

$$C_G^E = HC_L^E \tag{92}$$

where

C_G^E = gas-phase molar concentration in equilibrium with the liquid-phase concentration, kg/m^3

C_L^E = liquid-phase molar concentration in equilibrium with the gas-phase concentration, kg/m^3

H = Henry's law constant, mass concentration/mass concentration (dimensionless)

For efficient air stripping, the equilibrium between the liquid and gas phases is continuously destabilized by replenishing the air exhausted from the top with contaminant-free air entering at the bottom. By the time the water discharges from the column bottom, the contaminant in the liquid phase is reduced to a very low concentration. The higher the value of Henry's law constant, the more readily a VOC is air-stripped from water.

The rate of mass transfer of a VOC from water to air is proportional to the difference between the equilibrium concentration in solution and the existing concentration in solution.

$$J = K_L a(C_L^E - C_L) \tag{93}$$

where

J = rate of mass transfer per unit volume of packing, kg/m³ · s

K_La = overall mass transfer coefficient, s⁻¹

C_L^E = molar concentration in liquid phase in equilibrium with the gas-phase concentration, kg/m³

C_L = average molar concentration in liquid phase, kg/m³

The value of K_La depends on the geometry of the tower and packing, operation of the air-stripping system (e.g., the air-to-water ratio), and temperature.

The design of an air-stripping packed column for steady-state mass transfer is based on the following relationship:

$$Z = (\mathrm{HTU})(\mathrm{NTU}) \tag{94}$$

where

Z = depth of packing, m

HTU = height of a transfer unit, m

NTU = number of transfer units (dimensionless)

The height of a transfer unit (HTU) characterizes the mass transfer efficiency from the liquid to the gas phase.

$$\mathrm{HTU} = L/\rho_L \cdot K_La \tag{95}$$

where

L = water mass loading rate, kg/m² · s

ρ_L = water density, kg/m³

L/ρ_L = volumetric loading rate, m³/m² · s

K_La = overall mass transfer coefficient, s⁻¹

The number of mass transfer units (NTU) corresponds to the difficulty in removing the VOC from the liquid phase.

$$\mathrm{NTU} = \left(\frac{S}{S-1}\right)\ln\frac{(C_{in}/C_{out})(S-1)+1}{S} \tag{96}$$

where

S = stripping factor, (dimensionless)

C_{in} = VOC concentration in influent, kg/m³

C_{out} = VOC concentration in effluent, kg/m³

The stripping factor is defined as

$$S = H(Q_A/Q_w) \tag{97}$$

where

H = Henry's law constant, mass concentration/mass concentration (dimensionless)

Q_A = volumetric airflow rate, m^3/s

Q_W = volumetric water loading rate, m^3/s

Several mathematical models to calculate mass transfer coefficients have been proposed based on the two-film theory, which assumes that overall resistance to mass transfer is the sum of liquid- and gas-phase resistances. Lamarche and Droste [35] evaluated these models in packed-column air stripping of six VOCs. They also presented a laboratory technique for determining the value of Henry's law constant for VOCs at different temperatures.

The procedure for designing an air stripping tower starts with the selection of a packing. A stripping factor is selected between 2 and 5 (if high removal efficiency is required), and on the basis of this value, the air-to-water ratio is calculated. An allowable air pressure drop is selected. Data on the air pressure drop through a particular packing are generally available from the manufacturer. Operation at a high-pressure drop allows a smaller volume of packing, reducing the construction cost but increasing the operational costs. Various combinations of pressure drops and air-to-water ratios can be calculated to find the most cost-effective choice. Henry's law constant for the anticipated operating temperature is taken from the literature or determined by laboratory analysis. Selection of a mass transfer coefficient should preferably be from pilot-plant studies or based on experience in full-scale performance. Using these data, along with influent and effluent VOC concentrations, the required depth of packing can be calculated from Eqs. (94–97). The cross-sectional area of the tower is calculated from the quantity of water to be treated and the water loading.

Example 18

Determine the depth of packing and cross-sectional area for a countercurrent air-stripping tower to reduce the trichloroethylene from 200 μg/l to 2 μg/l (99% removal). The design water flow rate is 76 l/s, and the lowest operating temperature anticipated is 10°C, based on groundwater temperature and cooling in the tower. Henry's law constant for trichloroethylene is 0.30 at 10°C. The manufacturer of the proprietary random packing recommends a mass transfer coefficient of 0.017 s^{-1} based on pilot studies and an allowable pressure drop of 50 N/m$^2 \cdot$ m.

Solution: After discussions with the client and the manufacturer of the packing, the designer selected a loading of 10 l/m$^2 \cdot$ s (kg/m$^2 \cdot$ s) and a stripping factor of 3.6. Using Eq. (97),

$$\text{air-to-water ratio } (Q_A/Q_W) = 3.6/0.30 = 12 \text{ m}^3/\text{m}^3$$

$$\text{volumetric airflow rate} = 0.076 \text{ m}^3/\text{s} \times 12 \text{ m}^3/\text{m}^3 = 0.91 \text{ m}^3/\text{s}$$

Using Eq. (95),

$$HTU = \frac{10 \text{ kg/m}^2 \cdot \text{s}}{(1000 \text{ kg/m}^3)(0.017/\text{s})} = 0.59 \text{ m}$$

Using Eq. (96),

$$NTU = \left(\frac{3.6}{3.6 - 1}\right) \ln \frac{(200/2)(3.6 - 1) + 1}{3.6} = 5.9$$

Using Eq. (94),

$$Z \text{ (depth of packing)} = 0.59 \times 5.9 = 3.5 \text{ m}$$
$$\text{surface area of tower} = \frac{76 \text{ l/s}}{10 \text{ l/m}^2 \cdot \text{s}} = 7.6 \text{ m}^2$$
$$\text{diameter of cylindrical tower} = \left(\frac{7.6 \text{ m}^2}{\pi/4}\right)^{1/2} = 3.1 \text{ m}$$

SYNTHETIC ORGANIC CHEMICAL REMOVAL

Synthetic organic chemicals (SOCs) include pesticides (herbicides and insecticides), volatile organic chemicals, and DBPs. Trace concentrations of pesticides are found in runoff from agricultural lands, occasionally in groundwaters under agricultural lands, and in groundwaters contaminated by seepage from improper disposal of industrial wastes and spillage of chemicals. Conventional water treatment provides limited removal of organic chemicals. If adsorbed on particles or associated with large hydrophobic molecules, they can be taken out by coagulation–sedimentation–filtration. However, SOCs do not adsorb well to metal hydroxides and polymers, resulting in negligible removal. Adjustment of pH, changing coagulants or coagulant aids, and application of powdered activated carbon are options to be considered for improved treatment. In surface water treatment, these process variables are generally successful for greater removal of natural organic precursors to reduce subsequent formation of disinfection by-products.

41 ACTIVATED CARBON ADSORPTION

Activated carbon can be made from a variety of carbonaceous raw materials. Processing involves dehydration and carbonization by slow heating of a variety of substances such as lignite and bituminous coal, pine bark, and coconut shells in the absence of air followed by chemical activation to produce a highly porous structure. Powdered activated carbon (PAC) is often used in surface water treatment systems where it is applied in rapid mix or flocculation and subsequently removed in sedimentation and filtration. Granular activated carbon (GAC) is more commonly used either in the granular filter with sand or configured in a flow-through column as a post-filtration adsorbent. GAC must have good abrasion resistance, since GAC is subject to filter backwashing, conveyance as a slurry, and heat reactivation.

The activation process in manufacture creates a highly porous surface on the carbon particles with macropores and micropores down to molecular dimensions. Organic contaminants are adsorbed by attraction to and accumulation in pores of appropriate size; thus the pore structure is extremely important in determining adsorptive properties for particular compounds. Activation processes can be modified to produce activated carbons that are targeted for selective removal of particular organic compounds [36]. In general, GAC most readily adsorbs branch-chained high-molecular-weight organic chemicals with low solubility. These include pesticides, volatile organic chemicals, trihalomethanes, and NOM, although large NOM molecules may be size-excluded from smaller pores. Macropores are large enough for colonies of bacteria to grow and proliferate in them if biodegradable organic compounds are in the water. The benefits of microbial growth or potential risks to water quality are now being realized in biologically active filters following ozonation. GAC is reactivated thermally at a furnace temperature and retention time based on the volatility of the adsorbed chemicals. During each reactivation, 2–5% of the carbon is lost and must be replaced with fresh carbon.

Powdered activated carbon is a fine powder applied in a water slurry, which can be added at any location in the treatment process ahead of filtration. At the point of application, the mixing must be adequate to ensure dispersion and the contact time must be long enough for adsorption. The dosage for normal taste and odor control is usually up to 5 mg/l with a contact time of 10–15 min. Although PAC is an effective adsorber of organic compounds that cause taste and odor, this success is not repeated by the adsorption of SOCs. Poor adsorption is attributed to short contact time between the carbon particles and the dissolved organic chemicals, and interference by adsorption of other organic compounds. Efficiency in removal of SOCs requires a granular activated carbon filter to ensure close contact between the water and carbon for a sufficient time for adsorption to occur.

Adsorption Isotherms

Various methods are used to characterize activated carbon for a particular application. Most fundamental to this characterization is the equilibrium adsorption isotherm that shows the relationship between the adsorbate (contaminant to be removed) and the solid phase concentration of the adsorbate on the adsorbent (activated carbon). The water to be treated should be used when conducting the experiments that lead to the isotherm because it will then contain not only the contaminant but also any interfering substances that might degrade the process. Portions of the water are placed in vials with different concentrations of PAC. After sufficient contact time is allowed to establish equilibrium, the carbon is separated from the solution, and the concentration in the water is measured. It is assumed that reductions in the water concentration are attributed to the adsorption of the adsorbate on the activated carbon, although precautions may be required to prevent volatilization and biodegradation losses. The solid phase concentrations (sometimes referred to as the *loading*) are then calculated.

$$q = \frac{\text{mass of adsorbate on the activated carbon}}{\text{mass of activated carbon}} = \frac{(C_0 - C_e)V}{M} \qquad (98)$$

where

$$q = \text{solid phase concentration or loading, mg/g}$$

C_0 and C_e = concentration of adsorbate in water before adsorption and after equilibrium is attained, respectively, mg/l

V = volume of the vial containing the water and activated carbon, liters

M = mass of activated carbon in the vial, g

The data can be fit to a variety of models; the most often used and applied is the Freundlich model, given by

$$q = KC_e{}^b \tag{99}$$

where

K and b are coefficients for the model.

Example 19

Using the following isotherm results in the two left-hand columns of Table 18, determine the Freundlich model coefficients. The individual isotherm vials contained 200 ml of water, and the initial adsorbate concentration was 200 mg/l. Find the dose of PAC per liter of water to produce a concentration at equilibrium of 15 mg/l.

Solution: The solid phase concentrations for each vial can be determined from Eq. (98) and are shown in Table 18. The Freundlich model in Eq. (99) can be linearized with a log transform:

$$\log q = \log K + b \times \log C \tag{100}$$

Then the plot of the $\log q$ versus the $\log C$, shown in Figure 42, has a slope of 0.60, the value of b, and an intercept of 2.0, the value of the $\log K$. The model therefore is

$$q = 100C^{0.60}$$

TABLE 18   Equilibrium Isotherm Data

Mass of activated carbon (g)	Concentration of adsorbate (mg/l)	q (mg/g)	$\log q$	$\log C$
0.150	5	260	2.41	0.70
0.100	10	380	2.58	1
0.050	25	700	2.85	1.40
0.030	50	1000	3.00	1.70

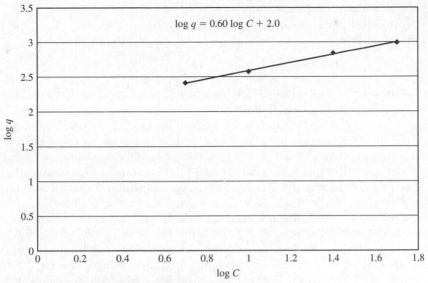

$$\log q = 0.60 \log C + 2.0$$

FIGURE 42   Freundlich plot for Example 19.

Using an equilibrium concentration of 15 mg/l in the above model gives $q = 508$ mg/g. Using Eq. (98) and recognizing that the dose of PAC is M/V gives

$$\text{Dose} = \frac{M}{V} = \frac{(C_0 - C_e)}{q} = \frac{(200 - 15)\text{mg/l}}{508 \text{ mg/g}} = 0.364 \text{ g/l}$$

Design of a GAC system requires pilot-plant tests for selection of the best carbon, determination of the required contact time and the effects of influent water quality variations, and establishment of the carbon loss during reactivation.

Pilot column tests make it possible to [37]

- Determine treatability
- Select the best carbon for the specific purpose based on performance
- Establish the required carbon dosage that, together with laboratory tests of reactivation, will determine the capacity of the carbon reactivation furnace or the necessary carbon replacement costs
- Determine the effects of influent water quality variations on plant operation

42   GRANULAR ACTIVATED CARBON SYSTEMS

The majority of new systems in water treatment to remove SOCs will use separate deep-bed contactors. GAC facilities require the following system components [37]

- Carbon contactors for the water to be treated for the length of time required to obtain the necessary removal of organics

- Reactivation or replacement of spent carbon
- Transport of makeup or reactivated carbon into contactors
- Transport of spent carbon from the contactors to reactivation or hauling facilities
- Facilities to backwash the GAC beds

A fixed-bed contactor has a GAC bed that remains stationary (fixed) during operation. Although the bed can be designed for downflow or upflow, downflow operation with provision for backwashing is more common. The GAC is not reactivated until chemical breakthrough; then the entire bed is removed and replaced. The design of a fixed-bed contactor is similar to that of a gravity granular-media filter or a pressure filter. In a surface water treatment plant, the conventional filter is retained to remove turbidity, and the fixed-bed contactor is added as a second stage. A postfilter contactor designed specifically to adsorb SOCs (without the necessity of turbidity removal) provides better use of the adsorptive capacity of the GAC and allows longer contact times. Adsorptive capacity can be significantly reduced by organic contaminants in an unfiltered water. Also, GAC suitable for filtration may not be optimum for adsorbing the contaminating organic chemicals. Contact time is expressed as empty bed contact time, calculated by dividing the volume of the bed by the flow rate. In conventional filtration, the empty bed contact time is usually 3–9 min, while in a GAC contactor it is 15–30 min or greater. A contactor following filtration also reduces the quantity of backwash water required and can be designed for easier removal of spent carbon and replacement. A gravity contactor is appropriate for removal of chemicals from a groundwater supply in a large plant. Pretreatment may be necessary to remove contaminants that can interfere with filtration through the GAC bed, for example, iron oxide deposits and growth of iron bacteria. For individual wells, the contactor may be a pressure vessel with discharge pressure from the well pump forcing the water through the bed.

REDUCTION OF DISSOLVED SALTS

Dissolved salts can be removed from water with chemical softening processes (Sections 15–17), RO and NF processes (Section 39), and ion exchange and distillation. Ion exchange processes are most often used for softening, but are now considered for selective removal of problematic contaminants such as nitrate, fluoride, and arsenic. Distillation is sometimes practiced to desalinate water.

43   ION EXCHANGE

Ion exchange is a mass transfer process whereby an ion or ions in the water are transferred to a solid phase ion exchanger while an ion previously associated with the solid phase is transferred to the water. The solid phase ion exchanger is a granular material made from a polymeric resin with fixed positive or negative charges (Figure 43a.) Fixed anionic sites attract mobile cations and are called cationic exchangers while fixed cationic sites attract mobile anions and are called anionic exchangers. The exchanger has presaturant ions that are associated with the fixed charges. These presaturant ions, such as sodium, are exchanged for ions such as calcium that remain on the exchange

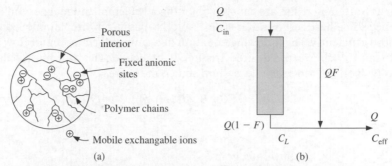

FIGURE 43   (a) Cationic ion exchange resin with fixed anionic sites and exchangeable mobile cations. (b) By-pass schematic.

resin and are thereby removed from the water. The ion exchange resin generally has a greater affinity for ions of a higher charge, so calcium will be selected over sodium in a cationic exchanger and sulfate will be selected over nitrate in an anionic exchanger. The ion exchange resin is fixed in a vessel, and water is passed through the bed while the exchange process proceeds.

The hardness-producing elements of calcium and magnesium are removed and replaced with sodium by a cation resin. Ion exchange reactions for softening may be written

$$Na_2R + \left.\begin{matrix} Ca \\ Mg \end{matrix}\right\} \left\{\begin{matrix} (HCO_3)_2 \\ SO_4 \\ Cl_2 \end{matrix}\right. \longrightarrow \left.\begin{matrix} Ca \\ Mg \end{matrix}\right\} R + \left\{\begin{matrix} 2\,NaHCO_3 \\ Na_2SO_4 \\ 2\,NaCl \end{matrix}\right. \tag{101}$$

where R represents the exchange resin. These reactions show that if a water containing calcium and magnesium is passed through an ion exchanger, these metals are taken up by the resin, which simultaneously gives up sodium in exchange.

After the ability of the bed to produce soft water has been exhausted, the unit is removed from service and backwashed with a solution of sodium chloride. This removes the calcium and magnesium in the form of their soluble chlorides and at the same time restores the resin to its original sodium condition. The bed is rinsed free of undesirable salts and returned to service. The governing reaction may be written

$$\left.\begin{matrix} Ca \\ Mg \end{matrix}\right\} R + 2\,NaCl \longrightarrow Na_2R + \left.\begin{matrix} Ca \\ Mg \end{matrix}\right\} Cl_2 \tag{102}$$

A majority of ion exchange softeners are the pressure type, with either manual or automatic controls. They normally operate at rates of 6–8 gpm/ft^2 of surface filter area. A water meter is usually employed on the inlet or outlet side. For manual-type operations, this meter can be set to turn on a light or sound an alarm at the end of the softening run. About 8.5 lb of salt is required to regenerate 1 ft^3 of resin and remove approximately 4 lb of hardness in a commercial unit. The reduction is directly related to the amount of cations present in the raw water and the amount of salt used to regenerate the resin bed.

Softening resins are capable of taking all calcium and magnesium from the water. Since some hardness in water is desirable, by-passing is often employed to use the resin more efficiently. The following equation determines the amount of flow that can be by-passed to achieve the desired treatment objective. This is a mass balance at mixing point P on the ion exchange system shown in Figure 43b.

$$QFC_{in} + Q(1 - F)C_L = QC_{eff} \tag{103}$$

where

Q = the flow rate, gpm

F = the fraction of the flow that is by-passed around the ion exchange column

C_{in}, C_L, and C_{eff} are the concentrations in the influent, leaking from the column, and in the effluent, respectively, mg/l

Dividing by the flow, Q, gives

$$FC_{in} + (1 - F)C_L = C_{eff} \tag{104}$$

The cost and use of salt to completely regenerate a softening column is often avoided; rather the regeneration is partial, allowing some leakage of calcium and magnesium from the column. Manufacturers of softening resins will give the leakage concentration as a function of regeneration. In Eq. (104) the effluent concentration is chosen to give the desired hardness in the water. When the influent concentration is known, the desired by-pass fraction can be determined.

Ion exchange systems designed to treat water for the removal of substances that have adverse health effects, such as nitrates and arsenic, do not have by-pass streams, as complete removal of these substances is desired.

44   DISTILLATION OF SEAWATER

Typical seawater has a salinity (total dissolved solids) of 35,000 mg/l, of which 30,000 mg/l is NaCl. The generally accepted quality standards for drinking water are 500 mg/l of total dissolved solids and 200 mg/l of chloride. Distillation is cost competitive for desalination of feedwater with a high salt content because the process operates virtually independent of influent solids concentration. Moreover, a product purity of less than 100 mg/l is easily attained [38].

Distillation involves heating feedwater to the boiling point and then boiling it into steam to form water vapor, which is then condensed to yield a salt-free water. The principal commercial processes are multistage flash distillation and thin-film multiple-effect evaporation. The prefix *multi-* in the names means that a series of evaporation–condensation units is employed to obtain multiple reuse of the energy content of the heated steam. There may be as many as 15–25 stages.

Multistage flash distillation is illustrated schematically in Figure 44. Seawater entering the plant is initially heated in a heat recovery unit in which the hot desalted product water and waste brine discharge are cooled. The warmed seawater is then blended with recycled brine and passed through a series of condenser tubes in the evaporator

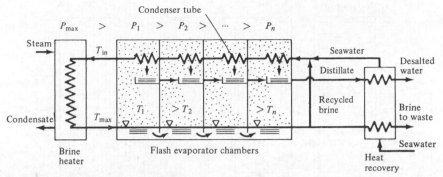

FIGURE 44   Multistage flash distillation.

chambers for further heating. In the process of condensing the steam to distillate (the desalted water), the temperature of the brine is increased in stages to temperature T_{in} as it enters the brine heater. In this unit, the temperature of the brine feed is raised by external thermal energy to just below the saturation temperature T_{max} under a pressure P_{max}. The hot brine is then discharged through the series of stages with progressively reduced pressure. The pressure $P_{max} > P_1$, $P_1 > P_2$, and so forth. Because of the reduction in pressure, a portion of the heated feed flashes to vapor in each stage to obtain equilibrium with the vapor condition prevailing in each individual stage. This results in a temperature drop in each stage (e.g., T_{max} drops to T_1, and T_1 drops to T_2), arriving at the minimum temperature T_n in the last stage. The total temperature drop is usually from a T_{max} of 250°F to a T_n of 100°F. The fraction of recirculating brine that can be flashed with each cycle is restricted to 0.10–0.15. Therefore, to produce the desired rate of distillate, the minimum brine recirculation rate must be in the range of 10, which is 6.6 times the production rate of desalted water. The brine wasted from the recycling feed line may contain approximately 70,000 mg/l for seawater input of 35,000 mg/l.

The controlling parameters for output of desalted water and energy consumption are the temperature drop allowed in each stage, the difference between the brine inlet temperature to the first stage and the discharge temperature at the last (overall flash range), and the stage heat transfer coefficients. The principal unavoidable heat losses result from imperfect heat transfer by the condenser tubes and heat exchangers. Other losses include poor venting resulting in vapor blanketing of the condenser tube surfaces and tube fouling as a result of scale formation. Energy consumption in distillation is always well in excess of the ideal theoretical minimum. For a particular installation, efficiency is related to design factors such as the number of stages.

Thin-film multiple-effect evaporation is the second process widely used for distillation of seawater. The steam generated in one effect condenses on the outside of long vertical tubes in the next effect, evaporating more water from a film of brine that runs down the inside of the tube. As shown in Figure 45, prime steam enters the shell of the first effect where it condenses on the outside of the tubes. The latent heat of condensation furnishes the energy required to evaporate a portion of the brine feed within the tubes. The partially concentrated brine proceeds to the second effect, which operates at a slightly lower pressure. The vapor leaving the first effect condenses on the tubing of the second effect, causing further evaporation of water from the brine. This process continues from

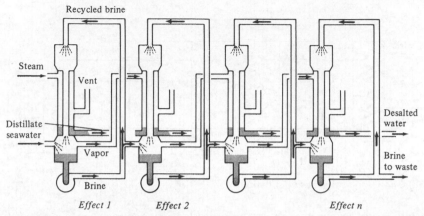

FIGURE 45   Thin-film multiple-effect evaporation with long vertical condenser tubes.

effect to effect until the lowest pressure vapor is condensed in a final condenser by giving up its latent heat to circulating cooling water. The combined condensate from all effects constitutes the product water from the plant. Using this same principle, several variations may be designed into the multiple-effect process. One modification is the use of horizontal rather than vertical tubes with the steam inside the tubes and the evaporating brine flowing in a film on the outside tube surfaces.

PROBLEMS

1 (a) Using atomic weights from the table of elements given in Table 7 in the Appendix, calculate the molecular and equivalent weights of alum (aluminum sulfate), ferric sulfate, and soda ash (sodium carbonate). The formulas of these compounds are given in Table 1. (b) Using atomic weights, compute the equivalent weights of the ammonium ion, bicarbonate ion, calcium carbonate, and carbon dioxide. Values are given in Table 2.

2 (a) Water contains 38 mg/l of calcium ion and 10 mg/l of magnesium ion. Express the hardness as mg/l of $CaCO_3$. (b) Alkalinity in water consists of 120 mg/l of bicarbonate ion and 15 mg/l of carbonate ion. Express the alkalinity in units of mg/l of $CaCO_3$.

3 Draw a milliequivalents-per-liter bar graph and list the hypothetical combinations for the following analysis of soft water:

$$Ca^{2+} = 36 \text{ mg/l} \qquad HCO_3^- = 208 \text{ mg/l}$$
$$Mg^{2+} = 14 \text{ mg/l} \qquad SO_4^{2-} = 14 \text{ mg/l}$$
$$Na^+ = 43 \text{ mg/l} \qquad Cl^- = 44 \text{ mg/l}$$
$$K^+ = 7 \text{ mg/l}$$

4 Draw a milliequivalents-per-liter bar graph for the following analysis of groundwater:

$$Ca^{2+} = 94 \text{ mg/l} \qquad HCO_3^- = 317 \text{ mg/l}$$
$$Mg^{2+} = 24 \text{ mg/l} \qquad SO_4^{2-} = 67 \text{ mg/l}$$
$$Na^+ = 14 \text{ mg/l} \qquad Cl^- = 24 \text{ mg/l}$$

5 Draw a milliequivalents-per-liter bar graph for the following water analysis:

$$\text{calcium hardness} = 185 \text{ mg/l} \qquad \text{alkalinity} = 200 \text{ mg/l}$$
$$\text{magnesium hardness} = 50 \text{ mg/l} \qquad \text{sulfate ion} = 58 \text{ mg/l}$$
$$\text{sodium ion} = 23 \text{ mg/l} \qquad \text{chloride ion} = 36 \text{ mg/l}$$
$$\text{potassium ion} = 20 \text{ mg/l} \qquad \text{pH} = 7.7$$

6 Calculate the pH of a solution of pure water containing 1.0 mg/l of sulfuric acid.

7 What is the dominant form of alkalinity in a natural water at pH 7? What are the forms present at pH 10.5?

8 Calculate points and sketch ideal output tracer curves (concentration versus normalized time) for a pulse tracer input for (a) a single completely mixed reactor and (b) a series of four equal-sized completely mixed reactors.

9 Flow through a baffled tank was analyzed by injecting a pulse of dye tracer into the influent and measuring the tracer concentrations in the effluent at time intervals of every 2 min after injection. The results are listed below. Sketch the tracer distribution curve by plotting C (mg/l) versus t (min) and locate the mean residence time. Calculate the number of completely mixed tanks in series represented by this residence time distribution.

t	C	t	C	t	C	t	C
0	0.00	6	0.10	12	0.40	18	0.05
2	0.00	8	0.35	14	0.22	20	0.00
4	0.00	10	0.65	16	0.11		

10 Flow through a compartmented aeration tank was analyzed by injecting a pulse of lithium chloride tracer in the influent. From the time and output concentration data listed, plot C (kg/m^3) versus t (min), the tracer response curve. Calculate the location of the mean residence time, $\bar{t}$, variance of the curve σ^2, and the number of completely mixed tanks in series that is represented by the distribution.

t	C	t	C	t	C	t	C
0	0	105	89.0	210	33.5	315	6.0
15	0	120	95.0	225	25.8	330	4.6
30	0	135	88.0	240	20.0	345	3.5
45	3.5	150	78.2	255	15.4	360	2.6
60	16.5	165	65.0	270	12.1	375	1.7
75	46.5	180	55.2	285	9.5	390	0.7
90	72.0	195	43.0	300	7.5	405	0

11 The residence time distribution of a cross-baffled serpentine chlorination tank was determined by injecting a pulse of 200 g of dissolved rhodamine dye into the influent. The tank is 9.4 m long and 6.7 m wide, with a longitudinal wall in the center. Each side has three baffle walls extending 2.5 m in from the outside wall and two extending in from the center wall to direct the serpentine flow pattern. The wastewater effluent enters through a channel near the top of the tank and discharges over an outlet weir. At the operating water depth of 2.55 m, the

liquid volume is 137 m^3 (excluding the volume occupied by the concrete walls). The test was conducted at the peak hourly flow rate of 10,100 m^3/d. Effluent sampling times in minutes after injecting the dye and corresponding dye concentrations are listed below. The dye concentrations were determined by measuring absorbance with a spectrophotometer at a wavelength of 550 μm. From these data, plot the tracer response curve C (mg/l) versus t (min). Calculate and locate the mean residence time $\bar{t}$ and the theoretical mean residence time t_R. In order to normalize the concentration test data, the value of C_0 must be determined. A portion of the dye adsorbed onto the walls of the tank and became trapped in stagnant water in the corners and near the bottom at the inlet and outlet. Therefore, C_0 must be based on the calculated quantity of dye recovered in the effluent rather than on the amount injected. To estimate the milligrams of dye discharged, determine the area under the C-versus-t tracer response curve in milligrams·minutes/liter and multiply this value by the flow rate in liters/minute. The C_0 value is this amount of dye divided by the volume of water in the tank, which is equal to 137 m^3. Calculate $\bar{t}/t_R$ and the peak normalized concentration C_{peak}/C_0.

t	C	t	C	t	C	t	C
0	0.00	10	0.97	19	0.92	40	0.08
2	0.00	11	1.01	20	0.83	44	0.06
3	0.00	12	1.08	22	0.72	48	0.04
4	0.00	13	1.12	24	0.60	52	0.06
5	0.00	14	1.15	26	0.49	56	0.00
6	0.04	15	1.17	28	0.42	60	0.00
7	0.45	16	1.06	30	0.33	64	0.00
8	0.67	17	1.06	32	0.22	68	0.00
9	0.83	18	0.92	36	0.11		

12 A reaction that proceeds by first-order irreversible kinetics is oxidizing chemical A in a wastewater treatment basin with a mean residence time of 1.5 hours. The reaction rate constant is 2.0 hr^{-1}. The basin is unbaffled and may be characterized as two completely mixed tanks in series. If the steady-state influent concentration is 30 mg/l, find the effluent concentration. If baffles are placed in the basin so that the basin may be characterized as four completely mixed tanks in series, and the mean residence time remains constant, find the effluent concentration.

13 What parameter dictates the rate of decrease in concentration of remaining reactant with time in (a) zero-order kinetics and (b) first-order kinetics?

14 The kinetics of a chemical reaction were analyzed by laboratory experiment. Lime was added to a water sample to precipitate reactant A as product P. While the water was continuously stirred, portions were withdrawn at 10-min intervals to measure the amount of A remaining. The data collected were as follows: $t = 0$, C_0 of A $= 100$ mg/l; $t = 10$ min, C of A remaining $= 55$ mg/l; $t = 20$ min, $C = 22$ mg/l; $t = 30$, $C = 8$; and $t = 40$, $C = 5$. Plot graphs as shown in Figure 3a and b. What are the kinetics of the reaction? What is the value of the reaction-rate constant?

15 The number of coliform bacteria is reduced from an initial concentration of 2,000,000 per 100 ml to 400 per 100 ml in a long, narrow chlorination tank under a steady wastewater flow with a hydraulic detention time of 30 min. Assuming first-order kinetics and ideal plug flow, calculate the reaction-rate constant. Using this rate constant, find the effluent concentration if the reactor is operated as a completely mixed reactor.

16 Alternative reactor systems are being considered to reduce the reactant in a steady liquid flow from an initial concentration of 100 mg/l to a final concentration of 20 mg/l. Assuming a first-order reaction-rate constant of 0.80 day^{-1}, calculate the hydraulic retention time required for each of the following reactor systems: (a) one plug flow reactor, (b) one completely mixed reactor, and (c) two equal-volume completely mixed reactors in series.

17 Define the terms *coagulation* and *flocculation* in reference to destabilization of colloidal suspensions. When these terms are used by an environmental engineer in reference to water treatment processes, what are their meanings?

18 The results from a jar test for coagulation of a turbid alkaline raw water are given in the table. Each jar contained 1000 ml of water. The aluminum sulfate solution used for chemical addition had such strength that each milliliter of the solution added to a jar of water produced a concentration of 8.0 mg/l of aluminum sulfate. (a) Based on the jar test results, what is the most economical dosage of aluminum sulfate in mg/l?

Jar	Aluminum Sulfate Solution (ml)	Floc Formation
1	1	None
2	2	Smoky
3	3	Fair
4	4	Good
5	5	Good
6	6	Very heavy

(b) If another jar had been filled with freshly distilled water and dosed with 5 ml of aluminum sulfate solution, what would have been the degree of floc formation?

19 In the coagulation reaction, commercial aluminum sulfate (alum) reacts with natural alkalinity or can be reacted with lime or soda ash if the water is deficient in alkalinity. Based on Eqs. (51–54), calculate the milligrams-per-liter amounts of alkalinity, lime as CaO, and soda ash as Na_2CO_3 that react with 1.0 mg/l of alum.

20 The removal of *Giardia* cysts from a soft, cold, low-turbidity water requires 15 mg/l of alum plus 0.10 mg/l of anionic polymer. (a) How many milligrams per liter of natural alkalinity are consumed in the coagulation reaction? How much carbon dioxide is released by this reaction? (b) What is the stoichiometric dosage of soda ash to react with the 15 mg/l of alum? This reduces loss of alkalinity but still produces carbon dioxide. How much carbon dioxide is released by this reaction? (c) Would a stoichiometric dosage of lime slurry be better than soda ash? Suggest a reason why lime slurry would not be used. How can carbon dioxide be removed from water?

21 A ferric chloride dosage of 40 mg/l and an equivalent dosage of lime are used to coagulate a water. (a) How many pounds of ferrous sulfate per million gallons are used? (b) How many pounds of hydrated lime per million gallons are used, assuming a purity of 70% CaO? (c) How many pounds of ferric hydroxide are theoretically produced per million gallons of water treated?

22 Treatment of a water supply requires 60 mg/l of ferric chloride as a coagulant. The natural alkalinity of the water is 40 mg/l. Based on theoretical chemical reactions, what dosage of lime as CaO is required to react with the ferric chloride after the natural alkalinity is exhausted?

23 The data listed below are from a pilot-plant study to determine turbidity and *Giardia* cyst removal from a cold, low-turbidity water (less than 1°C and 0.5 NTU in winter) by direct filtration using a cationic polymer as the coagulant. The filter was a dual-media coal-sand bed, 2 ft by 2 ft square, operated for most test runs at a loading of approximately 12 m^3/m$^2 \cdot$ h (4.9 gpm/ft^2) for durations in the range of 3–22 hr. During selected filter runs, *Giardia* cysts and coliform bacteria were injected into the raw water for 40–60 min and tested for presence in the filtered water. Calculate the percentages for *Giardia* cyst and coliform removals. Plot turbidity versus polymer dosage for both the raw water and filtered water on the same diagram. What is the least dosage of polymer for maximum turbidity removal? What appears to be an acceptable turbidity in the effluent to ensure 98%–99% (virtually 100%) *Giardia* cyst removal?

Filter Loading (m^3/m$^2 \cdot$ h)	Water Temp. (°C)	Polymer Dosage (mg/l)	Turbidity		*Giardia lamblia*		Coliforms	
			Inf. (NTU)	Eff. (NTU)	Inf. (Cysts/l)	Eff. (Cysts/l)	Inf. (Org/100 ml)	Eff. (Org/100 ml)
12.3	2.7	0	0.46	0.30				
8.0	0.3	0	0.45	0.22	340	69		
12.1	1.9	5	0.48	0.30				
12.2	0.3	10	0.60	0.05				
12.3	0.3	10	0.47	0.03				
11.4	0.3	12	0.45	0.03			360	9
12.3	0.3	12	0.48	0.04				
8.7	1.9	13	0.61	0.06	270	0.4	3900	580
12.3	0.3	13	0.47	0.03				
12.2	0.3	14	0.49	0.03				
11.9	8.3	18	0.65	0.07	3.2	0	8700	190
12.5	7.6	24	0.43	0.02	410	0	5800	300
12.3	0.2	24	0.48	0.02				

24 Presedimentation reduces the turbidity of a raw river water from 1500 mg/l suspended solids to 200 mg/l. How many pounds of dry solids are removed per million gallons? If the settled sludge has a concentration of 8% solids and a specific gravity of 1.03, calculate the sludge volume produced per million gallons of river water processed.

25 Sketch a preliminary process flow diagram for a water treatment plant to clarify and disinfect a turbid surface water at a design flow of 50 mgd. Use two identical, parallel, and separate processing lines with rapid mixing, flocculation, sedimentation, filtration, and clear-well storage. The flocculation and sedimentation processes for each line are in the same large rectangular concrete tank with paddle flocculators in baffled compartments ahead of the sedimentation section, and effluent "finger" channels extending into the tank from the outlet end. For each line, use four gravity dual-media coal-sand filters with deep filter boxes to prevent "air binding" and flow control by influent flow splitting for constant-rate filtration.

     On the flow diagram, show the chemicals to be added with alternate points of application. The raw water has a turbidity ranging from 10 to 40 NTU, and in the spring the water contains natural organic matter that creates bad taste and odor and forms trihalomethanes with prechlorination. The fluoride concentration is less than optimum. The treatment plant must meet the EPA rule for surface water disinfection as discussed in Section 28. Sketch a longitudinal cross-sectional view of the flocculation–sedimentation tank. List the design criteria for sizing the flocculation section and specifying paddle flocculators, sizing the sedimentation section and effluent channels, and sizing the filters. Sketch a plan view of the clear well to ensure compliance with the EPA disinfection rule.

26 The water defined by the analysis given below is to be softened by excess-lime treatment. (a) Sketch an meq/l bar graph. (b) Calculate the softening chemicals required. (c) Draw a bar graph for the softened water after recarbonation and filtration, assuming that 80% of the alkalinity is in the bicarbonate form.

$$CO_2 = 8.8 \text{ mg/l} \qquad Alk(HCO_3^-) = 135 \text{ mg/l}$$
$$Ca^{2+} = 40.0 \text{ mg/l} \qquad SO_4^{2-} = 29.0 \text{ mg/l}$$
$$Mg^{2+} = 14.7 \text{ mg/l} \qquad Cl^- = 17.8 \text{ mg/l}$$
$$Na^+ = 13.7 \text{ mg/l}$$

27 Settled water after excess-lime treatment, before recarbonation and filtration, contains 35 mg/l of CaO excess lime in the form of hydroxyl ion, 30 mg/l of $CaCO_3$ as carbonate ion, and 10 mg/l as $CaCO_3$ of $Mg(OH)_2$ in the form of hydroxyl ion. First-stage recarbonation precipitates the excess lime as $CaCO_3$ for removal by sedimentation, and second-stage recarbonation converts a portion of the remaining alkalinity to bicarbonate ion. Calculate the carbon dioxide needed to neutralize the excess lime and convert half of the alkalinity in the finished water to the bicarbonate form. Assume an excess of 20% of the calculated CO_2 is required to account for unabsorbed gas escaping from the recarbonation chamber.

28 For the water analysis given in Problem 5, calculate the additions of CaO, Na_2CO_3, and CO_2 needed for excess-lime softening. Sketch a bar graph for the finished water after two-stage precipitation softening by excess-lime treatment with intermediate and final recarbonation (Figure 13). Assume that three-quarters of the alkalinity in the finished water is in the bicarbonate form.

29 For the water analysis given in Problem 5, calculate the lime dosage required for selective calcium removal. The process flow scheme is a single-stage system of mixing, sedimentation, and filtration. Draw a bar graph for the finished water. Is this softening process recommended for this water?

30 A groundwater supply has the following analysis:

$$calcium = 94 \text{ mg/l} \qquad bicarbonate = 317 \text{ mg/l}$$
$$magnesium = 24 \text{ mg/l} \qquad sulfate = 67 \text{ mg/l}$$
$$sodium = 14 \text{ mg/l} \qquad chloride = 24 \text{ mg/l}$$

(a) Calculate the quantities of lime and soda ash for excess-lime softening, and the carbon dioxide reacted for neutralization by two-stage recarbonation. Assume that the practical limits of hardness removal for calcium are 30 mg/l as $CaCO_3$ and for magnesium are 10 mg/l as $CaCO_3$, and that three-quarters of the final alkalinity is converted to bicarbonate. Calculate the finished hardness and sketch the bar graphs for the raw and finished waters. (b) Calculate the chemical dosages for split-treatment softening, assuming a permissible magnesium hardness in the finished water of 40 mg/l. Follow the methods of solution in Example 8. Draw the bar graphs, after first-stage lime treatment, of the unreacted combined first-stage effluent and bypassed flow, and the finished water after reaction of soda ash. Calculate the finished water hardness.

(c) Calculate the chemical dosages for split-treatment softening using the method of solution in Example 9. Draw the bar graph after first-stage excess-lime–soda ash treatment and the finished water after reaction of the excess lime with the bypassed flow. Calculate the finished water hardness.

31 Compute the lime dosage needed for selective calcium-removal softening of the water described by the following analysis. What is the finished water hardness?

$$Ca^{2+} = 63 \text{ mg/l} \qquad CO_3^{2-} = 16 \text{ mg/l}$$
$$Mg^{2+} = 15 \text{ mg/l} \qquad HCO_3^- = 189 \text{ mg/l}$$
$$Na^+ = 20 \text{ mg/l} \qquad SO_4^{2-} = 80 \text{ mg/l}$$
$$K^+ = 10 \text{ mg/l} \qquad Cl^- = 10 \text{ mg/l}$$

32 Consider the split-treatment softening of water described by the analysis below. Use the criteria for the finished water given in Example 8. Draw a bar graph for the finished water after second-stage treatment with soda ash, sedimentation, and final filtration.

$$CO_2 = 15 \text{ mg/l as } CO_2 \qquad HCO_3^- = 200 \text{ mg/l as } CaCO_3$$
$$Ca^{2+} = 60 \text{ mg/l} \qquad\qquad SO_4^{2-} = 96 \text{ mg/l}$$
$$Mg^{2+} = 24 \text{ mg/l} \qquad\qquad Cl^- = 35 \text{ mg/l}$$
$$Na^+ = 46 \text{ mg/l}$$

33 Reconsider split-treatment softening of the water with the analysis given in Problem 32. Use the alternate method of solution given in Example 9. How does this finished water bar graph compare with the finished water bar graph determined in Problem 32? (Note: The equilibrium concentrations for $CO_3^=$ and HCO_3^- ions determined in these calculations are only approximate. In actual chemical reactions, the relationship of these ions depends on final pH.)

34 Sketch a preliminary process flow diagram for a split-treatment lime–soda ash water treatment plant to soften a design flow of 60 mgd. Use six equal-sized flocculator–clarifiers. The first-stage flow for excess-lime treatment is expected to be no greater than 50% of the raw water. Use eight gravity dual-media coal–sand filters with traditional flow control using rate-of-flow controllers. The preferred backwashing system is air scouring prior to water backwash. The clear-well capacity is 6.0 mil gal. The raw water has a hardness of approximately 230 mg/l, iron in the range of 0.2–0.3 mg/l, and a less than optimum concentration of fluoride. On the flow diagram, show the chemicals being added and their points of application. Sketch a cross-sectional view of the filter box showing the wash-water troughs, filter media, and underdrain system. List the design criteria for sizing the flocculator–clarifiers and filters.

35 The ionic characteristics of a fossil groundwater in an arid region are listed below. Draw a milliequivalents-per-liter bar graph and calculate total hardness and alkalinity. One recommendation for improving the quality of the water for domestic use is lime–soda ash softening to reduce hardness and total dissolved solids (TDS). Calculate the lime and soda ash additions for excess-lime treatment and draw the final bar graph after recarbonation. Calculate the theoretical total dissolved solids content by summing the weights of the ions (or hypothetical combinations) in the softened water. Was the recommendation of lime–soda ash softening appropriate?

$$Ca^{2+} = 108 \text{ mg/l} \qquad HCO_3^- = 146 \text{ mg/l} \qquad TDS = 900 \text{ mg/l}$$
$$Mg^{2+} = 44 \text{ mg/l} \qquad SO_4^{2-} = 110 \text{ mg/l}$$
$$Na^+ = 138 \text{ mg/l} \qquad Cl^- = 336 \text{ mg/l}$$

36 Sketch a meq/1 bar graph of the water described in Problem 26 after it is softened to zero hardness by cation exchange softening.

37 Consider the ion exchange softening of water described in Example 6. If 0.3 lb of NaCl is required to regenerate the resin bed per 1000 grains of hardness removed, calculate the salt required per million gallons of water softened. Sketch a meq/l graph for the ion-exchange-softened water. How does finished water from ion exchange softening differ from finished water produced in lime–soda softening?

38 A small community has used an unchlorinated well water supply containing approximately 0.3 mg/l of iron and manganese for several years without any apparent iron and manganese problems. A health official suggests that the town install chlorination equipment to disinfect the water and provide a chlorine residual in the distribution system. After initiating chlorination, consumers complain about water staining washed clothes and bathroom fixtures. Explain what is occurring due to chlorination.

39 The iron and manganese removal process for the well supply of a small community is mechanical aeration, the addition of potassium permanganate followed by detention in a contact tank, pressure filtration, and postchlorination. The construction specifications called for manganese-treated greensand; however, the actual filter medium provided was plain sand. Customers often complained that the treated water caused staining of bathroom fixtures and laundry. The common response of the plant operator was to increase the chemical dosage, which did not seem to improve the situation. The operator even tried prechlorination of the water in combination with potassium permanganate addition, but that appeared to increase the staining characteristics of the treated water. Discuss the most probable cause of the poor-quality finished water and your recommendations for improvement.

40 Untreated well water contains 1.2 mg/l of iron and 0.8 mg/l of manganese at a pH of 7.5. Calculate the theoretical dosage of potassium permanganate required for iron and manganese oxidation.

41 Iron and manganese are removed by aeration, chlorine oxidation, sedimentation, and sand filtration from a well water supply. The plant processes 3000 m^3/d with application of 2.5 mg/l chlorine. Calculate the usage in kilograms per month for each of the following chemicals: chlorine gas, 70% granular calcium hypochlorite, and 12% sodium hypochlorite solution. At the same pH of the chlorinated water, do all of these chemicals form the same kind of chlorine residual?

42 The results of a chlorine demand test on a raw water at 20°C are given in the following table.

Sample	Chlorine Dosage (mg/l)	Residual Chlorine After 10 Min of Contact (mg/l)
1	0.20	0.19
2	0.40	0.37
3	0.60	0.51
4	0.80	0.50
5	1.00	0.20
6	1.20	0.40
7	1.40	0.60
8	1.60	0.80

    (a) Sketch the chlorine demand curve.

    (b) What is the breakpoint chlorine dosage?

    (c) What is the chlorine demand at a chlorine dosage of 1.20 mg/1?

43 The practice of combined residual chlorination involves feeding both chlorine and anhydrous ammonia. Calculate the stoichiometric ratio of chlorine feed to ammonia feed for combined chlorination.

44 List the possible applications of ozone in water treatment. If ozone is applied for disinfection, may the use of chlorine be eliminated?

45 What is the suspected health risk of trihalomethanes (THMs) in drinking water, and how was this risk demonstrated? What is the origin of THMs in treated water? If the finished water from a river water treatment plant contains an excessive concentration of these chemicals during spring runoff, what remedial actions can be taken to reduce their formation?

46 Define the meaning of the $C \cdot t$ product. What factors affect the $C \cdot t$ value used in design and operation of a drinking water disinfection system? With reference to Tables 9 and 10, what kind of microorganism is most readily inactivated by free chlorine? What kind is the most difficult to inactivate? List the tabulated disinfectants in the order of most effective to least effective in disinfecting action.

47 What is the disease in humans caused by *Giardia lamblia* and *Cryptosporidium* species? In what manner do these protozoa infect humans and how are they transmitted to other humans by water? What are other modes of transmission? Describe the waterborne sources of these organisms.

48 Find the full tables for $C \cdot t$ values on the EPA web site. Plot the 3-log removal of *Giardia* by chlorine at 15°C as a function of pH. Plot the 4-log removal of viruses by chloramines as a function of temperature. Draw conclusions from these data and plots.

49 From Table 9, what is the $C \cdot t$ value for 99.9% (3.0-log) inactivation of *Giardia* cysts at a free chlorine residual of 1.0 mg/l, temperature of 10°C, and pH 7.0? How does a water temperature increase to 20°C affect the $C \cdot t$? How does a pH increase to 8.0 affect the $C \cdot t$?

50 A surface water treatment plant at a winter resort city has been designed to process cold, low-turbidity water by direct filtration based on the pilot-plant study described in Problem 23. The filtered water has a turbidity of less than 0.1 NTU, temperature of 10°C, and pH of 7.4 during the period of highest water consumption in the winter. Tracer analyses of the clear-well reservoir are illustrated in Figure 28. At the critical hourly flow of 3.0 mgd, $t_{10} = 90$ min. To comply with the EPA surface water disinfection regulation, what free chlorine residual must be maintained in filtered water at the outlet of the clear well? What would be the required dose of chlorine dioxide if it was used instead of chlorine?

51 Figure 46 illustrates surface water schemes of conventional water treatment and direct filtration treatment. Review data provided in Sections 28 and 29. Fill in the names of unit processes in the boxes and the numerical values of log removals required by the EPA in the blank spaces.

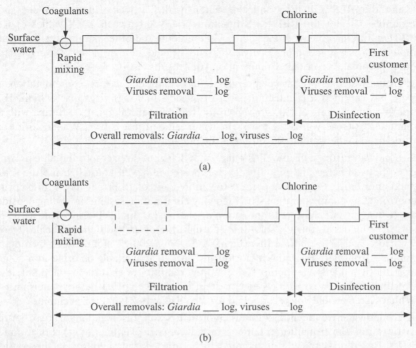

FIGURE 46   Surface-water treatment schemes listing the expected removals of
Giardia and viruses by (a) conventional water treatment; (b) direct filtration treatment.

52 A surface water treatment plant with coagulation, sedimentation, filtration, and effluent chlorination is being evaluated for compliance with the EPA surface water disinfection regulation. The critical time of the year is during peak demand in the summer when the finished water temperature is 10°C or greater, pH is 8.0 or less, and the turbidity is 0.2–0.3 NTU. Prechlorination cannot be practiced because of trihalomethane formation. Data from the tracer analysis at peak hourly flow through the clear well, which has been modified by installation of baffles to reduce short-circuiting, are given in Problem 9. After the clear well and prior to the first service connection, the finished water is transported through a pipeline for 4000 ft at a velocity of 5 fps. What chlorine residual is present in the water at the outlet of the pipeline?

53 The manufacturer of a UV disinfection unit has provided the following constants in the RED equation: $a = -0.80$, $b = -2.0$, $c = 0.18$, $d = 0.50$, $e = 0.85$. The following values apply to the water being treated: maximum UVA = 0.100 cm^{-1}, minimum $S/S_0 = 0.8$, maximum flow = 5 mgd. The validation factor for the model calibration with respect to *Cryptosporidium* is 1.8. How many banks of lamps will be required to disinfect this water to meet the requirements of the Long-Term 2 Enhanced Surface Water Treatment Rule?

54 Using the RED equation and the water quality values and flow values shown in Example 11, plot the RED as a function of UVA between UVA values of 0.05 and 0.30 cm^{-1} in increments of 0.05 cm^{-1} while holding the other parameters constant. Then plot RED as a function of Q between 2 and 10 mgd, in increments of 2 mgd holding all other parameters constant. Comment on your results.

55 A groundwater supply has been designated as vulnerable to fecal contamination, and the state has specified a disinfection level of 99.99% (4.0-log) virus inactivation. The peak hourly pumping rate is 2000 gpm from the well field through a 4200-ft pipe with a 16-in. diameter to a reservoir in the town. The water temperature is 10°C. What chlorine residual is required in the water at the outlet of the pipeline?

56 Groundwater from a deep well is pumped at 400 gpm directly into the pipe network of a city. The well pump and pipe fittings are located in a well house. During the seasons of maximum usage, the pump operates for an average of 18 hr per day, with chlorine feed controlled by pump operation. The following chlorination systems are being considered to apply 0.50 mg/l of chlorine to the pump discharge: (a) liquid chlorine from a 100-lb pressurized cylinder through a solution feed chlorinator; (b) sodium hypochlorite solution with 10% available chlorine (by weight) fed from a 200-gal storage tank by a diaphragm pump; (c) powdered calcium hypochlorite with 70% available chlorine in a 50-gal tank and fed by a diaphragm pump. Calculate the quantity of chlorine applied per 18-hr day. Calculate the number of days each system can feed chlorine before requiring renewal. Which system would you recommend for a cold climate? For a warm climate?

57 A groundwater treatment plant adds chlorine to oxidize iron and manganese for removal by filtration. The groundwater temperature during peak summer usage is 10°C and the pH is 7.8. Based on a tracer study, the t_{10} time from chlorine addition in the contact tank through filtration is 1.8 min. The t_{10} time in the clear well during peak pumpage is 8.0 min. The chlorine residual in the filter effluent is 0.8 mg/l and in the clear-well effluent is 0.4 mg/l. Is the disinfection adequate for 3.0-log inactivation of viruses?

58 What determines the occurrence and concentrations of different kinds of pathogens present in municipal wastewater? In general terms, to what degree are different kinds of pathogens removed in conventional wastewater treatment without effluent chlorination? With effluent chlorination?

59 A conventional activated-sludge treatment plant with effluent chlorination consistently produces a treated wastewater with a BOD less than 20 mg/l, suspended solids less than 30 mg/l, and fecal coliform count less than 200 organisms per 100 ml. The effluent has been described by the plant superintendent as clear "sparkling" water. You have been asked to evaluate the feasibility of using the effluent to irrigate the city's public park, which has playgrounds, and to apply to the state department of environmental control for permission to reuse the wastewater for this application. To introduce the idea and to allay the fears of an environmental citizens group, you have been asked to present a preliminary assessment of the situation to the city council. Outline the subjects that you would discuss in your presentation. (Refer to Sections 31 and 32).

60 What dosage of commercial fluosilicic acid is needed to increase the fluoride ion concentration from 0.3 to 1.0 mg/l? Use fluosilicic acid data from Table 16 and express the answers as mg/l and lb/mil gal.

61 A 4.0% sodium fluoride solution is applied to increase the fluoride concentration from 0.4 to 1.0 mg/l in a municipal water supply. (a) What is the application rate of NaF solution in gal/mil gal? (b) How many pounds of commercial-grade sodium fluoride are needed per million gallons?

62 What is the health risk of dietary intake of lead? Why are first-flush samples collected from consumers' faucets used to assess lead contamination of drinking water? What are recommended methods of controlling excessive lead concentrations?

63 List three possible methods for controlling crown corrosion in a large concrete sanitary sewer.

64 A distilled seawater contains 25 mg/l of sodium chloride. (Negligible amounts of magnesium, calcium, potassium, and sulfate are also present.) To stabilize this corrosive water, sufficient lime is applied to add 15 mg/l of calcium ion, and the hydroxide ion is converted to bicarbonate ion by applying carbon dioxide. (The equilibrium pH for stabilization is generally 8.5–8.7.) The desalinated stabilized water is transported to a blending plant where brackish groundwater is added prior to delivery to the water distribution system. The criterion for blending is a product water with not more than 250 mg/l chloride, 250 mg/l sulfate, or 100 mg/l of sodium. Based on the analysis of the groundwater listed below, what percentage of the blended water can be groundwater? Sketch milliequivalents-per-liter bar graphs for the distilled seawater, stabilized distilled water, and blended water.

$$Ca^{2+} = 220 \text{ mg/l} \quad Na^{1} = 580 \text{ mg/l} \quad SO_4^{2-} = 420 \text{ mg/l}$$
$$Mg^{2+} = 74 \text{ mg/l} \quad HCO_3^- = 210 \text{ mg/l} \quad Cl^- = 1030 \text{ mg/l}$$

65 Review Example 17. Evaluate the feasibility of operating this reverse-osmosis plant at a water recovery of 90%. (The $pK_2' - pK_s'$ value for a total dissolved-solids concentration above 10,000 mg/l can be assumed to remain essentially constant at 2.1.) If 90% recovery were to be performed, what process changes would be required?

66 The quality characteristics of a deep-well water in an arid region with a hot climate are

calcium hardness = 270 mg/l	pH = 8.1
magnesium hardness = 180 mg/l	alkalinity = 120 mg/l
sodium ion = 138 mg/l	sulfate ion = 110 mg/l
iron ion = 0.40 mg/l	chloride ion = 344 mg/l
manganese ion = 0.15 mg/l	fluoride ion = 1.4 mg/l
total dissolved solids = 830 mg/l	nitrate nitrogen = 15 mg/l
temperature = 27°	

(a) Is the water quality satisfactory for a municipal supply without treatment? Comment on any quality problems with respect to health and aesthetic standards.

(b) Propose a treatment scheme that will provide a water quality adequate to meet both health and aesthetic standards. Sketch a flow diagram showing the unit processes, chemical additions, and sources of wastes for disposal.

(c) Sketch an approximate bar graph of the treated water.

67 In Problem 35, lime–soda ash softening of the groundwater did not produce a treated water of drinking quality; filtrate a preliminary process flow diagram to treat this groundwater for potable use. On the flow diagram, show the chemicals being added and their points of application. Consider also the disposal of any process wastewaters.

68 What categories of chemicals are included in synthetic organic chemicals? In treatment of surface waters, how effective for removal of SOCs are conventional coagulation processes and the addition of powdered activated carbon for taste and odor control? What are the limitations in using aeration as a method for removal of VOCs from contaminated well water?

69 Determine depths of packing and surface areas between 4 m and 8 m for a countercurrent air-stripping tower to treat well water to reduce tetrachloroethylene from 100 μg/l to 2 μg/l, trichlorethylene from 25 to 2 μg/l, and *cis*-1,2-dichloroethylene from 70 to 2 μg/l. The design flow rate is 44 l/s, and the lowest temperature anticipated is 7°C, based on groundwater temperature and cooling in the tower. The following data are based on pilot-scale packed-column tests: (1) Henry's law constants for tetrachloroethylene, trichloroethylene, and *cis*-1,2,-dichloroethylene are 0.30, 0.21, and 0.094 at 7°C, respectively. (2) Assume the mass transfer coefficient for the most efficient and cost-effective commercial packing is 0.015 s^{-1} for all three compounds. (3) The optimum air-to-water ratio is 20:1.

70 A reverse-osmosis membrane has a k_w value of 2.5 × 10^{-4} $^{liters}/_{m^2 \cdot s \cdot bar}$ and an average k_s value of 3.5 × 10^{-4} $^{liters}/_{m^2 s}$ for TDS. Find the expected permeate TDS concentration of chloride if the feed concentration is 4500 mg/l and the system operates at a gauge pressure of 35 bar on the feed-concentrate side of the membrane. Assume that the permeate has negligible osmotic pressure and is at atmospheric pressure.

71 A low-pressure RO membrane system treating a brackish ground water is operating at 85% recovery. The rejection for both barium and sulfate is 90%. The feed water contains 0.05 mg/l of barium and 20 mg/l of sulfate, and the K_{sp} for $BaSO_4$ is 1 × 10^{-10}. Find the concentration of barium and sulfate in the concentrate and determine if the solubility of $BaSO_4$ is exceeded.

72 The following data were collected to establish an equilibrium isotherm for an SOC and a sample of activated carbon. The isotherm bottles contained 200 ml of water and the initial SOC concentration was 250 mg/l.

Mass of activated carbon (g)	0.25	0.12	0.075	0.050
Equilibrium SOC concentration (mg/l)	2	12	30	60

Find the Freundlich coefficients for the isotherm. Plot the Freundlich model and the data on the same set of axes to assess the fit of the calculated model. Find the carbon dose that would give an equilibrium SOC concentration of 50 mg/l.

73 Outlined below is the sequence of unit operations and chemical additions used in the treatment of a well water supply. Briefly state the function or purpose of each unit process and the reason for each chemical addition.

1. Mixing and flocculation with the addition of lime
2. Sedimentation
3. Recarbonation
4. Granular-media filtration
5. Postchlorination

74 Outlined below is the sequence of unit operations and chemical additions used in the treatment of a well water supply. Briefly state the function or purpose of each unit process and the reason for each chemical addition.

1. Prechlorination at the wells
2. Aeration over a tray aerator
3. Rechlorination
4. Detention in a settling basin
5. Granular-media filtration
6. Addition of anhydrous ammonia

75 Outlined below is the sequence of unit operations and chemical additions used in the treatment of a well water supply. Briefly state the function or purpose of each unit process and the reason for each chemical addition.

1. Prechlorination at the wells
2. Mixing–flocculation–sedimentation in flocculator–clarifiers using split treatment with lime and alum added to one leg and potassium permanganate to the other leg
3. Granular-media filtration
4. Postchlorination

76 Consider the following sequence of unit operations and chemical additions used in the treatment of a river water supply. Briefly state the function or purpose of each unit process and the reason for each chemical addition.

1. Presedimentation with polymer addition
2. Activated carbon available when needed
3. Mixing and flocculation with the addition of alum and polymer
4. Sedimentation
5. Addition of activated carbon
6. Granular-media filtration
7. Postchlorination

77 Outlined below is the sequence of unit operations and chemical additions used in the treatment of a reservoir water supply. Briefly state the function or purpose of each unit process and the reason for each chemical addition.

1. Intermittent applications of copper sulfate to the reservoir during summer and fall
2. Chlorine dioxide available when needed
3. Mixing and flocculation with the addition of alum and polymer
4. Sedimentation
5. Addition of activated carbon
6. Granular-media filtration
7. Postchlorination

78 Outlined below is the sequence of unit operations and chemical additions used in the treatment of a brackish groundwater. Briefly state the function or purpose of each unit process and the reason for each chemical addition.

1. Acidification with sulfuric acid
2. Addition of sodium hexametaphosphate
3. Cartridge filtration
4. High-pressure pumps
5. Reverse-osmosis modules
6. Degasification using stripping towers
7. Addition of sodium hydroxide
8. Addition of chlorine

REFERENCES

[1] *Standard Methods for the Examination of Water and Wastewater* (Washington, DC: Am. Public Health Assoc., 2005).

[2] O. Levenspiel, *Chemical Reaction Engineering* (New York: Wiley, 1972), 276.

[3] P. L. Bresonik, *Chemical Kinetics and Process Dynamics in Aquatic Systems* (Boca Raton, FL: CRC Press, 1994).

[4] W. J. Weber, Jr. and F. A. DiGiano, *Process Dynamics in Environmental Systems* (Wiley, 1996).

[5] H. E. Hudson, Jr., "Jar Testing and Utilization of Jar Test Data," *Water Clarification Processes Practical Design and Evaluation* (New York: Van Nostrand Reinhold, 1981), Chap. 3.

[6] *Enhanced Coagulation and Enhanced Precipitative Softening Guidance Manual,* EPA 815-R-99-012, (Washington, DC: Office of Drinking Water, U.S. Environmental Protection Agency, 1999).

[7] Committee Report, "Research Needs for the Treatment of Iron and Manganese," *J. Am. Water Works Assoc.* 79, no. 9 (1987): 119–122.

[8] *Alternative Disinfectants and Oxidants Guidance Manual,* EPA 815-R-99-014, (Washington, DC: Office of Drinking Water, U.S. Environmental Protection Agency, 1999).

[9] N. J. D. Graham, "Removal of Humic Substances by Oxidation/Biofiltration Processes – a Review," *Water Science and Technology*, 40, no. 9 (1999): 141–148.

[10] P. C. Singer, G. W. Harrington, G. A. Cowman, M. E. Smith, D. S. Schechter, and L. J. Harrington, *Impacts of Ozonation on the Formation of Chlorination and Chloramination By-products,* AWWA Research Foundation, Denver, CO (1999).

[11] *Ultraviolet Disinfection Guidance Manual for the Final Long Term 2 Enhanced Surface Water Treatment Rule*, EPA 815-R-07-007 (Washington, DC: Office of Drinking Water, U.S. Environmental Protection Agency, 2007).

[12] S. W. Krasner, M. J. McGuire, J. G. Jacangelo, N. L. Patania, K. M. Reagan, and E. M. Aieta, "The Occurrence of Disinfection By-Products in U.S. Drinking Water," *J. Am. Water Works Assoc.* 81, no. 8 (1989): 41–53.

[13] Z. Chen and R. Valentine, "Formation of N-Nitrosodimethylamine (NDMA) from Humic Substances in Natural Water," *Environmental Science and Technology,* 41, no. 17 (2007): 6059–6065.

[14] M. Edwards, "Predicting DOC Removal During Enhanced Coagulation," *J. Am. Water Works Assoc.* 89, no. 5 (1997): 78–89.

[15] "Treatment Techniques for the Control of DBP Precursors," *Code of Federal Regulations, Title 40, Part 141.135.*

[16] *LT1ESWTR Disinfection Profiling and Benchmarking Guidance Manual,* EPA 816-R-03-004 (Washington, DC: Office of Drinking Water, U.S. Environmental Protection Agency, 2003).

[17] *Guidance Manual for Compliance with the Filtration and Disinfection Requirements for Public Water Systems Using Surface Water Sources* (Washington, DC: Office of Drinking Water, U.S. Environmental Protection Agency, 1991).

[18] *Disinfection Profiling and Benchmarking Guidance Manual,* EPA 815-R-99-013 (Washington, DC: Office of Drinking Water, U.S. Environmental Protection Agency, 1999).

[19] Long Term 2 Enhanced Surface Water Treatment Rule, *Federal Register* 71, no. 3, (January 5, 2006): 782–783.

[20] Centers for Disease Control and Prevention, *Surveillance Summaries for Waterborne Disease Outbreaks*, U.S. Department of Health and Human Services.

[21] National Primary Drinking Water Regulations: Ground Water Rule, *Federal Register* 71, no. 216 (2006): 65573–65660.

[22] R. G. Feachem, D. J. Bradley, H. Garelick, and D. D. Mara, *Sanitation and Disease, Health Aspects of Excreta and Wastewater Management; World Bank Studies in Water Supply and Sanitation 3* (Chichester: Wiley, 1983).

[23] D. F. Striffler, W. O. Young, and B. A. Burt, "The Prevention and Control of Dental Caries: Fluoridation," in *Dentistry, Dental Practice, and the Community* (Philadelphia: Saunders, 1983), 155–199.

[24] J. R. Millette, A. F. Hammonds, M. F. Pansing, E. C. Hanson, and P. J. Clark, "Aggressive Water: Assessing the Extent of the Problem," *J. Am. Water Works Assoc.* 72, no. 5 (1980): 262–266.

[25] D. T. Merrill and R. L. Sanks, "Corrosion Control by Deposition of $CaCO_3$ Films," *J. Am. Water Works Assoc.* 69, no. 11 (1977): 592–599; 69, no. 12 (1977): 634–640; 70, no. 1 (1978): 12–18.

[26] L. S. McNeill and M. Edwards, "Iron Pipe Corrosion in Distribution Systems," *Am. Water Works Assoc.* 93, no. 7 (2001): 88–100.

[27] M. R. Schock, "Understanding Corrosion Control Strategies for Lead," *J. Am. Water Works Assoc.* 81, no. 7 (1989): 88–100.

[28] M. Edwards and L. S. McNeill, "Effects of Phosphate Inhibitors on Lead Release from Pipes," *J. Am. Water Works Assoc.* 94, no. 1 (2002): 79–90.

[29] R. G. Lee, W. C. Becker, and D. W. Collins, "Lead at the Tap: Sources and Control," *J. Am. Water Works Assoc.* 81, no. 7 (1989): 52–62.

[30] *Membrane Filtration Guidance Manual,* EPA 815-R-06-009, (Washington, DC: Office of Drinking Water, U.S. Environmental Protection Agency, 2006).

[31] W. A. Kelley and R. A. Olson, "Selecting MF to Satisfy Regulations," *J. Am. Water Works Assoc.* 91, no. 6 (1999): 52–63.

[32] A. Ko and D. B. Guy, "Brackish and Seawater Desalting," in *Reverse Osmosis Technology, Application for High-Purity-Water Production* (New York: Marcel Dekker, 1988), 185–277.

[33] H. F. Ridgway, Jr., "Microbial Adhesion and Biofouling of Reverse Osmosis Membranes," in *Reverse Osmosis Technology, Application for High-Purity-Water Production* (New York: Marcel Dekker, 1988), 429–481.

[34] Degremont, *Water Treatment Handbook*, 5th ed. (New York: Halsted Press, 1979), 878.

[35] P. L. Lamarche and R. L. Droste, "Air-Stripping Mass Transfer Correlation for Volatile Organics," *J. Am. Water Works Assoc.* 81, no. 1 (1989): 78–89.

[36] J. A. MacKenzie, M. Tennant, and D. Mazyck, "Tailored Granular Activated Carbon for the Control of 2-Methlyisoborneol," *J. Am. Water Works Assoc.* 97, no. 6 (2005): 76–87.

[37] *Handbook of Public Water Systems*, 2nd ed., "Activated Carbon Treatment," (New York: John Wiley & Sons, Inc., for HDR Engineering, Inc., 2001).

[38] A. Porteous, *Saline Water Distillation Processes* (London: Longman, 1975).

Biological Treatment Processes

Biological Treatment Processes

BIOLOGICAL CONSIDERATIONS

Biological treatment systems are "living" systems that rely on mixed biological cultures to break down waste organics and remove organic matter from solution. Domestic wastewater supplies the biological food, growth nutrients, and inoculum. A treatment unit provides a controlled environment for the desired biological process. Historically, civil engineers designed treatment systems on the basis of empirical rules. This practice has led to failures in sanitary design—not unsuccessful in the sense of collapse of a structure, but deficient in that the biological process did not function properly. Understanding the biological processes involved in wastewater treatment is essential to a design engineer.

1 BACTERIA AND FUNGI

Bacteria (singular, bacterium) are the simplest forms of plant life that use soluble food and are capable of self-reproduction. Bacteria are fundamental microorganisms in the stabilization of organic wastes and therefore are of basic importance in biological treatment. Individual bacterial cells range in size from approximately 0.5 to 5 μm, are shaped like rods, spheres, or spirals; and occur in a variety of forms, including individual, pairs, packets, and chains.

Bacteria reproduce by binary fission (the mature cell divides into two new cells). In most species, the process of reproduction—growth, maturation, and fission—occurs in 20–30 min under ideal environmental conditions. Certain bacterial species form spores as a means of survival under adverse environmental conditions. Their tough coating is resistant to heat, lack of moisture, and loss of food supply. Fortunately, only one spore-forming bacterium, *Bacillus anthracis*,* is pathogenic to humans. As the result of stringent public health measures, incidents of anthrax in humans are rare.

---

*Bacteria, like all other species, are named using a binominal system; that is, each species is given a name consisting of two words. The first word is the genus and the second is the name of the species.

Based on nutritive requirements, bacteria are classified as heterotrophic or autotrophic bacteria, although several species may function both heterotrophically and autotrophically.

Heterotrophic bacteria use organic compounds as an energy and carbon source for synthesis. Another term used instead of heterotroph is *saprophyte*, which refers to an organism that lives on dead or decaying organic matter. The heterotrophic bacteria are grouped into three classifications, depending on their action toward free oxygen. *Aerobes* require free dissolved oxygen to live and multiply. *Anaerobes* oxidize organic matter in the complete absence of dissolved oxygen. *Facultative bacteria* are a class of bacteria that use free dissolved oxygen when available but can also respire and multiply in its absence. *Escherichia coli*, a fecal coliform, is a facultative bacterium.

Autotrophic bacteria use carbon dioxide as a carbon source and oxidize inorganic compounds for energy. Autotrophs of greatest significance in sanitary engineering are the nitrifying, sulfur, and iron bacteria. Nitrifying bacteria perform the following reactions:

$$\text{NH}_3 \text{ (ammonia)} + \text{oxygen} \xrightarrow{\textit{Nitrosomonas}} \text{NO}_2^- \text{ (nitrite)} + \text{energy} \qquad (1)$$

$$\text{NO}_2^- \text{ (nitrite)} + \text{oxygen} \xrightarrow{\textit{Nitrobacter}} \text{NO}_3^- \text{ (nitrate)} + \text{energy} \qquad (2)$$

Autotrophic sulfur bacteria, *Thiobacillus*, convert hydrogen sulfide to sulfuric acid [Eq. (3)]. This bacterial production of sulfuric acid occurs in the moisture of condensation on side walls and crowns of sewers conveying septic wastewater. Since thiobacilli can tolerate pH levels less than 1.0, sanitary sewers constructed on flat grades in warm climates should be built using corrosion-resistant materials.

$$\text{H}_2\text{S (hydrogen sulfide)} + \text{oxygen} \rightarrow \text{H}_2\text{SO}_4 + \text{energy} \qquad (3)$$

True iron bacteria are autotrophs that oxidize inorganic ferrous iron as a source of energy. These filamentous bacteria occur in iron-bearing waters and deposit the oxidized iron, Fe(OH)_3, in their sheaths [Eq. (4)]. Not all species of the iron bacteria *Leptothrix* and *Crenothrix* may be strictly autotrophic; however, they are truly iron-accumulating bacteria and thrive in water pipes conveying water containing dissolved iron, where they form yellow- or reddish-colored slimes. When mature bacteria die, they may decompose, imparting foul tastes and odors to water.

$$\text{Fe}^{2+} \text{ (ferrous)} + \text{oxygen} \rightarrow \text{Fe}^{3+} \text{ (ferric)} + \text{energy} \qquad (4)$$

Fungi (singular, fungus) is a common term used to refer to microscopic nonphotosynthetic plants, including yeasts and molds. The most important group of yeasts for industrial fermentations is the genus *Saccharomyces*. *Saccharomyces cerevisiae* is the common yeast used by bakers, distillers, and brewers. *Saccharomyces cerevisiae* is single celled, is commonly 5–10 μm in size, and reproduces by budding, in which large, mature cells divide, each producing one or more daughter cells. Under anaerobic conditions, this yeast produces alcohol as an end product. *Saccharomyces cerevisiae* is facultative and performs the following reactions:

$$\textit{Anaerobic:} \quad \text{Sugar} \rightarrow \text{alcohol} + \text{CO}_2 + \text{energy} \qquad (5)$$

$$\textit{Aerobic:} \quad \text{Sugar} + \text{oxygen} \rightarrow \text{CO}_2 + \text{energy} \qquad (6)$$

Energy yield in the aerobic reaction is much greater than in the anaerobic fermentation.

Molds are saprophytic or parasitic filamentous fungi that resemble higher plants in structure, composed of branched, filamentous, threadlike growths called hyphae. Molds are nonphotosynthetic, multicellular, heterotrophic, and aerobic; reproduce by spore formation; and grow best in low-pH solutions (pH 2–5) high in sugar content. Molds are undesirable growths in activated sludge and can appear under low-pH conditions. The operation of an activated-sludge wastewater treatment system relies on gravity separation of microorganisms from the wastewater effluent. A large growth of molds creates a filamentous activated sludge that does not settle easily.

2   ALGAE

Algae (singular, alga) are microscopic photosynthetic plants. The process of photosynthesis is illustrated by the equation

$$CO_2 + 2H_2O \underset{\text{dark reaction}}{\overset{\text{sunlight}}{\rightleftharpoons}} \text{new cell tissue} + O_2 + H_2O \qquad (7)$$

The overall effect of this reaction is to produce new plant life, thereby increasing the number of algae. By-product oxygen results from the biochemical conversion of water.

Algae are autotrophic, using carbon dioxide (or bicarbonates in solution) as a carbon source. The nutrients phosphorus (as phosphate) and nitrogen (as ammonia, nitrite, or nitrate) are necessary for growth. Certain species of blue-green algae are able to fix atmospheric nitrogen. In addition, algae need certain trace nutrients, such as magnesium, sulfur, boron, cobalt, molybdenum, calcium, potassium, iron, manganese, zinc, and copper. In natural waters, the nutrients most frequently limiting algal growth are inorganic phosphorus and nitrogen.

Energy for photosynthesis is derived from sunlight. Photosynthetic pigments biochemically convert energy in the sun's rays to useful energy for plant synthesis. The most common pigment is chlorophyll, which is green in color. Other pigments or combinations of pigments result in algae of a variety of colors, such as blue-green, yellowish green, brown, and red. In the prolonged absence of sunlight, the algae perform a dark reaction—for practical purposes the reverse of synthesis. In the dark reaction, the algae degrade stored food or their own protoplasm for energy to perform essential biochemical reactions for survival. The rate of this endogenous reaction is significantly slower than the photosynthetic reaction.

Algae grow in abundance in stabilization ponds rich in inorganic nutrients and carbon dioxide released from bacterial decomposition of waste organics. Green algae *Chlorella* are commonly found in oxidation ponds. Certain genera of algae are identified with clean water, such as *Navicula*. Descriptions and pictorial representations of algae occurring in water and wastewater are given in *Standard Methods for the Examination of Water and Wastewater* [1].

---

3 PROTOZOANS AND HIGHER ANIMALS

Protozoans are single-celled animals that reproduce by binary fission. The protozoans of significance in biological treatment systems are strict aerobes found in activated sludge, trickling filters, and oxidation ponds. These microscopic animals have complex digestive systems and use solid organic matter as an energy and carbon source. Protozoans are a vital link in the aquatic chain because they ingest bacteria and algae.

Protozoans with cilia may be categorized as free swimming and stalked. Free-swimming forms move rapidly in the water, ingesting organic matter at a very high rate. The stalked forms attach by a stalk to particles of matter and use cilia to propel their heads about and bring in food. Another group of protozoans move by flagella. Long hairlike strands (flagella) move with a whiplike action, providing motility. *Amoeba* move and ingest food through the action of a mobile protoplasm.

Rotifers are the simplest multicelled animals. They are strict aerobes and metabolize solid food. A typical rotifer uses the cilia around its head for catching food. The name *rotifer* is derived from the apparent rotating motion of the cilia on its head. Rotifers are indicators of relatively clean water and are regularly found in streams and lakes.

Crustaceans are multicellular animals with branched swimming feet or a shell-like covering, with a variety of appendages (antennae). The two most common crustaceans of interest are *Daphnia* and *Cyclops*. Crustaceans are strict aerobes and ingest microscopic plants. The zooplankton population in a lake includes a wide selection of crustaceans that serve as food for fishes.

4 METABOLISM, ENERGY, AND SYNTHESIS

Metabolism (catabolism) is the biochemical process (a series of biochemical oxidation–reduction reactions) performed by living organisms to yield energy for synthesis, motility, and respiration to remain viable. In standard usage, metabolism implies both catabolism and anabolism—that is, both degradation and assimilative reactions.

The metabolism of autotrophic bacteria is illustrated in Eqs. (1) through (4). In these reactions, the reduced inorganic compounds are oxidized, yielding energy for synthesis of carbon from carbon dioxide, producing organic cell tissue. [In the case of algae, Eq. (7), the carbon source is carbon dioxide, but the energy is from sunlight.]

In heterotrophic metabolism, organic matter is the substrate (food) used as an energy source. However, the majority of organic matter in wastewater is in the form of large molecules that cannot penetrate the bacterial cell membrane. The bacteria, in order to metabolize high-molecular-weight substances, must be capable of hydrolyzing the large molecules into diffusible fractions for assimilation into their cells. Therefore, the first biochemical reactions are hydrolysis* of complex carbohydrates into soluble sugar units, protein into amino acids, and insoluble fats into fatty acids. Under aerobic conditions, the reduced soluble organic compounds are oxidized to end-products of

---

*Hydrolysis is the addition of water to split a bond between chemical units.

carbon dioxide and water [Eq. (8)]. Under anaerobic conditions, soluble organics are decomposed to intermediate end-products, such as organic acids and alcohols, while carbon dioxide and water are by-products [Eq. (9)]. Many intermediates, such as butyric acid, mercaptans (organic compounds with —SH radicals), and hydrogen sulfide, have foul odors.

Under anaerobic conditions, if excess organic acids are produced, the pH of the solution will drop sufficiently to "pickle" the fermentation process. This is the principle used for preservation of silage. Bacteria produce an overabundance of organic acids in the anaerobic decomposition of the green fodder stored in the silo, inhibit further bacterial decomposition, and preserve the food value of the fodder. However, if proper environmental conditions exist to prevent excess acidity from the production of organic acid intermediates, populations of acid-splitting, methane-forming bacteria will develop and use the organic acids as substrate [Eq. (10)]. The combined biological processes of anaerobic decomposition of raw organic matter to soluble organic intermediates and the gasification of the intermediates to carbon dioxide and methane are referred to as digestion.

$$Aerobic: \quad \text{Organics} + \text{oxygen} \rightarrow CO_2 + H_2O + \text{energy} \tag{8}$$

$$Anaerobic: \quad \text{Organics} \rightarrow \text{intermediates} + CO_2 + H_2O + \text{energy} \tag{9}$$

$$\text{Organic acid intermediates} \rightarrow CH_4 + CO_2 + \text{energy} \tag{10}$$

The growth and survival of nonphotosynthetic microorganisms are dependent on their ability to obtain energy from the metabolism of substrate. Biochemical metabolic processes of heterotrophs are energy-yielding, oxidation–reduction reactions in which reduced organic compounds serve as hydrogen donors and oxidized organic or inorganic compounds act as hydrogen acceptors. *Oxidation* is the addition of oxygen, removal of hydrogen, or removal of electrons. *Reduction* is the removal of oxygen, addition of hydrogen, or addition of electrons.

The simplified diagram of substrate dehydrogenation shown in Figure 1 is intended to illustrate the general relationship between energy yields of aerobic and anaerobic metabolism. Enzymatic processes of hydrogen transfer and methods of biologically conserving energy released are beyond the scope of this discussion. For students to understand fully the mechanisms illustrated in Figure 1, a knowledge of the biochemistry of microorganisms is necessary [2].

Energy stored in organic matter (AH_2) is released in the process of biological oxidation by dehydrogenation of substrate followed by transfer of hydrogen, or electrons, to an ultimate acceptor. The higher the ultimate hydrogen acceptor is on the energy (electromotive) scale, the greater will be the energy yield from oxidation of 1 mole of a given substrate. Aerobic metabolism using oxygen as the ultimate hydrogen acceptor yields the greatest amount of energy. Aerobic respiration can be traced in Figure 1 from reduced organic matter (AH_2) at the bottom, through the hydrogen and electron carriers, to oxygen. Facultative respiration, using oxygen bound in nitrates and sulfates, yields less energy than aerobic metabolism. The least energy yield results from strict anaerobic respiration, where the oxidation of AH_2 is coupled with reduction of B (an oxidized organic compound) to BH_2 (a reduced organic compound). The

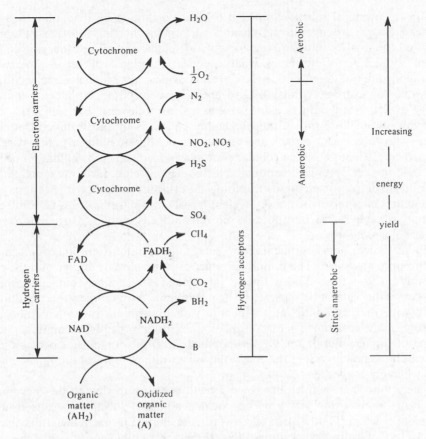

FIGURE 1   General scheme of substrate dehydrogenation for energy yield.
(FAD: flavin adenine dinucleotide; NAD: nicotinamide adenine dinucleotide.)

preferential use of hydrogen acceptors based on energy yield in a mixed bacterial culture is illustrated by the following equations:

$$Aerobic \quad AH_2 + O_2 \rightarrow CO_2 + H_2O + energy \quad (11)$$

$$AH_2 + NO_3^- \rightarrow N_2 + H_2O + \quad (12)$$

$$(Facultative) \; AH_2 + SO_4^{2-} \rightarrow H_2S + H_2O + \quad (13)$$

$$AH_2 + CO_2 \rightarrow CH_4 + H_2O + \quad (14)$$

$$Anaerobic \quad AH_2 + B \rightarrow BH_2 + A + energy \quad (15)$$

Decreasing energy yield

Hydrogen acceptors are used in the sequence of dissolved oxygen first, followed by nitrates, sulfates, and oxidized organic compounds, in this general order. Thus hydrogen sulfide odor formation follows nitrate reduction and precedes methane formation.

The biochemical reactions in Figure 1 are performed by oxidation–reduction enzymes. Enzymes are organic catalysts that perform biochemical reactions at temperatures and chemical conditions compatible with biological life. The coenzyme component of the enzyme determines what chemical reaction will occur. Coenzymes nicotinamide adenine dinucleotide (NAD) and flavin adenine dinucleotide (FAD) are responsible for hydrogen transfer. Cytochromes are respiratory pigments that can undergo oxidation and reduction and serve as hydrogen carriers.

Synthesis (anabolism) is the biochemical process of substrate utilization to form new protoplasm for growth and reproduction. Microorganisms process organic matter to create new cells. The cellular protoplasm formed is a combination of hundreds of complex organic compounds, including proteins, carbohydrates, nucleic acids, and lipids. Major elements in biological cells are carbon, hydrogen, oxygen, nitrogen, and phosphorus. On a dry-weight basis, protoplasm is 10%–12% nitrogen and approximately 2.5% phosphorus; the remainder is carbon, hydrogen, oxygen, and trace elements.

Relationships between metabolism, energy, and synthesis are important in biological treatment systems. The primary product of metabolism is energy, and the chief use of this energy is for synthesis. Energy release and synthesis are coupled biochemical processes that cannot be separated. The maximum rate of synthesis occurs simultaneously with the maximum rate of energy yield (maximum rate of metabolism). Therefore, in heterotrophic metabolism of wastewater organics, maximum rate of removal of organic matter for a given population of microorganisms occurs during maximum biological growth. Conversely, the lowest rate of removal of organic matter occurs when growth ceases.

The major limitation of anaerobic growth is energy, owing to the fact that in anaerobic decomposition a low energy yield per unit of substrate results from an incomplete reaction (Figure 2). In other words, the limiting factor in anaerobic metabolism is a lack of hydrogen acceptors. When the supply of biologically available energy is exhausted, the processes of metabolism and synthesis cease.

Aerobic metabolism is the antithesis of anaerobiosis, biologically available carbon being the limiting factor (Figure 3). Abundance of oxygen creates no shortage of hydrogen acceptors. But the supply of substrate carbon is rapidly exhausted through respiration of carbon dioxide and synthesis into new cells.

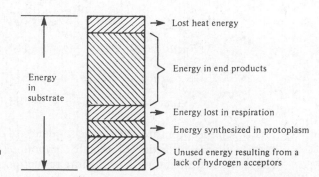

FIGURE 2   Energy conversions in anaerobic metabolism.

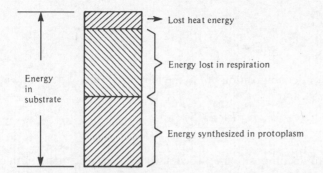

FIGURE 3 Energy conversions in aerobic metabolism.

The energy conversion diagrams shown schematically in Figures 2 and 3 illustrate the major features of anaerobic and aerobic metabolism. An anaerobic process has the following characteristics: incomplete metabolism, small quantity of biological growth, and production of high-energy products such as acetic acid and methane. An aerobic process results in complete metabolism and synthesis of the substrate, ending in a large quantity of biological growth.

5 ENZYME KINETICS

The reaction between an enzyme E and substrate S is postulated to be

$$E + S \underset{k_2}{\overset{k_1}{\rightleftharpoons}} ES \overset{k_3}{\rightarrow} E + \text{products} \tag{16}$$

In the first step, E combines with S to form ES by a reversible reaction where k_1 is the rate constant for formation of ES, and k_2 is the rate constant for dissociation of ES to E and S. After these combine to form ES, S is converted to products in the second step and E is released for combination with more S. The rate of conversion of ES to products is represented by k_3. An enzyme-catalyzed reaction can be experimentally performed by placing a small quantity of an enzyme in a substrate solution and measuring the decomposition of substrate with time. For example, sucrose is split into its two separate sugar rings of glucose and fructose by the enzyme *invertase* that performs this hydrolysis. The reaction in the form of Eq. (16) is written

Sucrose + *invertase* $\rightleftharpoons$ sucrose-*invertase*
$\rightarrow$ glucose + fructose + *invertase*

The first satisfactory mathematical analysis of the effect of substrate concentration on the rate of enzyme-catalyzed reactions was made in 1913 by Michaelis and Menten [3]. The derivation of their equation is based on Eq. (17), that is, the rate of decomposition of substrate is proportional to the concentration of the intermediate enzyme–substrate complex. For the reversible reaction $E + S \rightleftharpoons ES$, the dissociation constant of ES, defined as K_m, can be written as

$$K_m = \frac{(E - ES)S}{ES} \tag{17}$$

Rearranging the equation,

$$(ES) = \frac{(E)(S)}{K_m + S} \tag{18}$$

with k_3 the rate constant for decomposition of ES, the measured rate of decomposition of substrate r equals k_3 (ES), and

$$r = \frac{k_3(E)(S)}{K_m + S} \tag{19}$$

The maximum rate of decomposition r_m occurs when ES is at its maximum concentration—that is, when all of the enzyme is combined with substrate and ES = E. Therefore,

$$r_m = k_3(ES) = k_3(E) \tag{20}$$

Substituting r_m for $k_3(E)$ in Eq. (19) produces the Michaelis–Menten equation:

$$r = r_m\left(\frac{S}{K_m + S}\right) \tag{21}$$

or

$$K_m = S\left(\frac{r_m}{r} - 1\right) \tag{22}$$

Since K_m and r_m are constants, Eq. (21) is a rectangular hyperbola, as shown in Figure 4. Data from enzyme-catalyzed experiments by Michaelis and Menten are graphed to form this diphasic curve. From Eq. (22), when $r_m/r = 2$, the measured rate r is half the value of the limiting rate r_m and $K_m = S$. Therefore, the substrate concentration for attaining the half-maximum reaction rate is a characteristic constant K_m of an enzyme-catalyzed reaction, which is termed the *saturation constant*.

The substrate saturation phenomenon is a unique characteristic of enzymatic reactions and is the mathematical basis of kinetics in microbiology. For further explanation of this process, consider a batch experiment starting with a large amount of substrate relative to the concentration of enzyme. From Eq. (21), for a large S, K_m can be neglected and $r = r_m$. This can also be seen in Figure 4. The magnitude of r_m depends

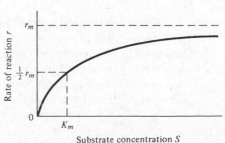

FIGURE 4   Theoretical curve of reaction rate versus substrate concentration for an enzyme-catalyzed reaction [Eq. (21)].

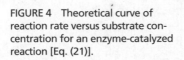

on the maximum rate at which the enzyme present can decompose the substrate. The rate is zero order; that is, the reaction proceeds at a rate independent of the concentration of substrate. As the quantity of substrate decreases, the concentration of enzyme remaining constant, the rate of reaction becomes increasingly dependent on the remaining substrate concentration. The rate at $\frac{1}{2}r_m$ corresponds to a substrate concentration equal to the saturation constant K_m. Below this substrate concentration, some of the enzyme molecules are not combined with substrate, resulting in a first-order reaction, which proceeds at a rate directly proportional to the substrate concentration. When S is much smaller than K_m, S can be neglected in Eq. (21) and $r = r_m S/K_m$.

6   GROWTH KINETICS OF PURE BACTERIAL CULTURES

A pure culture can be grown in a laboratory reactor by inoculating a sterile liquid medium with a small number of viable bacteria of a single species. The characteristic growth pattern for bacteria in such a batch culture is sketched in Figure 5. After a short lag period for adaptation to the new environment, the bacteria reproduce by binary fission, exponentially increasing the number of viable cells and biomass in the culture medium. The existence of excess substrate promotes this maximum rate of growth. The rate of metabolism in the *exponential growth phase* is limited only by the microorganisms' ability to process the substrate. With X representing the concentration of biomass and μ a proportionality constant, the biomass growth rate can be expressed as

$$\left(\frac{dX}{dt}\right)_g = \mu X \tag{23}$$

Dividing both sides of Eq. (23) by X yields

$$\mu = \frac{(dX/dt)_g}{X} \tag{24}$$

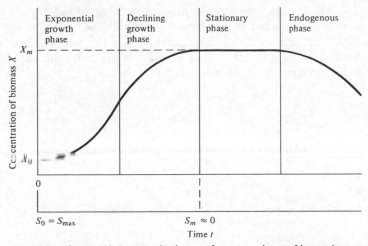

FIGURE 5   Characteristic growth phases of a pure culture of bacteria.

where

$$\mu = \text{specific growth rate (rate of growth per unit of biomass), time}^{-1}$$
$$(dX/dt)_g = \text{biomass growth rate, mass/unit volume} \cdot \text{time}$$
$$X = \text{concentration of biomass, mass/unit volume}$$

The *declining growth phase* is caused by an increasing shortage of substrate. The rate of reproduction decreases until the number of viable bacteria is stationary, which occurs when the rate of reproduction is equal to the rate of death. The total biomass exceeds the mass of viable cells since many of the microorganisms stopped reproducing owing to substrate-limiting conditions. Monod [4] studied the growth of bacteria in batch cultures in the laboratory. He found that growth was a function of both the concentration of microorganisms and the concentration of the growth-limiting substrate. The mathematical relationship proposed by Monod between the residual concentration of the growth-limiting substrate and the specific growth rate of biomass is the hyperbolic equation

$$\mu = \mu_m \left(\frac{S}{K_s + S} \right) \tag{25}$$

where

$$\mu = \text{specific growth rate, time}^{-1}$$
$$\mu_m = \text{maximum specific growth rate (at a concentration of the growth-limiting substrate at or above saturation), time}^{-1}$$
$$S = \text{concentration of growth-limiting substrate in solution, mass/unit volume}$$
$$K_s = \text{saturation constant (equal to the limiting substrate concentration at half the maximum growth rate), mass/unit volume}$$

As shown in Figure 6, Eq. (25) is similar in form to the Michaelis–Menten equation for enzyme-catalyzed reactions [Eq. (21) and Figure 4]. The constant K_s, similar in function to K_m in Eq. (22), is equal to the concentration of substrate S when the specific growth rate μ equals half the maximum growth rate μ_m.

The specific growth-rate relationship in Eq. (25) can be substituted for the proportionality constant in Eq. (23). The result is the following expression for biomass growth rate in a substrate-limiting solution:

$$\left(\frac{dX}{dt} \right)_g = \frac{\mu_m X S}{K_s + S} \tag{26}$$

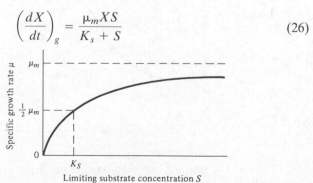

FIGURE 6   Specific growth rate versus substrate concentration for the exponential and declining growth phases of a bacterial culture.

where

$(dX/dt)_g$ = biomass growth rate, mass/unit volume · time
μ_m = maximum specific growth rate, time^{-1}
X = concentration of biomass, mass/unit volume
S = concentration of growth|hyphen|limiting substrate, mass/unit volume
K_s = saturation constant, mass/unit volume

The *growth yield Y* is defined as the incremental increase in biomass resulting from metabolism of an incremental amount of substrate [5]. The growth yield in a batch culture (Figure 5) is the biomass increase during the exponential and declining growth phases $(X_m - X_0)$ relative to the substrate used $(S_0 - S_m)$. Since growth is limited by depletion of the substrate, S_m is assumed to be zero. Therefore,

$$X_m - X_0 = YS_0 \tag{27}$$

If a series of batch cultures are grown starting with different initial substrate concentrations, a plot of X_m values versus their respective S_0 values is a straight line with slope Y (Figure 7). For bacterial cultures, when conditions are maintained constant, the growth yield is a constant reproducible value [4].

Growth yield can also be expressed in derivative form as

$$\left(\frac{dX}{dt}\right)_g = Y\left(\frac{dS}{dt}\right)_u \tag{28}$$

Substituting this into Eq. (26) results in an equation that defines the rate of substrate utilization in a solution in which the biomass growth rate is limited by the low concentration of substrate:

$$\left(\frac{dS}{dt}\right)_u = \frac{\mu_m X S}{Y(K_s + S)} \tag{29}$$

where

$(dS/dt)_u$ = substrate utilization rate, time^{-1}
μ_m = maximum specific growth rate, time^{-1}
X = concentration of biomass, mass/unit volume

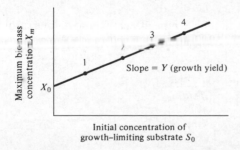

FIGURE 7   Growth yield for a series of four batch cultures (Figure 5) is determined by plotting X_m versus S_0.

S = concentration of growth-limiting substrate, mass/unit volume
Y = growth yield, mass/mass
K_s = saturation constant, mass/unit volume

In the *endogenous growth phase* (Figure 5), viable bacteria are competing for the small amount of substrate still in solution. The rate of metabolism is decreasing at an increasing rate, resulting in a rapid decrease in the number of viable cells. Starvation is evident when the rate of death exceeds the rate of reproduction. The total biomass decreases as cells utilize their own protoplasm as an energy source. Cells become old, die, and lyse, releasing nutrients back into solution. The action of cell lysis decreases both the number and mass of microorganisms.

The rate of biomass decrease during endogenous respiration is proportional to the biomass present. Thus,

$$\left(\frac{dX}{dt}\right)_d = -k_d X \tag{30}$$

where

$(dX/dt)_d$ = biomass decay rate, mass/unit volume · time
k_d = microbial decay coefficient, time^{-1}
X = concentration of biomass, mass/unit volume

To determine *net biomass growth rate* during the endogenous growth phase, Eq. (30) is combined with Eq. (26) and Eq. (28), resulting in the following equations:

$$\left(\frac{dX}{dt}\right)_g^{net} = \frac{\mu_m X S}{K_s + S} - k_d X \tag{31}$$

$$\left(\frac{dX}{dt}\right)_g^{net} = Y\left(\frac{dS}{dt}\right)_u - k_d X \tag{32}$$

The Monod relationship [Eq. (25)] modified to yield *net specific growth rate* is

$$\mu_{net} = \mu_m \frac{S}{K_s + S} - k_d \tag{33}$$

and the observed growth yield Y_{obs} accounting for the effect of endogenous respiration on the net biomass growth rate from the relationship in Eq. (28) is

$$Y_{obs} = \frac{(dX/dt)_g^{net}}{(dS/dt)_u} \tag{34}$$

7   BIOLOGICAL GROWTH IN WASTEWATER TREATMENT

Both fixed-film growth and suspended-solids growth systems are used in biological treatment of wastewater. In a fixed-growth process, organic matter is removed from wastewater as it flows over a biological film (slime layer) attached to a filter medium. Trickling filters use a variety of media, including stones, crushed rock, small plastic cylinders, and plastic vertical-sheet packing. A rotating biological contactor consists of a series of large-diameter plastic disks that slowly rotate in tanks conveying waste-water flow. In a suspended-growth process, active biological solids are mixed with the wastewater and held in suspension by aeration as the organic matter is taken out of solution by the microbial floc. The common name for this suspended-growth process is activated sludge.

Wastewater treatment relies on a mixed biological culture consisting of a variety of bacteria and protozoans. Microorganisms in the raw wastewater provide continuous inocula for the treatment process. The heterogeneous substrate content of a waste-water is expressed either as BOD or COD. The purpose of the treatment unit is to hold the biological culture in a controlled environment to promote growth of the microor-ganisms for extraction of colloidal and dissolved organics from solution.

The batch-culture growth pattern shown in Figure 5 is not directly applicable to biological treatment processes that are continuous-flow systems. For example, an acti-vated-sludge system is fed continuously, and excess microorganisms are withdrawn, either continuously or intermittently, to maintain the desired mass of microorganisms for metabolizing incoming organic wastes. A schematic diagram (Figure 8) illustrates the flow pattern for organic matter and microorganisms in an activated-sludge system. Influent wastewater is aerated with a mixed culture of microorganisms for a sufficient period of time to permit synthesis of the waste organics into biological cells. The microorganisms are then settled out of solution, removed from the bottom of the set-tling tank, and returned to the aeration tank to metabolize additional waste organics. Unused organic matter and nonsettleable microorganisms pass out in the system efflu-ent. Metabolism of the organic matter results in an increased mass of microorganisms in the system. Excess microorganisms are removed (wasted) from the system to

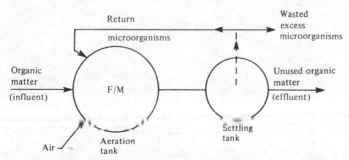

FIGURE 8   Schematic diagram of a continuous-flow activated-sludge process. (F/M: food/microorganism ratio.)

maintain proper balance between food supply and mass of microorganisms in the aeration tank. This balance is referred to as the *food-to-microorganism ratio* (F/M).

The F/M ratio maintained in the aeration tank defines the operation of an activated-sludge system. At a high F/M ratio, microorganisms are in the exponential growth phase, characterized by excess food and maximum rate of metabolism (Figure 9). Although the exponential growth phase is desirable for maximum rate of organic matter removal, distinct disadvantages make it undesirable for operation of an activated-sludge system. The microorganisms are in dispersed growth such that they do not settle out of solution by gravity. Consequently, the settling tank is not effective in separating microorganisms from the effluent for return to the aeration tank. Second, there is excess unused organic matter in solution that cannot be removed by sedimentation and passes out in the effluent. Operation at a high F/M ratio results in poor BOD removal efficiency.

At a low F/M ratio, overall metabolic activity in the aeration tank may be considered endogenous. Although initially there is rapid growth when the influent food and return microorganisms are mixed, competition for the small amount of food made available to the large mass of microorganisms results in near-starvation conditions for the majority of microorganisms within a short period of time. Under these conditions, continued aeration results in autooxidation of the microbial mass through cell lysis and resynthesis and also through the predator–prey activity where bacteria are consumed by the protozoans. Although the rate of metabolism is relatively low in the endogenous phase, metabolism of the organics is nearly complete and the microorganisms flocculate rapidly and settle out of solution by gravity. The good settling characteristics exhibited by activated sludge in the endogenous phase make operation in this growth period desirable where a high BOD removal efficiency is desired. Figure 9 summarizes the previous discussion and shows the range of operation for most activated-sludge treatment systems to be between the declining growth phase and the endogenous phase.

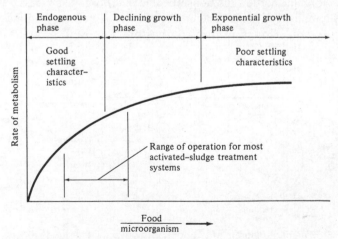

FIGURE 9   Rate of metabolism versus increasing food/microorganism ratio.

8   FACTORS AFFECTING GROWTH

Several factors affect the growth of microorganisms. The most important are temperature, pH, availability of nutrients, oxygen supply, presence of toxins, types of substrate, and, in the case of photosynthetic plants, sunlight. Growth with respect to both aerobic and anaerobic conditions and to the need for essential nutrients was discussed in Section 4.

   Bacteria are classified as psychrophilic, mesophilic, or thermophilic, depending on their optimum temperature range for growth. Of least significance to sanitary engineers are the *psychrophilic* (cold-loving) bacteria, which grow best at temperatures slightly above freezing (4°–10°C).

   Thermophilic (heat-loving) bacteria like an optimum temperature range of 50°–55°C. They are significant in sludge composting and attempts have been made to use a thermophilic temperature range for the anaerobic digestion of waste sludge. Thermophilic digestion has usually not been successful in practice because thermophilic bacteria are sensitive to small temperature changes, and it is difficult to maintain the required high operating temperature in a digestion tank.

   Mesophilic (moderation-loving) bacteria grow best in the temperature range 20°–40°C. The vast majority of biological treatment systems operate in the mesophilic temperature range. Anaerobic digestion tanks are normally heated to near the optimum level of 35°C (95°F). Aeration tanks and trickling filters operate at the temperature of the wastewater as modified by that of the air. Generally, this is in the range of 10°–20°C (50°–68°F) within outer maximums at a low of 5°C (41°F) and a high of 25°C (77°F). Higher wastewater temperature increases biological activity in the treatment process and can cause operating problems. At high temperatures, odor problems may be more pronounced at a wastewater plant.

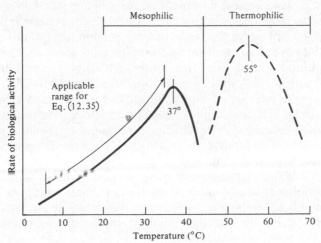

FIGURE 10   General effect of temperature on biological activity.

The rate of biological activity in the mesophilic range between 5° and 35°C doubles for every 10°–15°C temperature rise (Figure 10). The common mathematical expression for relating the change in the reaction-rate constant with temperature is

$$K = K_{20}\Theta^{T-20} \tag{35}$$

where

K = reaction-rate constant at temperature T
K_{20} = reaction-rate constant at 20°C
Θ = temperature coefficient
T = temperature of biological reaction, °C

The value of Θ is 1.072 if the rate of biological activity doubles with a 10°C temperature rise; the value of Θ is 1.047 if the rate doubles in 15°C. Above 40°C, mesophilic bacterial metabolism drops off sharply and thermophilic growth starts. Thermophilic bacteria have a range of approximately 45°–75°C, with an optimum near 55°C.

Cold wastewater can reduce BOD removal efficiency of biological processes. The efficiency of trickling filters is definitely decreased during cold weather and increased during warm periods. Trickling filters operating at 5°–10°C have poor BOD removals. However, low-loaded extended aeration systems operating at the same temperatures show good efficiencies. Extended aeration at a reduced BOD loading and resultant long aeration time compensates for the low metabolism rate of microorganisms. The biological treatment system most affected by cold winter temperature is the stabilization pond. Heat in the wastewater is not adequate to prevent formation of an ice cover in northern climates during winter.

The hydrogen ion concentration of the culture medium has a direct influence on microbial growth. Most biological treatment systems operate best in a neutral environment. The general range for operation of activated-sludge systems is between pH 6.5 and 8.5. At pH 9.0 and above, microbial activity is inhibited. Below 6.5, fungi are favored over bacteria in the competition for food. The methane-forming bacteria in anaerobic digestion have a much smaller pH tolerance range. General limits for anaerobic digestion are pH 6.7–7.4, with optimum operation at pH 7.0–7.1.

Biological treatment systems are adversely affected by toxic substances. Industrial wastes from metal-finishing industries usually contain toxic metal ions, such as nickel and chromium. Phenol is an extremely toxic compound found in chemical industry wastes. These and other inhibiting compounds are commonly removed by pretreatment at the industrial site prior to disposal of the industrial wastes to a municipal sewer.

Environmental conditions that adversely affect the desired microbial growth in an activated-sludge aeration tank can cause production of sludge with poor settling characteristics. This condition, resulting in excessive carryover of activated-sludge floc in the clarifier effluent (referred to as sludge bulking), is associated with filamentous growths and pinpoint floc with poor settleability.

9   POPULATION DYNAMICS

Previous sections described the important characteristics of each group of microorganisms (bacteria, fungi, algae, and protozoans) independently. In biological waste treatment systems, however, the naturally occurring cultures are mixtures of bacteria growing in mutual association and with other microscopic plants and animals. A general knowledge of the relationships, both cooperative and competitive, among various microbial populations in mixed cultures is essential to understanding biological treatment processes.

When organic matter is made available to a mixed population of microorganisms, competition arises for this food between the various species. Primary feeders that are most competitive become the dominant microorganisms. Under normal operating conditions, bacteria are the dominant primary feeders in activated sludge (Fig. 11).

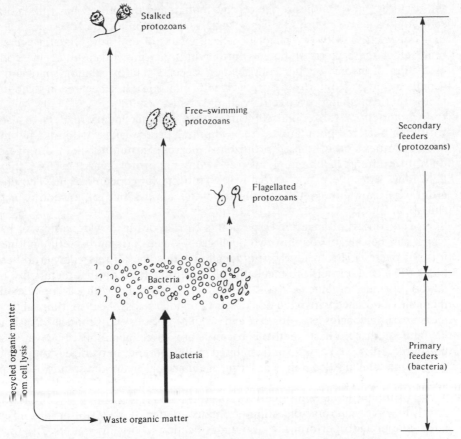

FIGURE 11   Schematic diagram of the population dynamics in activated sludge.

Saprobic protozoa, those that feed on dead organic matter (e.g., *Euglena*), are not effective competitors against bacteria.

Which species of primary bacteria dominate depend chiefly on the nature of the organic waste and environmental conditions in aeration tanks. Conditions adverse to bacteria, such as acid pH, low dissolved oxygen, and nutrient shortage, can produce a predominance of filamentous fungi, resulting in sludge bulking. These abnormal circumstances are rare in municipal activated-sludge systems treating wastewater that is chiefly from domestic sources. However, when bulking in an activated-sludge system does occur, sanitary engineers must be prepared to find the cause and recommend corrective action.

Primary bacteria in an activated-sludge system are maintained in the declining or endogenous growth phases. Under these conditions, the primary bacteria die and lyse, releasing their cell contents to solution. In this process, raw organic matter is synthesized and resynthesized by various groups of bacteria.

Holozoic protozoans, which feed on living organic matter, are common in activated sludge. They grow in association with the bacteria in a prey–predator relationship; that is, the bacteria (prey) synthesize the organic matter, and the protozoans (predators) consume the bacteria (Figure 11). For a single reproduction a protozoan consumes thousands of bacteria, with two major beneficial effects of the prey–predator action. First, removal of the bacteria stimulates further bacterial growth, resulting in accelerated extraction of organic matter from solution. Second, the flocculation characteristics of activated sludge are improved by reducing the number of free bacteria in solution, and a biological floc with improved settling characteristics results.

Competition for food also occurs between the secondary feeders. In a solution with high bacterial populations, free-swimming protozoans are dominant, but when food becomes scarce, stalked protozoans increase in numbers. Stalked protozoans do not require as much energy as free-swimming protozoans; therefore, they compete more effectively in a system with low bacterial concentrations. The photomicrographs shown in Figure 12 illustrate the appearance of a healthy activated sludge.

The process of anaerobic digestion is carried out by a wide variety of bacteria, which can be categorized into two main groups, acid-forming bacteria and methane-forming bacteria. (Protozoans do not function in the digester's strict anaerobic environment.) The acid formers are facultative or anaerobic bacteria that metabolize organic matter, forming organic acids as an end-product, along with carbon dioxide and methane (associated with oxidation of fats to organic acids). Acid-splitting methane formers use organic acids as a substrate and produce gaseous end-products of carbon dioxide and methane. These methane bacteria are strict anaerobes inactivated by the presence of dissolved oxygen and inhibited by the presence of oxidized compounds. The growth medium must contain a reducing agent such as hydrogen sulfide. Acid-splitting methane bacteria are sensitive to pH changes and other environmental conditions.

A simplified diagram (Figure 13) portrays the relationship between the two bacterial stages in anaerobic digestion of organic matter. Both major groups of bacteria must cooperate to perform the overall gasification of organic matter. The first stage creates organic acids for the second stage, where these organic acids are converted to gas, preventing excess acid accumulation. In addition to producing food for the methane bacteria, acid formers also reduce the environment to one of strict anaerobiosis by using the oxidized compounds and excreting reducing agents.

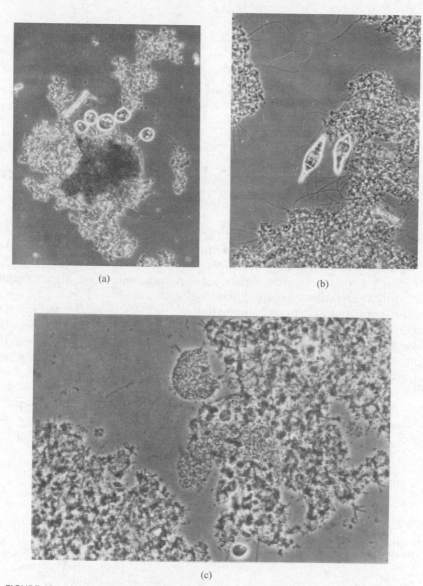

(a)

(b)

(c)

FIGURE 12   Photomicrographs of activated sludge. (a) Activated-sludge floc with stalked proto-zoans (100×). (b) Rotifers in activated sludge (100×). (c) Activated-sludge floc showing clusters of bacterial cells. Lower center flagellated protozoan (400×).

Problems in operating anaerobic treatment systems result when an imbalance occurs in the population dynamics. For example, if a sudden excess of organic matter is fed to a digester, acid formers very rapidly process this food, developing excess organic acids. The methane formers, whose population had been limited by a previous lower organic acid supply, are unable to metabolize the organic acids fast enough to prevent a drop in pH. When the pH drops, the methane bacteria are affected first, further

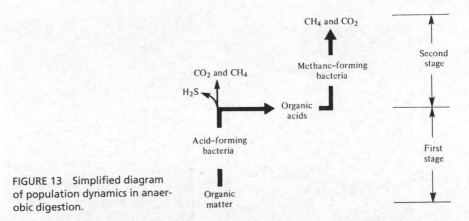

FIGURE 13　Simplified diagram of population dynamics in anaerobic digestion.

reducing their capacity to break down the acids. Under severe or prolonged overloading, the contents of the digester "pickles" in excess acids, and all bacterial activity is inhibited. In addition to organic overloading, the digestion process can be upset by a sudden increase in temperature, a significant shift in the type of substrate, or additions of toxic or inhibiting substances from industrial wastes.

A unique relationship exists between bacteria and algae in wastewater stabilization ponds (Figure 14). The bacteria metabolize organic matter for reproduction, releasing soluble nitrogen and phosphorus nutrients and carbon dioxide. Algae use these inorganic compounds, along with the energy from sunlight, for synthesis, releasing oxygen. The resulting dissolved oxygen in the pond water is taken up by the bacteria, thus closing the cycle. This type of association between organisms is referred to as *symbiosis*, a relationship in which two or more species live together for mutual benefit such that the association stimulates more vigorous growth of each species than if the growths were separate. The growth of algae replaces in part the organic matter decomposed by the bacteria. For this

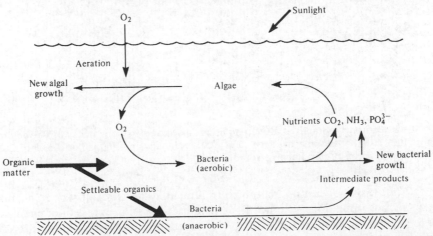

FIGURE 14　Schematic diagram of microbiological activity in a wastewater stabilization pond showing the symbiotic relationship between bacteria and algae and decomposition of organic matter by both aerobic and anaerobic bacteria.

reason, ponds do not always appear to provide satisfactory removal of organic matter. A variety of predators (protozoans, rotifers, and higher animals) that feed on the algae and bacteria are also present in pond water.

At the liquid depth commonly used in stabilization-pond design, bottom waters may become anaerobic while the surface remains aerobic. In terms of general oxygen conditions, these lagoons are commonly referred to as *facultative stabilization ponds* (Figure 14). During periods when the dissolved oxygen is at less than saturation level, the surface water is aerated through wind action. During the winter, both bacterial metabolism and algal synthesis are slowed by cold temperatures. The lagoon generally remains aerobic, even under a transparent ice cover. If the sunlight is blocked by a snow cover, the algae cannot produce oxygen, and the lagoon becomes anaerobic. The result is odorous conditions during the spring thaw until the algae becomes reestablished. This may take from a few days to weeks, depending on climatic conditions and the amount of organic matter accumulated in the lagoon during the winter.

CHARACTERISTICS OF WASTEWATER

Wastewater is defined as liquid wastes collected in a sewer system and conveyed to a treatment plant for processing. In most communities, storm runoff water is collected in a separate storm sewer system and conveyed to the nearest watercourse for disposal without treatment. A few large cities have a combined wastewater collection system where both stormwater and sanitary wastes are collected in the same pipe system. The dry-weather flow in the combined sewers is collected for treatment, but during storms the wastewater flow in excess of plant capacity may be stored for treatment later or, in some situations, is bypassed directly to the receiving watercourse.

Sanitary or domestic wastewater refers to liquid material collected from residences, commercial buildings, and institutions. The term *industrial wastes* refers to that from manufacturing plants. *Municipal wastewater* is a general term applied to liquid treated in a municipal treatment plant. Municipal wastewaters from towns frequently contain industrial effluents from dairies, laundries, bakeries, and factories, and those from large cities may have wastes from major industries, such as chemical manufacturing, breweries, meat processing, and metal processing.

10   FLOW AND STRENGTH VARIATIONS

The quantity of municipal wastewater flow varies from 50 to over 250 gal per capita per day (gpcd), depending on sewer uses of the community. A common value for sanitary flow is 120 gpcd (450 l/d). Per capita contribution of organic matter in domestic wastewater is approximately 0.24 lb (109 g) of suspended solids per day and 0.20 lb (91 g) of BOD per day in communities where a substantial portion of the household kitchen wastes are discharged to the sewer system through garbage disposals. These values are the population equivalents used to convert total pounds of solids or BOD of industrial wastewaters to equivalent population.

The actual quantities of flow and organic matter can differ significantly from these common values. The frequency distributions for per capita contributions of flow, suspended solids, and BOD based on analyses of data from 100 cities in Illinois, Indiana, Ohio, and Minnesota are graphed in Figure 15 [6]. The data show wide variations. Larger

Biological Treatment Processes

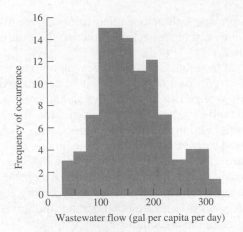

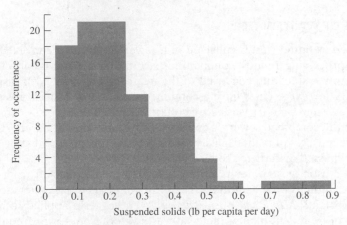

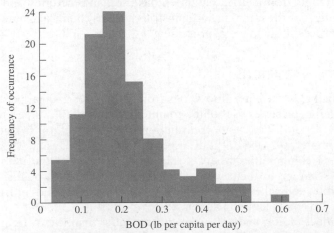

FIGURE 15 Histograms of average wastewater flow and quantities of suspended solids and BOD contributed per capita based on data from 100 cities in Illinois, Indiana, Ohio, and Minnesota. *Source:* From D. H. Stoltenberg, "Midwestern Wastewater Characteristics," *Public Works* 111, no. 1 (1980): 52–53.

cities have greater waste contributions per capita. For cities with populations greater than 100,000, mean flow was 194 gpcd, mean suspended solids were 0.40 lb/capita/day, and BOD was 0.30 lb/capita/day. For cities with populations less than 10,000, the values were 140 gpcd, 0.15 lb of suspended solids, and 0.14 lb of BOD. Geographic location and climate influence waste contributions, particularly flow in relation to the amount of infiltration and inflow. From a study of 700 Texas communities having populations less than 10,000, the average contributions per capita per day were 89 gal, 0.21 lb of suspended solids, and 0.16 lb of BOD [7].

The flows and loads entering a wastewater treatment plant during the year vary with climatic conditions, industrial production, domestic water use, and other factors. In a typical industrial community in a moderate climate, the summer average daily flow frequently exceeds winter flows by 20%–30%. Munksgaard and Young [8] analyzed operational data from 11 municipal plants in the range of 0.25–40 mgd to determine peak flows and loads. All the cities had separate sanitary sewers receiving less than 20% of the wastewater from industrial sources. The wastewater flows included normal infiltration expected in humid climatic areas with an annual precipitation in the range of 20–40 in. The peaking ratio equations derived for the average annual peak month and average annual peak day are

$$Q_m = Q\left(\frac{1.26}{Q^{0.0101}}\right) \tag{36}$$

$$B_m = B\left(\frac{1.91}{B^{0.0430}}\right) \tag{37}$$

$$S_m = S\left(\frac{2.18}{S^{0.0517}}\right) \tag{38}$$

$$Q_d = Q\left(\frac{1.96}{Q^{0.0360}}\right) \tag{39}$$

$$B_d = B\left(\frac{4.08}{B^{0.0732}}\right) \tag{40}$$

$$S_d = S\left(\frac{5.98}{S^{0.0716}}\right) \tag{41}$$

where

Q = average annual wastewater flow, mgd
B = average annual BOD load, lb/day
S = average annual suspended-solids load, lb/day
Q_m, B_m, S_m = average flow, BOD, and suspended-solids values during the peak month
Q_d, B_d, S_d = average flow, BOD, and suspended-solids values for the peak day

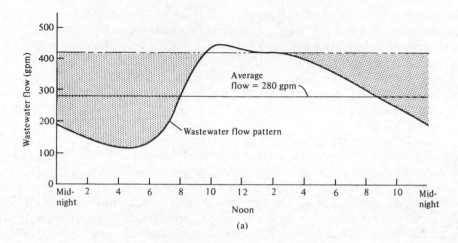

(a)

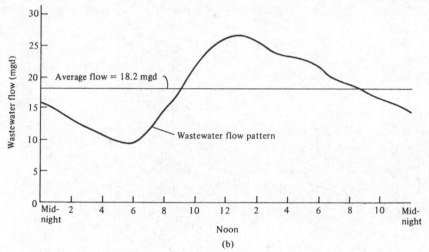

(b)

FIGURE 16   Diagrams of municipal wastewater flow showing hourly variations. (a) Flow diagram from a town with a population of 4500. (Shaded area is the typical recirculation flow for a high-rate trickling-filter plant at R = 0.5.) (b) Flow diagram from a city with a population of 150,000.

Diurnal flow variations depend primarily on the size of a municipality and industrial flows. Hourly flow rates range from a minimum of 20% to a maximum of 250% or more of the average daily rate for small communities and from 50% to 200% for larger cities. The wastewater flow diagrams in Figure 16 exemplify hourly flow variations for two municipalities of different sizes.

Example 1

The sanitary sewer system in a municipality located in a humid climate receives over three-quarters of the wastewater discharges from domestic and commercial sources. The average annual wastewater flow is 10.0 mgd, containing 16,700 lb of BOD and 20,000 lb of suspended solids. Calculate the average daily wastewater flow, BOD load, and suspended-solids load during the peak month of the year.

Solution: Applying Eqs. (36) through (38),

$$Q_m = 10 \left(\frac{1.26}{10^{0.0101}} \right) = 12.3 \text{ mgd}$$

$$B_m = 16,700 \left(\frac{1.91}{16,700^{0.0430}} \right) = 21,000 \text{ lb/day}$$

$$S_m = 20,000 \left(\frac{2.18}{20,000^{0.0517}} \right) = 26,100 \text{ lb/day}$$

11   COMPOSITION OF WASTEWATER

The data in Table 1 represent the approximate composition of domestic wastewater before and after treatment. BOD and suspended solids (nonfiltrable residue) are the two most important parameters used to define the characteristics of a domestic wastewater. A suspended-solids concentration of 240 mg/l is equivalent to 0.24 lb of suspended solids in 120 gal, and 200 mg/l of BOD is equivalent to 0.20 lb of BOD in 120 gal. Reduction of suspended solids and BOD in primary sedimentation is approximately 50% and 35%, respectively. Approximately 70% of the suspended solids are volatile, defined as those lost upon ignition at 550°C.

Total solids (residue on evaporation) include organic matter and dissolved salts; the concentration of the latter is dependent to a considerable extent on the hardness of the municipal water. The concentration of nitrogen in domestic waste is directly related to the concentration of organic matter (BOD). Approximately 60% of the total nitrogen is in solution as ammonia. If raw wastewater has been retained for a long time in

TABLE 1   Approximate Composition of Average Domestic Wastewater (mg/l)

	Before Sedimentation	After Sedimentation	Biologically Treated
Total solids	800	680	530
Total volatile solids	440	340	220
Suspended solids	240	120	30
Volatile suspended solids	180	100	20
BOD	200	130	30
Ammonia nitrogen as N	22	22	24
Total nitrogen as N	35	30	26
Soluble phosphorus as P	4	4	4
Total phosphorus as P	7	6	5

collector sewers, a greater percentage of ammonia nitrogen results from deamination of the proteins and urea in wastewater. Seven milligrams per liter of phosphorus is approximately equivalent to a 2-lb phosphorus contribution per capita per year.

The surplus of nitrogen and phosphorus in biologically treated wastewater reveals that domestic wastewater contains nutrients in excess of biological needs. The approximate BOD/nitrogen/phosphorus (BOD/N/P) weight ratio required for biological treatment is 100/5/1. The exact BOD/N/P ratio needed for treatment depends on the process and the biological availability of the nitrogen and phosphorus compounds in the wastewater. A minimum of 100/6/1.5 is commonly related to treatment of unsettled sanitary wastewater, while 100/3/0.7 is generally adequate for wastewater where the nitrogen and phosphorus are in soluble forms. The average domestic wastewater listed in Table 1 has a ratio of 100/17/3 before sedimentation and 100/23/5 after sedimentation, both of which values exceed the minimum 100/6/1.5. For biological treatment of industrial wastewater deficient in nutrients, soluble phosphorus can be supplied by adding H_3PO_4 and soluble nitrogen by adding NH_4NO_3.

Biodegradable organic matter in wastewater is generally classified in three categories: carbohydrates, proteins, and fats. *Carbohydrates* are hydrates of carbon with the empirical formula $C_nH_{2n}O_n$ or $C_n(H_2O)_n$. The simplest carbohydrate unit is known as a *monosaccharide*, although few monosaccharides occur naturally. Glucose is a common monosaccharide in the structure of polysaccharides. *Disaccharides* are composed of two monosaccharide units. Sucrose (table sugar) is glucose plus fructose. Common milk sugar is lactose, consisting of glucose plus galactose. *Polysaccharides* are long chains of monosaccharides, such as cellulose, starch, and glycogen. Cellulose is the common polysaccharide in wood, cotton, paper, and plant tissues. Starches are primary nutrient polysaccharides for plant growth and are abundant in potatoes, rice, wheat, corn, and other plant forms.

Proteins in simple form are long-chain molecules composed of amino acids connected by peptide bonds and are important in both the structural (e.g., muscle tissue) and dynamic aspects (e.g., enzymes) of living matter. Twenty-one common amino acids when linked together in long peptide chains form a majority of simple proteins found in nature. A mixture of proteins as a bacterial substrate is an excellent growth medium, since proteins contain all the essential nutrients. On the other hand, pure carbohydrates are unsuitable as a growth medium because they do not contain the nitrogen and phosphorus essential for synthesis.

Lipids, together with carbohydrates and proteins, form the bulk of organic matter of living cells. The term refers to a heterogeneous collection of biochemical substances having the mutual property of being soluble to varying degrees in organic solvents (e.g., ether, ethanol, hexane, and acetone) while being only sparingly soluble in water. Lipids may be grouped according to their shared chemical and physical properties as fats, oils, and waxes. A simple fat, when broken down by hydrolytic action, yields fatty acids. In sanitary engineering, the word *fats* in current usage apparently conveys the meaning of lipids. The term *grease* applies to a wide variety of organic substances in the lipid category that are extracted from aqueous solution or suspension by trichlorotrifluoroethane.

Actually, not all biodegradable organic matter can be classed into these three simple groupings. Many natural compounds have structures that are combinations of carbohydrates, proteins, and fats, such as lipoproteins and nucleoproteins.

Approximately 20%–40% of the organic matter in wastewater appears to be nonbiodegradable. Several organic compounds, although biodegradable in the sense that specific bacteria can break them down, are considered by sanitary engineers as only partially biodegradable because of time limitations in waste treatment processes. For example, lignin, a polymeric noncarbohydrate material associated with cellulose in wood fiber, is for all practical purposes nonbiodegradable. Cellulose itself is not readily available to the general population of domestic wastewater bacteria. Saturated hydrocarbons are a problem in treatment because of their physical properties and resistance to bacterial action. Alkyl benzene sulfanate (ABS synthetic detergent) is only partially biodegradable in wastewater treatment.

Example 2

Domestic wastewater contains 0.24 lb of suspended solids and 0.20 lb of BOD per 120 gal.

a. Using these values, calculate the suspended-solids and BOD concentrations in milligrams per liter.

b. What is the BOD equivalent population for an industry that discharges 0.10 mgd of wastewater with an average BOD of 450 mg/l? What is the hydraulic equivalent population of this wastewater?

Solution:

a.
$$BOD = \frac{0.20\ lb}{120\ gal} \times \frac{1,000,000\ gal}{8.34\ lb} = 200\ mg/l$$

$$suspended\ solids = \frac{0.24\ lb}{120\ gal} \times \frac{1,000,000\ gal}{8.34\ lb} = 240\ mg/l$$

b.
$$\left(\begin{array}{c} BOD\ equivalent \\ population \end{array}\right) = \frac{0.10\ mil\ gal \times 450\ mg/l \times 8.34\ lb/mil\ gal}{0.20\ lb/person} \frac{}{mg/l} = 1900$$

$$\left(\begin{array}{c} hydraulic\ equivalent \\ population \end{array}\right) = \frac{100,000\ gal/day}{120\ gal/person} = 830$$

Example 3

Wastewater from soluble coffee manufacturing is treated jointly with domestic wastewater in an activated-sludge process without primary settling. The mixture is 40% coffee wastewater and 60% domestic wastewater by volume. The characteristics of the coffee wastewater are 840 mg/l of BOD, 6.0 mg/l of total nitrogen, and 2.0 mg/l of total phosphorus. The domestic wastewater characteristics are as listed in Table 1.

   a. If the required BOD/N/P weight ratio is assumed to be 100/6.0/1.5 for activated-sludge processing, are the nitrogen and phosphorus concentrations in the combined wastewater adequate?

   b. If the nutrient content is not adequate, how many milligrams per liter of pure NH_4NO_3 and H_3PO_4 must be added to the wastewater?

Solution:

   a. BOD $= 0.40 \times 840 + 0.60 \times 200 = 456$ mg/l

   N $= 0.40 \times 6.0 + 0.60 \times 35 = 23.4$ mg/l

   P $= 0.40 \times 2.0 + 0.60 \times 7.0 = 5.0$ mg/l

	Available	Required	Need
BOD	456/4.56 = 100	100	—
N	23.4/4.56 = 5.1	6.0	0.9
P	5.0/4.56 = 1.1	1.5	0.4

   b. $NH_4NO_3 = 0.9 \times \dfrac{456}{100} \times \dfrac{80}{28} = 12$ mg/l

   $H_3PO_4 = 0.4 \times \dfrac{456}{100} \times \dfrac{98}{31} = 5.8$ mg/l

TRICKLING (BIOLOGICAL) FILTERS

Trickling filters are fixed-growth biological beds where wastewater is spread on the surface of media supporting microbial growths. Although the term *filter* is the accepted designation for this unit, no physical filtration occurs; contaminants are removed by biological action. The media placed in a tank under the wastewater distributor can be crushed rock, plastic-sheet packing formed into modules, or random plastic packing of various shapes. Trickling filters are preceded by primary clarifiers to remove settleable solids and are followed by final clarifiers to collect microbiological growths that slough from the media. The primary reasons for the popularity of trickling filters are their simplicity, low operating cost, and production of a waste sludge that is easy to process.

12   BIOLOGICAL PROCESS IN TRICKLING FILTRATION

The biological slime layers on filter media consist of bacteria, protozoans, and fungi. Frequently, noticeable populations of larger organisms such as sludge worms and rotifers are present. The top surface of a bed exposed to sunlight is coated with algae, and the lower portion of a deep filter can support nitrifying bacteria. Microorganisms near the surface of the bed where the food concentration is high are in a rapid growth phase, while the microorganisms near the bottom are in a state of starvation.

Figure 17 is a schematic diagram illustrating the general biological process at the surface of the medium. Although classified as aerobic treatment, the microbial film is

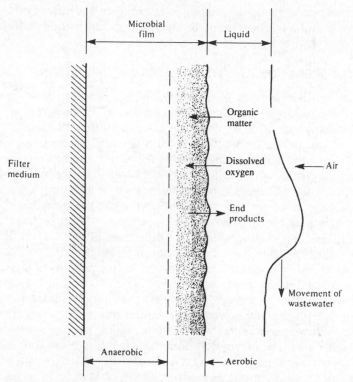

FIGURE 17 Schematic diagram showing the form of the biological process in a trickling filter.

aerobic to a depth of only 0.1–0.2 mm. The zone adjacent to the medium is anaerobic. As the wastewater flows over the microbial film, the soluble organic matter is metabolized and the colloidal organic matter is adsorbed on the film. Dissolved oxygen taken up in the liquid layer is replenished by reoxygenation from the surrounding air. Continuous passage of air through the bed is essential to prevent undesirable anaerobic conditions. The actual biological process is more complex than this simplified description and is poorly understood. Physical characteristics, such as media configuration, bed depth, and hydraulic loading, strongly influence the process. Several forms of manufactured media provide a high specific surface area with a corresponding large percentage of void volume. This permits substantial biological growth without inhibiting passage of air through the bed. A uniform medium also allows even loading distribution, and lightweight packing permits the construction of deep beds.

Problems with the biological process that can occur include poor effluent quality and emission of offensive odors, both associated with organic loading, industrial wastes, and cold-weather operation. The anaerobic zone of the film adjacent to the medium surface can produce odorous metabolic end products. If they are not oxidized while moving through the aerobic zone, they can be released and carried out in the airflow through the bed. Some industrial wastes have characteristic odors that are not easily oxidized by the microbial film. Cooling of the applied wastewater reduces the biological activity, allowing more organic matter to pass through the bed. In northern climates, the walls of deep filters can be insulated and covers can be placed over the tops to reduce cooling. Filter flies,

Psychoda, are a nuisance around filters during warm weather. They breed on the inside of the retaining walls and on the surface of the media around the margin of the bed.

13   TRICKLING-FILTER OPERATION AND FILTER MEDIA REQUIREMENTS

A cutaway view of a shallow trickling filter is shown in Figure 18. The major components are a rotary distributor, underdrain system, and filter medium. The distributor spreads the wastewater at a uniform hydraulic load per unit area on the surface of the bed. The arms are driven by the reaction of wastewater flowing out of the distributor nozzles, which usually requires a pressure head of 24 in. measured at the center column that supports the arms. The underdrain system, often vitrified clay blocks with entrance holes to drainage channels, carries away the effluent and permits circulation of air through the bed. The need for free passage of air controls the size of the openings in the underdrain. The filter media provide a surface for biological growth and voids for passage of air and water.

Traditionally, the common filter media have been crushed rock, slag, or field stone, since these are durable, insoluble, resistant to spalling (chipping), and often locally available. Stones, however, have the disadvantage of occupying the majority of the volume in a filter bed, thus reducing the void spaces for passage of air and limiting the surface area per unit volume for biological growth. Several forms of chemical-resistant plastic media are available that have much greater surface area per unit volume and a large percentage of free space. For shallow filters, the common types are random packing and high-density cross-flow media manufactured in handleable modules that can be cut and fitted into a circular tank. The common random packing is small (2–4 in.) cylinders with perforated walls and internal ribs made of plastic, as shown in Figure 19. The specific surface area is $30-40 \text{ ft}^2/\text{ft}^3$ ($100-130 \text{ m}^2/\text{m}^3$) with a void space of 91%–94%. The packing is placed by dumping it into a filter tank on top of the underdrains. Because of the random placement, the bed is efficient in distributing the applied wastewater to the media surfaces.

Biological towers are trickling filters with deep beds of 10–20 ft, usually in circular tanks with rotary distributors. The modules of packing with differing internal configurations are manufactured of polyvinyl chloride (PVC) in bundles 2 ft wide, 4 ft long, and 2 ft high. The module in Figure 20a is constructed of corrugated sheets

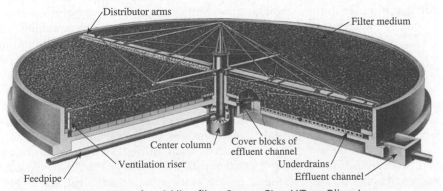

FIGURE 18   Cutaway view of a trickling filter. *Source:* GL + V/Dorr-Oliver Inc.

FIGURE 19 Random packing for both shallow and deep trickling filters. Each element is a plastic cylinder (3.5 × 3.5 in) with perforated walls and internal ribs.

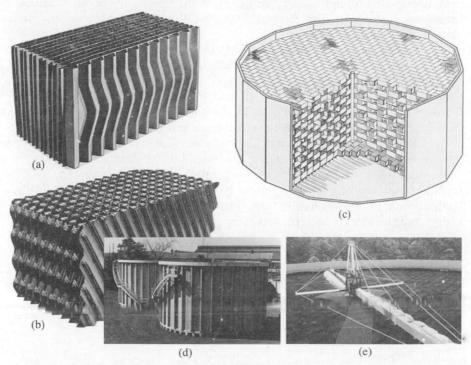

(a)

(b)

(c)

(d)

(e)

FIGURE 20 Biological tower media and construction. (a) Vertical-flow module with corrugated sheets bonded between flat sheets. (b) Cross-flow module with corrugated sheets assembled with adjacent sheets in a crossed pattern. (c) Cutaway view showing the construction of a circular biological tower. (d) Picture of two biological towers. (e) Distributor arm spreading wastewater on surface of tower media. *Source:* Courtesy of TLB Corporation, Newington, CT.

bonded between flat sheets. By preventing clear vertical openings, the wastewater passing down through the packing is distributed over the surfaces of the media. The specific surface is 26–43 ft²/ft³ (85–140 m²/m³), varying with manufacturer; the void space is about 95%. Cross-flow packing in Figure 20b is made of ridged corrugated sheets with ridges on adjacent sheets at 45° or 60° angles to each other and bonded together where the ridges contact. As wastewater flows down through the media, each contact point permits flow splitting and combining. Cross-flow wets the surfaces completely and slows the flow rate, resulting in an increased hydraulic residence time in the bed. The specific surface of low-density, cross-flow media is 27 ft²/ft³ (90 m²/m³), and that of the high-density media is 42 ft²/ft³ (140 m²/m³).

The modules have sufficient strength to support the packing with attached wet biological growth in towers of 20 ft in height. The media bundles are stacked to interlock for structural stability and can be cut to fit the edge modules in a circular tower equipped with a rotary distributor (Figure 20c, d, e).

14   TRICKLING-FILTER SECONDARY SYSTEMS

A trickling-filter secondary treatment system includes a final settling tank to remove biological growths that are washed off the filter media. These sloughed solids are commonly disposed of through a drain line from the bottom of the final clarifier to the head end of the plant. This return sludge flow is mixed with the raw wastewater and settled in the primary clarifier.

The raw wastewater in trickling filtration is diluted with recirculated flow so that it is reduced in strength and passes through the filter more than once. A typical filter design is illustrated in Figure 21. A return line from the final clarifier serves a dual function as a sludge return and a recirculation line. The combined flow $(Q + Q_R)$ through the filter is always sufficient to maintain a minimum hydraulic loading on the media and sufficient flow to turn the distributor arms.

The two most common recirculation patterns used in trickling filter systems are shown in Figure 22. The recirculation ratio is the ratio of recirculated flow to the quantity of raw wastewater. A common range for recirculation ratio values is 0.5–3.0. Recirculation may be done (1) only during periods of low wastewater flow, (2) at a rate proportional to raw-wastewater flow, (3) at a constant rate at all times, or (4) at two or more constant rates predetermined automatically or by manual control.

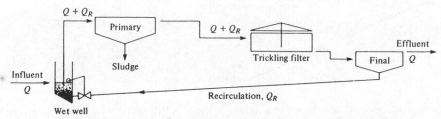

FIGURE 21   Profile of a typical single-stage trickling-filter plant with recirculation of underflow from the final clarifier to the head of the plant.

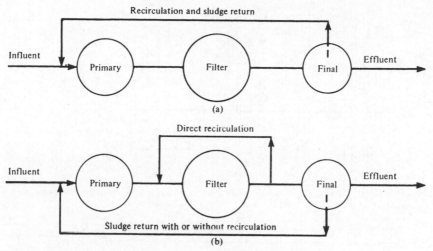

FIGURE 22 Typical recirculation patterns for single-stage trickling-filter plants. (a) Recirculation with sludge return. (b) Direct recirculation around the filter.

The gravity-flow-recirculation sludge-return system illustrated in Figures 21 and 22 is common for treatment of average-strength wastewater. The rate of recirculation flow is generally automatically regulated by the rate of raw-wastewater flow into the clear well. In this manner, the rate of return is increased during periods of low raw-wastewater flow and reduced, or even stopped, during high-flow periods. This kind of recirculation operation is shown graphically in Figure 16a. The shaded area represents recirculated flow. The average raw-wastewater flow is 280 gpm. Flow through the plant is 420 gpm, equal to $Q + Q_R$, except from 10 A.M. to 3 P.M., when the raw-wastewater flow exceeds 420 gpm. The recirculation ratio for this illustrated flow recirculation pattern is 0.5.

Direct recirculation, depicted in Figure 22b, is frequently used in the treatment of stronger wastewaters, where recirculation ratios of 2–3 are desirable. If high rates are used in pattern a, the primary clarifier must be sized for the increased flow rate created by the greater volume. In other words, if recirculation flow is routed through a clarifier during the peak hourly flows of the raw wastewater, the clarifier must be increased in size to prevent disturbance of the settled solids and resultant loss of removal efficiency in the sedimentation tank. Consider the flow diagram in Figure 16a, and assume that the shaded area is the flow in the sludge-return line shown in Figure 22b. Then apply a direct recirculation of 420 gpm around the filter using constant-speed pumps. The resultant ratio for the trickling filter is 2.0:0.5 from indirect recirculation (from the final to the head of the primary) and 1.5 from direct recirculation.

Two-stage trickling-filter secondary systems have two filters in series, usually with an intermediate settling tank. Two typical flow diagrams for two-stage filter installations are sketched in Figure 23. Two-stage filters are used where a high-quality effluent is required, for treatment of strong wastewater, and to compensate for lower bacterial activity in treating cold wastewater.

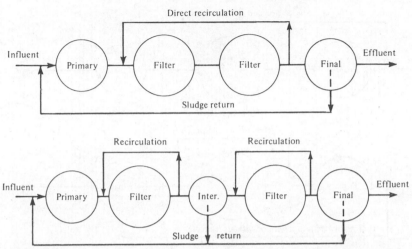

FIGURE 23 Typical recirculation patterns for two-stage trickling-filter plants without and with intermediate sedimentation.

Deep filters (biological towers) for treating municipal wastewater are generally single-stage units following primary sedimentation, although two stages are installed when processing strong wastewater resulting from industrial discharges. Direct recirculation is employed to maintain the desired flow through the tower. Sometimes a portion of the recirculation flow is drawn from the bottom of the final clarifier to develop a microbial floc in the wastewater circulating through the tower. Waste sludge accumulated in the final clarifier can be returned to the plant influent for settling in the primary clarifier.

15 EFFICIENCY EQUATIONS FOR STONE-MEDIA TRICKLING FILTERS

The BOD load on a trickling filter is calculated using the raw BOD in the primary effluent applied to the filter, without regard to the BOD in the recirculated flow. BOD loadings are expressed in terms of pounds of BOD applied per unit of volume per day. Common values are $20-40 \, \text{lb}/1000 \, \text{ft}^3/\text{day}$ ($320-640 \, \text{g/m}^3 \cdot \text{d}$) for single-stage filters and $40-60 \, \text{lb}/1000 \, \text{ft}^3/\text{day}$ ($640-960 \, \text{g/m}^3 \cdot \text{d}$) for two-stage filters based on the total media volume of both filters. The loadings apply to treatment of domestic wastewater (approximately 200 mg/l BOD) in the range of $15°-20°C$ ($59°-68°F$), with a minimum operating recirculation ratio of 0.5.

The hydraulic load is computed from the raw wastewater flow plus recirculated flow. Hydraulic loadings are expressed in terms of average flow in gpm applied per square foot of surface area per day. Recirculation flow is required to maintain an open, well-aerated bed by preventing excessive accumulation of biological growth in the voids and impeding the passage of water and air. The minimum recommended hydraulic loading is $0.16 \, \text{gpm/ft}^2$ ($9.4 \, \text{m}^3/\text{m}^2 \cdot \text{d}$). The maximum recommended is $0.48 \, \text{gpm/ft}^2$ ($28 \, \text{m}^3/\text{m}^2 \cdot \text{d}$). Above this, the flushing action is excessive and contact time of the wastewater with the filter media becomes too short. The recirculation ratio for this range of hydraulic loadings is usually between 0.5 and 3.0.

Trickling filters have a bed depth of 5–7 ft (1.5–2.1 m) for most efficient BOD removal per unit volume of stone or slag media. In the early development of filters, they were constructed as deep as 8 ft and as shallow as 3 ft. Experience showed that two 3-ft-deep filters in series were no more efficient than one 6-ft-deep filter, and that the filter media below 6 ft in a bed did not result in significant increased BOD removal.

General practice in trickling-filter design has been to use empirical relationships to find the required filter volume for a desired degree of wastewater treatment. Several of these associations have been developed from operational data collected at existing treatment plants. One of the first evolved was the National Research Council (NRC) formula, based on data collected from filter plants at military installations in the United States in the early 1940s [9].

The NRC formula for a single-stage trickling filter is

$$E = \frac{100}{1 + 0.0561 \, (w/VF)^{0.5}} \tag{42}$$

where

E = BOD removal at 20°C, %
w = BOD load applied, lb/day
V = volume of filter media, ft$^3 \times 10^{-3}$
F = recirculation factor
w/V = BOD loading, lb/1000 ft^3/day

The recirculation factor is calculated from the formula

$$F = \frac{1 + R}{(1 + 0.1R)^2} \tag{43}$$

where R is the recirculation ratio (ratio of recirculation flow to raw wastewater flow).

The NRC formula for the second stage of a two-stage filter is

$$E_2 = \frac{100}{1 + [0.0561/(1 - E_1)](w_2/VF)^{0.5}} \tag{44}$$

where

E_2 = BOD removal of the second stage at 20°C, %
E_1 = fraction of BOD removed in the first stage
w_2 = BOD load applied to the second stage, lb/day
w_2/V = BOD loading, lb/1000 ft^3/day

The effect of wastewater temperature on stone-filled trickling-filter efficiency may be expressed as

$$E = E_{20} \, 1.035^{T-20} \tag{45}$$

where

$$E = \text{BOD removal efficiency at temperature } T \text{ in } °C$$
$$E_{20} = \text{BOD removal efficiency at } 20°C$$

The BOD removal efficiencies computed by the NRC formulas include final settling of the filter effluent. In the empirical development of these formulas, the field procedure used in collecting data sampled the filter influent and final clarifier effluent. Therefore, in evaluating the efficiency of a trickling-filter secondary, the overflow rate and detention time of the final clarifier should be examined for adequacy of design.

For a two-stage filter secondary without an intermediate settling tank (Figure 23), the NRC formulas cannot be used to determine the efficiency of the first stage. In this case it is common to assume that the first-stage efficiency is 50% and find the efficiency of the second stage from Eq. (44).

Example 4

Calculate the BOD loading, hydraulic loading, BOD removal efficiency, and effluent BOD concentration of a single-stage trickling filter based on the following data:

$$\text{average raw wastewater flow} = 280 \text{ gpm}$$
$$\text{recirculation ratio} = 0.5$$
$$\text{settled wastewater BOD (primary effluent)} = 130 \text{ mg/l}$$
$$\text{diameter of filter} = 18.0 \text{ m}$$
$$\text{depth of media} = 2.1 \text{ m}$$
$$\text{wastewater temperature} = 18°C$$

Solution:

raw-wastewater flow = 280 gpm = 1530 m^3/d

recirculation flow = 0.50 × 1530 = 765 m^3/d

$$\text{BOD load} = 1530 \text{ m}^3/\text{d} \times 130 \text{ mg/l} \times \frac{\text{kg/m}^3}{1000 \text{ mg/l}} = 200 \text{ kg/d}$$

surface area of filter = $\pi(18.0)^2/4$ = 254 m^2

volume of media = 254 × 2.1 = 533 m^3

$$\text{BOD loading} = \frac{200,000 \text{ g}}{533 \text{ m}^3} = 375 \text{ g/m}^3 \cdot \text{d} = 23.5 \text{ lb}/1000 \text{ ft}^3/\text{day}$$

$$\text{hydraulic loading} = \frac{1530 \text{ m}^3/\text{d} + 765 \text{ m}^3/\text{d}}{254 \text{ m}^2} = 9.04 \text{ m}^3/\text{m}^2 \cdot \text{d} = 0.15 \text{ gpm/ft}^2 \cdot \text{d}$$

By Eqs. (43) and (42),

$$F = \frac{1 + 0.5}{(1 + 0.1 \times 0.5)^2} = 1.36$$

$$E_{20} = \frac{100}{1 + 0.0561(23.5/1.36)^{0.5}} = 81.1\%$$

Using Eq. (45),

$$E_{18} = 81.1 \times 1.035^{18-20} = 75.7\%$$
$$\text{Effluent BOD} = 130[(100 - 75.7)/100] = 32 \text{ mg/l}$$

Example 5

The design flow for a new two-stage trickling-filter plant is 1.2 mgd, with an average BOD concentration of 315 mg/l. Determine the dimensions of the sedimentation tanks and trickling filters (surface areas and depths) for the flow scheme shown in Figure 24. Calculate the volume of filter media based on a loading of 35 lb of BOD/1000 ft³/day, and divide the resulting volume equally between the primary and secondary filters. Estimate the BOD concentration in the plant effluent at 20°C.

Solution:

Primary Tank

Criteria are (1) 750-gpd/ft² overflow rate based on raw Q or 1500 gpd/ft² based on Q plus recirculation flow and (2) minimum depth of 10 ft. However, if accumulated

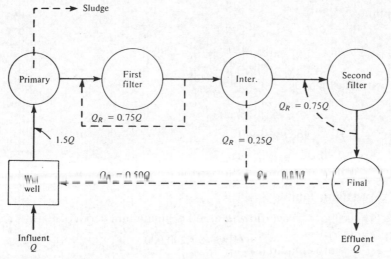

FIGURE 24   Flow scheme of the two-stage trickling-filter plant for Example 5.

sludge is to be retained in the bottom of the tank, increase the depth to accommodate the necessary sludge storage volume.

$$\text{area required} = \frac{1,200,000}{750} = 1600 \text{ ft}^2 \quad (\text{use})$$

or

$$\text{area required} = \frac{1.5 \times 1,200,000}{1500} = 1200 \text{ ft}^2$$

Estimate the daily sludge accumulation at 4% solids, assuming a sludge solids accumulation equal to 90% of the BOD load:

$$\text{volume} = \frac{0.9 \times 315 \times 1.2 \times 8.34}{0.04 \times 62.4} = 1138 \text{ ft}^3$$

$$\text{depth of sludge} = \frac{1138}{1600} = 0.7 \text{ ft}$$

Provide a side-wall depth of 11 ft plus freeboard.

$$\text{primary BOD removal} = 35\%$$

Trickling Filters

Criteria are (1) 35 lb/1000 ft^3/day BOD loading, and (2) 0.16–0.48 gpm/ft^2 hydraulic loading.

$$\text{volume required} = \frac{0.65 \times 315 \times 1.2 \times 8.34}{0.035} = 58,500 \text{ ft}^3$$

$$\text{volume of each filter} = 29,300 \text{ ft}^3$$

Try 6-ft depth:

$$\text{area} = \frac{29,300}{6.0} = 4880 \text{ ft}^2$$

Check the hydraulic loading:

$$\frac{(1.5 + 0.75)1,200,000}{4880 \times 1440} = 0.38 \text{ gpm/ft}^2 \quad (\text{OK})$$

Use 6-ft-deep filters with a 4880-ft^2 area.

Intermediate Settling Tank

Criteria are (1) 1000-gpd/ft^2 overflow rate, and (2) minimum depth of 10 ft.

$$\text{area required} = \frac{1.25 \times 1,200,000}{1000} = 1500 \text{ ft}^2$$

Use a side-wall depth of 10 ft plus freeboard.

Final Settling Tank

Criteria are (1) 800-gpd/ft^2 overflow rate, and (2) minimum depth of 8 ft.

$$\text{area required} = \frac{1,200,000}{800} = 1500 \text{ ft}^2$$

Use a side-wall depth of 8 ft plus freeboard.
Calculate BOD removal efficiency:

$$\text{primary tank} = 35\%$$

First-stage filter:

$$\text{BOD loading} = \frac{0.65 \times 315 \times 1.2 \times 8.34}{29.3} = 70 \text{ lb/1000 ft}^3/\text{day}$$

$$R = \frac{0.50Q + 0.75Q}{Q} = 1.25$$

$$F = \frac{1 + R}{(1 + 0.1R)^2} = \frac{1 + 1.25}{(1 + 0.125)^2} = 1.78$$

$$E_1 = \frac{100}{1 + 0.0561(70/1.78)^{0.5}} = 74\%$$

Second-stage filter:

$$\text{BOD loading} = 0.26 \times 70 = 18.2 \text{ lb/1000 ft}^3/\text{day}$$

$$R = \frac{0.25Q + 0.75Q}{Q} = 1.0$$

$$F = \frac{1 + 1.0}{(1 + 0.1 \times 1.0)^2} = 1.65$$

By Eq. (44),

$$E_2 = \frac{100}{1 + [0.0561/(1 - 0.74)](18.2/1.65)^{0.5}} = 58\%$$

The plant efficiency is

$$E = 100 - 100[(1 - 0.35)(1 - 0.74)(1 - 0.58)] = 93\%$$

The estimated effluent BOD is $0.07 \times 315 = 22$ mg/l.

---

16 EFFICIENCY EQUATIONS FOR PLASTIC-MEDIA TRICKLING FILTERS

The hydraulic profile for a typical biological tower is shown in Figure 25. Primary clarification is required to remove settleable and floating solids prior to filtration. Direct recirculation of the tower underflow is blended with the clarified raw wastewater to provide dilution and a greater flow through the media. In this way, the deep biological

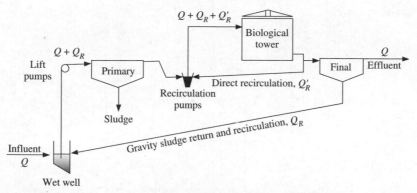

FIGURE 25 Profile of a typical biological tower with direct recirculation through tower and recirculation of underflow from the final clarifier to the inlet of the plant.

bed is more effectively used by vertical distribution of the BOD load throughout the depth of the media, and treatment is improved by passage of the wastewater through the filter more than once.

BOD loadings on biological towers with plastic media are usually 50 lb/1000 ft^3/day (800 g/m$^3 \cdot$ d) or greater with surface hydraulic loadings of 1.0 gpm/ft^2 (60 m^3/ m$^2 \cdot$ d, 0.68 l/m$^2 \cdot$ s) or greater. The design loading selected for treatment of a particular wastewater depends on BOD concentration, biodegradability, temperature, type and depth of media, and the ratio and pattern of wastewater circulation.

Plastic media, such as vertical-flow and cross-flow modules (Figure 20) and random packing (Figure 19), are manufactured with uniform geometric features of specific surface and shape. The objectives in design of these media are to provide a surface area that supports a continuous biological growth and distribution of the applied wastewater so that it flows uniformly over the biological growth. Based on this "definable" physical–biological system, several efficiency equations have been developed, modified, and refined in an attempt to find a suitable mathematical model. Nevertheless, no universal model exists to precisely describe substrate removal in a trickling filter. The following equations define a common model used in environmental engineering practice.

The residence time of applied wastewater in a filter bed is an important factor in BOD removal. The mean contact time between the wastewater and the biological film on the surface of the media can be related to filter depth, hydraulic loading, and the geometry of the media as

$$t = \frac{CD}{Q^n} \qquad (46)$$

where

$\qquad\qquad t$ = mean residence time, min
$\qquad C, n$ = constants related to specific surface and configuration of media
$\qquad\quad D$ = depth of media, ft (m)
$\qquad\quad Q$ = hydraulic loading, gpm/ft^2 (m^3/m$^2 \cdot$ h)

Constant C and exponent n are determined from pilot-plant studies using an experimental filter column packed with synthetic media to the depth of a full-scale unit. A minimum of three ports at different depths are installed to collect samples of the wastewater percolating down through the packing. Residence time is measured by adding a pulse tracer input, such as fluorescent dye, and observing the concentration of tracer in the effluent with respect to time. The mean residence time is when 50% of the tracer has passed out of the filter column. Since the thickness of the biological film affects the residence time, the experimental filter is acclimated to an applied wastewater feed for a sufficient period of time to establish dynamic equilibrium between the organic loading and microbial mass. Values of C and n are determined from a graph of the t and Q data plotted on logarithmic paper. From Eq. (46), t is proportional to Q^{-n}; therefore,

$$n = -\frac{\Delta \log t}{\Delta \log Q} \tag{47}$$

and $C = t/D$ when $Q = 1.0$.

The removal of soluble BOD in a plastic-media trickling filter, where the media supports a continuous biological growth and the wastewater is uniformly distributed, is as follows, based on first-order kinetics:

$$\frac{S_e}{S_0} = e^{-KD/Q^n} \tag{48}$$

where

S_e = soluble (filtered) BOD in effluent, mg/l

S_0 = soluble (filtered) BOD in influent, mg/l

e = 2.718(the Napierian base)

K = reaction-rate constant, gal/min/ft^3

D = depth of media, ft

Q = hydraulic loading, gpm/ft^2

n = empirical flow constant

This equation can be rewritten to include the specific surface area of the media by substituting $k_{20}A_s$ for K:

$$\frac{S_e}{S_0} = e^{-k_{20}A_s D/Q^n} \tag{49}$$

where

S_e = soluble (filtered) BOD in effluent, mg/l

S_0 = soluble (filtered) BOD in influent, mg/l

k_{20} = reaction-rate coefficient at 20°C, (gpm/ft^2)^n [(l/m$^2 \cdot$ s)^n]

A_s = specific surface area of media, ft^2/ft^3 (m^2/m^3)

D = depth of media, ft (m)

Q = hydraulic loading, gpm/ft^2 (l/m$^2 \cdot$ s)

n = empirical flow constant, often selected as 0.5 for vertical-flow and cross-flow media

The reaction-rate coefficient is corrected for temperature by the relationship

$$k = k_{20}\Theta^{T-20} \tag{50}$$

where

k = reaction-rate coefficient at temperature T, °C
k_{20} = reaction-rate coefficient at 20°C
Θ = temperature coefficient, normally selected as 1.035
T = wastewater temperature, °C

Equation (49) can be rewritten to include Eq. (50) as follows:

$$\ln\frac{S_0}{S_e} = \frac{k_{20}A_sD\Theta^{T-20}}{Q^n} \tag{51}$$

This is a linear equation that is convenient for analysis of experimental data. The value of k_{20} is determined graphically by plotting $\ln S_0/S_e$ versus $A_sD\Theta^{T-20}/Q^n$ on arithmetic paper. The value of k is the slope of a straight line originating from the origin and drawn as a best fit through the plotted data.

The BOD concentrations of the applied wastewater before and after dilution with clear recirculation flow is

$$S_0 = \frac{S_p + RS_e}{1 + R} \tag{52}$$

where

S_0 = soluble BOD in influent after dilution with recirculated flow, mg/l
S_p = soluble BOD in primary effluent before dilution with recirculated flow, mg/l
S_e = soluble BOD in effluent, mg/l
R = recirculation ratio, recirculated flow/primary effluent flow, Q_R/Q_P

Combining Eqs. (49), (50), and (52):

$$\frac{S_e}{S_p} = \frac{1}{(1 + R)\,e^{\phi} - R} \tag{53}$$

where

$\phi = k_{20}\Theta^{T-20}A_sD/(Q_p(1 + R))^n$
Q_p = hydraulic loading of primary effluent without recirculation flow, gpm/ft^2

This mathematical model is a simplification of complex biological–physical interactions that occur in trickling filters. The values for the reaction-rate coefficient k_{20} vary with media of different configurations with the same specific surface areas. The coefficient also varies with wastewater treatability and depth of media. The approximate range for k_{20} values for vertical-flow media is $0.0008-0.0016 \ (\text{gpm/ft}^2)^{0.5}$ $[0.0010-0.0020 \ (\text{l/m}^2 \cdot \text{s})^{0.5}]$, and for cross-flow media it is $0.0014-0.0023 \ (\text{gpm/ft}^2)^{0.5}$ $[0.0017-0.0028 \ (\text{l/m}^2 \cdot \text{s})^{0.5}]$, assuming $n = 0.5$. The k_{20} values for cross-flow media are greater than those for vertical-flow media, which is attributed to longer contact time and better wastewater flow distribution. Often manufacturers provide field data to verify reaction-rate coefficients for their media; however, where feasible, it is recommended that pilot studies using selected media be performed to determine the k_{20} for design.

Example 6 illustrates the application of these equations to determine the values of the reaction-rate constant K_{20} and the empirical flow constant n for random packing in a pilot-plant study. Example 7 presents the evaluation of data from a field study to determine the k_{20} for high-density cross-flow media in a shallow trickling filter.

Example 6

Balakrishnan, Eckenfelder, and Brown [10] demonstrated the feasibility of determining the constants for Eqs. (46) and (48), using data from a pilot-plant study.

The trickling filter was a 20-in.-diameter, 9-ft-long fiberglass cylinder with an air sparger to provide a uniform distribution of air from the bottom and distribution plates on top for uniform hydraulic loading. The filter was filled to a depth of 8 ft with 1.5-in.-diameter cylindrical random packing with a specific surface of 40 ft^2/ft^3 and 96% void space. Eight sampling ports were located at 1-ft intervals from the top of the filter bed.

The feed was settled domestic wastewater, containing filtered (soluble) BOD concentrations in the range of 65–90 mg/l, applied at hydraulic loadings of 0.20, 0.30, and 0.43 gpm/ft^2. After acclimation at each loading rate, samples were collected at various depths in the filter for laboratory analysis. The wastewater samples were settled for 30 min and filtered through Whatman No. 42 filter paper prior to BOD testing.

Solution:
Mean residence times of the wastewater in the filter were determined by measuring the time for concentrated doses of salt solution to flush through the column. The results, with and without the presence of biological slime growth, are graphed in Figure 26. The constant n for Eq. (46) is the negative slope of the line, and C is the intercept of the line at $Q = 1.0$ divided by the depth of media. With a biological growth coating the packing, the mean residence time was

$$ t = \frac{1.25D}{Q^{0.45}} $$

The mean residence time of clean packing, without slime, was

$$ t = \frac{0.24D}{Q^{0.43}} $$

A comparison of these equations shows the significant effect that slime growth has on the mean residence time.

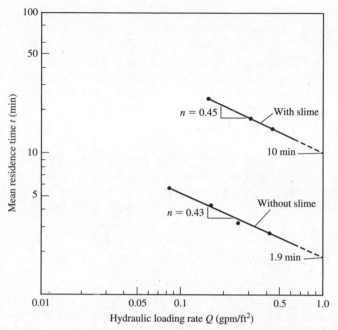

FIGURE 26   Relationship between hydraulic loading and mean residence time for Example 6. *Source:* Adapted from S. Balakrishnan, W. W. Eckenfelder, and C. Brown, "Organics Removal by a Selected Trickling Filter Media," *Water and Wastes Eng.* 6, no. 1 (1969): A.22–A.25.

Soluble BOD removal data are plotted in Figure 27 as the logarithm of BOD remaining, S_e/S_0, versus the depth D in the filter packing. From Eq. (48),

$$\log\left(\frac{S_e}{S_0}\right) = -\left(\frac{K}{2.3}\right)\left(\frac{D}{Q^n}\right) \tag{54}$$

Based on this equation, the slope of each line drawn through $\log(S_e/S_0)$ versus D data for a specific hydraulic loading is defined as

$$\text{slope} = \frac{\log(S_e/S_0)}{D} = -\left(\frac{K}{2.3}\right)Q^{-n} \tag{55}$$

The slopes in Figure 27a for hydraulic loadings of 0.20, 0.30, and 0.43 gpm/ft^2 are –0.059, –0.051, and –0.045, respectively.
Taking the logarithm of both sides of Eq. (55) yields

$$\log(\text{slope}) = -\, n \log Q + \log\left(-K/2.3\right) \tag{56}$$

which is the equation for a straight line of slope $-n$. Therefore, the slope of a line drawn through $\log(\text{slope})$ versus $\log Q$ data is $-n$. From the logarithmic plot in Figure 27b, $n = 0.39$ (Figure 26) (based on the slopes and hydraulic loadings given in Figure 27a.) Note: this is close to $n = 0.45$ from tracer analysis.

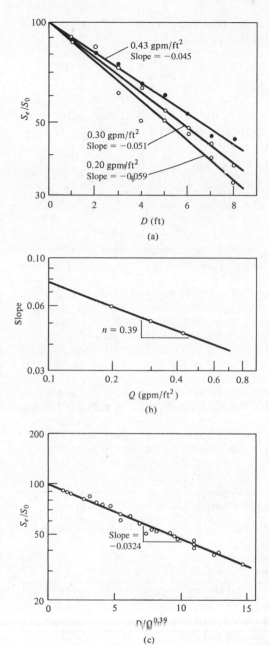

FIGURE 27 Plotted data for Example 6. (a) Relationship between filter depth and fraction of BOD remaining at various hydraulic loads. (b) Diagram for determination of n. (c) Diagram for determination of K. *Source:* Adapted from S. Balakrishnan, W. W. Eckenfelder, and C. Brown, "Organics Removal by a Selected Trickling Filter Media," *Water and Wastes Eng.* 6, no. 1 (1969): A.22–A.25.

Finally, the constant K is determined by plotting $\log(S_e/S_0)$ versus D/Q^n and determining the slope of the line drawn through the data, which from Eq. (54) equals $-(K/2.3)$. For the S_e/S_0 and $D/Q^{0.39}$ data plotted in Figure 27c, the slope of the line is -0.0324, and $K = -2.3 \times -0.0324 = 0.0745$ min^{-1}.

The average operating temperature of the pilot filter was 14°C. Correcting K to 20°C using Eq. (50), the reaction-rate constant at 20°C is

$$K_{20} = \frac{K}{(1.035)^{T-20}} = \frac{0.0745}{(1.035)^{14-20}} = 0.092 \text{ min}^{-1}$$

Substituting values of $K = 0.092$ and $n = 0.39$ in Eq. (48), the soluble BOD removal from a settled domestic wastewater for the specific filter packing tested is

$$\frac{S_e}{S_0} = e^{-0.092D/Q^{0.39}} \tag{57}$$

Example 7

Drury, Carmona, and Delgadillo [11] describe the rehabilitation of an old shallow stone-media trickling filter by installing plastic media to solve the problem of ponding due to plugging of voids in the bed.

High-density, cross-flow media with a specific surface area of 138 m^2/m^3 (42 ft^2/ft^3) and a depth of only 1.02 m (3.33 ft) was installed in the trickling-filter tank, which was 21.3 m (70 ft) in diameter. Before undertaking costly rehabilitation of the final settling tank, a study was performed to evaluate performance of the media and to establish a suitable loading for operation. The trickling filter was operated at a constant flow rate throughout the day (7 A.M.–midnight), with the primary effluent diluted by trickling-filter effluent returned to the wet well; the recirculation ratio ranged from 0.8 to 1.1. During the 8-hr period from 8 A.M.–4 P.M., the influent and effluent were composited and refrigerated by automatic samplers at 15-min intervals. The effluent sample was allowed to settle for 1 hr in a laboratory container to simulate clarification in a final settling tank, and the supernatant was decanted for analysis. The samples were tested for total BOD and dissolved BOD after filtration through a glass-fiber filter. The test results for the winter evaluation period are given in Table 2.

TABLE 2　Sampling Data and Calculated Values for Determination of Reaction-Rate Coefficient k_{20} in Example 7

$Q^{(a)}$ (l/m^2·s)	T (°C)	Influent BOD (mg/l)	S_0 (mg/l)	Effluent BOD (mg/l)	S_e (mg/l)	$\ln\dfrac{S_0}{S_e}$	$\dfrac{A_s D \theta^{T-20}}{Q^n}$ [(l/m^2·s)$^{-0.5}$]
0.49	20.0	75	44	32	18	0.89	201
0.54	20.5	50	29	23	13	0.80	195
0.49	20.0	73	38	27	14	1.00	201
0.49	18.5	53	22	22	9.5	0.84	191
0.59	18.5	64	34	32	17	0.69	174
0.49	19.0	45	30	24	12	0.92	195
0.31	23.0	80	33	16	9.2	1.28	280
0.35	21.5	66	37	18	12	1.13	251

$^{(a)}$includes recirculation flow.

Solution: For each set of Q, T, S_0, and S_e, calculate values for $\ln S_0/S_e$ and $A_s D\Theta^{T-20}/Q^n$. The following are sample calculations for the first set of data:

$$\ln \frac{S_0}{S_e} = \ln \frac{44}{18} = 0.89$$

$A_s = 138 \text{ m}^2/\text{m}^3$, $D = 1.02$ m, $\Theta = 1.035$, and $n = 0.5$:

$$\frac{A_s D\Theta^{T-20}}{Q^n} = \frac{138 \times 1.02(1.035)^{20.0-20}}{(0.49)^{0.5}} = 201$$

The calculated values for determining k_{20} are listed in Table 2 and plotted in Figure 28. The slope of the best-fit line through the plotted points is the reaction-rate coefficient k_{20} equal to 0.0047 $(1/\text{m}^2 \cdot \text{s})^{0.5}$.

This field evaluation demonstrated that high-density cross-flow media can be effectively used in shallow filters at high BOD loadings. The k_{20} was significantly greater than expected, based on other studies conducted of towers with much deeper media. Although the reason for this is not known, the authors speculated that the high BOD removal efficiency of a shallow bed may be related to improved oxygen transfer.

An allowable loading on the filter used in the study with high-density cross-flow media can be calculated based on the following parameters:

$$\text{Depth of media} = 1.02 \text{ m}$$
$$\text{Specific surface area} = 138 \text{ m}^2/\text{m}^3$$
$$k_{20} = 0.0047 \ (1/\text{m}^2 \cdot \text{s})^{0.5}$$

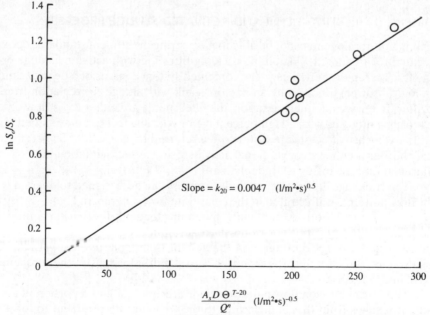

FIGURE 28   Plot of $\ln S_0/S_e$ versus $A_s D\Theta^{T-20}/Q^n$ to determine k_{20} for Example 7.

$$\text{Wastewater temperature} = 10°C$$
$$\text{Influent BOD with recirculation flow} = 70 \text{ mg/l}$$
$$\text{Soluble influent BOD} = 35 \text{ mg/l}$$
$$\text{Allowable effluent BOD} = 25 \text{ mg/l}$$
$$\text{Soluble effluent BOD} = 12.5 \text{ mg/l}$$

Rearranging Eq. (51),

$$Q = \left(\frac{k_{20} A_s D \Theta^{T-20}}{\ln(S_0/S_e)} \right)^2 \tag{58}$$

$$= \left(\frac{0.0047 \times 138 \times 1.02(1.035)^{10-20}}{\ln(35/12.5)} \right)^2 = 0.208 \text{ l/m}^2 \cdot \text{s}$$

Allowable BOD loading is

$$\left(Q \frac{1}{\text{m}^2 \cdot \text{s}} \right) \left(86,400 \frac{\text{s}}{\text{d}} \right) \left(\text{BOD} \frac{\text{mg}}{\text{l}} \right) \left(\frac{\text{g}}{1000 \text{ mg}} \right) \left(\frac{1}{A_s} \frac{\text{m}^2}{\text{m}^3} \right)$$

$$\tag{59}$$

$$= \frac{0.208 \times 86,400 \times 70}{1000 \times 1.02} = 1200 \text{ g/m}^3 \cdot \text{d} \ (77 \text{ lb/1000 ft}^3/\text{day})$$

---

17   COMBINED TRICKLING-FILTER AND ACTIVATED-SLUDGE PROCESSES

Trickling filters alone may not be able to meet stringent effluent standards occasionally specified for treatment. Combining trickling filtration with activated-sludge processes can increase removal efficiency. The combined system consists of a deep trickling filter (biological tower) followed by an aeration tank with sludge recirculation from a final clarifier. To ensure adequate aeration, the filter media are either cross-flow or vertical-flow plastic modules with a high percentage of void space. The aeration tank and final clarifier is an activated-sludge system often referred to as a solids contact process. The final clarifier is either a conventional activated-sludge sedimentation tank or one with a flocculation zone inside a large inlet baffle.

The trickling-filter activated-sludge process can be designed to operate with various flow patterns, as illustrated in the composite flow diagram in Figure 29. By providing direct recirculation for adequate hydraulic loading, the trickling filter can be operated independent of the second-stage aeration process. In this arrangement, the filter is called a *roughing* filter, and the system is suitable to treat variable-strength wastewaters. The filter absorbs shock loads to stabilize loading on the subsequent activated-sludge process.

The other common flow pattern includes recirculation of a portion of the settled biological solids from the final clarifier to the trickling-filter influent to form an activated sludge that recycles through both the filter and the aeration tank. [This process is

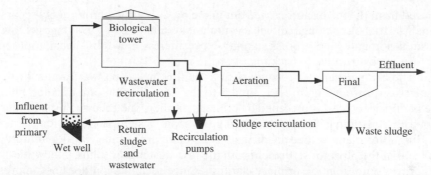

FIGURE 29   Profile of a combined trickling-filter activated-sludge process.

referred to by several names: activated biological filtration (ABF), activated biofiltration–activated-sludge, and trickling filtration–solids contact process.] This composite
system has the characteristics of both fixed-film and suspended-growth processes. The
mixed liquor in the aeration tank enhances removal of nonsettleable and dissolved
BOD in the filter effluent. Because of good process stability, a high-quality effluent can
be consistently produced. In a way, the biofilter in this process is acting as a static aerator; therefore, by increasing the hydraulic loading by recirculation, the transfer of oxygen is increased. However, if excess sludge solids are recirculated through the biofilter,
the oxygen demand exceeds the transfer capability of the media and limits BOD
removal.

     Equations to model the activated biofiltration–activated-sludge process have not
been successfully formulated because of the difficulty in analyzing the system. In
design, removal by the biofilter must be determined first so that the aeration tank and
associated aeration equipment can be properly sized. Arora and Umphres [12] evaluated the operation of 17 activated biofiltration–activated-sludge plants with redwood-
media filters. The following are the ranges of various design and operational
parameters of these treatment systems: percentage of the total volume (filter media
plus aeration tank) that is aeration tank volume, 40%–75%; system BOD loading
based on total volume, 20–50 lb/1000 ft^3/day (320–800 g/m$^3 \cdot$ d); biofilter loading,
50–110 lb/1000 ft^3/day (800–1800 g/m$^3 \cdot$ d); system food/microorganism ratio, 0.2–1.0
with the median at 0.5; and effluent BOD and effluent suspended solids, 5–25 mg/l. The
operating personnel at most of the plants believed the system was more stable than
conventional activated sludge and was better able to absorb shock loads.

18   DESCRIPTION OF ROTATING BIOLOGICAL CONTACTOR MEDIA AND PROCESS

A rotating biological contactor (RBC) consists of a shaft of circular plastic disks 12 ft
in diameter revolving at 40% submergence in a contour-bottom tank. The nominal
spacing between disks is 0.50–0.75 in. so that during submergence the wastewater can
enter between the surfaces. When rotated out of the tank, air enters the spaces while
the liquid trickles out over films of biological growth attached to the media. Alternat-
ing exposure to organics in the wastewater and oxygen in the air is similar to dosing a
trickling filter with a rotating distributor. Excess microbial solids are hydraulically

scoured from the media and carried out in the process effluent for gravity separation in a final clarifier. A rotating biological contactor system has the advantages of low power consumption and good process stability. Nevertheless, new RBC installations are rare because of cost relative to trickling filters.

The arrangement for secondary treatment of municipal wastewater by the RBC process, as shown in Figure 30, is similar to the flow diagram of a trickling-filter plant. The biological process is preceded by primary clarifiers and followed by secondary clarifiers. These settling tanks are sized using the same design criteria as for clarifiers in a trickling-filter plant. Settled solids that accumulate in the final clarifier are returned to the head of the plant for settlement with the raw-wastewater solids; thus, waste sludge is withdrawn only from the primary clarifiers. Since recirculation does not improve performance, the return flow is not designed to recycle wastewater through the RBC units.

Wastewater after sedimentation is applied to the first stage of a series of RBC chambers separated by baffles. In processing a wastewater that is essentially domestic in its characteristics, a series of four stages is usually employed to ensure adequate BOD reduction; additional stages can be added to initiate nitrification. Each stage acts as a completely mixed chamber, and the slow movement of wastewater through the system simulates plug flow. Biological solids sheared from the disk surfaces are hydraulically transported under the baffles separating the chambers and conveyed from the system suspended in the effluent.

Rotating biological contactors are sensitive to cold and must be protected from normal outdoor weather conditions—that is, precipitation, wind, and intense sunshine. Standard design procedure is either to enclose individual stages under insulated plastic covers or to house a series of units in a suitable building with adequate ventilation.

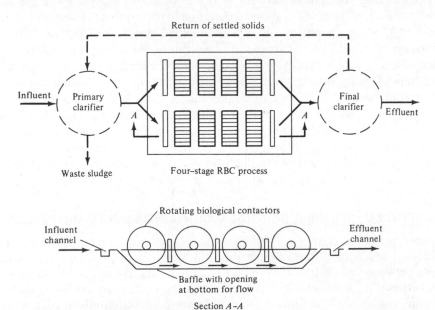

FIGURE 30   Flow diagram for a domestic wastewater plant using rotating biological contactors for secondary treatment.

Manufacturers' literature usually suggests design criteria based on operational performance of their full-scale installations. Typical recommendations follow for secondary treatment of domestic wastewater to yield an effluent of less than 30 mg/l of BOD and 30 mg/l of suspended solids:

1. Average loading based on total RBC surface area should be 1.5 lb/1000 ft^2/day of soluble BOD or 3.0 lb/1000 ft^2/day of total BOD (7.5 g/m$^2 \cdot$ d of soluble BOD or 15 g/m$^2 \cdot$ d of total BOD).
2. Maximum loading on the first stage should be 6 lb/1000 ft^2/day of soluble BOD or 12 lb/1000 ft^2/day of total BOD (30 g/m$^2 \cdot$ d of soluble BOD or 60 g/m$^2 \cdot$ d of total BOD).
3. A temperature correction for additional RBC surface area of 15% should be made for each 5°F below a design wastewater temperature of 55°F (15% for each 2.8°C below 13°C).

These recommendations are consistent with observed satisfactory performance at larger installations. For small plants, the safe upper limit is an average soluble BOD loading of approximately 1.0 lb/1000 ft^2/day (5 g/m$^2 \cdot$ d). Mathematical models to predict the performance of the RBC process reliably are still in the developmental stage [13].

Example 8

Calculate the RBC area required for secondary treatment of a raw domestic wastewater having 230 mg/l of BOD. The design flow is 2.0 mgd at a temperature of 50°F. The effluent quality specified is 30 mg/l of BOD.

Solution:

$$\text{primary effluent BOD concentration} = 0.65 \times 230 = 150 \text{ mg/l}$$

An appropriate average BOD loading to achieve an effluent BOD of 30 mg/l is 3.0 lb/1000 ft^2/day at 55°F. Therefore,

$$\text{RBC area at 55°F} = \frac{2.0 \times 150 \times 8.34}{3.0} = \frac{2500}{3.0} = 834,000 \text{ ft}^2$$

Correcting for a temperature of 50°F by a 15% area increase per 5°F,

$$\text{RBC area at 50°F} = 1.15 \times 834,000 = 959,000 \text{ ft}^2$$

Use RBC shafts manufactured with a nominal surface area of 60,000 ft^2 with 12-ft-diameter disks for installation in tanks with a length of 17 ft 4 in. Install four rows of four stages for a total of $16 \times 60,000 = 960,000$ ft^2.

BOD loading on the first stage based on a temperature of 55°F should not exceed 12 lb/1000 ft^2/day.

$$\text{first-stage loading at 55°F} = \frac{2500 \times 4}{(960/1.15)} = 12.0 \text{ lb/1000 ft}^2/\text{day} \quad \text{(OK)}$$

ACTIVATED SLUDGE

Activated-sludge processes are used for both secondary treatment and complete aerobic treatment without primary sedimentation. Wastewater is fed continuously into an aerated tank, where the microorganisms metabolize and biologically flocculate the organics (Figure 8). Microorganisms (activated sludge) are settled from the aerated mixed liquor under quiescent conditions in the final clarifier and returned to the aeration tank. Clear supernatant from the final settling tank is the plant effluent.

The primary feeders in activated sludge are bacteria; secondary feeders are holozoic protozoans (Figure 11). Microbial growth in the mixed liquor is maintained in the declining or endogenous growth phase to ensure good settling characteristics (Figure 9). Synthesis of the waste organics results in a buildup of the microbial mass in the system. Excess activated sludge is wasted from the system to maintain the proper food/microorganism ratio (F/M) and sludge age to ensure optimum operation.

Activated sludge is truly an aerobic treatment process because the biological floc are suspended in a liquid medium containing dissolved oxygen. Aerobic conditions must be maintained in the aeration tank; however, in the final clarifier, the dissolved-oxygen concentration can become extremely low. Dissolved oxygen extracted from the mixed liquor is replenished by air supplied to the aeration tank.

19   BOD LOADINGS AND AERATION PERIODS

General loading and operational parameters for the activated-sludge processes used in treatment of municipal wastewater in cool humid climatic regions are listed in Table 3.

"Allowable BOD loadings and performance of aeration processes depend on wastewater temperature, yet, few data from field studies of treatment plants are available to establish reliable design criteria based on temperature. Most of the design data listed in books [such as Table 3] are based on the operation of activated-sludge systems in cool humid climatic regions where wastewater temperature is in the range of 10° to 20°C (58° to 68°F). In this temperature climate, the concern is cooling of the wastewater below 10°C in winter. In a hot dry climate, the concern is the effect of warm water supplies

TABLE 3   General Loading and Operational Parameters for Activated-Sludge Processes

| Process | BOD Loading | | Sludge Age (days) | Aeration Period (hr) | Average Return Sludge Rates (%) |
	lb BOD/ 1000 ft^3/ day[a]	lb BOD/ day/lb of MLSS			
Step aeration	30–50	0.2–0.5	5–15	5.0–7.0	50
Conventional (tapered aeration)	30–40	0.2–0.5	5–15	6.0–7.5	30
Contact stabilization	30–50	0.2–0.5	5–15	6.0–9.0	100
Extended aeration	10–30	0.05–0.2	20+	20–30	100
High-purity oxygen	120+	0.6–1.5	5–10	1.0–3.0	30

[a]1.0 lb/1000 ft^3/day = 16 g/m$^3 \cdot$ d.

(particularly where the drinking water is warm groundwater or from distillation of seawater) that increase wastewater temperature to the range of 20° to 30°C or higher" [14].

The BOD load on an aeration tank is calculated using the BOD in the influent wastewater without regard to that in the return sludge flow. BOD loadings are expressed in terms of pounds of BOD applied per day per 1000 ft^3 of liquid volume in the aeration tank and in terms of pounds of BOD applied/day/lb of mixed-liquor suspended solids (MLSS) in the aeration tank. The latter, the F/M ratio, is expressed by some authors in terms of lb of BOD applied/day/lb of volatile mixed-liquor suspended solids (MLVSS).

The aeration period is the detention time of the raw-wastewater flow in the aeration tank expressed in hours. It is calculated by dividing the tank volume by the daily average flow without regard to return sludge. The activated sludge returned is expressed as a percentage of the raw-wastewater influent. For example, if the return sludge rate is 20% and the raw-wastewater flow into the plant is 10 mgd, the return sludge is 2.0 mgd.

BOD loadings per unit volume of aeration tank vary from greater than 50 to 10 lb of BOD/1000 ft^3/day, while the aeration periods correspondingly vary from 5 to 24 hr. The relationship between volumetric BOD loading and aeration period is directly related to BOD concentration in the wastewater. For example, converting the average BOD concentration of 200 mg/l into units of pounds per 1000 ft^3 yields a concentration of

$$200 \text{ mg/l} \times \frac{62.4 \text{ lb/1000 ft}^3}{1000 \text{ mg/l}} = 12.5 \text{ lb/1000 ft}^3$$

Therefore, 200 mg/l wastewater applied to an extended aeration system with a 24-hr (1-day) aeration period results in a BOD loading of 12.5 lb/1000 ft^3/day. If a high-rate aeration period of 6.0 hr is considered, the BOD loading becomes

$$12.5 \text{ lb/1000 ft}^3/\text{day} \times \frac{24 \text{ hr}}{6.0 \text{ hr}} = 50 \text{ lb/1000 ft}^3/\text{day}$$

Sludge age (mean cell residence time) relates the quantity of microbial solids in an activated-sludge process to the quantity of solids lost in the effluent and excess solids withdrawn in the waste sludge. Equation (60) establishes the sludge age in days on the basis of MLSS in the aeration tank relative to SS discharged in the effluent and SS in the waste sludge withdrawn daily:

$$\text{Sludge age} = \frac{\text{MLSS} \times V}{\text{SS}_e \times Q_e + \text{SS}_w \times Q_w} \tag{60}$$

where

sludge age = mean cell residence time, days
MLSS = mixed-liquor suspended solids, mg/l
V = volume of the aeration tank, mil gal (m^3/d)
SS$_e$ = suspended solids in effluent, mg/l
SS$_w$ = suspended solids in waste sludge, mg/l
Q_e = quantity of effluent wastewater, mgd (m^3/d)
Q_w = quantity of waste sludge, mgd (m^3/d)

Sludge age is also calculated using the MLVSS (volatile portion of the MLSS) and the VSS (volatile suspended solids) in the effluent and waste sludge. The argument is that the volatile portion of the suspended solids is more representative of the microbial masses, and thus the sludge age expresses the residence time of the microbial cells in the system more realistically.

The suspended-solids concentration maintained in the MLSS of conventional and step-aeration processes ranges from 1500 to 3000 mg/l. The concentration held in the operation of a particular system depends on the desired F/M and sludge age for the applied BOD load. High-rate completely mixed processes generally operate with higher MLSS concentrations of 3000–4000 mg/l. Because of the variety of extended aeration processes, MLSS values encompass the entire range of 1000 to greater than 5000 mg/l.

Solids retention in an activated-sludge system is measured in days, whereas the liquid aeration period is measured in hours. For example, a conventional activated-sludge process with an MLSS of 2500 mg/l in the aeration tank, treating an average domestic wastewater and operating at a 6-hr aeration period, has a sludge age of approximately 7 days. The suspended solids are cycled in the system from final clarifier back to aeration tank, while the liquid flows through the aeration tank and clarifier.

Effluent quality from well-operated activated-sludge processes in the BOD loading range of 30–50 lb BOD/1000 ft^3/day can reliably meet the secondary standards of average maximum BOD of 30 mg/l and suspended solids of 30 mg/l with the temperature of mixed liquor at 10°–20°C (50°–68°F). At loadings lower in the listed range, or mixed-liquor temperature in the upper range, the effluent quality is more likely to be nearer 20 mg/l BOD and 20 mg/l suspended solids. Biological activity doubles (or halves) for every 10°–15°C temperature change. Therefore, for processes in the loading range of 30–50 lb BOD/1000 ft^3/day, reducing the mixed-liquor temperature to 5°–10°C can adversely affect effluent quality. Conversely, in the range of 15°–25°C, the quality of the effluent is likely to improve, or the loading can be increased with no detriment to effluent quality. Because extended aeration systems operate in a lower range of 10–30 lb BOD/1000 ft^3/day, a decrease or an increase in mixed-liquor temperature has less influence on effluent quality. Selection of aeration equipment is to some extent dictated by this relationship between allowable BOD loading and operating temperature. In a cool climate, submerged diffused aeration is common to reduce cooling of the mixed liquor in winter operation. In a warm climate, surface aerators that spray the mixed liquor in the air to absorb oxygen can be used since cooling is not a major consideration.

The wide range of aeration periods and BOD loadings used in activated-sludge processes tends to contrast one process with another. Also, the variety of physical features, such as the aeration tank size and shape, used in the various processes tends to accent the differences. Actually all activated-sludge processes are biologically similar, as seen in the generalized activated-sludge diagram of Figure 31. BOD is removed in the process by assimilative respiration of microorganisms, and the new cell growth is reduced by endogenous respiration. Excess microbial growth is withdrawn from the system by wasting activated sludge. Oxygen is added to the process to maintain aerobic biological activity.

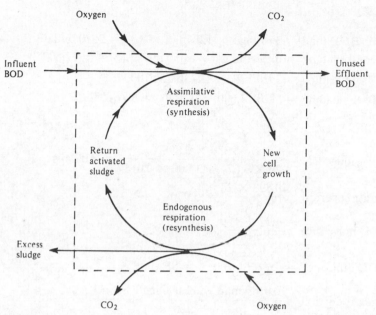

FIGURE 31 Generalized biological process reactions in the activated-sludge process.

Example 9

Data from a field study on a step-aeration activated-sludge secondary are as follows:

$$\text{aeration tank volume} = 120,000 \text{ ft}^3 = 0.898 \text{ mil gal}$$
$$\text{settled wastewater flow} = 3.67 \text{ mgd}$$
$$\text{return sludge flow} = 1.27 \text{ mgd}$$
$$\text{waste sludge flow} = 18,900 \text{ gpd} = 0.0189 \text{ mgd}$$
$$\text{MLSS in aeration tank} = 2350 \text{ mg/l}$$
$$\text{SS in waste sludge} = 11,000 \text{ mg/l}$$
$$\text{influent wastewater BOD} = 128 \text{ mg/l}$$
$$\text{effluent wastewater BOD} = 22 \text{ mg/l}$$
$$\text{effluent SS} = 26 \text{ mg/l}$$

Using these data, calculate the loading and operational parameters listed in Table 3 and the excess sludge production in pounds of excess suspended solids per pound of BOD applied.

Solution:

$$\text{BOD load} = 3.67 \text{ mgd} \times 128 \text{ mg/l} \times 8.34 = 3920 \text{ lb/day}$$
$$\text{MLSS in aeration tank} = 0.898 \text{ mil gal} \times 2350 \text{ mg/l} \times 8.34 = 17,600 \text{ lb}$$
$$\text{BOD loading} = 3920/120 = 32.7 \text{ lb/day/1000 ft}^3$$
$$\text{BOD loading} = 3920/17,600 = 0.22 \text{ lb/day/lb of MLSS}$$

Using Eq. (60),

$$\text{sludge age} = \frac{2350 \times 0.898}{26 \times 3.67 + 11,000 \times 0.0189} = 7.0 \text{ days}$$

$$\text{aeration period} = \frac{0.898 \times 24}{3.67} = 5.9 \text{ hr}$$

$$\text{return sludge rate} = \frac{1.27 \times 100}{3.67} = 35\%$$

$$\text{BOD efficiency} = \frac{(128 - 22)100}{128} = 83\%$$

$$\text{sludge production} = \frac{0.0189 \text{ mgd} \times 11,000 \text{ mg/l} \times 8.34}{3920}$$
$$= 0.44 \text{ lb SS wasted/lb BOD applied}$$

---

20   OPERATION OF ACTIVATED-SLUDGE PROCESSES

Operation of an activated-sludge treatment plant is regulated by (1) the quantity of air supplied to the aeration basin, (2) the rate of activated-sludge recirculation, and (3) the amount of excess sludge withdrawn from the system. Sludge wasting is used to establish the desired concentration of MLSS, food/microorganism ratio, and sludge age.

Field observations for monitoring an aeration system are the rates of wastewater influent, excess sludge wasting, and sludge recirculation; the dissolved-oxygen concentration in the mixed liquor; and the depth of the sludge blanket in the final clarifier. Laboratory tests are used to determine influent and effluent BOD, the concentration of suspended solids in the return sludge, and the concentration of MLSS in the aeration tank. From these data, BOD loadings, the aeration period, the return sludge rate, and the BOD removal efficiency can be calculated. The final clarifier operation is observed by testing for the concentration of suspended solids in the effluent and calculating the overflow rate and solids loading.

The degree of treatment achieved in an activated-sludge process depends directly on the settleability of the suspended solids in the final clarifier. If the biological floc agglomerate and settle rapidly by gravity, the overflow is a clear supernatant. Conversely, poorly flocculated particles (pin floc) and buoyant filamentous growths that do not separate by gravity contribute to BOD and suspended solids in the system effluent.

Excessive carryover of floc resulting in inefficient operation is referred to as sludge bulking. This can be caused by any one or a combination of the biological, chemical, and physical factors listed in Table 4. If an activated-sludge process is not functioning properly, the loadings on the aeration tank and final clarifier are calculated and

TABLE 4   Factors that Can Adversely Affect Settleability of Activated Sludge

Biological Factors

Species of dominant microorganisms (filamentous)
Ineffective biological flocculation
Denitrification in final clarifier (floating solids)
Excessive volumetric and food/microorganism loadings
Mixed-liquor suspended-solids concentration
Unsteady-state conditions (nonuniform feed rate and discontinuous wasting of excess activated sludge)

Chemical Factors

Lack of nutrients
Presence of toxins
Kinds of organic matter
Insufficient aeration
Low temperature

Physical Factors

Excessive agitation during aeration resulting in shearing of floc
Ineffective final clarification: inadequate rate of return sludge, excessive overflow rate or solids loading, or hydraulic turbulence

compared with established design criteria. Next, operational procedures are reviewed to ensure proper aeration, sludge recirculation, and sludge wasting. Special laboratory tests can be performed to determine detrimental chemical characteristics of the waste-water, such as a lack of nutrients or the presence of toxins. Microscopic examination of the activated sludge can reveal excessive filamentous growth [15].

21   ACTIVATED-SLUDGE TREATMENT SYSTEMS

Conventional Activated-Sludge Process

The conventional process diagrammed in Figure 32a is an outgrowth of the earliest acti-vated-sludge systems constructed, used for secondary treatment of domestic wastewater. The aeration basin is a long rectangular tank with air diffusers on one side of the tank bottom to provide aeration and mixing. Settled raw wastewater and return activated sludge enter the head of the tank and flow down its length in a spiral flow pattern. An air supply is tapered along the length of the tank to provide a greater amount of diffused air near the head where the rate of biological metabolism and resultant oxygen demand are the greatest. A conventional activated-sludge aeration tank is shown in Figure 33.

The conventional activated-sludge process uses bubble air diffusers set at a depth of 8 ft or more to provide adequate oxygen transfer and deep mixing. Several different bubble diffusers are manufactured; common kinds are stainless-steel or hollow-cylinder porous tubes 1–2 ft in length or porous disks about 6 in. in diameter. These individual diffusers are attached along a submerged air header about 10 ft in length attached to an air-supply hanger pipe. For maintenance of the diffusers, the hanger pipe can be designed with rotating joints (a swing-diffuser arm) so the header can be retracted using

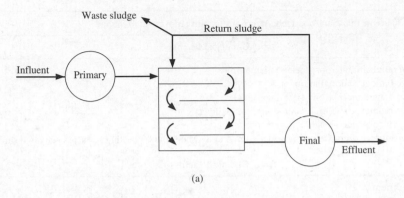

Waste sludge

Return sludge

Influent

Primary

Final

Effluent

(a)

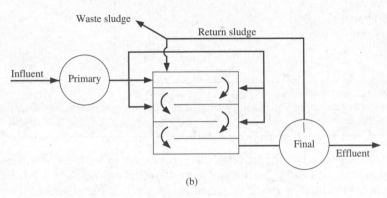

Waste sludge

Return sludge

Influent

Primary

Final

Effluent

(b)

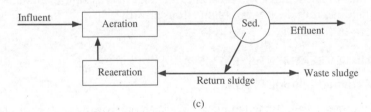

Influent

Aeration

Sed.

Effluent

Reaeration

Return sludge

Waste sludge

(c)

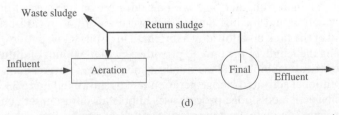

Waste sludge

Return sludge

Influent

Aeration

Final

Effluent

(d)

FIGURE 32   Flow diagrams for common activated-sludge processes. (a) Conventional activated-sludge process. (b) Step-aeration activated-sludge process. (c) Contact stabilization without primary sedimentation. (d) Extended aeration without primary sedimentation.

(a)

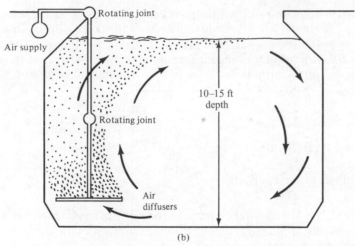

(b)

FIGURE 33 Conventional activated-sludge process. (a) Long rectangular aeration tank with submerged coarse-bubble diffusers along one side (Santee, CA). (b) Cross section of a typical aeration tank illustrating the spiral flow pattern created by aeration along one side.

a portable jack. The tops of swing-diffuser hanger arms can be seen in Figure 33a along the aeration tank.

Step-Aeration Activated-Sludge Process

The *step-aeration process* (Figure 32b) is a modification of the conventional process. Instead of introducing all raw wastewater at the tank head, this system introduced raw flow at several points along the tank length. Stepping the influent load along the tank produces a more uniform oxygen demand throughout. While tapered aeration attempts to supply air to match oxygen demand along the length of the tank, step loading provides a more uniform oxygen demand for an evenly distributed air supply.

Both step-aeration and conventional processes can use fine-bubble aeration. Fine-bubble diffusers produce bubbles with a diameter of approximately 2–5 mm (0.08–0.20 in.) in clean water. The three general categories of fine-pore media are ceramics, porous plastics, and perforated membranes. As illustrated in Figure 34, individual diffusers are mounted on holders attached to air piping on the tank bottom. Each membrane or ceramic disc, either 9 in. or 7 in. in diameter, is sealed to a holder by a screw-on retainer ring with an O-ring seal. With the diffusers over the entire floor area, the rising streams of fine bubbles mix and aerate the mixed liquor uniformly, keeping the microbial floc in suspension. The benefit of fine-bubble aeration is a power savings of 40%–60% when compared to coarse-bubble or mechanically aerated activated-sludge processes [16]. As a result of cost savings and system performance, use of fine-bubble aeration is now common in activated-sludge processes, particularly those with automated control. Automated aeration control is the manipulation of the aeration rate by computer to match the dynamic oxygen demand and maintain the desired residual dissolved-oxygen concentration in the mixed liquor.

Example 10

A step-aeration activated-sludge process is being sized for a settled wastewater flow of 7.40 mgd ($989,000$ ft^3/d) containing 7900 lb of BOD. The design maximum BOD loading is 40 lb/1000 ft^3/day, and the design minimum aeration period is 6.0 hr. (a) Calculate the dimensions for four identical aeration tanks. (b) Calculate the dimensions for four circular final clarifiers. (c) If the proposed minimum operating MLSS is 2000 mg/l, what is the calculated F/M at design loading?

Solution:

a. $V(\text{based on BOD loading}) = \dfrac{7900 \times 1000}{40} = 198,000 \text{ ft}^3$

$V(\text{based on aeration period}) = \dfrac{7,400,000 \times 6.0}{24 \times 7.48} = 247,000 \text{ ft}^3$

Use 247,000 ft^3 with an aeration period of 6.0 hr, which results in a BOD loading of 32 lb/1000 ft^3/day. Install four aeration tanks with 13 ft liquid depth and 24 ft width for fine-bubble aeration.

$$\text{length of each tank} = \dfrac{247,000}{4 \times 13 \times 24} = 198 \text{ ft}$$

b. From Section 10.11, use an overflow rate of 800 gpd/ft^2 and side-water depth of 11 ft to size 4 circular clarifiers.

$$\text{surface area} = \dfrac{7,400,000}{4 \times 800} = 2310 \text{ ft}^2 \quad (\text{diameter} = 54 \text{ ft})$$

$$\text{detention time} = \dfrac{2300 \times 11 \times 24}{989,000/4} = 2.5 \text{ hr}$$

c. F/M $= \dfrac{7900}{2000 \times 1.85 \times 8.34} = 0.26$ lb BOD/day/lb of MLSS

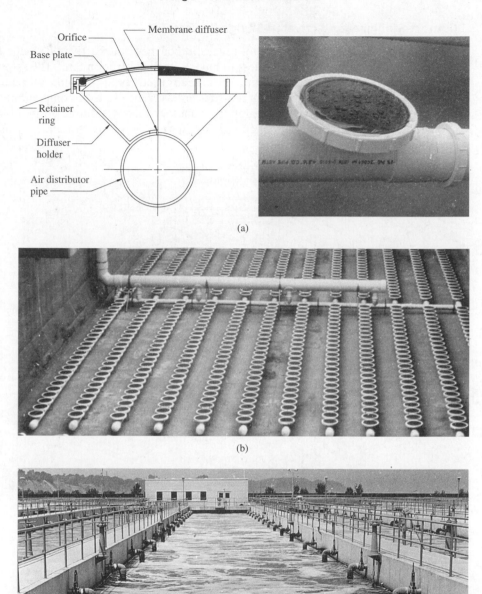

FIGURE 34 Fine-bubble diffuser for wastewater aeration. (a) A disc diffuser mounted on top of an air distributor pipe. (b) A grid of diffusers attached to air pipes mounted on the floor of an aeration tank. (c) Long rectangular aeration tank with uniform mixing and oxygenation by a grid of fine-bubble diffusers. *Source:* Sanitaire, a division of ITT Industries, Inc.

Contact-Stabilization Activated-Sludge Process

This process (Figure 32c) provides for reaeration of the return activated sludge from the final clarifier, allowing this process to have a smaller aeration tank. The sequence of aeration–sedimentation–reaeration has been used as a secondary treatment process in large plants but is rare in new design. Current use is of complete aerobic treatment without primary sedimentation in factory-built, field-erected plants with capacities of 0.05–0.5 mgd, as pictured in Figure 35. Using common walls for

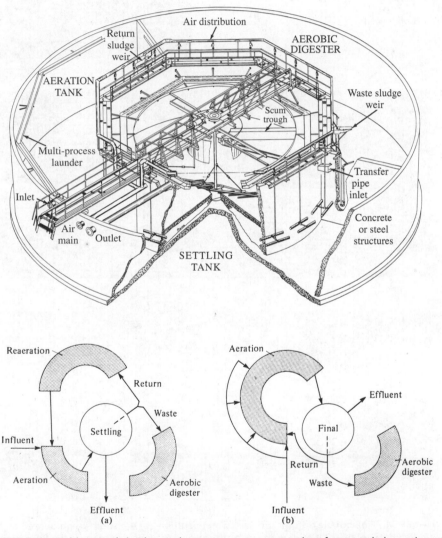

FIGURE 35   Field-erected circular steel wastewater treatment plant for extended-aeration, step-aeration, or contact stabilization processes. Drawing shows a cutaway view of the aeration tank and clarifier. (a) Contact stabilization (b) Extended or step aeration. *Source:* Sanitaire, a division of ITT Industries, Inc.

economical construction, the plant consists of two concentric circular tanks about 14 ft deep with the inner shell 15–30 ft in diameter and the outer tank 30–70 ft in diameter. The doughnut-shaped space between the two tanks is divided into three chambers for aeration, reaeration, and aerobic digestion. The circular chamber in the center is the final settling tank. The plant can also be segmented and constructed for extended aeration or step-aeration processes.

The sequence of operation for contact stabilization is aeration of the raw wastewater with return activated sludge, sedimentation to overflow clarified effluent, and reaeration of the settling tank underflow with a portion wasted to the aerobic digester. Supernatant drawn from the digester is returned to the aeration chamber. Periodically, aeration to the aerobic digester is stopped and suspended solids are allowed to settle so that gravity-thickened sludge may be withdrawn for disposal.

Example 11

A contact-stabilization plant, similar to the one diagrammed in Figure 35a, has compartments with the following liquid volumes:

$$\text{aeration chamber} = 85 \text{ m}^3$$
$$\text{reaeration chamber} = 173 \text{ m}^3$$
$$\text{aerobic digester} = 153 \text{ m}^3$$
$$\text{sedimentation tank} = 122 \text{ m}^3 \ (30.7\text{-m}^2 \text{ surface area})$$

If the plant is designed for an equivalent population of 2000 persons, calculate the BOD loading, aeration periods, and detention times.

Solution

$$\text{hydraulic load} = 2000 \times 450 \text{ l/person}$$
$$= 900,000 \text{ l/d} = 900 \text{ m}^3/\text{d}$$
$$\text{BOD load} = 2000 \times 91 \text{ g/person}$$
$$= 182,000 \text{ g/d}$$

$$\text{BOD loading on aeration tanks} = \frac{182,000}{85 + 173} = 705 \text{ g/m}^3 \cdot \text{d}$$
$$\text{aeration period (based on raw wastewater flow)} = \frac{85 \times 24}{900} = 2.3 \text{ h}$$
$$\text{reaeration period (based on raw wastewater flow)} = \frac{173 \times 24}{900} = 4.6 \text{ h}$$

The detention time for sedimentation (assuming 100% recirculation flow) is

$$\frac{122 \times 24}{2 \times 900} = 1.6 \text{ h}$$

The overflow rate on final clarifier (based on effluent flow) is

$$\frac{900}{30.7} = 29.3 \text{ m}^3/\text{m}^2 \cdot \text{d}$$

Extended-Aeration Activated-Sludge Process

The extended-aeration process (Figure 32d) is used primarily to treat wastewater flows from residential communities and small municipalities. The aeration period is 24 hr or greater, with complete mixing of the aeration tank and, because of low BOD loading, the activated-sludge process operates in the endogenous growth phase. As a result, the biological process is very stable and can accept variable loading. Waste sludge is discharged to an aerobic digester for stabilization prior to disposal. Final settling tanks are conservatively sized for a long detention time and a low overflow rate, generally in the range of 200–600 gpd/ft^2 for aeration tank volumes in the range of 5000–150,000 gal.

A well-known extended-aeration process is the closed-loop reactor, or oxidation ditch, aerated and mixed by horizontal rotors, as illustrated in Figure 36. The modern reactor is an elongated oval with vertical walls and a center dividing wall; earlier ditches had sloping side walls with a center island. In reactor design, the wastewater depth is up to 16 ft with 2-ft freeboard, and channel width is up to 31 ft, with the horizontal rotors spanning the full width of the channel. The flow diagram in Figure 36a shows parallel operation of two reactors, which can be changed to series operation by adjusting slide gates. Also, if one reactor is to be taken out of service temporarily for inspection, operation of the plant can continue, although at higher volumetric loading.

Dimensions of the reactor must conform to design criteria established by the manufacturer of the horizontal rotors. For example, for the horizontal rotor with individual blades illustrated in Figure 36b (Lakeside's *Magna Rotor*), the maximum liquid depth of channel is 16 ft, rotor diameter is 42 in. with minimum design immersion of 5 in., and available length is 5–30 ft. Manufacturers also provide design data on rate of oxygen transfer and installation requirements. As pictured, rotor covers are available to contain spray and to reduce cooling of the mixed liquor in low-temperature operation.

The *Carrousel*® system, similar in operation to an oxidation ditch, is a deep closed-loop aeration tank with vertical walls, as shown in the aerial view in Figure 37. However, in contrast, the aerators are vertical-shaft inverted open cones suspended from platforms constructed over the ends of the aeration channel. When treating unsettled municipal wastewater, the aeration period is generally 24 hr and the operating food/microorganism ratio less than 0.10 lb BOD/day/lb MLSS to operate at a long sludge age. Under these conditions with a warm mixed liquor, viable populations of nitrifying bacteria can be maintained in the activated sludge for nitrification.

The extended-aeration process can also be performed in a rectangular aeration tank aerated and mixed by mechanical aerators mounted on platforms supported by columns, as pictured in Figure 38. In order to have complete mixing, the length of the aeration tank is usually no greater than twice the width, with either two or four aerators. Mechanical aeration is often preferred to diffused aeration when the climate is sufficiently warm to prevent excessive cooling of the mixed liquor.

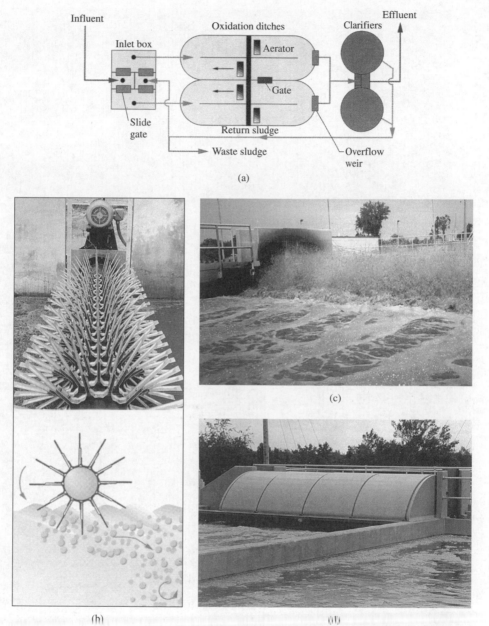

FIGURE 36 Closed-loop reactor (oxidation ditch) process. (a) Flow diagram of parallel operation of two reactors and clarifiers. Series operation is possible by closing two slide gates and the overflow gate of one reactor and opening the gate between ditches. (b) The horizontal rotor for aeration and moving the mixed liquor around the ditch. (c) Rotor operation showing aeration and mixing. (d) Rotor cover to contain spray and reduce icing in a cold climate. *Source:* Lakeside Equipment Corporation.

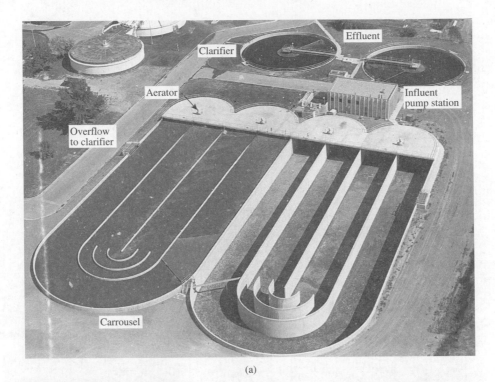

(a)

(b)

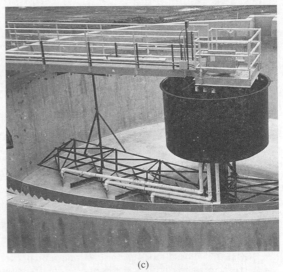

(c)

FIGURE 37   Aerial view of a *Carrousel*® activated-sludge plant. (a) Aeration and mixing is in oval serpentine aeration tanks with vertical walls followed by clarifiers for separation and return of activated sludge. (b) Low-speed vertical-shaft aerators are supported from a platform holding the drive motors and gear boxes. (c) Column-supported clarifier mechanisms have uptake pipes for rapid return of activated sludge. *Source:* EIMCO Process Equipment.

FIGURE 38   Platform-mounted low-speed mechanical aerator with an inverted open cone for high oxygen-transfer efficiency in an extended-aeration activated-sludge process. *Source:* EIMCO Process Equipment.

Example 12

Determine a preliminary layout for a closed-loop reactor plant to treat an unsettled wastewater flow of 240,000 gpd (32,100 ft³/d) with 400 lb of BOD (200 mg/l). (a) Calculate the dimensions for two oval closed-loop reactors with vertical walls, assuming a liquid depth of 5.0 ft. (b) Calculate the dimensions for two circular final clarifiers. (c) If the proposed minimum operating MLSS is 3000 mg/l, what is the operating F/M?

Solution: Use a layout of two reactors, as shown in Figure 36. For a typical domestic wastewater with a BOD of 200 mg/l, assume a design aeration period of 24 hr.

a. V (each reactor) $= 120{,}000 \text{ gal} = 16{,}000 \text{ ft}^3$

Assuming a liquid depth of 5.0 ft and channel width of 12 ft, each aeration tank would be 24 ft wide, with a straight length of 92 ft and total length, including circular ends, of 115 ft. Based on these dimensions, two 15-ft horizontal rotors could be installed in each tank.

The width and depth of the channel have to be confirmed by the manufacturer's recommendations for the installation of horizontal rotors for adequate aeration and velocity of flow in the channel. The rate of oxygen transfer must consider oxygen demand for both carbonaceous organic matter and nitrification. Because of the long sludge age, unintentional nitrification may occur, particularly in a warm mixed liquor.

b. Use an overflow rate of 400 gpd/ft^2 and side-water depth of 10 ft to size two circular clarifiers.

$$\text{surface area} = \frac{240,000}{2 \times 400} = 300 \text{ ft}^2 \quad (\text{diameter} = 20 \text{ ft})$$

$$\text{detention time} = \frac{300 \times 10 \times 24}{32,100/2} = 4.5 \text{ hr}$$

c. $\text{F/M} = \dfrac{400}{3000 \times 0.24 \times 8.34} = 0.06$ lb BOD/day/lb of MLSS

High-Purity-Oxygen Activated-Sludge Process

This process uses oxygen gas generated by cryogenic air separation or pressure-swing adsorption processes. A typical aeration tank, shown schematically in Figure 39, is divided into three or four stages by means of baffles to stimulate plug flow and is covered with a gas-tight enclosure. Raw wastewater, return activated sludge, and oxygen gas under a slight pressure are introduced to the first stage and flow concurrently through succeeding sections. Oxygen can be mixed with the tank contents by injection through a hollow shaft to a rotating sparger device, or a surface aerator installed on top of the mixer turbine shaft to contact oxygen gas with the mixed liquor. Successive aeration chambers are connected to each other so that the liquid flows through submerged ports, and head gases pass freely from one stage to the next with only a slight pressure drop. Exhausted waste gas is a mixture of carbon dioxide, nitrogen, and about 10%–20% of the applied oxygen. Effluent mixed liquor is settled in either a scraper-type or rapid-sludge-return clarifier, and the activated sludge is returned to the aeration tank.

Compared to air activated-sludge processes, high-purity-oxygen activated sludge has several advantages that are attributed to its higher oxygenation capacity [17]. If all of the nitrogen in air is displaced by oxygen, the partial pressure of oxygen is 100%,

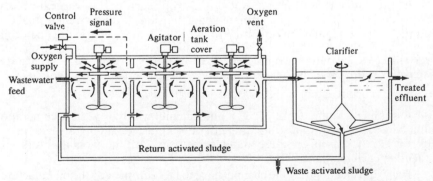

FIGURE 39   Schematic diagram of a high-purity-oxygen activated-sludge process with surface aerators in three stages.

resulting in a fivefold increase in the saturation value of dissolved oxygen in water. High efficiency is possible at increased BOD loads and reduced aeration periods by maintaining the food/microorganism ratio with MLSS concentrations of 4000–8000 mg/l. Even though the process simulates plug flow, shock organic loads do not produce instability, since extra oxygen is supplied to the first stage automatically on demand. Emission of foul odors is virtually eliminated because of the highly aerobic environment and reduced volume of exhaust gases. Covered tanks also help to reduce the cooling of the wastewater during cold-weather operation.

Example 13

A municipality has an average daily wastewater flow of 280 gpm with a peak hourly rate of 450 gpm. The average BOD concentration is 200 mg/l, except during several weeks when a seasonal industry increases the mean BOD to 250 mg/l. The city is considering installing a high-purity-oxygen system as in Figure 39 without primary clarification of the raw wastewater. Calculate (a) the volume of aeration tank capacity required, and (b) surface area and depth for a final settling tank. Recommended design criteria are a maximum BOD loading of 160 lb/1000 ft^3/day, a maximum food/microorganism ratio of 0.5 lb of BOD/day/lb of MLVSS, an operating MLSS concentration of 5500 mg/l (MLVSS of 4200 mg/l), and a highest overflow rate of 1200 gpd/ft^2 during peak flow.

Solution:

a.
$$\left(\begin{array}{c} \text{aeration tank volume} \\ \text{required at 250 mg/l of BOD} \end{array} \right) = \frac{280 \times 1440 \times 250 \times 8.34}{1,000,000 \times 0.160} = 5250 \text{ ft}^3$$

$$\left(\begin{array}{c} \text{aeration period} \\ \text{at average flow} \end{array} \right) = \frac{5250 \times 7.48 \times 24}{280 \times 1440} = 2.34 \text{ hr} \quad (\text{OK})$$

$$\left(\begin{array}{c} \text{BOD load at} \\ \text{200 mg/l of BOD} \end{array} \right) = \frac{280 \times 1440 \times 200 \times 8.34}{1,000,000 \times 5.25}$$

$$= 128 \text{ lb/1000 ft}^3\text{/day} \quad (\text{OK})$$

Check the F/M ratio for both BOD loadings (128 and 160 lb/1000 ft^3/day) at an MLVSS concentration of 4200 mg/l.

$$\text{At } \frac{128 \text{ lb of BOD/day}}{1000 \text{ ft}^3} : \frac{F}{M} = \frac{128/1000}{\dfrac{4200 \times 62.4}{1,000,000}} = 0.49 \frac{\text{lb of BOD/day}}{\text{lb of MLVSS}} \quad (\text{OK})$$

$$\text{At } \frac{160 \text{ lb of BOD/day}}{1000 \text{ ft}^3} : \frac{F}{M} = \frac{160/1000}{\dfrac{4200 \times 62.4}{1,000,000}} = 0.61 \text{ (slightly greater than 0.5)}$$

Therefore, use a three-stage aeration basin with a total volume of 5250 ft^3.

b. $\left(\begin{array}{c} \text{final clarifier surface area} \\ \text{required based on peak flow} \end{array} \right) = \dfrac{450 \times 1440}{1200} = 540 \text{ ft}^2$

$$\text{overflow rate at average flow} = \dfrac{280 \times 1440}{540} = 747 \text{ gpd/ft}^2$$

Assume the additional final clarifier design parameters of 8.0 ft minimum depth and 2.5 hr as the minimum detention time. Then the clarifier depth required for an overflow rate of 747 gpd/ft^2 is

$$\text{depth} = \dfrac{747 \text{ gal}}{\text{day} \times \text{ft}^2} \times \dfrac{\text{ft}^3}{7.48 \text{ gal}} \times 2.5 \text{ hr} \times \dfrac{\text{day}}{24 \text{ hr}} = 10.4 \text{ ft}$$

22   KINETICS MODEL OF THE ACTIVATED-SLUDGE PROCESS

The principles of growth kinetics from pure culture microbiology can be applied in suspended-growth wastewater treatment even though the processes differ significantly in relation to the method of growth (batch compared with continuous flow), microbial population (pure culture as opposed to mixed culture), and substrate content (uniform as opposed to a variety of organics). The shape of the wastewater processing curve in Figure 9 is similar to Monod's growth rate curve (Figure 6) and the Michaelis–Menten rate curve for an enzyme-catalyzed reaction (Figure 4). When plotted against substrate concentration, the reaction rates of enzyme, pure culture, and mixed culture reactions all follow the shape of a rectangular hyperbola where the substrate at one-half the maximum reaction rate is a characteristic constant of the reaction.

The following mathematical equations apply to completely mixed activated-sludge systems operating in a substrate-limiting condition (i.e., at a low F/M ratio). The fundamental relationships of growth kinetics used in the derivation of these equations are presented in Section 6.

The flow scheme for a completely mixed activated-sludge process is shown in Figure 40.

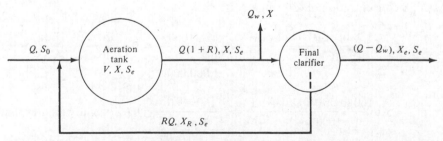

FIGURE 40   Flow scheme for the completely mixed activated-sludge system used in the derivation of the kinetics equations.

where

$$Q = \text{rate of influent flow}$$
$$Q_w = \text{rate of excess sludge wasting from aeration tank}$$
$$Q - Q_w = \text{rate of effluent flow}$$
$$R = \text{recirculation ratio } (Q_R/Q)$$
$$RQ = \text{rate of sludge recirculation}$$
$$Q(1 + R) = \text{rate of flow from aeration tank}$$
$$V = \text{volume of aeration tank}$$
$$X = \text{concentration of biomass in aeration tank (MLVSS)}$$
$$X_R = \text{concentration of biomass in recirculating sludge (VSS)}$$
$$X_e = \text{concentration of biomass in effluent (VSS)}$$

S_0 = concentration of substrate in influent flow (soluble BOD or COD)

S_e = concentration of substrate in effluent flow, recirculating sludge, and aeration tank (soluble BOD or COD)

The following conditions are assumed in the formulation of the mass balance equations:

1. Flows, biomass concentrations, and substrate concentrations are in a steady state.
2. All substrates are soluble (filtered BOD or COD).
3. The substrate concentration in the aeration tank equals the substrate concentration in the effluent after treatment.
4. Biological activity occurs only in the aeration tank.
5. No microorganisms are present in the influent wastewater.
6. The mean cell residence time is calculated based on the biomass in the aeration tank.
7. Excess activated sludge is wasted from the aeration tank rather than from the sludge recirculation line.
8. The aeration tank is complete mixing.

The aeration period (liquid detention time) is defined as

$$\theta = \frac{V}{Q} \tag{61}$$

where

$$\theta = \text{aeration period, time}$$

The mean cell residence time (sludge age) is the biomass (MLVSS) in the aeration tank divided by the sum of the biomasses in the waste sludge and effluent.

$$\theta_c = \frac{VX}{Q_wX + (Q - Q_w)X_e} \tag{62}$$

where

$$\theta_c = \text{mean cell residence time, time}$$

The definition of specific growth rate μ from Eq. (24) is the rate of growth per unit of biomass (time^{-1}). The inverse of μ is the biomass divided by the rate of growth, $X/(dX/dt)_g$. Therefore, under steady-state conditions, the mean cell residence time is

$$\theta_c = \frac{X}{(dX/dt)_g} = \frac{1}{\mu} \tag{63}$$

A mass balance for biomass around the entire activated-sludge system shown in Figure 40 is

$$\left(\begin{array}{c} \text{net rate of change} \\ \text{of biomass in system} \end{array} \right) = \left(\begin{array}{c} \text{net rate of growth} \\ \text{of biomass in system} \end{array} \right) - \left(\begin{array}{c} \text{rate of loss} \\ \text{of biomass from system} \end{array} \right)$$

Using the notation in Figure 40,

$$\left(\frac{dX}{dt} \right) V = \left(\frac{dX}{dt} \right)_g V - [Q_w X + (Q - Q_w)X_e] \tag{64}$$

At steady state, the rate of biomass growth equals the rate of biomass loss; hence, Setting Eq. (64) equal to zero and substituting the endogenous rate of growth from Eq. (32) for $(dX/dt)_g$ yields

$$\frac{1}{\theta_c} = Y \frac{(dS/dt)_u}{X} - k_d \tag{65}$$

Lawrence and McCarty [18] related the rate of substrate utilization both to the concentration of microorganisms in the aeration tank and to the concentration of substrate surrounding the organisms. The equation is

$$\left(\frac{dS}{dt} \right)_u = k \frac{XS_e}{K_S + S_e} \tag{66}$$

where

k = maximum rate of substrate utilization per unit mass of biomass, time^{-1}
X = concentration of biomass, mass/unit volume
S = concentration of substrate surrounding the microorganisms, mass/unit volume
K_S = saturation constant, equal to the substrate concentration when $(dS/dt)_u = k/2$, mass/unit volume

Equation (66), graphed in Figure 41, indicates that the functional relationship between substrate utilization rate and substrate concentration is continuous over the entire

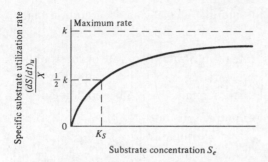

FIGURE 41   Specific substrate utilization rate versus substrate concentration surrounding the microorganisms based on Eq. (66).

range of substrate concentrations. It is similar in form to Eq. (29), with k replacing μ_m/Y.

Substituting Eq. (66) into Eq. (65) incorporates the term S_e.

$$\frac{1}{\theta_c} = Y\frac{k S_e}{K_s + S_e} - k_d \tag{67}$$

Rearranging terms gives the formula for S_e (effluent substrate concentration):

$$S_e = \frac{K_s(1 + k_d\theta_c)}{\theta_c\,(Yk - k_d) - 1} \tag{68}$$

The specific substrate utilization rate is defined as the substrate utilization rate divided by the concentration of biomass in the aeration tank. Hence,

$$U = \frac{(dS/dt)_u}{X} \tag{69}$$

where

$$U = \text{specific substrate utilization rate, time}^{-1}$$

This rate can be calculated from experimental data using the following formula:

$$U = \frac{Q(S_0 - S_e)}{V X} = \frac{S_0 - S_e}{\theta X} \tag{70}$$

Substituting the mathematical expression for specific substrate utilization rate, Eq. (69), into Eq. (65) gives the relationship

$$\frac{1}{\theta_c} = YU - k_d \tag{71}$$

where

θ_c = mean cell residence time, time
Y = growth yield, biomass increase-substrate metabolized, unitless
U = specific substrate utilization rate, time^{-1}
k_d = microbial decay coefficient, time^{-1}

A mass balance for substrate entering and leaving the aeration tank, as diagrammed in Figure 40, is

$$\begin{pmatrix} \text{net rate of change} \\ \text{of substrate} \\ \text{in aeration tank} \end{pmatrix} = \begin{pmatrix} \text{rate of substrate} \\ \text{entering} \\ \text{aeration tank} \end{pmatrix} - \begin{pmatrix} \text{rate of substrate} \\ \text{utilization} \\ \text{in aeration tank} \end{pmatrix}$$

$$- \begin{pmatrix} \text{rate of substrate} \\ \text{leaving} \\ \text{aeration tank} \end{pmatrix}$$

Using the notation in Figure 40,

$$\left(\frac{dS}{dt}\right)V = QS_0 + RQS_e - \left(\frac{dS}{dt}\right)_u V - Q(1 + R)S_e \tag{72}$$

At steady state, the rate of substrate entering the aeration tank equals the rate of substrate removal; hence, $(dS/dt)V = 0$. Setting Eq. (72) equal to zero and solving for the substrate utilization rate results in

$$\left(\frac{dS}{dt}\right)_u = \frac{Q(S_0 - S_e)}{V} = \frac{S_0 - S_e}{\theta} \tag{73}$$

Dividing both sides by X, Eq. (73) becomes

$$\frac{(dS/dt)_u}{X} = \frac{Q(S_0 - S_e)}{XV} \tag{74}$$

Substituting this expression for specific substrate utilization into Eq. (65) and rearranging, the equation for V (volume of the aeration tank) is

$$V = \frac{\theta_c YQ(S_0 - S_e)}{X(1 + k_d\theta_c)} \tag{75}$$

Equating the terms for $(dS/dt)_u$ from Eqs. (73) and (66), and dividing by X yields

$$\frac{S_0 - S_e}{\theta X} = k\frac{S}{K_s + S} \tag{76}$$

By inverting and linearizing Eq. (76),

$$\frac{X\theta}{S_0 - S_e} = \left(\frac{K_s}{k}\right)\left(\frac{1}{S_e}\right) + \frac{1}{k} \tag{77}$$

Substituting Eq. (70) for the left side of Eq. (77) gives

$$\frac{1}{U} = \left(\frac{K_s}{k}\right)\left(\frac{1}{S_e}\right) + \frac{1}{k} \tag{78}$$

where

U = specific substrate utilization rate, time^{-1}

K_s = saturation constant, mass/unit volume

k = maximum rate of substrate utilization per unit mass of biomass, time^{-1}

S_e = concentration of substrate in effluent, mass/unit volume

This presentation was limited to the kinetics model for completely mixed activated sludge. For a more detailed mathematical analysis of this system and discussions of models for other biological processes, the reader is referred to books by Benefield and Randall [19] and Grady and Lim [20].

23 LABORATORY DETERMINATION OF KINETIC CONSTANTS

The numerical values for the following kinetic constants must be determined by laboratory experiments before the model described in Section 22 can be used for design of completely mixed activated sludge:

Y = growth yield, mg VSS/mg BOD (or mg COD)

k_d = microbial decay coefficient, d^{-1}

K_s = saturation constant, mg/l of BOD (or COD)

k = maximum rate of substrate utilization per unit mass of biomass, d^{-1}

For design, additional required data include settling characteristics of the activated sludge and oxygen uptake rates during aeration of the wastewater.

A bench-scale activated-sludge unit as illustrated in Figure 42 is commonly used for laboratory evaluations. Operating conditions are the same as those assumed in the

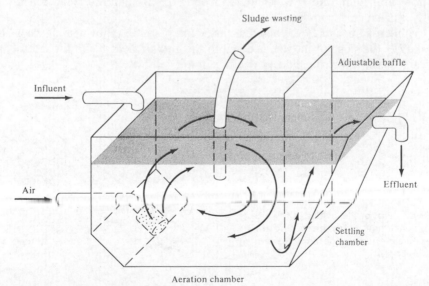

FIGURE 42 Bench-scale, continuous-flow, activated-sludge unit for laboratory testing of wastewater to determine kinetic constants.

derivation of the mass balance equations, which are listed at the beginning of Section 22. Essential for satisfactory results are a continuous influent flow rate with a constant substrate concentration and complete mixing in the aeration tank. To collect sufficient data, the unit is operated at several mean cell residence times for 3–20 days. Wasting the same quantity of suspended solids from the aeration tank maintains a constant θ_c, concentration of MLVSS, and F/M ratio. Ideally, the waste activated sludge is pumped out continuously; however, withdrawing batches of mixed liquor from the aeration tank at uniform time intervals may be practiced. Settleability of the activated sludge is tested by withdrawing a sample of the aerating mixed liquor and placing it in a settleometer; it may then be replaced or discarded as waste sludge. The length of time required for a test period, after steady-state conditions are established, is at least twice the mean cell residence time, with four residence times preferred. Temperature, pH, and dissolved oxygen concentration are held constant throughout the series of test runs.

Laboratory tests and operating conditions are generally recorded daily. The data required for calculating the operating parameters are as follows:

$$Q = \text{rate of influent flow, l/d}$$
$$Q_w = \text{rate of sludge wasting, l/d}$$
$$Q - Q_w = \text{rate of effluent flow, l/d}$$
$$V = \text{volume of aeration tank, l}$$
$$X = \text{concentration of MLVSS in the aeration tank, mg/l}$$
$$X_e = \text{concentration of VSS in effluent, mg/l}$$
$$S_0 = \text{soluble BOD (or COD) in influent, mg/l}$$
$$S_e = \text{soluble BOD (or COD) in effluent, mg/l}$$

From these data, the aeration period θ is calculated using Eq. (61), the specific substrate utilization rate U is calculated from Eq. (70), and the mean cell residence time θ_c is calculated from Eq. (62).

Values of $1/\theta_c$ and U for each test period are plotted as shown in Figure 43. Based on Eq. (71), the slope of the line is equal to the growth yield Y and the intercept with vertical axis is the microbial decay coefficient k_d.

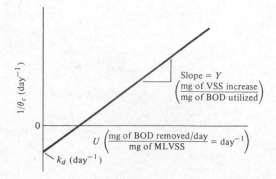

FIGURE 43   Plot of the inverse of the mean cell residence time versus the specific substrate utilization rate to determine Y and k_d based on Eq. (71).

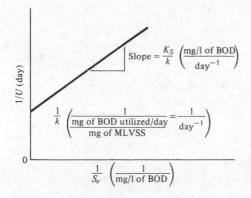

FIGURE 44   Plot of the inverse of the specific substrate utilization rate versus the inverse of concentration of substrate in the effluent to determine k and K_S based on Eq. (78).

TABLE 5   General Ranges of Magnitude for Kinetic Constants for Completely Mixed Activated-Sludge Processes Treating Municipal Wastewater at Approximately 20°C

Constant	Units	Range
Y	mg VSS/mg BOD	0.4–0.8
Y	mg VSS/mg COD	0.3–0.4
k_d	d^{-1}	0.04–0.08
K_S	mg/l of BOD	25–100
K_S	mg/l of COD	25–100
k	d^{-1}	4–8

A plot of $1/U$ and $1/S_e$ for each test period is shown in Figure 44. Based on Eq. (78), the slope of the line is equal to the saturation constant over the maximum rate of substrate utilization per unit mass of biomass K_s/k, and the intercept with the vertical axis is equal to $1/k$.

The general range of values for kinetic constants for completely mixed activated sludge treating municipal wastewaters is listed in Table 5.

Example 14

A municipal wastewater was tested to determine the kinetic constants using a laboratory apparatus similar to the bench-scale unit shown in Figure 42. The volume of the aeration chamber was 10 l. Wastewater feed was established at a constant rate of 34.3 l/d to provide a 7.0-hr aeration period for all of the test runs. A measured volume of sludge was wasted once a day from the tank. Determine the values for Y, k_d, k, and K_S from the following laboratory data.

Q (1/d)	S_0 (mg/l)	Q_w (1/d)	X (mg/l)	S_e (mg/l)	X_e (mg/l)
34.3	126	0.25	1730	5.2	9.4
34.3	126	0.35	1500	7.3	8.0
34.3	126	0.80	968	10.5	8.4
34.3	126	0.90	848	11.5	7.9

Solution: The following calculations are for the first test period. Using Eq. (62),

$$\theta_c = \frac{101 \times 1730 \text{ mg/l}}{0.25 \text{ l/d} \times 1730 \text{ mg/l} + (34.3 \text{ l/d} - 0.25 \text{ l/d})9.4 \text{ mg/l}} = 23 \text{ d}$$

The biomass growth rate per liter of aeration tank volume is

$$\left(\frac{dX}{dt}\right)_g = \frac{Q_w X + (Q - Q_w)X_e}{V}$$

$$\left(\frac{dX}{dt}\right)_g = \frac{0.25 \text{ l/d} \times 1730 \text{ mg/l} + (34.3 \text{ l/d} - 0.25 \text{ l/d})9.4 \text{ mg/l}}{101} = 75 \text{ mg/l} \cdot \text{d of VSS}$$

Checking the θ_c by Eq. (63) gives

$$\theta_c = \frac{1730 \text{ mg/l}}{75 \text{ mg/l}} = 23 \text{ d}$$

The soluble BOD utilization rate using Eq. (73) is

$$\left(\frac{dS}{dt}\right)_u = \frac{(34.3 \text{ l/d})(126 \text{ mg/l} - 5.2 \text{ mg/l})}{101} = 414 \text{ mg/l} \cdot \text{d}$$

The specific substrate utilization rate as defined by Eq. (69) is

$$U = \frac{414 \text{ mg/l} \cdot \text{d}}{1730 \text{ mg/l}} = 0.24 \text{ d}^{-1}$$

The following values are calculated for plotting the data:

$$\frac{1}{\theta_c} = \frac{1}{23 \text{ d}} = 0.043 \text{ d}^{-1}$$

$$\frac{1}{U} = \frac{1}{0.24 \text{ d}^{-1}} = 4.2 \text{ d}$$

$$\frac{1}{S_e} = \frac{1}{5.2 \text{ mg/l}} = 0.19 \text{ (mg/l)}^{-1}$$

The calculated data for all of the test runs are listed in Table 6.

TABLE 6 Data Calculated for Example 14 and Plotted in Figures 45 and 46 to Determine Kinetic Constants

θ_c(d)	$\left(\dfrac{dX}{dt}\right)_g$ (mg/l·d)	$\left(\dfrac{dS}{dt}\right)_u$ (mg/l·d)	$U(\text{d}^{-1})$	$1/\theta_c(\text{d}^{-1})$	$1/U(\text{d})$	$1/S_e[(\text{mg/l})^{-1}]$
23	75	414	0.24	0.0444	4.2	0.19
19	80	407	0.27	0.053	3.7	0.14
9.2	106	396	0.41	0.11	2.4	0.095
8.3	103	392	0.46	0.12	2.2	0.087

The plot in Figure 45 is to determine the values of Y and k_d. From the slope of the line, the growth yield $Y = 0.35$ mg VSS/mg BOD. The intercept on the vertical axis is a microbial decay coefficient of $k_d = 0.04$ d^{-1}.

The plot in Figure 46 is to determine the values of k and K_s. The intercept on the vertical axis is at $1/k = 0.25$ d; therefore, the maximum rate of substrate utilization per unit mass of biomass k is 4.0 d^{-1}. The slope of the line K_s/k is 22.5; hence,

$$K_s = 22.5 \text{ d} \cdot \text{mg/l} \times 4.0 \text{ d}^{-1} = 90 \text{ mg/l of BOD}$$

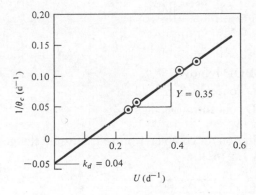

FIGURE 45 Plot of $1/\theta_c$ versus U to determine Y and k_d for Example 14.

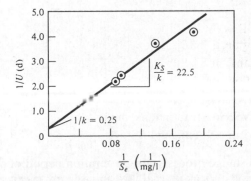

FIGURE 46 Plot of $1/U$ versus $1/S_e$ to determine k and K_s for Example 14.

24　APPLICATION OF THE KINETICS MODEL IN PROCESS DESIGN

The equations developed in Section 22 can be applied in the design of a completely mixed activated-sludge process based on kinetic constants determined by laboratory testing. Since the model is based on steady-state conditions that do not exist in full-scale systems, the selection of design parameters such as the mean cell residence time must account for the diurnal and random variations in wastewater loadings. Allowances must also be made for characteristics of the actual wastewater not taken into consideration in the theoretical equations. Rather than consisting solely of a soluble substrate, municipal wastewater contains suspended solids and an abundance of biological organisms. For example, the BOD of a treatment plant effluent includes oxygen demand from both the soluble organic matter and the volatile suspended solids. During the laboratory evaluation of wastewater treatability, both total BOD and filtered BOD analyses can be performed on the effluent from the bench-scale unit to correlate total and soluble substrate. Also, an evaluation of sludge settleability is necessary to establish design criteria for the final clarifier to ensure good gravity separation of the biological suspended solids.

　　The first step in process design is to select the desired concentration of effluent soluble BOD based on the allowable total effluent BOD and the anticipated performance in final clarification. Soluble BOD removal efficiency of the system is calculated by the following formula:

$$E = \frac{(S_0 - S_e)100}{S_0} \tag{79}$$

where

$$E = \text{efficiency of soluble BOD removal, \%}$$
$$S_0 = \text{influent soluble BOD concentration, mg/l}$$
$$S_e = \text{effluent soluble BOD concentration, mg/l}$$

　　The recommended loading criterion for completely mixed activated sludge is the mean cell residence time defined by Eq. (62):

$$\theta_c = \frac{VX}{Q_wX + (Q - Q_w)X_e}$$

where

$$\theta_c = \text{mean cell residence time, d}$$
$$V = \text{volume of aeration tank, m}^3$$
$$Q = \text{influent wastewater flow, m}^3\text{/d}$$
$$Q_w = \text{rate of excess sludge wasting, m}^3\text{/d}$$
$$X = \text{concentration of MLVSS in aeration tank, mg/l}$$
$$X_e = \text{concentration of VSS in effluent, mg/l}$$

　　A completely mixed activated-sludge process with an aeration period of 5–7 hr has a short θ_c of 3–5 d during the period of peak diurnal flow and is likely to exceed the effluent standards of 30 mg/l of total BOD and 30 mg/l of suspended solids. Under dispersed plug flow in long tanks (step aeration and conventional aeration), θ_c is in the range of 5–15 d and can provide a process efficiency resulting in an effluent of satisfactory uniform quality. A completely mixed extended-aeration process produces a high-quality effluent because of the long aeration period of 20–30 hr and θ_c of 20+ d. Selection of the mean cell residence time in design takes into consideration such factors as process efficiency, treatment reliability, and load variations.

Another common loading criterion is the food/microorganism ratio (F/M), which is defined for the kinetics model as

$$\text{F/M} = \frac{QS_0}{VX} = \frac{S_0}{\theta X} \tag{80}$$

where

F/M = food/microorganism ratio, g/d of soluble BOD applied per g of MLVSS in the aeration tank

Rearranging Eq. (70) allows one to express the specific substrate utilization rate as

$$U = \frac{QS_0}{VX} = \frac{S_0 - S_e}{S_0} \tag{81}$$

Then substituting the appropriate terms from Eqs. (79) and (80) gives a relationship between the food/microorganism ratio and the specific substrate utilization rate:

$$U = \frac{(\text{F/M})E}{100} \tag{82}$$

Replacing U in Eq. (71) with Eq. (82) relates θ_c and F/M such that

$$\frac{1}{\theta_c} = \frac{Y(\text{F/M})E}{100} - k_d \tag{83}$$

where

θ_c = mean cell residence time, d
Y = growth yield, unitless
F/M = food/microorganism ratio, g/d of soluble BOD per g of MLVSS
E = soluble BOD removal, %
k_d = microbial decay coefficient, d^{-1}

After establishing the desired effluent quality S_e and mean cell residence time θ_c, or the F/M, the required aeration tank volume can be calculated from Eq. (75):

$$V = \frac{\theta_c Y Q(S_0 - S_e)}{X(1 + k_d\theta_c)}$$

The choice of design flow Q and soluble influent BOD S_0 depends on the anticipated flow and strength variations, as discussed in Sections 10 and 11. Values of Y and k_d are determined from laboratory testing. Thus, the only remaining design parameter is X, the mixed-liquor volatile suspended solids to be maintained in the aeration tank.

Selection of an MLVSS concentration is based on a number of considerations, the most important of which are (1) the ability of the final clarifier to provide gravity separation of the activated-sludge suspended solids and (2) the oxygen transfer capacity of the aeration system. At a low design MLVSS the aeration period is long, resulting in an extended process time. A concentration of MLVSS that is too high produces a process characterized by poor soluble BOD removal efficiency and high suspended-solids concentration in the effluent, resulting from the limited aeration period and poor settleability of the microbial floc. In general, conventional secondary activated-sludge systems processing municipal wastewaters operate in the MLSS range of 1500–3000 mg/l with 70%–80% being volatile solids. In a typical design, therefore, the optimum MLVSS is within the range of 1200–2400 mg/l.

Waste sludge production in terms of volatile solids can be calculated based on the kinetics model. The observed growth yield Y_{obs}, as defined in Eq. (34), can be obtained by first substituting Eq. (32) for $(dX/dt)_g^{net}$ in the numerator and then replacing $(dS/dt)_u$ with UX from Eq. (69):

$$Y_{obs} = \frac{YU - k_d}{U} \qquad (84)$$

Substituting the relationship from Eq. (71) for U in Eq. (84) gives

$$Y_{obs} = \frac{Y}{1 + \theta_c k_d} \qquad (85)$$

where

Y_{obs} = observed growth yield, g of MLVSS/g of soluble BOD

Using this equation, Lawrence and McCarty [18] expressed the production of excess biomass in the waste-activated sludge as

$$P_x = \frac{YQ(S_0 - S_e)}{1 + \theta_c k_d} \qquad (86)$$

where

P_x = volatile solids in waste sludge, g/d

Example 15

A completely mixed activated-sludge process is being designed for a wastewater flow of 10,000 m³/d (2.64 mgd) using the kinetics equations. The influent BOD of 120 mg/l is essentially all soluble and the design effluent soluble BOD is 7 mg/l, which is based on a total effluent BOD of 20 mg/l. For sizing the aeration tank, the mean cell residence time is selected to be 10 d and the MLVSS 2000 mg/l. The kinetic constants from a bench-scale treatability study are as follows: $Y = 0.60$ mg VSS/mg BOD, $k_d = 0.06$ d^{-1}, $K_s = 60$ mg/l of BOD, and $k = 5.0$ d^{-1}.

Solution: From Eq. (79), the required soluble BOD efficiency is

$$E = \frac{(120 - 7)100}{120} = 94\%$$

Rearranging Eq. (83), one obtains the food/microorganism ratio for $\theta_c = 10$ d and $E = 94\%$:

$$\text{F/M} = \frac{(1/\theta_c + k_d)100}{YE} = \frac{(1/10 + 0.06)100}{0.60 \times 94} = 0.28 \frac{\text{g of soluble BOD}}{\text{g of MLVSS}}$$

The volume of the aeration tank, based on Eq. (75), is

$$V = \frac{10 \times 0.60 \times 10,000(120 - 7)}{2000(1 + 0.06 \times 10)} = 2100 \text{ m}^3 \ (74,800 \text{ ft}^3)$$

$$\theta = \frac{2100 \times 24}{10,000} = 5.0 \text{ hr}$$

From Eq. (68), the soluble BOD is

$$S_e = \frac{60(1 + 0.06 \times 10)}{10(0.60 \times 5.0 - 0.06) - 1} = 3.4 \text{ mg/l}$$

From Eq. (86), the excess volatile solids in the waste sludge are

$$P_x = \frac{0.60 \times 10,000(120 - 7)}{1 + 10 \times 0.06} = 420,000 \text{ g/d} = 420 \text{ kg/d}$$

---

25 OXYGEN TRANSFER AND OXYGENATION REQUIREMENTS

In activated-sludge processes, oxygen is supplied to the microorganisms by dispersing air into the mixed liquor by either diffused-air or mechanical surface aeration. Diffused-air systems use a variety of fine- and coarse-bubble diffusers. The two kinds of mechanical aerators, differentiated by the plane of rotation, are horizontal rotors and impellers mounted on vertical shafts.

The commonly accepted oxygen transfer scheme is diagrammed in Figure 47 Oxygen is dissolved in solution and then extracted from solution by the biological cells. Direct oxygen transfer from bubble to cell is possible if the microorganisms are adsorbed on the bubble surface. Bennett and Kempe [21] demonstrated direct oxygen transfer in a laboratory fermenter using a culture of *Pseudomonas ovalis* converting glucose to gluconic acid. The extent of direct oxygen transfer in activated-sludge systems is not known; however, it is generally felt to be secondary to oxygen transfer through the intermediate dissolved-oxygen phase.

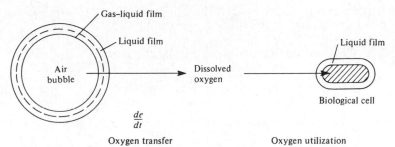

FIGURE 47   Schematic diagram of oxygen transfer in activated sludge.

The rate of oxygen transfer from air bubbles to dissolved oxygen in an aeration tank is expressed as

$$\frac{dc}{dt} = \alpha K_L a (\beta C_s - C_t) \tag{87}$$

where

dc/dt = rate of oxygen transfer, mg/l/hr
α = oxygen transfer coefficient of the wastewater
β = oxygen saturation coefficient of the wastewater
$K_L a$ = oxygen transfer coefficient, hr^{-1}
C_s = oxygen concentration at saturation, mg/l
C_t = oxygen concentration in the liquid, mg/l
$\beta C_s - C_t$ = dissolved-oxygen deficit, mg/l

Equation (87) without the α and β coefficients applies to clean water. The factors α and β depend on the characteristics of the wastewater being aerated, primarily the concentration of dissolved solids; $K_L a$ depends on the temperature and the aeration system features, such as the type of diffuser, depth of aerator, type of mixer, and tank geometry. In general, the rate of oxygen transfer increases with decreasing bubble size, longer contact time, and added turbulence. Methods for determining the coefficients $K_L a$, α, and β are discussed in Section 26.

The rate of dissolved-oxygen utilization by microorganisms in an activated-sludge system can be determined by placing a sample of mixed liquor in a closed container and measuring the dissolved-oxygen depletion with respect to time. The slope of the resultant curve r is the oxygen utilization rate. Figure 48 is a dissolved-oxygen depletion curve for a mixed liquor from a high-rate activated-sludge aeration tank. The r value depends on the microorganisms' ability to metabolize the waste organics based on such factors as the food/microorganism ratio, mixing conditions, and temperature. A general range for r in the mixed liquor of conventional and high-rate activated-sludge systems is 30–100 mg/l/hr.

Under steady-state conditions of oxygen transfer in an activated-sludge system, the rate of oxygen transfer to dissolved oxygen (dc/dt) is equal to the rate of oxygen

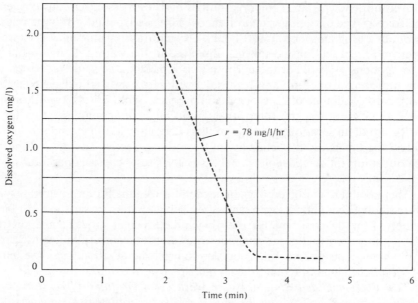

FIGURE 48 Oxygen utilization curve for a sample of mixed liquor from a high-rate activated-sludge aeration basin.

utilization (r). Substituting r in Eq. (87) for dc/dt and rearranging yields the following relationship:

$$\alpha K_L a = \frac{r}{\beta C_s - C_t} \tag{88}$$

where

$$r = \text{oxygen utilization rate by microorganisms in activated sludge, mg/l/hr}$$

The rate of aerobic microbial metabolism is independent of the dissolved-oxygen concentration above a critical (minimum) value. Below the critical value, the rate is reduced by the limitation of oxygen required for respiration. Critical dissolved-oxygen concentrations reported in the literature for activated-sludge systems range from 0.2 to 2.0 mg/l, depending on the type of activated-sludge process and characteristics of the wastewater. The most frequently referenced critical dissolved-oxygen value for conventional and high-rate aeration basins is 0.5 mg/l.

The aerator power required to satisfy microbial oxygen demand and to provide adequate mixing in an aeration tank depends on the type of activated-sludge process, BOD loading, and oxygen transfer efficiency of the aeration equipment. In the design of any activated-sludge system, the power requirements should be based on proven performance of the aeration equipment. The capacity of the aeration equipment must furnish sufficient air to meet peak BOD loads without the dissolved-oxygen concentration dropping below the critical level for aerobic metabolism.

Aeration systems are compared on the basis of mass of gaseous oxygen transferred to dissolved oxygen per unit of energy expended, pounds of oxygen per horsepower-hour (kilogram per kilowatt-hour). Oxygen transfer efficiency is expressed as the percentage of the mass of oxygen dissolved in the water relative to the applied mass of gaseous oxygen. For the purpose of comparison, the values specified for efficiency are based on operation in clean water with zero dissolved-oxygen concentration and standard conditions of 20°C and 1 atm pressure. Table 7 lists oxygen transfer efficiencies and oxygen transfer rates for different kinds of aeration systems. Of course, the selection of an aeration system in process design must also consider other factors, including the flexibility and reliability of operation, effective mixing, and the maintenance of equipment. An economic analysis encompasses capital, operation, and maintenance costs.

The amount of dissolved oxygen needed for treatment of a wastewater depends on the carbonaceous and nitrogenous oxygen demands that are satisfied. For biological oxidation of carbonaceous matter, the oxygen requirement varies from approximately 0.8 to 1.6 times the BOD of the applied wastewater for a corresponding food/microorganism loading range of extended aeration to high-rate aeration. The oxygen requirement for nitrification is 4.6 times the ammonia nitrogen oxidized to nitrate.

The *Recommended Standards for Wastewater Facilities, Great Lakes—Upper Mississippi River Board of State Public Health & Environmental Managers* [22] considers the following as minimum normal air requirements for diffused-air systems: conventional, step aeration, and contact stabilization 1500 ft^3 of air applied per lb of BOD aeration tank load; modified or high-rate 400–1500 ft^3/lb of BOD load; and extended aeration 2000 ft^3/lb of BOD load. These demands assume that the aeration equipment is capable of transferring at least 1.0 lb of oxygen to the mixed liquor per pound of BOD aeration tank loading. In any case, aeration equipment shall be capable

TABLE 7   Oxygen Transfer Data for Air Aeration Systems in Clean Water at 15-Ft Submergence

System	Oxygen Transfer Efficiency (%)	Oxygen Transfer Rate (lb/hp · hr)[a]
Fine-bubble diffusers, total floor coverage	20–32[b]	4.0–6.5
Fine-bubble diffusers, side-wall installation	11–15[b]	2.2–3.0
Jet aerators (fine bubble)	22–27[b]	4.0–5.0
Static aerators (medium-sized bubble)	12–14[b]	2.3–2.8
Mechanical surface aerators	—	2.5–3.5[c]
Coarse-bubble diffusers, wide-band pattern	6–8[c]	1.2–1.6
Coarse-bubble diffusers, narrow-band pattern	4–6[c]	0.8–1.2

[a] 1.0 lb/hp · hr = 0.61 kg/kW · h
[b] From manufacturers' bulletins and technical reports
[c] Common ranges for variations of these systems
Source: *Proceedings, Workshop Toward an Oxygen Transfer-Standard,* Environmental Protection Agency, EPA 600/9-78-021 (April 1979): 13.

of maintaining a minimum of 2.0 mg/l of dissolved oxygen in the mixed liquor at all times and ensuring thorough mixing of the mixed liquor.

Example 16

The following data were collected during field evaluation of a completely mixed activated-sludge secondary treatment of municipal wastewater. The aeration basin, with a diameter of 80 ft and a liquid depth of 17 ft, was mixed with four turbine mixers mounted above air sparge rings. Twenty-four-hour composite BOD analyses were run on the aeration basin influent, final clarifier effluent, and waste-activated sludge. The oxygen-utilization rate in the aeration basin was measured each hour throughout the 24-hr sampling period, and individual values were averaged for the oxygen utilization rate of the mixed liquor.

$$\text{influent wastewater flow} = 6.52 \text{ mgd}$$
$$\text{waste activated sludge} = 15,000 \text{ gpd}$$
$$\text{influent BOD} = 125 \text{ mg/l}$$
$$\text{effluent BOD} = 18 \text{ mg/l}$$
$$\text{waste sludge BOD} = 5300 \text{ mg/l}$$
$$\text{air supplied } (20°C \text{ and } 760 \text{ mm}) = 1650 \text{ cfm}$$
$$\text{minimum DO in mixed liquor} = 0.8 \text{ mg/l}$$
$$\text{average DO in mixed liquor} = 1.1 \text{ mg/l}$$
$$\text{temperature of mixed liquor} = 24°C$$
$$\text{oxygen utilization rate of mixed liquor} = 74 \text{ mg/l/hr}$$
$$\text{beta factor of mixed liquor} = 0.9$$

Use these data to calculate the following:

a. Pounds of BOD load.
b. Cubic feet of air applied per lb of BOD load.
c. Pounds of oxygen utilized per lb of BOD.
d. Oxygen transfer efficiency.
e. $\alpha K_L a$.

Solution:

a.   lb of BOD load = 6.52 mgd × 125 mg/l × 8.34 = 6800 lb/day

volume aeration tank = $\pi(40)^2 17 = 85,500 \text{ ft}^3$

BOD loading = 79.5 lb of BOD/1000 ft³/day

b.   air applied = $1650 \dfrac{\text{ft}^3}{\text{min}} \times 1440 \dfrac{\text{min}}{\text{day}} = 2,380,000 \text{ ft}^3$

$$\frac{\text{ft}^3 \text{ of air applied}}{\text{lb of BOD load}} = \frac{2,380,000}{6800} = 350 \frac{\text{ft}^3}{\text{lb of BOD}}$$

c. lb of oxygen utilized $= r \times$ volume of aeration tank $\times$ time

$$= 74 \frac{\text{mg/l}}{\text{hr}} \times 28.3 \frac{1}{\text{ft}^3} \times 85,500 \text{ ft}^3$$

$$\times \frac{\text{lb}}{453,600 \text{ mg}} \times 24 \frac{\text{hr}}{\text{day}}$$

$$= 9420 \text{ lb/day}$$

lb of BOD satisfied $=$ lb of BOD removed $-$ lb of BOD wasted

$$= 6.52(125 - 18)8.34 - 0.015 \times 5300 \times 8.34$$

$$= 5190 \text{ lb/day}$$

$$\frac{\text{lb of oxygen utilized}}{\text{lb of BOD satisfied}} = \frac{9420}{5190} = 1.82$$

$$\frac{\text{lb of oxygen utilized}}{\text{lb of BOD applied}} = \frac{9420}{6800} = 1.39$$

d. lb of oxygen applied $= 2,380,000 \dfrac{\text{ft}^3}{\text{day}} \times 0.0174 \dfrac{\text{lb of oxygen}}{\text{ft}^3}$

$$= 41,400 \text{ lb/day}$$

oxygen transfer efficiency $= \dfrac{9420}{41,400} \times 100 = 22.8\%$

e. From Eq. (88),

$$\alpha K_L a \text{ at } 24°C = \frac{74}{0.9 \times 8.5 - 1.1} = 11 \text{ hr}^{-1}$$

26   DETERMINATION OF OXYGEN TRANSFER COEFFICIENTS

In order to apply Eq. (87) in calculating the mass transfer of oxygen in the design of an activated-sludge process, the coefficients $K_L a$, α, and β must be experimentally determined.

The rate of oxygen transfer in clean water is defined as

$$\frac{dc}{dt} = K_L a(C_s - C_t) \tag{89}$$

where

$$dc/dt = \text{rate of oxygen transfer, mg/l/hr}$$
$$K_L a = \text{oxygen transfer coefficient, hr}^{-1}$$
$$C_s = \text{oxygen concentration at saturation, mg/l}$$
$$C_t = \text{oxygen concentration in liquid, mg/l}$$

The rate of oxygen dissolution is proportional to the dissolved-oxygen deficit $(C_s - C_t)$ and the area of the air–water interface per unit volume of water. K_La is the overall coefficient that incorporates the interfacial area a of diffusion and the liquid film coefficient K_L. The value of K_La depends on the hydrodynamics and turbulence at the interface between the air bubbles and the liquid; hence, it depends on the aeration system, geometry of the aeration tank, liquid characteristics, and temperature.

The efficiency of an aeration system to transfer oxygen is measured by conducting a non-steady-state test on a full-scale aeration basin or test tank using clean water [23, 24]. The clean aeration tank is filled with tap water at a temperature as close to 20°C as possible. Next, a cobalt chloride catalyst is dissolved in a small amount of warm water and added to the aeration tank; the concentration must be high enough to assure catalyzation of all of the sodium sulfite added. After operating the aerator for 20–30 min to achieve a steady-state mixing condition, the sodium sulfite is added to deoxygenate the water in the aeration tank as follows:

$$2\,Na_2SO_3 + O_2 \xrightarrow{\text{cobalt}} 2\,Na_2SO_4 \tag{90}$$

The sulfite addition is in excess of the theoretical requirement (7.88 mg/l of pure sodium sulfite per 1.0 mg/l of DO concentration) to allow a time lag for mixing before the dissolved oxygen starts to rise above zero. Simultaneously, sampling is initiated at several points in the aeration tank when the DO concentration begins to rise from zero and is continued at 1–3-min intervals, or at approximately every 1.0 mg/l increase in dissolved oxygen. At least six samples are collected at each point between the levels of 10% and 80% DO saturation. Water for sampling is continuously withdrawn by submersible pumps with sufficient capacity to limit the detention time between pump and sample outlet to 5–10 sec. Although oxygen concentrations are monitored and recorded by DO probes and meters, the standard test for dissolved oxygen is the Winkler titration method. Three replicate tests are normally conducted to determine the aeration efficiency for each operating condition.

Dissolved-oxygen data from each sampling point are plotted to determine the K_La value based on the following relationship, derived from Eq. (89):

$$K_La = \ln\left(\frac{C_s - C_2}{C_s - C_1}\right) \Big/ (t_2 - t_1) \tag{91}$$

Nonparallel slopes of the plots from different sampling points indicate poor mixing, and K_La values that differ significantly from the others are discarded. The saturation concentration C_s is the theoretical value at the temperature of the water during the test (Table 10 in the Appendix). In the case of diffused-air systems a correction factor for submergence of the bubbles is included in the pressure correction; this is normally taken as the pressure at one-half the depth of submergence of the diffusers. The K_La at test temperature in degrees Celsius is corrected to 20°C by the relationship

$$(K_La)_{20} = (K_La)_T \Theta^{20-T} \tag{92}$$

where Θ is commonly assumed to be 1.024. (The observed range is 1.01–1.05.)

The mass of oxygen dissolved in the water contained in a test tank per unit time at standard conditions (20°C, 1 atm pressure, and zero DO) is calculated as

$$N = 10^{-6} \, (K_L a)_{20} \, (C_s)_{20} W \tag{93}$$

where

N = rate of oxygen dissolution, lb/hr
$(K_L a)_{20}$ = oxygen transfer coefficient at 20°C, hr^{-1}
$(C_s)_{20}$ = oxygen concentration at saturation at 20°C, mg/l
W = weight of water in the test tank, lb
$10^{-6} \sim 1$ mg/l ~ 1 mg/1,000,000 mg

Oxygen transfer efficiency E in a diffused-aeration system is computed by

$$E = \frac{N \times 100}{A} \tag{94}$$

where

E = oxygen transfer efficiency, %
A = amount of oxygen applied (standard conditions), lb/hr

Determination of the applied oxygen requires accurate measurement of the air flow rate and adjustment of the observed rate to standard conditions of 20°C and 1 atm of pressure.

The oxygen transfer rate can be calculated for both diffused-air and mechanical aeration systems by the relationship

$$R_0 = \frac{N}{P} \tag{95}$$

where

R_0 = rate of oxygen transfer at standard conditions (20°C, 1 atm pressure, and zero DO), lb/hp · hr
P = power input, hp

The rate of oxygen transfer to a wastewater requires determining the alpha and beta coefficients in Eq. (87). The alpha coefficient is defined as the ratio of the oxygen transfer coefficient in wastewater to that in clean water,

$$\alpha = \frac{K_L a \text{ in wastewater}}{K_L a \text{ in clean water}} \tag{96}$$

The value of α is influenced by many conditions related to both the characteristics of the wastewater (temperature, soluble BOD, and concentration of suspended solids) and the aeration equipment (type of diffuser or mechanical aerator, mixing intensity, and aeration tank configuration). The magnitude can even change between the influent and effluent ends of a plug-flow aeration tank resulting from stabilization of the wastewater. Even though the most reliable method of measuring α is under field design conditions, it is often determined using a bench-scale aeration tank. Different laboratory units are designed to simulate diffused, mechanical-surface, and submerged-turbine aeration systems. The procedure involves conducting tests for K_La in the model aeration tank for both tap water and wastewater [23, 24]. Deoxygenation is performed by stripping the liquid in the tank with nitrogen gas. Conducting tests to determine alpha requires considerable expertise in oxygen transfer processes and laboratory techniques.

Alpha coefficients for municipal wastewater are generally in the range of 0.7–0.9; nevertheless, fine-bubble diffusers can have values as low as 0.4 and mechanical aerators as high as 1.1.

The beta coefficient in Eq. (87) is defined as the ratio of the DO saturation concentration in the wastewater to that in clean water.

$$\beta = \frac{\text{DO saturation concentration in wastewater}}{\text{DO saturation concentration in clean water}} \qquad (97)$$

The value of β is influenced by wastewater constituents, including dissolved salts, organics, and gases. To determine the saturation concentration in wastewater, a settled sample is aerated by vigorous hand mixing for several minutes in a half-full jar. The temperature and dissolved oxygen are then both measured, usually with a calibrated DO probe, for several minutes to ensure stable readings. Saturation for clean water is the theoretical value for the same temperature and is corrected for the barometric pressure (Table A.10). These two values are used in Eq. (97) to calculate β.

The magnitude of the beta coefficient for municipal wastewater typically equals 0.9 and is seldom less than 0.8.

Example 17

A coarse-bubble, diffused-aeration system was tested in a large tank to determine the oxygen transfer coefficient by the non-steady-state procedure in clean water. The diffusers were submerged 8.0 ft, and the atmospheric pressure on the day of the test was 720 mm Hg. Dissolved oxygen data from a sampling point at a depth of 4.0 ft are given in columns 1 and 3 of Table 8. The water temperature was 17°C.

The test tank was circular, with a diameter of 20.0 ft. The air supply during the test was 310 cfm (20°C and 760 mm) and the power input was 15 hp.

Determine the value of K_La and, based on this value and the above operating data, calculate the oxygen transfer efficiency and oxygen transfer rate.

Solution: The pressure at one-half the depth of submergence of the diffusers is

$$\frac{4.0 \text{ ft} \times 305 \text{ mm/ft}}{13.6 \text{ mm } H_2O/1.0 \text{ mm Hg}} = 90 \text{ mm Hg}$$

Therefore, the barometric pressure at mid-depth is equal to $720 + 90 = 810$ mm Hg. Using Table 10 from the Appendix,

$$C_s' = C_s \frac{P - p}{760 - p} = 9.7 \times \frac{810 - 15}{760 - 15} = 10.4 \text{ mg/l}$$

TABLE 8 Sampling Data and Calculated Values for Determination of the Oxygen Transfer Coefficient in Example 17

t (min)	C_s (mg/l)	C_t (mg/l)	$C_s - C_t$ (mg/l)	$\ln (C_s - C_t)$
1.2	10.4	2.3	8.1	2.1
2.8	10.4	4.6	5.8	1.8
5.0	10.4	6.7	3.7	1.3
8.0	10.4	8.2	2.2	0.8
0	10.4	9.4	1.0	0
16.0	10.4	10.0	0.4	-0.9
22.0	10.4	10.2	0.2	-1.6

This value for the oxygen concentration at saturation (17°C and 4.0 ft submergence) is entered in column 2 of Table 8 and is used to calculate the $C_s - C_t$ and $\ln(C_s - C_t)$.

The $\ln(C_s - C_t)$ versus time data are plotted in Figure 49. The slope of a straight line of best fit through the points between 20% and 80% DO saturation is $K_L a$, which is calculated using Eq. (91) as

$$K_L a = \frac{(2.0 - 0)60}{11.8 - 1.5} = 11.7 \text{ hr}^{-1}$$

Correcting $K_L a$ to 20°C by Eq. (92),

$$(K_L a)_{20} = 11.7(1.024)^{20-17} = 12.6 \text{ hr}^{-1}$$

The following parameters are calculated in order to use Eq. (93):

$$(C_s)_{20} = 9.2 \times \frac{810 - 18}{760 - 18} = 9.8 \text{ mg/l}$$

$$W = \pi(10)^2 \times 8.0 \times 62.4 = 157,000 \text{ lb}$$

Substituting into Eq. (93),

$$N = 10^{-6} \times 12.6 \times 9.8 \times 157,000 = 19.4 \text{ lb/hr}$$

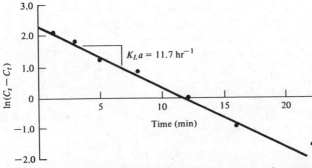

FIGURE 49 Plot of data from Table 8 to determine $K_L a$ for Example 17.

Calculating oxygen transfer efficiency by Eq. (94),

$$E = \frac{19.4 \text{ lb/hr} \times 100}{310 \text{ ft}^3/\text{min} \times 60 \text{ min/hr} \times 0.0174 \text{ lb of oxygen/ft}^3} = \frac{19.4 \times 100}{323} = 6.0\%$$

The rate of oxygen transfer from Eq. (95) is

$$R_0 = \frac{19.4}{15} = 1.3 \text{ lb/hp} \cdot \text{hr}$$

Example 18

A step-aeration activated-sludge process is being designed using the diffused-aeration system described in Example 17. The design criteria for the period of critical oxygen demand in the aeration basin are as follows:

$$\text{BOD loading} = 3.3 \text{ lb BOD/1000 ft}^3/\text{hr}$$
$$\text{oxygen transfer requirement} = 1.0 \text{ lb of oxygen/1.0 lb of BOD applied}$$
$$\text{temperature of mixed liquor} = 14°C$$
$$\text{minimum allowable DO} = 2.0 \text{ mg/l}$$
$$\text{beta coefficient} = 0.70$$
$$\text{alpha coefficient} = 0.90$$
$$\text{oxygen transfer coefficient } (K_La)_{20} = 12.0 \text{ hr}^{-1}$$
$$\text{oxygen transfer efficiency } E = 6.0\%$$
$$\text{pressure at mid-depth of diffusers} = 810 \text{ mm Hg}$$

Compare the rate of oxygen transfer dc/dt to the rate of oxygen utilization r, and calculate the volume of standard air required per pound of BOD applied. (One cubic foot of air at standard temperature and pressure, 20°C and 760 mm, contains 0.0174 lb oxygen.)

Solution: Using Table 10 from the Appendix for 14°C,

$$C_s = 10.4 \times \frac{810 - 12}{760 - 12} = 11.1 \text{ mg/l}$$

Correcting $(K_La)_{20}$ for 14°C,

$$K_La \text{ at } 14°C = (K_La)_{20} \, 1.024^{T-20} = 12.0(1.024)^{-6} = 10.4 \text{ hr}^{-1}$$

Substituting into Eq. (87), the rate of oxygen transfer is

$$\frac{dc}{dt} = 0.70 \times 10.4(0.90 \times 11.1 - 2.0) = 58 \text{ mg/l/hr}$$

Assuming 1.0 lb of oxygen is utilized per 1.0 lb of BOD applied, the rate of dissolved-oxygen utilization is

$$r = \frac{3.3 \text{ lb}}{1000 \text{ ft}^3 \cdot \text{hr}} \times \frac{453,600 \text{ mg}}{\text{lb}} \times \frac{\text{ft}^3}{28.3 \text{ l}} = 53 \text{ mg/l/hr}$$

The oxygen transfer rate of the aeration system is adequate since dc/dt exceeds r. (Refer to Figure 47.)

The efficiency of oxygen transfer is proportional to the rate of oxygen transfer; therefore,

$$E_{\text{actual}} = E\frac{\alpha(K_L a)(\beta C_s - C_t)}{(K_L a)_{20}(C_s)_{20}}$$

$$= 6.0 \times \frac{0.70 \times 10.4(0.90 \times 11.1 - 2.0)}{12.6 \times 9.8} = 2.8\% \qquad (98)$$

The volume of standard air required at an actual oxygen transfer efficiency of 2.8% per pound of BOD load, assuming 1.0 lb of oxygen utilized per 1.0 lb of BOD applied, is

$$\frac{1.0 \text{ lb of oxygen}}{0.0174 \text{ lb of oxygen/ft}^3 \times 0.028} = 2000 \text{ ft}^3/\text{lb of BOD applied}$$

Stabilization Ponds

Domestic wastewater can be effectively stabilized by the natural biological processes that occur in shallow ponds. Those treating raw wastewater are referred to as facultative ponds, lagoons, or oxidation ponds. Where small ponds are installed after secondary treatment, they are referred to as tertiary, maturation, or polishing ponds. Their purpose is to further reduce suspended solids, BOD, fecal microorganisms, and ammonia in the plant effluent.

Facultative ponds have a light BOD loading of 0.1–0.3 lb/1000 ft³/day, a normal operating water depth of 5 ft, and a long retention time of 50–150 days. Small ponds may be designed for complete retention with water loss only by evaporation. Tertiary polishing ponds generally have a retention time of only 10–15 days and are shallower, with water depths of 2–3 ft for better mixing and sunlight penetration.

A wide variety of microscopic plants and animals find the environment a suitable habitat. Waste organics are metabolized by bacteria and saprobic protozoans as primary feeders. Secondary feeders include protozoans and higher animal forms, such as rotifers and crustaceans. When the pond bottom is anaerobic, biological activity results in digestion of the settled solids. Nutrients released by bacteria are used by algae in photosynthesis. The overall process in a facultative stabilization pond (Figure 14) is the sum of individual reactions of the bacteria, protozoans, and algae.

27   DESCRIPTION OF A FACULTATIVE POND

A stabilization pond is a flat-bottomed pond enclosed by an earth dike (Figure 50). It can be round, square, or rectangular, with a length not greater than three times the width. The operating liquid depth has a range of 2–5 ft, with 3 ft of dike freeboard. A minimum of about 2 ft is required to prevent the growth of rooted aquatic plants. Operating depths greater than 5 ft can create odorous conditions because of anaerobiosis on the bottom.

Influent lines discharge near the center of the pond and the effluent usually overflows in a corner on the windward side to minimize short-circuiting. The overflow is generally a manhole or box structure with multiple-valved draw-off lines to offer flexible operation. Where the lagoon area required exceeds 6 acres, it is good practice to have multiple cells that can be operated individually, in series, or in parallel. If the soil is pervious, the bottom and dikes should be sealed to prevent groundwater pollution. A commonly used sealing agent is bentonite (clay). Dikes and areas surrounding the ponds are seeded with grass, graded to prevent runoff from entering the ponds, and fenced to preclude livestock and discourage trespassing. In the case of a multiple-pond installation,

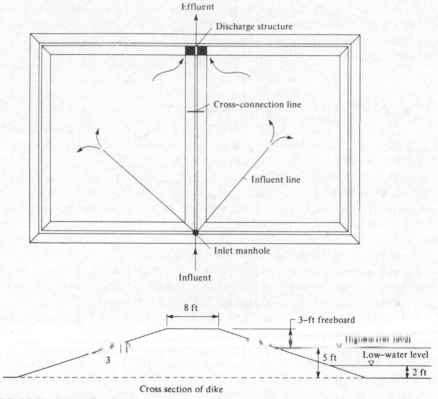

FIGURE 50   Two-cell stabilization pond.

the sequence of pond operation and liquid operating depth are regulated to provide control of the treatment system. Operating ponds in series generally increases BOD reduction by preventing short-circuiting. Conversely, parallel operation may be desirable to distribute the raw BOD load and avoid potential odor problems.

Where discharges of pond effluent in the winter result in pollution of the receiving stream, the operating level can be lowered before ice formation and gradually increased to 5 ft by retention of winter flows. The elevation can then be slowly lowered in the spring when the dilution flow in the receiving stream is high. Shallow operation can be maintained during the spring with gradually increasing depths to prevent emergent vegetation. In the fall, the level can again be lowered to hold winter flows.

Most stabilization ponds emit odors occasionally. This is the primary reason for locating them as far as practicable from present or future developed areas and on the leeward side so that prevailing winds are in the direction of uninhabited areas. Lagoons treating only domestic wastewater normally operate odor-free. Only for a short period of time in the early spring, when the ice melts and the algae are not flourishing, are offensive odors discharged. Lagoons treating certain industrial wastes, in combination with domestic wastewater, are often noted for their persistent obnoxious odors. The cause of these odors is most likely continuous or periodic overloading from industrial waste discharges or the odorous nature of the industrial waste itself. Unpleasant odors can be emitted from lagoons of small municipalities where poultry-processing wastes, slaughterhouse wastes, or creamery wastes are discharged to the municipal sewer without pretreatment.

28   BOD LOADINGS OF FACULTATIVE PONDS

Many efficiency equations have been proposed for modeling BOD removal in facultative ponds [25]. BOD reduction in a primary cell appears to follow a simple plug-flow hydraulic model with a first-order reaction rate; however, verification by comparison with actual performance data has been only marginally successful. More complex equations that include factors such as water temperature, light intensity, and dispersion are no more successful in predicting the efficiency of stabilization ponds. As a result, design of facultative ponds is commonly dictated by empirical rules based on the observation of pond performance in a region. Design guidelines may specify the maximum allowable BOD loading on primary cells, number of cells required for different-size pond systems, overall wastewater retention time, maximum and minimum water depths, and winter storage for a specified number of months. Example 20 illustrates the application of a typical set of design guidelines.

BOD loadings are usually expressed in pounds of BOD applied per acre of surface area per day (kg/ha · d or $g/m^2 \cdot d$). In northern states, loadings on primary cells are 25–35 lb BOD/acre/day ($2.8–3.9 \ g/m^2 \cdot d$), to minimize odor nuisance in the spring. In southern states, design loadings are about 40–50 lb BOD/acre/day. Total retention time for primary plus secondary cells is 3–6 months to allow seasonal storage and controlled discharge. Series operation reduces short-circuiting and, as a result, improves BOD and fecal coliform removals.

The degree of stabilization produced in a pond is influenced by climatic conditions. During warm, sunny weather, decomposition and photosynthetic processes flourish, resulting in rapid and complete stabilization of the waste organics. The pond water becomes supersaturated with dissolved oxygen during the afternoon. Suspended solids and BOD in the pond effluent are primarily from the algae. BOD reductions in the summer usually exceed 95%. During cold weather under ice cover, biological activity is extremely slow and the lagoon-treatment process is, for practical purposes, reduced to sedimentation. Anaerobic conditions can occur from a lack of reaeration by wind action and photosynthesis. Suspended solids and BOD in the pond effluent include organics from raw wastes and intermediate organics issuing from incomplete anaerobic metabolism. Under winter ice cover, BOD reductions are generally about 50%.

Warm pond water that is rich in plant nutrients, when exposed to sunlight, supports an abundance of algae, giving the water a green color. Because wastewater contains significant concentrations of carbon dioxide, inorganic nitrogen, and soluble phosphorus, the growth of algae is usually limited by shading caused by the high turbidity from the algae in suspension. Higher forms of aquatic animal life (i.e., zooplankton) that graze on the algae are also present. As a result of this natural biological activity, pond water during summer months contains 50–80 mg/l of suspended solids. Although this exceeds the effluent standard of 30 mg/l of suspended solids, most regulatory agencies have established higher limits for stabilization pond effluent, typically 60 mg/l, to allow summer and fall discharge. Where the effluent standard prohibits discharge to a watercourse, irrigation of nearby agricultural land appears to be the best solution. In a semiarid climate where evaporation exceeds rainfall by a wide margin, ponds serving a small community can be constructed large enough to provide complete retention. However, the land area needed for zero-discharge ponds is often prohibitive.

29 ADVANTAGES AND DISADVANTAGES OF STABILIZATION PONDS

A general list of items to be considered before selecting the stabilization pond process for treatment of a municipal wastewater is offered here. In general, stabilization ponds are suitable for small towns that do not anticipate extensive industrial expansion and where land with suitable topography and soil conditions is available for siting.

Advantages

1. The initial cost is probably lower than that of a mechanical plant.
2. Operating costs are lower.
3. Regulation of effluent discharge is possible, thus providing control of pollution during critical times of the year.
4. Treatment system is not significantly influenced by a leaky sewer system that collects storm water.

Disadvantages

1. Extensive land area is required for siting.
2. The assimilative capacity for certain industrial wastes is poor.
3. Odor problems are possible.
4. The expansion of the town and new developments may encroach on the lagoon site.
5. The effluent quality generally cannot meet the standard for suspended solids of 30 mg/l.

Example 19

Design population for a town is 1200 persons, and the anticipated industrial load is 20,000 gpd at 1000 mg/l of BOD from a milk-processing plant. Calculate the surface area required for a stabilization pond system, and estimate the number of days of winter storage available. Assume the following:

1. Wastewater flow of 100 gpcd with 0.17 lb of BOD per capita.
2. Design BOD loading of 25 lb of BOD/acre/day.
3. Water loss from evaporation and seepage of 60 in./yr.
4. Annual rainfall of 20 in./yr.

Solution:

BOD load (domestic + industrial)

$$= 1200 \times 0.17 + 0.020 \times 1000 \times 8.34 = 371 \text{ lb of BOD/day}$$

$$\text{stabilization pond area required} = \frac{371}{25} = 14.8 \text{ acres (use two ponds)}$$

volume available for winter storage between 2- and 5-ft depths

$$= (5 - 2)14.8 \times 43,560 = 1,930,000 \text{ ft}^3$$

water loss per day (evaporation + seepage − rainfall)

$$= \frac{(60 - 20)14.8 \times 43,560}{12 \times 365} = 5890 \text{ ft}^3/\text{day}$$

$$\text{wastewater influent per day} = \frac{1200 \times 100 + 20,000}{7.48} = 18,700 \text{ ft}^3/\text{day}$$

$$\text{winter storage available} = \frac{1,930,000}{18,700 - 5900} = 150 \text{ days}$$

Example 20

The design criteria for stabilization ponds specified by the state regulatory agency are that (1) the BOD loading in the primary cells shall not exceed 25 lb BOD/acre/day; (2) the minimum total water volume, based on influent flow and all cells at a water depth of 5 ft, shall not be less than 120 days; (3) the volume for winter storage between the water depths of 1.5 and 5.0 ft shall be sufficient so that no discharge is necessary for a 4-month period; and (4) the pond system shall have at least two primary cells and one or more secondary cells that cannot receive raw wastewater. Size the ponds for a community with an average daily wastewater discharge of 160,000 gpd with a BOD of 220 mg/l. Based on available data, the net water loss (evaporation plus seepage minus precipitation) during the storage months is 1.0 in./month.

Solution:

$$\text{area of primary ponds} = \frac{0.160 \times 220 \times 8.34}{25}$$

$$= 11.7 \text{ acres}$$

$$\text{construct two primary cells each} = 5.9 \text{ acres}$$

$$\text{minimum total water volume required} = 120 \times 0.160 = 19.2 \text{ mil gal}$$

$$\text{volume of primary cells} = 11.7 \times 5 \times 0.326$$

$$= 19.1 \text{ mil gal} \quad (\text{OK})$$

$$\text{wastewater inflow during 4 months} = 0.160 \times 3.07 \times 4 \times 30 = 58.9 \text{ acre-ft}$$

$$\text{pond area required for storage} = \frac{\text{inflow} - \text{water loss}}{\text{difference in water levels}}$$

$$\text{pond area} = \frac{58.9 - \text{pond area} \times \frac{4}{12}}{5.0 - 1.5}$$

$$\text{pond area} = 15.4 \text{ acres}$$

$$\text{area of secondary cell} = 15.4 - 2 \times 5.9 = 3.6 \text{ acres}$$

30　COMPLETELY MIXED AERATED LAGOONS

Aerated ponds for pretreatment of industrial wastes or first-stage treatment of municipal wastewaters are commonly completely mixed lagoons 8–12 ft deep with floating or platform-mounted mechanical aeration units. A floating aerator consists of a motor-driven impeller mounted on a doughnut-shaped float with a submerged intake cone (Figure 51). Inspection and maintenance are performed using a boat, or by disconnecting the restraining cables and pulling the unit to the edge of the lagoon. Platform-mounted aerators are placed on piles or piers extending into the pond bottom (Figure 38). The impeller is held beneath the liquid surface by a short shaft connected to the motor mounted on the platform. A bridge may be constructed from the lagoon dike to the aerator for ease of inspection and maintenance.

Complete mixing and adequate aeration are essential environmental conditions for a lagoon biota. Selection and design of mixing equipment depend on manufacturers' laboratory test data and field experience. Aerators are spaced to provide uniform blending for the dispersion of dissolved oxygen and suspension of microbial solids. Their oxygen transfer capability must be able to satisfy the BOD demand of the waste while retaining a residual dissolved-oxygen concentration. Figure 52 illustrates the general relationships between power required for mixing and that required for

(a)

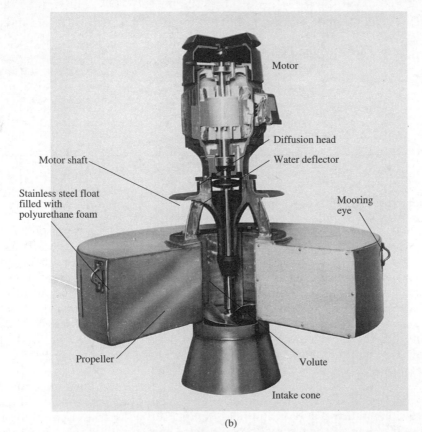

(b)

FIGURE 51　Floating aerator. (a) Picture of an aerator in operation. (b) Cutaway section showing aerator design with propeller directly connected to motor that is fastened to the float. Water drawn up through the intake cone is deflected by the diffusion head for aeration by dispersion. *Source:* Aqua-Aerobic Systems, Inc., Rockford, IL.

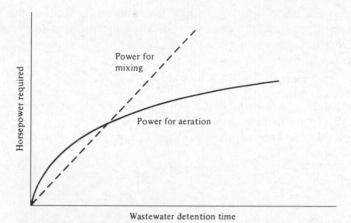

FIGURE 52   General relationships between the power required for mixing and that needed for aeration relative to wastewater detention time for mechanical aerators in completely mixed lagoons.

aeration. Only one detention time exists for a given wastewater strength where both stirring and aeration functions are at an optimum. Thus, deviations in loadings should be considered in the design selection and operational control of mechanical aeration units.

Organic stabilization depends on suspended microbial floc developed within the basin, since no provision is made for settling and returning activated sludge. BOD removal is a function of detention time, temperature, and nature of the waste, primarily biodegradability and nutrient content. The common relationships are

$$\frac{L_e}{L_0} = \frac{1}{1 + kt} \tag{99}$$

$$k_T = k_{20°C} \Theta^{T-20} \tag{100}$$

where

L_e = effluent BOD, mg/l
L_0 = influent BOD, mg/l
k = BOD-removal-rate constant to base e, day^{-1}
t = detention time, days
T = temperature, °C
Θ = temperature coefficient

The value of k relates to degradability of the waste organics, temperature, and completeness of aeration mixing. At 20°C, k values have been found to range from 0.3 to over 1.0; the precise value for a particular waste must be determined experimentally. The coefficient Θ is a function of biodegradability and generally falls between 1.035 and 1.075, with 1.035 being the most common value.

Biological oxygen utilization is equal to assimilative plus endogenous respiration, as in the activated-sludge process. However, with the low concentration of microbial suspended solids in the aerating wastewater, oxygen uptake can be simply related to BOD removal by the relationship

$$\text{lb of oxygen/day} = a \times \text{lb of BOD removed/day} \qquad (101)$$

The magnitude of a is determined by laboratory or field testing the particular wastewater to be treated. Values are from 0.5 to 2.0, 1.0 being typical.

Oxygen transferred by surface-aeration units can be computed by

$$R = R_0 \frac{\beta C_s - C_t}{9.2} \times 1.02^{T-20}(\alpha) \qquad (102)$$

where

R = actual rate of oxygen transfer, lb of oxygen/hp·hr

R_0 = rate of oxygen transfer of manufacturer's unit under standard conditions (water at 20° C, 1 atm pressure, and zero dissolved oxygen), lb of oxygen/hp·hr

β = oxygen saturation coefficient of the wastewater

C_s = oxygen concentration at saturation, mg/l

C_t = oxygen concentration existing in liquid, mg/l

T = temperature of lagoon liquid, °C

α = oxygen transfer coefficient

9.2 = saturation oxygen concentration of pure water at 20°C, mg/l

The manufacturer's oxygen transfer rate R_0 is guaranteed performance based on aerator test data stated in terms of standard conditions. The α and β factors are discussed in Section 26.

A facultative, aerated lagoon results if insufficient mixing permits deposition of suspended solids. BOD removal cannot be predicted with certainty in a nonhomogeneous system. Anaerobic decomposition of the settled sludge can cause emission of foul odors, particularly in treating certain industrial wastes. Facultative conditions often result from overloaded completely mixed lagoons or may derive from poorly designed systems with inadequate mixing. To ensure odor-free operation, pond contents must be thoroughly stirred, with dissolved oxygen available throughout the liquid. Aeration equipment installed should be of proven performance and purchased from a reputable manufacturer.

Significant increases in effluent BOD can occur from reducing detention time since the biological process is time dependent. Cooling-water discharges and shock loads of relatively uncontaminated water, for example, storm runoff, should be diverted around the lagoon to the secondary ponds. Sudden, large inputs of biodegradable or toxic wastes resulting from industrial spills can also upset the process. Pretreatment and control systems at industrial sites should be furnished to prevent taxing the lagoon's equalizing capacity. Biodegradability studies are essential for municipal wastewater containing measurable amounts of industrial discharges to determine such design parameters as BOD removal-rate constant, influence of temperature, nutrient requirements, oxygen utilization, and sludge production.

Example 21

Size an aerated lagoon to treat a domestic plus industrial waste flow of 0.30 mgd with an average BOD of 600 mg/l (1500 lb of BOD/day). The temperature extremes anticipated for the lagoon contents range from 10°C in winter to 35°C in summer. Minimum BOD reduction through the lagoon should be 75%. The surface aerators to be installed carry a manufacturer's guarantee to transfer 2.5 lb of oxygen/hp · hr under standard conditions. During laboratory treatability studies, the wastewater exhibited the following characteristics: $k_{20°C} = 0.68$ per day, $\Theta = 1.047$, $\alpha = 0.9$, and $\beta = 0.8$.

Solution: The required detention time at a critical temperature of 10°C is found using Eqs. (99) and (100):

$$k_{10°C} = 0.68 \times 1.047^{10-20} = 0.43 \text{ per day}$$

$$\frac{L_e}{L_0} = 1 - 0.75 = \frac{1}{1 + 0.43t}$$

$$t = 7.0 \text{ days}$$

$$\text{lagoon volume} = 0.30 \text{ mgd} \times 7.0 \text{ days} = 2.1 \text{ mil gal} = 280{,}000 \text{ ft}^3$$

Use a 10-ft depth with earth sides sloped appropriately for soil conditions. Oxygen utilization using $a = 0.8$:

At 10°C:

$$\text{BOD removal} = 0.75 \times 1500 = 1120 \text{ lb of BOD/day}$$

$$\text{oxygen required} = \frac{1120 \times 0.8}{24} = 37 \text{ lb of oxygen/hr}$$

At 35°C:

$$k = 0.68 \times 1.047^{35-20} = 1.35 \text{ per day}$$

$$\text{BOD removal} = 1500 - \frac{1500}{1 + 1.35 \times 7.0} = 1360 \text{ lb of BOD/day}$$

$$\text{oxygen required} = \frac{1360 \times 0.8}{24} = 45 \text{ lb of oxygen/hr}$$

Aerator power requirements using Eq. (102) at a minimum of 2.0 mg/l of dissolved oxygen ($C_s = 11.3$ mg/l at 10°C and 7.1 mg/l at 35°C):

$$R_{10°C} = \frac{2.5(0.8 \times 11.3 - 2.0)}{9.2} 1.02^{10-20} \times 0.9 = 1.4 \text{ lb of oxygen/hp} \cdot \text{hr}$$

$$\text{power required} = \frac{37 \text{ lb of oxygen/hr}}{1.4 \text{ lb of oxygen/hp} \cdot \text{hr}} = 26 \text{ hp}$$

$$R_{35°C} = \frac{2.5(0.8 \times 7.1 - 2.0)}{9.2} 1.02^{35-20} \times 0.9 = 1.2 \text{ lb of oxygen/hp} \cdot \text{hr}$$

$$\text{power required} = \frac{45}{1.2} = 38 \text{ hp}$$

Power requirements at 35°C control design: Use four 10-hp surface aerators.

ODOR CONTROL

Increased urbanization has resulted in wastewater treatment plants being situated in close proximity to housing areas and commercial developments. This has caused complaints about odors and, in serious situations, led to lawsuits against municipalities operating the disposal systems. Although the problem of foul odors emitting from treatment plants is not new, only in recent years have political and legal pressures forced processing facilities to consider abatement.

31   SOURCES OF ODORS IN WASTEWATER TREATMENT

Principal odors are hydrogen sulfide and organic compounds generated by anaerobic decomposition. The latter include mercaptans, indole, skatole, amines, fatty acids, and many other volatile organics. Often, industrial wastes in a municipal sewer create odors inherent in the raw materials being processed or the manufactured products (poultry processing, slaughtering and rendering, tanning, and manufacture of volatile chemicals). With the exception of hydrogen sulfide, it is very difficult to distinguish specific odor-producing substances. Weather conditions, such as temperature and wind velocity, influence the intensity and prevalence of emissions.

Frequently, the initial evolution of malodors is from septic wastewater in the sewer collection system. Flat sewer grades, warm temperatures, and high-strength wastes lead to anaerobiosis. The first sources at the treatment plant are the wet well and grit chamber. Turbulent flow and preaeration of raw waste strip dissolved gases and volatile organics, discharging them into the atmosphere. Odors also may arise from the liquid held in primary clarifiers, particularly if excess activated sludge is returned to the head of the plant, resulting in an active microbial seed being mixed with the settleable raw organic matter. Sludge taken from these tanks has an obnoxious smell. Pumping it into uncovered holding tanks releases the scent previously confined under the water cover. Polymers do not neutralize the olfactory compounds prior to mechanical dewatering; therefore, the air drawn through the sludge cake picks up volatile compounds and carries them to the atmosphere. The use of ferric chloride and lime for conditioning chemicals significantly reduces odors, but for most municipal wastes, polymers provide more economical operation. The process of anaerobic digestion takes place in enclosed tanks, while digested sludge is dewatered either mechanically or on drying beds. The smell of well-digested sludge is earthy, but if the digestion process is not complete, intermediate aromatic compounds may be released during drying.

Secondary biological processes also yield odors, particularly stone-media trickling filters. Although referred to as aerobic devices, filters are actually facultative, since the microbial films are aerobic on the surface and anaerobic adjacent to the medium. Because of this potential for anaerobic decomposition, filters under heavy organic loading can reek. Odors are not as likely to be created in biological towers because of thinner biological films and improved aeration. Activated-sludge processes yield a relatively inoffensive musty odor carried by the air passing through the mixed liquor. Foul smells are rare, since microbial flocs in the aeration basin are completely surrounded by liquid containing dissolved oxygen.

32   METHODS OF ODOR CONTROL

Modern treatment plant design incorporates odor prevention [26]. When choosing the location for a plant, it is prudent to provide a reasonable buffer zone to prevent encroachment of other activities in which people will be offended by the presence of a treatment plant.

The first step in analyzing an existing problem is to determine the cause of odorousness and attempt to isolate the sources. Special attention must be paid to industrial wastes entering the sewer system. Overloading often increases malodors; however, expansion of facilities is no guarantee that the situation will change dramatically. Foul emissions can be given off by properly loaded units if the design is poor, if they are not maintained properly, or when the waste includes organics with an inherent smell. Typical problems are hydrogen sulfide and other volatile odorous compounds being stripped out of solution and dispersed in air from the wet well, grit chamber, or primary clarifiers. Warm septic wastewater can release extremely offensive odors. Anaerobiosis can occur in poorly vented trickling filters. In sludge processing, foul odors are most likely to be released from raw sludge in holding tanks and in ventilation exhaust from buildings housing mechanical dewatering equipment. The sources of odors can be difficult to locate precisely. For example, convection can lift odorous air up and transport it a considerable distance before it descends.

Chemicals can sometimes be used to oxidize odorous compounds, particularly hydrogen sulfide. Chlorination of the wastewater in main sewers, or prior to primary settling, may prove beneficial. Using lime and ferric chloride as chemical sludge conditioners reduces bacterial activity and oxidizes many products of anaerobic decomposition.

The best method for preventing odorous emissions is to contain the foul air and process it through an air pollution control system. Fiberglass and aluminum covers and domes can be constructed over grit chambers, primary clarifiers, sludge-holding tanks, sludge conveyors, and trickling filters for containment. For a deep wet well, an exhaust pipe can be installed to withdraw air from above the wastewater inflow. Exhaust hoods are commonly placed over sludge dewatering equipment (e.g., belt filter presses and centrifuges) to reduce indoor air pollution and to treat the released air. In activated-sludge plants, contained or exhausted foul air can be cleansed effectively by using the air as a portion of the air supply to the aeration tanks [27].

The common air pollution control system is a countercurrent packed-tower scrubber where a chemical solution, usually hypochlorite or permanganate, is used to oxidize airborne odorous compounds. The foul air flows up through the packing, passes through a mist eliminator, and exhausts to the atmosphere. The scrubbing chemical solution is sprayed down on the packing, flows over the packing, and is collected in the bottom of the tank for recirculation. The purpose of the packing is turbulent mixing of the solution and air to increase the rate of gas–liquid mass transfer. Fresh chemical is automatically added to maintain solution strength and a small amount of spent solution is wasted. While some contaminants like hydrogen sulfide are readily adsorbed, organic compounds such as amines and aldehydes are less effectively removed. The main advantages of the packed-tower scrubber are the ability to process large air flows in an economically sized system and to treat effectively a rapid increase in concentration of hydrogen sulfide. A similar process is a mist scrubber, which does not contain packing. A strong chemical solution is introduced through air-atomizing nozzles to create very fine droplets that adsorb airborne odors by gas–liquid contact.

An activated-carbon adsorber is a bed through which odorous air is passed to remove contaminants. After degradation, the carbon has to be replaced or regenerated. Since activated carbon is most effective in removing many organic molecules, an adsorber may follow a packed-tower scrubber to remove organic sulfur and volatile organic compounds.

A biofilter is a bed of organic bulk material used to adsorb and biologically oxidize airborne contaminants, including sulfur compounds, ammonia, and hydrocarbons. After collection from various treatment processes, the foul air is blown out of perforated pipes buried in the bed. Biofiltration can remove a wide variety of air contaminants to a level not achievable with packed-tower scrubbing or other absorption systems with chemical treatment. The disadvantages are the large amount of space, extensive piping, and energy required to force the foul air through the bed.

INDIVIDUAL ON-SITE WASTEWATER DISPOSAL

33   SEPTIC TANK–ABSORPTION FIELD SYSTEM

Approximately 30% of the population in the United States live in unsewered areas and rely on on-site systems for wastewater treatment and disposal. Almost one-third of the housing units use septic tanks or cesspools; the majority of the remainder, usually in remote locations, use pit privies.

The installation of a septic tank and absorption field, sketched in Figure 53, has the advantages of low cost and underground disposal of effluent. The septic tank is an underground concrete box sized for a liquid detention time of approximately 2 days. With garbage grinders and automatic washers, the recommended minimum capacity is 750 gal (2.8 m^3) for a two-bedroom house, 900 gal (3.4 m^3) for three bedrooms, 1000 gal (3.8 m^3)

for four bedrooms, and 250 gal (1.0 m^3) for each additional bedroom. Inspection and cleaning ports are accessible for maintenance by removing the 1-ft-thick earth cover. Inlet and outlet pipe tees, or baffles, prevent clogging of the openings with scum that accumulates on the liquid surface. The functions of a septic tank are settling of solids, flotation of grease, and anaerobic decomposition and storage of sludge. Retention of large solids and grease is essential to prevent plugging of the absorption field. Under normal loading, the accumulated sludge (septage) must be pumped from the tank every 3–5 yr.

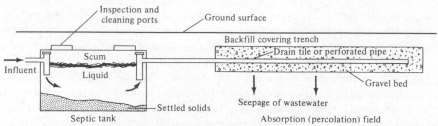

FIGURE 53   A typical septic tank–absorption field system for on-site disposal of household wastewater.

A typical absorption field consists of looped or lateral trenches 18–24 in. wide and at least 18 in. deep. Drain tile or perforated pipe in an envelope of gravel distributes the wastewater uniformly over the trench bottom. Organics decompose in the aerobic-facultative environment of the bed and the water seeps downward into the soil. Air enters the gravel bed through the backfill covering the trenches and by ventilation through the drain tile from the house plumbing stack. The percolation area required depends on soil permeability. For a four-bedroom dwelling, the area needed is in the range of 300–1300 ft^2 (30–120 m^2). Trench area for a particular location can be determined by subsurface soil exploration and percolation tests; however, most state environmental control agencies and county health departments have guidelines for installations based on local conditions.

The most frequent complaints in the operation of septic tank–absorption field systems involve plumbing stoppages and odorous seepage appearing at or near the ground surface. Plugging of the influent is often the result of excessive accumulation of solids due to either overloading or neglecting to pump out the sludge every few years. When cleaning a tank, leave a small amount of the black digesting sludge in the tank to ensure adequate bacterial seeding to continue solids digestion. Obstruction of percolation can result for any of the following reasons: construction in soils of low permeability that are inadequate for the seepage, high-water-table conditions that saturate the soil profile during the wet-weather season, inadequate design resulting in hydraulic and organic overloading, and improper cleaning of the septic tank.

Soils with a high infiltration rate, although advantageous for effluent disposal, often do not have the capacity to absorb contaminants. The result can be serious groundwater pollution, either limited to the area immediately surrounding an absorption field or widespread, depending on the density of housing units. Nearby wells can be polluted with disease-producing microorganisms, particularly viruses. The most common pollutants, however, are mobile substances like detergents, and ions such as chloride and nitrate.

MARINE WASTEWATER DISPOSAL

34 OCEAN OUTFALLS

An ocean outfall is a pipeline that extends thousands of feet from the shore to relatively deep water. At the end of the pipe, a diffuser discharges the wastewater through a series of ports spaced to provide initial dilution. After reaching the sea surface, or an intermediate equilibrium level, this mixed plume tends to move with the prevailing currents to provide secondary dispersion. Data collected for design of an outfall include physical, chemical, biological, and geological conditions. Of particular concern is a comprehensive oceanographic study to predict dilution and diffusion of the wastewater.

The general water quality objective in marine disposal is to maintain the indigenous marine life and a healthy and diverse marine community. Relevant considerations are contamination of shellfish with pathogens, toxicity of aquatic life, accumulation of sediments that impair benthic life, and aesthetics of the ocean surface.

The beneficial uses of ocean waters to be protected are water contact and non-contact recreation, commercial and sport fishing, marine habitat, shellfish harvesting (mussels, clams, and oysters), and industrial water supply.

Effluent requirements, based on samples collected from the outfall pipeline, limit both major constituents and toxins for protection of aquatic life and human health. As listed in Table 9, the major constituents limited by the state of California are grease and oil, suspended solids, settleable solids, turbidity, pH, and acute toxicity [28]. The limitations of specific toxins, mostly heavy metals and pesticides, are listed separately, and BOD is included for domestic wastewater. For municipal wastewaters, these limitations can be achieved by pretreatment of industrial wastewaters at industrial sites and conventional biological treatment with chlorination for effluent disinfection. Fish bioassays for acute toxicity are conducted with the threespine stickleback. The test species for chronic toxicity bioassays preferably include a fish, an invertebrate (shrimp or oyster), and an aquatic plant (red algae or giant kelp). Effluent quality limitations for chemicals for protection of human health are based on calculated initial dilution as determined from a mathematical model. The characteristics of the outfall for inputs to the model include length of diffuser, number and spacing of ports, port diameter and angle from the horizontal, average depth of ports under mean sea level, and rate of wastewater discharge.

Water quality in the zone of initial dilution (Figure 54) is determined from samples collected at boat stations. The physical characteristics of the ocean water in this zone should be no visible floating particulates, grease or oil, and no aesthetically undesirable discoloration of the ocean surface. Natural light penetration shall not degrade biological benthic communities. Chemical changes are not to decrease dissolved oxygen more than 10%, lower the pH more than 0.2 units, increase dissolved sulfide concentration, increase the concentration of degrading substances in sediments, or increase nutrients causing objectionable aquatic plant growths. The biological

TABLE 9   Effluent Quality Limits of Major Wastewater Constituents for Ocean Discharge to Protect Marine Aquatic Life

Parameter	Monthly (30-Day Average)	Weekly (7-Day Average)	Maximum at Any Time
Grease and oil, mg/l	25	40	75
Suspended solids, mg/l	60 with a minimum removal of 75%		
Settleable solids, ml/l	1.0	1.5	3.0
Turbidity, NTU	75	100	225
pH	within limits of 6.0–9.0 at all times		
Acute toxicity, TUa[a]	1.5	2.0	2.5

[a]$TUa = \dfrac{100}{96\text{-hr } LC_{50}}$

where
TUa = toxicity units acute
LC = lethal concentration, 50%
Source: California Ocean Plan, Ocean Waters of California, State Water Resources Control Board (Sacramento, CA: 2001).

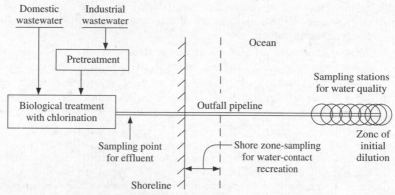

FIGURE 54   Schematic diagram of marine discharge of wastewater.

water quality changes shall not degrade vertebrate, invertebrate, or plant species; alter the natural taste, odor, or color of fish or shellfish for human consumption; or increase the bioaccumulation of toxins in fish or shellfish to a level harmful to human health.

Water quality in the shore zone for water-contact recreation is monitored by collecting samples for coliform testing from the shoreline into the ocean for a distance of 1000 ft or to the 30-ft depth contour, whichever is further. The typical standard is an average of fewer than 1000 total coliforms per 100 ml in any 30-day period, with no single sample exceeding 10,000 per 100 ml. For fecal coliforms, the standard is not to exceed a geometric mean of 200 per 100 ml, with no more than 10% exceeding 400 per 100 ml in a 60-day period [28]. In areas where shellfish are being harvested for human consumption, the median total coliform concentration is not to exceed 70 per 100 ml, with no more than 10% exceeding 230 per 100 ml.

PROBLEMS

1   (a) How do autotrophic bacteria gain energy? (b) Why do some bacteria convert ammonia to nitrate [Eqs. (1) and (2)], whereas others reduce nitrate to nitrogen gas [Eq. (12)]? (c) Hydrogen sulfide emitted by septic wastewater and sludge is too weak an acid to cause significant corrosion, yet when hydrogen sulfide is present, concrete deteriorates and iron corrodes. Explain this phenomenon. (d) What promotes the growth of iron bacteria in water pipes distributing well water? How do these bacteria contribute foul tastes and odors to the water?

2   List the major nutritional and environmental conditions necessary to culture algae in a laboratory container.

3   A fresh wastewater containing nitrate ions, sulfate ions, and dissolved oxygen is placed in a sealed jar without air. In what sequence are these oxidized compounds reduced by the bacteria? Why is dissolved oxygen the preferred hydrogen acceptor? When do obnoxious odors appear?

4   Discuss the relationships among metabolism, energy, and synthesis and the effect of these on growth under aerobic and anaerobic conditions. (a) Include comments on growth rates,

extent of metabolism, and limiting factors under the two environments. (b) Why is bacterial synthesis for the same quantity of substrate greater in an aerobic environment than under anaerobiosis?

5   What are the relationships between biomass and substrate in the exponential growth and declining growth phases of a pure bacterial culture? List the characteristics of the endogenous growth phase.

6   What is the mathematical relationship for growth kinetics of a pure bacterial culture under substrate-limited growth conditions proposed by Monod and graphed in Figure 6? How does this relate to enzymatic reactions as defined by Michaelis and Menten?

7   A series of fermentation tubes containing varying concentrations of glucose in a nutrient broth were inoculated with a pure bacterial culture. The concentrations of cells in the broth media were determined after 16 hr of incubation at 37°C. Rates of growth and initial glucose concentrations are listed below. Plot growth rate expressed as cell divisions per hour versus initial glucose concentration. Estimate the maximum growth rate and the saturation constant (glucose concentration at one-half the maximum growth rate). Write an equation in the form of Eq. (25), and draw the curve for this equation on the graph with the plotted data. Does the growth of this pure culture appear to be a hyperbolic function as defined by the Monod relationship?

Glucose (moles $\times 10^{-4}$)	Cell Divisions (per hr)	Glucose (moles $\times 10^{-4}$)	Cell Divisions (per hr)
0.1	0.23	0.8	0.94
0.1	0.28	1.6	1.06
0.2	0.32	3.2	1.15
0.4	0.71		

8   How is growth yield determined in pure bacterial cultures?

9   (a) How does temperature affect biological processes? (b) The rate of BOD reduction in aeration of a synthetic wastewater decreased 25% when the temperature of the laboratory fermentation tank was lowered from 20° to 15°C. Using Eq. (35), calculate the temperature coefficient. How many degrees of temperature drop are required to reduce the rate of BOD reduction by one-half?

10   State the two main reasons why an activated-sludge system is operated at a relatively low food/microorganism ratio.

11   Why are bacteria rather than protozoans the primary feeders in activated sludge?

12   Why is impending failure of an anaerobic digestion process forecast by an increase in the percentage of carbon dioxide in the gas produced?

13   (a) Describe the role of algae in biological stabilization of wastewater in a stabilization pond. (b) Describe what is wrong with the following statement: "The key to waste stabilization in a pond is the algal growth; overloading kills the algae, whereas they thrive on a reasonable supply of organic matter."

14   The average annual wastewater flow of a municipality is 24 mgd, with an average BOD concentration of 200 mg/l and suspended-solids concentration of 220 mg/l. Based on the equations in Section 10, estimate the average annual peak month and average annual peak day of wastewater flows, BOD loads, and suspended-solids loads.

15   The average wastewater flow and strength anticipated during the maximum month of the year are often used for design. If the annual average wastewater flow and characteristics

are estimated to be 32,000 m³/d with 250 mg/l of BOD and 280 mg/l of suspended solids, what are the values likely to be for the peak month, using the equations in Section 10?

16 The wastewater from a synthetic textile manufacturing plant is discharged to a municipal treatment plant for processing with domestic wastewater. The characteristics of the synthetic textile wastewater are 1500 mg/l BOD, 2000 mg/l SS, 30 mg/l nitrogen, and no phosphorus. The characteristics of the domestic wastewater are listed in Table 1. If the required BOD/N/P weight ratio is 100/5/1, what is the minimum quantity of domestic wastewater required per 1000 gal of textile wastewater to provide adequate nutrients for biological treatment?

17 The wastewater from the manufacture of synthetic chemicals produces a wastewater flow of 779 m³/d containing 4300 mg/l of BOD, 1200 mg/l of suspended solids, 70 mg/l of nitrogen, and negligible phosphorus. You are asked to recommend dosages of pure NH_4NO_3 and H_3PO_4 to be applied for activated-sludge treatment. After the biological process is stabilized, how would you determine whether your recommended dosages were correct?

18 A pharmaceutical wastewater needs a minimum BOD/N/P of 100/3.0/0.7 for biological treatment. The wastewater characteristics are BOD = 740 mg/l, suspended solids = 250 mg/l, *soluble nitrogen* = 24 *mg/l*, and soluble phosphorous = 12 mg/l. What ammonium nitrate and phosphoric acid additions would you recommend to ensure adequate nutrients for a daily flow of 28 m³/d?

19 A dairy that processes about 250,000 lb of milk daily produces an average of 65,100 gpd of wastewater with a BOD of 1400 mg/l. The principal operations are bottling milk and making ice cream, with limited production of cottage cheese. Compute the flow and BOD per 1000 lb of milk received, and the BOD and hydraulic equivalent populations of the daily wastewater discharge.

20 A meat-processing plant discharges 10,000 m³/d of wastewater containing 1300 mg/l of BOD, 960 mg/l of suspended solids, 2500 mg/l of COD, and 460 mg/l of grease. Calculate the BOD equivalent population and the hydraulic equivalent population.

21 The domestic and industrial waste from a community consists of 100 gpcd from 7500 persons; 65,000 gpd from a milk-processing plant with a BOD of 1400 mg/l; and 90,000 gpd containing 450 lb of BOD from potato-chip manufacturing. Calculate the combined wastewater flow, BOD concentration in the composite waste, and BOD equivalent population.

22 The combined wastewater flow from a community includes domestic waste from a sewered population of 2000 and industrial wastes from a dairy and a poultry-dressing plant. The poultry plant discharges 125 m³/d and 136 kg of BOD/d. The dairy produces a flow of 190 m³/d with a BOD concentration of 900 mg/l. Estimate the total combined wastewater flow from the community and the BOD concentration in the composite discharge.

23 A town with a sewered population of 4000 has a daily wastewater flow (including industrial wastewaters) of 1600 m³ and an average BOD of 280 mg/l. The industrial discharges to the municipal sewers are 60 m³ at 1800 mg/l BOD from a meat-processing plant and 100 m³ at 400 mg/l BOD from a soup-canning plant. Determine the contribution of domestic flow in liters per person and the BOD in grams per person based on the town's wastewater, excluding the industrial wastewaters.

24 The municipal wastewater flow from a town is 1890 m³/d with an average BOD of 280 mg/l. Assuming 35% BOD removal in the primary, calculate the size required for one single-stage trickling filter. Use a depth of 2.1 m, a BOD loading of 480 g/m³·d, and minimum required hydraulic loading. Compute the BOD concentration in the effluent at 20°C and 15°C, using the NRC formula and temperature correction relationship in Eq. (25).

25 A single-stage trickling-filter plant (Figure 21) is proposed for treating a dilute wastewater with a BOD concentration of 170 mg/l. The plant is located in a warm climate and the minimum wastewater temperature anticipated is 16°C. Using a recirculation ratio of 0.5, what

is the maximum allowable BOD loading for a stone-media filter to achieve an average effluent BOD of 30 mg/l?

26 The sizing of primary clarifiers is generally based on the average weekday flow during the time of the year of greatest flow. If the plant is a trickling-filter system, gravity return of underflow from the final clarifier to the wet well is performed for recirculation during periods of low influent flow (Figure 21). This recirculation flow, usually $0.5Q$ or less as diagrammed in Figure 16a, is necessary to maintain rotation of the distributor arm at night and to provide adequate hydraulic loading of the filter media. Should the size of primary clarifiers be increased to account for this low-flow recirculation? Explain.

27 Estimate the effluent BOD for the two-stage trickling-filter plant designed in Example 5 for a wastewater flow of 1.2 mgd with a BOD concentration of 250 mg/l.

28 Determine the NRC BOD removal efficiency for a two-stage trickling-filter plant based on the following: primary clarification with 35% BOD reduction, first-stage filters loaded at 80 lb/1000 ft^3/day, intermediate settling, second-stage filters sized identical to the first-stage units, an operating recirculation ratio of 1.0 for all filters, final clarification of the effluent, and a wastewater temperature of 18°C.

29 An existing single-stage trickling-filter plant cannot meet the effluent limitation of 30 mg/l BOD during cold weather. In operation under the design loading with the wastewater temperature at 15°C, the plant influent BOD is 240 mg/l, the primary effluent BOD equals 155 mg/l, and the plant effluent averages 55 mg/l. The proposed modification is the addition of a second-stage trickling filter and final clarifier to reduce the effluent BOD from 55 to 30 mg/l with a wastewater temperature of 15°C. Under normal operation, the recirculation flow in the second-stage filtration is to be one-half of the average wastewater flow entering the plant. Calculate the design BOD loading that should be used to determine the volume of stone media needed in the proposed second-stage filter.

30 Plot the recirculation factor in the NRC formulas for trickling filters as a function of the recirculation ratio. Discuss the relationship between these two values. Why is the recirculation factor used instead of the recycle ratio in the NRC formulas?

31 The following are design data for the town of Nancy, with a sewered population of 7600. Design flows are as follows: the average daily flow is 0.84 mgd, the peak hourly flow is 1.25 mgd, and the minimum hourly flow is 0.12 mgd. Design average BOD equals 1740 lb/day and average suspended solids equal 1530 lb/day. Calculate the following: equivalent population based on 0.20 lb of BOD per capita; design flows in units of gpm, ft^3/sec, m^3/min, and m^3/d; mean BOD and SS concentrations in mg/l.

32 Consider the feasibility of treating the wastewater from the town of Nancy (Problem 31) in a single-stage stone-media trickling-filter plant as diagrammed in Figure 21. The treated wastewater is required to meet the effluent standards of 30 mg/l of BOD and 30 mg/l of suspended solids at a wastewater temperature of 15°C. Assume a primary BOD removal efficiency of 35%. Size the trickling filters based on a BOD loading of 35 lb/1000 ft^3/day, recirculation ratio of 0.5, and a stone-media depth of 7.0 ft. Calculate the volume of filter media required, filter surface area, hydraulic loading with recirculation in gallons per minute per square foot, and effluent BOD concentration using the NRC formula.

33 Consider the feasibility of treating the wastewater from the town of Nancy (Problem 31) in a two-stage stone-media trickling-filter plant with intermediate clarification. The treated wastewater is required to meet the effluent standards of 30 mg/l of BOD and 30 mg/l of suspended solids at a wastewater temperature of 15°C. Assume a primary BOD removal efficiency of 35%. Calculate the volume of filter media required at a BOD loading of 35 lb/1000 ft^3/day and divide the resulting volume equally between the first-stage and second-stage filters. Use a filter media depth of 7.0 ft. Assuming a recirculation ratio of 0.5 for both filters, determine the effluent BOD concentration using the NRC formulas.

34 Consider the feasibility of treating the wastewater from the town of Nancy (Problem 31) in a single-stage trickling-filter plant, as diagrammed in Figure 21, using high-density cross-flow media with a specific surface area of 42 ft^2/ft^3. Use the same filter surface area as calculated for stone-media filtration in Problem 31 ($A = 4600$ ft^2) and a recirculation ratio of 0.5. The design wastewater temperature is 15°C. As determined from laboratory testing, the soluble (filtered) BOD of the primary effluent is 100 mg/l or less, compared to the unsettled unfiltered BOD of 160 mg/l. The soluble effluent BOD concentration of trickling-filter plants treating similar wastewaters is approximately 50% of the unfiltered BOD concentration. From pilot-plant studies and full-scale experience, the manufacturer of the cross-flow media recommends a reaction-rate coefficient at 20°C of 0.0030 $(gpm/ft^2)^{0.5}$ for a media depth of 6.6 ft (2.0 m). From these data, calculate the soluble effluent BOD and double this value for the estimated effluent BOD.

35 A single-stage, trickling-filter plant consists of a primary clarifier, a trickling filter 70 ft in diameter with a 7-ft depth of random packing, and a final clarifier. The raw-wastewater flow is 0.80 mgd with 200 mg/l of BOD and a temperature of 15°C. The constants for the random plastic media are an n of 0.44 and K_{20} of 0.090 min^{-1}. Assuming 35% BOD removal in the primary, calculate the effluent BOD concentration (a) without recycle and (b) with an indirect recirculation to the wet well of 0.40 mgd and direct recirculation of 0.80 mgd.

36 A single-stage, high-rate trickling-filter plant treating wastewater with 200 mg/l of BOD cannot meet the effluent standard of less than 30 mg/l of BOD. Primary settling removes 35% of the raw-wastewater BOD and the 7-ft-deep filters have an efficiency of 75% under a loading of 40 lb/1000 ft^3/day of BOD and a hydraulic loading of 0.18 gpm/ft^2 without recirculation. This provides average effluent BODs of 30–35 mg/l during the summer and 40–45 mg/l during the winter. One proposal is to replace the stone media with the random packing described in Example 6, which has constants $n = 0.39$ and $K_{20} = 0.120$ min^{-1}; cover the filters with fiberglass domes to prevent the wastewater from cooling below 16°C in winter; and modify the plant to provide both direct and indirect recirculation. Calculate the effluent BOD at 16°C for the filters packed with the random plastic media at $R = 1.0$.

37 Using Eq. (57) developed in Example 6, plot the filtered BOD remaining versus depth in a filter with 20 ft of random packing. Assume an applied filtered BOD of 100 mg/l and a hydraulic loading of 0.35 gpm/ft^2.

38 A tracer analysis was performed on a pilot trickling filter packed with a 10-ft depth of plastic media. The time to the appearance of the peak of the tracer concentration was recorded as a function of the hydraulic loading rate. The following data were collected:

Hydraulic loading rate (Q) gpm/ft²	0.2	0.6	0.9	1.2
Time to peak of tracer conc., min	28	21	15	14

Find the coefficients C and n in the model shown in equation 46.

39 A pilot-scale study was conducted to determine the reaction-rate coefficient for cross-flow media treating a settled municipal wastewater. The tower was 1.2 m by 1.2 m square with a 6.0-m depth of media, which had a specific surface area equal to 98 m^2/m^3. From the following data, plot a graph as shown in Figure 27 and determine k_{20}. Assume $n = 0.5$ and $\Theta = 1.035$.

Q (l/m²·s)	T (°C)	Influent		Effluent	
		BOD (mg/l)	S_0 (mg/l)	BOD (mg/l)	S_e (mg/l)
1.03	18	92	54	25	14
0.64	23	90	52	18	10
0.47	21	104	54	17	9
1.06	19	72	48	23	12
0.97	24	77	43	20	10
0.70	20	85	45	17	11

40 A biological tower has vertical-flow packing with a $k_{20} = 0.0014$ (gpm/ft²)$^{0.5}$, $n = 0.50$, and $A_s = 36$ ft²/ft³. The tower is cylindrical, with a diameter of 32 ft and depth of packing of 16 ft. The primary effluent is 0.60 mgd with 80 mg/l of soluble BOD at a temperature of 14°C. Direct recirculation is 400 gpm and the final clarifier is properly sized. Calculate the soluble BOD loading, hydraulic loading, and soluble effluent BOD using Eq. (53).

41 A biological tower with high-density, cross-flow packing has a surface area of 480 ft² and a depth of 0 ft. The packing has a specific surface area of 42 ft²/ft³, $n = 0.5$, and $k_{20} = 0.0035$ (gpm/ft²)$^{0.5}$. The effluent from the primary clarifier is 600,000 gpd with a total BOD of 126 mg/l and soluble BOD of 62 mg/l. The wastewater temperature is 18°C and the recirculation ratio is 1.0. Calculate the effluent soluble BOD and estimate the effluent total BOD, assuming the ratio of soluble BOD to total BOD is the same as in the primary effluent.

42 A stone-media trickling filter with a depth of 7.0 ft cannot produce an effluent with an average BOD equal to or less than 30 mg/l, as specified in the discharge permit. From a field study, the operational data for the filter and final clarifier were as follows: hydraulic loading on the filter from primary clarifier = 0.35 gpm/ft²; settled wastewater from the primary clarifier BOD = 126 mg/l and soluble BOD = 68 mg/l; final clarified effluent BOD = 48 mg/l and soluble BOD = 26 mg/l; wastewater temperature = 18°C; and recirculation ratio of 1.0. Since the stone media were in poor condition and causing plugging of the voids, one of the recommendations for remedial action was to install high-density cross-flow packing with a specific surface area = 42 ft²/ft³, $n = 0.50$, and $k_{20} = 0.0035$ (gpm/ft²)$^{0.5}$. Using Eq. (53), calculate the effluent BOD for cross-flow packing based on field-study data for hydraulic loading, influent soluble BOD, temperature, and recirculation ratio. Assume that the effluent BOD would have the same fraction of soluble BOD as in the field study, 26/48 = 0.54.

43 Calculate the required surface area and the minimum required recirculation ratio based on the following: cross-flow media with $k_{20} = 0.0018$ (gpm/ft²)$^{0.5}$, $A_s = 42$ ft²/ft³, $n = 0.5$, and $D = 20$ ft; settled wastewater flow $Q_p = 0.50$ mgd; minimum wetting rate = 0.7 gpm/ft²; influent BOD = 162 mg/l, $S_p = 80$ mg/l, and temperature = 15°C; and effluent BOD = 20 mg/l and $S_e = 10$ mg/l. For the calculated surface area, what is the BOD loading in pounds per 1000 ft³ per day?

44 Calculate the RBC surface area required for secondary treatment of wastewater for the town of Nancy (Problem 31). Assume 35% BOD removal in the primary, a required effluent quality of 30 mg/l of BOD, and wastewater temperature of 50°F.

45 A community with a wastewater flow during the peak month of the year of 2.0 mgd at 15°C is considering constructing a new treatment plant. The composition of the raw wastewater is as shown in Table 1, and the effluent limits are 30 mg/l of BOD, 30 mg/l of suspended solids, and fecal coliform count of less than 200 per 100 ml. Sketch flow diagrams for the treatment systems listed below, showing the arrangement of unit processes (i.e., tanks, pumping stations, and division boxes) and major pipelines (i.e., for wastewater, recycle, and sludge). Assume sludge stabilization is by anaerobic digestion and dewatering by belt filter presses. Duplication of treatment units is necessary, so if any unit is out of service for maintenance the wastewater can still be processed through the plant, although the effluent quality may be reduced. No pipelines are allowed to bypass raw or settled wastewater to the plant outlet. Standby generators are provided for emergency operation during electrical power outage. List numerical design guidelines for sizing each treatment unit, except pumps and sludge processing.

(a) Preliminary treatment with constant-speed pumps

(b) Preliminary treatment with variable-speed pumps

(c) Two-stage trickling-filter plant with stone-media filters

(d) Trickling-filter plant with single-stage biological towers

46 The following are average operating data from a conventional activated-sludge secondary: wastewater flow = 7.7 mgd, volume of aeration tanks = 300,000 ft^3 = 2.24 mil gal, influent total solids =600mg/l, influent suspended solids = 120 mg/l, influent BOD = 173 mg/l, effluent total solids = 500 mg/l, effluent suspended solids = 22 mg/l, effluent BOD = 20 mg/l, mixed-liquor suspended solids = 2500 mg/l, recirculated sludge flow = 2.7 mgd, waste sludge quantity = 54,000 gpd, and suspended solids in waste sludge = 9800 mg/l. Based on these data, calculate the following: aeration period; BOD loading in lb/1000 ft^3/day; F/M ratio in lb BOD/day/lb MLSS; total solids, suspended solids, and BOD removal efficiencies; sludge age; and return sludge rate.

47 The general loading and operational parameters for activated-sludge processes in Table 3 are for a continental climate with cold, snowy winters and short, warm, humid summers, and for a temperate climate with mild rainy winters and warm, humid summers or mild, rainy summers. In the northern United States, the concern is wastewater cooling below 10°C toward 5°C in activated-sludge processes; hence, aeration is by submerged air diffusers to prevent cooling (e.g., Figures 33 and 34). In the southern United States, where the air temperature stays above freezing, aeration may be by mechanical surface aerators (e.g., Figure 38). For regions with moderate air temperatures, mechanical aeration systems that have housing or covers over the aerators can minimize cooling of the mixed liquor (e.g., Figures 36 and 37).

Wastewater temperatures of 20°–30°C in hot, arid climates have significant influence on the sizing of an activated-sludge aeration tank and the capacity of aeration supply. (a) Commonly recommended loading criteria for a secondary step-aeration activated-sludge process (Figure 32b) for a minimum wastewater temperature of 10°C is a maximum of 40 lb BOD/1000 ft^3/day (640 kg BOD/m^3·d), a minimum aeration period of 6.0 hr, and an operating F/M of 0.26 lb BOD/day/lb of MLSS (0.26 kg BOD/kg MLSS·d). Using Eq. (35), calculate the rate of biological activity increase for a wastewater temperature increase from 15° to 25°C, assuming doubling with a 15°C temperature rise (θ = 1.047). For the rise in biological activity, calculate new values of volumetric BOD loading, aeration period, and F/M ratio. (b) Higher wastewater temperature also affects oxygen transfer in the mixed liquor because the rate of transfer is directly related to the dissolved oxygen deficit [Eq. (87)]. Calculate the values of $\beta C_s - C_t$ at 15°C and 25°C, assuming β = 0.9 and C_t = 2.0 mg/l, which is a common minimum dissolved-oxygen concentration recommended in design. Determine C_s from Table 10 in the Appendix for zero chloride concentration. What is the percentage reduction in the rate of oxygen transfer when the temperature of the mixed liquor increases from 15°C to 25°C? (c) "At wastewater temperatures lower than 15°C, nitrification (oxidation of ammonia to nitrate) is limited in activated-sludge aeration. In contrast nitrification during aeration of wastewater with a temperature higher than 25°C cannot be prevented" [14]. For the wastewater characteristics in Table 1, calculate the BOD oxygen demand, which is 1 lb of oxygen per lb of BOD (Section 25) and the nitrogen oxygen demand, which is 4.6 lb of oxygen per lb of nitrogen oxidized to nitrate. Based on these data, how much oxygen demand should be considered in design for aeration of a warm wastewater?

48 Data from a field study on a step-feed activated-sludge secondary are as follows:

$$\text{Aeration tank volume} = 2800 \text{ m}^3$$
$$\text{Settled wastewater flow} = 13,900 \text{ m}^3/\text{d}$$
$$\text{Wastewater temperature} = 20°C$$
$$\text{Return sludge flow} = 4800 \text{ m}^3/\text{d}$$
$$\text{Waste sludge flow} = 72 \text{ m}^3/\text{d}$$
$$\text{MLSS in aeration tank} = 2350 \text{ mg/l}$$
$$\text{SS in waste sludge} = 14,000 \text{ mg/l}$$
$$\text{Influent wastewater BOD} = 128 \text{ mg/l}$$
$$\text{Effluent wastewater BOD} = 22 \text{ mg/l}$$
$$\text{Effluent SS} = 26 \text{ mg/l}$$

Using these data, calculate the BOD loading and F/M ratio, operational parameters of sludge age, aeration period and return sludge rate, and BOD removal efficiency. Calculate the excess sludge production in kilograms of excess suspended solids per kilogram of BOD applied.

49 A conventional activated-sludge system treats 11,000 m^3/d of wastewater with a BOD of 180 mg/l in an aeration tank with a volume of 3400 m^3. The operating conditions are an effluent suspended solids of 20 mg/l, an MLSS concentration maintained in the aeration tank of 2500 mg/l, and an activated-sludge wasting rate of 160 m^3/d containing 8000 mg/l. From these data, calculate the aeration period, volumetric BOD loading, F/M loading, and sludge age.

50 Determine the activated-sludge aeration volume required to treat 2.64 mgd with a BOD of 120 mg/l based on the criteria of a maximum BOD loading of 40 lb/1000 ft^3/day and a minimum aeration period of 5.0 hr. Assuming an operating F/M of 0.20 lb BOD/day per lb of MLSS, calculate the MLSS to be maintained in the aeration tank. Estimate the operating sludge age (mean cell residence time), assuming an effluent suspended solids of 30 mg/l. Determine the diameter and side-water depth of two identical final clarifiers for this activated-sludge system.

51 Determine the volume of three identical activated-sludge tanks following primary clarification to aerate 36,000 m^3/d with a BOD concentration of 180 mg/l at a BOD loading of 560 $\text{g/m}^3 \cdot \text{d}$. What is the aeration time? For an F/M of 0.35, what MLSS concentration should be maintained in the aeration tanks? Estimate the operating sludge age, assuming an effluent suspended solids of 30 mg/l. If the waste sludge has a concentration of 10,000 mg/l, what is the calculated volume of sludge to be wasted each day? Determine the dimensions of three identical rectangular clarifiers (length, width, and side-water depth) with a 2:1 length-to-width ratio.

52 A treatment plant has two oxidation-ditch activated-sludge systems, as illustrated in Figure 36. Each ditch has a liquid volume of 35,000 ft³ and is equipped with two horizontal-rotor aerators with capacity to transfer 1150 lb of oxygen per day at normal submergence. Each system has a clarifier with a diameter of 30 ft, a 9.0 ft side-water depth, and a single weir set on a diameter of 30 ft. The effluent chlorination tank has a volume of 2200 ft³. The design flow is 0.54 mgd: 0.35 domestic and commercial, 0.02 industrial, and 0.17 infiltration and inflow. The design BOD and suspended solids are both 740 lb/day. During heavy rains, the peak hydraulic loading anticipated is 800 gpm for 2–3 hr. Calculate (a) the BOD concentration at design flow and (b) at design flow, the aeration period, volumetric BOD loading, and F/M at 2500 mg/l. How do these compare with values listed in Table 3? (c) How many pounds of oxygen can be transferred to the mixed liquor per pound of BOD aeration tank loading? (d) Calculate the overflow rate and weir loading at the peak hydraulic loading. How do these values compare with recommended design values? (e) What is the detention in the chlorination tank at peak hydraulic flow? At twice the design flow? How do these values compare with the recommended detention time for chlorination of wastewater effluent?

53 The high-purity-oxygen process illustrated in Figure 39 is being considered for treatment of an unsettled domestic wastewater flow of 1.40 mgd with an average BOD of 200 mg/l. Compute the aeration volume required based on a maximum allowable BOD loading of 130 lb/1000 ft³/day and minimum aeration period of 1.8 hr. For this system, what is the F/M ratio in terms of lb of BOD/day/lb of MLVSS, assuming an MLSS of 5500 mg/l, that is 75% volatile?

54 Size an extended aeration system for the town of Nancy (Problem 31). Provide two identical activated-sludge aeration tanks with diffused aeration and final clarifiers. The treated wastewater is required to meet the effluent standards of 30 mg/l of BOD and 30 mg/l of suspended solids at a wastewater temperature of 15°C. The sludge is to be stabilized by aerobic digestion and dewatered on drying beds.

55 Refer to the instructions given in Problem 45. (a) Sketch a flow diagram showing the arrangement of unit processes and major pipelines for a treatment system of primary sedimentation followed by a step-aeration secondary and sludge stabilization by anaerobic digestion. (b) Sketch a flow diagram for a treatment system of extended aeration with aerobic sludge digestion. For both systems, list numerical design guidelines for sizing the unit processes, except preliminary treatment and sludge processing.

56 List the major assumptions made in the derivation of the mathematical model for biological kinetics of the activated-sludge process. What are the limitations in applying the kinetics equations given in Section 22?

57 A municipal wastewater containing both domestic and food-processing wastewaters was tested to determine the kinetic constants using a laboratory apparatus similar to the bench-scale unit shown in Figure 42. The volume of the aeration chamber was 10 l, and the wastewater feed was established at a constant rate of 30.0 l/d to provide an 8.0-hr aeration period for all of the test runs. A measured volume of sludge was wasted once a day from the tank. Determine Y, k_d, k, and K_s from the following laboratory data using the procedure in Example 14:

Q (l/d)	S_0 (mg/l)	Q_w (l/d)	X (mg/l)	S_e (mg/l)	X_e (mg/l)
30.0	150	0.31	2460	2.5	7.7
30.0	150	0.53	1690	3.3	6.5
30.0	150	0.98	1320	4.4	5.6
30.0	150	1.27	1080	5.9	5.0

58 Example 15 illustrates the application of the kinetics model in sizing the aeration volume required for a completely mixed activated-sludge process. What operating parameters must be assumed in the design procedure?

59 A completely mixed activated-sludge process is being designed for a wastewater flow of 3.0 mgd using the kinetics equations. The influent BOD of 180 mg/l is essentially all soluble and the design effluent soluble BOD is 10 mg/l. For sizing the aeration volume, the mean cell residence time is selected to be 8.0 days and the MLVSS 2500 mg/l. The kinetic constants from a bench-scale treatability study are as follows: $Y = 0.60$ lb VSS/lb BOD, $k_d = 0.06$ day^{-1}, $K_s = 60$ mg/l, and $k = 5.0$ day^{-1}.

60 The aeration tank for a completely mixed aeration process is being sized for a design wastewater flow of 7500 m^3/d. The influent BOD is 130 mg/l with a soluble BOD of 90 mg/l. The design effluent BOD is 20 mg/l with a soluble BOD of 7.0 mg/l. Recommended design parameters are a sludge age of 10 d and volatile MLSS of 1400 mg/l. Selection of these values takes into account the anticipated variations in wastewater flows and strengths. The kinetic constants from a bench-scale treatability study are $Y = 0.60$ mg VSS/mg soluble BOD and $k_d = 0.06$ per day. Calculate the volume of the aeration tank, aeration period, food/microorganism ratio, and excess biomass in the waste-activated sludge.

61 A step-aeration activated-sludge system at a loading of 40 lb of BOD/1000 ft^3/day requires an air supply of 1200 ft^3/lb of BOD applied to maintain an adequate dissolved-oxygen level. The measured average oxygen utilization of the mixed liquor is 36 mg/l/hr. Calculate the oxygen transfer efficiency. (Assume 0.0174 lb of oxygen per cubic foot of air, which is the amount at 20°C and 760 mm pressure.)

62 An air supply of 1000 ft^3 of air is required per pound of BOD applied to a diffused aeration basin to maintain a minimum DO of 2.0 mg/l. Assuming that the installed aeration equipment is capable of transferring 1.0 lb of oxygen to dissolved oxygen per pound of BOD applied, calculate the oxygen transfer efficiency of the system. (One cubic foot of air at standard temperature and pressure contains 0.0174 lb of oxygen.)

63 A 10-hp surface aerator was tested in a tank filled with 9200 ft^3 of tap water at 22°C by the non-steady-state procedure. The dissolved-oxygen saturation was assumed to be the standard value of 8.8 mg/l from Table 10 in the Appendix. Based on the following time and dissolved-oxygen data, determine the value of $K_L a$ corrected to 20°C. Also calculate the oxygen transfer rate in pounds per horsepower-hour.

t (min)	C_t (mg/l)	t (min)	C_t (mg/l)
0	0	8.0	5.5
2.0	3.0	11.0	6.3
4.0	4.3	14.0	7.1
6.0	5.0	17.0	7.6

64 A 40-hp surface aerator was tested in a 120-ft-diameter tank with a water depth of 8.0 ft. Cobalt chloride catalyst and sodium sulfite were added to the tap water in the tank to remove the dissolved oxygen. The water temperature was 21.9°C, and the dissolved-oxygen saturation was 8.7 mg/l. During the test, the average electric power usage was 33.1 kW, which at 90% efficiency is equivalent to 40.0 hp. From the following time and dissolved-oxygen data, determine the value of $K_L a$ corrected to 20°C, and calculate the oxygen transfer rate in pounds per horsepower-hour.

t (min)	C_t (mg/l)	t (min)	C_t (mg/l)
0	0	23	6.5
2	1.0	28	7.1
4	1.9	33	7.5
6	2.7	38	7.7
8	3.1	43	7.9
13	4.9	48	8.0
18	5.9	58	8.3

65 Calculate the surface area required for a stabilization pond to serve a domestic population of 1000. Assume 80 gpcd at 210 mg/l of BOD. Use a design loading of 20 lb of BOD/acre/day. If the average liquid depth is 4 ft, calculate the retention time of the wastewater based on influent flow. The effluent is spread on grassland by spray irrigation at a rate of 2.0 in./week (54,300 gal/acre/wk). Compute the land area required for land disposal. In these computations, assume no evaporation or seepage losses from the ponds.

66 Facultative stabilization ponds with a total surface area of 6.0 ha (1 ha = 10,000 m²) serve a community with a waste discharge of 530 m³/d at a BOD of 280 mg/l. Calculate the BOD loading and days of winter storage available between the 0.6- and 1.5-m depths, assuming a daily water loss of 0.30 cm by evaporation and seepage.

67 Stabilization pond computations are required for the town of Nancy (Problem 31). (a) Calculate the lagoon area required for a design loading of 40 lb of BOD/acre/day. (b) Determine the percentage of the average design flow that appears as effluent from the lagoons, assuming a water loss from the ponds of 60 in./yr (seepage plus evaporation minus precipitation). (c) Using the water-balance data from part (b), calculate the BOD removal efficiency if the average BOD concentrations in the influent and effluent are 250 mg/l and 25 mg/l, respectively. (d) How many acres of cropland are needed to dispose of the effluent by spray irrigation if the application rate is 2.0 in./week year-round?

68 Design a layout of stabilization ponds for the town of Nancy (Problem 31) based on the following criteria: (1) BOD loading in the primary cells cannot exceed 25 lb/acre/day, (2) minimum total water volume with the ponds full to a 5.0-ft depth in primary cells and 8.0-ft depth in secondary cells cannot be less than 120 days times the design flow, (3) volume for winter storage above water depths of 1.5 ft should be sufficient so that no discharge is necessary for a 4-month period when the net water loss (evaporation plus seepage minus precipitation) is 1.0 in./month, and (4) the system should have at least two primary cells and at least two secondary cells that cannot receive raw wastewater.

69 The wastewater flow from a small town is 240 m³/d with a BOD of 180 mg/l and SS of 210 mg/l. Size and sketch a layout for a stabilization pond arrangement consisting of two identical primary cells, which can be operated in parallel, and one secondary cell. The primary cells can have a maximum water depth of 1.5 m, and the secondary cell can have a maximum depth of 2.5 m. The minimum operating water depth in all cells is 0.5 m. Determine the dimensions of the ponds based on the following criteria: (1) The BOD loading on the primary cells cannot exceed 4.0 g/m^2·d. (2) The water storage capacity considering all three cells must be at least 120 d between the minimum and maximum water levels, with allowance for a water loss of 2.0 mm/d by evaporation and seepage.

70 A completely mixed aerated lagoon is being considered for pretreatment of a strong industrial wastewater with $k = 0.70$ at 20°C and $\Theta = 1.035$, using a detention time of 4 days. What is the BOD reduction at 20°C based on Eqs. (99) and (100)? If the wastewater temperature is 10°C, compute the detention time required to achieve the same degree of treatment.

71 A manufacturer's specified oxygen transfer capacity of a surface-aeration unit is 3.0 lb of oxygen/hp·hr. Using Eq. (102), calculate the oxygen transfer capability of this unit for an $\alpha = 0.9$, $\beta = 0.8$, a temperature of 20°C, and a dissolved-oxygen level of 2.0 mg/l in the lagoon water.

72 The rate of oxygen transfer for a surface aerator is specified by the manufacturer as 4.2 lb/hp·hr at standard conditions. Calculate the actual rate of transfer for a 40-hp aerator in a lagoon using a beta coefficient = 0.8, alpha, coefficient = 0.9, and residual oxygen concentration = 2.0 mg/l at wastewater temperatures of 25°C and 15°C. If the efficiency of the electric drive motor is 90%, what is the electric power usage for the 40-hp aerator?

73 An aerated lagoon with a 10-ft depth and liquid volume of 175,000 cu ft treated an average of 0.20 mgd of wastewater with a BOD of 550 mg/l (920 lb of BOD/day). The anticipated temperature extremes of the aerating wastewater range from 10°C in winter to 30°C in summer. The two 15-hp surface aerators recommended for adequate mixing and oxygenation have the manufacturer's guarantee to provide an oxygen transfer of 2.5 lb/hp·hr under standard conditions. Based on laboratory treatability studies, the wastewater has the following characteristics: $k_{20} = 0.68$ per day, $\Theta = 1.047$, $\alpha = 0.9$, $\beta = 0.8$, and an oxygen utilization rate of 1.0 lb of oxygen to satisfy 0.8 lb of BOD removal. Is the lagoon adequately sized? For a minimum BOD reduction of 75%, is the aeration capacity adequate?

74 A completely mixed aerated lagoon with a volume of 1.0 mil gal treats a daily wastewater flow of 250,000 gal with a BOD of 400 mg/l. The liquid temperature ranges from 4°C in the winter to 30°C in the summer. There are four 5.0-hp surface aerators rated at 2.0 lb of oxygen/hp·hr. The wastewater characteristics are $\Theta = 1.035$, $\alpha = 0.9$, $\beta = 0.9$, $k = 0.80$ per day at 20°C, and $a = 1.0$ lb of oxygen utilized/lb of BOD removed. The designer states that this system will remove at least 400 lb of BOD/day and maintain a dissolved-oxygen concentration greater than 2.0 mg/l. Verify or disprove these claims by appropriate calculations.

75 Design a layout for an aerated lagoon followed by two secondary facultative ponds to treat a combined food-processing and domestic wastewater. The design flow is 200,000 gpd containing 1100 lb of BOD. The water temperatures in the aerated lagoon are expected to range from 2°C in winter to 25°C in summer. Determine the size and shape of the aerated lagoon and the number and horsepower of the surface aerators based on the following parameters: $\alpha = 0.9$, $\beta = 0.8$, $k = 0.90$ per day at 20°C, $a = 1.0$ lb of oxygen required per lb of BOD removed, a minimum of 80% BOD removal, and an aerator oxygen transfer rate $R_0 = 2.33$ lb of oxygen/hp·hr. The BOD loading on the two facultative ponds receiving the aerated wastewater is limited to 20 lb BOD/acre/day, and the storage volume of the ponds between the minimum water depth of 1.5 ft and maximum of 5.0 ft must be equal to or greater than 4 months of wastewater discharge at design flow.

76 The superintendent of a conventional activated-sludge plant receives complaints from nearby residents and businesses about odors, particularly in the summer. After a comprehensive field investigation, the major sources were found to be emissions of predominantly hydrogen sulfide from the grit chamber and primary clarifiers. Apparently, in the summer, convection lifts the foul air over the bushes and trees in the buffer zone and in the summer people are more likely to be outside or have their windows open. Recommend alternative schemes for containing and cleansing the foul air before it is released to the atmosphere.

77 Recommend the minimum wastewater treatment processes to produce an effluent to meet the standards specified by the state of California for ocean discharge. What steps should be taken if toxicity limits are exceeded?

REFERENCES

[1] *Standard Methods for the Examination of Water and Wastewater* (Washington, DC: Am. Public Health Assoc., 1995).

[2] G. J. Tortora, B. R. Funke, and C. L. Case, *Microbiology* (Menlo Park, CA: Benjamin/Cummings, 1982).

[3] L. Michaelis and M. L. Menten, "Die Kinetik der Invertinwirkung," *Biochemische Zeitschrift*, Neunundvierzigster Band (Vol. 49) (Berlin: Springer-Verlag, 1913): 333–369.

[4] J. Monod, "The Growth of Bacterial Cultures," *Ann. Rev. Microbiol.* 3 (1949): 371–393.

[5] S. J. Pirt, *Principles of Microbe and Cell Cultivation* (New York: Halsted Press Book, Wiley, 1975).

[6] D. H. Stoltenberg, "Midwestern Wastewater Characteristics," *Public Works* 3, no. 1 (1980): 52–53.

[7] N. W. Classen, "Per Capital Wastewater Contributions," *Public Works* 98, no. 5 (1967): 81–83.

[8] D. G. Munksgaard and J. C. Young, "Flow and Load Variations at Wastewater Treatment Plants," *J. Water Poll. Control Fed.* 52, no. 8 (1980): 2131–2144.

[9] "Sewage Treatment at Military Installations," Report of the Subcommittee on Sewage Treatment in Military Installations, National Research Council, *Sewage Works J.* 18, no. 5 (1946): 787–1028.

[10] S. Balakrishnan, W. W. Eckenfelder, and C. Brown, "Organics Removal by a Selected Trickling Filter Media," *Water and Wastes Eng.* 6, no. 1 (1969): A.22–A.25.

[11] D. D. Drury, J. Carmona III, and A. Delgadillo, "Evaluation of High Density Cross Flow Media for Rehabilitating an Existing Trickling Filter," *J. Water Poll. Control Fed.* 58, no. 5 (1986): 364–367.

[12] M. L. Arora and M. B. Umphres, "Evaluation of Activated Biofiltration and Activated Biofiltration/Activated Sludge Technologies," *J. Water Poll. Control Fed.* 59, no. 4 (1987): 183–190.

[13] Proceedings, First National Symposium on Rotating Biological Contactor Technology (Pittsburgh: University of Pittsburgh, 1980).

[14] M. J. Hammer, *Wastewater Treatment in Dry Climates (Desert or Desert with Some Rain)* (Alexandria, VA: Water Environment Federation, 2001).

[15] "The Causes and Control of Activated Sludge Bulking and Foaming," U.S. Environmental Protection Agency, Center for Environmental Research Information, EPA 625/8-87-012 (Cincinnati, OH: July 1987).

[16] *Design Manual, Fine Pore Aeration Systems*, EPA/625/1-89/023, U.S. Environmental Protection Agency, Technology Transfer (September 1989).

[17] *Oxygen Activated-Sludge Wastewater Treatment Systems*, U.S. Environmental Protection Agency, Technology Transfer (August 1973).

[18] A. W. Lawrence and P. L. McCarty, "Unified Basis for Biological Treatment Design and Operation," *Proc. Am. Soc. Civil Engrs., J. San. Eng. Div.* 96 (SA3) (1970): 757–778.

[19] L. D. Benefield and C. W. Randall, *Biological Process Design for Wastewater Treatment* (Upper Saddle River, NJ: Prentice Hall, 1980).

[20] C. P. Grady, Jr., and H. C. Lim, *Biological Wastewater Treatment* (New York: Dekker, 1980).

[21] G. F. Bennett and L. L. Kempe, "Oxygen Transfer in Biological Systems," *Proc. 20th Industrial Waste Conf., Purdue Univ. Ext. Service* 49, no. 4 (1965): 435–447.

[22] *Recommended Standards for Wastewater Facilities, Great Lakes—Upper Mississippi River Board of State Public Health & Environmental Managers* (Albany, NY: Health Research, Inc., Health Education Services Div., 1990).

[23] American Society of Civil Engineers, *ASCE Standard: Measurement of Oxygen Transfer in Clean Water* (New York: Am. Soc. Civil Eng., 1984).

[24] "Development of Standard Procedures for Evaluating Oxygen Transfer Devices," U.S. Environmental Protection Agency, Municipal Environmental Research Laboratory, EPA 600/2-83-002 (Cincinnati, OH: 1983).

[25] E. J. Middlebrooks, "Design Equations for BOD Removal in Facultative Ponds," *Water Science Tech.* 19, no. 12 (1987): 187–193.

[26] "Odor and Corrosion Control in Sanitary Sewerage Systems and Treatment Plants," U.S. Environmental Protection Agency, Technology Transfer, Center for Environmental Research Information, EPA 625/1-85/018 (Cincinnati, OH: 1985).

[27] R. P. G. Bowker, "Cleaning the Air on an Overlooked Odor Control Technique," *Water Environment & Treatment, Water Environment Federation*, 11, no. 2 (1999): 30–35.

[28] *California Ocean Plan, Water Quality Control Plan, Ocean Waters of California*, State Water Resources Control Board (Sacramento, CA: California Environmental Protection Agency, 2001).

Processing of Sludges

SOURCES, CHARACTERISTICS, AND QUANTITIES OF WASTE SLUDGES

Mathematical relationships for estimating the specific gravity and computing the sludge volume appear first, as they are fundamental calculations applicable to all sludges. Then the characteristics and methods for estimating sludge quantities are presented separately for wastewater and water treatment plant residues.

1 WEIGHT AND VOLUME RELATIONSHIPS

The majority of sludge solids from biological wastewater processing are organic, with a 60%–80% volatile fraction. The concentration of suspended solids in a liquid sludge is determined by straining a measured sample through a glass-fiber filter. Nonfilterable residue, expressed in milligrams per liter, is the solids content. Since the filterable portion of a sludge is very small, sludge solids are often determined by total residue on evaporation (i.e., the total deposit remaining in a dish after evaporation of water from the sample and subsequent drying in an oven at 103°C). Volatile solids are determined by igniting the dried residue at 550°C in a muffle furnace. Loss of weight upon ignition is reported as milligrams per liter of volatile solids, and the inerts remaining after burning are reported as fixed solids. Waste from chemical coagulation of a surface water contains both organic matter removed from the raw water and mineral content derived from the chemical coagulants. Most solids are nonfilterable and have a volatile fraction of 20%–40%. Precipitate from treated well water is essentially mineral.

The specific gravity of solid matter in a sludge can be computed from the relationship

$$\frac{W_s}{S_s\gamma} = \frac{W_f}{S_f\gamma} + \frac{W_v}{S_v\gamma} \tag{1}$$

where

$$W_s = \text{weight of dry solids, lb}$$
$$S_s = \text{specific gravity of solids}$$
$$\gamma = \text{unit weight of water, lb/ft}^3 \text{ (lb/gal)}$$
$$W_f = \text{weight of fixed solids (nonvolatile), lb}$$
$$S_f = \text{specific gravity of fixed solids}$$
$$W_v = \text{weight of volatile solids, lb}$$
$$S_v = \text{specific gravity of volatile solids}$$

The specific gravity of organic matter is 1.2–1.4, while the solids in chemically coagulated water vary from 1.5 to 2.5. The value for a solids slurry is calculated from

$$S = \frac{W_w + W_s}{(W_w/1.00) + (W_s/S_s)} \tag{2}$$

where

$$S = \text{specific gravity of wet sludge}$$
$$W_w = \text{weight of water, lb}$$
$$W_s = \text{weight of dry solids, lb}$$
$$S_s = \text{specific gravity of dry solids}$$

Consider a waste biological sludge of 10% solids with a volatile fraction of 70%. The specific gravity of the solids can be estimated using Eq. (1) by assuming values of 2.5 for the fixed matter and 1.0 for the volatile residue.

$$\frac{1.00}{S_s} = \frac{0.30}{2.5} + \frac{0.70}{1.0} = 0.82$$

$$S_s = \frac{1}{0.82} = 1.22$$

Then the specific gravity of the wet sludge, by Eq. (2), is 1.02:

$$S = \frac{90 + 10}{(90/1.00) + (10/1.22)} = 1.02$$

These calculations demonstrate that for organic sludges of less than 10% solids the specific gravity may be assumed to be 1.00 without introducing significant error. Example 1 illustrates that even for mineral residue a high concentration of precipitate is required to increase the specific gravity of a slurry above 1.0.

The volume of waste sludge for a given amount of dry matter and concentration of solids is given by

$$V = \frac{W_s}{(s/100)\gamma S} = \frac{W_s}{[(100 - p)/100]\gamma S} \tag{3}$$

where

V = volume of sludge, ft^3 (gal)[m^3]

W_s = weight of dry solids, lb [kg]

s = solids content, %

γ = unit weight of water, 62.4 lb/ft^3 (8.34 lb/gal)[1000 kg/m^3]

S = specific gravity of wet sludge

p = water content, %

In this formula the volume of a sludge is indirectly proportional to the solids content. Thus, if a waste is thickened from 2% to 4% solids, the volume is reduced by one-half, and if consolidation is continued to a concentration of 8%, the quantity of wet sludge is only one-fourth of the original amount. During this concentration process, water content is reduced from 98% to 92%. In applying Eq. (3), specific gravity of the sludge S is normally taken as 1.0 and therefore not included in computations, as demonstrated in Example 2.

Example 1

Coagulation of a surface water using alum produces 10,000 lb (4540 kg) of dry solids/day, of which 20% are volatile. Both the settled sludge following coagulation and filter backwash water are concentrated in clarifier–thickeners to a solids density of 2.5%. Centrifugation can be used to increase the concentration to 20%, a consistency similar to soft wet clay, or the clarifier–thickener underflow can be dewatered to a 40% cake by pressure filtration. (a) Estimate the specific gravities of the thickened sludge, concentrate from centrifugation, and filter cake. (b) Calculate the daily sludge volumes from each process.

Solution:

a. Applying Eq. (1), one has

$$\frac{1.00}{S_s} = \frac{0.80}{2.50} + \frac{0.20}{1.00} = 0.52$$

$$S_s = \frac{1}{0.52} = 1.9$$

From Eq. (2),

$$S(\text{thickened sludge}) = \frac{97.5 + 2.5}{(97.5/1.0) + (2.5/1.9)} = 1.0$$

$$S(\text{centrifuge discharge}) = \frac{80 + 20}{(80/1.0) + (20/1.9)} = 1.1$$

$$S(\text{filter cake}) = \frac{60 + 40}{(60/1.0) + (40/1.9)} = 1.2$$

b. Substituting these values into Eq. (3) with $W_s = 10{,}000$ lb/day gives

$$V(\text{thickened sludge}) = \frac{10{,}000}{(2.5/100)8.34 \times 1.0} = 48{,}000 \text{ gpd}$$

$$= \frac{4540 \text{ kg}}{(2.5/100)1000 \text{ kg/m}^3 \times 1.0} = 182 \text{ m}^3/\text{d}$$

$$V(\text{centrifuge discharge}) = \frac{10{,}000}{(20/100)8.34 \times 1.1} = 5400 \text{ gpd } (20.6 \text{ m}^3/\text{d})$$

$$V(\text{filter cake}) = \frac{10{,}000}{(40/100)8.34 \times 1.2} = 2500 \text{ gpd } (9.5 \text{ m}^3/\text{d})$$

Example 2

Estimate the quantity of sludge produced by a trickling-filter plant treating 1.0 mgd of domestic wastewater. Assume a suspended-solids concentration of 220 mg/l in the raw wastewater, a solids content in the sludge equivalent to 90% removal, and a sludge of 5.0% concentration withdrawn from the settling tanks.

Solution:

$$\text{solids in the sludge} = 1.0 \times 220 \times 8.34 \times 0.90 = 1650 \text{ lb/day}$$

$$\text{volume of sludge } [\text{using Eq.(3)}] = \frac{1650}{0.05 \times 62.4} = 530 \text{ ft}^3/\text{day}$$

---

2   CHARACTERISTICS AND QUANTITIES OF WASTEWATER SLUDGES

The purpose of primary sedimentation and secondary aeration is to remove waste organics from solution and concentrate them in a much smaller volume to facilitate dewatering and disposal. The concentration of organic matter in wastewater is approximately 200 mg/l (0.02%), while that in a typical raw-waste sludge is about 40,000 mg/l (4%). Based on these approximate values, treatment of 1.0 mil gal of wastewater produces about 4000 gal of sludge. This raw, odorous, and putrescible residue must be further processed and reduced in volume for land disposal or incineration. Common methods include gravity or mechanical thickening, biological digestion, and mechanical dewatering after chemical conditioning.

The quantity and nature of sludge generated relates to the character of the raw wastewater and processing units employed. Daily sludge production may fluctuate over a wide range, depending on the size of the municipality, contribution of industrial wastes, and other factors. Both maximum and average daily sludge volumes are considered in designing facilities. A limited quantity of solids can be stored temporarily in clarifiers and aeration tanks to provide short-term equalization of peak loads. Mechanical thickening and dewatering units may be sized to handle sludge quantities as high as double the daily average. Other processes, such as conventional anaerobic digestion, have substantial equalizing capacity and are designed on the basis of maximum average monthly loading. Often, selection of conservative design parameters and liberal estimates of sludge yield take into account anticipated quantity variations. In this manner, designers disguise the fact that the maximum sludge yield is being considered in sizing unit processes. For example, in designing a trickling-filter plant, the dry solids may be calculated assuming 0.24 lb/capita/day when the actual amount realized in the treatment process is closer to 0.15 lb/capita/day. Furthermore, the required digester volume may be computed using a conservative figure of 5 ft^3/population equivalent.

Primary sludge is a gray-colored, greasy, odorous slurry of settleable solids, accounting for 50%–60% of the suspended solids applied, and tank skimmings. Scum is usually less than 1% of the settled sludge volume. Primary precipitates can be dewatered readily after chemical conditioning because of their fibrous and coarse nature. Typical solids concentrations in raw primary sludge from settling municipal wastewater are 4%–6%. Overpumping during sludge withdrawal can result in a thinner sludge by drawing in wastewater from above the settled solids, and biological activity in warm wastewater can result in gas production, decreasing solids concentration in the settled sludge. The portion of volatile solids varies from 60% to 80%.

Trickling-filter humus from secondary clarification is dark brown in color, flocculent, and relatively inoffensive when fresh. The suspended particles are biological growths washed from the filter media. Although they exhibit good settleability, the precipitate does not compact to a high density. For this reason and because sloughing is irregular, underflow from the final clarifier containing filter humus is returned to the wet well for mixing with the inflowing raw wastewater. Thus humus is settled with raw organics in the primary clarifier. The combined sludge has a solids content of 4%–5%, which is slightly thinner than primary residue with raw organics only.

Waste-activated sludge is a dark-brown, flocculent suspension of active microbial masses that is inoffensive when fresh, but it turns septic rapidly because of biological activity. Mixed-liquor solids settle slowly, forming a rather bulky sludge of high water content. The thickness of return activated sludge is 0.5%–1.5% suspended solids, depending on the rate of recirculation pumping, with a volatile fraction of 0.7–0.8. Excess activated sludge in most processes is wasted from the return sludge line. A high water content, resistance to gravity thickening, and the presence of active microbial floc make this residue difficult to handle. Routing of waste-activated sludge to the wet well for settling with raw wastewater is not recommended. Carbon dioxide, hydrogen sulfide, and odorous organic compounds are liberated from the settlings in the primary basin as a result of anaerobic decomposition, and the solids concentration is rarely greater than 4%. Waste-activated sludge can be thickened effectively by gravity belt thickening and dissolved-air flotation with chemical addition to ensure high solids capture in the concentration process.

Anaerobically digested sludge is a thick slurry of dark-colored particles and entrained gases, principally carbon dioxide and methane. When well digested, it dewaters rapidly on sand-drying beds, releasing an inoffensive odor resembling that of garden loam. Substantial additions of chemicals are needed to coagulate a digested sludge prior to mechanical dewatering, owing to the finely divided nature of the solids. The dry residue is 30%–60% volatile, and the solids content of digested liquid sludge ranges from 3% to 12%, depending on the mode of digester operation.

Aerobically digested sludge is a dark-brown, flocculent, relatively inert waste produced by long-term aeration of sludge. The suspension is bulky and difficult to gravity-thicken, thus creating problems of ultimate disposal. Since decanting clear supernatant can be difficult, the primary functions of an aerobic digester are stabilization of organics and temporary storage of waste sludge. The solids concentration in thickened, aerobically digested sludge is generally in the range 1.0%–2.0% as determined by digester design and operation. The thickness of aerobically digested sludge can be less than that of the influent, since approximately 50% of the volatile solids are converted to gaseous end products. Stabilized sludge is often disposed of by spreading on land for its fertilizer value, particularly at small treatment plants. For these reasons, aerobic digestion is limited to treatment of waste-activated sludge from aeration plants without primary clarifiers.

Mechanically dewatered sludges vary in characteristics based on the type of sludge, chemical conditioning, and unit process employed. The density of dewatered cakes ranges from 15% to 40%. The thinner cake is similar to a wet mud, while the latter is a chunky solid. The method of ultimate disposal and economics dictate the degree of moisture reduction necessary.

Biosolids refer to liquid and dewatered sludges that have been suitably processed for land application as agricultural fertilizer and soil conditioner. To control the concentration of heavy metals and other toxins in the sludge, industrial wastewaters are pretreated prior to discharge to the sewer collection system. The common sludge treatment is anaerobic or aerobic digestion to reduce pathogenic microorganisms and to stabilize the organic matter. Quality standards for application of biosolids are established by EPA regulations [1].

Waste solids production in primary and secondary processing can be estimated using the following formulas:

$$W_s = W_{s_p} + W_{s_s} \tag{4}$$

where

W_s = total dry solids, lb/day

W_{s_p} = raw primary solids, lb/day

W_{s_s} = secondary biological solids, lb/day

$$W_{s_p} = f \times \text{SS} \times Q \times 8.34 \tag{5}$$

where

W_{s_p} = primary solids, lb of dry weight/day

f = fraction of suspended solids removed in primary settling

SS = suspended solids in unsettled wastewater, mg/l

Q = daily wastewater flow, mgd

8.34 = conversion factor, lb/mil gal per mg/l

$$W_{s_s} = k \times \text{BOD} \times Q \times 8.34 \tag{6}$$

where

$$W_{s_s} = \text{biological sludge solids, lb of dry weight/day}$$

k = fraction of applied BOD that appears as excess biological growth in waste-activated sludge or filter humus, assuming about 30 mg/l of BOD and suspended solids remaining in the secondary effluent

BOD = concentration in applied wastewater, mg/l

Q = daily wastewater flow, mgd

The first expression states that the total weight of dry solids produced equals the sum of the primary plus secondary residues. Settleable matter removed in primary clarification can be considered a function of the suspended-solids concentration [Eq. (5)]. For typical municipal wastewaters, the value for f is between 0.4 and 0.6. The settleable fraction of suspended solids in a fresh domestic wastewater is about 0.5, but septic conditions and industrial waste contributions are likely to decrease the portion of settlings in a wastewater. For example, many food-processing discharges are high in colloidal matter and exhibit BOD/suspended-solids ratios of 2:1 or greater. Thus, a combined wastewater may exhibit an f value that is considerably less than the average 0.5 for domestic waste.

Organic matter entering secondary biological treatment is colloidal in nature and best represented by its BOD value. Most is synthesized into flocculent biological growths that entrain nonbiodegradable material. Therefore, excess activated-sludge solids from aeration and humus from biological filtration can be estimated by Eq. (6), which relates residue production to BOD load. The coefficient k is a function of process food/microorganism ratio and biodegradable (volatile) fraction of the matter in suspension. For trickling-filter humus, k is assumed to be in the range 0.3–0.5, with the lower value for light BOD loadings and the larger number applicable to high-rate filters and rotating biological contactors. The k for secondary activated-sludge processes can be estimated using Figure 1 by entering the diagram along the ordinate with a known food/microorganism ratio.

Excess solids production for activated-sludge processes treating unsettled wastewater can be estimated using Eq. (7) (based on influent BOD), without considering suspended solids input, by increasing the calculated quantity by 100%. Thus, for aeration systems without primary clarifiers, the k factor is the value determined from Figure 1 multiplied by 2.0.

$$W_{as} = 2.0k \times \text{BOD} \times Q \times 8.34 \qquad (7)$$

where

W_{as} = total dry solids from activated-sludge processing without primary sedimentation, lb/day of dry weight

The design of a sludge-handling system is based on the volume of wet sludge as well as dry solids content. Once the dry weight of residue has been estimated, the volume of sludge is calculated by applying Eq. (3).

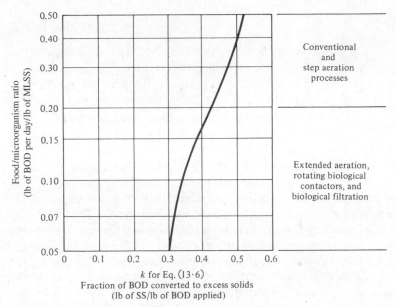

FIGURE 1   Hypothetical relationship between the food-to-microorganism ratio
and the coefficient *k* in Eqs. (6) and (7).

The foregoing formulations are reasonable for sludge quantities from processing domestic wastewater at average daily design flow. Real sludge yields may differ
considerably from anticipated values when a municipal discharge contains substantial
contributions of industrial wastes and when loading or operational conditions create
unanticipated peak sludge volumes.

Peak loads must be assessed for each treatment plant design based on local
conditions such as seasonal industrial discharges, anticipated trends in per capita solids
contribution, and the type of unit operations employed in wastewater processing. A
rule-of-thumb approach assumes that the maximum weekly dry solids yield will be
approximately 25% greater than the yearly mean. Variations in daily sludge volumes
may be considerably greater, owing to changes in moisture content. For example, if the
concentration of settlings drawn from primary clarifiers shifts from 6% to 4%, the total
quantity of wet sludge increases 50% for the same amount of dry solids. These deviations
are normally taken into account by selecting conservative design criteria in sizing
biological digesters. Where mechanical dewatering is practiced, increased quantities of
sludge can be handled by applying higher chemical dosages and by extending the time
of operation each day. Perhaps the most difficult parameter to predict is the solids
concentration of waste-activated sludge. Bulking can easily reduce the solids content
by one-half, say, from 15,000 mg/l to 7500 mg/l, thus doubling the volume. Processing of
this larger quantity must be evaluated by the designer. One guideline is to size mechanical
thickeners at 200% of the estimated volume during normal operation in order to
ensure consolidation of the diluted slurry. Provisions are required for the addition of
coagulants to aid in concentrating waste-activated sludge.

Example 3

One million gallons of municipal wastewater with a BOD of 260 mg/l and suspended solids of 220 mg/l are processed in a primary plus secondary activated-sludge plant. Estimate the quantities and solids contents of the primary, waste-activated, and mixed sludges. Assume the following: 60% SS removal and 40% BOD reduction in clarification, a water content of 94.0% in the raw sludge, and an operating F/M ratio of 1:3 in the aeration basin; the solids concentration of 15,000 mg/l in the waste-activated sludge is increased to 45,000 mg/l by gravity belt thickening. If the sludges are blended, calculate the consolidated sludge volume.

Solution: The primary sludge solids and volume based on Eqs. (5) and (3) are, respectively,

$$W_{s_p} = 0.60 \times 220 \times 1.0 \times 8.34 = 1100 \text{ lb}$$

$$V = 1100/[(100 - 94)/100]8.34 = 2200 \text{ gal}$$

To determine k for Eq. (6), enter Figure 1 with F/M = 0.33, and read 0.48 lb of SS produced/lb of BOD applied.

The thickened waste-activated sludge, based on Eq. (6), is

$$W_{s_s} = 0.48 \times 260 \times 0.60 \times 1.0 \times 8.34 = 620 \text{ lb}$$

$$V = \frac{620}{0.045 \times 8.34} = 1650 \text{ gal}$$

The blended sludge volume, solids content, and solids concentration are, respectively,

$$V = 2200 + 1650 = 3850 \text{ gal}$$

$$W_s = 1100 + 620 = 1720 \text{ lb}$$

$$s = \frac{1720 \times 100}{3850 \times 8.34} = 5.4\%$$

Example 4

The rational formulas for waste solids production [Eqs. (4)–(6)] can be used to predict future sludge yields, provided the characteristics of the wastewater are not expected to change significantly.

Listed in columns 1–5 of Table 1 are average monthly operating data for a conventional activated-sludge plant treating a municipal wastewater containing discharges from several industries. The average suspended solids removal in primary sedimentation is 50% ($f = 0.33$) and the BOD removal is 22%, leaving an average of 490 mg/l in the settled wastewater. The current solids concentration in the combined waste sludge varies from 4.0% to 4.5%. The sludge is dewatered by belt filter presses 5 days per week using a sludge holding tank for storing weekend production.

Develop equations to calculate the average annual weekday sludge solids production and the average weekday solids production during the maximum month. Calculate these values and sludge volumes at 4.0% solids concentration for a future raw wastewater flow of 3.0 mgd with 600 mg/l suspended solids and 580 mg/l BOD.

TABLE 1   Operating Data and Calculated Values of Solids Production for Example 4

		Measured Values			Calculated Values	
Month	Flow (mgd)	Suspended Solids in Unsettled Wastewater (mg/l)	BOD in Settled Wastewater (mg/l)	Sludge Solids Produced from Wastewater (mg/l)	Sludge Solids Production from Eq. (8) (mg/l)	Percentage Difference of Columns 5 and 6 (%)
Feb.	2.3	480	480	340	410	−17
Mar.	2.5	620	460	530	480	10
Apr.	2.5	640	500	660	500	32
May	2.3	780	600	460	610	−24
June	2.5	740	400	580	520	11
July	2.4	870	550	450	640	−30
Aug.	2.4	600	430	450	460	−2
Sept.	2.5	460	480	520	400	30
Mean	2.4	650	490	500	500	

Solution: The average solids production expressed in milligrams per liter of wastewater processed is

$$W_s = W_{s_p} + W_{s_s} = f \times SS + k \times BOD$$

We substitute the mean measured values from Table 1 and solve for k:

$$500 \text{ mg/l} = 0.53 \times 650 + k \times 490$$

$$k = 0.32$$

The equation for average annual weekday sludge solids production in milligrams per liter of wastewater processed is then

$$W_s = 0.53 \times SS + 0.32 \times BOD \tag{8}$$

Using this equation, the sludge solids production is calculated for each month and listed in column 6 of Table 1. The percentage difference between the measured and calculated solids production values is computed and listed in column 7 by subtracting the numbers in column 6 from those in column 5, dividing the resultants by the numbers in column 6, and multiplying by 100 to yield percentages.

Based on Eq. (8), the equation for average annual weekday sludge solids production in pounds based on a 5-day work week is

$$W_{s_d} = (7/5)(Q)(8.34)(0.53 \times SS + 0.32 \times BOD)$$

The results in column 7 of Table 1 show that the average weekday solids production during the maximum month is 30% greater than the average; therefore,

$$W_{s_m} = 1.3 W_{s_d}$$

For a future raw-wastewater flow of 3.0 mgd with 600 mg/l suspended solids and 580 mg/l of BOD (settled BOD of 0.78 × 580 = 450 mg/l), the average annual values are

$$W_{s_d} = (7/5)(3.0)(8.34)(0.53 \times 600 + 0.32 \times 450) = 16,000 \text{ lb}$$

$$V_{s_d} = \frac{16,000}{0.04 \times 8.34} = 48,000 \text{ gal}$$

The average weekday values during the maximum month are $W_{s_m} = 20,000$ lb and $V_{s_m} = 61,000$ gal.

---

3   CHARACTERISTICS AND QUANTITIES OF WATER-PROCESSING SLUDGES

The characteristics and quantities of water treatment plant residuals vary greatly depending on the water source and kinds of treatment processes; the most common plants are coagulation–filtration systems to remove turbidity and pathogens and precipitation softening to reduce hardness [2]. Water treatment residuals are derived from sedimentation and filtration of chemically conditioned water. Surface supplies yield wastes containing colloidal matter removed from the raw water and chemical flocs, while groundwater-processing precipitates are mineral with little or no organic material. Sludges vary widely in composition, depending on character of the water source and chemicals added during treatment. A typical method of handling a turbid river supply includes presedimentation for reduction of settleable solids, lime softening for hard water, alum coagulation, and filtration for removal of colloids, plus the addition of activated carbon for taste and odor control, and chlorination for disinfection. The presedimentation deposit is silt plus detritus; settling-basin sludge is a mixture of inerts, organics, and chemical precipitates, including metal hydroxides; and filter backwash water contains floc from agglomerated colloids and unspent coagulant hydroxides. Lake and reservoir waters are often dosed with alum and flocculation aids, plus activated carbon. Settlings during the summer may include significant quantities of algae. Precipitates from lime–soda ash softening are predominantly calcium carbonate and magnesium hydroxide with traces of other minerals, such as oxides of iron and manganese.

Sludge storage capacity and the time intervals between withdrawals are governed by the installation design, the type of water processing, and operations management. Clarifiers equipped with mechanical scrapers discharge sludge either continuously at a low rate or intermittently, often daily. Settled sludge is allowed to accumulate and consolidate in plain rectangular or hopper-bottomed basins. These tanks are cleaned at time intervals varying from a few weeks to several months by draining and removing the compacted sludge. Backwashing of filters produces a high flow of dilute waste-water for a few minutes, usually once a day for each filter. Obviously, any system for handling water treatment wastes must consider temporary storage and thickening of wash water.

Alum coagulation sludge is dramatically influenced by the gelatinous nature of the aluminum hydroxides formed in the reaction with raw-water alkalinity. Particles entrained in the floc and other coagulation precipitates do not suppress the jellylike consistency that makes an alum slurry difficult to dewater. Coagulation settlings and backwash water normally can be gravity thickened to a liquid with 2%–3% solids, although polymers may be needed to achieve this consolidation. Studies have shown that centrifugal dewatering can concentrate this waste to a truckable semisolid with 10%–15% solids with a consistency similar to a soft wet clay. Pressure filtration will produce a 30%–40% cake with the consistency of stiff clay that breaks easily. Complete dehydration by drying or freezing results in a granular material that does not revert to its original gelatinous form if again mixed with water. Enmeshed water of hydration, not water of suspension, causes the original jelly consistency. Iron coagulants yield slightly denser sludges that are somewhat easier to handle.

Surface water wastes are highly variable, owing to changes in raw-water quality. High turbidities during spring runoff and periods of high rainfall result in a decreased percentage of aluminum hydroxide solids. The result is a precipitate that settles better and is easier to dewater. Water temperature changes affect algal growth in surface supplies, the rate of chemical reactions in treatment, and filterability of the sludge. In designing a waste-handling system, changes in raw-water quality and accompanying variations in sludge characteristics must be investigated by long-term studies of daily and seasonal records.

Sludge production from surface water treatment can be estimated from chemical additions and raw-water characteristics. Based on empirical data, 1 mg of commercial alum applied as a coagulant produces 0.44 mg of aluminum precipitate, which is nearly double the 0.26 theoretical amount. The observed relationship between turbidity of the raw water, expressed in nephelometric turbidity units (NTU), and weight of impurities removed varies from 0.5 to 2.0 mg/NTU, with an average value of 0.74. The following equation for estimating dry sludge solids production from alum coagulation is based on these data:

Total sludge solids (lb/mil gal)
$$= 8.34(0.44 \times \text{alum dosage} + 0.74 \times \text{turbidity}) \qquad (9)$$

The majority of sludge solids settle by gravity in the sedimentation basins; the remainder are removed by subsequent filtration. The nonsettleable portion depends on the kinds of impurities in the water and chemicals applied in coagulation. The sludge withdrawn from sedimentation basins is 1%–2%, and the solids content of filter wash water is less than 0.05%. Gravity thickening of settled sludge and backwash water from alum coagulation can be thickened in a clarifier–thickener to 2%–6%.

Coagulation–softening sludges result from processing hard, turbid surface waters, such as those found in Midwestern rivers. A typical treatment plant flow arrangement is presedimentation followed by two-stage or split treatment; lime softening and coagulation with alum or iron salts; and filtration. Solids concentration in settled sludges varies with turbidity in the raw water, ratio of calcium to magnesium in the softening precipitate, type and dosage of metal coagulant, and filter aids used. In general, filter wash water gravity thickens to about 4%, alum–lime sludges have densities of up to 10%, and lime–iron precipitates range between 10% and 20%, with a consistency of a viscous liquid. The quantity of sludge produced is difficult to predict because the chemical treatment varies with hardness and turbidity of the river water. In-plant modifications to help even out fluctuations in sludge yield may include applying polymers in coagulation, closer pH control to reduce the amount of magnesium hydroxide produced in softening, and providing flexibility to thicken sludges separately or combined.

Lime–soda ash softening sludges produced in treating groundwaters contain calcium carbonate and to a lesser extent magnesium hydroxide. Aluminum hydroxides and other coagulant aids may be present if added in water processing. The quantity of $Mg(OH)_2$ depends on magnesium hardness in the raw water and the softening process employed. In general, dry solids are 85%–95% $CaCO_3$. The residue is stable, dense, inert, and relatively pure, since groundwater does not contain colloidal inorganic or organic matter. Calcium carbonate compacts readily, while magnesium hydroxide, like aluminum hydroxide, is gelatinous and does not consolidate as well nor dewater as easily. Slurry wasted from flocculator–clarifiers (upflow units) has a solids content in the range of 2%–5%. Stoichiometrically, from Eq. (10), 3.6 lb of calcium carbonate is precipitated for each pound of lime applied. However, in actual practice, the dry solids yield from softening is closer to 2.6 lb/lb of lime applied, owing to incomplete chemical reaction, impurities in commercial-grade lime, and precipitation of variable amounts of magnesium.

$$CaO + Ca(HCO_3)_2 = 2\,CaCO_3 + H_2O \tag{10}$$

Iron and manganese oxides removed from groundwater by aeration and chemical oxidation are flocculent particles with poor settleability. The amount of sludge produced in the removal of these metals without simultaneous precipitation softening is relatively small. The majority of hydrated ferric and manganic oxides pass through sedimentation tanks, are trapped in the filters, and appear in the dilute backwash water.

Filter wash water is a relatively large volume of wastewater with a low solids concentration of 100–400 mg/l. The exact amount of water used in backwashing is a function of the type of filter system, cleansing technique, and quality and source of the raw water being treated. Generally, 2%–3% of the water processed in a plant is used for filter washing. The fraction of total waste solids removed by filtration depends on efficiency of the coagulation and sedimentation stages, type of treatment system, and characteristics of the raw water. The amount may be a substantial portion, say, 30% of the dry solids resulting from treatment.

Example 5

A reservoir water supply with a turbidity of 10 units in the summer is treated by applying an alum dosage of 30 mg/l. For each million gallons of water processed, estimate the total solids production, volume of settled sludge, and quantity of filter wash water. Assume a settled sludge concentration of 1.5% solids, a filter solids loading of 26 lb/mil gal, and a backwash water with 400 mg/l of suspended solids; also assume that Eq. (9) is applicable. Compute the composite sludge volume after the two wastes are gravity thickened to 3.0% solids.

Solution: By Eq. (9),

$$\text{Total sludge solids} = 8.34(0.44 \times 30 + 0.74 \times 10) = 172\ \text{lb/mil gal}$$

$$\begin{aligned} \text{Sedimentation basin solids} &= \text{total sludge solids} - \text{solids to filters} \\ &= 172 - 26 = 146\ \text{lb/mil gal} \end{aligned}$$

Applying Eq. (3) yields

$$V \text{ of settled sludge} = \frac{146}{0.015 \times 8.34} = 1170 \text{ gal}$$

$$V \text{ of wash water} = \frac{26}{(400/1,000,000)8.34} = 7800 \text{ gal}$$

$$V \text{ of thickened sludge} = \frac{172}{0.030 \times 8.34} = 690 \text{ gal}$$

Example 6

The lime–soda ash softening process requires a lime dosage of 2.7 meq/l CaO and a soda ash addition of 1.2 meq/l of Na_2CO_3. Based on the appropriate chemical reactions, calculate the calcium carbonate residue produced in the softening of 10^6 m³ of water, assuming the practical limit of $CaCO_3$ precipitation is 0.60 meq/1 (30 mg/l).

Solution: The 0.4 meq/l of CO_2 is precipitated by addition of 0.4 meq/l of lime to form 0.4 meq/l of $CaCO_3$:

$$Ca(OH)_2 + CO_2 = CaCO_3\downarrow + H_2O$$

The 2.3 meq/l of $Ca(HCO_3)_2$ reacts with 2.3 meq/l of lime to form 4.6 meq/l of $CaCO_3$:

$$Ca(HCO_3)_2 + Ca(OH)_2 = 2CaCO_3\downarrow + 2H_2O$$

Finally, 1.2 meq/l of soda ash precipitates 1.2 meq/l of $CaCO_3$,

$$CaSO_4 + Na_2CO_3 = CaCO_3\downarrow + Na_2SO_4$$

The residue is theoretically equal to the stoichiometric quantities of $CaCO_3$ formed minus the practical limit of treatment (solubility):

$$0.4 + 4.6 + 1.2 - 0.6 = 5.6 \text{ meq/l}$$
$$5.6 \times 50 = 280 \text{ mg/l of } CaCO_3$$

and
$$280 \text{ g/m}^3 \times 10^6 \text{ m}^3 \times 10^{-3} \text{ kg/g} = 280,000 \text{ kg/10}^6 \text{ m}^3$$

ARRANGEMENT OF UNIT PROCESSES IN SLUDGE DISPOSAL

Many processes for sludge handling are applied to both wastewater sludges and water treatment plant residues. Individual unit operations are discussed in the latter sections of this chapter, with comments relative to their method of operation and application. Under this heading, selection and arrangement of units are outlined to illustrate how they integrate with each other. Referring to these discussions while studying the individual operations will help relate them to complete sludge-disposal schemes.

4   SELECTION OF PROCESSES FOR WASTEWATER SLUDGES

Techniques selected for processing waste sludges are a function of the type, size, and location of the wastewater plant, the unit operations employed in treatment, and the method of ultimate solids disposal [3]. The system adopted must be able to accept the primary and secondary sludges produced and economically convert them to a residue that is environmentally acceptable for disposal.

Methods for storage, treatment, and disposition are listed in Table 2. Settled raw solids may be stored in the bottom of primary clarifiers during the day, or perhaps over a weekend, and then pumped directly to a processing unit. In small plants, sludge is transferred to anaerobic digesters either once or twice a day. Belt filter presses and centrifuges require a steady flow of sludge during the operating period, which may extend from 4 to 24 hr/day. Separate holding tanks can be used to receive and blend primary and secondary sludges. Primary sludge may be pumped intermittently using an automatic time-clock control, while secondary sludge wasting may be either continuous

---

TABLE 2   Processes for Storage, Treatment, and Disposal of
Wastewater Sludges

Storage prior to processing
   In the primary clarifiers
   Separate holding tanks
   Sludge lagoons
Thickening prior to dewatering or digestion
   Gravity settling in tanks
   Gravity belt thickening
   Dissolved-air flotation
   Centrifugation
Conditioning prior to dewatering
   Stabilization by anaerobic digestion
   Stabilization by aerobic digestion
   Chemical coagulation
   Heat treatment or wet oxidation
Mechanical dewatering
   Belt filter pressure filtration
   Plate-and-frame pressure filtration
   Centrifugation
Composting
Air drying of digested sludge
   Sand drying beds
   Shallow lagoons
Disposal of liquid or dewatered digested sludge
   Spreading as biosolids on agricultural land
   Application on dedicated surface disposal site
Disposal of dewatered raw or digested solids
   Codisposal in municipal solid-waste landfill
   Burial in dedicated sludge landfill
   Incineration
   Production of bagged fertilizer and soil conditioner

---

or periodic. Aerated holding tanks for accumulating and biologically stabilizing waste from aeration plants are called *aerobic digesters*.

The economics of chemical conditioning and biological treatment are directly related to the sludge density. As a general rule, the solids content of settled waste must be at least 4% for feasible handling. Primary precipitates and mixtures of primary and secondary settlings are amenable to thickening by sedimentation; therefore, gravity tank thickeners are used to increase the concentration of sludges withdrawn from either clarifiers or holding tanks. Because of the flocculent nature of waste-activated sludge, separate thickening is performed by either dissolved-air flotation or gravity belt thickening. The float or thickened sludge is then blended with primary waste and directed to holding tanks or the next dewatering or treatment step.

The purpose of anaerobic digestion is to convert bulky, odorous, and putrescible raw sludge to a well-digested material that can be rapidly dewatered without emission of noxious odors. In addition to stabilizing and gasifying the organic matter, the process significantly reduces the volume of residue by withdrawal of supernatant from digesters to thicken the sludge. Aerobic digestion is almost exclusively used to treat excess sludge from plants without primary clarifiers. Although it stabilizes the organic matter, solids thickening and dewatering are troublesome, owing to the bulky nature of overaerated sludge. Chemical coagulation with polymers or other coagulants is required for mechanical dewatering of both raw and digested wastes.

Heat treatment and wet oxidation are less commonly applied than other methods of sludge conditioning prior to dewatering because of higher costs of operation and maintenance. This conditioning sterilizes, deodorizes, and prepares the waste for mechanical dewatering without addition of chemicals. Processes using heat treatment apply steam to heat the reactor vessel to about 300°F under a pressure of 150 psi or greater. Sludge from the reactor is discharged to a decant tank, from which the underflow is withdrawn for dewatering. The supernatant contains high concentrations of water-soluble organic compounds and must therefore be returned to the treatment plant for processing. This is a serious drawback in handling some sludges, since it can result in cycling of solids through the heating process back to the treatment plant, which extracts them and returns them again to the heat treatment. Wet oxidation can be achieved under high pressure at elevated temperatures. Liquid sludge with compressed air is fed into a pressure vessel, where the organic matter is stabilized. Inert solids are separated from the effluent by dewatering in lagoons or by mechanical means.

Belt filter presses in small and medium-sized plants and centrifuges in large plants are the most common methods of dewatering chemically conditioned sludges. Belt presses are effective in dewatering a wide range of waste concentrations from raw primary to thin aerobically digested sludges. In operating performance, the main advantages are low energy consumption, high cake density, and clarity of filtrate. Centrifuges dewater digested sludges to a high cake density. Economy in centrifugation results from high-capacity machines that require much less space than an equivalent capacity of belt filter presses. Polymers are applied to sludges for chemical conditioning prior to dewatering by both belt filter presses and solid-bowl decanter centrifuges. Plate-and-frame filter presses are rarely used to dewater wastewater sludges because of the high installation cost. Their operation is a batch process with a cycle of filling with sludge, pressure dewatering, discharging of cake, and washing of filter cloths. The sludge is chemically conditioned with lime and ferric chloride, which are chemicals that are more difficult to store and feed than polymers are. For very small treatment plants, any kind of mechanical dewatering may not be economical because of the minimum available sizes of dewatering units. The smallest belt filter press can dewater the sludge production from a population of 5000. The minimum size of centrifuges restricts their application to even larger treatment plants serving a population greater than 100,000.

The oldest technique for drying digested sludge is on open sand beds contained by short concrete walls. Well-digested slurry is drained or pumped onto the surface of the bed to a depth of 8–12 in. Moisture leaves by evaporation and seepage; the latter is collected in underdrain piping for return to the plant influent. In current design, the beds have vertical draw-off pipes to decant supernatant after the solids settle and paved surfaces that gently slope to a narrow strip of sand bed with an underdrain located along the center line of the bed. This construction allows cleaning with a small front-end loader, since manual cleaning with hand shovels is no longer economical. Shallow lagoons can also be used for air drying of digested sludge. This permits the use of front-end loaders or buckets on draglines, but operations can be disrupted by inclement weather.

Liquid and dewatered digested sludges (biosolids) are commonly spread on and tilled into agricultural land as a fertilizer and soil conditioner. Farmland application is often originated by the operator of a small plant to avoid codisposal in a municipal solid-waste landfill. Currently, many large plants digest and dewater sludges for application on agricultural land, with a sludge management firm acting as the intermediary to sell and haul the biosolids to applicators and to ensure that the quality meets EPA requirements. Where agricultural land is not available, the sludge can be applied on a dedicated surface disposal site.

Dewatered solids, both raw and digested, can be disposed of in municipal solid-waste or dedicated-sludge landfills. Dried anaerobic cake and incinerator ash are relatively inoffensive, but cake composed of raw solids putrefies and may contain pathogens. The latter type must be covered every day to prevent nuisance odors and to control health hazards. Incineration is much more costly than land disposal, yet in highly urbanized areas it is often the only feasible alternative. Rather than burning, digested sludge may be dried and bagged as soil conditioner.

The following process flow diagrams graphically illustrate the selection and arrangement of common sludge-processing layouts. Figure 2 is typical for communities with a population of less than 10,000. Raw solids and filter humus are settled and stored in the primary clarifiers. Once or twice a day, sludge and scum are pumped to anaerobic digesters, and supernatant is withdrawn and returned to the treatment plant influent. Stabilized and thickened sludge accumulates in the digesters for withdrawal when weather conditions permit disposal. These biosolids can be applied as liquid digested sludge on agricultural land or dried on sand beds or in lagoons and then hauled to a landfill for burial.

The optimum sludge-process scheme for an activated-sludge plant, shown in Figure 3a, thickens the waste-activated sludge separately prior to blending with the primary sludge. (Activated-sludge plants that return waste-activated sludge to the plant influent commonly experience serious difficulties resulting from anaerobiosis and

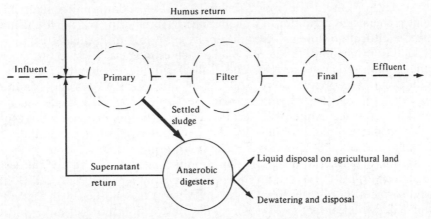

FIGURE 2   Typical sludge-handling scheme for a trickling-filter plant serving a community of fewer than 10,000 people.

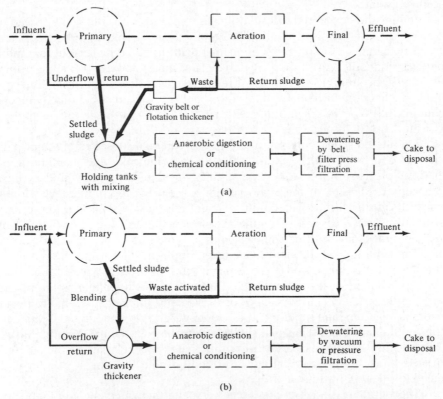

FIGURE 3   Alternative schemes for processing activated-sludge plant wastes by thickening in advance of conditioning and dewatering. (a) Separate thickening of waste-activated sludge before mixing with primary sludge. (b) Gravity thickening of combined raw primary and waste-activated sludges.

thinning of settled sludge in the primary clarifier.) The waste-activated sludge is concentrated independently by gravity belt thickening or dissolved-air flotation, processes that give reliable and effective results. Water of separation is returned for reprocessing, while the thickened sludge is pumped along with a primary sludge to a mixed blending tank. If the sludge is anaerobically digested, the dewatered biosolids are likely to be applied to land as a fertilizer and soil conditioner. If the blended raw sludge is dewatered without prior digestion, the blending tank is sized so that sludge can accumulate when not being dewatered, and the installed mixing impellers are adequate to ensure a homogeneous feed for mechanical dewatering. Unless the retention time of the blended sludge is relatively short by continuous removal, the tank may release foul odors. The active microbial floc in the waste-activated sludge decomposes the raw organic matter in the primary sludge under anaerobic conditions, releasing hydrogen sulfide and other reduced volatile organic compounds. Dewatered raw solids are disposed of by burial in a landfill or incineration.

An alternative arrangement, shown in Figure 3b, blends waste-activated and raw sludges in a gravity thickening tank. Consolidation of this waste mixture by gravity settling may yield only marginal results because of carryover of flocculent solids, thus providing poor solids capture. Assuming good operation and chemical additions, performance at the allowable solids loading can recover (capture) up to 90% of the solids. The thickened underflow is likely to be only in the range of 4%–6% solids (Section 6). Supernatant from the thickener is returned to the plant inlet and underflow sludge is pumped for processing and disposal.

Aerobic processing of wastewater without primary sedimentation often utilizes aerobic digestion for stabilization (Figure 4). Decanting chambers for return of supernatant, installed in the digesters of package plants, rarely provide efficient solids separation. However, tanks with separate controls for aeration and decanting can be effective in concentrating aerobically digested solids. The most common method for eliminating the liquid stabilized sludge is to spread it on farmland.

Designing a sludge-processing system requires a thorough understanding of the characteristics of the waste being produced and the most feasible method for solids disposal. Selection of the latter is dictated by local conditions and practices. Intermediate steps of thickening, treatment, and dewatering must be integrated so that each

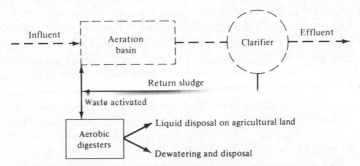

FIGURE 4   Common disposal methods for waste-activated sludge from small treatment plants without settling prior to aeration.

relates to the prior operation and prepares the residue for subsequent handling. A scheme should have flexibility to allow alternative modes of operation, since actual conditions may differ from those assumed at the time of design. Too often, built-in rigidity, by limiting piping and pumping facilities, does not permit plant personnel to vary operations to meet changing conditions. The practice of sanitary design requires both knowledge and foresight to consider all available options.

The following list illustrates typical sludge-processing and disposal problems that have confronted plant operators:

1. Returning excess activated sludge to the head of the treatment plant with no alternative for separate thickening or disposal. The result can be upset primary clarifiers, reduced efficiency, thin sludge, and higher chemical costs for conditioning prior to mechanical dewatering.

2. Employing gravity thickeners to concentrate combined primary and waste-activated sludges Figure 3b or waste-activated sludge alone. This results in limited thickening of the sludges, and the thickener overflow returns to the head of the plant a substantial quantity of suspended solids that are then recycled through the system.

3. Returning poor-quality digester supernatant to the head of a treatment plant, thereby increasing the BOD load and recycling of suspended solids.

4. Having excessive concentrations of heavy metals in biologically stabilized sludges that limit their application as biosolids on agricultural land.

5. Being forced to incinerate sludge when an alternate method would be much less expensive if facilities were available.

6. Providing only sand drying beds for dewatering anaerobic or aerobically digested sludges at small plants with no provision for spreading on adjacent grassland or farmland. Plant operators usually modify the piping and buy a tank wagon or truck for liquid disposal because of the labor involved in scooping up dried cake from the beds.

5   SELECTION OF PROCESSES FOR WATER TREATMENT SLUDGES

The pollution of surface waters and groundwaters from the discharge of residuals from water treatment is controlled by state regulations under authorization from the EPA. In general, clarified waters like settled backwash water from filters and overflow from solids-separation processes can be discharged to flowing waters, provided that in-stream water quality standards are not violated. After separation of supernatant, the sludge is often disposed of by land application. Water treatment plants may also discharge to a sanitary sewer or directly to a wastewater plant, provided that the wastewaters comply with pretreatment requirements for industrial wastewater.

Water treatment processes can be modified to change the characteristics and reduce the quantities of residuals. Polymers as coagulant aids lower the required dosages of alum and auxiliary chemicals. The result is less sludge that is easier to dewater because of the reduced content of hydroxide precipitate. Polymers also enhance presedimentation of turbid river waters, thus controlling carryover of solids to subsequent chemical coagulation. The addition of specially manufactured clays can be used to aid flocculation of relatively clear surface supplies by producing a denser floc that settles more rapidly. Coagulant aids with alum should be considered as a cost-effective technique for modifying sludge-handling processes at surface water plants. Groundwater softening plants can also change their mode of operation to lessen the volume of waste sludge. Emphasis is placed on preventing magnesium hydroxide precipitation because it inhibits dewaterability and the feasibility of processing sludge for recovery of lime. Also, hardness reduction can be limited to produce less solid material while still supplying a moderately soft water acceptable to the general public.

The common processes for storage, treatment, and disposal of water treatment sludges are listed in Table 3. Each waterworks is unique so that local conditions and existing facilities tend to dictate techniques applied in processing and disposing of waste solids [4].

Modern clarifiers equipped with mechanical scrapers discharge sludge at regular intervals, usually daily. Separate holding tanks can be installed to accumulate this slurry prior to dewatering. Filter backwash can be stored in clarifier–flocculators that serve as both temporary holding tanks and wash-water settling basins. Equalization and settling are generally the only prerequisites if sludges are discharged to a sewer for processing at the municipal wastewater treatment plant.

A typical system for thickening coagulation waste and filter wash water is shown schematically in Figure 5. The two primary sources of waste are sludge from the clarifier, following chemical coagulation, and wash water from backwashing filters. The

TABLE 3   Processes for Storage, Treatment, and Disposal of Water Treatment Sludges

Storage prior to processing
    Sedimentation basins
    Separate holding tanks
    Flocculator–clarifier basins
Thickening prior to dewatering
    Gravity settling
Chemical conditioning prior to dewatering
    Polymer application
    Lime addition to alum sludges
Mechanical dewatering
    Centrifugation
    Pressure filtration
Air drying
    Shallow lagoons
    Sand drying beds
Disposal of dewatered solids
    Codisposal in municipal solid-waste landfill
    Burial in dedicated landfill
Disposal of liquid and dewatered sludge
    Spread on agricultural land
    Application on dedicated surface disposal site

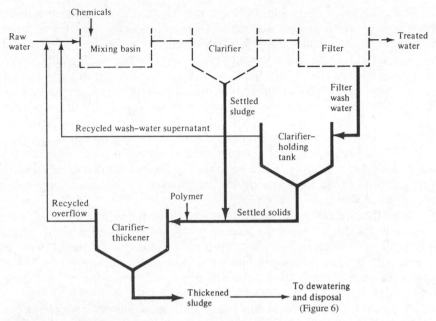

FIGURE 5   Thickening coagulation waste and filter wash water in preliminary handling of water treatment plant sludges.

latter is discharged to a clarifier holding tank for gravity separation of the suspended solids and flow equalization. Settled solids consolidate to a sludge volume less than one-tenth of the wash-water volume. Supernatant is withdrawn slowly and recycled to the plant inlet. After a sufficient portion has been drained, the holding tank is able to receive the next backwash surge. Settled sludges from both the wash-water tanks and in-line clarifiers are given second-stage consolidation in a clarifier–thickener. Polymer is normally added to enhance solids capture, overflow is recycled, and thickened sludge withdrawn for further dewatering and disposal.

    Recycled wash-water supernatant and recycled overflow without treatment can return microorganisms, organic precursors, and disinfection by-products to the influent raw water. Figure 5 satisfies the EPA Filter Backwash Recycling Rule that requires treatment of recycled flows and their point of return ahead of coagulation (i.e., before the rapid mix/coagulant process preceding clarification and/or filtration). The primary objective of this regulation is to ensure the removal of 99% of *Cryptosporidium* oocysts in treatment of surface water. This rule applies to all recycled flows including filter backwash, supernatant from sludge thickening, and wastewater from sludge dewatering.

    Mechanical dewatering of chemical sludges can be accomplished by centrifugation or plate-and-frame pressure filtration and in some instances by belt filter pressure filtration (Figure 6). A major advantage of a solid-bowl decanter centrifuge is operational flexibility. Machine variables, such as speed of rotation, allow a range of moisture content in the discharged solids varying from a dry cake to a thickened slurry. Feed rates, sludge solids content, and chemical conditioning are also variables that influence

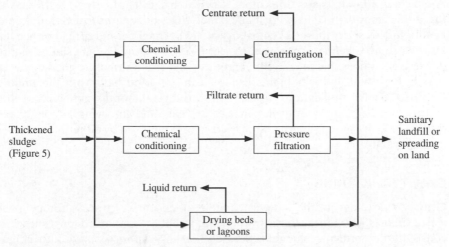

FIGURE 6   Alternative methods for disposal of water treatment sludges by dewatering, drying, or chemical recovery of thickened chemical coagulation wastes.

performance. Polymers or other coagulants are normally applied with the slurry feed to enhance solids capture. Lime sludges compact readily, producing a cake with 50% or greater solids from a feed of 5%–10%. Alum sludges do not dewater as readily and discharge with a toothpaste consistency suitable for either further processing or transporting by truck to a disposal site. Gravity-thickened sludge containing about one-half aluminum hydroxide slurry can be concentrated to 10%–15% solids, while one-quarter hydrate slurry can be dewatered to 20% or greater. Removal of solids by centrifugation varies over a broad range, depending on operating situations and chemical conditioning; in general, solids recovery and density of cake are related to polymer dosage.

A plate-and-frame filter press is particularly advantageous for dewatering alum sludges if a high solids concentration in the filter cake is desired. Aluminum hydroxide wastes are often conditioned with lime to improve their filterability. The filter medium is precoated with either diatomaceous earth or fly ash before applying sludge solids. Precoat protects against blinding of the filter cloth by fines and ensures easy cake discharge without sticking. With proper chemical conditioning, alum sludges can be pressed to a solids content of about 30%–40%, which can be handled as a chunky solid rather than the paste consistency associated with a 15% density. Belt filter presses can dewater alum sludges to 15%–20% and lime sludges to 50% or greater with polymer conditioning.

Lagooning is a common method for dewatering, thickening, and temporary storage of waste sludge where suitable land area is available [4]. The diked pond area needed relates to character of the sludge, climate, design features such as underdrains and decanters, and method of operation. Clarified overflow may be returned to the treatment plant, particularly if filter wash water is directed to the lagoons without prior thickening. Sludges from lime softening consolidate to about 50% solids after drying by evaporation and can be removed by a scraper or dragline and hauled to land burial.

Alum sludge dewaters and dries more slowly to a density of only 10%–15%. Although the surface may dry to a hard crust, the underlying sludge turns to a viscous liquid upon agitation. This slurry must be removed, usually by dragline, and spread on the banks to air dry prior to hauling. Freezing enhances the dewatering of alum sludge by breaking down its gelatinous character. Neither lime nor alum sludges make a good, stable landfill. Air drying at small water plants can be done on sand beds with tile underdrains. Repeated sludge applications over a period of several months can be made in depths up to several feet. Dewatering action is by drainage and air drying, although operation may include decanting supernatant. Dried cake is removed by either hand shoveling or mechanical means.

GRAVITY THICKENING

Gravity thickening is the simplest and least expensive process for consolidating waste sludges. Thickeners in wastewater treatment are employed most successfully in consolidating primary sludge separately or in combination with trickling-filter humus. When raw primary and waste-activated sludges are blended and concentrated, results are often marginal because of poor solids capture. Water treatment wastes from both sedimentation and filter backwashing can be compacted effectively by gravity separation.

6   GRAVITY SLUDGE THICKENERS IN WASTEWATER TREATMENT

The tank of a gravity thickener resembles a circular clarifier except that the depth–diameter ratio is greater and the hoppered bottom has a steeper slope. The three settling zones are the clear supernatant on top, feed zone characterized by hindered settling, and compression near the bottom where consolidation occurs. Figure 7 is a schematic diagram with the main components labeled. Influent sludge is applied continuously. However, if this is not practical, sludge application can be intermittent at frequent intervals. The circular inlet baffle is partly submerged but not so deep as to disturb the sludge blanket. The discharge weir is peripheral for maximum length. Although not always installed, a skimmer can be used to push scum over the weir with

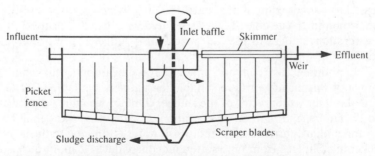

FIGURE 7   Schematic diagram of a gravity sludge thickener.

the overflow or down a pipe for separate collection. Thickened sludge is scraped to a central outlet for continuous or intermittent discharge. Withdrawal is often governed by the operation of the feed pump to the next processing step (e.g., anaerobic digestion). Attached to the scraper arms are picket fences consisting of vertical rods or pickets that are slowly pulled along. Gentle agitation of the settled solids increases consolidation by dislodging gas bubbles and preventing the bridging of solids. A properly designed picket fence is considered essential in thickening of organic waste [5].

The principal design criterion is solids loading expressed in units of pounds of solids applied per square foot of bottom area per day (lb/ft^2/day or kg/m$^2 \cdot$ d). Typical loading values and thickened-sludge concentrations based on operational experience are listed in Table 4. These data assume good operation and chemical additions, such as chlorine, if necessary to inhibit biological activity. Solids recovery in a properly functioning unit is 90%–95%, with perhaps the exception of a unit handling primary plus waste activated where it is difficult to achieve this degree of solids capture. Most continuous-flow thickeners are designed with a side-water depth of approximately 10 ft to provide an adequate clear-water zone, sludge-blanket depth, and space for temporary storage of consolidated waste. Sludge-blanket depths (feed plus compaction zones) should be 3 ft or greater to ensure maximum compaction, using a suggested solids retention time of 24 hr. This is estimated by dividing the volume of the sludge blanket by the daily sludge withdrawal; values vary from 0.5 to 2 days, depending on operation. Overflow rates should be 400–900 gpd/ft^2 (16–37 m^3/m$^2 \cdot$ d) and are defined by the quantity of sludge plus supplementary dilution water applied. Dilution water blended with sludge feed increases the overflow rate to carry out fine solids in the supernatant to enhance thickening and reduce the emission of foul odors from anaerobiosis.

Gravity thickeners are normally sized to handle the maximum anticipated seasonal or monthly sludge yield. Peak daily sludge production often requires storage in the thickener or other sludge-processing units. Low liquid overflow rates result in malodors from septicity of the thickener contents. A common remedy is to feed dilution water to the thickener along with the sludge to increase hydraulic loading. An alternative is to apply chlorine to reduce bacterial activity. The design of pumps and piping should be sufficiently flexible to allow regulation of the quantity of dilution water and have the capacity to transport viscous, thickened sludges.

TABLE 4   Gravity Thickener Design Loadings and Underflow Concentrations for Wastewater Sludges

Type of Sludge	Average Solids Loading (lb/ft^2/day)[a]	Underflow Concentration (% solids)
Primary	20	8–10
Primary plus filter humus	10	6–8
Primary plus activated sludge	8	4–6

[a]1.0 lb/ft^2/day $=$ 4.88 kg/m$^2 \cdot$ d

Example 7

The daily quantity of primary sludge from a trickling-filter plant contains 1130 lb of solids at a concentration of 4.5%. Size a gravity thickener based on a solids loading of 10 lb/ft^2/day. Calculate the daily volumes of applied and thickened sludges, assuming an underflow of 8.0% and 95% solids capture. What is the flow of dilution water required to attain an overflow rate of 400 gpd/ft^2? If the blanket of consolidated sludge in the tank has a depth of 3.0 ft, estimate the solids retention time.

Solution:

$$\text{tank area required} = \frac{1130}{10} = 113 \text{ ft}^2$$

$$\text{diameter} = \left(\frac{113 \times 4}{\pi}\right)^{1/2} = 12.0 \text{ ft}$$

Use a depth of 10.0 ft.

$$\text{volume of applied sludge} = \frac{1130}{0.045 \times 62.4} = 402 \text{ ft}^3/\text{day}$$

$$= 3010 \text{ gpd}$$

$$\text{overflow rate of applied sludge} = \frac{3010}{113} = 27 \text{ gpd/ft}^2$$

$$\text{supplemental dilution flow to attain 400 gpd/ft}^2 = (400 - 27)113 = 42,000 \text{ gpd}$$

$$\text{volume of thickened sludge} = \frac{1130 \times 0.95}{(8.0/100)62.4} = 215 \text{ ft}^3/\text{day}$$

$$\text{solids retention time} = \frac{3 \times 113 \times 24}{215} = 38 \text{ hr}$$

7   GRAVITY SLUDGE THICKENERS IN WATER TREATMENT

The performance of thickeners processing water treatment plant wastes varies with the character of the water being treated and the chemicals applied. Alum sludges from surface water coagulation settle to a density in the range of 2%–6% solids. Coagulation–softening mixtures from the treatment of turbid river waters gravity thicken approximately as follows: alum–lime sludge, 4%–10%; iron–lime settlings, 10%–20%; alum–lime filter wash water, about 4%; and iron–lime backwash, up to 8%. The density achieved in gravity thickening relates to the calcium–magnesium ratio in the solids, quantity of alum, nature of impurities removed from the raw water, and other factors. Calcium carbonate residue from groundwater softening consolidates to 15%–25% solids. In most cases, special studies have to be conducted at a particular water works to determine settleability of solids in waste sludges and wash water. Flocculation aids are used to improve clarification in most cases.

Relatively dense chemical slurries are thickened in tanks similar to the one shown in Figure 7. Thin sludges and backwash waters may be concentrated in clarifier–thickeners that have an inlet well equipped with mixing paddles, where the feed can be flocculated with polymers or other coagulants. Holding tanks are used to dampen hydraulic surges of filter wash water. These units can be plain tanks with mixers or clarifiers equipped for removing settled solids and decanting clear supernatant.

Evaluating the performance of a thickener often involves mass balance calculations. Overflow plus underflow solids equals influent solids. Also, the sum of overflow and underflow volumes is equal to the quantity of applied sludge and supplementary dilution water. These values can be calculated using Eq. (3), as illustrated in Example 8.

Example 8

An alum–lime slurry with 4.0% solids content is gravity thickened to 20% with a removal efficiency of 95%. Calculate the quantity of underflow per 1.0 m^3 of slurry applied and the concentration of solids in the overflow. Assume a specific gravity of 2.5 for the dry solids.

Solution:

$$\text{solids applied} = 1.0 \text{ m}^3 \times 1000 \text{ kg/m}^3 \times 0.04 = 40 \text{ kg}$$

$$\text{underflow solids} = 0.95 \times 40 = 38 \text{ kg}$$

The specific gravity of underflow using Eq. (2) is

$$S = \frac{80 + 20}{(80/1.0) + (20/2.5)} = 1.14$$

$$\text{volume of underflow [Eq. (3)]} = \frac{38}{0.20 \times 1000 \times 1.14} = 0.17 \text{ m}^3$$

$$\text{volume of overflow} = 1.0 - 0.17 = 0.83 \text{ m}^3$$

From Eq. (3), the concentration of solids in the overflow is

$$s = \frac{0.05 \times 40 \times 100}{0.83 \times 1000 \times 1.0} = 0.24\% = 2400 \text{ mg/l}$$

GRAVITY BELT THICKENING

The stand-alone gravity belt thickener is an outgrowth of the development of the belt filter press (Section 20), which has a gravity drainage zone for initial thickening prior to the pressure dewatering zone. After flocculation of a sludge, conveyance on a continuous porous belt supported horizontally on an open framework allows the separated water to drain freely through the belt. In addition to mechanical development, success of gravity belt thickening is attributable to the availability of improved polymers for flocculation of sludge solids to release bound water. The common application is separate thickening of waste-activated sludge prior to blending with primary sludge for anaerobic digestion.

8   DESCRIPTION OF A GRAVITY BELT THICKENER

The feed sludge is conditioned by applying a polymer solution through an injection ring ahead of a variable orifice venturi mixer that discharges into the bottom of a feed retention tank. Adequate conditioning is necessary to ensure flocculation by agglomerating the solids to reduce their affinity to water so that drainage can occur. After flowing up through the retention tank to allow formation of larger floc and free water, the flocculated sludge is uniformly applied across the belt through a chute.

As illustrated in Figure 8, the porous belt moves horizontally across the drainage zone to the drive roller where the thickened sludge slurry is discharged. It then passes underneath where the belt is washed, maintained in alignment by a steering roller, and returns to the top by passing over the belt tensioning roller. In the drainage zone, the belt is supported by bars that wipe the underside of the belt, and sludge is prevented from flowing off the sides of the belt by retainers and rubber seals. To open channels in the sludge layer being conveyed along the belt, plastic drainage elements are supported just above the belt surface. The filtrate is collected in a pan under the drainage zone and discharged below the machine. The belt is fabricated of monofilament polyester, with the mesh design, porosity, and tensile properties based on the kind of sludge being thickened. The effective dewatering length (horizontal travel distance of the belt) varies with manufacturer from 12 to 14 ft (3.8 to 4.3 m). The effective widths of belts are 1.0, 1.5, 2.0, and 3.0 m.

The thickened sludge, usually in the range of 5%–8% solids, is a loose, wet slurry subject to splashing; therefore, the scraper blade and discharge hopper are surrounded by a shield. The rubber-covered drive roller that provides traction to pull the belt is powered by an electric motor with a drive train for variable speed up to 100 fpm. Since woven monofilament polyester fabrics have visible clear openings, solids can penetrate the pores of the fabric, requiring washing with a high-pressure water spray. The spray containment housing has a wash tube with jet nozzles and an internal brush with a hand-wheel for cleaning nozzles during operation. The steering assembly monitors the position of the belt and shifts the steering roller to maintain belt alignment. A sensing unit in contact with the edge of the belt signals the roller positioning unit, which can be either a hydraulic or a pneumatic system. Variable belt tension is established and controlled by a roller held in a yoke tensioned by either hydraulic or pneumatic cylinders.

9   LAYOUT OF A GRAVITY BELT THICKENER SYSTEM

A complete separate system of auxiliary equipment, as shown in Figure 9, is recommended for each gravity belt thickener. The sludge feed must be applied at a uniform rate by a plunger pump or a progressing cavity pump, or at higher feed rates by a centrifugal pump. A variable-speed drive is necessary with a maximum pumping capacity greater than the design hydraulic loading. The polymer preparation and feed equipment is designed with flexibility to allow for variations in feed rate and use of different kinds of polymers. Dry flake or microbead polymer has greater than 95% active solids and is commonly prepared for feed at a concentration of 0.2% total solids; emulsion forms are 25%–50% active solids and prepared at 0.5%; and liquid forms are 2%–8% active solids prepared at 2.0%. For accuracy in polymer addition,

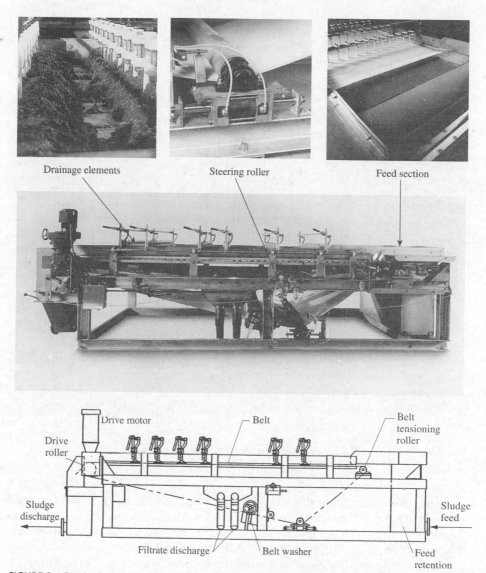

FIGURE 8   Gravity belt thickener. Sludge feed after polymer injection overflows a retention tank onto the porous belt for gravity drainage. Elements positioned close to the belt open channels for free drainage and to decelerate the agglomerated sludge solids. The thickened sludge slurry is released from the belt by a discharge blade. *Source:* Komline-Sanderson, Peapack, NI

the metering pump is positive displacement with a speed regulator. The sludge mixed with polymer is applied to the belt after upward flow through the feed retention tank.

Shown at the top of Figure 9 are the air compressor or hydraulic unit, which controls the belt tension cylinder and steering mechanism, and the wash-water booster pump. The supply of wash water is 15–20 gpm/m $(1-1.3\,\text{l/s}\cdot\text{m})$ at a pressure of

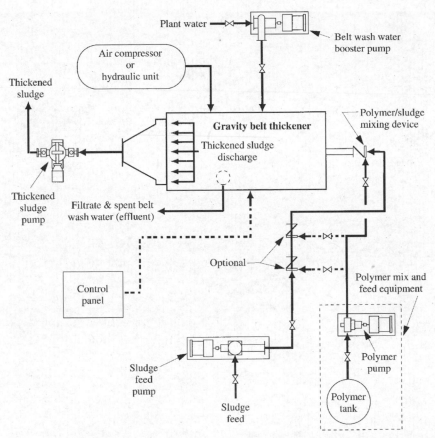

FIGURE 9   Schematic layout showing the major components of a gravity thickener system. *Source:* Komline-Sanderson, Peapack, NJ.

80–100 psi. For cleaning the belt, either clear plant effluent or potable water can be used as a supply. The electric control panel provides for automatic, sequenced start-up and shut-down, with monitoring at each step in the cycle to provide prewetting of the belt prior to sludge application and discharge of sludge slurry and belt washing upon shut-down. Alarm conditions shut down the system in case of serious belt misalignment, low air or hydraulic pressure, low wash-water pressure, or broken belt or belt drive. All auxiliary equipment for each press is controlled from one panel. For return to the plant inlet, the filtrate and belt wash water are collected in a drain under each machine. The thickened sludge is pumped for further processing.

10   SIZING OF GRAVITY BELT THICKENERS

The main operating parameters of a gravity belt thickener are hydraulic loading, solids loading, and polymer dosage. Hydraulic loading is expressed in gallons per minute per meter of belt width (cubic meters per meter per hour). Solids loading is expressed as the pounds of total dry solids feed per meter per hour (kilograms per meter per hour). Polymer dosage is calculated as pounds applied per ton of total dry solids in the sludge feed (kilograms per tonne). The key performance parameter is concentration of dry solids by weight in the thickened sludge expressed as a percentage.

Thickened sludge is usually in the range of 5%–8% solids when the feed is conditioned with sufficient polymer and solids capture is 95% or more. Underdosing produces unstable floc formation and poor drainage, resulting in reduced solids concentration, lower solids capture, and the necessity to reduce the feed rate. Overdosing, though giving the appearance of improved operation by better drainage and higher solids concentration, can, after an extended period of operation, prevent proper drainage by blinding the porous belt as the excess polymer forms a skin on the surface of the belt. Maintaining optimum polymer feed rate is important for cost-effective operation.

Drainage belts are available in various porosities affecting drainage rate and solids capture. Design selection is based on documented experience at other plants thickening a sludge with similar characteristics. Similarly, hydraulic loading and speed of the belt are based on the kind and concentration of waste solids and dewaterability after polymer conditioning. To account for seasonal and operational variations in the volume of sludge produced, a conservative capacity is normally selected in design. The maximum weekly production of dry solids may be greater than 25% of the annual average, and the water content may increase as much as 50% to double the sludge volume. The maximum hydraulic capacity of a gravity belt thickener is usually 50%–80% greater than the design rating to allow increased loading of conditioned sludge at increased belt speed. Conversely, decreasing capacity can be achieved by reducing hydraulic loading, polymer feed rate, and belt speed. The minimum capacity is normally 25% of design rating. Since the horizontal travel distance between sludge application and discharge is fixed, belt speed affects the time allowed for drainage. At higher belt speed, the thickened sludge solids concentration is likely to decrease, while at slower speed, the solids content is likely to increase.

Design of a thickening facility considers the size of the treatment plant and desired flexibility of operation. The selection of belt filters depends on the quantity of sludge production, design feed rate, and operating time. Gravity thickeners are manufactured with active belt widths of 1.0, 1.5, 2.0, and 3.0 m. Unless adequate storage is available in sludge treatment units, at least two machines are installed so one can operate while the other is out of service for maintenance. In a small plant, the operating time may be 7 hr/day, whereas in a larger plant, operating time may be for a period of 15 or 23 hr/day. These schedules allow 1 hr for start-up and shut-down. Approximate operating parameters for gravity belt thickening of two kinds of sludge are listed in Table 5. Because published operational data are limited, these listed values should not be relied on for design without verification. For a machine fashioned by a particular manufacturer, operating experience at other installations thickening a sludge of similar characteristics is essential. In general, belt filter capacity should be prudently selected for new installations to account for the probable inaccuracy in projecting performance and peak sludge volume.

TABLE 5   Approximate Results from Gravity Belt Thickening of Polymer Flocculated Wastewater Sludges

Type of Sludge	Feed Solids (%)	Hydraulic Loading (gpm/m)[a]	Solids Loading (lb/m/hr)[b]	Thickened Sludge Solids (%)	Active Polymer Dosage (lb/ton)[c]
Waste activated	0.5–2	150–250	600–2000	5–8	4–8
Anaerobically digested primary plus waste activated	2.5–5	100–150	2000–3000	6–10	5–10

[a] 1.0 gpm/m = 0.225 m^3/m · h
[b] 1.0 lb/m/hr = 0.454 kg/m · h
[c] 1.0 lb/ton = 0.500 kg/tonne

Example 9

As originally constructed, a conventional activated-sludge plant was piped to return waste-activated sludge to the plant inlet or blend it with primary sludge. Returning the waste sludge to the inlet upset the primary clarifiers, resulting in floating solids, foul odors, and thinner sludges. After the waste-activated and primary sludges were blended, the mixture was less than 3% solids, which was too low for good operation of anaerobic digestion. The proposed solution is to modify the sludge processing system by installing gravity belt thickeners to concentrate the solids in the waste-activated sludge and a blending tank to mix this thickened sludge with the primary sludge prior to digestion, as diagrammed in Figure. 3a. If the waste-activated sludge were thickened to 5%–8%, the mixed sludge would be in the range of 6%–7%.

Size two gravity belt thickeners to increase the solids content of the waste-activated sludge to 5%–8% at the plant design load of 15.0 mgd. During the maximum month, the average plant wastewater load is 10.9 mgd. Normal operation of the activated-sludge process produces an average of 72,000 gpd with a solids concentration of 1.12% (11,200 mg/l). Poor operation, which may periodically last for one or two weeks, results in an average of 102,000 gpd with 0.81% solids.

Solution: Assuming similar operating conditions at design load, the volume of waste-activated sludge production would be as follows:

$$\text{Volume with normal operation} = (15.0/10.9)72,000$$
$$= 99,100 \text{ gpd}$$
$$\text{Volume with poor operation} = (15.0/10.9)102,000$$
$$\doteq 140,000 \text{ gpd}$$

Design operation of the gravity belt thickeners is to be 7 days per week for a maximum of 7 hr/day. During normal operation, assume a conservative hydraulic loading of 150 gpm/m from Table 5 to calculate the required belt width and solids loading.

$$\text{Belt width required at 150 gpm/m} = \frac{99,100}{150 \times 7 \times 60} = 1.57 \text{ m}$$

$$\text{Solids loading at 150 gpm/m} = 150 \times 8.34 \times 0.0112 \times 60$$
$$= 840 \text{ lb/m/hr}$$

During poor operation, calculate the required belt widths and solids loadings for both the lower hydraulic loading limit of 150 gpm/m and the upper limit of 250 gpm/m from Table 5.

$$\text{Belt width required at 150 gpm/m} = \frac{140,000}{150 \times 7 \times 60} = 2.22 \text{ m}$$

$$\text{Solids loading at 150 gpm/m} = 150 \times 8.34 \times 0.0081 \times 60$$
$$= 608 \text{ lb/m/hr}$$

$$\text{Belt width required at 250 gpm/m} = \frac{140,000}{250 \times 7 \times 60} = 1.33 \text{ m}$$

$$\text{Solids loading at 250 gpm/m} = 250 \times 8.34 \times 0.0081 \times 60$$
$$= 1010 \text{ lb/m/hr}$$

Installation of two 1.5-m gravity belt thickeners satisfies both the hydraulic and solids loading ranges given in Table 5 during the maximum month with one unit in operation. During normal activated-sludge process operation,

$$\text{Hydraulic loading} = \frac{99,100}{1.5 \times 7 \times 60} = 157 \text{ gpm/m}$$

$$\text{Solids loading} = 157 \times 8.34 \times 0.0112 \times 60 = 880 \text{ lb/m/hr}$$

During poor activated-sludge process operation,

$$\text{Hydraulic loading} = \frac{140,000}{1.5 \times 7 \times 60} = 222 \text{ gpm/m}$$

$$\text{Solids loading} = 222 \times 8.34 \times 0.0081 \times 60 = 900 \text{ lb/m/hr}$$

For the few weeks of poor operation, both thickeners could be operated for 7 hr or less using the combined belt width of 3.0 m to lower the hydraulic loading to 150 gpm/m. Alternately, if one thickener were out of service, the other one could be operated for 10.4 hr at 150 gpm/m.

FLOTATION THICKENING

Air flotation is applicable in concentrating waste-activated sludge and pretreatment of industrial wastes to separate grease or fine particulate matter. Fine bubbles to buoy up particles may be generated by air dispersed through a porous medium, by air drawn from the liquid under vacuum, or by air forced into solution under elevated pressure followed by pressure release. The latter, called *dissolved-air flotation*, is the process used to thicken waste-activated sludge.

11   DESCRIPTION OF DISSOLVED-AIR FLOTATION

The major components of a typical flotation system are sludge pumps, chemical feed equipment to apply polymers, an air compressor, a control panel, and a flotation unit. Figure 10 is a schematic diagram of a dissolved-air system. Influent enters near the tank bottom and exits from the base at the opposite end. Float is continuously swept from the liquid surface and discharged over the end wall of the tank. Effluent is recycled at a rate of 30%–150% of the influent flow through an air dissolution tank to the feed inlet. In this manner, compressed air at 60–80 psi is dissolved in the return flow. After pressure release, minute bubbles with a diameter about 80 μm pop out of solution. They attach to solid particles and become enmeshed in sludge flocs, floating them to the surface. The sludge blanket, varying from 8 to 24 in. thick, is skimmed from the surface. Flotation aids are introduced in a mixing chamber at the tank inlet.

The operating variables for flotation thickening are air pressure, recycle ratio, detention time, air/solids ratio, solids and hydraulic loading rates, and application of chemical aids. The operating air pressure in the dissolution tank influences the size of bubbles released. If they are too large, they do not attach readily to sludge particles, while too fine a dispersion breaks up fragile floc. Generally, a bubble size less than 100 μm is best; however, the only practical way to establish the proper rise rate is by conducting experiments at various air pressures.

Recycle ratio is interrelated with feed solids concentration, detention time, and air/solids ratio. Detention time in the flotation zone is not critical, providing that particles rise rapidly enough and the horizontal velocity does not scour the bottom of the sludge blanket. An air/solids ratio of 0.01–0.03 lb of air per lb of solids is sufficient to achieve acceptable thickening of waste-activated sludge. Optimum recycle ratio must be determined by on-site studies.

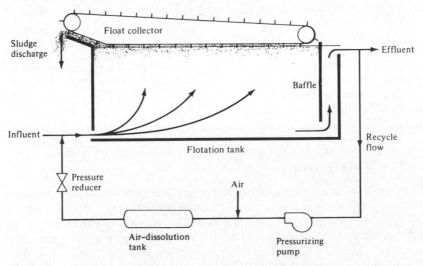

FIGURE 10   Schematic diagram of a dissolved-air flotation system.

Operating data from plant-scale units indicate that solids loadings of $2-4$ lb/ft^2/hr, with hydraulic flows of about 1 gpm/ft^2, can produce floats of 4%–8% solids. Without polymer addition, solids capture is 70%–90%. However, removal efficiency increases to a mean of 97%, with an active polymer dosage of approximately 10 lb/ton of dry suspended solids. This is the reason most wastewater installations use polymers as flotation aids.

12   DESIGN OF DISSOLVED-AIR FLOTATION UNITS

Wherever possible, laboratory and pilot-scale tests are recommended to help determine specific design criteria for a given waste. Notwithstanding, the suggested design criteria for flotation thickening of typical waste-activated sludges are listed in Table 6. A conservative solids design loading is 2 lb/ft^2/hr (10 kg/m$^2 \cdot$ h) with the use of flotation aids. From actual operating data, at least 3 lb/ft^2/hr can be expected, and most thickeners have a built-in capacity for $4-5$ lb/ft^2/hr loadings. While a 4% minimum float concentration is specified for design purposes, 5%–6% solids can normally be expected. Flotation without polymers generally results in a concentration that is about 1 percentage point less than with chemical aids. Removal efficiency varies from 90% to 98% with polymer addition. The maximum hydraulic loading for design is set at 0.8 gpm/ft^2 (0.54 l/m$^2 \cdot$ s); this is equivalent to applying a waste with a solids concentration of 5000 mg/l at a loading of 2 lb/ft^2/hr. Lower solids levels or higher hydraulic loadings result in lower removal efficiencies and/or float densities.

The typical design values recommended in Table 6 apply to anticipated average sludge production. This procedure provides a significant safety factor and permits flexibility in operations. Peak solids loads at municipal treatment plants can usually be accommodated, since these conservative design criteria allow a maximum loading of

TABLE 6   Design Parameters for Dissolved-Air Flotation of Waste-Activated Sludge with Addition of Polymer Flotation Aids

Parameter	Typical Design Value	Anticipated Results
Solids loading (lb/ft^2/hr)[a]	2	3–5
Float concentration (%)	4	5–6
Removal efficiency	90–95	97
Polymer addition		5–10
(lb/ton of dry solids)	10	
Air/solids ratio		
(lb of air/lb of solids)	0.02	
Effluent recycle ratio		
(% of influent)	40–70	
Hydraulic loading		
(gpm/ft^2)	0.8 maximum	

[a] 1.0 lb/ft^2/hr = 4.88 kg/m$^2 \cdot$ h

nearly 100% greater than the average without a serious drop in performance. Perhaps the most critical condition is during a period of sludge bulking when the waste mixed liquor is more difficult to thicken and maximum hydraulic loading is applied to the flotation unit.

Sizing of flotation units for an existing plant can be calculated from available data on sludge quantities, characteristics, and solids concentrations. For new plant design, raw wastewater is often assumed to contain 0.24 lb of dry solids/capita/day. A portion of these solids is removed in primary settling, and a conservative estimate for secondary activated-sludge production is 0.12 lb/capita/day. The actual amount is likely to be closer to one-half of this value, because of biological decomposition. Solids yield in an activated-sludge process without primary settling may be safely assumed to be 0.20 lb/capita/day for domestic wastewater. If the waste sludge from such a system is aerobically digested, the concentration of solids is reduced by about 35%.

Operating hours of a flotation unit depend on the size of the plant and the working schedule. Although a unit does not require continuous operator attention, periodic checks of a system are scheduled. Generally, a 48-hr week is adequate for plants with capacities of less than 2 mgd. For systems of 2–5 mgd, two shifts 5 days per week establishes an operating period of 80 hr/week. Treatment plants handling more than 20 mgd have operators on duty continuously, and thickening units are run on a schedule appropriate for sludge dewatering and disposal.

Example 10

A dissolved-air flotation thickener is being sized to process waste-activated sludge based on the design criteria given in Table 6. The average waste flow is 33,600 gpd at 15,000 mg/l (1.5%) suspended solids, and the maximum daily quantity contains 50% more solids at a reduced concentration of 10,000 mg/l. What is the peak daily hydraulic loading that can be processed? Base all computations on a 14-hr/day operating schedule.

Solution: The flotation tank surface area required for the average daily flow at a design loading of 2.0 lb/ft^2/hr for a 14-hr/day schedule is

$$\text{area} = \frac{33{,}600 \times 0.015 \times 8.34}{2.0 \times 14} = \frac{4200}{28} = 150 \text{ ft}^2$$

Check the solids loading and overflow rate at maximum daily sludge production:

$$\text{maximum solids loading} = \frac{1.5 \times 4200}{150 \times 14} = 3.0 \text{ lb/ft}^2/\text{hr} \quad (\text{OK})$$

$$\text{maximum sludge volume} = \frac{1.5 \times 4200}{0.01 \times 8.34} = 75{,}500 \text{ gpd}$$

$$\text{maximum hydraulic loading} = \frac{75{,}500}{150 \times 14 \times 60} = 0.60 \text{ gpm/ft}^2 \quad (\text{OK})$$

$$\text{peak hydraulic loading based on } 0.80 \text{ gpm/ft}^2 = 0.80 \times 150 \times 14 \times 60$$
$$= 100,000 \text{ gpd}$$

BIOLOGICAL SLUDGE DIGESTION

Biological digestion of sludge from wastewater treatment is widely practiced to stabilize the organic matter prior to ultimate disposal. Anaerobic digestion is used in plants employing primary clarification followed by either trickling-filter or activated-sludge secondary treatment. Aerobic digestion stabilizes waste-activated sludge from aeration plants without primary settling tanks. The end product of aerobic digestion is cellular protoplasm, and growth is limited by depletion of the available carbon source. The end products of anaerobic metabolism are methane, unused organics, and a relatively small amount of cellular protoplasm. Growth is limited by a lack of hydrogen acceptors. Anaerobic digestion is basically a destructive process, although complete degradation of the organic matter under anaerobic conditions is not possible.

13 ANAEROBIC SLUDGE DIGESTION

Anaerobic digestion consists of two distinct stages that occur simultaneously in digesting sludge. The first consists of hydrolysis of the high-molecular-weight organic compounds and conversion to organic acids by acid-forming bacteria. The second stage is gasification of the organic acids to methane and carbon dioxide by the acid-splitting, methane-forming bacteria.

Methane bacteria are strict anaerobes and very sensitive to conditions of their environment. The optimum temperature and pH range for maximum growth rate are limited. Methane bacteria can be adversely affected by excess concentrations of oxidized compounds, volatile acids, soluble salts, and metal cations and also show a rather extreme substrate specificity. Each species is restricted to the use of only a few compounds, mainly alcohols and organic acids, whereas the normal energy sources, such as carbohydrates and amino acids, are not attacked. An enrichment culture developed on a feed of acetic or butyric acid cannot decompose propionic acid. The sensitivity exhibited by methane bacteria in the second stage of anaerobic digestion, coupled with the rugged nature of the acid-forming bacteria in the first stage, creates a biological system in which the population dynamics are easily upset. Any shift in environment adverse to the population of methane bacteria causes a buildup of organic acids, which in turn further reduces the metabolism of acid-splitting methane formers.

Pending failure of the anaerobic digestion process is evidenced by a decrease in gas production, a lowering in the percentage of methane gas produced, an increase in the volatile acids concentration, and eventually a drop in pH when the accumulated volatile acids exceed the buffering capacity created by the ammonium bicarbonate in solution. Therefore, the operation of a digester can be monitored by any of the following methods: plotting the daily gas production per unit of raw sludge fed, the percentage of carbon dioxide in the digestion gases, or the concentration of volatile acids in the digesting sludge. A reduction in gas production, an increase in carbon dioxide percentage, and a rise in volatile acids concentration all indicate reduced activity of the acid-splitting methane-forming bacteria. Digester failure may be caused by any of the following: a significant increase in organic loading, a sharp decrease in digesting sludge volume (i.e., when digested sludge is withdrawn), a sudden increase in operating temperature, or the accumulation of a toxic or inhibiting substance.

The EPA specifies processing requirements for application of digested sludge as biosolids on agricultural land [1]. Anaerobic digestion reduces pathogens so that public health is not threatened, provided site restrictions minimize the potential for human and animal contact until after natural die-off reduces any remaining pathogens. The criteria for adequate digestion are a solids retention time (mean cell residence time) and temperature between 15 days at 35°C (95°F) and 60 days at 20°C (68°F). Stabilization for vector reduction is at least 38% reduction in volatile solids. Of the 10 toxic metals controlled, cadmium is of greatest concern since it is suspected of being taken up by plants to enter the human food chain.

General conditions for mesophilic sludge digestion are given in Table 7.

TABLE 7   General Conditions for Sludge Digestion

Temperature	
Optimum	97°F (36°C)
General range of operation	85°–100°F (29°–38°C)
pH	
Optimum	7.0–7.1
General limits	6.7–7.4
Gas production	
Per pound of volatile solids added	8–12 ft^3 (230–340 l)
Per pound of volatile solids destroyed	16–18 ft^3 (450–510 l)
Gas composition	
Methane	65%–69%
Carbon dioxide	31%–35%
Hydrogen sulfide	Trace
Volatile acids concentration as acetic acid	
Normal operation	200–800 mg/l
Maximum	Approx. 2000 mg/l
Alkalinity concentrations as CaCO$_3$	
Normal operation	2000–3500 mg/l
Minimum solids retention times	
Single-stage digestion	25 d
High-rate digestion	15 d
Volatile solids reduction	
Single-stage digestion	50%–70%
High-rate digestion	50%

14   SINGLE-STAGE FLOATING-COVER DIGESTERS

The cross section of a floating-cover digestion tank is shown in Figure 11. Raw sludge is pumped into the digester through pipes terminating either near the center of the tank or in the gas dome. Pumping sludge into the dome helps to break up the scum layer that forms on the surface.

Digested sludge is withdrawn from the tank bottom. The contents are heated in the zone of digesting sludge by pumping them through an external heater and returning the heated slurry through the inlet lines. The tank contents stratify with a scum layer on top and digested thickened sludge on the bottom. The middle zones consist of a layer of supernatant (water of separation) underlain by the zone of actively digesting sludge. Supernatant is drawn from the digester through any one of a series of pipes extending out of the tank wall. Digestion gas from the gas dome is burned as fuel in the external heater or wasted to a gas burner.

The weight of the cover is supported by sludge, and the liquid forced up between the tank wall and the side of the cover provides a gas seal. Gas rises out of the digesting sludge, moves along the ceiling of the cover, and collects in the gas dome. The cover can float on the surface of the sludge between the landing brackets and the height of the overflow pipe. Rollers around the circumference of the cover keep it from binding against the tank wall.

Three functions of a single-stage floating-cover digester are (1) anaerobic digestion of the volatile solids, (2) gravity thickening, and (3) storage of the digested sludge. A floating-cover feature of the tank provides for a storage volume equal to approximately one-third that of the tank. The unmixed operation of the tank permits gravity thickening of sludge solids and withdrawal of the separated supernatant. Anaerobic digestion of the sludge solids is promoted by maintaining the digesting sludge near optimum temperature and stirring it through the recirculation of heated sludge. The rate of biological

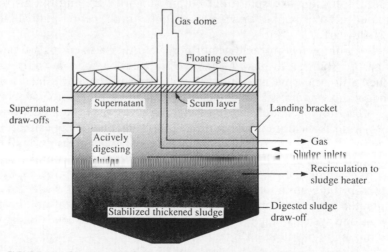

FIGURE 11   Cross-sectional diagram of a floating-cover anaerobic digester.

activity is inhibited by the lack of mixing; on the other hand, good mixing would prevent supernatant formation. Therefore, in single-tank operation, the biological process is compromised to allow both digestion and thickening to occur in the same tank.

In the operation of an unmixed digester, raw sludge is pumped to the digester from the bottom of the settling tanks once or twice a day. Supernatant is withdrawn daily and returned to the influent of the treatment plant. It is normally returned by gravity flow to the wet well during periods of low raw-wastewater flow, or, in the case of an activated-sludge plant, it may be pumped to the head end of the aeration basin. Because of the floating cover, supernatant does not have to be drawn off simultaneously with the pumping of raw sludge into the digester.

Digested sludge is stored in the tank and withdrawn periodically for disposal. Spreading of liquid sludge from smaller plants on grassland or cropland is common practice in agricultural regions. In larger plants, it is mechanically dewatered and used as a fertilizer and soil conditioner or hauled to land burial. In either case, weather often dictates the schedule for digested sludge disposal. In northern climates, the cover is lowered as close as possible to the corbels (landing brackets) in the fall of the year to provide maximum volume for winter sludge storage.

15   HIGH-RATE (COMPLETELY MIXED) DIGESTERS

The biological process of anaerobic digestion is significantly improved by complete mixing of the digesting sludge, either mechanically or by use of compressed digestion gases. Mechanical mixing is normally accomplished by an impeller suspended from the cover of the digester (Figure 12a). Three common methods of gas mixing are the injection of compressed gas through a series of small-diameter pipes hanging from the cover into the digesting sludge (Figure 12b); the use of a draft tube in the center of the tank, with compressed gas injected into the tube to lift recirculating sludge from the bottom and spill it out on top (Figure 12c); and the distribution of compressed gas to a number of diffusers mounted in the center at the bottom of the tank (Figure 12d).

A completely mixed digester may be either a fixed- or a floating-cover tank. Digesting sludge is displaced when raw sludge is pumped into a fixed-cover digester. When a floating cover is used, tank volume is available for the storage of digesting sludge, and withdrawals do not have to coincide with the introduction of raw sludge.

The homogeneous nature of the digesting sludge in a high-rate digester does not permit formation of supernatant. Therefore, thickening cannot be performed in a completely mixed digester. High-rate digestion systems normally consist of two tanks operated in series (Figure 13). The first stage is a completely mixed, heated, floating- or fixed-cover digester fed as continuously as possible, whose function is anaerobic digestion of the volatile solids. The second stage may be heated or unheated, and it accomplishes gravity thickening and storage of the digested sludge. Two-stage systems may consist of two similar floating-cover tanks with provisions for mixing in one tank.

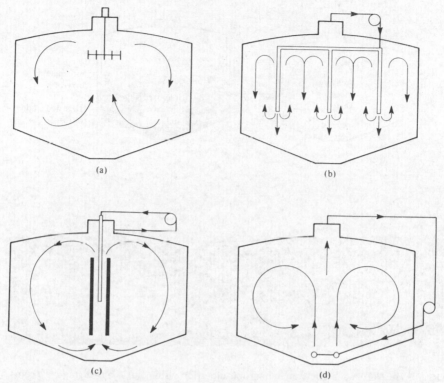

FIGURE 12   High-rate digester-mixing systems. (a) Mechanical mixing. (b) Gas mixing using a series of gas discharge pipes. (c) Gas mixing using a central draft tube. (d) Gas mixing using diffusers mounted on the tank bottom.

16   VOLATILE SOLIDS LOADINGS AND DIGESTER CAPACITY

Typical ranges of loadings and detention times employed in the design and operation of heated anaerobic digestion tanks treating domestic waste sludge are listed in Table 8. Values given for volatile solids loading and digester capacity for conventional, single-stage digesters are based on the total sludge volume available in the tank (i.e., the volume with the floating cover fully raised). Figures given for high-rate digestion apply only to the volume needed for the first-stage tank. There are no established design standards for the tank capacity required in second-stage thickening and supernatant separation.

The loading applied to a digester is expressed in terms of pounds of volatile solids applied per day per cubic foot of digester capacity. Detention time is the volume of the tank divided by the daily raw-sludge pumpage. Digester capacity in Table 8 is given in terms of cubic feet of tank volume provided per design population equivalent of the treatment plant.

The *Recommended Standards for Wastewater Facilities, Great Lakes–Upper Mississippi River Board of State Public Health & Environmental Managers* [6]

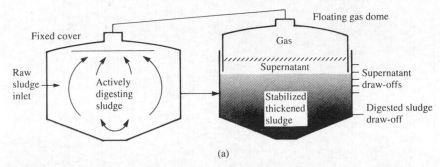

(a)

(b)

FIGURE 13   Sketch of a two-stage anaerobic digestion system. (a) The first stage is a completely mixed high-rate digester with a fixed cover. The second stage is a thickening and storage tank covered with a dome for collecting and storing gas. (b) Photograph of two-stage digesters, Lincoln, NE.

TABLE 8   Loadings and Detention Times for Heated Anaerobic Digesters

	Conventional Single-Stage (Unmixed)	First-Stage High-Rate (Completely Mixed)
Loading (lb/ft^3/day of VS)^a	0.02–0.05	0.1–0.2
Detention time (days)	30–90	15
Capacity of digester (ft^3/population equivalent)^b		
Primary only	2–1	0.4–0.6
Primary and secondary	4–6	0.7–1.5
Volatile solids reduction (%)	50–70	50

^{a}1.0 lb/ft^3/day = 16.0 kg/m^3/d
^{b}1.0 ft^3 = 0.0283 m^3

recommends a maximum loading of 0.08 lb/ft³/day of VS (1.3 kg/m³ · d) for high-rate digestion and a maximum of 0.04 lb/ft³/d(0.6 kg/m³/d) of VS loading for single-stage operation. These loadings assume that the raw sludge is derived from domestic wastewater, the digestion temperature is in the range of 85°–100°F (29°–38°C), volatile solids reduction is 40%–50%, and the digested sludge is removed frequently from the digester.

The capacity required for a single-stage floating-cover digester can be determined by the formula

$$V = \frac{F + A}{2} \times T_1 + A \times T_2 \qquad (11)$$

where

V = total digester capacity, ft³ (m³)
F = volume of average daily raw-sludge feed, ft³/d (m³/d)
A = volume of daily digested sludge accumulation in tank, ft³/day (m³/d)
  = $F - S$
S = daily supernatant withdrawal, ft³/day (m³/d)
T_1 = period required for digestion, days [approximately 25 days at a temperature of 85°–100°F (29°–38°C)]
T_2 = period of digested sludge storage, days (normally 30–120 days)

Figure 14 is a pictorial representation of Eq. (11).

Predicting daily volumes of raw sludge produced and the digested sludge accumulated as required in Eq. (11) is often difficult. Therefore, the capacity of conventional digesters frequently is based on empirical values relating digester capacity to the equivalent population design of the plant (Table 8). Values of 5 and 6 ft³/capita (0.14 and 0.17 m³/capita) are frequently used for high-rate trickling-filter plants and activated-sludge plants, respectively.

The minimum detention time for satisfactory high-rate digestion at 100°F (38°C) is approximately 15 days. In general, this limiting period depends on the minimum time required to digest the grease component of raw sludge. Also, too little detention time results in depletion of the methane-bacteria populations, since they are washed out of the digester. The maximum volatile solids loadings, at a 15-day detention time, vary

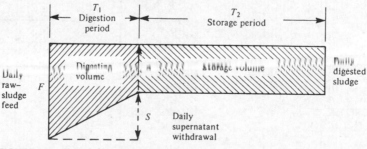

FIGURE 14   Pictorial presentation of Eq. (11).

from 0.1 to 0.2 lb/ft^3/day (1.6–3.2 kg/m$^3 \cdot$ d) for adequate volatile solids destruction and gas production. For larger treatment plants with uniform loading conditions, design values of a 15-day minimum detention time and maximum 0.15 lb/ft^3/day of VS loading appear to be satisfactory. Digesters for small treatment plants with wider variations in daily sludge production should be planned using more conservative loading rates.

The capacities required for a high-rate digestion system can be determined by the following equations:

$$V_{\mathrm{I}} = F \times T \tag{12}$$

where

V_{I} = digester capacity required for first-stage high-rate, ft^3 (m^3)
F = volume of average daily raw sludge feed, ft^3/day (m^3/d)
T = period required for digestion, days

and

$$V_{\mathrm{II}} = \frac{F + A}{2} \times T_1 + V_2 \times T_2 \tag{13}$$

where

V_{II} = digester capacity required for second-stage digested sludge thickening and storage, ft^3(m^3)
F = volume of digested sludge feed = volume of average daily raw sludge, ft^3/day (m^3/d)
A = volume of daily digested sludge accumulation in tank, ft^3/day (m^3/d)
T_1 = period required for thickening, days
T_2 = period of digested sludge storage, days

Figure 15 explains Eqs. (12) and (13).

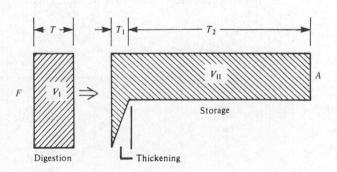

FIGURE 15   Diagrams for
Eqs. (12) and (13).

Example 11

A high-rate trickling-filter plant treats a domestic wastewater flow of 0.48 mgd. Determine the digester capacities required for a single-stage floating-cover digestion system. Digested sludge is to be dried on sand beds, and the longest anticipated storage period required is 90 days.

Solution:

$$\text{Equivalent population} = 4000 \text{ at } 0.24 \text{ lb per capita}$$

Assume the following:

$$\text{water content in raw sludge} = 96\%$$
$$\text{volatile solids in raw sludge solids} = 70\%$$
$$\text{water content of digested sludge} = 94\%$$
$$\text{volatile solids reduction} = 50\%$$

The volume of raw sludge, from Eq. (3), is

$$V = \frac{4000 \times 0.24}{[(100 - 96)/100]62.4} = 385 \text{ ft}^3/\text{day}$$

The volume of digested sludge is

$$V = \frac{0.30(4000 \times 0.24) + 0.70 \times 0.50(4000 \times 0.24)}{[(100 - 94)/100]62.4} - 167 \text{ ft}^3/\text{day}$$

Substituting into Eq. (11) yields

$$V = [(385 + 167)/2]25 + 167 \times 90 = 21{,}900 \text{ ft}^3$$

Check the volatile solids loading:

$$\frac{0.70 \times 4000 \times 0.24}{21{,}900} = 0.031 \text{ lb/ft}^3/\text{day of VS}$$

Verify the digester capacity per capita:

$$\frac{21{,}900}{4000} = 5.5 \text{ ft}^3/\text{population equivalent}$$

(This value is in the range of the empirical design figure of 4–6 ft^3/population equivalent given in Section 16.)

Example 12

A high-rate digester operating at a minimum temperature of 30°C with a volume of 2800 m^3 is fed 180,000 l/d of raw sludge with 7400 kg of solids that are 70% volatile. Calculate the concentration of solids in the raw sludge and in the digested sludge, assuming 50% volatile solids destruction, the volatile solids loading, and the detention time. Compare the loading and detention times with those given in Table 8.

Solution:

$$\text{raw sludge solids} = \frac{7400 \times 100}{180,000} = 4.1\%$$

$$\text{digested sludge solids} = \frac{(0.30 \times 7400 + 0.50 \times 0.70 \times 7400)100}{180,000} = 2.7\%$$

$$\text{volatile solids loading} = \frac{0.70 \times 7400}{2800} = 1.85 \text{ kg/m}^3 \cdot \text{d}$$

$$\text{detention time} = \frac{2800}{180} = 15.6 \text{ days}$$

Values in Table 8 are 1.6–3.2 kg/m^3 · d and 15 d.

---

17   AEROBIC SLUDGE DIGESTION

The function of aerobic digestion is to stabilize waste sludge solids by long-term aeration, thereby reducing the BOD and destroying volatile solids. The most common application of aerobic digestion is in handling waste activated sludge. Customary methods for disposal of the digested sludge are spreading on farmland, lagooning, and drying on sand beds.

The EPA specifies the degree of aerobic digestion and quality of the biosolids for application on agricultural land [1]. For pathogen reduction, the solids retention time and temperature must be between 40 days at 20°C (68°F) and 60 days at 15°C (59°F). (This range of 800–900 degree-days appears to be excessive for aerobic digestion of waste-activated sludge, without the addition of raw primary sludge, since the sludge age in the aeration tank is usually already 20 days or more prior to transfer to the aerobic digester.) For vector attraction reduction, the volatile solids reduction during sludge treatment must be at least 38%. If this is not achieved, the digested sludge can be tested in a bench-scale batch digester to determine whether the stability is adequate. The additional volatile solids reduction at 20°C is to be less than 15%. The concentrations of 10 toxic metals in the solids are limited for land application.

Aerobic digestion is accomplished in one or more tanks mixed by diffused aeration. Since dilute solids suspensions have a low rate of oxygen demand, the need for effective mixing rather than microbial metabolism usually governs the air supply required. The volume of air supplied for aerobic digestion is normally in the range of 15–30 cfm/1000 ft^3 of digester.

Design criteria vary with the type of activated-sludge system, BOD loading, and the means provided for ultimate disposal of the digested sludge. Small activated-sludge plants (e.g., package and factory-built, field-erected plants) without primary sedimentation are generally provided with 2–3 ft^3 (57–85 l) of aerobic digester volume per design population equivalent of the plant. This provides a conservative loading in the range of 0.01–0.02 lb/ft^3/d (0.16–0.32 kg/m^3 · d) of volatile solids loading. For stabilizing waste-activated sludge with a suspended-solids concentration of 1%–2%, the volatile solids loading should be limited to 0.04–0.08 lb/ft^3/d (0.64–1.28 kg/m^3 · d), and the aeration period should be 200–300 degree-days, computed by multiplying the digesting temperature in degrees Celsius times the sludge age. This equates to a minimum aeration period of 10 days at 20°C or 20 days at 10°C. Volatile solids and BOD reductions at these loadings are in the range of 30%–50%, and the digested sludge can be disposed of without causing odors or other nuisance conditions.

Long-term aeration of waste-activated sludge creates a bulking material that resists gravity thickening. The solids concentration of aerobically digested sludge is usually in the range of 1.0%–2.0%. The maximum concentration in a well-operated system is not likely to exceed 2.5%. This poor settleability frequently creates problems in disposing of the large volume of sludge produced. Thickening or dewatering by mechanical methods is often too expensive for incorporation in small treatment plants. Therefore, plant design should consider storage of aerobically digested sludge for hauling to land disposal.

An aerobic digester is operated as a semibatch process with continuous feed and intermittent supernatant and digested sludge withdrawals. The contents of the digester are continuously aerated during filling and for a specified period after the tank is full. Aeration is then discontinued, allowing the stabilized solids to settle. Supernatant is decanted and returned to the head of the plant, and a portion of the gravity-thickened sludge is removed for disposal. In practice, aeration and settlement may be a daily cycle with feed applied early in the day and clarified water decanted later in the day. Digested solids are withdrawn when the sludge in the tank does not gravity thicken to provide a supernatant with adequate clarity.

Example 13

Calculate the cubic meters of aerobic digester volume provided per design population equivalent, and estimate the volatile solids loading on the aerobic digester.

Solution: The data are

$$\text{volume of aerobic digester} = 153 \text{ m}^3$$
$$\text{design population of plant} = 2000$$

Therefore,

$$\text{volume provided} = \frac{153,000}{2000} = 76 \frac{\text{liters of digester volume}}{\text{design population equivalent}}$$

$$\text{BOD load on plant} = 182 \text{ kg/d}$$

Assuming a BOD loading of 0.20 g of BOD/g of MLSS applied to the aeration tank, the estimated excess sludge produced per day from Figure 1 is 0.42 g of SS/g of BOD load. For the digester volume of 153 m^3 and assuming 70% of the SS as volatile, the estimated volatile solids loading applied to the aerobic digester is $2.0(182 \times 0.70 \times 0.42)/153 = 0.70 \text{ kg/m}^3 \cdot \text{d}$.

Example 14

The wastewater treatment plant serving a resort community in a warm climate is an extended aeration system without primary clarifiers. Processing of the waste-activated sludge is by gravity thickening in basins without mechanical scrapers. After settling for about 12 hr, supernatant is drawn off and returned to the plant inlet and thickened sludge is discharged to open sand drying beds. This method of sludge processing has proven to be unsatisfactory for several reasons: high temperature of the waste-activated sludge with biological activity reduces settleability, resulting in significant overflow of solids in the supernatant; thickened sludge has only 1.5%–1.8% total solids; foul odors are emitted from the drying beds; and drying time is excessive. Thus, for several years, the majority of waste sludge has had to be hauled away as a liquid for disposal.

The wastewater flows currently exceed plant capacity during most of the tourist season, while during the off-season when the weather is cool the flows decrease by more than one-half. The proposed plant expansion to meet the high-season flows is to double the aeration capacity, construct aerobic digesters to stabilize and thicken the waste-activated sludge, and install belt presses to dewater the digested sludge. Laboratory and operations reports from the tourist season were studied for the past five years. From this study, the following data were established as values during the maximum month to be used for design of the expanded plant:

$$\text{Design flow} = 22{,}500 \text{ m}^3/\text{d}$$

$$\text{Design BOD load} = 10{,}100 \text{ kg/d } (450 \text{ mg/l})$$

$$\text{Total volume of aeration tanks} = 26{,}800 \text{ m}^3$$

$$\text{Operating MLSS in aeration tanks} = 4000 \text{ mg/l}$$

$$\text{Wastewater temperature} = 20° \text{ to } 25°\text{C}$$

$$\text{Effluent BOD} = {<}15 \text{ mg/l}$$

$$\text{Effluent suspended solids} = 15 \text{ mg/l}$$

$$\text{Waste-activated sludge volume} = 552 \text{ m}^3/\text{d}$$

$$\text{Waste-activated sludge solids} = 6900 \text{ kg/d } (1.25\%)$$

$$\text{Waste-activated sludge temperature} = 20°\text{C}$$

Perform preliminary calculations to determine the number and size of aerobic digesters required and discuss the general method of operation.

Solution: An aerobic digestion tank should be deep enough for gravity settling of solids with aeration off so that the underflow of sludge is thickened for dewatering and the supernatant is clear enough to return to the plant inlet. Minimum thickening requires zone settling with a compression depth of 1–2 m. Zone settling is represented by clear supernatant over a hindered settling layer underneath. Compression of settled solids occurs near the bottom of the tank. Adequate depth is also necessary to mount nonclog air diffusers for complete mixing and good oxygen transfer. For draw-and-fill batch operation, several identical tanks are necessary to allow aeration between raw sludge additions to stabilize the solids before withdrawal.

Four tanks are proposed to operate on a 4-day cycle. After adding raw sludge, the tank is aerated continuously for 3 days. On the fourth day, aeration is turned off and the solids are allowed to settle for several hours before withdrawal of digested sludge and draw-off of supernatant. Upon completion, waste-activated sludge is withdrawn from the wastewater aeration system to refill the digester.

Design criteria for the digesters are as follows:

$$\text{minimum aeration period for solids} = 240 \text{ degree-days}$$

$$\text{maximum volatile solids loading} = 1.28 \text{ kg/m}^3 \cdot \text{d}$$

$$\text{total solids reduction during digestion} = 30\%$$

$$\text{solids concentration in settled digested sludge} = 2.50\%$$

Consider four tanks, each 15 m square, side-water depth of 4.0 m plus 0.5 freeboard, and a hopper bottom with slopes toward a draw-off of approximately 1:3. The liquid volume of each tank is 1100 m^3 with 200 m^3 of this in the hopper.

$$\text{volatile solids loading} = \frac{0.70 \times 6900}{4 \times 1100} = 1.10 \text{ kg/m}^3 \cdot \text{d} \quad \text{(OK)}$$

$$\text{liquid detention time} = \frac{4 \times 1100}{552} = 8.0 \text{ d}$$

To increase solids stabilization, the sludge age is increased by retaining the maximum solids concentration in the tank. After aeration, the raw solids are reduced by 30%; therefore,

$$\text{digested solids remaining} = 0.70 \times 6900 = 4830 \text{ kg}$$

$$\text{volume of sludge withdrawn} = \frac{4830}{0.025 \times 1000} = 193 \text{ m}^3$$

Resulting from the withdrawal of this volume of sludge,

$$\text{liquid level in the tank lowers} = \frac{193}{15 \times 15} = 0.86 \text{ m}$$

To add 552 m^3 of raw sludge,

$$\text{supernatant draw-off required} = 552 - 193 = 359 \text{ m}^3$$

$$\text{liquid level in the tank lowers} = \frac{359}{15 \times 15} = 1.60 \text{ m}$$

$$\text{liquid remaining in the tank} = 1100 - 193 - 359$$
$$= 548 \text{ m}^3$$

$$\text{liquid level above the hopper} = 4.0 - 0.86 - 1.60$$
$$= 1.54$$

For ideal solids retention, the upper boundary of zone settling with a 2.5% solids concentration would be at the top of liquid level, but this would be an unrealistic expectation. Instead, assume the top of the zone settling is 0.5 m below the liquid surface, then

volume of settled sludge in tank

$$= (15 \times 15)(1.54 - 0.5) + 200(\text{in hopper}) = 434 \text{ m}^3$$
$$\text{dry weight of solids in tank} = 434 \times 1000 \times 0.025$$
$$= 10,900 \text{ kg}$$

Total solids in each tank before sludge withdrawal is this amount plus the digested solids resulting from the addition of raw waste solids after withdrawal of sludge and supernatant.

$$\text{total solids} = 10,900 + 0.70 \times 6900 = 15,700 \text{ kg}$$
$$\text{sludge age} = \frac{\text{solids in 4 tanks}}{\text{solids withdrawn}} = \frac{15,700 \times 4}{0.70 \times 6900} = 13.0 \text{ d}$$
$$\text{aeration period of solids} = 13.0 \times 20$$
$$= 260 \text{ degree-days} \quad (\text{OK})$$

---

18   OPEN-AIR DRYING BEDS

Historically, small communities have dewatered digested sludge on open beds because these systems are much simpler than more complex mechanical systems. The disadvantages include poor drying during damp weather, potential odor problems, large land area required, and labor for removing the dried cake. In construction of outmoded drying beds, the entire surface area was a level layer of coarse sand supported on a bed of graded gravel. Tile or perforated pipe underdrains were spaced about 20 ft apart in the bottom gravel layer to collect and return drainage to the treatment plant influent. Cleaning dried sludge cake from the beds was a laborious job. The cake had to be lifted from the surface of the sand by hand shoveling and taken off in wheelbarrows for loading in a truck. Attempts to use mechanical equipment resulted in excessive loss of sand and disturbance of the gravel underdrain.

In modern design, drying beds are constructed to permit the use of tractors with front-end loaders to scrape up the sludge cake and dump it into a truck. The main features as illustrated in Figure 16 are (1) watertight walls extending 18–24 in. above the surface of the bed; (2) an end opening in the wall, sealed by inserting planks, for entrance of a front-end loader; (3) centrally located drainage trenches filled with a coarse sand bed supported on a gravel filter with a perforated pipe underdrain; (4) paved areas on both sides of the trenches with a 2%–3% slope for gravity drainage; and (5) a sludge inlet at one end and supernatant draw-off at the opposite end. For this illustrated bed, the width is 40 ft and the length 100 ft. The operating procedure is to apply digested sludge to a depth of 12 in. or more, draw off supernatant after the solids settle, and allow the sludge to dry. A well-digested sludge forms a cake 3–5 in.

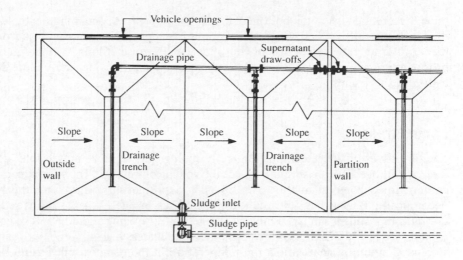

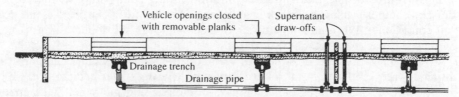

FIGURE 16   Open-air beds for drying digested sludge with paved surfaces to allow mechanical removal of dried cake. Water is separated by decanting supernatant, draining to trenches, and evaporation. *Source*: HDR Engineering, Inc.

thick that is thoroughly dry and black in color, and that has cracks resulting from horizontal shrinkage. Paved drying beds have been constructed with more limited drainage than shown in Figure 16; however, climatic conditions must be very favorable since the major water loss is by evaporation.

Rational design for sludge beds is difficult, owing to the multitude of variables that affect drying rate. These include climate and atmospheric conditions, such as temperature, rainfall, humidity, and wind velocity; sludge characteristics, including degree of stabilization, grease content, and solids concentration; depth and frequency of sludge application; and condition of the sand stratum and drainage piping. The bed area furnished for desiccating anaerobically digested sludge is from 1 to 2 ft^2/BOD design population equivalent of the treatment plant. Solids loadings average about 20 lb/ft^2/yr (100 kg/m^2 y) in northern states, while unit loading may be as high as 40 lb/ft^2/yr in southern climates. Drying time ranges from several days to weeks, depending on drainability of the sludge and suitable weather conditions for evaporation. Dewatering may be improved and exposure time shortened by chemical conditioning, such as addition of a polymer.

Air drying of digested sludge may be practiced in shallow lagoons where permitted by soil and weather conditions. Water removal is by evaporation, and the groundwater table must remain below the bottom of the lagoon to prevent contamination by seepage. Sludge is normally applied to a depth of about 2 ft and residue removed by a front-end loader after an extended period of consolidation. Because of long holding times, odor problems are more likely to occur. Design data and operational techniques are defined by local experience.

19   COMPOSTING

The objectives of sludge composting are to biologically stabilize putrescible organics, destroy pathogenic organisms, and reduce the volume of waste [7]. The optimum moisture content for a compost mixture is 50%–60%; less than 40% may limit the rate of decomposition, while over 60% is too wet to stack in piles. Volatile solids reduction during composting is similar to biological digestion, averaging about 50%. The compost product is a moist, friable humus with a water content less than 40%. For most efficient stabilization and pasteurization, the temperature in the compost piles should rise to 130°–150°F (55°–65°C) but not above 176°F (80°C). Moisture content, aeration rates, size and shape of pile, and climatic conditions affect composting temperature. The finished compost, although too low in nutrients to be classified as fertilizer, is an excellent soil conditioner. When mixed with soil, one advantage of the added humus content is increased capacity for retention of water.

The main products of biological metabolism in aerobic composting are carbon dioxide, water, and heat. Anaerobic composting produces intermediate organics, such as organic acids, and gases including carbon dioxide and methane. Since anaerobic decomposition has a higher odor potential and releases less heat, most systems are designed for aerobic composting. Nevertheless, all forms of composting have the potential for problems such as odors and dust.

Dewatered sludge cake, usually with a moisture content in the range of 70%–85%, is too wet to maintain adequate porosity for aeration. If it is not mixed with another substance, a pile of sludge cake tends to slump and compact to a dense mass with a wet, anaerobic interior and a dried exterior crust. Figure 17 is a generalized

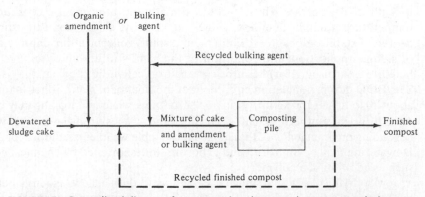

FIGURE 17   Generalized diagram for composting dewatered wastewater sludges.

diagram for composting organic sludges. Dewatered cake is mixed with either an organic amendment (e.g., dried manure, straw, or sawdust) or a recoverable bulking agent (e.g., wood chips) to reduce the unit weight and increase air voids. Finished compost may also be recycled and added to the wet cake. Although composting can be performed in an enclosed reactor, the common processes use outdoor piles either exposed or sheltered under a roofed structure. Compost may be placed in either windrows agitated by periodic turning for remixing and aeration or static piles with forced aeration. The choice between these two processes is based on several factors, including climate, environmental considerations, the availability of a bulking agent, and economics.

In the windrow system, mixed compost material is arranged in long parallel rows. These windrows are turned at regular intervals by mobile equipment to restructure the compost. The piles may be triangular or trapezoidal in shape and may vary in height and width, as determined by the equipment used for turning and the characteristics of the composting material. The height of windrows is usually 4–8 ft and the width 8–12 ft.

Windrow composting is used in agricultural regions where manure from confined feeding of cattle is available for an amendment. The manure is aged and dried by stacking in the feedlot. The wastewater sludge is unstable (raw) filter cake collected immediately after mechanical dewatering with polymer conditioning. Combined in approximately equal portions, the wet cake and dried manure are mixed using a modified manure spreader with the back beaters reversed so that the compost is deposited on the ground in a row rather than being thrown upward by the back beaters for widespread distribution. A large machine straddling the rows, equipped with an auger-type agitator between the outboard wheels, forms the shaped windrows; the same machine performs periodic turning. With weekly turning, stabilization requires 4–6 weeks in good weather. In northern climates, the windrows may freeze on the outside and be covered with snow for several weeks, preventing turning and slowing the rate of decomposition. The finished compost is stored and applied at appropriate times on grassland and cropland.

In the aerated static-pile process, oxygen is supplied by mechanically drawing air through the pile. Porosity is maintained by wood chips or a similar recyclable bulking agent, which also reduces the initial water content by absorption. The ratio of sludge to wood chips on a volumetric basis is in the range of 1:2 to 1:3. After a base of wood chips is prepared over perforated aeration piping, the mixture is placed on a pile 8–10 ft high. This is layered with finished compost to form a cover. Air is then drawn through the pile for a period of about 3 weeks by a blower operating intermittently to prevent excessive cooling. Exhaust air is vented and deodorized through a pile of finished compost. After stabilization, the mixture is cured and dried for several weeks either in the original pile or after moving to a stockpile. The wood chips are separated from the compost by vibrating screens for reuse.

PRESSURE FILTRATION

Sludges can be dewatered by pressure filtration using either a belt filter press or a plate-and-frame filter press. The belt filter press consists of two continuous porous belts that pass over a series of rollers to squeeze water out of the sludge layer compressed between the belts. A filter press consists of a series of recessed plates with cloth filters and intervening frames held together to form enclosed filter chambers. Sludge pumped under high pressure into these chambers forces water out through the cloth filters, filling the chamber with dewatered cake. At the end of the feed and pressure cycles, the plates are separated to remove the sludge cake. This type of pressure filter is noted for producing a dry cake.

20   DESCRIPTION OF BELT FILTER PRESS DEWATERING

The two-belt filter press shown in Figure 18 illustrates the basic operational steps. Before wet sludge is distributed on the top of the upper belt, it is conditioned with polymer to aggregate the solids. Initial dewatering takes place in the gravity drainage zone where the belt is supported on closely spaced small-diameter bars to allow separated water to drain freely through the belt into a collection pan. Some presses use an open framework or grid to support the belt. Small adjustable plastic drainage elements (cones, plows, or vanes, depending on the manufacturer) are supported just above the belt surface to open channels in the sludge to aid the release of free water. Depending on the characteristics of the applied sludge, up to one-half of the water is removed in the gravity zone; thus, the solids content is nearly doubled and the sludge volume halved. After dropping onto the lower belt, the sludge is gradually compressed between the two belts as they come together in the low-pressure, cake-forming zone. This wedge zone terminates with the two belts wrapping over the first of a series of rollers. Some machines have uniform diameter rollers, while on others the subsequent rollers decrease in diameter to gradually increase pressure on the cake. As the belts pass over these rollers, the confined sludge layer is subjected to both compression and shearing action caused by the outer belt being a greater distance from the center of the roller than the inner belt. Depending on the manufacturer, the rollers may be perforated stainless steel cylinders or plain carbon steel with a coating for protection against corrosion. The belt tension, alignment, and drive rollers have a rubber coating to increase frictional resistance and prevent slippage. The cake is scraped from the belts by doctor blades held against the belts.

Belts are made from several fabrics of synthetic fibers. Monofilament polyester woven fabrics with visible clear openings are used in dewatering wastewater sludges. As a result, solids pressed tightly on the surface can penetrate the pores of the fabric and belts can require washing with a high-pressure water spray. To confine and collect the wash water, the nozzles are housed in enclosures through which the belts pass. These wash boxes are located on both the upper and lower belts after cake discharge. Belt tensioning is performed by pressing one roller against each belt using hydraulic or pneumatic cylinders connected to the roller shaft. A tension that is too low results in belt slippage, while excess pressure can extrude sludge from between the belts. Each belt is kept centered on its rollers, using a steering assembly consisting of a device that senses the track of the belt and signals adjustment by an alignment roller. By actuating a hydraulic cylinder attached to one end of the shaft, this roller swivels, causing the track of the belt to move along the axis of the roller.

The option of a separate belt for the gravity drainage zone allows a longer time for water separation through a more porous belt than those used for the pressure zone.

Feed section   Belt support bars   Drainage elements

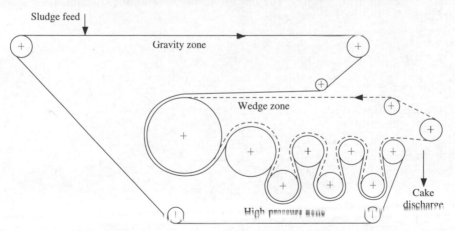

FIGURE 18   Two-belt filter press with a gravity drainage zone, wedge zone, and high-pressure zone. *Source:* Komline-Sanderson, Peapack, NJ.

Nevertheless, many two-belt presses are used in dewatering sludges where an independent gravity zone is not of additional benefit. In a three-belt press as diagrammed in Figure 19, the independent upper belt conveys wet sludge in the gravity zone and drops it on the lower belt of a two-belt press that compresses the sludge through the wedge zone and the high-pressure zone.

The layout of a belt filter press system is similar to that of a gravity belt thickener, shown in Figure 9 (Section 9), with one major exception. The wet cake from dewatering sludge at solids concentrations of 15%–25% is more like a semisolid than the liquid slurry of a thickened sludge of 5%–8% solids. Therefore, the cake is transported away from the belt press by a belt conveyor, screw conveyor, or cake pumps.

21   APPLICATION OF BELT FILTER DEWATERING

The most significant variables that affect dewatering performance of a belt filter press are the sludge characteristics, polymer conditioning, sludge feed rate, belt tension, and belt speed. The characteristics of greatest importance in wastewater sludges are the solids concentration, the nature of the solids, and prior biological or chemical conditioning. A press is limited to a hydraulic capacity essentially independent of solids concentration less than about 4%. For thin sludges, the recommended maximum loading is 50 gpm (11.4 m^3/h) per meter of belt width. For solids with contents greater than about 6%, the capacity of a press is restricted by solids loading. The nature of the solids influences both polymer flocculation and mechanical dewatering. Fibrous solids, commonly associated with primary clarifier settlings, are much easier to dewater than the fine, bulky biological solids wasted from secondary activated-sludge processing.

A polymer is applied to flocculate a sludge, forming aggregates of the particles to allow easier release of the water. The dosage of polymer applied per mass of solids

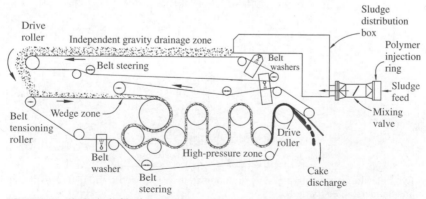

FIGURE 19   Three-belt filter press with one belt for the independent gravity zone for drainage of the flocculated sludge followed by two belts in the high-pressure zone for dewatering sludge confined between the belts. *Source:* Komline-Sanderson, Peapack, NJ.

dewatered depends essentially on the sludge characteristics and machine loading, which is in turn directly related to belt speed (detention time in the gravity dewatering zone). Besides inadequate flocculation, the maximum sludge feed rate can be governed by poor solids recovery, too wet a cake, or excessive polymer dosage. If sludge loading is too high, the detention time in the gravity drainage section cannot provide sufficient water release. The result is the extrusion of fine solids through the fabric and from between the belts at the edges. Excessive belt tension can also cause extrusion of solids. In actual plant operation, the acceptable loading is based on the economy of operation, the two major costs being the polymer consumption and hours of operation. A logical sequence for adjusting processing variables at a given sludge loading rate is to select a polymer dosage, adjust the belt speed, set the belt tension, and then readjust these three settings to achieve the desired cake dryness and solids recovery with the minimum polymer dosage.

The main performance parameters of a belt filter press are the hydraulic and solids loading rates, polymer dosage, solids recovery, cake dryness, wash-water consumption, and wastewater discharge. Hydraulic loading is expressed in gallons per minute of sludge feed per meter of belt width (cubic meters per meter per hour). Solids loading is expressed as the pounds of total dry solids feed per meter per hour (kilograms per meter per hour). The polymer dosage is calculated as the pounds applied per ton of total dry solids in the sludge feed (kilograms per tonne). Although the fraction of solids recovery is the quantity of dry solids in the cake divided by the dry solids in the feed sludge, it is often calculated based on the suspended solids in the wastewater (filtrate plus wash water) as follows:

$$\text{solids recovery} = \frac{\left(\begin{array}{c}\text{total solids}\\\text{in feed sludge}\end{array}\right) - \left(\begin{array}{c}\text{suspended solids}\\\text{in wastewater}\end{array}\right)}{\text{total solids in feed sludge}} \tag{14}$$

Cake dryness is expressed as the percentage of dry solids by weight in the cake. For easy comparison with hydraulic sludge loading, wash-water consumption and wastewater discharge are usually expressed in units of gallons per minute per meter of belt width (cubic meters per meter per hour). Example 15 illustrates the calculation of these parameters.

Example 15

A belt filter press with an effective belt width of 2.0 m is used to dewater an anaerobically digested sludge. The machine settings during operation are a sludge feed rate of 18.2 m³/h (80 gpm), polymer dosage of 1.8 m³/h (8.0 gpm) containing 0.20% powdered polymer by weight, belt speed of 6.1 m/min, belt tension of 4.7 kN/m of roller, and wash-water application of 15.4 m³/h (68 gpm) at 550 kN/m². Based on laboratory analyses, total solids in the feed sludge equal 3.5%, total solids in the cake are 32%, wastewater from belt washing contains 2600 mg/l suspended solids, and filtrate production measures 17.7 m³/h (78 gpm) with a suspended solids concentration of 550 mg/l. From these data calculate the hydraulic loading rate, solids loading rate, polymer dosage, and solids recovery. Comment on the production water usage and wastewater generated relative to the hydraulic sludge feed.

Solution:

$$\text{hydraulic loading rate} = \frac{18.2}{2} = 9.1 \text{ m}^3/\text{m} \cdot \text{h (40 gpm/m)}$$

$$\text{solids loading rate} = \frac{18.2 \text{ m}^3/\text{h} \times 1000 \text{ kg/m}^3 \times 0.035}{2 \text{ m}}$$

$$= 320 \text{ kg/m} \cdot \text{h (700 lb/m/hr)}$$

$$\text{polymer dosage} = \frac{1.8 \text{ m}^3/\text{h} \times 0.002 \times 1000 \text{ kg/m}^3 \times 1000 \text{ kg/t}}{320 \text{ kg/m} \cdot \text{h} \times 2.0 \text{ m}}$$

$$= 5.7 \text{ kg/t (11.4 lb/ton)}$$

wastewater suspended solids

$$= \text{wash-water solids} + \text{filtrate solids}$$

$$= \frac{15.4 \text{ m}^3/\text{h} \times 2600 \text{ g/m}^3 + 17.7 \text{ m}^3/\text{h} \times 500 \text{ g/m}^3}{2 \text{ m} \times 1000 \text{ g/kg}}$$

$$= 24 \text{ kg/m} \cdot \text{h (54 lb/m/hr)}$$

(Note that approximately 80% of the waste solids are in the wash water.)

$$\text{solids recovery} = \left(\frac{320 - 24}{320}\right)100 = 93\%$$

Wash-water consumption equals 7.7 m^3/m · h and the polymer feed is 0.9 m^3/m · h for a total of 8.6 m^3/m · h, and hence the process water added very nearly equals the 9.1 m^3/m · h sludge feed. Wastewater production is 16.5 m^3/m · h, composed of 7.7 m^3/m · h wash water and 8.8 m^3/m · h filtrate from the sludge and polymer solution water. This equals 1.8 times the sludge feed rate of 9.1 m^3/m · h.

22   SIZING OF BELT FILTER PRESSES

Belt widths of presses range from 0.5 to 3.0 m, with the most common sizes between 1.0 and 2.5 m. Some manufacturers supply only 1.0- and 2.0-m machines, while others build 1.5- and 2.5-m units. The selection during design of a sludge dewatering facility depends on such factors as the size of the plant, the desired flexibility of operations, anticipated conditions of dewatering, and economics. Typical results from filter pressing of wastewater sludges are listed in Table 9. The solids loading rates relate to both the feed solids concentration and hydraulic loading. For example, in the first line, a 4%

TABLE 9   Approximate Results from Belt Filter Press Dewatering of Polymer Flocculated Wastewater Sludges

Type of Sludge	Feed Solids (%)	Hydraulic Loading (gpm/m)[a]	Solids Loading (lb/m/hr)[b]	Cake Solids (%)	Active Polymer Dosage (lb/ton)[c]
Anaerobically digested primary only	4–6	40–60	1000–1600	20–28	4–8
Anaerobically digested primary plus waste activated	2–4	40–60	500–1000	16–22	6–12
Aerobically digested without primary	1–3	30–45	200–500	12–16	8–14
Raw primary and waste activated	3–6	40–50	800–1200	18–24	4–10
Thickened waste activated	3–5	40–50	800–1000	14–16	6–10
Extended aeration waste activated	1–3	30–45	200–500	12–16	8–14

[a]1.0 gpm/m = 0.225 m^3/m · h
[b]1.0 lb/m/hr = 0.454 kg/m · h
[c]1.0 lb/ton = 0.500 kg/tonne

feed at 50 gpm/m yields a solids loading of 1000 lb/m/hr. Also, the cake solids percentage decreases and the polymer dosage increases with greater dilution of the sludges and for those containing waste-activated sludge. Since performance of filter pressing depends on the character of the sludge, sizing of presses for new treatment plants without an existing sludge to test must be based on operating experience at other installations. While such data are more reliable than the values given in Table 9, new installations should be conservatively sized to account for the probable inaccuracy in projecting performance.

Design of a belt filter press installation at an existing facility can be reliably done by conducting field testing using a narrow-belt machine enclosed in a mobile trailer. Most manufacturers use a full-scale 0.5- or 1.0-m press that is representative of their larger machines. During the preliminary design phase, a rented trailer unit can be used to determine the dewaterability of the sludge and to establish testing criteria for the performance specifications. After sizing and design of the press facility, selection of the press manufacturer can be based on both competitive bidding and qualification testing using trailer units, either individually, with the lower bidder's press first, or as a group of several proprietary machines operating in parallel. This procedure reduces the risk in design by demonstrating that the selected manufacturer's press can achieve the results required by the performance specifications. This testing does not replace acceptance testing after construction, when the installed presses are evaluated to ensure compliance with the specifications.

Example 16

An existing wastewater treatment plant is going to install belt filter presses to dewater anaerobically digested sludge prior to stockpiling and spreading on agricultural land. The current system of lagooning and disposal of liquid sludge is expensive and has created environmental problems. Past sludge production records were studied to determine the following values for design. The average annual sludge quantity equals 80,000 gpd, with an average solids concentration of 5.0%. The design quantity during the peak month is 130,000 gpd at 4.0% solids, which contain 30% more dry solids than the annual average. The digesters have sufficient capacity to equalize the variations in raw-sludge feed during the peak month.

Field testing using a trailer-mounted press resulted in the following performance data. When the sludge feed had a solids concentration of 4.0%, the allowable hydraulic loading was 50 gpm/m (solids loading of 1000 lb/m/hr), producing a cake with a solids content of 22% with a polymer dosage of 9.6 lb/ton. At 5.0% sludge feed, acceptable operation was a hydraulic loading of 45 gpm/m (solids loading of 1100 lb/m/hr), producing a 24% cake with a polymer dosage of 8.1 lb/ton. Solids recoveries for all tests were between 94% and 96%. The polymer solution was 0.20% dry powder by weight, and wash-water usage was 32 gpm/m.

The design operating schedule is a maximum of 12 hr/day during the peak month. A minimum of two machines is desired so that sludge can be continuously dewatered if one unit is out of service. Based on these criteria, size the belt filter presses and determine the operating times under design conditions. For the average annual sludge quantity, calculate the polymer usage and weight of cake produced and estimate the wastewater generated.

Solution: The belt width required based on peak month operation is

$$\frac{130{,}000 \text{ gal}}{50 \text{ gpm/m} \times 60 \text{ min/hr} \times 12 \text{ hr}} = 3.6 \text{ m}$$

or

$$\frac{130{,}000 \text{ gal} \times 8.34 \times 0.040}{1000 \text{ lb/m/hr} \times 12 \text{ hr}} = 3.6 \text{ m}$$

Specify two belt filter presses with effective belt widths of 2.0 m. For these units, the operating time at the peak monthly load is

$$\frac{130{,}000 \text{ gal}}{2 \times 2.0 \text{ m} \times 50 \text{ gpm/m} \times 60 \text{ min/hr}} = 10.8 \text{ hr/day}$$

with both presses operating; with one unit operating, the time required is 21.6 hr/day. The operating time at the average annual load is

$$\frac{80{,}000}{2 \times 2.0 \times 45 \times 60} = 7.4 \text{ hr/day}$$

with both presses operating. Polymer usage at the average daily annual load is

$$\frac{80{,}000 \text{ gal} \times 8.34 \times 0.05 \times 8.1 \text{ lb/ton}}{2000 \text{ lb/ton}} = 140 \text{ lb/day}$$

The weight of cake produced is

$$\frac{80{,}000 \times 8.34 \times 0.05}{0.24 \times 2000} = 70 \text{ tons/day}$$

The flow of wastewater generated equals the wash water plus filtrate. The filtrate can be estimated by subtracting the theoretical volume of sludge cake from the sludge feed plus polymer solution.

$$\text{sludge feed} = 45 \text{ gpm/m}$$

polymer solution feed

$$= \frac{1100 \text{ lb/m/hr} \times 8.1 \text{ lb/ton}}{60 \text{ min/hr} \times 2000 \text{ lb/ton} \times 0.002 \text{ lb/lb} \times 8.34 \text{ lb/gal}} = 4 \text{ gpm/m}$$

theoretical flow of sludge cake

$$= \frac{1100 \text{ lb/m/hr}}{60 \text{ min/hr} \times 0.24 \text{ lb/lb} \times 8.34 \text{ lb/gal} \times 1.05} = 9 \text{ gpm/m}$$

$$\text{filtrate} = 45 - 4 - 9 = 32 \text{ gpm/m}$$

$$\text{wash water} = 32 \text{ gpm/m}$$

Therefore, the wastewater flow is $32 + 32 = 64$ gpm/m. The quantity of wastewater at the average daily annual load is

$$64 \text{ gpm/m} \times 4.0 \times 60 \text{ min/hr} \times 7.4 \text{ hr} = 110{,}000 \text{ gpd}$$

---

23 DESCRIPTION OF FILTER PRESS DEWATERING

The two types of plate-and-frame filter presses are the fixed-volume press and the variable-volume diaphragm press. Removal of dewatered cake from a fixed-volume press is done by manually separating the press frames and loosening the layers of cake from the recessed plates with a wooden paddle if they do not drop by force of gravity. The diaphragm press is designed for automatic operation. After opening, the cakes are forcefully discharged and the filter cloths are automatically washed before the press closes for another cycle.

Compared with belt presses, filter presses are more expensive, have higher operating costs, and are substantially larger machines for the same sludge processing capacity. In this system, dewatering of wastewater sludge requires lime and ferric chloride conditioning; polymer flocculation is not suitable. High cake dryness is the principal advantage of pressure filtration with cake solids content greater than 35% and up to 40%–50% possible.

A pressure filter consists of depressed plates held vertically in a frame for proper alignment and pressed together by a hydraulic cylinder (Figure 20). Each plate is constructed with a drainage surface on the depressed portion of the face. Filter cloths are

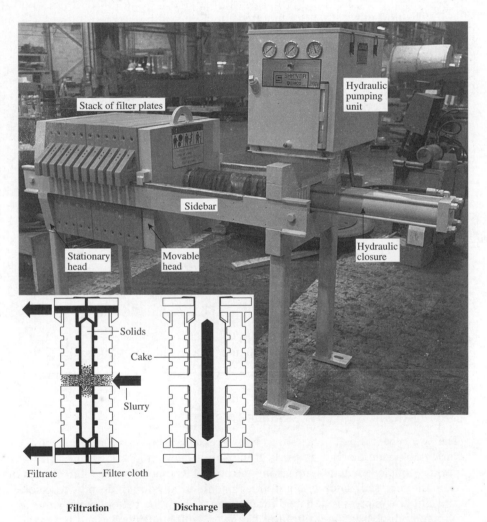

FIGURE 20   Pressure filter for dewatering waste slurries from water and wastewater processing. The two major components of the filter press are the skeleton frame and plate stack. With the plates clamped together, as shown on the left, waste slurry is pumped under pressure into the cavities between the plates and filtrate passes through the filter cloths to discharge as the cavities fill with solids. The cake is released, as shown on the right, by opening the plates. *Source*: EIMCO Process Equipment.

caulked onto the plate and peripheral gaskets seal the frames when the press is closed. Influent and filtrate ports are formed by openings that extend through the press. Sludge is pumped under pressure into the chambers between the plates of the assembly, and water passing through the media drains to the filtrate outlets. Solids retained form cakes between the cloth surfaces and ultimately fill the chambers. High pressure consolidates the cakes by applying air to the sludge inlet at about 225 psi (1550 kN/m^2). After this filter cycle, which requires from 2 to 3 hr, compressed air blows the feed sludge remaining in the influent ports back to a holding tank. The filter plates are separated and dewatered cakes drop out of the chambers into a hopper equipped with a conveyor mechanism. Cake release is assisted by introducing compressed air behind the filter cloths and by manually prodding with a paddle if necessary.

Chemical conditioning improves sludge filterability by flocculating fine particles so that the cake remains reasonably porous, allowing passage of water under high pressure. Dosages for conditioning wastewater sludges, expressed as percentages of dry solids in the feed sludge, are commonly 10%–20% CaO and 5%–8% $FeCl_3$. Precoating the media with diatomaceous earth or fly ash helps to protect against blinding and ensures easy separation of the cake for discharge. Filter aid for the precoat is placed by feeding a water suspension through the filter before applying sludge. In some cases, the aid may be added to the conditioned sludge mixture to improve porosity of the solids as they collect. Solids capture in pressure filtration is very high, commonly measuring 98%–99%. The organic sludge solids content in a typical cake is 35%. If the application of conditioning chemicals were 20%, the cake would have a total solids concentration, including chemicals, of 40%.

24   APPLICATION OF PRESSURE FILTRATION

Water treatment plant wastes are suited to pressure filtration because they are often difficult to dewater, particularly alum sludges and softening precipitates containing magnesium hydroxide. Figure 21 shows a schematic flow diagram for a pressure filtration process. Gravity-thickened alum wastes are conditioned by the addition of lime slurry. A precoat of diatomaceous earth or fly ash is applied prior to each cycle, and conditioned sludge is then fed continuously to the pressure filter until filtrate ceases and the cake is consolidated under high pressure. A power pack holds the chambers closed during filtration and transports the movable head for opening and closing. An equalization tank provides uniform pressure across the filter chambers as the cycle begins. Prior to cake discharge, excess sludge in the inlet ports of the filter is removed by air pressure to a core separation tank. Filtrate is measured through a weir tank and recycled to the inlet of the water treatment plant. Cake is transported by truck to a disposal site.

Alum sludges are conditioned using lime and/or fly ash. Lime dosage is in the range of 10%–15% of the sludge solids. Ash from an incinerator, or fly ash from a power plant, is applied at a much higher dosage, approximately 100% of dry sludge solids. Polymers may also be added to aid coagulation. Fly ash and diatomaceous earth

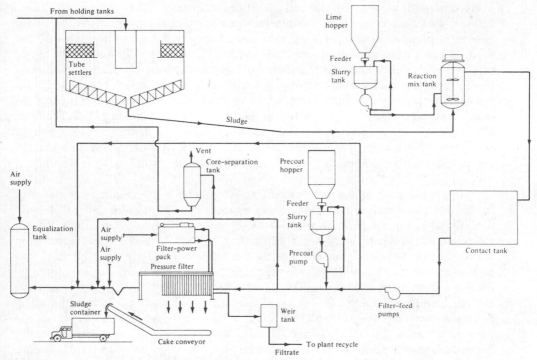

FIGURE 21   Schematic flow diagram for conditioning and filter-press dewatering of alum sludge from surface water treatment. *Source:* G. P. Westerhoff and M. P. Daly, "Water-Treatment-Plant Waste Disposal," *J. Am. Water Works Assoc.* 66, no. 7 (1974): 443. Copyright 1974 by the American Water Works Association, Inc.

are used for precoating; the latter requires about 5 lb/100 ft^2 of filter area. Under normal operation, cake density is 40%–50% solids and has a dense, dry, textured appearance.

Wastewater sludges are amenable to dewatering by pressure filtration after conditioning with ferric chloride and lime or fly ash. Minimum ferric chloride and lime dosages are 5% and 10%, respectively, for a waste concentration of 5% solids or greater. Conditioning with fly ash requires 100%–150% additions. Either diatomaceous earth or fly ash is used for precoating the filter media.

CENTRIFUGATION

Solid-bowl decanter centrifuges are used to dewater waste sludges from both wastewater and water treatment plants. Dewatering of wastewater sludge by centrifugation is an economic choice in large plants (usually greater than 40 mgd) where costs of machines and a facility building, operating costs, and disposal of drier cake are less than for an equivalent belt filter press system. For water treatment plant wastes, the advantages are thickening sludges from which pore water is difficult to separate (e.g., alum coagulation residues) and for which high solids concentration is desirable (e.g., lime-softening precipitates prior to recalcining).

25   DESCRIPTION OF CENTRIFUGATION

The basic operating principles of a solid-bowl decanter centrifuge are illustrated in Figure 22. A centrifuge is like a clarifier with the base wrapped around a center line so that its rotation generates gravitational force of 1000–4000 times the force of gravity. The greater the rotational speed, the more rapidly the solids in the sludge are spun out against the rotating bowl wall. While the separated water forms a concentric inner layer and overflows the adjustable plate dam, the settled solids are compacted and moved onto a conical drainage area for further dewatering. The scroll (helical screw conveyor) pushing the solids operates at a higher rotational speed than the bowl.

The solid-bowl decanter centrifuge is the best kind of centrifuge to provide centrate clarity and cake dryness for a wide variety of granular, fibrous, flocculent, and gelatinous solids in sanitary sludges. The cutaway view in Figure 23 shows the construction of an actual centrifuge, including feed input, conveyor, bowl, and adjustable plate dam. Feed slurry enters at the center and is spun against the bowl wall. Settled solids are moved by the conveyor to one end of the bowl and out of the liquid for drainage before discharge, while clarified effluent discharges at the other end over a dam plate. This system is best suited for separating solids that compact to a firm cake and can be conveyed easily out of the water pool. If solids compact poorly, moving a soft cake causes redispersion, resulting in poor clarification and a wet concentrate. Flocculent solids are made scrollable by chemical conditioning of the sludge.

A major advantage of scroll dewatering is operational flexibility. Machine variables include pool volume, bowl speed, and conveyor speed. The depth of liquid in the bowl and the pool volume can be controlled by an adjustable plate dam. Pool volume adjustment varies the liquid retention time and changes the drainage deck surface area in the solids-discharge section. The bowl speed affects gravimetric forces on the settling particles, and conveyor rotation controls the solids retention time. The driest cake results when the bowl speed is high; the pool depth is the minimum allowed, and the differential speed between the bowl and conveyor is the maximum possible. Flexibility of operation allows a range of densities in the solids discharge varying from a dry cake to a thickened liquid slurry. Feed rates, solids content, and prior chemical conditioning can also be varied to influence performance.

The performance of centrifuge dewatering for given feed and machine-operating conditions depends on the dosage of polymers and other chemical coagulants. Suspended-solids removal and usually cake dryness is increased with greater chemical additions, while carryover of solids in the centrate decreases. There is, however, a saturation point at which flocculent dosage does not significantly improve centrate clarity. Optimum chemical conditioning without overdosing can be determined most reliably by full-scale or pilot-plant tests. For some wastes, centrate recycling can improve overall suspended-solids removal, but for others it may cause upset, owing to an accumulation of fine particles.

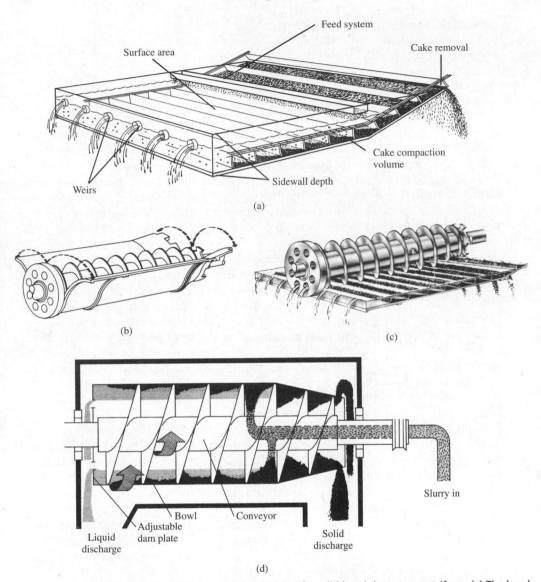

FIGURE 22   Diagrams illustrating the operating principle of a solid-bowl decanter centrifuge. (a) The bowl represents a clarifier with defined surface area and retention time with overflow weirs. (b) The bottom of the clarifier is wrapped around a centerline to form a bowl that rotates to increase the gravitational force for sedimentation. (c) The liquid flows through the long narrow channel formed by the helical screw conveyor against the bowl and out over the weirs. (d) As the liquid discharge flows out over the weir (adjustable dam plate), the settled solids are moved by the conveyor out of the liquid onto a conical drainage area for dewatering prior to discharge. *Source*: Alfa Laval Sharples, Alfa Laval Separation, Inc.

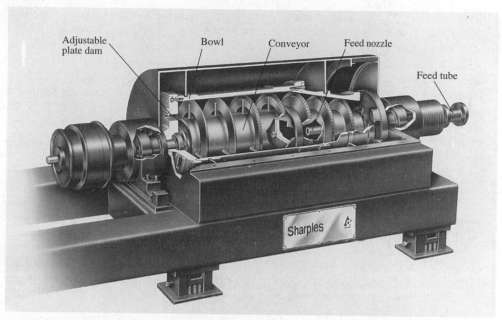

FIGURE 23   Solid-bowl decanter centrifuge. *Source:* Alfa Laval Sharples, Alfa Laval Separation, Inc.

26   APPLICATIONS OF CENTRIFUGATION

The characteristics of a wastewater sludge to be dewatered determine the centrifugation capacity, chemical conditioning, cake dryness, and solids recovery. The ratio of primary to waste-activated solids in a sludge has a significant effect. For illustration, consider the following typical performance data in dewatering different kinds of sludges by using an adequate polymer dosage for a minimum of 90% solids recovery: raw primary, cake solids of 28%–34%, and polymer dosage of 2–4 lb/ton of dry solids; raw primary plus waste-activated sludge, cake solids of 18%–25%, and polymer dosage of 6–14 lb/ton; and raw waste-activated sludge, cake solids of 14%–18%, and polymer dosage of 12–20 lb/ton [3]. Usually, the cake solids can be increased a few percentage points by applying an excessive polymer dosage. Machine loadings have notable influence on performance. Underloading allows reduced polymer dosage and produces a drier cake. As the loading increases toward the capacity of the centrifuge, the required polymer dosage increases and the cake becomes wetter. Therefore, to be cost effective, dewatering must take into account machine loading relative to hours of operation per day and the operational cost of standby centrifuge capacity.

The number of centrifuges and operating hours are designated in design. An installation requires at least one standby machine. More may be required depending on availability of maintenance service and alternative methods of disposal. For example, wastewater plants under 20 mgd should have two full-sized machines (one + one standby); plants between 20–100 mgd should have a minimum of three machines (two + one); and those over 250 mgd should have a minimum of six machines (four + two) [3]. The designer's performance specification designates the sludge characteristics (raw or digested, solids concentrations, ratio of primary to waste activated, and temperature) and performance requirements (sludge flow rates, minimum cake solids, minimum solids recovery, and polymer dosage). The design engineer does not normally select the actual model and size of the centrifuges unless on-site testing has been conducted. Field tests of two or more machines are run concurrently so that all are dewatering sludge with the same characteristics. The testing range of flow and solids loadings should be adequate to fully evaluate plant operations. The test machines must represent the full-scale centrifuges that will be provided by the manufacturer for installation.

Water treatment plant wastes are also amenable to centrifuge dewatering. For alum sludges from surface water treatment, centrifugation performance must be verified by testing at each plant, since sludge characteristics vary considerably. In general, aluminum hydroxide slurries from coagulation settling and gravity-thickened backwash waters can be concentrated to a truckable pasty sludge of about 20% solids. The removal efficiency in a scroll centrifuge ranges from 50% to 95%, based on operating conditions and polymer dosage, and the centrate is correspondingly turbid or clear. Lime-softening precipitates compact more readily than alum floc. A gravity-thickened sludge of 15%–25% solids can be dewatered to a solidified cake of 65%. Solids recovery is often 85%–90% with polymer flocculation.

Example 17

A conventional activated-sludge plant mixes primary and thickened waste-activated sludges prior to high-rate anaerobic digestion. Currently, the digested sludge is stored and thickened in sludge lagoons. Using a dredge, the bottom layer of sludge with a solids concentration of about 8% is pumped into tank trucks and hauled to a dedicated land disposal site. This method of disposal has resulted in complaints about truck traffic, foul odors, potential environmental problems, and high cost of hauling. Because of these factors and the steady increase in raw wastewater flow into the plant, installation of a biosolids dewatering facility using centrifugation has been proposed. An environmental solid-waste management company would be hired under contract to haul and sell the biosolids to local farmers for fertilizer and soil conditioner, with a portion of the profit applied to treatment plant expenses.

Table 10 lists the current and design wastewater flows, BOD and suspended-solids loads, waste solids produced based on existing records, and projected digested-solids production for 15 years in the future when the plant is expected to reach design flow. Outline the primary considerations for design of a biosolids dewatering facility using centrifugation.

Solution:

Equalization of Digested Sludge Feed

Because of existing structures on the plant site, the biosolids dewatering building, load-out structure, and truck parking area must be sited remote from the anaerobic digesters. Therefore, the digested sludge must be pumped to a location near the dewatering facility and stored in feed tanks. Based on design maximum volume of digested

TABLE 10 Current and Design Wastewater Flows, BOD and Suspended-Solids Loads, and Projected Anaerobically Digested Sludge Production for Example 17

Parameter	Current Annual Average	Current Maximum Month	Design Annual Average	Design Maximum Month
Wastewater flow (mgd)	150	190	220	260
BOD load (lb/d)	260,000	310,000	450,000	670,000
Suspended-solids load (lb/d)	210,000	260,000	400,000	450,000
Primary solids (lb/d)	140,000	—	—	—
Waste-activated solids (lb/d)	100,000	—	—	—
Total solids (lb/d)	240,000	—	—	—
Digested-solids production (lb/d)	170,000	—	—	—
Digested-solids concentration (%)	2–3	—	—	—
Digested-sludge volume at 2.0% (gal/d)	1,020,000	—	—	—
Projected digested-solids production (lb/d)	—	—	250,000	330,000
Projected digested-solids concentration (%)			2.0	2.0
Projected digested-sludge volume at 2.0% (gal/d)			1,500,000	2,000,000

sludge (Table 10), four 250,000-gal storage tanks are needed for a half-day retention time. This storage time with mixing at a 30-min turnover rate is to maintain uniform conditions to moderate changes in solids concentration, since even a minor change in concentration can reduce consistency of the cake discharged from the centrifuges. Screening of the feed sludge between the storage tanks and centrifuges should be considered.

Size and Number of Centrifuges

Selecting the size of centrifuges is based on estimated costs, operation, and service experience. Mid-size machines are chosen, rather than large, because they have been in service for a much longer operating record. Although capacities vary somewhat with manufacturers, typical recommended design values of flow rate and solids loading for mid-size centrifuges are as follows: flow rate of 200–300 gpm (up to 450 gpm maximum) and solids loading of 2400–5500 lb/hr (up to 8000 lb/hr maximum). The centrifuges are to be operated continuously, since the plant is staffed 24 hr/d for 7 d/wk and significant cost savings result from continuous operation. The sludge cake hoppers are to provide 2 days' storage so that biosolids do not have to be trucked away on the weekend.

The following calculations determine the required number of operating centrifuges based on data given in Table 10, assuming a median flow rate of 250 gpm to each centrifuge.

$$\text{At current annual average: } \frac{1,020,000}{250 \times 1440} = 2.8 \text{ centrifuges}$$

$$\text{Solids loading with three centrifuges} = \frac{170,000}{3 \times 24} = 2400 \text{ lb/hr}$$

$$\text{At design annual average:} \frac{1,500,000}{250 \times 1440} = 4.2 \text{ centrifuges}$$

$$\text{Solids loading with four centrifuges} = \frac{250,000}{4 \times 24} = 2600 \text{ lb/hr}$$

$$\text{At design maximum month:} \frac{2,000,000}{250 \times 1440} = 5.6 \text{ centrifuges}$$

$$\text{Solids loading with six centrifuges} = \frac{330,000}{6 \times 24} = 2300 \text{ lb/hr}$$

Two additional machines are to be added, one for standby and one for maintenance. Therefore, at design capacity of the treatment plant, the recommended number of mid-size centrifuges is eight.

Polymer Feed System

Polymers are available in dry-powder or granular form and in concentrated liquid as emulsion or solution. Figure 24 is a day tank system for feeding either dry or liquid polymers. The components to prepare a diluted aged polymer solution from dry forms are bulk storage for a 20–30-day supply, volumetric feeder calibrated to deliver the required amount per batch, mixed aging tank to improve activation, and transfer pump to day tank. Liquid polymers require little or no aging time and can be pumped

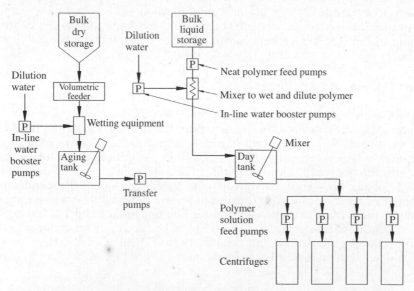

FIGURE 24   Polymer feed system with a day tank for diluted solution from either dry or liquid forms of polymer. *Source:* HDR Engineering, Inc.

through a mixing unit for dilution to a day tank. Since activated polymers are unstable after 2–3 days, the diluted polymer solution should be used daily. Consideration should be given to installing only one polymer feed system with space provided for future installation of the other. Polymer solution is fed to each centrifuge by a positive displacement pump.

The expected performance in dewatering the dilute anaerobically digested sludge is as follows: active polymer dosage of 13 lb/ton with an operating range of 9–17 lb/ton, cake solids of 28% with an operating range of 25%–32%, and solids capture of 95% with an operating range of 95%–98%.

Cake Conveyance and Loadout

Cake can be conveyed by belt conveyors, augers, and cake pumps. The belt conveyor is a continuous revolving belt supported by a framework of rollers and is most effective in long straight runs. The auger is a rotating screw that pushes solids along the bottom of a U-shaped trough that can be covered to contain spillage and odors. The cake pump is a hydraulically driven high-pressure positive-displacement twin-cylinder reciprocating piston pump capable of pushing semisolid cake through a pipeline. Thus, the solids are enclosed, preventing spillage and emission of odors.

The cake conveyance system recommended is a combination of augers and cake pumps. Figure 25 is a schematic plan view showing the installation locations of eight centrifuges with additional spaces for future installation of four more machines. An inclined auger receives the cake discharge from each centrifuge and conveys it to one of two horizontal augers. Each inclined auger is sized for 40 gpm, which is the maximum volume of cake discharge of 5500 lb/hr of dry solids at a solids concentration of 25%. Although normal operation is for each horizontal conveyor to transport cake discharge from only two centrifuges, the design capacity is 160 gpm for receiving cake from four centrifuges. The cake pumps are located at each cake hopper for a total of six pumps, each with a pumping rate of 120–160 gpm with discharge pressure up to 600–800 psi for a maximum discharge pipe length of 200–250 ft. The pipes terminate at the top of the loadout hoppers 50 ft above ground level.

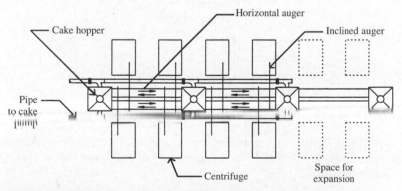

FIGURE 25 Plan view of eight installed centrifuges showing locations of machines, inclined augers, horizontal augers, cake hoppers, and piping to cake pumps. *Source:* HDR Engineering, Inc.

The loadout structure is to have two truck bays each with two hoppers, for a total 2-day cake storage capacity of 40,000 ft^3 weighing 2,600,000 lb. The hopper configuration is cylindrical, with slide gates and openings with splash protection. Loadout operations are to be designed for an 8-hr shift. The truck loading time is assumed to be 10–15 min. With a maximum truck load of 45,000 lb and two bays in operation, 64–96 loads can be hauled away in an 8-hr period.

CYCLING OF WASTE SOLIDS IN TREATMENT PLANTS

Centrate (the liquid removed in centrifugation) from dewatering sludge is returned to the head of a treatment plant, contributing suspended solids and BOD to the raw-wastewater influent. In addition to centrate from centrifuges, other recycled flows from sludge processes are supernatant from anaerobic or aerobic digesters, flow from gravity thickeners, and filtrate from belt presses and pressure filters. Consequently, poor solids capture in sludge thickening and dewatering contribute to the load on the plant and cycling of solids within the system. Being colloidal in nature, many of the finer solids pass through primary sedimentation for capture in biological aeration and return in the waste secondary sludge for thickening and dewatering again. Cycling solids can lead to overloading and upset of all treatment processes. However, their presence is normally first noticed by a thinner primary sludge and an increase in the oxygen demand of biological aeration.

27   SUSPENDED-SOLIDS REMOVAL EFFICIENCY

A relatively easy method of estimating solids capture by a sludge-thickening or dewatering unit is to measure solids concentrations in the process flows. The relationship is developed as follows. The solids mass balance is given in Eq. (15), and the liquid volumetric balance in Eq. (16):

$$M_S = M_R + M_C \tag{15}$$

$$Q_S = Q_R + Q_C \tag{16}$$

where

M_S, Q_S = mass of solids and quantity of flow of feed sludge
M_R, Q_R = mass of solids and quantity of return flow
M_C, Q_C = mass of solids and quantity of flow of thickened sludge or cake

Without introducing significant error, the specific gravity of all flows can be assumed to be 1.00. Hence, the mass of solids M in a process flow stream is the rate of flow Q times the solids concentration S.

$$M = Q \times S \tag{17}$$

Combining these equations results in the following relationships:

$$\frac{M_C}{M_S} = \frac{S_C(S_S - S_R)}{S_S(S_C - S_R)} \tag{18}$$

where

M_C/M_S = fraction of solids removal (solids capture)
S_C = solids concentration in thickened sludge or cake
S_S = solids concentration in feed sludge
S_R = solids concentration in return flow

$$\frac{Q_R}{Q_S} = \frac{S_C - S_S}{S_C - S_R} \tag{19}$$

where

Q_R/Q_S = fraction of feed sludge appearing as return flow

The solids concentrations S can be either total solids (residue upon evaporation) or suspended solids (nonfilterable residue). Testing for suspended solids by the standard laboratory technique of filtration through a glass filter is feasible for dilute suspensions where dissolved solids are a major portion of the total solids. In contrast, wastes with high solids contents are difficult to test accurately by laboratory filtration. Therefore, suspended-solids analysis of a sludge sample is performed by a total-solids test that is corrected by subtracting an estimated dissolved-solids concentration. The procedure does not create significant error since the filterable solid content usually amounts to less than 5% of the total solids in the sludge samples.

Example 18

A scroll centrifuge dewaters an alum–lime sludge containing 8.0% solids at a feed rate of 20 gpm. The cake produced has a solids concentration of 55% and the centrate contains 9000 mg/l. Calculate the solids removal efficiency and the centrate flow.

Solution: From Eq. (18),

$$\text{solids removal} = \frac{M_C}{M_S} = \frac{55(8.0 - 0.9)}{8.0(55 - 0.9)} = 0.90\ (90\%)$$

Substituting into Eq. (19) yields

$$Q_R = 20\ \text{gpm} \times \frac{55 - 8.0}{55 - 0.9} = 17.4\ \text{gpm}$$

Example 19

The operation of a vacuum filter dewatering wastewater sludge was analyzed by sampling and testing the feed sludge and cake for total-solids content and the filtrate for both total-solids and suspended-solids concentrations. The presence of conditioning chemicals was ignored, since the polymer addition amounted to only 3% of the solids content in the sludge. Based on the following laboratory results, estimate the suspended-solids capture and the fraction of flow of feed sludge appearing as filtrate.

	Total Solids (mg/l)	Suspended Solids (mg/l)
Sludge	36,600	
Cake	158,000	
Filtrate	10,800	8700

Solution: Calculate the dissolved solids in the filtrate:

$$DS = TS - SS = 10{,}800 - 8700 = 2100 \text{ mg/l}$$

Applying this value to the sludge and cake, one sees that suspended-solids concentrations for all three flows are

$$S_C = 158{,}000 - 2100 = 156{,}000 \text{ mg/l}$$
$$S_S = 36{,}600 - 2100 = 34{,}500 \text{ mg/l}$$
$$S_R = 8700 \text{ mg/l}$$

Substituting into Eqs. (18) and (19) yields

$$\text{solids removal} = \frac{M_C}{M_S} = \frac{156{,}000 \times (34{,}500 - 8700)}{34{,}500 \times (156{,}000 - 8700)} = 0.79 \ (79\%)$$

$$\frac{\text{filtrate flow}}{\text{sludge feed}} = \frac{Q_R}{Q_S} = \frac{156{,}000 - 34{,}500}{156{,}000 - 8700} = 0.82 \ (82\%)$$

The recommendation is to replace the vacuum filters with belt filter presses during the next treatment plant renovation.

FINAL DISPOSAL OR USE

Table 11 summarizes the estimated final disposition of waste solids from municipal wastewater treatment plants. Spreading on agricultural land as a fertilizer and soil conditioner is the fastest growing method of use, currently amounting to approximately two-thirds of land-applied biosolids. Codisposal with municipal solid waste accounts for the disposal of about one-third of waste sludge. Nevertheless, because of the difficulty in burying wet sludge and high cost of preparing an environmentally safe landfill, treatment plants are often encouraged to process waste sludge to produce biosolids for land application. Where land is economically available, often near the plant, a site may

TABLE 11 Estimated Final Disposal or Use of Waste Sludge Based on Survey Data of the Majority of Municipal Wastewater Treatment Plants.[a]

Method of Ultimate Disposal or Use	Treatment Plants		Quantity of Sludge	
	Number	Percentage (%)	Dry Solids (1000 tons)	Percentage (%)
Land application on agricultural land, forest, and reclamation sites	4700	49	1600	35
Codisposal in municipal solid waste sites	3000	32	1600	35
Surface disposal by burial or injection at dedicated sites	1400	15	600	13
Incineration in furnaces and other incinerators	400	4	800	17
Ocean disposal	0	Ocean Dumping Ban Act of 1988		

[a]Adopted from [1].

be dedicated solely for the purpose of sludge disposal by burial, impoundment in lagoons, or subsurface injection.

Land application, codisposal, and surface disposal are discussed separately in subsequent sections.

Incineration involves drying sludge cake to evaporate the water and burning for complete oxidation of the volatile solids at high temperature to deodorize exhaust gases. Natural gas or fuel oil is frequently needed for complete combustion. The fuel value of sludge solids is low; they are usually unable to sustain combustion because of heat absorbed for evaporation of water and losses in stack gases and radiation through furnace walls [4]. Incineration is rarely used where land disposal or use is possible; hence, most sludge burning is done in large metropolitan areas. The survey data in Table 11 estimate that 4% of the treatment plants dispose of 17% of waste sludge by incineration.

Water treatment plant waste solids are commonly disposed of in municipal solid waste sites and burial in monofills at dedicated sites. As a result of increasing regulatory and environmental constraints, surface application on agricultural land, dedicated sites, and for land reclamation is increasing as a disposal option. Comprehensive quantitative data on final disposal or use of water treatment plant wastes are not available.

28 LAND APPLICATION

The EPA Standards for the Use and Disposal of Sludge define the quality parameters for biosolids applied on land as a soil conditioner and fertilizer. The key concerns are selected metals, vector attraction (the attraction of disease vectors such as flies), and human pathogens. Sludge samples are tested for the following 10 metals: arsenic, cadmium, chromium, copper, lead, mercury, molybdenum, nickel, selenium, and zinc. For each metal, numerical limits are established for the maximum concentration expressed in milligrams of metal per kilogram of biosolids and annual loading rate in kilograms of metal applied per hectare of land. Vector attraction limits and pathogen reductions are applied to two categories of biosolids, Class A and Class B.

Class A biosolids can be applied in land areas open to the public and sold in bag or container form. To reduce vector attraction and pathogen levels, disinfection treatment for production of Class A is usually by thermal treatment defined by time and temperature or high-pH, high-temperature alkaline treatment. The levels of pathogens cannot exceed one plaque-forming unit (PFU) of enteric virus and cannot exceed one viable helminth ovum in 4 g of total-sludge biosolids (dry weight). The level of bacteria must be less than 3 most probable number (MPN) of *Salmonella* spp in 4 g of total-sludge biosolids (dry weight) or less than 1000 MPN of fecal coliforms per 1 g of total-sludge biosolids (dry weight) [8].

Class B biosolids can be applied on agricultural land for fodder, fiber, and seed crops and selected food crops with different site restrictions imposed for harvesting, animal grazing, and public contact based on the particular crop. The common sludge treatment processes for Class B are biological digestion for a minimum volatile-solids reduction at a defined temperature and mean cell residence time for anaerobic digestion (Section 13) and aerobic digestion (Section 17). The pathogen requirement for application of digested sludge on agricultural land is a fecal coliform density in sludge solids not to exceed 2 million CFU (colony forming units) or MPN (most probable number) per gram of total-sludge biosolids (dry weight) [8]. The monitoring procedure for Class B requires that the average geometric mean fecal coliform density of seven treated sludge samples be less than 2 million CFU or MPN per gram of total-sludge biosolids (dry weight).

Biosolids contain plant macronutrients of nitrogen and phosphorus and micronutrients such as boron, copper, iron, manganese, molybdenum, and zinc. The organic matter is a valuable soil conditioner, making clayey soils more friable and increasing the water-holding capacity of sandy soils.

Approximately two-thirds of biosolids are applied to cropland planted with corn, soybeans, cotton, small grains, and forages like alfalfa and clover. The typical rate of application is 5 ton/ac/yr (10 tonne/ha · y); thus, a large land area is needed to spread biosolids from a large plant. Also, application scheduling must be compatible with planting, harvesting, and weather conditions. Since the farmland is usually privately owned, conditions of application and storage of biosolids on farm sites are included in an agreement between the farmers and the municipality or contract hauler.

Spreading on forest land accounts for only a few percent of biosolids applied to land. The major constraints are the cost of long-haul distances and, in the forest, limited-access roads and uneven terrain. Yet, newly established plantations and recently cleared land prior to planting may be advantageous sites for nearby treatment plants.

Reclamation sites, usually owned by mining firms or governmental agencies, account for about one-tenth of biosolids application. Renovation of unsightly and often useless land areas has a positive environmental impact. Biosolids improve the poor soils by providing nutrients, pH buffering, water retention, and organic matter.

Approximately one-fifth of biosolids are sold or given away in a bag or other container for application on public parks, highway median strips, golf courses, and private lawns and gardens. The limitations on toxic metals and pathogens for this use are stricter than for agricultural use because of potential human contact and lack of direct control in application. For necessary reduction of pathogens, the biosolids are often thermally treated for a specific time–temperature regime (e.g., heat drying to reduce moisture to 10% or lower at a temperature exceeding 80°C). The bag or container must be labeled giving the nitrogen concentration and allowable application rate information so the user does not exceed the annual pollutant-loading rate for metal contaminants.

Agricultural Land Application

The main environmental and health concerns with regard to application of biosolids on agricultural land are the degree of stabilization of the organic matter, reduction of pathogenic organisms, and presence of toxic chemicals. EPA regulations have been promulgated to specify reduction of pathogens, limitation of toxic chemicals, application of nitrogen to no more than the agronomic rate, and management practices to protect the environment [1, 2].

The variety and numbers of bacteria, viruses, and parasitic organisms that are pathogenic to humans and animals and that are found in wastewater relate to the state of health of the contributing community. Although treatment processes reduce their numbers, often considerably, the effluent and sludge still contain the species present in the wastewater. The certainty of pathogens being present in raw sludge is the reason for spreading only stabilized sludges on agricultural land. The effectiveness of reducing pathogenic populations during sludge stabilization is a subject of considerable controversy. In general, anaerobic or aerobic digestion of sludge is effective in reducing the numbers of viruses and bacteria, but not in reducing roundworm and tapeworm ova or other resistant parasites. Being the most fragile microorganisms, bacteria and viruses are inactivated by sunlight, drying, and competition in the soil environment. In contrast, parasitic ova are more resistant and may persist in soils or on vegetation for several weeks or months. Even though the risk of infecting livestock is not great, farmers are usually advised to allow 30 days or more after sludge application before grazing animals or harvesting a fodder crop. Regarding human health, despite the possibility of communicable disease transmission, the lack of epidemiological evidence suggests that the current practice of sludge disposal to land is safe [8].

Anaerobic and aerobic digestion are the common processes for reducing the organic content in sludges. Besides eliminating unaesthetic conditions, particularly offensive odors, stabilization reduces the attraction of disease vectors like flies and rodents. Although disease transmission in an agricultural setting is unlikely, vectors can be a nuisance and do have the potential of carrying pathogens from sludge. Digestion processes also substantially reduce the numbers of enteric bacteria and viruses. The adverse environments and passage of time during storage and spreading on the land contribute significantly to continued die-off of pathogens.

The cultivation of fodder, fiber, and seed crops is unrestricted when digested sludge is applied on farmland. In contrast, food crops with harvested parts that contact the soil–biosolids mixture and with harvested parts underground cannot be harvested for more than a year after application of biosolids. Animals should be prevented from grazing for 30 days after application. For land with high potential for public exposure, such as parks, public access is restricted for 1 yr after applying biosolids. For private farmland, public access is restricted for 30 days [1].

Haul distance, climate, and availability of storage facilities are key factors in land application of sludge. At large plants, mechanical dewatering is used to reduce the sludge mass and cost of hauling. The cake can be distributed by a spreader with back-beaters that throw the solids outward from the rear of a wagon or truck-mounted box. Disk cultivators are used to incorporate the sludge solids into the surface soils. Biolog-ically stabilized cake can be stockpiled at farm sites between planting seasons and during winter months. Storage sites are prepared to prevent pollution of air, groundwater, and surface waters. At small plants, liquid sludge is often transported in a tank truck or tractor-drawn wagon for spreading on fields. Storage can be provided at the plant in digesters or holding tanks. Also, drying beds can be used for dewatering and storage of sludge when spreading is not feasible.

Liquid biosolids can be applied by a vehicle equipped with a rear splash plate for surface spreading or by chisel plows for subsurface incorporation. The flexibility of vehic-ular hauling allows application at a variety of locations, often privately owned farmlands. Spraying from fixed or portable irrigation nozzles can be practiced where odor and insects are not problems. Subsurface injection is the most environmentally acceptable method, since the sludge is incorporated directly into the soil, eliminating exposure to the atmosphere. A tractor pulls an injection unit that is supplied with liquid biosolids through a trailing hose. Several injectors are mounted on spring-loaded chisel plow shanks with wide cultivator sweeps. As a sweep passes through the soil, a cavity is formed approxi-mately 6 in deep for injecting the sludge. Sludge is supplied to the injection unit directly from a remote holding tank through underground piping and a flexible delivery hose. Another means of incorporating sludge, which is less effective in covering the liquid, is disk plowing with hoses discharging sludge ahead of each disk. Valves and sludge pumps located near the holding tank are operated by radio control from the tractor.

The environmental concerns of chemicals in sludge spread on agricultural land are surface water and groundwater pollution and contamination of soil and crops with toxic substances. Laboratory analyses of a sludge normally include solids content; nitrate, ammonia, and organic nitrogen; soluble and organic phosphate; potassium; and metals of arsenic, cadmium, chromium, copper, lead, mercury, molybdenum, nickel, selenium, and zinc. These 10 toxic metals are regulated as maximum allowable concen-trations in biosolids applied to agricultural land [1]. Cadmium is the heavy metal of greatest concern to human health, since it can be taken up by plants to enter the human food chain. The movement of cadmium to groundwater is very unlikely at pH values greater than 6.0 that are commonly associated with agricultural soils. The primary chronic health effect of excessive dietary intake is kidney damage.

The cadmium content of agricultural soils ranges from near zero to several hun-dred milligrams per kilogram of soil contaminated by industrial wastes. In addition to sludge, many phosphate fertilizers contain cadmium. Predicting plant uptake from soils with accumulated cadmium is difficult because of interactive controlling conditions. Soil pH is an important chemical factor, but the kind of plant species is just as important. Within plants, the highest amounts of cadmium absorption occur in the fibrous roots, followed by the leaves; the lowest concentrations are in fruits, seeds, and storage organs. Potential high-risk food plants for humans are leafy vegetables (e.g., lettuce and spinach). Fodder crops and cereal grains appear to present the least risk. Davis and Coker [9] have written a comprehensive literature review and discussion of the distribution of cadmium, plant uptake, and hazards associated with sludge used in agriculture.

Example 20

A municipal wastewater contains 200 mg/l of BOD, 220 mg/l of suspended solids, 35 mg/l of nitrogen, and 0.016 mg/l of cadmium. Wastewater processing is primary sedimentation and secondary activated sludge, with the waste sludge anaerobically digested prior to spreading on agricultural land. The plant effluent is discharged to a river. Based on operational data, 25% of the influent cadmium appears in the 110 mg of digested sludge solids produced per liter of wastewater processed. The fertilizer value of the dried sludge solids is 4.0% available nitrogen.

    a. Calculate the concentration of cadmium in the plant effluent in milligrams per liter. If the concentration limit of cadmium in the river water is 0.0013 mg/l to protect aquatic life, what dilution ratio of plant effluent to cadmium-free river water is needed?

    b. Calculate the concentration of cadmium in the dry biosolids in units of milligrams per kilogram. Compare this value to the maximum allowable concentration of 85 mg/kg. The digested sludge is being applied to land cultivated for growing soybeans with a recommended agronomic nitrogen application rate of 220 kg/ha. Calculate the maximum allowable biosolids application rate for nitrogen uptake in tonnes per hectare.

    c. Ferric chloride (waste pickle liquor) added to the wastewater for increasing phosphorus removal in treatment also increases the cadmium removal to 70%. What dilution ratio of plant effluent to cadmium-free river water is needed? Calculate the concentration of cadmium in the dry biosolids.

Solution:

    a. The cadmium in effluent amounts to $0.75 \times 0.016 = 0.012$ mg/l. Assume the dilution ratio is X (i.e., when the effluent flow is 1, the river flow is X). Then

$$X \times 0 + 1 \times 0.012 = (1 + X) \times 0.0013$$

$$X = \text{flow of river/flow of wastewater discharge} = 8.2$$

    b. The concentration of cadmium in sludge solids equals

$$\frac{0.25 \times 0.016 \text{ mg}}{110 \text{ mg} \times 10^{-6} \text{ kg/mg}} = 36 \text{ mg/kg } (<85 \text{ mg/kg})$$

The nitrogen content of the sludge solids equals

$$\frac{110 \text{ mg/l} \times 0.04 \times 1000 \text{ kg/t}}{110 \text{ mg/l}} = 40 \text{ kg/t}$$

The maximum allowable biosolids application rate equals

$$\frac{220}{40} = 5.5 \text{ t/ha}$$

    c. The cadmium in effluent is $0.30 \times 0.016 = 0.0048$ mg/l. Therefore, the dilution ratio required is 2.7. The concentration in the sludge is 100 mg/kg, which exceeds the maximum allowable concentration of 85 mg/kg. The maximum allowable sludge application rate based on nitrogen is 5.5 t/ha.

These computations illustrate that treatment for removal of phosphate by chemical precipitation also increases the removal of cadmium. Therefore, although the effluent quality improves, the contamination of the sludge is greater.

---

29   CODISPOSAL IN A MUNICIPAL SOLID-WASTE LANDFILL

Sludge cake disposed of with household refuse can be either dewatered raw or digested sludge [10, 11]. The estimated percentage of sludge buried in municipal landfills for final disposal is 35% (Table 11).

    The methods of codisposal can be to mix the wet sludge cake with either solid waste or soil. In a sludge–solid-waste operation, sludge is deposited on top of a layer of solid waste at the working face of the landfill and mixed as thoroughly as possible. Using bulldozers and landfill compactors, each mixed layer is then spread, compacted, and covered with a layer of soil. If the sludge is too wet, it is difficult to confine on the working face and equipment can slip and become stuck. Application of sludge should not exceed the absorptive capacity of the refuse. If difficulties persist, the sludge must be dewatered to a higher solids content or the quantity of sludge accepted by the landfill must be reduced. The recommended design bulking ratios (weight of refuse to weight of wet sludge) for various sludge solids contents are as follows: 6 tons of refuse for 1 wet ton of sludge at 10%–17% solids content, 5 for 1 at 17%–20%, and 4 for 1 at 20% or greater [10]. Water treatment plant sludges are buried in codisposal landfills in a similar manner [2].

    In a sludge–soil mixture operation, the sludge is mixed with soil and placed as intermediate layers between layers of refuse and as a final cover. Although this method is not strictly landfilling, it is a viable option with the advantage of removing sludge from the working face where difficulties with equipment occur. A final cover of sludge–soil mixture promotes growth of vegetation over the fill area to minimize wind and water erosion, without the need for fertilizer.

    Codisposal regulations for municipal solid-waste landfills define wastewater sludges and water treatment plant residuals as nonhazardous wastes. If toxicity is suspected, testing for controlled toxic substances is advisable. A key restriction in codisposal applies to liquids to reduce the amount of landfill leachate. Using conventional dewatering processes, the solids contents of wastewater and water wastes are usually adequate.

30   SURFACE LAND DISPOSAL

Surface disposal is the placement of sludges on land at high application rates for final disposal rather than as a beneficial soil amendment [10]. Of the approximately 13% of wastewater sludge (Table 11) disposed of in surface sites, about one-half is placed in dedicated sites, one-quarter in monofills, and one-quarter in other sites. Water treatment plant residuals are usually buried in monofills [2].

Dedicated sites are where liquid wastewater sludge is injected below the surface using a chisel plow injector unit or spread on the surface by tank truck or sprayed by an irrigation system. Because of the high rate of disposal, dedicated sites do not qualify as land application even though some are designated as beneficial use sites to grow a vegetative cover.

Monofills are burial sites where raw or digested wastewater sludges or water treatment residuals as semisolids are spread and covered with soil. On sites with deep groundwater or bedrock, trenches can be excavated with a layer of stratum or soil between the deposited sludge and the top of the groundwater or bedrock. The sludge mass is usually dumped from the transport trucks directly into the trenches and on-site equipment is used for trench excavation and covering. The other method of monofill construction is an area fill, with sludge placed on the ground surface and the fill built as a mound with a soil cover. Area fills are better for sites with shallow groundwater or bedrock.

Other surface disposal methods are piles and impoundments. Sludge piles are uncovered mounds of stabilized cake used for storage prior to final disposal. Surface impoundments are above-ground or below-ground ponds for storage of liquid sludges, such as anaerobically digested wastewater sludge and water treatment plant clarifier and backwash waters. In order to maintain a constant liquid depth, an overflow pipe drains supernatant back to the treatment plant. Seepage is controlled by either a liner or a leachate system. Settled solids accumulate until the impoundment is either dredged or covered and closed.

PROBLEMS

1 The settled sludge from coagulation of a surface water is 1.5% solids, of which 30% are volatile. Compute the specific gravity of the dry solids and specific gravity of the wet sludge. Assume specific gravity values of 2.5 for the fixed matter and 1.0 for the volatile. What is the volume of waste in cubic meters per 1000 kg of dry solids?

2 A primary wastewater sludge contains 6.0% dry solids that are 65% volatile. Calculate the specific gravities of the solid matter and the wet sludge. If this residue is thickened to a cake of 22.0% solids, what is the specific gravity of the moist cake?

3 Compute the volume of a waste sludge with 96% water content containing 1000 lb of dry solids. If the moisture content is reduced to 92%, what is the sludge volume?

4 An activated-sludge wastewater plant with primary clarification treats 10 mgd of wastewater with a BOD of 240 mg/l and suspended solids of 200 mg/l. (a) Calculate the daily primary and waste-activated sludge yields in pounds of dry solids and gallons, assuming the following: 60% SS removal and 35% BOD reduction in primary settling; a primary sludge concentration of 6.0% solids; an operating food/microorganism ratio of 1:3 in the aeration basin; and a solids concentration of 15,000 mg/l (70% volatile) in the waste-activated sludge. (b) What would be the solids content of the sludge mixture if the two waste volumes were blended together? (c) If the waste activated is thickened separately to 4.5% solids before blending, what would be the combined sludge volume and solids content?

5 Estimate the excess solids production of an extended aeration process treating unsettled wastewater with a BOD of 200 mg/l and suspended solids concentration of 240
mg/l, assuming $k = 0.35$. Express the answer in milligrams per liter of wastewater
treated.

6 A municipal wastewater with 220 mg/l of BOD and 260 mg/l of suspended solids is
processed in a two-stage trickling-filter plant. Calculate the following per 1.0 m^3 of wastewater treated: (a) the dry solids production in primary and secondary treatment, assuming
50% SS removal and 35% BOD reduction in primary settling and a k value of 0.40 applicable for the trickling-filter secondary; (b) the daily sludge volume, both primary and secondary solids, assuming 5.0% solids content. (A specific gravity of 1.0 can be assumed for
the wet sludge.)

7 What is the estimated waste-activated sludge generated from a conventional aeration
process treating 29,000 m^3/d with 173 mg/l of BOD after primary settling? The operating
F/M is 0.24 g BOD/day per gram MLSS. Assume a suspended-solids concentration of 9800
mg/l in the waste sludge.

8 A river water treatment plant coagulates raw water having a turbidity of 12 units with an
alum dosage of 40 mg/l. (a) Estimate the total sludge solids production in lb/mil gal of
water processed. (b) Compute the volumes of waste from the settling basins and filter
backwash water, assuming that 70% of the total solids are removed in sedimentation and
30% in filtration, the settled sludge solids concentration is 1.2%, and the solids content is
600 mg/l in the filter wash water. (c) Calculate the composite sludge volume after the two
wastes are gravity thickened to 3.5% solids.

9 A water plant treats a surface water with a mean turbidity of 18 NTU by applying an average of 19.8 mg/l of alum. From plant records, the sludge yield from the sedimentation
basins averages 1400 m^3 per Mm^3 of water treated with a solids content of 1.4%. The filter
wash water, at a volume of 3.2% of the water treated, contains an average of 160 mg/l of
solids. Determine the total dry solids produced per 1.0 Mm^3 of water treated and compare
this value with the total sludge solids calculated by using Eq. (9).

10 Based on the appropriate chemical reactions, both precipitation softening and recarbonation removal of excess lime, calculate the total residue produced per million gallons of
water processed.

11 Based on the appropriate chemical reactions, calculate the precipitate produced per million gallons of water processed.

12 The superintendent of a water treatment plant requests your assistance in calculating the
dissolved mineral solids removed in the lime softening of a well water and the sludge
solids produced. He wants to present these data to the city council to emphasize the
improvement in water quality resulting from treatment. The plant processes 0.45 mgd by
the addition of 300 mg/l of hydrated lime, which is 74% CaO by weight, followed by recarbonation. The lime treatment also removes iron and manganese from the water. Analyses
of the well water and treated water are listed below. (a) Tabulate the ionic concentrations,
calculate the milliequivalents per liter, and sketch milliequivalent-per-liter bar graphs. Calculate the dissolved minerals (calcium, magnesium, iron, manganese, and bicarbonate)
removed in pounds per day for the 0.45 mil gal of water treated. (c) Calculate the dry
sludge solids produced per day and the weight of the wet sludge, assuming a solids concentration of 5%.

Well Water				Treated Water			
(All values are given in milligrams per liter, except pH.)							
Ca	94	HCO$_3$	390	Ca	21	HCO$_3$	107
Mg	24	SO$_4$	73	Mg	14	SO$_4$	64
Na	27	Cl	2	Na	23	Cl	6
Fe	0.7	F	0.3	Fe	0	F	0.2
Mn	0.4			Mn	0		
Total hardness = 332				Total hardness = 112			
pH = 7.2				pH = 7.7			

13 The purpose of this problem is to view conventional wastewater treatment as a thickening process where pollutants removed from solution are concentrated in a small volume convenient for ultimate disposal. Figure 3(a) is a schematic diagram of conventional wastewater treatment. Starting with 120 gpcd of average domestic wastewater, show in step-by-step calculations how 120 gal of wastewater is reduced to one-half pint of filter cake with 20% solids. Assume 35% solids reduction in anaerobic digestion. List your assumptions. (1 gal = 8 pints.)

14 The proposed sludge-processing scheme for a conventional step-aeration activated-sludge plant is as follows: return of waste-activated sludge to the head of the plant, withdrawal of the combined sludge (raw and waste activated) from the primary clarifier, concentration in a gravity thickener, application of plant effluent to the thickener for dilution water, return of the thickener overflow to the plant inlet, and mechanical dewatering of the thickened underflow. Briefly comment on the operating problems you would anticipate with this system. What type of sludge handling and thickening would you recommend to replace the proposed scheme?

15 As originally constructed, a conventional activated-sludge plant cannot thicken the waste-activated sludge before mixing with the primary sludge. The combined sludge has an average solids concentration of 2.5%, which is too low for good operation of anaerobic digestion. The proposed solution is to modify the sludge-processing system by installing gravity belt thickeners to concentrate solids in the waste-activated sludge before mixing with the primary sludge, which has a solids concentration averaging 3.5%. If the waste-activated sludge were thickened to 6%, the mixed sludge would have a solids concentration of 4.0% to 4.5%, which is considered the minimum for satisfactory anaerobic digestion. Currently, during the maximum month, the average plant wastewater load is 41,000 m^3/d. Normal operation of the activated-sludge process produces an average of 270 m^3/d, with a solids concentration of 1.12% (11,200 mg/l). Poor operation, which may periodically last for one or two weeks, results in an average of 380 m^3/d with 0.81% solids. Determine the size of two gravity belt thickeners to increase solids content of the waste-activated sludge to the 6% at the plant design load of 57,000 m^3/d of wastewater.

16 Outline the alternative methods for processing and disposal of alum-coagulation wastes from treatment of a surface water. If two lagoons are used for storage and dewatering the waste slurry, what is your recommended method for operation of the lagoons? If the sludge in the lagoon is a viscous liquid at the time a lagoon must be emptied, how can the sludge be dewatered for disposal in a landfill?

17 A gravity thickener handles 33,000 gpd of wastewater sludge, increasing the solids content from 3.0% to 7.0% with 90% solids recovery. Calculate the quantity of thickened sludge.

18 A waste sludge flow of 40 m³/day is gravity thickened in a circular tank with a diameter of 6.8 m. The solids concentration is increased from 4.5% to 7.5% with 85% suspended-solids capture. Calculate the solids loading in $kg/m^2 \cdot d$ and the quantity of thickened sludge in m^3/d.

19 Size a gravity thickener based on 10 lb/ft²/day for a waste sludge flow of 25,000 gpd with 5.0% solids. Assume a side-water depth of 10.0 ft. After installation, operation at design flow yields an underflow of 8.0% with 90% solids removal. What is the flow of dilution water needed to maintain an overflow rate of 400 gpd/ft²? If the consolidated sludge blanket in the tank is 4.0 ft thick, compute the estimated solids retention time in the thickener.

20 An activated-sludge treatment plant without primary sedimentation processing a warm wastewater has two aeration basins with a total volume of 6730 m³ and two clarifiers with scraper mechanisms to push the settled solids to a central hopper. Each aeration basin is prismoidal in shape, with the length twice the width and completely mixed by pedestal-mounted mechanical aerators. The waste-activated sludge is discharged to prismoidal thickening and holding tanks with a maximum liquid depth of 3.9 m and designed for fill-and-draw operation. Before withdrawing supernatant, the suspended solids thicken by hindered settling, and at least some compression, for several hours. The underflow of thickened sludge is discharged to open-air sand drying beds for dewatering and the supernatant is returned to the plant inlet. The loading on the plant is 13,000 m³/d with 260 g/m³ of BOD, is and the effluent contains 7 mg/l of BOD and 13 mg/l of suspended solids. The operating MLSS is 2300 mg/l, and the mixed liquor is normally 20°C or greater. The waste-activated sludge averages 340 m³/d with 0.80% solids. The designer assumed the waste sludge would thicken to 3.0% solids and drying time on the sand beds would be 32 d. In actual operation, the performance of the sludge processing system was a failure. The solids concentration in the thickened sludge averaged 1.8%, which is 67% greater in volume than a concentration of 3.0%. Furthermore, the wet sludge required two to three times longer than 32 d to dry sufficiently for removal from the sand beds. Since the cake remained moist on the bottom and did not shrink sufficiently to open cracks, the organic solids adhered to the sand grains, sealing the pores on the surface of the bed. Foul odors were emitted during drying. As a result, most of the settled sludge is hauled away in tank trucks for disposal in a dedicated landfill, which is a costly operation.

(a) How would you classify this activated-sludge process? Keep in mind the high temperature of the wastewater.

(b) Calculate the sludge age and multiply it by 20°C. Compare this to the aeration period of 200–300 degree-days given in Section 17. What does this value indicate?

(c) Could the solids concentration of 0.80% in the waste-activated sludge have been improved by installing different clarifier mechanisms? Could the return sludge rate in operation of the activated-sludge process influence the solids concentration in the waste sludge?

(d) Why doesn't the waste-activated sludge thicken to 3.0% by plain sedimentation? (Refer to Section 2.)

(e) Why is the thickened waste-activated sludge difficult to dewater on sand drying beds?

(f) What sludge processing and disposal system would you recommend for this treatment plant?

21 Settled sludge and filter wash water from water treatment are thickened in clarifier–thickeners prior to mechanical dewatering. The settled sludge volume is 1150 gpd with 1.0% solids, and the backwash is 9800 gpd containing 500 mg/l of suspended solids. Calculate the daily quantity of thickened sludge, assuming a concentration of 3.0% solids.

22 Lagoon disposal of alum sludge is being considered for a water treatment plant processing 10,000 m^3/d. The proposed site can accommodate four lagoon cells, each with a surface area of 800 m^2 and depth of 3.0 m. Sludge from the sedimentation basins averages 15 m^3/d and contains 1.4% solids; the quantity of filter wash water is 400 m^3/d and contains 160 mg/l of suspended solids. The wash water is to be gravity thickened to greater than 1% with polymer addition before discharging to the lagoons. The plan of operation is to discharge from the sedimentation basins and thickeners to fill one cell at a time, withdrawing supernatant and allowing consolidation and air drying for at least one year after filling before cleaning. This aging period is expected to enhance dewatering by subjecting the sludge to freeze–thaw cycles during the winter months. Based on field studies, this procedure will shrink the sludge layer to a depth of less than one meter with an average solids content of 10%. Is this proposed plan likely to be successful?

23 After expansion of an activated-sludge plant, the production of waste-activated sludge during the maximum month is 500 m^3/d with 0.80% solids. The old existing flotation thickeners are to be replaced by gravity belt thickeners. Determine the size of two identical units to increase the solids content to a minimum of 5%. Assume that operation is to be 7 d/wk for a maximum of 7 hr/d; design hydraulic loading of 34 m^3/m · h and maximum solids loading of 270 kg/m · h. If the polymer solution is 0.20% dry powder by weight, what is the solution feed rate for a polymer dosage of 3.0 kg/tonne?

24 Waste-activated sludge from a biological aeration system is 293,000 gpd with 1.0% solids consisting of 70% volatile solids. The sludge is thickened to 4% with a 98% solids capture by gravity belt thickening. The thickened sludge is digested, without withdrawal of supernatant, in high-rate anaerobic digestion (Section 15) resulting in a 50% volatile solids reduction. The sludge is then dewatered by belt filter pressing (Section 20) to 18% solids concentration with a 95% capture of solids. Calculate the solids concentration and flow at each step in the process, including the wastewater flow recycled from gravity belt thickening and filtrate from the pressure dewatering.

25 A flotation thickener processes 250 m^3 of waste-activated sludge in a 16-hr operating period. The solids content is increased from 10,000 mg/l to 40,000 mg/l with 92% solids capture. Calculate the quantity of float in cubic meters per 16-hr period. If the solids loading is 12 kg/m^2 · hr, what is the hydraulic loading in m^3/m^2 · d?

26 Waste-activated sludge processed by dissolved-air flotation is concentrated from 9800 mg/l to 4.7% with 95% suspended-solids capture. During a 24-hr operating period, 50,000 gal of sludge was applied with a polymer dosage of 32 mg/l. The thickener surface area is 75 ft^2. Calculate the solids loading, volume of float produced in 24 hr, and polymer addition in lb/ton of dry solids.

27 A single-stage anaerobic digester has a capacity of 13,800 ft^3, of which 10,600 ft^3 is below the landing brackets. The average raw waste sludge solids fed to the digesters are 580 lb of solids/day. (a) Calculate the digester loading in lb of volatile solids fed/ft^3 of capacity below the landing brackets/day. Assume that 70% of the solids are volatile. (b) Determine the digester capacity required based on Eq. (11), using the following data:

$$\text{average daily raw-sludge solids} = 580 \text{ lb}$$
$$\text{raw-sludge moisture content} = 96\%$$
$$\text{digestion period} = 30 \text{ days}$$

solids reduction during digestion = 45%

digested-sludge moisture content = 94%

digested-sludge storage required = 90 days

28 Calculate the digester capacity in cubic meters required for conventional single-stage anaerobic digestion based on the following parameters:

daily raw-sludge solids production = 630 kg

volatile solids in raw sludge = 70%

moisture content of raw sludge = 95%

digestion period = 30 days

volatile solids reduction during digestion = 50%

moisture content of digested sludge = 93%

storage volume required for digested sludge = 90 days

29 The design wastewater loading for a proposed two-stage trickling-filter plant is 1200 m³/d containing 260 mg/l BOD and 310 mg/l suspended solids. (a) Calculate the required capacity of a conventional digester based on a raw-sludge concentration of 4.5%, digested-sludge solids concentration of 8.0%, total solids reduction during digestion of 40%, an f value of 0.50 for Eq. (5), a k value of 0.40 for Eq. (6), and a storage period for digested sludge of 90 days. (b) Compute the digester capacity per population equivalent load on the treatment plant.

30 The average daily quantity of thickened raw waste sludge produced in a municipal treatment plant is 15,000 gal containing 10,000 lb of solids. The solids are 70% volatile. (a) Calculate the percentage of moisture in the thickened sludge. (b) Determine the volume required for a first-stage high-rate digester based on the following criteria: a maximum loading of 100 lb of volatile solids per 1000 ft³/day and a minimum detention time of 15 days. (c) If the volatile solids reduction in the completely mixed digester is 60%, what is the percentage of moisture in the digested sludge?

31 The waste sludge production from a trickling-filter plant is 12.5 m³/d containing 620 kg of solids (70% volatile). The proposed anaerobic digester design to stabilize this waste consists of two floating-cover heated tanks, each with a volume of 480 m³ when the covers are fully raised and a volume of 310 m³ with the covers resting on the landing brackets. (a) Calculate the digester volume per equivalent population with the covers fully raised. Assume 100 g of solids production per capita. (b) Calculate the digester loading in terms of kg volatile solids fed/m³ of tank volume below the landing brackets/day. (c) Calculate the digested-sludge storage time available between lowered and raised cover positions. Assume a volatile solids reduction of 60% during digestion and a digested-sludge moisture content of 93%.

32 A domestic wastewater plant using rotating biological contactors for secondary treatment has a two-stage anaerobic digestion system (Figure 13). The first stage is a heated, completely mixed fixed-cover digester with a liquid volume of 15,500 ft³. The second stage is an unheated and unmixed digester with a liquid volume of 15,500 ft³ equipped with a gas-dome cover and supernatant draw-offs. Alum is added to the RBC effluent ahead of the final clarifiers to precipitate phosphate. (The plant was retrofitted with alum feeders and new final clarifiers after original construction to meet a revised effluent standard for phosphorus.) The average wastewater flow is 0.63 mgd. Influent characteristics are 166 mg/l of BOD, 128 mg/l of suspended solids, and 7.1 mg/l of inorganic phosphorus. Effluent

characteristics are 7 mg/l of BOD, 16 mg/l of suspended solids, and 1.3 mg/l of inorganic phosphorus. Alum addition is 405 lb/day. The quantity of raw sludge produced averages 2400 gpd with 4.4% solids, which are 67% volatile. The quantity of digested sludge accumulated in the second-stage tank averages 1500 gpd with 4.3% solids, which are 45% volatile. The total gas production from digestion is 4200 ft^3/day. (a) Calculate the volatile solids loading and liquid detention time of the first-stage digester. How do these values compare with those in Table 8? (b) Calculate the digestion gas production per pound of volatile solids added and per pound of volatile solids destroyed. Compare these values with those in Table 6. (c) Estimate the total dry solids sludge yield as the sum of raw primary solids [Eq. (5)], biological sludge solids [Eq. (6)], and alum precipitate as aluminum phosphate. How does this compare with actual sludge solids yield?

33 The two-stage anaerobic digesters at a trickling-filter plant are a fixed-cover tank for first-stage high-rate sludge stabilization with a liquid volume of 42,000 ft^3 and a floating-cover second-stage storage and thickening tank with a volume of 70,000 ft^3 between the lowered and fully raised cover positions. The quantity of raw sludge applied is 2800 ft^3/day containing 5.0% solids that are 70% volatile. (a) If 60% of the volatile solids in the raw sludge is reduced by digestion, calculate the solids concentration in the digested sludge leaving the first-stage digester. (b) Estimate the daily methane production in first-stage digestion. (c) If the digested, thickened sludge contains 7.0% solids, compute the maximum number of days of digested-sludge storage available. (d) Assume the first-stage digester has been operated at a digesting sludge temperature of 35°C for several weeks. How would the gas production change if the operating temperature were decreased slowly to 25°C? How would gas production be affected by a slow increase in operating temperature from 35° to 45°C?

34 A wastewater sludge is stabilized and thickened in anaerobic digestion. The daily raw-sludge feed is 100,000 lb containing 5500 lb of dry solids. Forty percent of the matter applied is converted to gases during digestion, and the digested residue is increased to 10% solids by supernatant withdrawal. Calculate the volumetric reduction of wet sludge achieved in the digestion process.

35 The raw sludge pumped to an anaerobic digester contains 5.0% solids that are 65% volatile. The digested sludge withdrawn from the tank has 6.5% solids that are 40% volatile. Based on these data, estimate by calculations (a) the percentage of volatile solids converted to gas during digestion and (b) the quantity of supernatant withdrawn for every 1000 gal of raw sludge fed to the digester.

36 A new two-stage anaerobic digestion system is being sized for an activated-sludge plant with primary sedimentation. Based on an average raw wastewater flow during the maximum month of 50,000 m^3/d containing 280 mg/l of suspended solids and 240 mg/l of BOD, primary waste solids are calculated to be 7000 kg/d and waste-activated sludge solids are calculated to be 3900 kg/d for a total of 10,900 kg/d with a volatile solids content of 70%. Both sludges are to be thickened so that the solids concentration will be 5.0% for a volume of 218 m^3/d. For a solids retention time in the first-stage tank of 20 d, calculate the volatile solids loading. If digestion reduces the volatile solids by 50%, what is the calculated concentration of solids in the digested sludge flowing into the second-stage tank? If 50 m^3/d of reasonably clear supernatant can be withdrawn from the second tank, what is the estimated concentration of digested solids in the thickened sludge withdrawn from the second tank?

37 Aerobic digesters with a total capacity of 50,000 ft^3 stabilize waste-activated sludge from an extended-aeration treatment plant without primary clarification. The average daily sludge flow pumped to the digestion tanks is 32,000 gal with 1.5% solids, of which 65% are volatile. The estimated solids production per capita is 0.17 lb of VS/person/day. Calculate the sludge detention time in the digesters, VS loading lb/ft^3/day and volume provided per capita.

38 A waste-activated sludge with a total solids concentration of 12,500 mg/l and volatile solids content of 8800 mg/l is applied to an aerobic digester with a detention time of 25 days. The volatile solids destruction is 50% during digestion. Calculate the volatile solids loading in units of kg/m$^3 \cdot$d and the solids content of the digested sludge, assuming no supernatant is withdrawn. If the solids content at the bottom of the digester can be increased to 1.5% by quiescent settling, what percentage of the waste sludge can be decanted as supernatant?

39 The activated-sludge treatment plant without primary sedimentation described in Problem 20 is recommended for expansion to process a wastewater flow of 19,500 m³/d by adding one more aeration basin and clarifier. Using a waste activated sludge of 510 m³/d with 0.80% solids, determine the dimensions of three aerobic digesters using the same design data (except for waste-activated sludge volume and solids concentration) and criteria listed in Example 14.

40 The design wastewater flow for a small community is 400 m³/d, containing 200 mg/l BOD and 240 mg/l suspended solids. The proposed treatment is extended aeration without primary sedimentation. After aerobic digestion, the waste sludge can be taken directly from the aerobic digesters for spreading on agricultural land or pumped into a large asphalt-lined storage basin for winter storage. (a) Calculate the required capacity for the aerobic digesters assuming the F/M loading on the aeration tank is 0.15 g BOD/d per gram MLSS, the waste-activated sludge solids content is 1.5% (70% volatile), and the criteria for sizing the aerobic digesters are a maximum VS loading of 0.60 kg/m³·d and a minimum digestion period of 15 days. (b) How large must the storage basin be to hold a 90-day volume of digested sludge, assuming that the total solids reduction during aerobic digestion is 25% of the total solids in the applied sludge and the solids concentration in the storage basin can be increased to 2.0% by withdrawing supernatant?

41 What are the reasons for mixing either an organic amendment or a recoverable bulking agent with dewatered sludge cake before composting?

42 A treatment plant produces an average of 75,000 gpd of primary sludge with a solids concentration of 6.0% and 230,000 gpd of waste-activated sludge having a water content of 99.0%. (a) If the waste-activated sludge is thickened to 4.0% solids by flotation and then combined with the primary sludge prior to dewatering, what are the quantity and solids content of the blended sludge? (Assume 100% solids capture in flotation thickening.) (b) If belt filter presses dewater the sludge to 23% solids, how many 8-ton truckloads of cake must be hauled to land burial each day? (Assume 100% solids capture in filtration and negligible weight added by chemical conditioning.)

43 The smallest belt filter press manufactured for sludge dewatering has an effective belt width of 1 m. Estimate the equivalent population that can be served by this unit assuming 0.20 lb of dry solids/capita/day of sludge production, a solids loading of 100 lb/m/hr, and a 7-hr operating period each day.

44 A belt filter press with an effective belt width of 1.5 m dewaters anaerobically digested sludge at a sludge feed rate of 70 gpm. The polymer dosage is 6.0 gpm containing 0.20% polymer by weight, and the wash-water usage is 50 gpm. Based on laboratory analyses, total solids in the feed sludge are 4.0%, total solids in the cake are 35%, and suspended solids in the wastewater (filtrate, polymer feed, and wash water) are 1800 mg/l. Calculate the hydraulic feed rate, solids loading rate, polymer dosage, and solids recovery. Compare these values with those listed in Table 9.

45 A belt filter press with an effective belt width of 2.0 m dewaters 100 gpm of anaerobically digested sludge with a solids content of 6.5%. The polymer dosage is 6.4 gpm, containing 0.20% powdered polymer by weight. The wash-water consumption for belt cleaning is 60 gpm. The cake solids content is 30% and the suspended-solids concentration in the wash water measures 1800 mg/l. Calculate the hydraulic loading rate, solids loading rate, and polymer dosage and estimate the solids recovery.

46 A belt filter press housed in a mobile trailer was used to test the dewaterability of an anaerobically digested sludge. The effective width of the belt was 0.50 m. The operating data were a sludge feed rate of 4.5 m^3/hr, polymer dosage of 0.45 m^3/hr containing 0.20% powdered polymer by weight, and wash-water flow of 1.07 1/s. Based on laboratory analyses, total solids in the feed sludge equaled 3.5%, total solids in the cake equaled 32%, wastewater from belt washing contained 2600 mg/l suspended solids, and the filtrate was 1.20 1/s with 500 mg/l of suspended solids. Calculate the hydraulic loading, solids loading, polymer dosage, and solids recovery.

47 Recommend the size of belt filter presses and schematic layout for dewatering the aerobically digested sludge in Problem 43.

48 At an existing treatment plant, the practice of hauling away liquid digested sludge for spreading on farmland is being replaced by belt filter presses to dewater anaerobically digested sludge prior to stockpiling and spreading on agricultural land. The design sludge production, which is the average quantity during the maximum month of the year plus 25% for future plant expansion, equals 90,000 gpd with an average solids concentration of 5.0%. Using a trailer-mounted press, the performance data for dewatering the 5.0% sludge were a hydraulic loading of 45 gpm/m, cake solids content of 24%, polymer dosage of 4.0 gpm/m with a concentration of 0.20% powdered polymer, wash-water usage of 32 gpm/m, and wastewater production of 64 gpm/m containing 2200 mg/l of suspended solids. Calculate the following: solids loading, polymer dosage, wash-water usage and wastewater production per 1000 gal of sludge dewatered, solids recovery, and daily cake production. For a design operating schedule of 12 hr/day with two presses, recommend the size of the presses for installation.

49 An alum sludge is dewatered by pressure filtration. A daily volume of 40 m^3 of slurry is pressed from 2.0% solids concentration to a cake of 40% solids, after conditioning with 10% lime. Calculate the volume of filtrate and weight of the cake produced per day. (The 40% concentration of cake solids includes the alum precipitate and the lime addition.)

50 A diaphragm plate-and-frame filter press is used to dewater alum sludge from a water treatment plant. Each chamber of the press has a filtering area of 36 ft^2. During normal operation, the total cycle time (feed, compression, discharge, and wash) is 20 min. The volume of alum sludge applied per chamber per cycle is 300 gal, and the lime dosage as CaO is 10% of the alum solids. The alum sludge feed averages 3.6% solids, and the sludge cake

is 38.5% solids, including the lime. Solids capture can be assumed to be 100%, since the filtrate contains less than 200 mg/l of suspended solids. Calculate the cake production per gallon of alum sludge in pounds, assuming a specific gravity of 1.0, and the filter yield in pounds per square foot per hour based on applied alum solids.

51 Refer to Example 17. Why were centrifuges selected for dewatering the sludge from this plant rather than belt filter presses? Why is equalization of feed sludge important in centrifuge dewatering? What were the selected methods of cake conveyance?

52 A solid-bowl centrifuge dewaters an anaerobically digested blend of primary and waste-activated sludges at a flow rate of 8.0 l/s with a polymer addition of 10 kg per 1000 kg of dry solids. The sludge feed contains 2.4% solids, the cake averages 19%, and the suspended-solids concentration in the centrate is 3200 mg/l. Calculate the solids recovery and centrate flow rate.

53 A lime precipitate from a water-softening plant is concentrated in a scroll centrifuge from 10% to 60%. The suspended-solids capture is 90%. Calculate the suspended-solids concentration in the centrate and the volumetric reduction of the waste slurry as a percentage of the feed.

54 **(a)** Compare the required processing and quality for biosolids sold in bulk for agricultural land application with biosolids sold in bags for application on private lawns and gardens.

(b) Compare the required processing and quality for biosolids sold in bulk for agricultural land application with dewatered sludge buried by codisposal in a municipal solid-waste landfill.

55 Anaerobically digested sludge dewatered by belt filter press is tested for fecal coliform density by the CFU (colony-forming units) method as specified by EPA for application of biosolids on agricultural land (Section 28). The results of seven sludge samples collected and tested on consecutive days expressed in number of fecal coliforms per gram of total solids (dry weight) are as follows: 140,000; 320,000; 130,000; 330,000; 300,000; 220,000; and 305,000. Calculate the average density based on geometric mean for these data. (Geometric mean of a number is the logarithm to base 10.) Does this sludge meet the pathogen reduction for Class B biosolids?

REFERENCES

[1] "Process Design Manual, Land Application of Sewage Sludge and Domestic Septage," U.S. Environmental Protection Agency, Office of Research and Development, EPA/625/R-95/001 (Cincinnati, OH: September 1995).

[2] *Management of Water Treatment Plant Residuals*, AWWA Technology Transfer Handbook (Denver, CO: Am. Water Works Assoc., 1996).

[3] "Design Manual, Dewatering Municipal Wastewater Sludges," U.S. Environmental Protection Agency, Office of Research and Development, EPA/625/1-87/014 (September 1987).

[4] *Handbook of Public Water Systems* 2nd edn Chapter 23, "Residuals Management," HDR Engineering, Inc. (New York: John Wiley & Sons, 2001).

[5] G. Hoyland, A. Dee, and M. Day, "Optimum Design of Sewage Sludge Consolidation Tanks," *J. Inst. Water Env. Manage.* vol. 3 no. 5, (1989): 505–516.

[6] *Recommended Standards for Wastewater Facilities, Great Lakes–Upper Mississippi River Board of State Public Health & Environmental Managers* (Albany, NY: Health Research Inc., Health Education Services Division, 1978).

[7] "Composting of Municipal Wastewater Sludges," U.S. Environmental Protection Agency, Technology Transfer, EPA 625/4-85-014 (August 1985).

[8] "Control of Pathogens and Vector Attraction in Sewage Sludge," U.S. Environmental Protection Agency, Office of Research and Development, EPA/625/R-92/013, http://www.epa.gov/ORD/NRMRL (October 1999).

[9] R. D. Davis and E. G. Coker, *Cadmium in Agriculture With Special Reference to the Utilization of Sewage Sludge on Land*, Water Research Centre, Stevenage Laboratory, England, TR 139 (June 1980).

[10] "Process Design Manual, Surface Disposal of Sewage Sludge and Domestic Septage," U.S. Environmental Protection Agency, Office of Research and Development, EPA 625/R-95/002 (Washington, DC: September 1995).

[11] "Process Design Manual, Municipal Sludge Landfills," U.S. Environmental Protection Agency, Office of Solid Waste, EPA 625/1-78-010 SW-705 (October 1978).

Appendix

TABLE 1   Weights and Measures

Length

	cm	m	in.	ft	yd	mi
1 cm = 1		0.01	0.3937008	0.03280840	0.01093613	6.213712×10^{-6}
1 m = 100		1	39.37008	3.280840	1.093613	6.213712×10^{-4}
1 in. = 2.54		0.0254	1	$0.08333333\ldots$	$0.02777777\ldots$	1.578283×10^{-5}
1 ft = 30.48		0.3048	12	1	$0.3333333\ldots$	$1.893939\ldots \times 10^{-4}$
1 yd = 91.44		0.9144	36	3	1	$5.681818\ldots \times 10^{-4}$
1 mi = 1.609344×10^5		1.609344×10^3	6.336×10^4	5280	1760	1

Area

	cm²	m²	in.²	ft²	acre	mi²
1 cm² = 1		10^{-4}	0.155003	1.076391×10^{-3}	2.5×10^{-8}	3.861022×10^{-11}
1 m² = 10^4		1	1550.003	10.76391	2.5×10^{-4}	3.861022×10^{-7}
1 in.² = 6.4516		6.4516×10^4	1	6.944444×10^{-3}	1.59×10^{-7}	2.490977×10^{-10}
1 ft² = 929.0304		0.09290304	144	1	2.3×10^{-5}	3.587007×10^{-8}
1 acre = 40.47×10^6		4047	6.27×10^6	43,560	1	1.56×10^{-3}
1 mi² = 2.589988×10^{10}		2.589988×10^6	4.014490×10^9	2.78784×10	640	1

Volume

	ml	l	in.³	ft³	gal	acre·ft
1 cm³ = 1	1	10^{-3}	0.06102374	3.531467×10^{-5}	2.641721×10^{-4}	8.1×10^{-10}
1 l = 1000	1000	1	61.02374	0.03531467	0.2641721	8.1×10^{-7}
1 in.³ = 16.38706	16.38706	0.01638706	1	5.787037×10^{-4}	4.329004×10^{-3}	1.33×10^{-8}
1 ft³ = 28,316.85	28,316.85	28.31685	1728	1	7.480520	2.3×10^{-5}
1 gal (U.S.) = 3785.412	3785.412	3.785412	231	0.1336806	1	3.07×10^{-6}
1 acre·ft = 1.23×10^9	1.23×10^9	1.23×10^6	75.3×10^6	43,560	325,851	1

Mass

	g	kg	oz	lb	ton
1 g = 1	1	10^{-3}	0.03527396	2.204623×10^{-3}	1.102311×10^{-6}
1 kg = 1000	1000	1	35.27396	2.204623	1.102311×10^{-3}
1 oz (avdp) = 28.34952	28.34952	0.02834952	1	0.0625	5×10^{-4}
1 lb (avdp) = 453.5924	453.5924	0.4535924	16	1	0.0005
1 ton = 907,184.7	907,184.7	907.1847	32,000	2000	1

Système International d'Unités (SI)

The SI metric system is based on meter-kilogram-second units. The principal units applicable to water and wastewater engineering are listed in Tables 2 and 3. Derived SI units are consistent, since the conversion factor among various units is unity (e.g., 1 joule = 1 newton $\times$ 1 meter). Prefixes given in Table 4 may be added to write large or small numbers and thus avoid the use of exponential values of 10. Groups of three digits, on either side of the decimal point, are separated by spaces. Tables 5 and 6 list common conversion factors from customary units to SI metric. [Reference: *Units of Expression for Wastewater Management*, Manual of Practice No. 6 (Washington, DC: Water Pollution Control Federation, 1982).]

Acceleration of gravity $g = 32.174$ ft/s^2 = 9.806 65 m/s^2.

TABLE 2   Basic SI Units

Quantity	Unit	Symbol
Length	meter	m
Mass	kilogram	kg
Thermodynamic temperature	Kelvin	K
Time	second	s
Molecular weight	mole	mol
Plane angle	radian	rad

TABLE 3   Derived SI Units

Quantity	Unit	Symbol	Formula
Energy	joule	J	$N \cdot m$
Force	newton	N	$kg \cdot m/s^2$
Power	watt	W	J/s
Pressure	pascal	Pa	N/m^2

TABLE 4   Multiples and Submultiples of SI Units

Multiplier		Prefix	Symbol
1 000 000	= 10^6	mega	M
1000	= 10^3	kilo	k
0.001	= 10^{-3}	milli	m
0.000 001	= 10^{-6}	micro	μ

TABLE 5   Conversion Factors from English Units to SI Metric Units

Customary Units			Metric Units	
	Symbol	Multiplier	Symbol	
Description	Multiply...	By...	To Obtain...	Reciprocal
Acre	acre	0.404 7	ha	2.471
British thermal unit	Btu	1.055	kJ	0.947 0
British thermal units per cubic foot	Btu/ft^3	37.30	J/I	0.026 81
British thermal units per pound	Btu/lb	2.328	kJ/kg	0.429 5
British thermal units per square foot per hour	Btu/ft^2/hr	3.158	J/m$^2 \cdot$ s	0.316 7
Cubic foot	ft^3	0.028 32	m^3	35.31
Cubic foot	ft^3	28.32	l	0.035 31
Cubic feet per minute	cfm	0.471 9	l/s	2.119
Cubic feet per minute per thousand cubic feet	cfm/1000 ft^3	0.016 67	l/m$^3 \cdot$ s	60.00
Cubic feet per second	cfs	0.028 32	m^3/s	35.31
Cubic feet per second per acre	cfs/acre	0.069 98	m^3/s $\cdot$ ha	14.29
Cubic inch	in.^{3}	0.016 39	l	61.01
Cubic yard	yd^3	0.764 6	m^3	1.308
Fathom	f	1.839	m	0.546 7
Foot	ft	0.304 8	m	3.281
Feet per hour	ft/hr	0.084 67	mm/s	11.81
Feet per minute	fpm	0.005 08	m/s	196.8
Foot-pound	ft $\cdot$ lb	1.356	J	0.737 5
Gallon, U.S.	gal	3.785	l	0.264 2
Gallons per acre	gal/acre	0.009 35	m^3/ha	106.9
Gallons per day per linear foot	gpd/lin ft	0.012 42	m^3/m $\cdot$ d	80.53
Gallons per day per square foot	gpd/ft^2	0.040 74	m^3/m$^2 \cdot$ d	24.54
Gallons per minute	gpm	0.063 08	l/s	15.85
Grain	gr	0.064 80	g	15.43
Grains per gallon	gr/gal	17.12	mg/l	0.058 41
Horsepower	hp	0.745 7	kW	1.341
Horsepower-hour	hp $\cdot$ hr	2.684	MJ	0.372 5
Inch	in.	25.4	mm	0.039 37
Knot	knot	1.852	km/h	0.540 0
Knot	knot	0.514 4	m/s	1.944
Mile	mi	1.609	km	0.621 5
Miles per hour	mph	1.609	km/h	0.621 5
Million gallons	mil gal	3 785.0	m^3	0.000 264 2
Million gallons per day	mgd	43.81	l/s	0.022 82

(*Continued*)

TABLE 5   (Continued)

| Customary Units | | | Metric Units | |
Description	Symbol Multiply...	Multiplier By...	Symbol To Obtain...	Reciprocal
Million gallons per day	mgd	0.043 81	m^3/s	22.82
Ounce	oz	28.35	g	0.035 27
Pound (force)	lbf	4.448	N	0.224 8
Pound (mass)	lb	0.453 6	kg	2.205
Pounds per acre	lb/ha	1.121	kg/ha	0.892 1
Pounds per cubic foot	pcf	16.02	kg/m^3	0.062 42
Pounds per foot	lb/ft	1.488	kg/m	0.672 0
Pounds per horsepower-hour	lb/hp · hr	0.169 0	mg/J	5.918
Pounds per square foot	lb/ft^2	0.047 88	kN/m^2	20.89
Pounds per square inch	psi	6.895	kN/m^2	0.145 0
Pounds per thousand cubic feet per day	$lb/1000 \ ft^3/day$	0.016 02	$kg/m^3 \cdot d$	62.43
Square foot	ft^2	0.092 90	m^2	10.76
Square inch	$in.^2$	645.2	mm^2	0.001 550
Square mile	mi^2	2.590	km^2	0.386 1
Square yard	yd^2	0.836 1	m^2	1.196
Ton, short	ton	0.907 2	t	1.102
Yard	yd	0.914 4	m	1.094

Acceleration of gravity $g = 32.174 \ ft/s^2 = 9.806 \ 65 \ m/s^2$.

TABLE 6   Selected English–Metric Conversion Factors

	English Unit	Multiplier	Metric Unit
Mass	lb	0.453 6	kg
Length	ft	0.304 8	m
Area	ft^2	0.092 90	m^2
	acre	4047	m^2
	acre	0.404 7	ha
Volume	gal	0.003 785	m^3
	gal	3.785	l
	ft^3	0.028 32	m^3
	ft^3	28.32	l
Velocity	fpm	0.005 08	m/s
Flow	mgd	3785	m^3/d
	gpm	5.450	m^3/d
	gpm	0.063 09	l/s
	cfs	0.028 32	m^3/s
BOD loading	lb/1000 ft^3/day	16.02	$g/m^3 \cdot d$
	lb/acre/day	1.121	$kg/ha \cdot d$
Solids loading	lb/ft^2/day	4.883	$kg/m^2 \cdot d$
	lb/ft^3/day	16.02	$kg/m^3 \cdot d$
Hydraulic loading	gpd/ft^2	0.040 75	$m^3/m^2 \cdot d$
	gpm/ft^2	0.679 0	$l/m^2 \cdot s$
Concentration	lb/mil gal	0.119 8	mg/l

	Metric Unit	Multiplier	English Unit
Mass	kg	2.205	lb
Length	m	3.281	ft
Area	m^2	10.76	ft^2
	m^2	0.000 247	acre
	ha	2.471	acre
Volume	m^3	264.2	gal
	m^3	35.31	ft^3
	l	0.264 2	gal
	l	0.035 31	ft^3
Velocity	m/s	196.8	fpm
Flow	m^3/d	0.000 264 2	mgd
	m^3/d	0.183 5	gpm
	m^3/s	35.31	cfs
	l/s	15.85	gpm
BOD loading	$g/m^3 \cdot d$	0.062 43	lb/1000 ft^3/day
	$kg/ha \cdot d$	0.892 1	lb/acre/day
Solids loading	$kg/m^2 \cdot d$	0.204 8	lb/ft^2/day
	$kg/m^3 \cdot d$	0.062 42	lb/ft^3/day
Hydraulic loading	$m^3/m^2 \cdot d$	24.54	gal/ft^2/day
	$l/m^2 \cdot s$	1.473	gpm/ft^2
Concentration	mg/l	8.345	lb/mil gal

TABLE 7 Relative Atomic Weights

Name	Symbol	Atomic Number	Atomic Weight	Name	Symbol	Atomic Number	Atomic Weight
Actinium	Ac	89	—	Mercury	Hg	80	200.59
Aluminum	Al	13	26.9815	Molybdenum	Mo	42	95.94
Americium	Am	95	—	Neodymium	Md	60	144.24
Antimony	Sb	51	121.75	Neon	Ne	10	20.183
Argon	Ar	18	39.948	Neptunium	Np	93	—
Arsenic	As	33	74.9216	Nickel	Ni	28	58.71
Astatine	At	85	—	Niobium	Nb	41	92.906
Barium	Ba	56	137.34	Nitrogen	N	7	14.0067
Berkelium	Bk	97	—	Nobelium	No	102	—
Beryllium	Be	4	9.0122	Osmium	Os	76	190.2
Bismuth	Bi	83	208.980	Oxygen	O	8	15.9994
Boron	B	5	10.811	Palladium	Pd	46	106.4
Bromine	Br	35	79.904	Phosphorus	P	15	30.9738
Cadmium	Cd	48	112.40	Platinum	Pt	78	195.09
Calcium	Ca	20	40.08	Plutonium	Pu	94	—
Californium	Cf	98	—	Polonium	Po	84	—
Carbon	C	6	12.01115	Potassium	K	19	39.102
Cerium	Ce	58	140.12	Praseodymium	Pr	59	140.907
Cesium	Cs	55	132.905	Promethium	Pm	61	—
Chlorine	Cl	17	35.453	Protactinium	Pa	91	—
Chromium	Cr	24	51.996	Radium	Ra	88	—
Cobalt	Co	27	58.9332	Radon	Rn	86	—
Copper	Cu	29	63.546	Rhenium	Re	75	186.2
Curium	Cm	96	—	Rhodium	Rh	45	102.905
Dysprosium	Dy	66	162.50	Rubidium	Rb	37	85.47
Einsteinium	Es	99	—	Ruthenium	Ru	44	101.07
Erbium	Er	68	167.26	Samarium	Sm	62	150.35
Europium	Eu	63	151.96	Scandium	Sc	21	44.956
Fermium	Fm	100	—	Selenium	Se	34	78.96
Fluorine	F	9	18.9984	Silicon	Si	14	28.086
Francium	Fr	87	—	Silver	Ag	47	107.868
Gadolinium	Gd	64	157.25	Sodium	Na	11	22.9898
Gallium	Ga	31	69.72	Strontium	Sr	38	87.62
Germanium	Ge	32	72.59	Sulfur	S	16	32.064
Gold	Au	79	196.967	Tantalum	Ta	73	189.948
Hafnium	Hf	72	178.49	Technetium	Tc	43	—
Helium	He	2	4.0026	Tellurium	Te	52	127.60
Holmium	Ho	67	164.930	Terbium	Tb	65	158.924
Hydrogen	H	1	1.00797	Thallium	Tl	81	204.37
Indium	In	49	114.82	Thorium	Th	90	232.038
Iodine	I	53	126.9044	Thulium	Tm	69	168.934
Iridium	Ir	77	192.2	Tin	Sn	50	118.69
Iron	Fe	26	55.847	Titanium	Ti	22	47.90
Krypton	Kr	36	83.80	Tungsten	W	74	183.85
Lanthanum	La	57	138.91	Uranium	U	92	238.03
Lead	Pb	82	207.19	Vanadium	V	23	50.942
Lithium	Li	3	6.939	Xenon	Xe	54	131.30
Lutetium	Lu	71	174.97	Ytterbium	Yb	70	173.04
Magnesium	Mg	12	24.312	Yttrium	Y	39	88.905
Manganese	Mn	25	54.9380	Zinc	Zn	30	65.37
Mendelevium	Md	101	—	Zirconium	Zr	40	91.22

Source: "Report of the International Commission on Atomic Weights—1961," *J. Am. Chem. Soc.* 84 (1962): 4192.

TABLE 8 Properties of Water in English Units

Temperature ($^\circ$F)	Specific Weight γ (lb/ft^3)	Mass Density ρ (lb$\cdot$sec^2/ft^4)	Absolute Viscosity μ ($\times 10^{-5}$ lb$\cdot$sec/ft^2)	Kinematic Viscosity ν ($\times 10^{-5}$ ft^2/sec)	Vapor Pressure p_v(psi)
32	62.42	1.940	3.746	1.931	0.09
40	62.43	1.938	3.229	1.664	0.12
50	62.41	1.936	2.735	1.410	0.18
60	62.37	1.934	2.359	1.217	0.26
70	62.30	1.931	2.050	1.059	0.36
80	62.22	1.927	1.799	0.930	0.51
90	62.11	1.923	1.595	0.826	0.70
100	62.00	1.918	1.424	0.739	0.95
110	61.86	1.913	1.284	0.667	1.24
120	61.71	1.908	1.168	0.609	1.69
130	61.55	1.902	1.069	0.558	2.22
140	61.38	1.896	0.981	0.514	2.89
150	61.20	1.890	0.905	0.476	3.72
160	61.00	1.896	0.838	0.442	4.74
170	60.80	1.890	0.780	0.413	5.99
180	60.58	1.883	0.726	0.385	7.51
190	60.36	1.876	0.678	0.362	9.34
200	60.12	1.868	0.637	0.341	11.52
212	59.83	1.860	0.593	0.319	14.70

TABLE 9 Properties of Water in SI Metric Units

Temperature ($^\circ$C)	Specific Weight γ (kN/m^3)	Mass Density ρ (kg/m^3)	Absolute Viscosity μ ($\times 10^{-3}$ kg/m$\cdot$s)[a]	Kinematic Viscosity ν ($\times 10^{-6}$ m^2/s)	Vapor Pressure p_v(kPa)
0	9.805	999.8	1.781	1.785	0.61
5	9.807	1000.0	1.518	1.518	0.87
10	9.804	999.7	1.307	1.306	1.23
15	9.798	999.1	1.139	1.139	1.70
20	9.789	998.2	1.002	1.003	2.34
25	9.777	997.0	0.890	0.893	3.17
30	9.764	995.7	0.798	0.800	4.24
40	9.730	992.2	0.653	0.658	7.38
50	9.689	988.0	0.547	0.553	12.33
60	9.642	983.2	0.466	0.474	19.92
70	9.589	997.8	0.404	0.413	31.16
80	9.530	971.8	0.354	0.364	47.34
90	9.466	965.3	0.315	0.326	70.10
100	9.399	958.4	0.282	0.294	101.33

[a]N$\cdot$s/m^2

TABLE 10 Saturation Values of Dissolved Oxygen in Water Exposed to Water-Saturated Air Containing 20.90% Oxygen Under a Pressure of 760 mm Hg[a]

| | Chloride Concentration in Water (mg/l) | | | | | |
| | 0 | 5000 | 10,000 | | | |
Temperature (°C)	Dissolved Oxygen (mg/l)			Difference per 100 mg Chloride	Temperature (°C)	Vapor Pressure (mm)
0	14.6	13.8	13.0	0.017	0	5
1	14.2	13.4	12.6	0.016	1	5
2	13.8	13.1	12.3	0.015	2	5
3	13.5	12.7	12.0	0.015	3	6
4	13.1	12.4	11.7	0.014	4	6
5	12.8	12.1	11.4	0.014	5	7
6	12.5	11.8	11.1	0.014	6	7
7	12.2	11.5	10.9	0.013	7	8
8	11.9	11.2	10.6	0.013	8	8
9	11.6	11.0	10.4	0.012	9	9
10	11.3	10.7	10.1	0.012	10	9
11	11.1	10.5	9.9	0.011	11	10
12	10.8	10.3	9.7	0.011	12	11
13	10.6	10.1	9.5	0.011	13	11
14	10.4	9.9	9.3	0.010	14	12
15	10.2	9.7	9.1	0.010	15	13
16	10.0	9.5	9.0	0.010	16	14
17	9.7	9.3	8.8	0.010	17	15
18	9.5	9.1	8.6	0.009	18	16
19	9.4	8.9	8.5	0.009	19	17
20	9.2	8.7	8.3	0.009	20	18
21	9.0	8.6	8.1	0.009	21	19
22	8.8	8.4	8.0	0.008	22	20
23	8.7	8.3	7.9	0.008	23	21
24	8.5	8.1	7.7	0.008	24	22
25	8.4	8.0	7.6	0.008	25	24
26	8.2	7.8	7.4	0.008	26	25
27	8.1	7.7	7.3	0.008	27	27
28	7.9	7.5	7.1	0.008	28	28
29	7.8	7.4	7.0	0.008	29	30
30	7.6	7.3	6.9	0.008	30	32

[a]Saturation at barometric pressures other than 760 mm (29.92 in.), C'_σ is related to the corresponding tabulated values C_s by the equation

$$C'_\sigma = C_s \frac{P - p}{760 - p}$$

where

C'_σ = solubility at barometric pressure P and given temperature, mg/l
C_s = saturation at given temperature from table, mg/l
P = barometric pressure, mm
p = pressure of saturated water vapor at temperature of the water selected from table, mm

Index

739